THE COLONIAL
HOUSES OF WORSHIP
IN AMERICA

Harold Wickliffe Rose

THE COLONIAL
HOUSES OF WORSHIP
IN AMERICA

Built in the English Colonies

before the Republic,

1607-1789,

and still standing

Ad Majorem Gloriam Dei

by

HAROLD WICKLIFFE ROSE

with photographs and maps by the author

HASTINGS HOUSE, PUBLISHERS

NEW YORK

Published simultaneously in Canada
by S. J. Reginald Saunders, Publishers, Toronto 2B.

Library of Congress Catalog Card Number: 63-19175

Printed in the United States of America
Designed by Al Lichtenberg

To

FREDERICK WILLIAM and CARRIE SPERRY BEINECKE

with affection and deep gratitude

for their inspiration and confidence

which encouraged me to go forward

with this work

CONTENTS

		Page
	Acknowledgements	XI
	Introduction	XIII
Chapter 1	The Colonial Houses of Worship	1
	1. The British Colonies in America	1
	2. The Colonial Period	6
	3. Types of Houses of Worship	8
	4. Regional Distribution	9
Chapter 2	The Church of England and the South	13
	1. Virginia	13
	2. Maryland	18
	3. Carolina	21
	4. Georgia	23
Chapter 3	The Colonial Catholics	27
Chapter 4	The Dissenters and New England	37
Chapter 5	The Colonial Jews	44
Chapter 6	The Protestants and the Mid-Atlantic	53
	1. Dutch Reformed	54

2. German Reformed 57

3. German Lutherans 58

4. Swedish Lutherans 60

5. Presbyterians 63

6. Friends 70

7. Mennonites 75

8. Dunkards 76

9. Seventh Day German Baptists 77

10. Baptists 77

11. Moravians 78

12. Methodists 82

13. Shakers 85

14. Anglicans 87

Chapter 7   Brick 91

Chapter 8   Wood 99

Chapter 9   Stone 105

Chapter 10   Their Names 110

State Summaries, State Maps, Photographs, Accounts (Each building identified by a serial number on map, photograph, references in text, and list Appendix I) 113

Connecticut	Serial Nos.	1-12	114-129
Delaware		13-27	130-143
Georgia		28-30	144-148
Maine		31-37	149-157
Maryland		38-86	158-201
Massachusetts		87-113	202-237
New Hampshire		114-130	238-258
New Jersey		131-167	259-291
New York		168-197	292-325
North Carolina		198-201	326-332
Pennsylvania		202-259	333-399
Rhode Island		260-273	400-419

			Page
South Carolina	274-290		420-442
Vermont	291-292		443-445
Virginia	293-344		446-524
West Virginia	345		525-526

Appendix I   Buildings in Order of Date
                by Name, Location, Serial Number, Original
                Denomination, and Material 529

Appendix II   Summary of Buildings
                by Denomination and Region 536

Appendix II A   Summary of Buildings in the South
                by Denomination and State 536

Appendix II B   Summary of Buildings in New England
                by Denomination and State 537

Appendix II C   Summary of Buildings in Mid-Atlantic
                by Denomination and State 537

Appendix III   Summary of Buildings
                by Material, Region, State 538

Appendix IV   British Sovereigns and
                American Colonial History 539

Appendix V   Some Firsts Among
                Colonial Houses of Worship 540

Bibliography 543

Index 551

ACKNOWLEDGEMENTS

Friends and strangers alike have undertaken with enthusiasm to help in the search for these colonial houses of worship during the thirty years of the project. Ministers and members of the active parishes have responded well in looking up records and providing information, even though some of the more famous churches receive many such inquiries, and their patience and assistance is appreciated. The historical societies have been an important source; when it has not been possible for me to do some research in person, they have been accommodating in looking up information and copying it for me, even though their staffs are limited in number. Also the libraries of towns, cities, states, the Federal Government, colleges, seminaries, and church denominations, have been consulted widely and have been helpful both on visits and by correspondence.

Some errors of dates and data probably are perpetuated here, but the true picture presented by these parishes does not depend on accuracy of detail. While I was a trustee of the Philadelphia Museum of Art, we had an exhibition of over four hundred works of art by Henri Matisse. He sent four drawings of himself, all different but obviously the same person, to illustrate his point that "exactitude is not truth." One of the difficult features of research in this field arises from local pride. It is human nature to want to be connected with the best, the first, the only, or the oldest, and claims for the old churches sometimes reflect stronger motives of that kind than desire for historical accuracy. It has not been practical for me to search original records in all cases; it has already been done thoroughly in many cases, and in some the records no longer exist (see Bibliography and the note on documentation). I have had to reconcile conflicting claims in the published evidence and among various accounts; in some cases it has been possible to resolve conflicts, and in a few to correct errors and mistaken claims. For those interested in "firsts," Appendix V lists some of them compiled from this complete work. With the buildings listed in chronological order and by denomination and material, in Appendix I, it is easy to see at a glance which were first in various categories.

The American Guide Series, covering all the states, the Federal Writers Project of the Works Progress Administration, was a "good," blown by the wind of the depression. It was a source for locating many of the buildings, and while the books omitted a number of those in this collection and they contain some errors, by the Matisse criterion they still present a true picture of America, and they make fascinating reading. Among the books listed in the Bibliography, a number of the authors were consulted and their helpful responses are appreciated.

Only once was a request for information refused. That was by a man in a New England village, who was referred by the church in question as the town historian. He considered local history to be private domain, and he refused to part with any more information, on the ground that in the past it had been published without his name. I only wish it were practical to acknowledge by name all the people to whom I am grateful for their help in this work. Special thanks go to the following:

Baltimore Yearly Meeting of Friends; Berkshire Athenaeum, Pittsfield, Mass.; The Rev. George MacLaren Brydon, D.D., Historiographer of the Diocese of Virginia; Brooklyn Town Library Association, Brooklyn, Conn.; Samuel J. Bunting, Jr., Philadelphia, Pa.; Carolina Art Association, Charleston, S. C.; Carroll County Historical Society, Md.; The Century Association, Library, New York, N. Y.; Church Historical Society (Episcopal), Philadelphia, Pa.; Dropsie College, Philadelphia, Pa. (Sephardic Jews); Episcopal Divinity School, Library, Philadelphia, Pa.; Essex Institute, Salem, Mass.; Miss Adelaide Friese, Archivist, Moravian Church in America, Winston-Salem, N. C.; Friends Historical Association, Dr. Frederick B. Tolles, President, Swarthmore, Pa.; Friends Historical Library, Swarthmore College, Swarthmore, Pa.; Germantown Historical Society, Germantown, Pa.; Hamilton Library, Carlisle, Pa.; The Historical Societies of Connecticut, Maine, Maryland, Massachusetts, New Hampshire, New Jersey, New York, Pennsylvania, Rhode Island, South Carolina, Vermont, and Virginia; Historical Society of Berks County, Reading, Pa.; Jamestown Historical Society, Jamestown, R. I.; Lenox Library, Lenox, Mass.; Library of Congress, Washington, D. C.; Longmeadow Historical Society, Longmeadow, Mass.; Lutheran Seminary Library, Germantown, Pa.; Mason Library, Great Barrington, Mass.; The Rev. Arthur Pierce Middleton, Ph. D. in Colonial History, Rector of St. James' Parish, Great Barrington, Mass.; Richmond P. Miller, Philadelphia Yearly Meeting of Friends; New Hampshire State Library, Concord, N. H.; New Jersey Department of Education, Trenton, N. J.; Newport Historical Society, Newport, R. I.; New York Yearly Meeting of Friends; Old Colony Historical Society, Taunton, Mass.; Old Fort Niagara Association, Youngstown, N. Y.; Philadelphia Bibliographical Center and Union Library Catalogue; Philadelphia Fellowship Commission Library; Pennsylvania Historical and Museum Commission, Harrisburg, Pa.; Presbyterian Historical Society, Library, Philadelphia, Pa.; Salem Historical Society, Salem, N. H.; Schoharie County Historical Society, Schoharie, N. Y.; Society for the Preservation of New England Antiquities, Boston, Mass.; Samuel G. Stoney, Charleston, S. C.; Tucker Library, Henniker, N. H.; United States Department of the Interior, National Park Service, Historical Buildings Survey; Virginia State Commission on Conservation and Development; Virginia State Library, Historical Division, Richmond, Va.; Yale University Library, James T. Babb, University Librarian, and staff.

To my wife, Elizabeth Leeming Rose, I am particularly grateful for sharing the photographing expeditions, inspiring my work, with understanding and patience guarding my isolation in the library, and giving constructive criticism on the manuscript.

H. W. R.

INTRODUCTION

Early in 1946, soon after World War II, I had occasion to travel widely in Japan, as a member of the Textile Mission. After they had learned that the Occupation was benevolent, two attitudes of the Japanese people were found to be quite prevalent: first, they rejoiced at their liberation from the military clique, who had seized the government, brought on the war, and at the end had tried to carry the nation to complete destruction; second, they sought to learn how such a tragic mistake could be avoided in the future. The same question in many forms was asked me, as it was of many members of the Occupation: "What are democracy and Christianity?" "What does our country lack, that such a terrible mistake could be made?" "What is the spirit in you which has prevailed?" In their question, it is interesting that they consistently coupled Christianity and democracy, assuming that the two had an affinity.

It was a sobering experience. I returned with determination to learn more about our country — what we are, and why we are what we are. I was learning that if one wants to understand Christianity and democracy, one should try giving them to others. In 1943, during a very dark time in World War II, in his book *Education for a World Adrift,* Sir Richard Livingstone set forth a vivid contrast between the integrity of science and the wasteland of shaken beliefs and shattered standards in the realm of morals and religion. Two years later, scientists achieved the release of atomic energy, and although it was instrumental in bringing World War II to an end, mankind entered the atomic age of anxiety. The disintegration of standards continued, the Korean War was fought, and the Cold War was impinged upon the world with the implication that it is to be a permanent way of life. Under these conditions, there has been much evidence of a spiritual revival, as people through faith seek to find stability in "a world adrift." They have been trying to get their roots down, or to discover where they are rooted.

When I returned from Japan, with the sobering questions of the Japanese still in mind, I began to find the nature of our democracy unfolding in the histories of the colonial settlements and their parishes. To my surprise I found that my image of the American Republic was distorted by inadequate knowledge, some false assumptions, and a few legends. (I was reminded of the remark to the effect that history is the recording of the misconceptions fashionable at the time.) Great diversity was found among the various colonies and colonists, forming a complex web of races, nationalities, religion, denominations, political backgrounds, and social patterns. In all this heterogeneous society, what was the source of the nation's strength? What had made this a land of promise for the peoples of Europe, many of whom had been driven from their land? What has been the spirit in us which has prevailed?

I had started photographing colonial churches in 1935. Of the first three churches photographed, two were found not to be colonial, much to my surprise. The third, the meeting house in Dedham, Massachusetts (built in 1762, No. 101 in the collection) not only was colonial, but the print was awarded second prize in a salon of 300 at New York, with Edward Steichen heading the committee of judges, and it appeared in *U. S. Camera: 1936*. At that stage I found myself bitten by the question, "What is a colonial church?" There was no one source for the answer; the research and the photographing expeditions took me farther and farther afield, until I had covered all the British colonies. The first book in my library on the subject had been given to me "For Second of the Fifth Form, St. Albans School, June 7, 1915." It is *Early American Churches*, by Aymar Embury II, 1914. Now, many books, many miles, and many years later, this present book is my answer to the compelling question.

The restoration of Williamsburg, the colonial capital of Virginia, has made it a living page of history, which is visited with delight by thousands every year. The restoration there not only included the Bruton Parish Church in Williamsburg, but it inspired the restoration of the Wren Chapel at the College of William and Mary; St. Peter's Church, New Kent; and the Old Brick Church, Isle of Wight; all of which are in this collection. A number of other colonial houses of worship have been restored to their colonial design, after alterations had been made, and there is growing appreciation of these historical buildings and the importance of preserving them. Like Williamsburg, they are all pages of the nation's colonial history, and they form an open book to be seen and enjoyed. A by-product of my photographing expeditions has been that they took me off the highways into byways and back country, which otherwise I would never have seen. Every one who visits Charleston knows St. Michael's and most of those who drive there know Goose Creek Church, for it is near a highway, but one must have the definite objective to find the way through the semitropical forest and winding sand roads to Strawberry Chapel and Pompion Hill Chapel.

The work involved has been absorbing, and it has been an education as well as a delight for me. I hope that this presentation may inspire others to discover for themselves the fascinating stories in our heritage. In his *Civilization on Trial* (1948), Arnold J. Toynbee makes it evident that history itself is ecumenical, and not parochial; and he gives one the breadth of view which enables one to sense history's all-embracing flow, broader than the current or eddy of the country in which one happens to have been born. In the course of research to discover what common line of inheritance comes to us through the colonial parishes, one principle was found to have persisted from ages before the time of Christ. The principle of "the one in many" was central to the philosophy of Plato. Aristotle, who spent twenty years with Plato, impressed it on his young pupil, Alexander. In the course of conquering all of the civilized world that he could reach, and in his capacity as a demigod, Alexander sought to unify the world of diverse nations and peoples under one emperor-god. The Greek and then the Roman civilizations went a long way toward establishing one in the many, and the civilization of both was ecumenical. Judaism was an expression of the principle in Palestine, in captivity, and in Diaspora. When the Roman Empire adopted Christianity as the official religion, the one Church and one emperor embraced the many. With the crowning of Charlemagne by Pope Leo III in St. Peter's at Rome on Christmas Day, 800 A. D., the Holy Roman Empire embraced many kingdoms, principalities, and peoples of Western Europe in all their diversity. That empire endured in name until the time of Napoleon, who officially abolished it in order to replace it with his own union of Europe — his personal dream of the one in many. Meanwhile, amidst the splintering of the empire into many European nations, and of the one Church into many Protestant denominations and sects, the English colonies in America were born, and the Republic was founded.

The principle of the one in many did not come to an end with the founding of the United States, and it still lives also in the United Nations. The new Republic adopted the principle "E Pluribus Unum" as a motto. This confederation of states embraced under one government all the diverse colonial elements, but it differed fundamentally from the governments from which those elements had been derived — Church and State were clearly separated. Freedom of worship replaced conformation, and this became the world's first republic to be founded on that principle. Although there has been a general misconception to the contrary, the accounts here reveal that the colonies were *not* all settled for freedom of worship, and that it took the entire colonial period to develop the principle among the varied colonists to the point where it could be incorporated in the Constitution. In this new Republic there has been room for all faiths, religions, denominations, sects, and tastes, and in all this diversity there has been strength. Freedom is a principle of the spirit, and in all this history of man's activity that led to the founding of the colonies, religion — the realm of the spirit — was man's principal concern.

These colonial houses of worship reveal that the colonies were a product of the Reformation. The Reformation is still with us, and the splintering of the Church has kept Christians separated for half a millenium. The United States has proved, however, that people in all their diversity can be united in spirit. In 1962, Pope John XXIII convened the Vatican Council for the purpose of bringing closer in Christian brotherhood the separated Christians of the world. It can be done without reuniting them under a new Holy Roman Empire, and without destroying the diversity in Christianity. It is possible to attain the goal, if Christians learn the lessons of history and permit the strength in freedom to prevail in Christendom. An ecumenical Christian brotherhood can give strength in the complex life of the world through a true sense of the brotherhood of mankind, and to the extent that progress is made in that direction, the atomic age of anxiety will give way to the ecumenical age of understanding.

H. W. R.
"Meadowood"
Great Barrington, Mass.

1

THE COLONIAL HOUSES OF WORSHIP

1. The British Colonies in America

The Republic of the United States of America was founded by a confederation of states that had been colonies of Great Britain, after they had developed through the colonization efforts of three countries — England, Holland, and Sweden. The English began the colonization in Virginia and continued it in New England; the Dutch colonized in New York, New Jersey, and Delaware; and the Swedes colonized in Delaware, West Jersey, and up the Delaware River to the area of Philadelphia. Into these colonies also came groups of people as settlers from various other parts of Western Europe, including Scotland, Northern Ireland, Wales, France, Switzerland, Moravia, Austria, and Germany. Among all this variety of peoples there was one strong motivating force in common — they were Protestants. Even the French who settled in these colonies were Huguenots — French Protestants. The settling of these colonies was a Protestant phenomenon. This colonization was a result of the Reformation on the continent of Europe and in England, and it was not allowed to begin until the forces in that struggle had passed a climax in the Battle of the Armada.

Colonization on the Atlantic coast of North America did not begin until after the close of the sixteenth century. In that century there developed the culmination of the forces of the Renaissance, the age of exploration and discovery, the Reformation, and the rise of nationalism. In that order the movements took place and had a part in the founding of the United States. The four interrelated movements respectively represent learning, trade, religion, and government; and the four are inseparable in the history of Europe and America.

In the early part of the fifteenth century, Portugal opened the great age of exploration, and Spain brought it to a dramatic peak in 1492, with the discovery of the

New World. Spain then proceeded to colonize the West Indies, Central America, and Peru, and the Portuguese colonized Brazil. Upon each new discovery the land was claimed in the names of the Roman Catholic Church and the sovereign of the country. The Pope was the world authority who awarded the territories so claimed, and settled lines of demarcation in the Atlantic Ocean between the zones of Spanish and Portuguese dominion. From the moment that Christopher Columbus first set foot on an island of the West Indies, the colonial history of America was involved with the history of religion. In 1500, at the dawn of colonization in the Western Hemisphere, the Holy Roman Empire held together various kingdoms and principalities of Europe within one empire and one church under one Pope. But the empire was waning, and in 1600, when Protestants were about to begin colonizing in North America, independent nations were replacing it.

During that century while the Spanish were colonizing the West Indies and Central and South America, efforts were made by Protestants to settle on the Atlantic Coast of North America, but they were unsuccessful. The first effort was made by Huguenots, who sought a refuge from persecution in Roman Catholic France. In 1562, under Jean Ribaut, their expedition crossed the Atlantic to a site near the present Beaufort, South Carolina, and there they built Fort Charles at Port Royal Harbor, now Port Royal Island. After two years of hardships and no supplies from France, the survivors abandoned the settlement and returned to their home country. In 1564 another company of Huguenots under the same direction tried again, this time at the mouth of the St. John's River in Florida. There they built Fort Caroline, but a year after their arrival they came into conflict with the Spanish. In 1565, Don Pedro Menendez de Aviles landed with a company of Spaniards and started the settlement of St. Augustine. Within a few months, he headed an expedition north thirty-five miles to the St. John, where he conquered Fort Caroline and put the inhabitants to the sword. Ribaut, who had returned from France to visit the settlement at this tragic moment, was lured ashore by false promises of safety, and he and his companions were killed. Spain and France were not at war, but Menendez accounted for his action by having a monument erected with the inscription, "I do not do this as to Frenchmen, but as to Lutherans." There in a few words was the situation involving the settlement of North America. In France only five years later, in 1572, French Catholics slaughtered an estimated 50,000 Huguenots in the massacre of St. Bartholomew. The persecution of Huguenots in France a century later, particularly after the Revocation of the Edict of Nantes in 1685, caused many of them to emigrate to South Carolina, then an English colony, where they settled successfully (see Pompion Hill Chapel, No. 276). In South Carolina all of the Huguenot churches, except the one in Charleston, merged with the Church of England during the colonial period. (The Huguenot Church in Charleston is not a colonial building and is not in this collection.)

Another unsuccessful attempt to colonize on the Atlantic Coast was made by English Protestants. The colony at Roanoke Island, on the coast of North Carolina, was sent out in 1584 by Sir Walter Raleigh, under a patent for colonization granted to him by Queen Elizabeth I. In 1591, when an English ship returned to the island, there was no trace of the inhabitants, except the name "Croatan" carved on a tree. Other evidence also indicates that the surviving settlers were absorbed by the local Indian tribe of that name.

Around the territory that became the British colonies, from Florida and the Gulf of Mexico to the St. Lawrence River, the Roman Catholics of Spain and France staked their claims. Spaniards from the West Indies and Mexico established missions and settlements from Florida westward across the Gulf Coast and up into California. Frenchmen explored and discovered territory from the Gulf up the Mississippi, and from the Atlantic up the St. Lawrence. By right of discovery, the French claimed all the territory drained by the two great rivers and the Great Lakes, and they proceeded to establish Roman Catholic missions, forts, and settlements from New Orleans to Quebec. Pressure by the Spanish and the French was maintained on the southern, western, and northern frontiers of the British colonies during the colonial period, and it was a major factor in their development. The French and Indian War was an expression of it; and Georgia, the last of the British colonies to be chartered, was established as a buffer against the Spanish and the French on the south and southwest. Old Fort Niagara, at the northwestern tip of New York, on Lake Ontario, was built by the French as one in a chain of strongholds through their dominion of New France. In the French Castle there, the Jesuit Chapel is the only French colonial house of worship that survives within these British colonies (see No. 197). The Spanish colonial missions and churches were all outside the British colonies. English Roman Catholics in Maryland developed quite a different story in colonial history, which is outlined in Chapter III.

Colonization in America by Protestants depended upon the outcome of the long rivalry between Philip II, the devout Catholic King of Spain, and the determined Protestant Queen of England, Elizabeth I. That rivalry resulted from the new situation of the Church of England, after Henry VIII had broken with the Pope over his divorce of Catherine of Aragon. The Church of England had become independent of Rome, and the English sovereign had become its head. The complex relationship between Spain and England was one of international power politics, involving marriage and intermarriage in the royal families of the two countries. The family saga, in which colonization in North America was determined, is briefly outlined as follows:

Ferdinand V (1452-1516) and Isabella (1451-1504), "the Catholic," who were cousins, married and thereby united the thrones of Castile and Leon and Aragon, preparing the way for the unification of Spain. In 1492, Isabella raised the curtain on the America story by sponsoring the voyage of Columbus. At the same time the sovereigns reconquered Granada, the last remaining Moorish kingdom in Spain, and Isabella lowered the curtain on the Jews in Spain and Portugal (see Chapter 5), by dispersing them as well as the Moors; and the Inquisition was instituted to convert or eliminate all heretics among their subjects. To extend their political power, their daughter, Catherine of Aragon, became the first wife of Henry VIII of England.

Charles (1500-1558) was a grandson of Ferdinand and Isabella, and a nephew of Catherine. He married his first cousin, Isabella of Portugal. He was Charles V as the Emperor of the Holy Roman Empire and Charles I as King of Spain. He inherited from his father the Netherlands, which won independence from his son and played an important part in the history of Protestantism and the founding of the United States. While they were both in the Netherlands, Charles, with the hope of using England to improve his relations with France and Germany, arranged the marriage between his son, Philip II, and Mary Tudor of England. Charles himself had been betrothed to Mary when she was a girl of nine years. She was the daughter of Henry VIII and Catherine of Aragon and so was the cousin of Charles and the cousin once removed of Philip. Mary was the seventh child of the union of Henry and Catherine and the only one to live. Of the previous six, two were males who would have been princes had they lived. Because she did not produce a male heir for the throne, Henry divorced Catherine and was excommunicated, whereupon Henry had himself made juridicial head of the Church of England through the Act of Supremacy, in 1534.

During her reign Mary I tried to restore the Roman Catholic Church and the power of the Pope in England. Through her persecution of Protestants as heretics, nearly three hundred of whom were burned, she became known as "Bloody Mary." The persecutions drove many English Protestants to the Continent, particularly to Geneva, where they became attracted to Calvinism; and this contact with the "new religion" was to have a profound effect on the history of religion in England and America. In line with his father's original purpose in the marriage alliance, Philip persuaded his wife to wage war on France, but the result was the loss of Calais by England. When Mary died a few months later, she was childless and Philip had abandoned her.

Mary was succeeded by her half sister, Elizabeth I, the daughter of Henry and his second wife, Anne Boleyn. Elizabeth immediately undertook a policy of an independent England, and she restored the Church of England to its independent Protestant status. Her action was confirmed by a papal bull that excommunicated her and her Church. The Geneva exiles returned to England and developed the puritan party within the Church, seeking to free it from all its Roman features, and there was general relief at the ending of the persecutions.

Philip was anxious to regain England for Spain's zone of influence. Spain was at her height of world power, having recently conquered Portugal and defeated the French at the Azores; but Protestantism was growing in the Netherlands and it had returned to England, and Philip had Isabella's fanatical zeal for forcing conformity to the Roman Church. As a crusader he began organizing for an invasion of England. There was a plot to murder Queen Elizabeth. The English Catholics were to rise and proclaim Mary Stuart (Queen of Scots) as queen. Roman Catholicism and papal power would be restored. Persisting in the original policy of his father, it was Philip's expectation that Mary, being half French and a devout Roman Catholic, would improve his relations with France; stem the rise of Protestantism in the Netherlands, which Elizabeth was aiding; and improve his relations also with Germany, where his father had been Emperor, but where the Reformation was growing.

Elizabeth got wind of the plot against her. In 1587, the year before the Armada sailed against England, she permitted Mary Stuart to be executed, on the charge of participating in Roman Catholic plots against her. She alerted three naval men on Spain's plan for invasion — Francis Drake, John Hawkins, and Martin Frobisher. They had gained years of experience in fighting the Spanish at sea, in the West Indies and elsewhere, and they knew how to design and to sail ships that would outmaneuver the large and unwieldy Spanish galleons.

In 1588 the rivalry between Philip and Elizabeth came to a climax in the Battle of the Armada. The Spanish fleet was decisively defeated in the mouth of the Channel between England and France. As a result, England continued as a Protestant stronghold, as did the Netherlands and Germany. Spain declined as a world power thereafter, but Philip continued intermittently to plot invasion against Elizabeth for the remaining ten years of his life. In his dedicated faith, he was blind to the decline in the power of the Roman Church to hold the peoples of Europe together as one holy empire, and he failed to see that the Renaissance and the Reformation had stimulated the rise of nationalism. It was an irony that a few months before he died at the Escorial, in 1598, the Edict of Nantes was proclaimed, giving religious liberty to the Huguenots, the Protestant subjects of the French King, Henry IV.

Still the wilderness of the American coastal region had to await the dawn of colonization. It was not until after both of the antagonists had died — Elizabeth five years after Philip, in 1603 — that Spain would permit Protestants to settle in North America. When James VI of Scotland, the son of Mary Stuart, Queen of Scots, succeeded Elizabeth as James I of Great Britain and Ireland, he immediately appointed a commission to negotiate a treaty of peace, amity, and commerce with Spain. (See Davenport, *European Treaties Bearing on the History of the United States and its Dependencies to 1648*, vol. I) It was the intention of James to gain the right for Englishmen to trade and settle in Spanish dominions; he authorized one concession only, that they would not settle where Spaniards were planted. He signed the treaty in 1604, and the King of Spain signed it in 1605. The only reference to religion provides that English traders in the Spanish dominions should not be molested "for cause of conscience . . . so that they give not scandal unto others." The delicate question of permitting Protestants to settle in Spanish dominions was not mentioned in the treaty itself. After much negotiation on the question, it was left to the interpretation of both parties, in the light of existing treaties and their precedents. The interpretation of King James was reflected in the grants that were made for the settlement of Virginia — to the Plymouth Company for North Virginia and to the Virginia Company of London for South Virginia. Full rights were granted for settlement of territory "not actually possessed by any Christian prince or people." Spain did not like this invasion of North America, but on the one hand she was by then too weak to resist, and on the other she was far more interested in colonizing to the south of the continent, where gold had been found in the old civilizations.

In 1606 the Virginia Company of London dispatched its first expedition to establish a colony in Virginia, under the command of Captain John Smith. Three vessels made the voyage, the *Susan Constant,* the *God Speed,* and the pinnace *Discovery.* After a storm had blown them to the West Indies, in May of 1607 they landed on a point which they named Cape Henry. Then they sailed up the Powahatan River, which they called the James, and on a marshy island near the north shore they made a settlement and named it James Town, in honor of the King. This was the first permanent settlement of Protestants in America (see the Brick Church, Jamestown, No. 293).

Within the territory that they covered, the present work intends to include all the houses of worship that were built in the colonies during the colonial period and still stand. The western boundaries of the colonies were vague and unknown. The original charters for Virginia and Carolina were granted for provinces extending westward to the "Southern Sea." Many houses of worship were built, before the Republic was founded, in what are now Tennessee, West Virginia, Kentucky, and Ohio. Few of them were of lasting materials, however, and it is not surprising that in nearly every case these pioneer structures either did not endure or were replaced. The building in this collection farthest to the west is the Rehoboth Church in Monroe County, West Virginia. It is a plain log cabin built by Methodists among the hills far from any town. For many years it has been protected from the weather by a tin shed which stands above the entire structure (see No. 345).

2. The Colonial Period

It would seem to be an easy matter to define the colonial period, but the term is used in a number of different senses. It is used quite generally to mean a period of architecture or of furniture, and such usage has led to "colonial" becoming a style as well as a period of time.

Historians, architects, and antiquarians have divided the country's history variously into periods, such as the Colonial, the Post-Colonial, the Federal, and the Republic. For defining the colonial houses of worship, we find it appropriate to recognize only two periods, the Colonial and the Republic; it remains only to decide the dividing date. Regardless of what date we choose, there are many interesting houses of worship that were built immediately thereafter, which constitute a temptation to extend the dividing date in order to include them (we succumbed in the cases of two buildings and included them as special exceptions, as noted at the end of Appendix I).

The question now is, when did our colonial period end? Was it with the Declaration of Independence in 1776, or with the beginning of the Revolution? Was it with the end of the Revolution, marked by the capitulation of General Cornwallis in 1781, or the Treaty of Peace with Great Britain, which was ratified in 1783? It might have ended with the Ordinance of July, 1787, which was the foundation of the American system of state and territorial government. Again, it could be considered to have ended in September of the same year, when the Constitutional Convention adjourned, after drafting the constitution that was offered to the states; or it might have been in 1788, when the Constitution was ratified by the ninth state, New Hampshire.

Rather than on any of these dates, each of which marked a decisive step in the transition from colonial status to the confederation of states and the Republic, we will assume simply that the colonial period ended when the Republic began. George Washington was inaugurated as the first President of the United States in 1789. For the purposes of this collection, therefore, any house of worship begun in or before 1789 is considered to be colonial. There was no change in church architecture between 1776 and 1789 to affect this selection of date. The next change in church architecture was the Classic Revival, which took place after 1789. That style was used extensively during the first half of the nineteenth century, in building new churches and in remodeling colonial churches and meeting houses. It accounts for the many white pillared porticos seen in this collection, particularly among the New England buildings, which commonly are mistaken for colonial.

Next comes the question of how the buildings are dated. Wherever it is known, the year in which construction began is the date assigned to the building. The problem of the Julian and the Gregorian calendars frequently arises, and often it is not clear which style is used in a record or publication. If the date used here is one year off of that given elsewhere, the difference might be accounted for by the old and new styles. In many cases, dated cornerstones give the year in which construction began. For many of the New England frame meeting houses, the date of the raising of the frame identifies the beginning of the construction; there are cases, however, in which the drawing and hewing of timbers began in the autumn, and the raising did not take place until the spring of the following year, and in such cases the earlier date is used. The dates of completion of colonial houses of worship were quite variable, in some cases many years or even decades after the beginning of construction. In common practice the date of completion is used to identify buildings, but here it is used only if the beginning date is not known, or as additional information. "Finishing" a building usually meant not "completion," but flooring, pewing, trimming, plastering, and furnishing. As many of the houses of worship were used for services before they were finished, the finishing date here usually is given only as additional information. Many buildings had towers and spires added later; they are treated here as alterations rather than completions — some that had towers were never completed with spires, as in the case of King's Chapel, Boston (No. 95). A date in a brick wall might mean that the brickwork was completed at that time; the date is used here for identification only if it is known that the building was begun in the same year, otherwise as additional information. Churches often are given the date of dedication for identification; but dedication was not practised by all denominations, nor consistently by any, during the colonial period. An Anglican church cannot be consecrated, given to God, until it is free of debt and in position to be given, and then it must be consecrated by a bishop; but as there was no bishop in America during the colonial period, and consecration took place only after the Revolution, consecration is of value only for its historical interest.

3. Types of Houses of Worship

Among the colonial houses of worship in this collection, there are churches, chapels, meeting houses, manor houses, Mass houses, halls, cloisters, and a synagogue.

There are Anglican churches and chapels. The parish church frequently was supplemented by chapels of ease, for the convenience of parishioners in remote parts of the parish.

The Methodists began as a sect within the Church of England. They built chapels for their separate worship, while they continued for years to take Communion in Anglican churches. After the Methodist Church had become an independent denomination, some of their chapels became known as churches, but not all of them.

Roman Catholics were not allowed by the Maryland charter, under the laws of England and its Established Church, to build and own public houses of worship, but they were permitted to worship in private as they wished. Their early houses of worship in Maryland and Pennsylvania, therefore, were private chapels at residences. Some were in the homes of lay people and others in residences of the priesthood. Where priests owned a manor, the chapel originally was in the manor house; if a priest owned a more modest farm house, it was called the priest's house, or Mass house. As the principle of religious freedom became established, the right for Roman Catholics to build houses for public worship was recognized, and such chapels appeared during the late colonial period in Maryland and Pennsylvania.

Lutheran congregations, both German and Swedish, built churches, as did the Reformed congregations, both Dutch and German. In Frederick, Maryland, there is a Reformed church which was retained as a chapel to serve the new parish church (see Trinity Chapel, No. 65).

The Pilgrims and Puritans in New England built meeting houses. Congregationalism became established as the official religion in New England, except in Rhode Island, and the meeting house accommodated both town and religious meetings. The Town was one organized body, and the Church Society was another. When the Society built an independent house of worship, it generally became the Congregational church, and the old meeting house became the town house. In this collection we find examples of all three — meeting houses, churches, and town houses (or town halls).

Presbyterians built both meeting houses and churches in the colonial period.

The Baptists originally built meeting houses. Only in later years did their houses of worship become known as churches.

In Germantown, Pennsylvania, the Mennonites built a meeting house that still stands (No. 213), while in the same neighborhood the Church of the Brethren (Dunkard) built a church (No. 214).

Friends have always called their house of worship the meeting house. Their organization is the meeting. Meetings for worship usually originated in private homes and were held there until a meeting house could be built. In the meeting house, meetings for worship and business meetings are held.

There are three cloistered communities represented in the collection. The Moravian Community at Bethlehem, Pennsylvania, built first a *Gemeinhaus*, or "common house." Later they built a chapel attached to it (No. 244), and still later a church was built across the street. At Bethabara, North Carolina, which was a settlement but not a cloister, the Moravians built a church (No. 201). At Ephrata, Pennsylvania, there is the Cloister, which was built by a new sect of Seventh Day German Baptists (No. 248). The Sister House (on the left in the photograph) was used by the sisters for prayers during the night hours. Attached to it is the Saal, a multi-floored building in which the large hall on the ground floor was used for community meetings and worship. The third cloistered community was at Mount Lebanon, New York, where we find a colonial Shaker meeting house (No. 189). In this multi-floored building, as in that at Ephrata, the large hall on the ground floor was used for worship.

The one Jewish house of worship is the Touro Synagogue in Newport, Rhode Island (No. 271). It was built by a community of Sephardic Jews, Congregation Jeshuat Israel (see Chapter 5).

4. Regional Distribution

The colonial houses of worship are grouped in three different regions — the South, New England, and the Mid-Atlantic. In each region of the three, a different polity, or form of government, predominated among the religious organizations that built these houses of worship. In each region also a different building material predominated.

Maryland is included in the South and Delaware in the Mid-Atlantic. The boundary between Maryland and Pennsylvania was in dispute for many years between the Lords Baltimore and the Penns. The dispute began when Pennsylvania was granted to William Penn in 1681, and it was not settled until after the Mason and Dixon Line had been surveyed between 1763 and 1767. Delaware was in the disputed territory, and it was set off as a separate state, on a boundary with Maryland which was surveyed by the same two English astronomers.

In the South, Episcopalianism predominated. The Church of England was brought to Virginia by the first settlers at Jamestown. There it was the Established Church, as it was in England, and it became established in the same sense in each of the other colonies in the South — South Carolina, North Carolina, Maryland, and Georgia. Of the 345 colonial houses of worship in this collection, 126 are in the South. Of that number, 53 were in Virginia (1 of them is now in West Virginia), 49 in Maryland, 17 in South Carolina, 4 in North Carolina, and 3 in Georgia. The 126 buildings in the South were built by 11 different denominations. Anglicans built 95 of the total. The next largest number was 8, built by Friends. In the South the vast majority of the houses of worship in this collection were built of brick, 100 of the total 126. (See Appendices II and III for details.)

In New England, the second region where colonization began, Congregationalism predominated. It was the religion established by law, known as the "Established Order," in all the New England colonies except Rhode Island. Of the 345 houses of worship in this collection, 79 are in New England, the smallest total of the three regions. Of that number, 50 were built by Congregationalists, 10 by Anglicans, and 9 by Friends. The vast majority of these buildings were built of wood, 72 out of the 79.

The Mid-Atlantic was the third region to be colonized. Although it includes only four states — New York, New Jersey, Pennsylvania, and Delaware — it contains more houses of worship than either of the other two regions, 140 of the 345. The largest number in any one state is 58 in Pennsylvania, while New Jersey with 37 and New York with 30, each have more than any New England state. In this region there is also the largest number of denominations that built the houses of worship, 15 of the total 20 in the collection. We find that while Episcopalianism was established and prevalent in the South, and Congregationalism was established and prevalent in New England, no one polity was established in the Mid-Atlantic, though Presbyterianism was prevalent. The largest number of the houses of worship in this collection were built by Friends, 56 of the 140. While Friends controlled the government of Pennsylvania in the time of William Penn, as they did for a time in New Jersey and Rhode Island, they did not make Quakerism the official religion by law. Anglicans built 25 of the 140, and Presbyterians 23. The polity of the Reformed churches, both Dutch and German, was Presbyterian, and the 8 Reformed churches in the Mid-Atlantic should be added to the 23, giving a total of 31 with Presbyterian polity, the number second largest to that of the Friends. As to the polity of the Society of Friends, it was democratic, with a system of subordinated meetings similar in some respects to Presbyterian organization. It might be said then, without dogmatic implications, that Presbyterianism was the outstanding polity in the Mid-Atlantic region. As for building material in that region, almost half of the houses of worship, 69 of 140, were built of stone.

To summarize, and to put it another way, we find in the three regions the following situation among the colonial houses of worship. In the South, where the Church of England was established by the Crown, the polity was Episcopalian and royal. In New England, where Congregationalism prevailed in dissent and separation from the Church of England, the polity was democratic. Between the two, in the Mid-Atlantic region, where Presbyterianism was widespread and influential, the polity was representative, or republican.

In the following chapters, each of these categories will be outlined. It was not by coincidence that the denominations were so grouped in these three regions, but by the character of the colonization. We find also that the principal material used in each region was determined by the geology, geography, and climate, while the building styles were determined by the denominations.

All through these accounts will be found origins of colleges. In the colonial days colleges were founded to educate preachers, and preachers kept bright the lamp of learning, as did the clergy during the Middle Ages. Again in each of the three regions we find that colleges originated within each of the three ecclesiastical polities.

The earliest example in the South is the College of William and Mary at Williamsburg (see the Wren Chapel, No. 295). It was founded in 1693, the second oldest in the colonies, by a royal charter from King William III and Queen Mary II, as an Anglican seminary in the colonies. The presidents of the College were priests of the Church of England, and eight of them have been rectors of Bruton Parish Church (No. 294). The Archbishop of Canterbury and the Bishop of London alternated as chancellors of the College, and the members of the faculty also were Anglican priests. English and Indian youths were taught, and it was hoped that Indians would enter the ministry, but there is no record that any did so.

In New England, Harvard College was founded in 1636, the first in the colonies, by an appropriation of the General Court of the Puritan colony. John Harvard (1607-1638) was a Puritan minister recently arrived from Emmanuel College, Cambridge, England, who bequeathed half of his modest estate and 300 books to the new College (see Holden Chapel, No. 97). On the gates to Harvard Yard are carried the words from a letter of the times, expressing the intentions of the founders: "After God had carried us safe to New England, and wee had builded our houses, provided necessaries for our liveli-hood, rear'd convenient places for Gods worship, and setled the Civill Government; One of the next things we longed for, and looked after was to advance *Learning*, and perpetuate it to Posterity; dreading to leave an illiterate Ministry to the Churches, when our present Ministers shall lie in the Dust." The charter gives as the purpose of the College "the advancement of all good literature, arts, and sciences," and "the education of the English and Indian youth . . . in knowledge and goodlynes." The College began under the control of the clergy, and among these colonial parishes in New England we find that many graduates of Harvard served as ministers. Unitarianism, which brought about a revolution in the Congregational parishes of the New England region in the early nineteenth century, originated at Harvard, with considerable encouragement from the pastor of the Old Ship Meeting House at Hingham (No. 87).

Yale College was founded by ten Congregational clergymen, all graduates of Harvard, who were conservative and leaned more toward Presbyterianism than the liberal and radical Congregationalism developing at Harvard. The first president of the College, the Reverend Abraham Pierson, Jr., represented that trend in theology, for he was pastor of the First Church at Newark, New Jersey (No. 132), when it changed from Congregational to Presbyterian.

That same church, together with the First Presbyterian Church at Elizabeth, New Jersey (No. 133), had a part also in founding Princeton University. At both churches, in succession, was located the College of New Jersey, which originated in the Log College at Neshaminy Church in Pennsylvania (No. 238), and which was moved later to Princeton. In the account of Neshaminy Church will be found a list of fifty-one Presbyterian colleges, which stemmed from the Log College of William Tennent and his four sons, all famous Presbyterian preachers.

Also in the Mid-Atlantic region is another example of a college founded by a church with Presbyterian polity. In connection with the Reformed Dutch Church at

Hackensack, New Jersey (No. 131), we find that Queens College, now Rutgers, was founded by the Dutch Reformed Church. These are only examples of the many colleges founded in colonial times by clergymen, as religion and learning were woven into the colonial life of the colonies that became the United States.

2

THE CHURCH OF ENGLAND AND THE SOUTH

1. Virginia

Virginia was the name given by Sir Walter Raleigh to the whole country, when from London he was trying, unsuccessfully, to found a colony on the Atlantic coast of North America. The Virginia Company of London was granted rights of trade and settlement in South Virginia, Between 34° and 41° North latitude, that is, from the present Columbia, South Carolina, to the Hudson River above Manhattan. Captain John Smith, under whose command the original expedition had sailed to James Town, and who in 1608 was made head of government for the colony, from 1614 to 1616 explored the coast of North Virginia from Penobscot Bay to Cape Cod. In his book, *A Description of New England* (1616), he gave the territory its present name (see First Parish Meeting House, Cohasset, Mass., No. 88, which region he discovered in 1614).

North and South Virginia had another bond in the beginning — their first permanent settlements were founded by puritans. We have seen that the persecution of Protestants under Mary I had driven many of them to the Continent, and particularly to Geneva, the source of Calvinism, and that upon their return to England under Elizabeth I, they had formed a school of thought which sought to "purify" the Church of England of every vestige of the Roman Church. The more radical members of the sect became Separatists and left the national Church, some during the reign of Elizabeth, but more under James I. The first presbytery in England was formed by 1572. A group of these Separatists were called Brownists and Barrowists, and later they adopted the name "Independents." As this group was punished for severe criticism of the ritual of the Church of England, some of them fled to Leyden, Holland, and their congregation became the Pilgrim Fathers. Members of this congregation sailed for America in the *Mayflower* and made the first permanent settlement in New England at Plymouth (see Chapter 4).

The Separatists left a larger number of puritans in the Church, who kept in touch with Geneva, particularly through Oxford and Cambridge and students who took graduate courses in Geneva. They strove to modify the Church along the lines of early Christian ideals. Edwin Sandys (1561-1629), son of the Archbishop of York, was such a puritan. As Sir Edwin, he was a member and became the executive officer of the Virginia Company, and it was he who put the colony on its firm course of growth. As a member of Parliament, he was one of the leaders of the puritan party, and he did his best to have the Pilgrim Fathers go to the colony in South Virginia, instead of to the Jersey coast for which they sailed, or to Cape Cod and Plymouth where they eventually landed.

Together with Sir Edwin Sandys, all the leaders of the Virginia Company brought the influence of Geneva to bear on the Virginia colony. That influence was constructive in the early years of the colony, with the possible exception of the tyrannical rule of Deputy-Governor Samuel Argall, whose puritanism was severe (see Argall's Church, Jamestown, No. 293). The Geneva polity was representative, as in Presbyterianism, and the principle was introduced into the earliest government of Virginia. The original four divisions of government — the corporations of James City, Elizabeth City, the City of Henricus (or Henrico), and Charles City, in which we find many of the churches in this collection — were reflections of the free city of Geneva, whose government, Sir Edwin said, "was made in heaven." Each successive charter of the Company brought liberal features to Virginia, including the House of Burgesses, with members elected to represent each of the plantations.

The Plantation period came to an end in 1624, however, when King James had the Company's charter annulled and took full control of the colony under the Crown. The rule of the Church in Virginia then passed from the puritan party to the conservative Church party, and thereafter the doctrine, discipline, and loyalty to the king were made to conform to the orthodoxy of the mother Church.

Puritans continued to live in Virginia in harmony, until the Rebellion in England, which brought to power Oliver Cromwell, Parliament, and the "Puritans," who by then had formed a definite party. These Puritans waged war on the Crown and the Church; but Virginia remained loyal to both, proclaimed allegiance to Charles II after the execution of Charles I, defied Cromwell, and governed herself independently during the period of the Commonwealth. In Nansemond County the Puritans were concentrated, the most prominent of them being Richard Bennett (see Bennett's Creek Church, known as the Glebe Church, No. 302). In 1642, the year when the Rebellion started in England, the Puritans of Nansemond requested Massachusetts to send them three Puritan preachers. The governor and council ordered them to return to Massachusestts, and passed an act requiring that "all ministers whatsoever which reside in this Colony are to be comfortable to the orders and constitution of the Church of England and the laws therein established; and not otherwise to be admitted to teach or preach publicly or privately." The fear was that the Puritans of

Massachusetts and Virginia were to unite and prepare the way for colonial control by Cromwell. Lord Baltimore invited the Puritans of Virginia to migrate, and in 1649 over three hundred of them moved to Maryland. While Parliament forbad the use of the Prayer Book, Virginia passed an Act in 1647 ordering its use in every parish every Sunday. When William Laud, Archbishop of Canterbury, was executed and the Church of England collapsed, many loyal clergymen, known as Cavaliers, who were deprived of their parishes by the Puritans, came to Virginia. Here they were welcomed, and particularly so because under the conditions in England, no new priests could be ordained. While Cromwell was in power he sent a commission, with Bennett as a member, to demand the submission of Virginia under threats of force. The commission was met by a fleet in the James River and an armed militia, and the articles that subsequently were drawn up granted Virginia greater privileges than ever before. As Virginia continued on her independent course, the use of the Prayer Book was maintained through the period of the commonwealth and until the Revolution.

As noted in the account of the Brick Church at Jamestown (No. 293), the colonists held services immediately upon landing, and took steps to build their first Anglican church under the direction of Captain John Smith. As the settlements grew and spread, the territory was divided into shires and then subdivided into counties. In many cases, parishes and counties were laid out simultaneously in the same act. Throughout the colonial period, as settlements were established farther inland, a parish usually was coextensive with the county, until it was subdivided to accommodate the growing settlements and congregations. In the accounts of churches in Virginia, therefore, the changes in county and parish boundaries are given where they are of historical interest in the account of a church and its connection with churches and chapels. The county-parish relationship in Virginia is comparable with the town-parish relationship in New England, and both were influenced by the Calvin polity at Geneva.

Government of the Church of England in Virginia and all the American colonies differed in a fundamental respect from that of the Church in the home country. Anglican churches in America came under the jurisdiction of the Bishop of London. No American bishop was consecrated before the Revolution, and no bishop was sent from England to the colonies. This meant that priests could not be ordained in America, but had to be sent to England for ordination, or English priests were sent to the colonies as missionaries. William Laud, who served as Bishop of London and later as Archbishop of Canterbury, was largely to blame for making no provision for American bishops. He refused to recognize the forces of change growing within and around the Church in England and in the colonies, and his uncompromising policy led to the militant rise of the Puritans and the execution of Charles and himself. As we find in the account of Ware Church (No. 317), after the Restoration, King Charles II nominated the rector of that church to be consecrated as Bishop of Virginia; but the rector died soon after the nomination, and nothing came of the movement for an American episcopacy. No Anglican bishop set foot on American soil before the Revolution, and consequently, not only could no priest be ordained in

America, but new members could not be confirmed, and churches could not be consecrated. Samuel Seabury was consecrated as the first American bishop in 1784, after the Revolution. Even then the English bishops, although they seem to have tried for a year, were unable to find legal means for consecrating an American bishop, and Seabury had to go to Scotland. There he was consecrated by Non-Jurors, those who had remained loyal to the Stuart line, after the deposition of James II, and had not sworn allegiance to the King of England (see account of St. Paul's Church, Woodbury, Conn., No. 11). The lack of bishops in America retarded the development of the Anglican colonies, and dependence on England in this respect was one of the causes of the War of Independence.

Instead of bishops, the Bishop of London sent "bishop's commissaries" to oversee the many parishes of the several provinces. One such bishop's commissary was James Blair (1656-1743), an able Scottish churchman who served in that capacity for the Province of Virginia. He afforded a counterbalance to the arbitrary government in Virginia that caused Bacon's Rebellion (1676), and he became the founder and first president of the College of William and Mary (see St. John's, Richmond, No. 312, and Wren Chapel, Williamsburg, No. 295).

Another bishop's commissary, who had an important part in the establishment of Anglican churches in America, was Thomas Bray (1656-1730). He was an English churchman educated at Oxford. In 1696 the Bishop of London appointed him as his commissary to organize the Anglican Church in Maryland, where thirty parishes had been established four years previously (see Section 3, this chapter). He had a deep understanding of the intellectual poverty in the wilderness, as he worked among the Indians and the settlers. As a result of his work and reports, in 1701 the Society for the Propagation of the Gospel in Foreign Parts was chartered in London. During all of the colonial period until the Declaration of Independence, the S.P.G. (the Society, the Honorable Society, or the Venerable Society, as it variously was called) sent clergymen to serve as missionaries, either as itinerant preachers or as settled rectors of parishes. Dr. Bray had been active in collecting and sending libraries of books to various parishes in the English world, such as that at St. Paul's, Edenton, North Carolina (No. 199). The result was a charter, in 1699, founding the Society for the Promotion of Christian Knowledge. By that time, Bray had sent books to Charleston, Maryland, William and Mary College, New York, Boston, and points as far apart as Bermuda and Bengal. The S.P.C.K. has continued to carry on that important function of the Anglican Church.

Missionaries of the S.P.G. appear in various accounts of the Anglican churches in this collection. One of the most influential and active was George Keith (1638-1716), who came to America in 1702 as the first missionary of the Society. Raised as a Presbyterian in Scotland, he had been a Quaker in Freehold, New Jersey. He created a schism in the Society of Friends with proposals such as the introduction of Sacraments, and he was disowned by the Society in London. He then became a priest in the Church of England and returned to America. Back at Freehold, he converted members of his old Friends Meeting and organized St. Peter's Church (No. 147). He then proceeded to travel through America from New England to Virginia, challenging Quakers, preaching, inspiring congregations, and organizing Anglican churches. In his *Journal*, a detailed account of his mission in America, 1702-1704, he noted, for example, that he preached on Sunday, May 2, 1703, "at Kicketan Church by James River" (see St. John's, Hampton, No. 310).

In addition to the Puritans, Friends, and Baptists in Nansemond County, there were other Protestants in Virginia during the colonial period. Governor Spotswood brought in German Lutherans to work his iron industry, and they built the Hebron Church (No. 339). More Friends from Pennsylvania settled in the northwest corner of Virginia, where they built Hopewell Friends Meeting House (No. 340) and Goose Creek Friends Meeting House (No. 341). Presbyterians from the Cumberland Valley, Pennsylvania, pioneered in the Shenandoah Valley region, where we find their Augusta Church (No. 343) and Timber Ridge Presbyterian Church (No. 344). The first presbytery in Virginia was founded in Hanover County (see account of the Anglican Fork Church, No. 315), and it was vigorous in its opposition to the Established Church. We find also a Baptist church in the Blue Ridge, at Hamburg, the Mill Creek Church (No. 342).

In the eastern part of Virginia, the landed gentry of the plantation economy were in control of the established parishes, while dissenting congregations generally arose among overseers, tradesmen, and the working class. As the Revolution brewed, feeling increased against the Church of England as well as the king. When the war was over, and the Anglican Church had been disestablished, in 1785, there followed a long period of decline. The Diocese of Virginia was organized in 1785, and the Protestant Episcopal Church was organized in 1789 at Philadelphia (see Christ Church, No. 205), but the new Church went through a period of hard times and discouragement that extended well into the nineteenth century. In Virginia the dissenting churches demanded the property of the Anglican churches, and the movement was successful. In 1802 the Virginia legislature passed an act ordering the glebe lands to be sold for the benefit of the poor and for educational institutions. (This act is the subject of Chap. XXIII of Brydon's *Virginia's Mother Church.*) The Glebe Church (No. 302) gets its name as a result of that act. In this collection we find in Virginia a number of colonial Anglican churches and chapels being used by other denominations, which were acquired during those difficult years.

For the Tricentennial of the Jamestown settlement in 1907, many of the colonial church buildings in Virginia were restored. As Virginia was the first colony, the accounts of the Virginia houses of worship should be seen first, but as the photographs and accounts are arranged alphabetically by states, Virginia will be found at the end of the book. There it is revealed that, of the fifty-two colonial houses of worship still standing in Virginia, forty-six were built by the Church of England. Because of its colonial association with the Church of England, the population of the Protestant Episcopal Church in America is still centered in the area of the British colonies. Although the Revolution ended the jurisdiction of the Church of England over the churches in America, the membership of the communicants of the American churches in the Anglican Communion has never been interrupted. These American churches have always been "in communion with" the English churches.

2. Maryland

The second province to be settled in the South was Maryland. In 1632 (after colonization had been begun by the English in Massachussetts, the Dutch in New York, and the Swedes in Delaware) the Maryland charter was issued. In 1634 the first settlers under the charter arrived, with Leonard Calvert in charge; the company included two Roman Catholic priests. As the charter was granted to the Roman Catholic Cecilius Calvert, Lord Baltimore, the brother of Leonard, special conditions governed the Province of Maryland, which are outlined in the following chapter. Even though the Proprietary of the province was Roman Catholic, the charter required that Maryland be governed by the laws of England, which included the Church of England.

In 1629, before the charter had been issued, an Anglican settlement had been made in Maryland under the authority of the Virginia Company of London, and the Company was a strenuous opponent of the charter, on the ground that it infringed their territorial rights. Captain William Claiborne (who was to become a member of Cromwell's commission to Virginia, mentioned in the preceding chapter) settled a Virginia plantation on Kent Island, a large island in the Chesapeake Bay at the mouth of the Chester River, which borders the present Kent County. The hundred people of his company were members of the Church of England, and in 1631 Claiborne brought from Hampton, Virginia, a priest of the Church of England, Richard James; in that wilderness of the province the first Christian services were held.

Although records are not available for the first congregation at the first capital of the province, St. Mary's City, there is some evidence that the original church there, St. Mary's Chapel, was used for worship both by Roman Catholics and Anglicans. Built between 1634 and 1638, we only know that it was a brick building in the form of a Latin cross, with mullion brick separating the casements of the windows. The foundation was excavated in 1938. St. Mary's City, according to Henry Chandler Forman in his book *The Architecture of the Old South* (1948), had many two-storied brick buildings about 1640, when Plymouth was still a settlement of wooden cabins. There is evidence that St. Mary's City was more imposing than Jamestown. Today at the site of that first capital of Maryland, as at Jamestown, there is no town, and none of the colonial buildings remain. In 1630 Anglicans worshipped in a hut. In 1642 they built Trinity Church, on Smith's Creek, and later they moved to a lot near the present rectory. In 1695 the government was moved from St. Mary's City to Annapolis, and, as was the case at Jamestown, the first capital began to decline and finally vanished. The cruciform brick courthouse was given to St. Mary's Parish (one of the thirty Anglican parishes established in 1692). The courthouse was torn down in 1829, and the pressent Trinity Church was built from the colonial brick; near by stands a modern reconstruction of the courthouse. In the churchyard stands the Leonard Calvert Monument, marking the site where the original settlers from the *Ark* and the *Dove* assembled and heard Calvert read the royal charter, in accordance with the "Instruction" from Lord Baltimore, his brother in London.

Freedom of religion was a guiding principle in the development of Maryland, as it was in Rhode Island in New England, and in Pennsylvania in the Mid-Atlantic region. In Maryland there were from the beginning, Anglicans, Roman Catholics, and Nonconformists. With the Puritans and Parliament in control in England, in 1649 the Assembly of Maryland passed the famous Act of Religious Toleration. All forms of Christian faith were protected; it is interesting that it was forbidden to reproach any one by calling him a "Heretick, Schismatic, Idolator, Puritan, Presbyterean, Independent, Papist Priest, Jesuit, Jesuited Papist, Lutheran, Calvinist, Anabaptist, Brownist, Antinomian, Barrowist, Roundhead, Separatist," and "reproachfull speeches, words, or language, concerning the Holy Trinity" were punishable by death, and such utterances against the saints by fine or banishment. During the Commonwealth period, the Puritans had more success in Maryland than they did in Virginia. Led by those whom he had invited from Virginia, as noted above, they took control of the government from Lord Baltimore, and in 1654 they guaranteed freedom of conscience, "Provided such liberty be not extended to Popery or Prellacy."

Following the Restoration in England the Puritans' militant power waned, and in Maryland the dissenting bodies began to emerge as organized denominations. There were settled Meetings of Friends in 1661, and in 1672 George Fox, a founder of the Society of Friends in England, organized the Maryland Yearly Meeting; it was the second in America, following that in Rhode Island (see Newport Friends Meeting House, No. 266). The Third Haven Friends, on the Eastern Shore of Maryland, were mentioned by Fox in his account of his visit in the province, and the present Third Haven Friends Meeting House (No. 76), built in 1682, is the second oldest frame house of worship in America.

Presbyterians on the Eastern Shore of Maryland petitioned for a minister, and in 1683 Francis Makemie came from Northern Ireland. He founded congregations, and his church at Rehoboth (No. 83) is the oldest Presbyterian church building in America. He was the leader in forming the first presbytery to be founded by Presbyterians in America, at Philadelphia, as noted in Chapter 6, Section 5.

The Methodists developed as a sect within the Church of England. They clung to their membership in the Anglican Communion as long as possible, but finally, in 1784, at Baltimore in their Lovely Lane Chapel, the Methodist Church in America was organized. Unfortunately the chapel with the romantic name does not survive (see Barratt's Chapel, Del., No. 24).

The English Revolution of 1688, which deposed James II, and ended his efforts to reestablish the power of the Roman Catholic Church in England, also brought to an end the government in Maryland of the Roman Catholic Lord Baltimore. The Church of England was made the Established Church of Maryland in 1692, when

William and Mary brought to a close the proprietary period under the Calverts, and opened the royal period of government. Lionel Copley, the new governor and an Anglican, proceeded in that year to divide the province into thirty parishes. The Act of 1692, "An act for the service of Almighty God and the Establishment of the Protestant religion within this province," ordered that "the book of Common Prayer as then established be read each Sunday and Holy Day, and the Blessed Sacrament administered according to the rites of the Church of England." The accompanying table lists thirty parishes, by county, and the twenty-eight colonial Anglican churches that still

THIRTY ANGLICAN PARISHES CREATED IN MARYLAND IN 1692 AND THIRTY SURVIVING CHURCHES

Original Parish of 1692	County	Surviving Church	Serial
St. Paul's	Kent	St. Paul's	72
	Kent	Emmanuel	73
Kent Island	Kent		
North Sassafras	Cecil	St. Mary's, North East	71
South Sassafras, or Shrewsbury	Cecil		
St. Paul's	Talbot	St. Luke's, Wye	75
	Talbot	St. Luke's, Church Hill	74
St. Michael's	Talbot		
St. Peter's	Talbot	St. Peter's, White Marsh	77
Great Choptank	Dorchester		
Dorchester	Dorchester	Trinity	78
Somerset	Somerset	St. Andrew's	82
Coventry	Somerset	Rehoboth	84
Stepney	Somerset	Green Hill	79
	Somerset	Spring Hill	80
Snow Hill	Somerset (later in Worcester)	All Hallows, Snow Hill	85
	Somerset	St. Martin's	86
William and Mary	St. Mary's		
	St. Mary's	St. George's, Valley Lee	40
King and Queen	St. Mary's	Christ Church, Chaptico	42
St. Paul's	Calvert (later in Prince George)	St. Paul's, Baden	49
	Calvert (later in Prince George)	St. Thomas'	50
	Calvert (later in Prince George)	St. Barnabas	51
All Faith	Calvert (later in St. Mary's)	All Faith	43
	Calvert (later in St. Mary's)	St. Andrew's	41
Christ Church	Calvert	Christ Church	52
	Calvert	Middleham Chapel	53
All Saints	Calvert		
William and Mary	Charles	Christ Church, Wayside	45
Port Tobacco	Charles		
Durham	Charles	Durham Church	44
Piscataway, or St. John's	Charles (later in Prince George)	St. John's	48
	Charles (later in Prince George)	Christ Church, Accokeek	47
St. Margaret's, Westminster	Anne Arundel		
St. Anne's, or Middleneck	Anne Arundel		
All Hallows. or South River	Anne Arundel	All Hallows	55
St. James', Herring Creek	Anne Arundel	St. James', Herring Creek	54
St. George's, or Sepsutia	Baltimore		
St. John's, or Gunpowder	Baltimore	St. James', My Lady's Manor	59
St. Paul's, or Patapsco	Baltimore	St. Thomas', Garrison Forest	58

stand and are in this collection. Colonial churches do not survive from the two earliest settlements, on Kent Island and at St. Mary's City. The summary at the beginning of the Maryland photographs reveals that of the forty-nine in the state, thirty-one were built by Anglicans, six by Friends, and five by Roman Catholics. In addition, one Baptist and two Presbyterian churches make five denominations of British settlers in colonial Maryland. Germans from Pennsylvania brought two more Protestant denominations, German Lutheran and German Reformed. From a Reformed congregation in Baltimore, a new sect was founded, the United Brethren in Christ (see the Otterbein Church, No. 62).

3. Carolina

We have noted that the first attempt to colonize on the Atlantic Coast, which was unsuccessful, was made by French Huguenots in 1562, on what is now Port Royal Island, near Beaufort, South Carolina. The first permanent settlement in Carolina was made by Englishmen in 1670, on the Ashley River; and on the point between that river and the Cooper River, Charles Town was developed. Charles I and again Charles II granted territory that comprised the Province of Carolina. While officially it was all one province, the north and the south regions had separate governments during most of the colonial period, and their communities were so far apart that they developed as separate provinces, even though the boundary between them was not defined until 1815.

Into South Carolina came Englishmen direct from the home country and from Barbados, and French Huguenots revived their dream of a haven from religious persecution. In and near Charleston, the Huguenots built their own churches and used the French language. The English settlers included both Anglicans and Dissenters, for the original constitution, while declaring the national religion of England for the province, granted freedom of worship to "every church or profession" so long as its members believed in God and His public worship and bore witness to the truth (see St. Michael's Church, No. 274). When political representation was provided in 1693, by dividing the legislature and establishing a house of elected representatives, controversy arose among the English between the Anglicans and the Dissenters. The colony was in close touch with the islands, and a congregation of Barbadians on Goose Creek, known as the "Goose Creek Men" (see Goose Creek Church, No. 275), were the backbone of the party that established the Church of England in the province. In 1706 an Act of Assembly, known as the Church Act, made the Church of England the Established Church in Carolina, and it created nine parishes in Tidewater South Carolina. In those parishes, seven colonial houses of worship survive and are found in this collection: St. James' Parish, Goose Creek Church (No. 275); St. Thomas' Parish, Pompion Hill Chapel (No. 276); St. John's Parish, Berkeley, the Biggin Church (No. 277) and Strawberry Chapel (No. 278); St. Andrew's Church (No. 279); Christ Church (No. 281); and St. James', Santee (No. 282).

Within the Anglican Parish of St. Thomas was a French settlement and the Huguenot Church of St. Denis (the patron saint of France), another of the nine parishes named in the Church Act. Here the peculiar situation of a parish within a parish was recognized by calling it the Parish of St. Thomas and St. Denis (see No. 276). The Huguenots used the Liturgy of the Church of England but the French language. An Act of 1708 provided that when the language of their church became English, the church would take its place in the parish in the normal Anglican manner. Eventually all the French congregations became Anglican, except the Huguenot Church in Charleston, which is the only one of the denomination in the country.

The summary at the beginning of the South Carolina photographs reveals that, of the seventeen colonial houses of worship in the state, fifteen were built by Anglicans, one by Congregationalists and one by Presbyterians. As in Tidewater Virginia, in the Low Country of South Carolina the plantation economy, the ocean trade, and the government were controlled by Anglicans, and the Church of England continued as the established religion until the Revolution. In Charleston, as well as in Williamsburg, there developed among this Anglican ruling class, a spirit of independence of action that was expressed by the leaders of the Revolution and an understanding of the political principles that they incorporated into the foundation of the Republic. The persistent independence of Charlestonians carried over into the next century, when they started the secession from the Union and the Civil War. Also in both colonies the Presbyterians, of Scottish and Scotch-Irish stock, pushed inland and pioneered in opening new territory and new opportunity. In the port of Charleston, as in the other thriving ports, there was a congregation of Sephardic Jews, who were in close touch with the congregation at Newport, Rhode Island (see Touro Synagogue, No. 271, and Chapter 5).

The northern region of Carolina (above the Cape Fear River) was first called Albemarle. Following the unsuccessful attempt of Sir Walter Raleigh, in England, to found a colony on the coast of this region commencing in 1585, it was not until about 1660 that the first permanent colony was established at Albemarle by Englishmen from Virginia. The proprietary period in North Carolina was marked by religious controversy, even though the peaceful influence of Quakers was present in the province. Dissenters objected to the Church of England becoming established, as it was in South Carolina. The rebellion started in 1708 by Thomas Carey, the deputy-governor, ended in failure in 1711, when the Church of England was established as the official religion in the northern province, five years after it was established in the southern province. At the same time, Quakers were deprived of the privilege of holding public office or serving on juries. The Church of England continued as the Established Church until the Revolution.

In a wilderness on the bank of the Brunswick River, just south of the Cape Fear River in the southeastern tip of North Carolina, with pines growing between its brick walls, stands the ruin of St. Philip's Church (No. 200). As at Jamestown and St. Mary's City, here the town of Brunswick thrived for a time as the capital of the province, only to decline and die after the government had been removed. St. Philip's was the official church of the governor and his administration, until the mosquito drove the inhabitants to higher ground at the present city of Wilmington.

For a time the capital was located at Bath, another seaport town. It also has declined since the government was removed, but it has not died. There we find the oldest church in North Carolina, St. Thomas' (No. 198). Governor Eden officially attended services at St. Thomas'. He was in league with the pirate Blackbeard, Edward Teach, who used Bath as his home port. Bath was the scene of the Tuscarora massacre, which occurred in 1711, the year in which the Church of England was established, and the victims lie buried beneath the brick floor of St. Thomas' Church. After their defeat, the Tuscaroras migrated to upper New York, where they joined the Five Nations and became the sixth nation of the Iroquois (see French Chapel, Old Fort Niagara, N.Y., No. 197).

Edenton is another port that served as the capital, when the assembly met there occasionally. St. Paul's Church (No. 199) was the official church, and Governor Charles Eden, for whom the town was named, was buried in the churchyard. Daniel Earle served as rector throughout the Revolution, adhering to the Church of England while fostering revolutionary activities. He presided over a mass meeting protesting the Boston Port Act, and the Test, signed by the vestry in June of 1776, was an ecclesiastical declaration of independence.

The remaining colonial church, of the four in North Carolina, is the Moravian Church at Bethabara (No. 201). Members of this oldest Protestant church in the world (other than the Eastern Churches), came from Bohemia and Moravia to Saxony, Germany, thence to Georgia and Pennsylvania, and from Bethlehem they migrated to North Carolina and settled in the wilderness. Their settlement of Salem has grown into the twin city of Winston-Salem.

4. Georgia

In 1733, exactly a century after the first settlers under Lord Baltimore's charter had landed in Maryland, the last of the British colonies was founded. In that year the ship *Anne*, with General James Edward Oglethorpe and his comany of settlers, arrived on the Savannah River and started settling the town of Savannah. During the 126 years since the first settlement at Jamestown, the Church of England had become the established religion in each of the colonies in the south. Now the royal charter for Georgia (named for King George II) granted religious freedom for all but Roman Catholics, provided that none were offensive to the government. The English in Carolina, in 1686, had forced the Spanish to withdraw to the St. Mary's River, the present border between Georgia and Florida; and now the principal mission of Oglethorpe was to establish a buffer colony between Carolina and the Roman Catholics of Spain in Florida and of France in Louisiana. Even though freedom of worship was beginning to be granted to Roman Catholics in other colonies, it was feared that to do so in Georgia would be to invite spies for the Spanish, French, and Indians. Otherwise, none of the colonies began with a more cordial welcome to all faiths and conditions of people. In order to colonize rapidly after such a late start, and also to provide a haven for the oppressed and the persecuted Protestants of Europe, in whom he was deeply interested, Oglethorpe invited the indigent and the imprisoned debtors of England and the exiled Protestants of the Continent, as well as Sephardic Jews who had been dispersed, to emigrate; and the trustees of the colony offered as inducements, free passage and provisions until a crop could be made in the new land.

As a result of the purpose and the means of founding Georgia, the composition of the settlement was different from that of any other colony. In addition to Englishmen, there came from the Continent German Lutherans (Salzburgers), Piedmontese, Scots, Swiss, and Portuguese Jews. After 1752 there was also a considerable migration from Virginia and Carolina into Georgia. While the economic policy under the trustees, who administered the colony for twenty-two years, was a failure, for the debtors and the improvident proved to be inadequate for pioneering, the policies of religious freedom for Protestants and Jews and the bulwark erected against the Spanish and the French were successful. Oglethorpe brought with him an Anglican clergyman on the first voyage, and he became the first minister in the colony. Christ Church Parish was organized immediately in Savannah, and about 1740 the first building of a church was begun. Savannah served as the capital of Georgia until it was captured by the British in 1778, and the Anglican Church was made the Established Church by the Act of 1758, but no colonial church of the denomination survives.

The development of colonial history of religion in the South is revealed in the contrast between Virginia, the first colony, and Georgia, the last. From the beginning in Virginia, the Church of England was the Establishment, which dominated the life of the colony until the Revolution and the disestablishment. In Georgia the story was one of Christian concern for the needy and the oppressed, and of liberty of conscience for all groups from the time of their arrival. An old Protestant denomination, the Moravian Church, was represented by a group among the first settlers, and the Wesleys were there when they were groping for the faith on which a new denomination, the Methodist Church, was to be founded. The first orphanage and the first Sunday school were founded here, and strong currents of religious thought flowed through Georgia, which inspired various denominations throughout the colonies and aroused the greatest spiritual revival in colonial times. Although we do not find in Georgia colonial houses of worship representing all of these subjects, they are outlined below to provide a framework for viewing the buildings in other colonies that resulted from, or were affected by, these events.

It was on the voyage to Georgia that John Wesley had the religious experience that showed him the way to Methodism. On Oglethorpe's second voyage, in 1736, he was accompanied by the Wesleys, who were Anglicans, and a group of Moravians from Herrnhut, Saxony (sometimes called "Herrnhutters"). John had a mission to convert Indians, and Charles came as Secretary of Indian Affairs. The Moravians, of the Unity of Brethren (*Unitas Fratrum*) as their Church was called, were among the first to assume the evangelization of the heathen as a duty of the Church. This third mission of theirs to leave Germany — after one to the slaves in the West Indies and another to the Eskimos — was similar to that of the Wesleys. On the voyage to Georgia a raging storm frightened John and gave him grave concern for the safety of the ship, its company, and his own life; but through it all he observed that the Moravians were calm and unperturbed. He was in the phase of seeking a religious life, as a puritan within the Church of England, with the ideal of the simplicity of primitive Christianity. In subsequent conversations with the Brethren, he found a well of faith. It had originated with John Huss of Bohemia, the "Reformer before the Reformation," who had been influenced by John Wycliffe, had offered the Bible as the standard of faith and practice, and had died at the stake in 1415, a century before Martin Luther posted his theses on the church door at Wittenberg. In 1467 two priests of the Brethren had been consecrated as bishops in apostolic succession, and the Unity thus became a Protestant Episcopal Church before the Reformation. John Wesley was inspired by what he learned, and the Moravians continued to teach and influence him in Savannah, in England, and on a visit to Herrnhut, their refuge and headquarters on the estate of Count Zinzendorf in Saxony. Wesley went on to found the Methodist Church, and in England the Moravians were so influential that, in 1749, Parliament recognized the Brethren as "an ancient Protestant Episcopal Church." Thus in Savannah the old passed the torch on to the new.

In Europe members of the Unity had taken up arms in the Thirty Years War between Catholics and Protestants, and had been defeated and executed. In Georgia they faced again the necessity of taking up arms, this time to fight the Spanish, and the Brethren decided not to risk extinction again. Abandoning their hard-earned mission in 1740, they migrated to Pennsylvania under the leadership of Peter Bohler who had converted the Wesleys in England, and there, in the following year they founded the Moravian Community of Bethlehem (No. 244).

As a missionary, John Wesley preached to the inhabitants and Indians in and about Savannah and out on the Sea Islands, indoors or out under the live oaks. As a priest of the Church of England he served as the third rector of Christ Church, where he founded the first Sunday school (half a century before the more famous one of Robert Raikes in England), which is still in existence.

Another Christian concern of John Wesley was aroused as he observed the growing number of orphans in the new and struggling colony, as fever and failures carried off the parents. He persuaded another Anglican priest, George Whitefield, to come to Georgia, and when Whitefield saw the conditions he started an orphanage. The Bethesda Orphanage Asylum, which Whitefield established in 1740, about eight miles from Savannah, was the first orphanage in the colonies. Raising money for its support became the central motive in Whitefield's travels throughout the colonies and Great Britain. He preached to throngs of thousands from every denomination, with an astounding schedule of one or more sermons a day for the rest of his life. On his seventh tour in America in 1770, he died at Newburyport, Massachusetts, and there he was laid to rest in the crypt of Old South Church (No. 112), which had been organized as a result of his preaching on an earlier visit. It was his preaching that identified him as a founder of Methodism, although he never ceased to be an Anglican priest and left organization to others. He preached in many colonial Anglican churches and was involved in controversy with others. His preaching stimulated new theological thought and considerable emotion, and as a result the Presbyterian churches divided into New Side and Old Side factions. It stimulated a spiritual revival in colonial America, which became known as the Great Awakening, and which was fostered in New England by Jonathan Edwards. Whitefield preached in many of the churches in this collection.

Another orphanage was founded in Georgia by Salzburgers at Ebenezer. In Salzburg, a duchy of Austria bordering on German Bavaria, Protestants were being persecuted by the Roman Catholic Church. Through the intercession of William I of Prussia, they were permitted to emigrate in 1731 and 1732. In 1734 a company of seventy-eight Salzburgers accepted the invitation of Oglethorpe and went from Bavaria to Georgia. In a pine woods near the Savannah River, twenty-five miles above the city, their brick Jerusalem Church (No. 28), built in 1767, is the only remaining building of their town of Ebenezer.

The church of another denomination is found at Appling, the Kiokee Church (No. 29), organized in 1772 by George Marshall, an Anabaptist preacher. He was arrested for violating the Act of 1758, which established the Church of England in Georgia. He was tried, but he won over the officials and was allowed to continue his ministry until his death in 1784.

The Midway Church (No. 30), was built by Congregationalists. They had a long continuity from England to Massachusetts to South Carolina to Georgia, using the name Dorchester at each place. St. John's Parish, which included Midway Church, was the center of dissent in Georgia, and there the Revolution was fomented by the congregation as though they were in Old South Meeting House, Boston, while in the rest of Georgia about half of the inhabitants were loyal. The Midway Church was a good example of Congregationalism with Presbyterian leanings, reflecting the influence of Geneva on the puritans in the Church of England during the reign of Elizabeth I and James I; but it is surprising to find a New England meeting house in the deep South, the one farthest south in the collection. It has the effect of bringing to full circle the puritan element in the original Jamestown colony.

3

THE COLONIAL
CATHOLICS

Roman Catholics surrounded the English colonies — the Spanish from Florida to California and the French from Quebec to New Orleans — and during all of the colonial period the English struggled to keep them out. The only house of worship left by either of those groups is the Jesuit Chapel in the French Castle at Old Fort Niagara, New York (No. 197). As mentioned earlier, that strong point was a trading post in a chain of fortified posts established by the French through the wilderness of their New France. It was captured by the English as a part of the New York colony. Today at the fort there fly the three flags of France, England, and the United States that were contemporary with their respective periods of occupation. The only Roman Catholics permitted by the English to colonize in America came from England to Maryland under a royal charter granted to Lord Baltimore, a Catholic. These English Catholics, as they are called by most historians, are not to be confused with the English who were members of the Church of England. In that branch of the Apostolic Church, as well as in the whole Anglican Communion, the members have adhered to the Catholic faith of Christianity, and they have never ceased to declare their faith in the Holy Catholic Church, as stated in the ancient Christian creeds. The two branches of the Church, the Roman and the English, were separated when papal authority was brought to an end by Henry VIII, who was made "Protector and Supreme Head of the English Church and Clergy."

In respect to religion, Maryland was unique, as were her charter and its author, George Calvert (c. 1580-1632), the first Lord Baltimore. Maryland was the first colony to be founded on the principle of freedom of religion for all Christians. It was the fruition of a scheme for the colonization of Roman Catholics in the New World, which had been cherished by Sir George for many years, but which he did not live to see. He became the link that connected England with the colonies, in the long struggle between the Roman Catholicism of Spain and the Protestantism of England. In Parliament, under James I, he was regarded with suspicion for favoring the alliance with Spain and the marriage of the Infanta to Prince Charles, who was to become King Charles I. In 1623 the proposed marriage and the hope of alliance with Spain failed, and Calvert saw that England would continue to be Protestant. He withdrew from public office in 1625, declared himself a convert to Roman Catholicism, and was created Baron Baltimore of Baltimore. Thereafter he devoted his life to the founding of a haven for Catholics in the colonies. In 1621 he had established the settlement of Avalon in Newfoundland, for which King James had granted him a charter in 1623. In 1627 he took his first son, Cecilius, who then was nineteen years of age, on an expedition to Avalon. Also with him were a secular priest to serve the Catholic colonists, and a Protestant priest to care for the Protestant members of the expedition, thereby revealing the principle of religious freedom which he was to incorporate in the Maryland charter, and which was to guide his son in its administration. The climate and soil of Newfoundland were hostile to plantation, and he went to Jamestown, where he applied for permission to settle. There the oaths of allegiance and supremacy were required, and while he could take the former, as a Roman Catholic he had to decline the latter, and he returned to England. There he was successful in his application to Charles I for a charter. It granted to him a province that would fulfill his dream, and he gave it the name of the Virgin Mary and of the Queen Mary who had tried in vain to restore Roman Catholicism as the national religion of England. Lord Baltimore died in 1632, after the charter had been granted but shortly before it had passed the great seal; his son and heir, Cecilius Calvert, became the second Lord Baltimore and the grantee of the charter.

The territory granted by the charter was nearly double that of the present Maryland. It included what is now Delaware, a wide strip of Southern Pennsylvania, and the land between the two branches of the Potomac — territory that was long in dispute between the Penns and the Lords Baltimore as the result of conflicting grants by the Crown. The charter was unique, in that it made Maryland a palatinate, with all the royal and viceregal rights of that exceptional type of government, which then existed in the Bishopric of Durham. It gave to the proprietary the most comprehensive civil and political authority ever granted by the English Crown. The proprietary appointed the governor and all civil and military officers; he had the power of granting land and creating manors, whose grantees had the same rights as those in England; he had the patronage of churches and the advowsons (in English law, the patronage of a church living); he could initiate laws and he had the power of life and death over the inhabitants in regard to punishment.

With such royal power vested in the proprietary, who had the avowed purpose of founding a Roman Catholic haven, why is it that of the forty-nine colonial houses of worship still standing in Maryland, thirty-one were built by Anglicans, six by Friends, and only five by Roman Catholics, and that of the five, only two were churches and the others were private chapels in residences? The answer lies in the charter itself, in the policy of Lord Baltimore in administering it, and in the religious struggle that characterized the colonial history of Maryland. That history is divided into three periods — the proprietary or Catholic period of religious freedom for all Christians; the period of usurpation, when the Puritans took the government from the proprietary and tried to eliminate both the Church of England and Roman Catholicism in the province; and the royal period, starting with the seizure by William and Mary of all civil and political authority and, in 1692, the establishment of the Church of England, and ending with the Revolution, during which period a series of restrictive laws were passed against Roman Catholics.

The Calverts ruled Maryland in succession as Lord Baltimore. Cecilius Calvert, the second Lord Baltimore and the first proprietary, remained in England and sent his brother Leonard to settle and govern the province. Philip Calvert, another brother, served for a period of two years as governor. Upon the death of Cecilius, in 1675, his son Charles became the third Lord Baltimore, the second proprietary, and the governor; it was he who was deprived of the civil and political authority granted in the charter. When he died in 1715, his son Benedict Leonard Calvert became the fourth Lord Baltimore and the third proprietary of the lands, which the family had been permitted to retain. Benedict had renounced the Roman Catholic faith before his father's death, and his father had cut off his allowance. He conformed to the Church of England and applied to Queen Anne for an allowance, and the Queen ordered an annuity to be paid from the revenue of the province. His son, Charles II, who had conformed with his father, succeeded as the fifth Lord Baltimore and the fourth proprietary, and from Queen Anne he received the governorship, a different matter from being governor as Lord proprietary. (The Baltimore oriole does not get its name from association with the city, but from the colors in the Baltimore coat of arms.)

The charter gave the proprietary the power to make laws, "Provided neverthelesse, that the said Lawes be consonant to reason, and be not repugnant or contrary, but as neere as conveniently may be, agreeable to the Lawes, Statutes, Customes, and Rights of this our Kingdome of England." In anticipation of doubts and questions concerning religion, the Church of England was protected by the following passage, which appears near the end of the charter: "Provided always, that no Interpretation be admitted thereof, by which Gods Holy and Truely Christian Religion, or the Allegiance due unto us, Our Heirs and Successors, may in any thing suffer any prejudice, or diminuation."

When Cecilius Calvert, Lord Baltimore, Lord of the Province of Mary Land and Avalon, found that he would be unable to make the voyage with the *Ark* and the *Dove* in 1633, he addressed a document of "Instruction" to his "well beloved Brother Leonard Calvert, Esq.", who was to head the expedition and serve as governor of the province. He wanted the conditions of plantation (used in the sense of planting people) to be understood by all from the beginning. In England there was opposition to the charter from the Virginia Company of London, and also in Virginia by the colonists, who considered it to be an infringement of their territorial rights. After hearing both parties, the committee of the Privy Council on American plantations decided "to leave the Lord Baltimore to his charter, and the Protestants to their remedy at law."

The first article of the Instruction was designed to avoid giving offence in the practice of worship, as follows:

"1. His Lord proprietary requires his said Governor and Commissioners that in their voyage to Mary Land they be very carefull to preserve unity and peace amongst all passengers on Shipp-board, and that they suffer no scandall nor offence to be given to any of the Protestants, whereby any just complaint may hereafter be made, by them, in Virginia or in England, and that for that end, they cause all Acts of Romane Catholique Religion to be made as privately as may be, and that they instruct all Romane Catholiques to be silent upon all occasions of discourse concerning matters of Religion; and that the said Governor and Commissioners treate the Protestants with as much mildness and favor as Justice will permitt. And this to be observed at Land as well as at sea."

Religion was considered to be of primary importance also in the statement of purposes, as follows:

"6. That when they have made choice of the place where they intend to settle themselves and that they have brought their men ashore with all their provisions, they do assemble all the people together in a fitt and decent manner and then cause his majestic letter pattents to be publikely read by his Lord proprietary's [written Lop.ps] Secretary John Bolles, and afterwards his Lord proprietary's Commission to them, and that either the Governor or one of the Commissioners presently after make some short declaration to the people of his Lord proprietary's intentions which he means to pursue in this his intended plantation, which are first the honor of God by endeavoring the conversion of the savages to Christianity, secondly the augmentation of his majesties Empire and Dominions in those parts of the world by reducing them under the subjection of his Crowne, and thirdly by the good of such of his Countrymen as are willing to adventure their fortunes and themselves in it, by endeavoring all he cann, to assist them, that they may reape the fruites of their charges and labors according to the hopefulnes of the thing, with as much freedome comfort and incouragement as they can desire . . ."

He instructed further, as follows:

"9. That where they intend to settle the Plantation they first make choice of a fitt place, and a competent quantity of ground for a fort within which or neere unto it a convenient house, and a church or a chappel adjacent may be built, for the seate of his Lord proprietary or his Governor or other Commissioners . . . that they likewise make choice of a fitt place neere unto it to seate a towne."

In November of 1633, the *Ark* and the *Dove* sailed from Southampton and stopped at Cowes, Isle of Wight, to take aboard two Jesuits, including Father Andrew White, who was to become known as the "Apostle of Maryland." The company of twenty gentlemen, all Roman Catholics except possibly one, and about two hundred fifty artisans, mechanics, laborers, and servants, most of whom were Protestants, then sailed across the Atlantic to the Chesapeake Bay and landed on St. Clements Island. Father White relates in his account of the expedition, *Relatio Itineris in Marylandiam*, "On 25 March, 1634, we celebrated Mass for the first time in the island. This had never been done before in this part of the world." The party came ashore to what is now St. Mary's County, on the tip of Southern Maryland at the mouth of the Potomac River.

There Governor Calvert purchased a large tract of land from the Piscataway Indians, who gave them a village for temporary shelter, and the chief's bark hut, known as a witchott, for the use of the priests as a residence and chapel. The settlers then enjoyed a period of peaceful development, while they built St. Mary's City and St. Mary's Church, as noted in the previous chapter.

William Claiborne, who established a trading post on Kent Island in the Chesapeake before the Maryland charter, was a member of the Council of Virginia. At his settlement Anglican services were held before the arrival of Lord Baltimore's expedition — the first Christian services to be held in Maryland. Claiborne had a license from Governor Harvey of Virginia to trade with the Indians. He held no patent of land, but he opposed the Maryland charter and refused to acknowledge the authority of Lord Baltimore and submit to his rule; he referred the question to the Virginia Council and was upheld. Governor Calvert thereupon reduced the island to submission. Claiborne organized an expedition to recapture the island, but he was defeated; he escaped and continued for the rest of his life as an active foe of the Calverts and their Roman Catholic province. He encouraged Richard Ingle, a pirate, to make a raid on the province in 1644. Ingle descended on St. Mary's with the ship *Reformation*; captured, plundered, and burned the city; forced Governor Calvert, two Jesuit priests, and other inhabitants to flee to Virginia; and took Father White in chains to London, where it was expected that he would be condemned to death as a returned Jesuit. Father White escaped death, on the plea that his return was involuntary. Under these trying conditions, Lord Baltimore wrote Leonard to save what he could and abandon the colony; but the Governor returned to Maryland, drove out the raiders, and reestablished his authority.

While Cecilius Calvert, the proprietary, thus was confronted by enemies from outside the province, he became embarrassed by the infringement of the privileges of his charter by the Jesuits within the province. As proprietary, he had exclusive authority for the disposal of lands in his territory, and there was no other source for granting titles during all of the colonial period. A few years after their landing, the Jesuits received the plantation of Metapannay (now Mattapany) as a gift from the Indian King of Patuxent. Other gifts or cessions of land also were made by the Indians to the missionaries for the Society of Jesus. Lord Baltimore took strong exception to such illegal acquiring of land. He became so alarmed by the implications of this encroachment, and the threat to his charter and the whole enterprise, that he protested the actions to the *Congregatio de Propaganda Fide* at Rome, and petitioned for the recall of the Jesuit missionaries and the sending of secular priests in their place.

In 1642 the Jesuits stated their view that in Maryland there were those who "have not feared to violate the immunities of the Church, by using their endeavors that laws of the kind formerly passed in England and unjustly observed there, may obtain like force here, to wit: it shall not be lawful for any person or community, even ecclesiastical, in anywise, even by gift, to acquire or possess any land unless the permission of the Civil Magistrate first be obtained." Lord Baltimore was clear in his intention that the province would be governed in accordance with the laws of England

and the provisions of his charter, and the complaint of the Jesuits was against both. In fact, they sought the privileges and exemptions that were enjoyed by Catholic orders in Catholic countries, ignoring the fact that England no longer was a Catholic country. The case was referred by Rome to London, where Father Henry More, then Provincial of the Society of Jesus in England, granted the justice of Lord Baltimore's position and decided against the Jesuits. He ordered the release of all lands obtained from the Indians, and upheld the title of Lord Baltimore to the land. He also renounced all claims to immunity from the laws of the province and agreed that no priest should be sent to Maryland without the approval of Lord Baltimore. Dom Rosetti, titular Archbishop of Tarsus, was appointed prefect, the priests who had caused the dispute were recalled, and two secular priests were sent out. There was objection to the new arrivals on the part of the Jesuits who continued the missionary work in Maryland, on the ground that they were there first and had endured hardships on behalf of the province, but the case was closed.

The firm hand with which Cecilius Calvert ruled the province from London, for nearly forty years, steered a straight course between the Churches of Rome and England. To prevent any recurrence of the situation, he withdrew from his deputy, Governor Leonard Calvert, the power to grant land to any religious body and reserved that authority for himself. He went further and drew up new conditions of plantation, by which the English statutes of *mortmain* (the "dead hand" of a church holding property out of the economic life of the country) were extended to Maryland; and the acquiring of land by any society or corporation, temporal or spiritual, was prohibited. The result was that Maryland became the only state of the United States in which no religious body could acquire land by any means, except a small tract for a church, without the approval of the legislature, no bequest or devise to a minister of religion was valid without such approval, and no minister of religion could be a member of the legislature.

In accordance with the authority granted the proprietary to initiate laws, in 1649 the famous Act of Toleration was passed unanimously by the General Assembly of Maryland, most of the members of which were Roman Catholics. Drafted by Cecilius Calvert, the law clearly states the policy which had originated with his father, as follows:

> "And whereas the enforcing of the conscience in matters of religion hath frequently fallen out to be of dangerous consequence in those commonwealths where it hath been practised, and for the more quiet and peaceable government of the province and the better to preserve mutual love and amity amongst the inhabitants thereof: Be it therefore enacted that noe person or persons whatsoever within this province ... professing to believe in Jesus Christ, shall henceforth be in any waies troubled, molested or discountenanced for or respect of his or her religion or in the free exercise of any other religion against his or her consent."

In his *History of the United States*, Hubert Howe Bancroft gives Cecilius Calvert the honor of "being the first in the annals of mankind to make religious freedom the basis of the State."

Others outside of Maryland were welcome to come and enjoy this freedom. It has been noted in the previous chapter that a large number of Puritans in Virginia were invited to settle in Maryland, after the Act of 1643 of Virginia had required strict conformity with the Church of Virginia. When they arrived in Maryland, the governor gave them a large tract of land on the Severn River, and there they made a settlement, which they called Providence (now Annapolis). It was ironical that this same group of Puritans in 1650, during the Rebellion in England, started a local rebellion against the authority of the Catholic proprietary. They seized the government and convened an illegal General Assembly from which Catholics were excluded, and they repealed the Act of Toleration of 1649 and replaced it. Their Act Concerning Religion provided, "That none who profess and exercise the Papistic, commonly known as Roman Catholic religion, can be protected in this province." The Catholic Church suffered during the following several years, as the chapels and mission houses were raided and their property destroyed. Jesuit priests fled to Virginia, where, as we have noted, the Anglicans defied Cromwell, and only one remained in Maryland. In 1658, two years before the Restoration in England with the coronation of Charles II, the government of Maryland was restored to Lord Baltimore. Immediately the Act of Toleration of 1649 was reenacted, and it continued in effect until the Protestant Revolution of 1689. During that interval of peace, the Jesuits returned and resumed their missionary labors. Most of the Catholics during that period, of a total probably not exceeding five thousand, were in St. Mary's and Charles counties, where they were served by two or three Jesuits and two Franciscans who had arrived in 1673.

When Cecilius Calvert died, in 1675, and his son and heir, Charles, became the third Lord Baltimore, the second proprietary, and the governor of Maryland, immediately the new proprietary was caught up in the Anglican reaction to the Puritan usurpation. In 1676 pressure was brought on him to provide support for the Church of England by taxation, but he refused to do so without the approval of the inhabitants. The Catholic government was denounced in a proclamation that demanded its overthrow and the appointment of a royal governor. An armed body was gathered in Calvert County, but Governor Notley suppressed the uprising while Sir Charles was in England. Another movement was organized later, under the resounding title of "The Protestant Association in arms to defend the Protestant religion." They spread false but alarming rumors, declaring that the Catholics were going to join with the Indians to massacre the Protestants, and the reality of the French and Indian War gave the rumors credibility. The English Revolution of 1688, in which James II was deposed for his Roman Catholicism, took place while Lord Baltimore was away defending his territory against the claims of William Penn. His opponents in Maryland took advantage of the situation, and the government of the proprietary was replaced by a Committee of Safety, which was recognized by the new sovereigns. In 1692 William and Mary took over the government of the province and made it a royal colony. William III was Prince of Orange, of the line of Protestants in the Netherlands, and Mary II was the Protestant elder daughter of James II. The Act of Religion of the same year established the Church of England in Maryland and laid out the thirty parishes listed in the previous chapter. It declared all the penal laws in force against Catholics in England to be in force in Maryland, and Episcopal clergymen were given jurisdiction in testamentary causes.

As Anglicans were a small minority, while Dissenters, Quakers, and Catholics formed a large majority, provisions of the law were repugnant to the majority. By an Act of 1702 all Dissenters were given exemptions from the law, leaving only Roman Catholics subject to its full pains and penalties. The Test Oath of 1692 debarred Catholics from practising law in Maryland, and the Act of 1704 outlawed the Catholic religion and debarred priests from the practice of it; and priests and parents were forbidden the teaching of it to children. There is no evidence that Confirmation was ever performed in Maryland before the Revolution. Freedom of religion did not return to Maryland until it was established by the Constitution of the United States.

Under these difficult conditions, during the century and a half of Maryland's colonial history, the Roman Catholics struggled to make it a haven in America. Lord Baltimore used the manorial system provided in the charter to enable the Jesuits to establish their missions. In 1651 he laid off 10,000 acres near Calverton Manor for the Indian converts under the care of the fathers, the first fund established for Indian missions in the English colonies.

The first durable house of worship was the third to be built in the province. It was a chapel built on an acre and a half of land in St. Mary's County, given to the Jesuits by William Bretton and his wife, Temperance, who had acquired the manor of Little Bretton in 1637. At St. Inigoes the present St. Ignatius Church (No. 39), built in 1785, was the third building of the church.

The land of St. Thomas' Manor, in St. Mary's County, was claimed in the name of Thomas Copley, who brought settlers into Maryland. Father Philip Fisher managed the property as the headquarters of the Jesuits and built a chapel here in 1662. By 1700, after the destructive period of the Puritan usurpation, and after the establishment of the Church of England, this chapel and the one at St. Inigoes Manor were the only Catholic brick chapels left in Maryland. The Manor (No. 46) was built in 1741.

Another manor in St. Mary's County was Newton Manor. In 1668 part of its land was acquired by the Jesuits, and on it they built a chapel dedicated to St. Francis Xavier. The present church of that name (No. 38) was built in 1767 by Father Ashley.

The two remaining Roman Catholic colonial houses of worship in Maryland are extremes in contrast. One is a farmhouse in Harford County overlooking Deer Creek. A Jesuit mission was established there in 1747. The land was deeded in 1764 to Father Bennett Neale. He erected the present house in 1764, during the royal period when the public practice of his religion was prohibited. The central hall was furnished as a chapel, and the building became known as Priest Neale's Mass House (No. 68). The other is one of the most beautiful colonial manor houses in the country, Doughoregan Manor (No. 56). At one end of the 300-foot façade, a small private chapel is attached as an ell. It was the home of the Carrolls, one of the outstanding Roman Catholic families in America.

The first in a line of three Charles Carrolls, a man of Irish descent, came to Maryland in 1688, from England where Catholics were being persecuted. He served as attorney general under the third Lord Baltimore, who shortly was deprived of his political authority when Maryland was made a royal colony. His son, Charles Carroll of Annapolis (1703-1783), was a wealthy landowner, and it was he who built Doughoregan Manor. His son, Charles Carroll of Carrollton (his estate in Frederick County) was born in Annapolis in 1737, and died in 1832 at Doughoregan Manor. In the house where he was born were held the earliest Catholic services of worship in Annapolis, the second capital of the province. The father was bitterly opposed to the restrictions against Catholics, and in 1752 he went to France seeking a grant of land in Louisiana for a refuge, but he was refused. Some Catholics were moving to Pennsylvania, where the laws were not as hard on Catholics as they were becoming in Maryland. He wrote his son that Maryland no longer was a fit place for a Catholic to reside, and he was inclined to sell out and move away. The son dissuaded him, and went on in public life to work for greater religious freedom. As a patriot he served on various committees leading to the Revolution, and he signed the Declaration of Independence. As a member of the Constitutional Convention he used his influence, particularly among Catholics, in founding a stable central government for the new Republic, with freedom of religion written into the Constitution. He then continued to serve his state and country as a United States Senator.

Charles Carroll of Carrollton and his cousin John Carroll (1735-1815) attended school at the Jesuit mission of Bohemia, on Harmon's Manor in Cecil County. (The colonial church at Bohemia burned and was replaced by a post-colonial building.) In 1776 the Continental Congress sent the two Carrolls with Benjamin Franklin and Samuel Chase on an unsuccessful mission to win the French Canadians as allies in the Revolution. A positive result of the mission was the friendship developed between Franklin and John Carroll. John became a Jesuit priest and went on to become the outstanding person in the Roman Catholic Church in the United States. Upon Franklin's recommendation, John was named prefect apostolic, the American church being recognized as an independent church in 1784. With Baltimore as the episcopal seat, John Carroll was chosen as the first bishop of the Roman Catholic Church in America. Georgetown University, the oldest Catholic literary establishment in the United States, was founded in 1789. Education was a primary function of the Jesuits, but restrictions made it impossible for them to found a school at St. Mary's City, and much of their educational work was done in secret. The school at Bohemia inspired John Carroll to found Georgetown College and the seminary at that University.

Also from Bohemia went the Jesuit missionaries who brought Roman Catholicism to Pennsylvania. The first Catholic mission in that colony was established as a farm, on a hill overlooking the Little Conewago Creek in Adams County. There the first Catholic services in Pennsylvania were conducted, in a large stone house which still stands (No. 254). In 1741 a log chapel was built onto the stone farmhouse, to avoid the restrictions on Catholic churches. Beside the house is the stone Church of the Sacred Heart, built in 1785.

When Joseph Greaton, a Jesuit priest, went from Bohemia to Philadelphia and founded St. Joseph's Chapel, he went disguised as a Quaker, the common dress of the day in Penn's province. There he built a residence in the seclusion of Willing's Alley, and in it a room was furnished as St. Joseph's Chapel. There the issue of freedom of worship by Roman Catholics was brought to the test. The result, in 1734, was a triumph of religious freedom under Penn's Charter, won for Pennsylvania and ultimately for the United States. A record of it on a tablet at St. Joseph's Chapel was unveiled in a ceremony on May 21 and 22, 1956, which reads as follows:

"When in 1733
St. Joseph's Roman Catholic Church
was founded and
dedicated to the guardian of the Holy Family
it was the only place
in the entire English speaking world
where public celebration of
the Holy Sacrifice of the Mass
was permitted by law
In 1734
the Provincial Council of Pennsylvania
defended the liberty of worship
granted by William Penn to this colony
successfully withstood
the demand of the Governor of the Province
that this church be outlawed and such liberty suppressed
Thus was established permanently
in our nation
the principle of religious freedom
which was later embodied into
the Constitution
of
the United States of America"

St. Mary's Church (No. 210) was built near St. Joseph's as a chapel, and in that connection appears an account of St. Joseph's. The third and last Catholic colonial house of worship in Pennsylvania is St. Paul's Chapel at Bally (No. 246). The number of their houses of worship was small, as was the relative number of Catholics at any one time, but against great odds they played an important part in establishing the principle of religious freedom for the United States.

4

THE DISSENTERS AND
NEW ENGLAND

As Episcopalianism became the established religion in all colonies of the South, so Congregationalism became the established religion in all of New England, except Rhode Island. Of the three major religious polities, the contrast between these two was one of extremes, while the third, Presbyterianism, which became the prominent polity in the Mid-Atlantic, stood between the two both politically and geographically. The Episcopalianism of the South was a royal polity, established by the government under the king. The Congregationalism that was brought first to New England by the Pilgrim Fathers at Plymouth, was a religion of Dissenters and Separatists from the Church of England; the polity was purely democratic, government by the voice of individuals in a congregation. The Congregationalism brought to New England by the Puritans of the Massachusetts Bay Colony became theocratic and autocratic; as it led to autocratic government in England during Cromwell's Commonwealth, so Puritanism led to the Bible Commonwealth in Massachusetts, in which the practice and discipline of religion was established and enforced by law and was made a condition of citizenship.

Congregationalism in New England developed from the earliest urge in England for reform in the national Church. The Holy Roman Empire had developed a hierarchy in Europe, during the millenium and a half of Christendom — a rigid system of great vested interests, and a liturgy and lavish ritual that was determined and administered by the clergy, with a minimum of participation and understanding by the people. Such an establishment as the Church of England was considered by many Christians of that country to be a barrier in the relationship of the individual Christian to God through Christ. By 1384, when John Wycliffe died, he had become the leading advocate of the principles of the Lollards, a large and growing group of Englishmen who sought simplification in religion and a return to primitive Christian fundamentals. Wycliffe inspired John Huss in Bohemia, who was martyred in 1415 for having advocated reforms, and Huss preceded by about a century Martin Luther, whose proposals of reform launched the Reformation. In his *England in the Age of Wycliffe*, George Macauley Trevelyan wrote, in the Note following the text: "In a Bohemian psalter of 1572 appears a symbolical picture representing Wycliffe striking the spark, Huss kindling the coals, and Luther brandishing the lighted torch. To some extent this truly represents the case; for it is scarcely too much to say that the works of Huss were repetitions or paraphrases of Wycliffe's writings."

The Lollards were absorbed into the English Reformation. The process in England was a long, bitter, and complex struggle, in which many advocates of reform were driven out of the church, jailed, burned or hanged as heretics, or were exiled. Out of that struggle emerged several religious lines of inheritance and new denominations that had a part in founding the United States. Congregationalism grew from the ideals of the Lollards and their quest of primitive Christianity, the form that prevailed during the first two and a half centuries. It evolved among the puritans in the Church of England who sought to purify the Church from within, but who found that the only prospect for accomplishing their goal was to leave the Church; thus they became Separatists. The first statement of Congregationalism in England was written, in 1570, by Richard Fitz, Minister, in a manifesto, *The True Marks of Christ's Church*, etc. It contains three statements of principles — that the Glorious word and Evangel should be preached "freely and purely," and not in "bondage and subjection" as they considered it to be under the hierarchy of Episcopacy; "Secondly, to have the Sacraments ministered purely, only and altogether according to the institution and good worde of the Lord Jesus, without any tradition or invention of man"; finally, to do without canon law, and to practice only a discipline that was agreeable to the word of Jesus Christ.

The first prominent Separatist was Robert Browne (1550-1638), who established Congregationalism as a polity distinct from both Episcopacy and Presbyterianism; subsequent variants of Congregationalism adhered to his principles. Henry Barrowe (c. 1550-1593) promulgated a variation on the theology, but at the end of the Elizabethan period and the beginning of the reign of James I, when colonization in North America was about to begin, "Brownists" and "Barrowists" were all Separatists and forerunners of the Congregationalists.

About 1606 (when the Virginia Company and the Plymouth Company were chartered) two branches were divided out of a church that had originated a few years before at Gainsborough — one branch met at Gainsborough and the other at Scrooby Manor House. In 1607 the Gainsborough branch moved to Holland, to Amsterdam, where it played a part in originating the Baptist wing of Congregationalism. In 1608 the Scrooby branch moved to Amsterdam, and then to Leiden in the following year. Under John Robinson, who had joined the congregation originally in Gainsborough, the church at Leiden became the origin of both English and American Congregationalism. From Leiden a company returned in the *Speedwell* to England, in 1620, and they were the Pilgrim Fathers who sailed in the *Mayflower* and settled the Plymouth Colony.

Meanwhile, in 1616, Henry Jacob had founded a church at Southwark, across the Thames from the City of London, which is considered to be the mother church of the Independent (Congregationalist) denomination as it now exists. Jacob and Robinson both progressed through Puritanism and Separatism to Congregationalism and the concept of an "independent" church. The divergence of their Congregationalism from that of the Puritans is found in their church Covenant, "to walk together in all God's ways and ordinances, according as He had already revealed, or should further make known to them." The looking forward to more truth and light, "yet to break forth of his Holy Word," kept the minds of the Plymouth Congregationalists open and tolerant, while those of the Puritans in England and Massachusetts were closed and intolerant. This difference was evident between the colonies of Plymouth and Massachusetts Bay. Plymouth Congregationalism remained Trinitarian, while after the end of the Puritan's Bible Commonwealth, Unitarianism divided many of the Congregational churches of Massachusetts, and led to the organization of the American Unitarian Association at Boston in 1825.

The congregation at West Barnstable on Cape Cod is directly descended from that founded by Jacob at Southwark. John Lothrop, who worked with Jacob and succeeded him as leader of the congregation, was jailed in 1632 with about forty of his followers. After nearly three years in jail, he was released and banished; and in 1634, with thirty-four members of his congregation, he sailed in the ship *Griffin* for New England. The party landed at Boston and settled at Scituate, in the Plymouth Colony. Five years later, Lothrop and his followers moved to Barnstable, where they built a meeting house on what has been known since as Lothrop Hill. The present meeting house (No. 91) was built in the West Parish in 1717, and there the congregation continues to worship in the Trinitarian faith that came to them from one of the earliest Congregational groups.

Members of the Plymouth Colony were instrumental in founding, in Rhode Island, the Baptist Church of America. As noted above, the Baptist Church was derived from the Gainsborough branch of Congregationalism. By saving Roger Williams (c. 1604-1684) from banishment and persuading him to settle in their territory of Rhode Island, the Plymouth Congregationalists were instrumental in introducing religious freedom into that territory. Williams was a pioneer in individualism and religious liberty. While he was serving as teacher (assistant minister) of the church in Salem, where the Puritans had first established their Massachusetts Bay Colony, Williams held that the civil authorities had no jurisdiction over the consciences of man. Such views were against the law, and they caused the Puritan authorities in Boston to try him. In 1635 Williams was convicted and sentenced to banishment. Just before he was to be deported to England, officials of the Plymouth Colony arranged for him to escape to their territory, and there he settled on a site which he named Providence. He then took the steps that founded the Baptist Church in America (see First Baptist Church, Providence, R.I., No. 260). In the same colony, two Baptist sects subsequently were formed — the Six Principle Baptist Church (see Elder Ballou Meeting House, No. 264), and the Seventh Day Baptist Church (see Sabbath Day Meeting House, No. 268).

Attracted by the principles of individualism and freedom of religion in Rhode Island, Quakers settled there in 1657, and about 1661 they held the first General Meeting of Friends in America at Newport (see Old Newport Friends Meeting House, No. 266). In this liberal colony Quakers thrived and eventually governed it, while in Massachusetts the Puritans persecuted them, hung some of them on Boston Common, and drove others to move to the more liberal Plymouth Colony (see Pembroke Friends Meeting House, near Scituate, No. 90). A liberal policy is aided greatly by a sense of humor. On an occasion when the governors of New England tried to persuade the governor of Rhode Island to join with them in outlawing Quakers, an interesting sidelight on Rhode Island's toleration was reflected in the governor's response. He said that, as the Quakers thrived on martyrdom, it had been decided to ignore them, with the expectation that they then would leave Rhode Island. During the colonial period in that colony, religious freedom did not include Roman Catholics, but it was extended to Jews, as outlined in the next chapter.

Puritanism developed in England under considerable influence from Calvinism and Presbyterianism. During the Protectorate, Presbyterians were in favor, together with Independents and Baptists. After the Restoration, the reestablished Church of England considered both Presbyterians and Congregationalists to be Nonconformists, and the rejection drew them closer together. At one time they were referred to interchangeably as "Presbyterians or Independents." After the Toleration Act of 1689, an attempt was made in the London area to unite the two, incorporating features of both in what was known as the New England Way. The result in both England and New England was a Congregationalism with strong Presbyterian leanings. A good example of it is found in this collection, in the story of the congregation that went from Dorchester, England, to settle Dorchester, Massachusetts, and thence to Dorchester, South Carolina (see No. 280), and finally to Dorchester, Georgia (see No. 30). In Georgia, where Dr. Abiel Holmes, the father of Oliver Wendell Holmes was pastor, the congregation was as New England as if they were still in Massachusetts, and on occasion they had Presbyterian preachers.

In the long struggle between the Puritans and the Crown, the situation in New England was the reverse of that in Virginia. In the southern colony, the Anglicans defied Cromwell and the Puritans during the Rebellion, and maintained their Episcopal worship throughout the colonial period. In Massachusetts the Puritans defied the efforts of the Crown to introduce the Church of England. The Puritan Bible Commonwealth, with its intolerance, restrictions, and death penalties in matters of religion, was well entrenched. Under those conditions, the Book of Common Prayer was excluded, and Anglicans were denied citizenship. In 1688, Sir Edmund Andros was sent over to unite New Jersey and New York with the New England colonies into the Dominion of New England, and to introduce the Church of England. He ordered the congregation of Old South Church, Boston (No. 94), to permit their meeting house to be used for worship by the Anglicans, until Queen's Chapel (later King's Chapel, No. 95) could be built, the first Anglican church in New England. The first building of the chapel was started that year, while the Anglicans attended services in the Congregational meeting house on Sunday afternoons, amidst considerable tension. In 1689 Boston revolted and put Andros in prison. The result was that Massachusetts was given a new charter by William and Mary in 1691, which ended the long colonial independence of both the Plymouth Colony and the Puritan Bible Commonwealth of Massachusetts and united them under one royal governor. The new charter eased the Puritan abuses of religious requirements for office and franchise, and provided liberty of conscience for all but Roman Catholics. Thus William and Mary ended the Puritan period in Massachusetts at the same time that they ended the Catholic period in Maryland, and made royal colonies of both. After King's Chapel had introduced the Church of England into New England, the first Anglican parish in Rhode Island was founded in 1688 by Sir Francis Nicholson. He was serving in New York as deputy of Andros, governor of the Dominion of New England, (see Trinity Church, Newport, No. 267).

Another Anglican church of New England is of particular historical interest. It was at the Glebe House of St. Paul's Church, Woodbury, Connecticut, that a conference of ten of the fourteen Anglican priests in the colony in 1783 elected Samuel Seabury, the rector of that church, to go to England and seek consecration as Bishop of Connecticut, the first in America (see No. 11). After being refused by the Church of England, he finally was consecrated by Scottish bishops at Aberdeen in 1784.

The new charter united Maine and Massachusetts, and Congregationalism was the established religion in the whole region. In the Berkshire Hills of western Massachusetts, Dutch traders from the Hudson River and Mohawk valleys settled, but English settlers came up through the Connecticut River Valley and established Congregationalism on that frontier (see Old Parish Church, Sheffield, No. 108). The colony of Connecticut was founded, not by royal charter originally, but by English settlers from Massachusetts as a buffer against the Dutch, who thereby were contained in the Hudson Valley of New York.

The Congregationalism that became the established religion in Connecticut was conservative and Calvinistic, as was that of the founders of Yale College. Throughout these colonial parishes in New England we find pastors who were graduated from Harvard or Yale. Harvard College (see Holden Chapel, No. 97), was founded by Puritans, but the civil magistrates removed the first president, Henry Dunster, for questioning infant baptism. During the subsequent years, the trend of theology at the College was liberal, and the orthodox Puritans, with Increase and Cotton Mather leading the reaction, tried to gain control through the Board of Overseers. After they had failed, the reactionaries, with Cotton Mather exerting a strong influence, founded Yale College. The conservative Congregationalism of the new College, with strong Presbyterian influence, was evident from the beginning in the appointment of the first president. We find his story outlined in connection with the First Presbyterian Church, Newark, New Jersey (No. 132). There the Reverend Abraham Pierson, Jr., had succeeded his father as the second pastor. He had gone with his father from Branford, Connecticut, to New Jersey, and it was during his pastorate that the congregation of the church at Newark had changed from Congregational to adopt a Presbyterian form. Back at Branford, a group of ten clergymen, all Harvard graduates, founded the new College in 1701, and elected Pierson its first rector, or president. While the conservative secession at Yale developed, Harvard went further into radical theology; in 1805 a Unitarian, Henry Ware, pastor of the First Parish of Hingham (see Old Ship Meeting House, No. 87), was elected Hollis Professor of Divinity, amidst considerable controversy.

Harvard was founded to bring Christian education to the Indians as well as to the English colonists. Within a decade of its founding, work among the Indians was undertaken by John Eliot and Thomas Mahew. Eliot translated the Scriptures into their language, and by 1675 there were about four thousand converts in six Indian churches. In this collection we find the Old Indian Church at Mashpee, on Cape Cod (No. 92). The church originally was Congregational, but the congregation did not always enjoy the privileges of that established religion, and an Indian preacher, "Blind Joseph Amos," helped them to become Baptists under a special act of the legislature.

Another example of the close relationship between Congregationalism and Presbyterianism in Massachusetts was the Old South Church at Newburyport (No. 112). It was associated from its beginning with the Great Awakening, for it was organized under the inspiration of George Whitefield, the evangelist who not only was a founder of Methodism, but inspired the "New Side" Presbyterians in opposition to the conservative "Old Side" faction, and who continued to be a priest of the Church of England as long as he lived. As noted earlier, he first came to America when John Wesley invited him to Georgia, and after preaching all over the British colonies on seven visits from England, he died at Newburyport in 1770, and was buried in the crypt of the church which he had founded. While the religion of the church was Presbyterian from the beginning, it was not until 1802 that the Presbyterian polity was formally adopted.

Jonathan Edwards (1703-1758) was the preacher who carried the torch with Whitefield and led the revival in New England. He was a moving preacher in a spiritual awakening that was characterized by emotion. At Enfield, Connecticut, we find that in the Congregational Church (see No. 9) during the Great Awakening, Edwards preached one of his most stirring and famous sermons, "Sinners in the Hands of an Angry God."

Puritans from New England migrated westward as pioneer settlers, carrying with them the democracy of their town meeting and the Calvinism of their religion. In this collection we find that they moved from Connecticut and the Connecticut River Valley in Massachusetts to settle in New Jersey, from Newark to West Jersey on the lower Delaware River. Carrying their names with them (in much the same way as the Dorchester communities mentioned earlier), they founded the First Presbyterian congregation of Connecticut Farms (No. 134), the Presbyterian Church at Springfield (No. 135), the Fairfield Presbyterian Church at New England Cross Roads (No. 150), and the Presbyterian Church at Deerfield (No. 152).

In New England, democracy in its purest form survives in the town meeting. There every voting citizen has a voice in the government of the town. In the Established Order under Puritan rule, all voting citizens were members of the Congregational Church, and Anglicans among others were barred from citizenship. The meeting house was the public place of meeting for civic business as well as for church business and worship. In it were held elections and church services. It was a common custom in elections for the candidates to put their hats in a ring on the clerk's table in the meeting house, where they served as ballot boxes. Among the colonial meeting houses in this collection, a number will be found that are now serving only as town houses, or town halls as they generally are called today. In its early years a town had only one meeting house. When the town grew, and the church society built a meeting house of its own, the original building was confined to town government and civic functions.

In summary, of the seventy-nine colonial houses of worship in New England, fifty were built by Congregationalists and five by Presbyterians, ten were Anglican churches, and nine were Friends meeting houses. Most of the Friends meeting houses are in Rhode Island. Also in that state there are three Baptist meeting houses — one was built by the mother church in America, and the others by two different Baptist sects. And in Rhode Island there is at Newport the one colonial Jewish synagogue in the United States (No. 271). At Waldoboro, Maine, at the northeastern extremity of the collection, stands a colonial meeting house of German Lutherans (No. 35).

5

THE COLONIAL JEWS

The story of the colonial Jews in America, like that of America itself, goes back to 1492 and the Catholic sovereigns of Spain, Ferdinand and Isabella. The Jews who came to America during the colonial period were Sephardim. These Sephardic Jews were descended from those in Spain and Portugal, where many had gone in the Great Dispersion, after the capture of Jerusalem by Titus in the year 70. The Jews everywhere in Diaspora, following the Babylonian captivity and the Great Dispersion, suffered persecution sooner or later and in varying degrees. On the Iberian Peninsula, the main persecution came later, after 1492 when the Catholic sovereigns reconquered the last of the Moorish kingdoms in Spain. Meanwhile, even though there were four outbursts of persecution by the Church during the fifteenth century, the Jews in Spain enjoyed three centuries of freedom that made it a golden age in the history of their people; it was comparable to that of their gaonate in Babylonia under Persian rule, a thousand years after the captivity. As a result of the development of their culture during those centuries of freedom in Spain and Portugal, the Sephardic Jews, who came to America during the colonial period, were different from the Ashkenazim (the Jews of Germany and northern Europe), who came to America after the Revolution as refugees from generations of living in ghettos.

Sepharad was a place mentioned in the Old Testament in connection with the captivity. Verse 20 of Obadiah says, ". . . and the captivity of Jerusalem, which is in Sepharad, shall possess the cities of the south." All that we know about Sepharad is that it must have been in Asia Minor. As it was in Babylonia that Israel was purified and reformed, the lost haven of Sepharad assumed mystical significance, like that of Shangri La in James Hilton's *Lost Horizon*; and after the golden age in Spain and Portugal, the Jews who had enjoyed it were called Sephardim.

In the history of the Jews, the second great period began with Alexander the Great and his conquest of Asia Minor. This period is important in the history of Christendom, for it is the Hellenic period, during which Greek culture dominated the civilized world of the Mediterranean and prepared the way for Christianity. The period began with a concept that has influenced the history of the Western world, from Aristotle and Plato through Alexander, the world Community of Jews, and the Holy Roman Empire, to the United States — *E Pluribus Unum*, "One Out of Many." Alexander, a disciple of Aristotle, took this idea, which became central to the philosophy of Plato, and as a demi-god, attempted to unite the many conquered states and peoples of his world into one empire under one god-emperor, while leaving each state and people their individuality. St. Paul stated the principle in his First Epistle to the Corinthians, 12:13-14. The Holy Roman Empire was based on the same concept, with the different states and peoples united under one emperor, with Christianity as the one religion under one pope. In America the concept had evolved to the point where the one was the government, while the many included the different states, peoples, races, religions, faiths, denominations, sects, and all the different tastes within a parish. Two thousand years of struggle were involved in the efforts of emperors and kings to enforce conformity to one religion — from Alexander's conquest, more than three centuries before Christ, to the American Revolution. The complex struggle finally resulted, in 1789, in the formation of the world's first republic in which complete religious freedom was guaranteed, with state and church separate. In this Republic, "*E Pluribus Unum*" is the motto for the many different but united states, and "In God We Trust" is the motto for the many different religious faiths among the diverse but united peoples under one God.

That Hellenic period in the history of the Jews lasted for four centuries. It ended in A.D. 70, with the fall of Jerusalem, the destruction of the Temple, and the abolition of the priesthood. Titus, who conquered Jerusalem, was the son of Vespasian, who had been ordered by Nero to put down a rebellion and civil war between rival factions in Palestine. Within a short time after the appointment, Nero died, and Vespasian had been proclaimed emperor. He turned over his command to Titus, and after the fall of Jerusalem the Jews were allowed civil and religious freedom under their rule.

Sixty-five years later, however, in A.D. 135, a war to free Jerusalem from Roman domination ended in complete disaster. Hundreds of thousands of lives were lost in fighting, fire, and famine, and political nationalism of the Jews was annihilated. Then the dispersion of Jews to Europe, which already had begun, was greatly accelerated. The loss of the Temple at Jerusalem and the priesthood had led to the establishment of Jewish life as a world community. Babylonia, which had been the scene of the captivity a thousand years before, now under Persian rule became a new Palestine, and at Nehardea, which was to the Jews as a new Jerusalem, a new principle was formulated that enabled them to live in foreign lands with accommodation — "The law of the government is the law."

Jerusalem was rebuilt by the Roman Emperor Hadrian, and the Temple of Jehovah was replaced by a Temple of Jupiter, but Roman laws gave Jews civil rights. When Christianity replaced the pagan gods as the official religion of the empire, civil rights for the dispersed Jews continued under the Christian emperors. The Church's increasing fear of the growth and intrusion of Judaism, however, led to the imposition of increasingly severe legal restrictions on Jews.

Mohammed introduced a new religion which borrowed from both Judaism and Christianity, but it excluded both Jews and Christians as infidels. The Jews then entered upon an amazing paradox — they came to live a freer life under the Crescent than under the Cross. The Christian Empire officially granted liberties to Jews but practiced increasing intoleration, while Islam officially was intolerant and had no place for Jews, but in practice the Jews became allies and equals of the Mohammedans in the Moorish kingdoms of Spain.

There were Jews in Spain before the conquest by the Moors, as there had been since the Dispersion also in Byzantium, Greece, and Rome. However, with the conquest of Spain in A.D. 711, by the Arabs, Syrians, and Berbers, who became known collectively as Moors, a great migration of Jews took place. In North Africa, the Arab had swept away the Roman fiscal system and had substituted a system of raising revenue by poll tax and land tax. With the prospect of taxing Christians, the Arab's interest in Spain was economic rather than religious, and he welcomed the Jews who eagerly joined the conquest. The Jewish Community was dispersed over the civilized world, forming a natural framework for a system of trade, and the Jews in Europe became the princes of international trade. Charlemagne, the first emperor of the Holy Roman Empire, encouraged the Jews in the development of trade, at the very time that the famous Moslem, Harun al-Rashid, was persecuting both Jews and Christians, but in general throughout the Middle Ages in Europe the situation was the reverse, and Jews were encouraged more by Moslems than by Christians. In Spain, from the beginning of the Moorish conquest, the Jews rose to high places in the state, and between A.D. 711 and 1492 they developed a culture that was comprehensive and deep. From the Mohammedans in free association, the Jews absorbed philosophy, science, and poetry, and developed men who were outstanding in learning, literature, and science, as well as in medicine, statecraft, and general affairs. An outstanding product of this Spanish-Jewish culture in the Middle Ages was Rabbi Moses Ben Maimon (1135-1204), known as Maimonides. He matured in Spain at a time when a fanatical revival of Islam was threatening Judaism in that country, and his wide learning, philosophy, and teaching inspired a revival of Jewish faith. His writings contributed to the philosophy of Baruch Spinoza (1632-1677), the philosopher who was born in Amsterdam of Sephardic Jewish parents, who had fled to that liberal haven of Holland to escape persecution by the Christian Church.

During the crusades, the Jews in Spain suffered at the hands of the Christians, who fought the Mohammedans in that country and swept across it on their way to Palestine. When the Almohades, the fanatical Islamic sect of North Africa and Spain, threatened invasion in 1212, a crusade against them was waged by the kings of Castile, Aragon, Navarre, and Portugal; and the defeat of the Mohammedans left Spain open to the Christians. After 1265 the Mohammedans held only Granada and the ports around the cape to Cadiz. The Jews suffered under the brutal Almohades, and they aided King Ferdinand III in the reconquest of Andalusia. As a result, the King maintained confidence in them. The freedom of the Jews continued until Ferdinand and Isabella completed the reconquest of Spain by taking Granada in 1492. It was this long period, commencing with the reign of Ferdinand III (1217-1252) and ending with that momentous date in history, 1492, that constituted the golden age for the Jews in Spain. The whole period of 781 years of the Moors and Jews in Spain ended in 1492, and then their expulsion or absorption into Christianity began.

The marriage of Ferdinand and Isabella in 1469 had united the crowns of Castile and Aragon and prepared the way for the unification of Spain. The Catholic sovereigns undertook the Christianizing of the kingdoms, and by their ruthless methods, that proved to be easier than unification. There was to be no toleration and no compromise for non-Christians or heretics, and the Spanish Inquisition, independent of the Roman Church, was instituted by Ferdinand and Isabella, in 1480, as a national royal instrument to enforce conformity. The principle of "One in Many" was invoked by the Catholic sovereigns, to unify the diverse states under one government, with all subjects in one Christian Church, even though Jews and Mohammedans comprised a large part of the population, roughly estimated at nearly one-half. Under persecution by the Church, the practice of Marranism developed, and in both Spain and Portugal many Marranos, or Christianized Jews, retained their old faith in secret. The Inquisition generated a spirit of intolerance that inaugurated the ghetto period in northern Europe, and in Spain led to the expulsion of the Jews in 1492 by Isabella, the Catholic.

On the first voyage with Columbus there was a Sephardic Jew serving as navigator. By a happy coincidence, that same Catholic sovereign who dispersed the Spanish Jews, in the same year sponsored the voyage that discovered the New World, and opened new lands for the eventual settlement of oppressed and persecuted peoples of Europe.

This new age of discovery was preceded by a century of exploration and colonizing by the Portuguese. Their expansion by sea was forced by the situation of the Spanish kingdoms on the land routes into Europe. As they opened new routes down the African coast and around that continent, the Jews participated in developing new trade. The story of the Jews in Portugal was distinct but similar in many respects to that of the Spanish Jews. They developed in trade, finance, and wealth; they became the tax collectors for the sovereign; they were envied and resented and were persecuted in the name of the Church; they were taxed on nearly every business transaction, and with a special poll tax in the amount that Judas had received for the betrayal of Christ; and through the centuries in Portugal they developed a comprehensive culture. Their learning contributed to all seven branches of medieval scholasticism, and their knowledge of mathematics and astronomy was such that they contributed to exploration through navigation and the development of instruments for it. During the fifteenth century, as the Portuguese gained a world monopoly in international trade, the Jews participated as financiers and traders, and they comprised a middle class that was essential to the economy of Portugal.

In 1496 the course of Portugal's history was altered. Pursuing a policy of intermarriage with the royal families of Castile and Aragon, to unify the kingdoms of Spain and Portugal, Emanuel I was to marry Isabella, the daughter of Ferdinand and Isabella. As a condition of the marriage, however, he was required to purge Portugal of all Jews by the end of October, 1497. In order to avoid the economic consequences to his country at the height of her world power, all Jews were forcibly baptized, and the converted Christians, Marranos, then were forbidden to leave the country before 1507. Following a riot and the massacre of the majority of the Jews in Lisbon in 1506, the Marranos were protected during Emanuel's reign, and were allowed to emigrate. Most of the Jews in Portugal took advantage of the opportunity to flee the country, and their exodus in this new dispersion was an important factor in the decline of Portugal as a world power.

Sephardic Jews emigrated to Holland, and they became as active with the Dutch in trade and colonization as they had been with the Portuguese and the Spanish. Holland had become a haven of religious freedom after a war of independence against the same royal families that had expelled the Jews from Spain and Portugal. The frequency of intermarriage weakened those families with epilepsy and madness and contributed to the decline of the two countries. Ferdinand and Isabella were cousins, for example, as were their grandchildren, Charles I (as King of Spain) and V (as Emperor of the Holy Roman Empire) and his wife Isabella, daughter of Isabella and Emanuel I of Portugal.

Charles V was born and raised in the Netherlands, which he inherited from his father, Philip of Burgundy. Upon his abdication at Brussels in 1555 he resigned the Netherlands to his son Philip, who in the following January became also Philip II of Spain and the American colonies. At the same time, Charles arranged the marriage of Philip and Mary Tudor of England, a cousin. In 1559, Philip left Brussels for Spain and Madrid, and he never returned. He revived the religious fanaticism of his great-grandparents, Ferdinand and Isabella, and on the ancient interpretation that "one in many" meant all dependencies united under the Roman Church, he waged war on heresy in the Netherlands, where Protestantism was growing, using the army, the navy, and the Inquisition in the campaigns.

William of Nassau, Prince of Orange, became a Lutheran and then formally entered the Calvinistic Communion. The Calvinist preachers fomented such a frenzied resistance to the Roman Church that, for a time, mobs raided churches and destroyed property. The result was bloody reprisals from the Spanish armies under the Duke of Alva, and the independence movement led by William was set back. The conditions for which William led the fight were laid down in 1574, and they were far-reaching in their influence on the colonial history of America. It is interesting to note that the first of the three concerned religion: (1) Freedom of worship and liberty to preach the gospel according to the Word of God; (2) the restoration of all ancient charters, liberties, and privileges of the land; (3) the removal of all Spaniards and other foreigners from public offices, civil and military. The climax of the struggle for independence came in 1577, when Don Juan of Austria, brother of Philip, who had been sent as governor-general of the Netherlands, withdrew from Brussels, and William of Orange was proclaimed leader of all the Netherlands. The Catholic nobles of the south, however, adhered to the royalist cause, to become the separate country of Belgium. In 1579 the Union of Utrecht bound together the northern provinces in a confederacy, which became the independent Protestant country of Holland.

Thus Holland became a haven of religious independence, nine years before the Battle of the Armada settled the rivalry between Catholic Philip II of Spain and Protestant Elizabeth I of England. Elizabeth aided William in the liberation of the Netherlands, and with Protestantism as a mutual bond, the two countries maintained a close relationship. Elizabeth brought to England many artisans and craftsmen from the Low Countries. The best example of their craftsmanship to be found among these colonial houses of worship in America is the brickwork in Flemish bond, which is prevalent in the colonial churches of Virginia. Another is the corbie, or stepped, gable found on the Old Brick Church, Isle of Wight County, Virginia (No. 297). The principle of freedom of conscience attracted to Holland various Protestant groups of the Reformation and Sephardic Jews. Holland became a point of departure for various religious groups that settled in America. We have seen that Separatists went from England to Holland and then sailed to New England. In the next chapter is an account of the Dutch Reformed and German Reformed groups, which came from Holland to America.

The Sephardic Jews made Amsterdam their headquarters, and in the Jewish community of that city they built the mother synagogue. They went to London and became established in England. One of the most famous Sephardic Jews in England was Benjamin Disraeli, first Earl of Beaconsfield and Prime Minister in the reign of Queen Victoria; like his father, Isaac D'Israeli, he was also an author of literary works. [In America a well-known Sephardic Jew was Associate Justice of the Supreme Court of the United States—Benjamin Nathan Cardozo (1870-1938).] In the West Indies and South America, Sephardic Jews settled in Dutch and English colonies, and in North America they settled in the ports and engaged in ocean trade, as they had been doing for a thousand years. Quite logically, their first community in North America was settled in New Amsterdam, where the Dutch established their first colony. During the colonial period in America, substantial and wealthy Sephardic Jews settled in the Atlantic ports, in addition to New York, at Savannah, Charleston, Richmond, Baltimore, Philadelphia, and Newport. Of all their communities, the only colonial synagogue to survive in the United States is Touro Synagogue at Newport, Rhode Island (see No. 271). During the colonial period the Jews of other colonies came to regard Congregation Jeshuat Israel at Newport as the mother congregation.

Much is found at Touro Synagogue that establishes the connections of Congregation Jeshuat Israel with the world Community of Sephardic Jews. In the graveyard the inscriptions are in Hebrew, Latin, Spanish, Portuguese, and English. The community was the second in the colonies, after that at New York, and its synagogue, built in 1759, not only is the oldest, but is considered to be the loveliest in the country. It is antedated in the Western Hemisphere only by the Mikveh Israel Synagogue in Curaçao (Dutch West Indies), consecrated in 1732, and the Zedek ve Shalom

Synagogue in Paramaribo, Surinam (Dutch Guiana), dedicated in 1737. The first synagogue in North America was built in New York in 1730, but the building was torn down and replaced in that ever-changing city. The New York community contributed about one-tenth of the cost of the building at Newport, and contributions came also from Congregation Shaar Hashamayim in Jamaica, Congregation Shaar Hashamayim in London, Congregation Mikveh Israel in Curaçao, and Congregation Neveh Shalom in Surinam. The architecture of the building, which was designed by Peter Harrison of Newport, is in the Spanish style, with features of the Sephardic synagogues derived from the mother synagogue in Amsterdam (1675). In that tradition the seats are arranged, not facing the Ark, but at right angles to it, along the north and south walls (see No. 271, interior). The space is clear between the reading desk in the center and the Ark at the east end. Also in keeping with the synagogue at Amsterdam and that at London (1701) is the location of the "banco," or seat for the *Parnas Presidente*, the presiding officer, at the middle of the north wall.

To Rhode Island as to Holland, the Sephardic Jews were attracted by the principle of religious freedom on which the government of the colony was founded. The earliest evidence of their presence in Newport is a document of 1658. Some of the congregation were Marranos, such as Abraham Lopez, who was born in Lisbon, Portugal. There he was christened as Michael, was married to Joanna, in the Roman Catholic Church, and they had three sons who were given the Christian names of Edward, Joseph, and John. Threatened by the Inquisition, the family emigrated to America; here the parents were remarried under the Jewish law, and changed their names to Abraham and Abigail, and the names of the children became Moses, Samuel, and Jacob. Free to live their lives to the best of their abilities, as they had been during the golden age in Spain and Portugal, the Jews in Newport prospered and took part in the cultural life of the city. They owned seven vessels, which were active in intercolonial and foreign trade, and they engaged in manufacturing. They worked as silversmiths and in iron and brass foundaries. The Rivera family, in the 1740's, established the first spermaceti candle factory; and it was reminiscent of their Iberian origin that, in 1761, James Lucena introduced the manufacture of Castile soap. In the cultural life of the city these Jews took part in the Philosophical Society, and when it was succeeded by the Redwood Library, three of its members, in 1747, were Abraham Hart, Moses Lopez, and Jacob Rodriguez Rivera of this congregation.

As the religious freedom guaranteed in Pennsylvania by the charter of William Penn was tested by the Roman Catholics and proved valid for all time, so was that established by Roger Williams in Rhode Island tested by the Jews of Newport and proved valid. The code of laws drafted in 1647, eleven years after Williams had founded the colony, concluded with the words, ". . . All men may walk as their consciences persuade them, every one in the name of his God. And let the saints of the Most High walk in this colony without molestation in the name of Jehovah their God, forever and ever." Thirty-seven years later, in 1684, in the early days of the Jewish community, the protection promised in that statement was threatened, and it was tested by two members of the congregation, Simon Mendez and David Brown, in a petition to the General Assembly. That body responded by declaring that "... they may expect as good protection here as any strangers being not of our nation residing among us, in His Majesty's Colony, ought to have, being obedient to His Majesty's laws."

The colonial Jews in America, like the Roman Catholics, played a part in the founding of the United States that is out of all proportion to their numbers. That part is revealed in an exchange of communications between the Congregation Jeshuat Israel and President George Washington. In 1790, the year after his inauguration, Washington visited Newport in the course of a tour to inspire the people of the United States with their responsibilities as citizens of this new Republic. He was presented with an address by Moses Seixas on behalf of the Hebrew Congregation, which read in part as follows:

"Deprived as we heretofore have been of the invaluable rights of free citizens, we now (with a deep sense of gratitude to the Almighty Dispenser of all Events) behold a Government erected by the majesty of the people, a Government which gives to bigotry no sanction, to persecution no assistance; but generously affording to all liberty of conscience and immunities of citizenship, deeming everyone, of whatever nation, tongue, or language, equal parts of the great Governmental machine."

Washington replied on August 21, 1790, in a letter which reads as follows:

To the Hebrew Congregation in Newport
Rhode Island

Gentlemen.

While I receive with much satisfaction your Address replete with expressions of affection and esteem; I rejoice in the opportunity of assuring you, that I shall always retain a grateful remembrance of the cordial welcome I experienced in my visit to Newport, from all classes of Citizens.

The reflection on the days of difficulty and danger which are past is rendered the more sweet, from a consciousness that they are succeeded by days of uncommon prosperity and security. If we have wisdom to make the best use of the advantages with which we are now favored, we cannot fail, under the just administration of a good Government, to become a great and a happy people.

The Citizens of the United States of America have a right to applaud themselves for having given to mankind examples of an enlarged and liberal policy: a policy worthy of imitation. All possess alike liberty of conscience and immunities of citizenship. It is now no more that toleration is spoken of, as if it was by the indulgence of one class of people, that another enjoyed the exercise of their inherent natural rights. For happily the Government of the United States, which gives to bigotry no sanction, to persecution no assistance requires only that they who live under its protection should demean themselves as good citizens, in giving it on all occasions their effectual support.

It would be inconsistent with the frankness of my character not to avow that I am pleased with your favorable opinion of my Administration, and fervent wishes for my felicity. May the Children of the stock of Abraham, who dwell in this land, continue to merit and enjoy the good will of the other Inhabitants, while every one shall sit in safety under his own vine and figtree, and there shall be none to make him afraid. May the father of all mercies scatter light and not darkness in our paths, and make us all in our several vocations useful here, and in his own due time and way everlastingly happy.

G. Washington

In recognition of the part played by the members of the Hebrew Congregation in the growth of religious freedom, as a basic principle in the foundation of the United States, and in the development of life as a whole among the American people, Touro Synagogue was dedicated on August 31, 1947, by the National Park Service, Department of the Interior, as a National Shrine.

6

THE PROTESTANTS AND THE MID-ATLANTIC

The Mid-Atlantic region was the third in which colonization began, following the settlement of Anglicans in Virginia and the Pilgrim Congregationalists at Plymouth. With the Church of England established in all colonies of the South, and Congregationalism in all New England colonies except Rhode Island, the societies of those two regions was relatively homogeneous. In the Mid-Atlantic, however, it was decidedly heterogeneous. Not only were there Dissenters from New England, but there were Quakers and Presbyterians from Great Britain, and Protestants of various denominations and sects from a variety of countries, principalities, and duchies of Europe. In this region, colonies were established by the Dutch and the Swedes. They were followed from Europe by the English, French Huguenots, Germans, Swiss, Welsh, Scots, and Scotch-Irish — all Protestants — and Sephardic Jews. A liberal policy toward Protestants was pursued by the various governments in each of the colonies in the region, with the result that there are fifteen denominations in the region, of the total of twenty in the collection (for summary see Appendix II).

While Episcopalianism dominated in the South and Congregationalism in New England, Presbyterianism was the prevailing polity in the Mid-Atlantic. It came in with the Dutch Reformed, the German Reformed, the Calvinistic Puritans from New England, and the Scottish and Scotch-Irish Presbyterians. The Quakers brought a polity of subordinated meetings ruled by elders that was presbyterian in character, and the Moravians one that was both episcopalian and presbyterian. In general, this presbyterian polity in the Mid-Atlantic was republican, in the conduct of general affairs through elected representatives.

1. Dutch Reformed

The Reformed Dutch Church originated in the teachings of the Swiss reformer, Ulrich Zwingli (1484-1531), and was developed and formulated by John Calvin (1509-1564), the French Protestant who, at Geneva, became the leader of the new religion. Calvin's dispute with the Lutherans respecting the Lord's Supper led to the separation of the evangelical Protestants into two great sections, the Lutherans and the Reformed. The Reformed shared Calvin's faith in a virtual presence of the body and blood of Christ in the Eucharist, and spiritual participation through faith, while the Lutherans held that the body and blood of Christ are objectively and consubstantially present and are actually partaken. Thus the Reformed or Calvinistic churches repudiated both the transubstantiation of the Roman Church and the consubstantiation of the Lutheran churches. The Dutch established in their American colony the first settlement of the Reformed faith in the New World.

In 1623 the Dutch founded the province of New Netherland, under the management of the Chamber of Amsterdam, after the granting of a charter in 1621 that gave to the West India Company a monopoly of Dutch trade for the entire coast of America, from Newfoundland to the Straits of Magellan. In 1624 the Chamber of Amsterdam sent the ship *New Netherland* across the Atlantic with the first permanent Dutch colonists, thirty families, most of whom were Walloons. These people were from the southern provinces of the Netherlands, which became Belgium. Originally the Walloons had been Protestant refugees from France and Flanders. The Walloon Church was a Protestant church using the *Geneva Catechism* of the faith of Calvin.

New Netherland originally extended from the Delaware to the Connecticut River, and the company that arrived in the ship *New Netherland* bracketed the entire territory with their settlements, not only at Manhattan where the ship landed, and up the Hudson at the site of the present Albany, but also on the Delaware River and at the site of the present Hartford on the Connecticut. In Chapter 4, it was noted that Connecticut was established by the English colonists of Massachusetts to contain the Dutch in the Hudson Valley. The Dutch period in New Netherland extended until the English took over in 1664. Under British rule, toleration was granted to the Dutch Reformed Church and all other Protestants. Charles II then created a province of the area from the Delaware to the Connecticut River, and granted it to his brother James, Duke of York and Albany, and New Netherland became New York. At the same time the Duke of York began the separation of New Jersey from the province, by granting the area between the Delaware and the Hudson rivers to John, Lord Berkeley and Sir George Carteret. The new province was given the name *Nova Caesarea*, or New Jersey, for the Channel island where Carteret, its governor, had sheltered the Duke during the Puritan Parliament in England. After a decade, the Dutch recaptured New York temporarily, but in 1674 the English took permanent possession. After 1683, when the province of New York was divided into twelve counties, two of them passed to Massachusetts, and New York became confined to the Hudson Valley and westward.

The "Church in the Fort" at Fort Amsterdam, Manhattan, was the first Dutch Reformed church to be organized in America. The congregation is now the Collegiate Church of New York, but no church building of the colonial period survives. At Fort Orange, now Albany, was located the earliest Dutch settlement, and there the second oldest congregation of the Dutch Reformed Church in America was organized in 1642. The present building of that congregation, the First Dutch Reformed Church or the North Dutch Church, is the fourth (begun in 1797 and not included in this collection). As the Dutch West India Company was interested only in colonizing for trade and profit, education of the people and their religious life was left entirely to the Church, a situation quite different generally from that in New England and the South.

The West India Company offered patroonships, or large grants of land, on the condition of settling fifty colonists within four years. One of the most important patroonships to be established was Rensselaerswyck, a vast tract on the Hudson and Mohawk rivers that included the site of Albany. This was the center of the fur trade with the Indians, and we find colonial churches along both rivers. As the fur trade diminished, the patroons divided their manors into farms, which were worked by tenant farmers under leasehold, as subjects of the lord of the manor. In the Hudson Valley, the three most important manors below Rensselaerswyck were Philipsburgh Manor, Van Cortlandt Manor, and Livingston Manor. Each of the three had a colonial church associated with it, each built by a different denomination. The Sleepy Hollow Dutch Reformed Church (No. 178), at Scarborough, was built in 1699 by Frederick Philipse as the church of the Manor of Philipsburgh. Washington Irving, who recorded vividly the life of the Dutch people on the Hudson, made the church famous in the *Legend of Sleepy Hollow*. At Van Cortlandtville, near the Van Cortlandt Manor house, St. Peter's Church (No. 179) was built by Anglicans in 1767. The third is the Evangelical Lutheran Church of St. Peter the Apostle (No. 188), which was built in 1730 by German Lutherans who worked on Livingston Manor. At Fishkill stands the Old Dutch Church (No. 182), built in 1731, the only other Dutch church on the Hudson to survive the colonial period.

West of Albany, in the Mohawk and Schoharie valleys, stand four Dutch Reformed churches. Two are on the Mohawk — the Fort Herkimer Dutch Church (No. 194), built in 1730, and the Dutch Reformed Church at Stone Arabia (No. 191), built in 1788. The other two are on Schoharie Creek. Like the one in Herkimer County, the Dutch Reformed Church in the town of Schoharie (No. 195), built in 1772, became a fort for defense in Indian raids; it was known as Old Stone Church, Old Stone Fort, and Lower Fort. The Upper Fort was at Middleburg, upstream on the Schoharie, and there the Dutch Reformed Church (No. 196) was built in 1786. These Dutch Reformed congregations west of Albany were more German than Dutch. As noted in Section 2 below, the Dutch Reformed Church developed in Holland with Germans participating, and the German Reformed Church was not a separate body in America until after the Revolution. In the Schoharie and Mohawk valleys, there were congregations of Low Dutch, High Dutch, Dutch Reformed, and Lutheran churches; there was a minister at Schoharie, for example, who preached in German at one church and in Dutch at another each Sunday.

About the same time that Henry Hudson, an Englishman employed by the Dutch, was exploring up the river that was named for him, Samuel de Champlain led a French expedition down from the St. Lawrence to the lake that was named for *him*. In all of the territory west along Lake Ontario to the Niagara River, the French were rivals of the Dutch and the British for the trade with the Indians. As a trading post on the shore of the lake at the mouth of the Niagara, the French built the French Castle in 1726, which became Fort Niagara. In it they built a Jesuit chapel (No. 197), in honor of St. Joseph and Francis Xavier (who brought Christianity to Japan in 1549), the patron saints of the Jesuit mission among the Hurons. The chapel served the traders and the Iroquois, the Indians of the Six Nations. It is the only Roman Catholic house of worship of the French to survive the colonial period in the British colonies. The English captured Fort Niagara in 1759, and replaced the Jesuit chapel with an Anglican chapel built on the parade ground in front of the French Castle, but it has vanished.

The first church in New Jersey was the Dutch Reformed Church that was organized in 1662 at Bergen. The First Reformed Dutch Church at Hackensack, a colonial building which still stands (No. 131), was organized in 1686 by Petrus Taschemaker. He had been ordained in Holland in 1679, had preached at the Bergen church the same year, had gone to the congregation at New Castle, Delaware, in 1680, and had returned to found the church at Hackensack. The original congregation was joined by a number of French Huguenots, who had abandoned their church in the neighborhood; they brought with them the stones from their building and used them in the building at Hackensack. After serving as pastor of this church for three years, Taschemaker was called to the church in Schenectady, New York, where he and his household were killed in the Schenectady massacre. The ministry of Dominie Taschemaker covered approximately the extent of the Dutch territory of New Netherland, from South River (the Delaware) to North River (the Hudson).

The next pastor at Hackensack was Guilliem Bertholf, who had been serving as the *voorseler*, or clerk, of the Dutch church at Haarlem (now the Harlem section of New York City). He was ordained, in 1693, after preaching his trial sermon before the Classis at Flushing, Holland, and returned to assume pastoral care of the congregation at Hackensack and Acquackanock (Passaic). His service was important in the colonial history of the region, for he was the first Pietist to come to America.

Pietism had begun in Germany in an effort among Lutherans to restore Christian faith to the heart, where Luther had centered it. In the next section, on German Reformed, there is an account of Michael Schlatter, another prominent Pietist, who visited the Reformed congregations of America at the direction of the Dutch Reformed Synods of Holland (see First Reformed Church, Easton, Pa., No. 245). In the section on German Lutherans, a third prominent Pietist is mentioned, Henry Melchior Muhlenberg, who was "Patriarch" of the German Lutherans in America (see Trappe Church, Pa., No. 231). Another Pietist who had a prominent part in establishing a Protestant denomination in this region was Count Zinzendorf, a leader of the Moravian Church and a founder of the Moravian Community at Bethlehem, Pennsylvania (see No. 244). The Moravian Church had its origin *before* the Reformation, as outlined in the section of this chapter on Moravians. Thus we find represented among these Pietists, reform before the Lutheran Reformation, reform within the Lutheran Church, and the Reformed Church separated from the Lutherans.

For many years, Bertholf was the only Dutch Reformed pastor north of the Raritan River. In the 1690's he founded the Raritan Church, and New Brunswick became a center for educating ministers and teachers. Queens College, the forerunner of Rutgers, was founded there in 1766 by the Dutch Reformed Church; it was the only colonial church to become a state college.

The Calvinism brought into New York and New Jersey by the Dutch was introduced also into their settlements in Delaware. At New Castle the congregation of the Old Presbyterian Church (No. 17), built in 1707, grew from the Dutch Reformed congregation that built Fort Casimir in 1651. Services were held in the fort until their first church could be built in 1657. In Section 5 below it is noted further that Presbyterians from New Castle pioneered up the Susquehanna River into the Cumberland Valley of Pennsylvania, and thence into the Shenandoah Valley of Virginia.

2. German Reformed

Many Germans went to Holland during the Pietist movement, and there they found in Calvinism the basis for the reform they sought. Since Pietism was a reform by return to original Lutheran doctrine, it became known as the second Reformation. In the American colonies there were both Dutch and German Reformed churches. We have seen that the Dutch Reformed congregations in the Mohawk and Schoharie valleys were composed of both Dutch and German people. In Schoharie there was also a German Lutheran congregation during the colonial period, of which no colonial church survives. The Reformed churches, Dutch and German, were closely related in the Synods of Holland, and it was not until 1793, after the United States had begun operating as a republic, that the German Reformed Church in America met at Lancaster, Pennsylvania, to adopt a constitution that established its independence from Holland. Meanwhile, in the early years, the congregations of upper New York shared ministers and co-operated closely. As time went on and the settlements grew, theological skirmishes became increasingly frequent between the different factions — Low Dutch, High Dutch, Dutch Reformed, German Reformed, and German Lutheran — and the denominations and sects gradually became distinct.

The Germans of upper New York, where there were also Dutch people, kept in close touch with the Germans to their southwest in Pennsylvania, where there were few Dutch. There the Germans became known as "Pennsylvania Dutch," not as Hollanders, but because the word for "German" is "Deutsch." At Easton, Pennsylvania, a Dutch Reformed church was organized in a congregation of Germans (see First Reformed Church, No. 245). The congregation was founded in 1745. In the following year it was visited by Michael Schlatter (1716-1790), a Swiss and a Pietist who had been sent by the Dutch Reformed Synods of Holland to visit American colonists of the Reformed faith. The present building of the church in Easton, erected in 1775, is the only colonial German Reformed church in Pennsylvania.

Germans from Pennsylvania moved over the border into Maryland, where there are two colonial German Reformed churches — Trinity Chapel at Frederick (No. 65), and the Zion German Reformed Church at Hagerstown (No. 66).

In Baltimore stands the mother church of a denomination, or rather a sect, that was derived from the German Reformed Church. The Otterbein Evangelical United Brethren Church (No. 62) was organized originally, in 1774, by a German Evangelical Reformed congregation. The first pastor, Philip William Otterbein (1726-1813) came from Germany and served first in a German Reformed congregation near Frederick. In 1789, with Martin Boehm, who had been a Mennonite bishop (see Section 7), he founded a new Church, the United Brethren in Christ. Otterbein was acclaimed the first bishop of the new Church, and the church at Baltimore, which carries his name, is the mother church of the sect. Otterbein was a Pietist.

3. German Lutherans

By the time when emigration of Germans to the American colonies began on a large scale, the Evangelical, or Lutheran, churches were varied in polity and creed. Several countries established a national Lutheran Church, Sweden among them. The national churches maintained the episcopate, and in each state (as is the case in the Church of England since the Act of Supremacy) the sovereign continues to be the *summus episcopus*, the supreme bishop or temporal head of the Church. In Germany, where the Reformation started, a number of different Lutheran churches developed. Their *Book of Concord* contained nine different creeds, the *Augsburg Confession*, and Luther's two *Catechisms*. Most of those Lutheran bodies that rejected the *Book of Concord* became Calvinistic (Reformed). The others adopted a variety of principles, with the *Augsburg Confession* and Luther's *Short Catechism* being held in common by all Evangelical Lutherans. The church polity is not episcopalian, as there are no bishops, but consistorial, a form of church government that permits great latitude of detail among the many different constitutions. As there is the same latitude in liturgy, the result is that there is no uniform Lutheran liturgy.

Most of the Germans who emigrated to America during the colonial period came to the Mid-Atlantic colonies. They settled mainly in New York and Pennsylvania, and there were some in New Jersey (see Zion Lutheran Church, Oldwick, No. 139). We have seen also that one group of Lutherans established a community at Waldoboro, Maine (No. 35), another group in Madison County, Virginia (No. 339), and a third group at Ebenezer, Georgia (No. 28). Germans from Pennsylvania moved south into Maryland, and at Frederick they founded the Evangelical Lutheran Church, of which the original stone building still stands (No. 64).

Germans from the Palatinate, a region of the upper Rhine, came into New York in three major migrations — 1708, 1710, and 1722. Among them were both Lutherans and Reformed. The second of these migrations was the greatest. In 1710, after a year in London during the reign of Queen Anne, who sheltered them in their flight from oppression, a number of Palatines settled in the Hudson Valley about ninety miles north of New York, on Livingston Manor. Under contract with the British government to repay their expenses and passage, they operated in producing naval stores from the pine forest, one of the few industries permitted under British colonial policy. In the course of time the industry there proved to be less economical than that using southern pine, and the British government released them from their contract. As the Germans became frustrated by the medieval leasehold system, which demanded uneconomic rents with no ownership of their farms, they moved up the Hudson and into the Mohawk and Schoharie valleys. Meanwhile, however, Lutherans built the Evangelical Lutheran Church of St. Peter the Apostle at Red Hook (No. 188). The land was donated by Gilbert Livingston for the use of the church forever, but the Germans abandoned it when they moved to the Mohawk, and now there is no other relic of their community.

In the Mohawk Valley these Lutherans revealed their origin in naming their Palatine Church (No. 192), located between Palatine Bridge and St. Johnsville. It is the second of the two colonial Lutheran churches still standing in New York.

Among the Palatines who moved up from Livingston Manor was John Conrad Weiser. In 1713 he led a large group of Germans to the Schoharie, where he settled the town of Weiser's Dorf, now Middleburg (see the Reformed Dutch Church, Middleburg, No. 196), one of seven Palatine settlements in the region. His son, Conrad Weiser, was adopted as a son by a Mohawk chief, and he became the famous Indian interpreter in Pennsylvania who aided the negotiation of important treaties with the Indians (see First Presbyterian Church, Carlisle, No. 256). He became a member of the society at the Cloister of Ephrata (see No. 248). He founded Reading, Pennsylvania, and his home near that city is now a historic landmark, Conrad Weiser Park. His daughter, Anna Maria Weiser, become the wife of Henry Melchior Muhlenberg, the outstanding leader of the Lutherans in colonial America.

The Germans of upper New York, Pennsylvania, and Maryland kept in close touch through the ministrations of Muhlenberg (1711-1787), who traveled extensively between their congregations, preaching, teaching, and visiting with them, until he became known as the "Patriarch of the Lutheran Church in America." He was a Pietist, who was sent to America from Halle, Germany, the center of Pietism. As a

Pietist, he had less sympathy with orthodox Lutherans than with the Reformed congregations. He shared liberal theological views with William Tennent and his sons of the New Side faction of Presbyterians (see Neshaminy Church, No. 238), and with George Whitefield, who inspired the Great Awakening which had its origin in Pietism. Thus we find that the Lutheranism introduced into the American colonies was another liberal theology that played an important part in the founding of the United States. For an account of the Muhlenbergs, see Old Trappe Church, Trappe, Pennsylvania (No. 231). Of the eleven children of Henry Melchior and Anna Weiser Muhlenberg, four sons became clergymen, and one of the four, Peter, became a famous general in Washington's army. Another son, Augustus, was the first speaker of the House of Representatives and the first functioning head of the United States government, when he presided over the House in New York for the month preceding the inauguration of George Washington as the first President.

The Old Trappe Church, Augustus Lutheran Church, was built by Henry Muhlenberg in 1743, soon after his arrival from the Orphanage and Missionary Training School at Halle, Saxony. He gave the church the name "Augustus" in honor of August Hermann Francke, who was the founder of the Orphanage and a co-founder of the University of Halle with Jacob Spener, the founder of Pietism; it was Francke's son who had persuaded Muhlenberg to accept the mission in America. The church is unique in its architecture, which stands in its original form. It is the oldest of four Lutheran churches in Pennsylvania. The second is the beautiful Evangelical Lutheran Church of the Holy Trinity at Lancaster (No. 249). Another son, Gotthilf Henry Ernst Muhlenberg, served there as pastor from 1780 until his death in 1815. The third is St. Peter's Lutheran Church at Middletown (No. 259), and the fourth is Falckner's Swamp Lutheran Church in Hanover Township (No. 232).

4. Swedish Lutherans

Sweden was one of the countries that adopted Lutheranism as the national religion. The Swedish Lutheran Church maintained bishops, while the Evangelical Lutherans in Germany did not. The episcopacy of the Swedish Lutheran Church afforded a bond with the Church of England. The two enjoyed close relations in America during the colonial period, and after the Revolution the Swedish Lutheran churches merged into the Protestant Episcopal Church.

The Swedes established their only American colony on the Delaware River, the southern limit of the Dutch colony of New Netherland. The river was discovered by Henry Hudson in 1609, when he was employed by the Dutch East India Company. He then sailed the *Half Moon* further north and discovered the river that carries his name. The Dutch, however, called the first the South River and the second the North River, a name which the Hudson still carries as it flows past New York, amidst some confusion because it is *west* of Manhattan. A year after the discovery of South River,

Captain Samuel Argall, of the Jamestown colony (see Argall's Church, No. 293), sailed into the bay in the pinnace *Discovery*, one of the three vessels on the original voyage to Jamestown. He named the river and the cape in honor of Lord de la Warr, Sir Thomas West, governor of Virginia (see Westover Church, Va., No. 311), whose province included this region, and under whom Argall served as deputy-governor.

The Dutch showed more interest in shrewd trade and immediate profit than in the colonization of New Netherland for the long term. A member of the Dutch West India Company, William Usselinx, withdrew in 1624 and persuaded the King of Sweden, Gustavus Adolphus, and his chancellor, the great statesman, Count Axel Oxenstjerna, to take an interest in colonizing in America. The result, in 1637, was the formation of the New Sweden Company, popularly known as the South Company. The young Queen Christina, who reigned through a regent, with Oxenstjerna still in office and actively interested in the colony, was its patroness. The first expedition was under the direction of Peter Minuit, a Dutchman who also had become discontented with the policies of his country's company. Half the funds for the expedition were raised in Holland, and the first expedition of two ships, the *Kalmar Nyckel* (Key of Kalmar) and the *Grip*, with both Swedes and Dutchmen in the company, sailed from Gothenburg that same year. In March of 1638, after a ten-day refreshing period at Jamestown, they sailed up the Delaware and landed at "The Rocks," the site of the present Wilmington. A fort was built and named for the young Queen, as was the Christina Kill, which flows into the Delaware at that point. In the fort were held the first Swedish Lutheran services in America.

The first priest of the Swedish Lutheran Church in New Sweden was Reorus Torkillus, who arrived with the expedition of 1640. The first church of the Swedes was built at Christina in 1641-42. The Cranehook (Tranhook) Church building was erected in 1667, at a site now marked by a stone monument near the Marine Terminal in Wilmington. Perhaps "erected" is not technically accurate, for the structure was of horizontal logs and is commonly called a log cabin. The type became famous, as the pioneers pushed westward into the wilderness. It is significant that it was introduced into America first by the Swedes, and not earlier by the English, for it had been used for ages in Sweden, whereas in England it had not been in use at all (see Chapter 8). In 1697, Erik Björck (1668-1740) arrived from Sweden and became pastor of the Cranehook Church. He began at once preparing for the building of a new church, and in 1698 work was begun on the present stone building of *Heliga Trefaldighets Kyrka*, or Holy Trinity Church, known affectionately as Old Swedes (No. 13).

The land purchased from the Minquas Indians by Peter Minuit, known as New Sweden, extended up the Delaware to the mouth of the Schuylkill. In 1643, Governor Johan Printz, who had been sent out by the Swedish sovereign, arrived in the colony. He proceeded to establish a settlement on Tinicum Island at the site of the present Essington, Pennsylvania, and he made it the capital of New Sweden. Among other buildings of the settlement were his residence, a fort, and a Swedish Lutheran church, but nothing remains of the town, which was burned more than once. The first ordained minister to preach at the church at Tinicum was Jacobus Fabritius.

In 1672 two parishes were organized, the lower parish at Crane Hook, and the upper parish in Wicaco, near the mouth of the Schuylkill. In 1677, Fabritius became the pastor at Wicaco. As it lay outside the Swedish settlement that was to become Philadelphia, Wicaco was fortified, and Fabritius used as his church the old blockhouse, which had been converted for the purpose. The present Gloria Dei Church (No. 202), which also is known as Old Swedes, replaced the blockhouse on the same site. Gloria Dei was begun in 1697, the year before work began on Old Swedes, Wilmington, which makes the church in Philadelphia the oldest Swedish Lutheran church in America.

Two new parishes grew from Gloria Dei, both west of the town of Philadelphia. In 1760, St. James' Church (No. 203) was built at Kingsessing, now in West Philadelphia. In the same year, Christ Church, also called Old Swedes (No. 204), was built at Bridgeport in Upper Merion Township, on the Schuylkill.

Most of the Swedish settlements were on the west side of the Delaware. The Swedes had territory also on the east side, in West Jersey. At the town of Raccoon, now Swedesboro, there was a congregation who attended services for many years by crossing the Delaware to Christina. In 1703, over the objections of the congregation at Christina, they built their first church of logs. In 1784 they replaced it with the present fine brick Trinity Church (No. 157).

In 1655 Fort Christina was captured from the Swedes by the Dutch under Peter Stuyvesant, and in 1664 the English took New Netherland from the Dutch, including the territory in the Delaware Valley. Under British government, the Swedish inhabitants continued to thrive. The Swedish mission to America was active for nearly a century. It supplied the Swedish Lutheran churches in the colonies, as the English supplied the Anglican churches through the Society for the Propagation of the Gospel. The Swedish mission began under British rule in 1697, when three priests arrived, and it lasted until 1789, when the Republic of the United States began. The three priests were Andrew Rudman, Erik Björck, and Jonas Aureen. Rudman was pastor of Gloria Dei when he died in 1708. He was in close touch with the Anglican rectors of the region: He took charge of Christ Church, Philadelphia (No. 205), while the rector was in England; he preached a sermon at the opening of Immanuel Church, New Castle (No. 16); and, in addition to his own congregation, he administered for about two years to Trinity Church, Oxford (No. 209), located about eight miles north of Gloria Dei, which distance he walked for a time until he bought a horse. Björck, who was pastor of Old Swedes, Wilmington, preached at the opening service at Gloria Dei. The Swedish mission was supervised by the Archbishop and Consistory of Uppsala, Sweden, and a close relationship was maintained with the S.P.G. in London. English gradually became the dominant language on the Delaware, and in time some Swedes began attending Anglican churches when the Swedish pastor could not speak good English. By 1774 the pastor of Gloria Dei had an English-speaking assistant. Some Swedes were attracted to the New Light congregations and to the Moravian Church, and others were carried away by the "enthusiasm" of the Great Awakening. The conservatives, however, remained Episcopalian. In 1789, when the Republic began and the Protestant Episcopal Church was organized, the Swedish mission in America was withdrawn, and the Swedish clergymen were permitted, by Archbishop Uno von Troil, of Uppsala, to return home. By agreement, the remaining Swedish churches became Episcopalian. The last to retain at least nominal Swedish Lutheranism were the three churches of the Philadelphia area, which remained in the care of the beloved Dr. Nicholas Collin, until his death in 1831.

As seen in the photographs, the architecture of the Swedish Lutheran churches also had much in common with the Anglican churches. Gloria Dei, however, shows distinctive Swedish character in the steep pitch of its roof, the small square belfry, and the small spire.

5. Presbyterians

Presbyterianism entered the colonies in a number of different forms and in all three regions, but it was most prevalent in the Mid-Atlantic. It came first to America in the South with the French Huguenots, who tried unsuccessfully to settle on the coast of South Carolina in the sixteenth century, and in the following century established settlements in and around Charleston. It came to New England in the Puritanism of the Massachusetts Bay Colony. It came to the Mid-Atlantic colonies in various forms — through the Huguenots on Staten Island and the Hackensack River; the Reformed Churches, both Dutch and German, in New York, New Jersey, and Pennsylvania; the Puritans from New England on Long Island, in New Jersey, and at Philadelphia; Scottish Covenanters in New Jersey; and Scotch-Irish Presbyterians in Delaware and Pennsylvania.

Presbyterianism has a polity of ecclesiastical rule by the elders of the congregation, and as it goes back to the ancient Israelites, it is the oldest of the colonial American church polities. God said to Moses in Egypt, "Go, and gather the elders of Israel together . . ." (Exodus 3:16) "And Moses and Aaron went and gathered together all the elders of the children of Israel" (Exodus 4:29). The polity developed among the earliest Christians from the time of the Apostles, as they formed their communities and adopted the Jewish form of oversight and rule by elders. As it has evolved through the Reformation and Calvinism, both the minister and the elders of a congregation are presbyters, and they comprise the only spiritual order. In the Presbyterian Church, a session is the council for governing a congregation; the presbytery (or classis in the Reformed Churches) is a council composed of the ministers and selected ruling elders from the congregations in a district; the synod is a provincial council of a number of presbyteries; and the general assembly is representative of the whole Church. Communicants have the rights of membership, and they elect the presbyters. The system, therefore, is republican, or representative. In this political sense, as well as through their religious doctrines and their passion for independence, which had its source in Geneva, Presbyterianism and its faithful had a profound influence in the founding of the United States. The Presbyterian spirit of independence is fostered in a body of churches that are *interdependent*, as compared to Congregational churches, which are independent and so have been called the Independent churches.

Calvinism had a major part in the transition from a medieval Europe, dominated by the Roman Church, to a Europe in which a reformed Reformation gave the individual a voice in ecclesiastical affairs, and ruled the faithful without a hierarchy of ministers. Calvinism became an international movement — broad, complex, appealing, and effective. It was greater than the man, and involved the thoughts of many men, including Aristotle, Augustine, Thomas Aquinas, Martin Luther, Martin Bucer of Strasbourg, and Zwingli of Zurich; but John Calvin (1509-1564) was the central inspiration for the movement. His work in education, organization, and administration at Geneva, as well as his theology, inspired others and pointed the way. Outside of Lutheran Germany, Calvinism became the dominant influence of the Reformation. Not only did it lead to the organization of the various presbyterian churches, but English Puritanism, in close touch with Zurich and Geneva, merged with the movement while maintaining its own identity.

Calvin was a French reformer and prophet of the new religion, who had to flee for his life to escape persecution and possible martyrdom in France. The first French Protestant congregation was organized in 1546 at Meaux, along the lines of the church at Strasbourg, where Calvin was pastor during his three years of banishment. A French Catholic paid the new church the tribute of saying that it had brought back Christianity in its primitive innocence — the very goal that the reformers were seeking. In 1559 the Synod of Paris, the first in France, met in the face of danger from persecution. Its organization was based on the constitution initiated by Calvin in Geneva, which was also the basis of all the presbyterian churches to come. The persecution of the Huguenots (so called because, like St. Hugo, they came out at night) forced many of them to flee their country and seek refuge in America. In addition to the settlements in South Carolina, the Huguenots established a settlement on Staten Island, at Richmond. Although the Huguenot Church was derived from Calvinism, their churches in America were close to the Church of England in a friendly relationship. At Richmond the Huguenots had a church before the Anglicans, and for four years after the arrival of a priest of the Church of England, he was allowed to conduct services on Sunday afternoons in their church, until the Anglicans built their own St. Andrew's Church (No. 169). There is no Huguenot church in America today except the one at Charleston, where the congregation adheres to the ancient forms.

There were more Puritan Presbyterian churches outside of New England than there were in that region. On Long Island, where the territory for a time belonged to Connecticut, nine such churches were established between 1640 and 1670. Suffolk County was settled by Puritans, and at Setauket, on Long Island Sound, the Puritan Presbyterian church was there before the Anglicans had a church. In 1685 there was a protest in town meeting against the "minister of the town" using the Book of Common Prayer. The Anglican parish was finally organized in Setauket in 1723 (see Caroline Church, No. 175). In the same county, the congregation of the First Presbyterian Church was organized at Huntington in 1665. The present building, the third, was erected in 1784 (No. 174), and it is the only Presbyterian colonial house of worship to survive in New York.

In New Jersey, where eight of the thirty-seven colonial houses of worship are Presbyterian, the New England influence is even more evident. The Puritans of Connecticut were more Presbyterian than those of Massachusetts, as mentioned earlier, and many of them migrated to New Jersey. In 1666 the First Church at Newark (No. 132) was organized by the Puritan founders of Newark from Branford, Connecticut, originally as a Congregational church. It is the oldest organized Christian congregation in New Jersey; services of the Dutch Reformed Church were held before that date, but they had no organized churches in New Jersey. During the ministry of Abraham Pierson, Jr., who had accompanied his father from Branford to New Jersey, and had assisted him and then succeeded him as the second pastor, the church adopted the Presbyterian form, amidst considerable controversy. Subsequently, Pierson was elected the first president of Yale College, which was founded in 1701 on principles of Calvinistic Puritanism. About 1718 the church at Newark became fully and formally Presbyterian, during the pastorate of Joseph Webb, the sixth pastor.

The present building of "Old First Church," as the First Church of Newark is called, is the third building. The second building stood across the street, and in it the College of New Jersey was organized, in 1748, after a few months at Elizabeth. Later it was moved to Princeton, where it became Princeton College. Aaron Burr, the father of the third Vice President of the United States and the seventh pastor of Old First Church, became the second president of the College. (His wife was the daughter of Jonathan Edwards, the famous Calvinist and leader of the spiritual revival in New England.) The College of New Jersey had begun operating at Elizabeth the previous autumn, with classes in a building on the grounds of the First Presbyterian Church of Elizabeth (No. 133). This church also had been founded by Connecticut Puritans, and it had become fully Presbyterian at nearly the same time as the church at Newark. The pastor of the church, Jonathan Dickinson, became the first president of the College of New Jersey, but he died four months later. When the pastor of the Newark church was elected to succeed him, the College was moved to Newark, where Burr organized it and the curriculum, and the first commencement was held there. The College of New Jersey was derived from the Log College at Neshaminy Church, in Pennsylvania (No. 238), as outlined below in this section.

At Union, New Jersey, stands another colonial church founded by New England Puritans. The settlement of Connecticut Farms (now Union) was made by families from Connecticut in 1667, among whom were Abraham Pierson and his son, who later moved to Newark. The settlers attended church at Elizabeth, four or five miles away until 1730, when they organized their separate First Presbyterian Congregation of Connecticut Farms (No. 134), as Union then was called. The first pastor, Simon Horton, who had just graduated from Yale in 1731, was born in Southold, Long Island, where there was a church which had been organized by Puritans in 1640 and became fully Presbyterian in the early eighteenth century; that congregation and the one at Southampton are among the oldest Calvinistic congregations in the country. The church and most of the town of Connecticut Farms were burned by the British in 1780, on their return along this route from a battle in near-by Springfield. The pastor, James Caldwell, returned from the battle where he had served as chaplain, to find the town burned and his wife shot dead in the parsonage. At Springfield, which originally was in the parish of Connecticut Farms, stood the First Presbyterian Church, which was being used as a depot for military stores. The battle was fought around the meeting house and through the village, and as they retired the British troops burned the church. After the war, services were held in the barn of the parsonage at Springfield, until the meeting house was rebuilt on the old foundations (No. 135).

Another Presbyterian church further south is associated with a more important battle of the Revolution. The Tennent Church, Monmouth County (No. 146), was organized not by New Englanders, but by Scottish Covenanters, in 1692. It was called the Scots Church until 1859, when it was named for two of its pastors, William Tennent, Jr. and John Tennent, two of the four sons of the pastor of Neshaminy Church in Pennsylvania (No. 238), all of whom were educated at the Log College and became Presbyterian preachers. William, Jr., who was a strong supporter of the Revolution, served as pastor from 1733 to 1777, and he was buried beneath the floor of the meeting house. The Battle of Monmouth, between the armies of General George Washington and General Sir Henry Clinton, was fought around the church on June 28, 1778. Several bullets pierced the meeting house, which was used after the battle as a hospital, and many of the soldiers were buried in the graveyard here.

Near Princeton, on what was the Great Highway between Philadelphia and New York, a Presbyterian meeting house was built about 1698 at the post village of Maidenhead. The present building of the Maidenhead Presbyterian Church was built in 1764 (No. 143). It has been the Presbyterian Church of Lawrenceville since the town was renamed, in 1816, in honor of Captain James Lawrence, whose dying words as the British were taking his command, the *Chesapeake*, in 1813, were, "Don't give up the ship!" In 1810 the Lawrenceville School, a preparatory school for boys, was founded by the church, in the continuing concern of Presbyterians for the education of youths.

Two other colonial Presbyterian churches still stand in New Jersey, both reflecting New England heritage in their names. In 1695, Thomas Bridge, together with other Calvinists from Fairfield County, Connecticut, settled in southern New Jersey near the Delaware, at Cohansey between Deerfield and Greenwich. At Deerfield, in Cumberland County, the Deerfield Stone Church was built in 1771 (No. 152). The village is a shipping center for the potato crop, in this great area of rich farmland that makes New Jersey the "Garden State." In the same county, about five miles from Bridgeton, is the town of New England Cross Roads, and there stands the Fairfield Presbyterian Church (No. 150), a stone building erected in 1780.

Other New England Presbyterians were sent as missionaries across the river into Delaware and Pennsylvania. Benjamin Woodbridge went to Philadelphia in 1698, followed soon after by Jedidiah Andrews, who organized the first Presbyterian church there in 1701 (see Pine Street Presbyterian Church, No. 211). In 1698, John Wilson became pastor of the Presbyterian Church at New Castle (No. 17). Samuel Davis preached at Lewes, Delaware, as early as 1692, and another New England missionary in the area was Nathaniel Taylor. In 1706 the ministers of the Delaware Valley, including those on the Jersey side, met in Philadelphia and, with Francis Makemie as moderator, organized the Presbytery of Philadelphia, the first in America.

Francis Makemie was not a New Englander, but a Presbyterian of Scottish descent from the Presbytery of Laggan in Northern Ireland. He was sent to the Eastern Shore of Maryland in 1683, at the request of Colonel William Stevens, of the Governor's Council, to administer to the community of Presbyterians on his Rehoboth plantation, located on the Pocomoke River. There Makemie organized in that year the Rehoboth Church, the first in America to be organized by Presbyterians as such, rather than by Puritan Calvinists or other branches of Calvinism. In 1706, the same year in which he served as the leader in founding the first presbytery, Makemie built the present Rehoboth Church, which is known affectionately as Makemie's Church (No. 83).

With the Presbyterian Church firmly planted through the Presbytery of Philadelphia, it grew rapidly and spread west to the area of the present Harrisburg. In 1716 the Presbytery of Philadelphia became a synod by dividing into four subordinate meetings of presbyteries. At New Castle the Presbyterian Church (No. 17) grew from the Dutch Reformed congregation who held their first services in Fort Casimir when it was built in 1651. With the assistance of Makemie, the present church was built in 1707, replacing the Dutch church of 1657. Many Scotch-Irish immigrants entered the colonies at New Castle, and the church there, through the Presbytery of New Castle, became the mother church of many others as the Presbyterians moved inland. Among them was the First Presbyterian Church in St. George's Hundred, near Odessa at Drawyers Creek, and known as Old Drawyers (No. 18). The Donegal Presbyterian Church (No. 251), as the name indicates, was settled by Scotch-Irish Presbyterians from the north of Ireland, who moved from New Castle up the Susquehanna and settled on its east bank in Lancaster County, Pennsylvania. The Donegal Presbytery, which was organized by the Synod of Philadelphia, was composed of five ministers and eight churches; it held its first meeting in the Donegal Church on October 11, 1732. From there the pioneers continued to press through the wilderness up the Susquehanna, and in 1734 they crossed over into the Cumberland Valley. There they made settlements at five springs, and at each built Presbyterian churches under the Donegal Presbytery. The present First Presbyterian Church at Carlisle (No. 256) was built in 1757 by a congregation that had settled and built the first meeting house here, at what then was called Meeting House Springs. The present Silver Spring Presbyterian Church (No. 257) was built in 1783 by a congregation who had settled in 1734 at the spring named for James Silver, the original settler and large land holder. As noted earlier in the account of Virginia, Scotch-Irish pioneers of this same movement pressed on down the Cumberland Valley and into the Shenandoah Valley of Virginia, and there west of the Blue Ridge they built the Augusta Church (No. 343) and the Timber Ridge Church (No. 344). Some of the Presbyterian pioneers remained on the east side of the Susquehanna and settled the present Harrisburg, and Paxtang a few miles east. In Paxtang stands the beautiful stone Paxton Presbyterian Church (No. 258). The first item of business at the first meeting of the Presbytery of Donegal in 1732, mentioned above, was a call for William Bertram to serve as pastor of the Paxton and Derry congregations. Derry, another name reflecting the Irish origin of these Presbyterians (found also at a Presbyterian Church in New Hampshire, No. 122), is now the town of Hershey, made famous by one man and his chocolate.

The evangelistic preaching of George Whitefield in the colonies, which in 1740 and 1741 aroused the Great Awakening, caused considerable controversy and led to schisms in several denominations. In the Presbyterian Church, the younger generation of American-born liberals, known as the "New Lights," separated from the older generation who were known as the "Old Lights." The congregations took sides, and the liberal churches became known as "New Side," as compared to the conservative "Old Side" churches.

Gilbert Tennent became active in the controversy, favoring the preaching of Whitefield, and the Tennent family of preachers together with their Log College became involved. As a result, the Presbytery of New York joined with the Tennents in 1745, and established the Synod of New York, which was New Side, while the Synod of Philadelphia continued to be Old Side. William Tennent, Sr., a cousin of James Logan (who was the secretary of William Penn), had been an Anglican clergyman in Northern Ireland, but in Pennsylvania he became a Presbyterian. In 1726 he organized the Neshaminy Presbyterian Church (No. 238), in Bucks County at the Forks of the Neshaminy. Near by he established the Log College, to educate for the ministry his four sons and other youths, and it became so famous that his church became known as the Log College Church. An act of the Synod in 1738 was directed against the Log College, by declaring that candidates for the ministry must be educated in New England or Great Britain. As a result, after the schism in the Presbyterian Church, the New Side established the College of New Jersey at Elizabeth, as noted above, and it became Princeton College.

So influential was the Log College, and so active were the Presbyterians in pioneering in the fields of religion and education, that a long list of colleges grew from that modest beginning. At the site of the Log College there is a monument erected in honor of William Tennent, a granite shaft on which there are three bronze tablets. The middle tablet is headed by the Latin motto, *Lux In Tenebris*, followed by a bas-relief of the Log College, beneath which is the following inscription: *Here in the life of a pioneer teacher sound learning endued with spiritual passion wrought to vitalize knowledge, glorify truth, enrich life, and in due time call forth, to the glory of God and the welfare of American youth, these many Christian colleges.* The side panels name the fifty-one Presbyterian colleges that have sprung from this humble beginning, with their dates in the order of their establishment, as follows:

1746	Princeton	1869	Wilson
1771	Queens	1872	Arkansas
1776	Hampden-Sidney	1875	Park
1787	Washington and Jefferson	1875	Parsons
1794	Tusculum	1875	Southwestern
1812	Hamilton	1880	South Carolina
1819	Centre	1881	Coe
1819	Maryville	1882	Hastings
1826	Lafayette	1882	Emporia
1827	Hanover	1883	Huron
1827	Lindenwood	1883	Jamestown
1829	Illinois	1884	Grove City
1832	Wabash	1885	Macalester
1836	Davidson	1886	Alma
1842	Cumberland	1887	Occidental
1842	Mary Baldwin	1889	Daniel Baker
1846	Carroll	1889	Agnes Scott
1849	Westminster, Mo.	1890	Whitworth
1849	Austin	1891	Buena Vista
1850	Waynesburg	1891	College of Idaho
1852	Dubuque	1893	College of Ozarks
1853	Western	1894	Belhaven
1854	Lincoln University	1895	Tulsa
1855	Elmira	1896	Flora McDonald
1857	Blackburn	1901	James Millikin
		1902	Texas Presbyterian

In 1734 William Tennent was granted permission by the Presbytery of Philadelphia to preach once a month at Newtown, east of Neshaminy Church. There a log church was built and used for thirty-five years, until the present Newtown Presbyterian Church (No. 239) was built in 1769. In addition to the Tennent Church in New Jersey, where William, Jr. and John Tennent preached (as noted above), the Presbyterian Church at New Castle (No. 17) had Gilbert Tennent for a short time, and Charles Tennent served as pastor of the Blackwater Presbyterian Church in Delaware (No. 26).

About 1738, four years after William Tennent, Sr. began preaching at Newtown, a congregation composed mostly of people from Northern Ireland was organized as the Tinicum Presbyterian Church (No. 240), with James Campbell from Scotland as pastor. They were located in upper Bucks County near the Delaware, and they maintained close relations with the church at Newtown.

The oldest Presbyterian church building in America is the Norriton Presbyterian Meeting House (No. 230), built in 1698 in Montgomery County, Pennsylvania. The original settlers were Hollanders, who came there between 1660 and 1670. Among the oldest gravestones there are inscriptions in Dutch and in German.

6. Friends

The principle of freedom of conscience and religious liberty, on which the United States was founded, was introduced by one man into each of the three regions. In the South it was introduced by Lord Baltimore, a Roman Catholic, in the Maryland charter. In New England it was introduced by Roger Williams when he founded Rhode Island and the Baptist Church. And in the Mid-Atlantic it was introduced by William Penn, the Quaker, in the charters for his two provinces of West Jersey and Pennsylvania. The guarantee of religious liberty in the Penn Charter for Pennsylvania was tested and upheld in the case of the Roman Catholic St. Joseph's Chapel at Philadelphia, as outlined in Chapter 3. The principles of Quakerism, on which Penn organized and administered his colonial territories, were such a vital force that his colonization was called a holy experiment, and his principal city was given the name "Philadelphia," meaning "City of Brotherly Love."

Of the 345 houses of worship in this collection, 73 or 21 per cent are Friends meeting houses. The number may be disproportionate in some respects but not in the influence of Quakerism in the founding of the United States. It was in the City of Brotherly Love that the Constitution was drafted and the early capital of the new Republic was located. There were Quakers in various of the colonies, and at one time they governed New Jersey and Rhode Island as well as Pennsylvania. Of the fifty-six colonial Friends meeting houses in the Mid-Atlantic, twenty-six are in Pennsylvania, eighteen are in New Jersey, where Penn had his other province, ten are in New York, and two are in Delaware. In New England there are nine, of which six are in Rhode Island, two in Massachusetts, and one in New Hampshire. In the South there are eight, of which six are in Maryland, where the Friends were close to those in Pennsylvania, and two are in Virginia, where they went from Pennsylvania. This distribution is in proportions that fairly represent the spread of Quakerism in the colonies.

The Quakers came early to America. The movement was launched in England by the preaching of George Fox in 1647, and only nine years later, in 1656, Mary Fisher and Ann Austin appeared in Boston. They were imprisoned for heresy and then banished, as were eight others that year. In the years following, severe laws and penalties were enacted against Quakers in Massachusetts, who rushed into the colony welcoming trials and martyrdom. All during the period of the Puritan Commonwealth in England, Quakers were persecuted and prosecuted under a variety of laws, but mainly as Nonconformists, and conditions were similar in the Puritan Commonwealth of Massachusetts. Unlike other Nonconformists, the Quakers always met in open meeting with strangers welcome, and not in secret.

In such an environment during the early years, the peculiarities of Quakers and their obstinate opposition to the Established Order, overshadowed much of their inner faith and the principles which later caused the Society of Friends to grow. They did not have paid ministers; they had no creed, but based their faith on the ministry of all believers, who were in direct communication with God through the inward light in each individual, man or woman; they did not have set prayers, but worshiped in silent communion, or spoke in meeting as the spirit moved the individual; they did not use outward and visible sacraments of baptism and Communion, but believed that the acts of ordinary life could be sacramental, in the washing away of sin and in remembrance of the Lord Jesus Christ, who was identified with the inward light in each individual. These basic principles of the colonial Quakers, in matters of faith and practice, have continued with only minor variations in the Quakerism practised today.

The polity of the Society of Friends is presbyterian in character, as it is a system of subordinated meetings. There is a Meeting of Ministers and Elders, who appoint persons to have oversight of a Meeting for Worship, which is a congregation. Like a presbytery, a monthly meeting is composed of several meetings in a section, and it conducts business and owns property. Like a synod, the quarterly meeting is composed of several monthly meetings in an area. The yearly meeting is composed of all the quarterly meetings in a large territory.

The Quaker meeting houses were designed to fill only the bare necessities. They were deliberately plain and even austere; there was no altar, no pulpit, no choir or provision for music in the colonial period. The auditorium was furnished with plain wooden benches, usually without cushions. Many of them had a gallery, which usually was used by the children. Two entrances were provided in one wall, which enabled the men and women to enter their separate meetings for business simultaneously. A movable partition down the middle of the auditorium separated the two meetings, and it could be removed to open the auditorium as one room for meetings for worship. At the end of the room, there were facing benches on a raised level for those who had been appointed to have oversight of the meeting and those accustomed to speak in meeting. Decoration, ornamentation, and features of comfort were avoided, as being worldly and diverting from a spiritual attitude. In general these features have been retained in current practice. In many meeting houses however, modern facilities for heat and light have been installed, and rooms have been added for school and other functions.

After years of persecution by the Puritans of England and New England, the Quakers began to look for unoccupied land in the colonies, where they could settle and live their own lives in peace. George Fox was in the colonies from 1671 to 1673, preaching and visiting from Carolina to Rhode Island. The first General Meeting of Friends in America was held in Newport about 1661, and Fox visited there in 1672 (see Newport Friends Meeting House, No. 266). The first substantial settlement of Quakers, however, was made in 1677-78 on the east side of the Delaware River, in the new Province of West Jersey. In 1674, Lord Berkeley sold a large portion of New Jersey to Quakers. John Fenwicke received land in trust for Edward Byllinge, and with a large company of Quakers Fenwicke sailed up the Delaware in 1675, and settled on a tract which he named Salem (see Salem Friends Meeting House, No. 154). Byllinge could not meet his debts, and in that same year he placed his lands in the hands of trustees, including William Penn, who then offered them for sale. It was just the opportunity the Quakers had been looking for, and the largest purchasers were companies of Quakers in London and Yorkshire. Thus William Penn, Gawen Lawry, and Nicholas Lucas, together with two other Friends, John Eldridge and Edmund Warner, became masters of West Jersey. The boundary setting it off as a separate province ran "from the east side of Little Egg Harbor, straight through the country, to the utmost branch of Delaware River." The five proprietors appointed three commissioners and gave them instructions, in 1676, to settle disputes, to purchase more land, and to build a town. In 1677-78 five ships brought eight hundred immigrants to West Jersey. The first ship was the *Kent*, whose Quaker passengers settled the town of Beverly, now Burlington.

William Penn, who had not yet come to America, drafted the constitution of West Jersey. It included the principle of democratic equality and complete freedom of conscience, which he was to incorporate later in his charter for Pennsylvania. The liberality of the laws attracted many Quakers to West Jersey. The first legislative assembly, formed four years after the founding of the province, was composed mostly of Friends. In 1679, East Jersey also came under Quaker control. The two provinces of East and West Jersey operated separately until 1699, when they were reunited as a royal colony under one governor. Burlington served meanwhile as the capital of West Jersey.

Burlington also became the center of Quakerism, from which meetings grew on both sides of the Delaware. The first Monthly Meeting was set up at Burlington in 1678. Four years later, in 1682, the year in which William Penn first came to America, the first Burlington Friends meeting house was built. Even after Philadelphia had developed as a Quaker center, the Yearly Meeting was held alternately at Burlington and Philadelphia, until 1760 when it was confined to Philadelphia.

While the Friends meetings were multiplying in New Jersey, as witnessed by the many accounts in this collection, the Society of Friends was growing even faster and stronger in Pennsylvania. In 1681, upon his request to the Crown for settlement of a debt owed his father by Charles II, a royal grant was signed making William Penn master of the Province of Pennsylvania. He suggested the name "Sylvania," and the King prefixed the "Penn" in memory of William's father, who had served as a British admiral. How long and to what extent Penn retained his interest in West Jersey is not certain, but it is clear that his interest in Pennsylvania became absorbing.

When he sailed up the Delaware in 1682, Penn landed at the Swedish settlement of Upland, now Chester (see Chester Friends Meeting House, No. 216). There the first meeting of Friends in Pennsylvania had been held, in 1675, at the home of Robert Wade. The assembly met immediately after Penn's arrival, and the "Great Law of Pennsylvania" was enacted in December of that year. It was based on the concept of Pennsylvania as a Christian state with Quaker principles. Quakerism thus became established in the government of the province, but not to the exclusion of other religions. The Quaker supremacy continued until about 1764, when the rising tide of Scotch-Irish immigration and their pioneering into the western wilderness, noted earlier in the account of Presbyterians, began to demand adequate defense for the frontier. Penn had developed friendly relations with the Indians, through his Quaker policy of love and non-violence, but during the eighty years since his appearance in the province, the population had been growing and spreading, and frontier settlements were under pressure from the French and Indians in Ohio. In 1776 the first state constitution was put through by the Radical party, ending Quaker control of the government.

The spread of Quakers in Pennsylvania, Delaware, and adjacent Maryland can be traced through the accounts in this collection. An important group of Quakers were the Welsh who settled west of Philadelphia and south of the Schuylkill. While they were in Wales, they purchased 40,000 acres of land which they wanted intact as one barony, but it was divided into tracts in Pennsylvania and Delaware. The Welsh settled in large numbers in Chester, Delaware, and Montgomery Counties, and they spread over into Lancaster County, and into what is now the State of Delaware. In the Welsh Tract, or Welsh Barony, west of Philadelphia, they settled three townships among which they rotated Friends meetings — Merion, Haverford, and Radnor. The settlers at Merion arrived in 1682, the year in which Penn came to the province. They named the township Meirion (Merion) for their home county in northern Wales, Meirionydd (Merionethshire). In 1695 they built the Merion Friends Meeting House, the oldest in Pennsylvania and one of the three oldest Friends meeting houses in America (for details see Merion, No. 229; Haverford, No. 219; Radnor, No. 221).

The spread of the Religious Society of Friends in the colonies is revealed in the following list of yearly meetings:

The first General Meeting of Friends in America was held in Newport, Rhode Island, in 1661, under London Yearly Meeting.

New England Yearly Meeting was established in 1683.

Philadelphia Yearly Meeting was established in 1683, the year after William Penn arrived there.

New York Yearly Meeting was established in 1695.

Virginia Yearly Meeting was established in 1696.

North Carolina Yearly Meeting was established in 1698.

Baltimore Yearly Meeting was established in 1790; meanwhile the meetings of that province were under Philadelphia.

One of the Friends meeting houses is different from all the rest. In Philadelphia at Fifth and Arch Streets stands the Free Quakers Meeting House. In the gable end is a marble tablet bearing the inscription, "By General Subscription for the Free Quakers Erected in the year of our Lord 1783 of the Empire 8." At the time it was not known what form the government of the new nation would take. The Free Quakers were also known as the "Fighting Quakers," for they held themselves free to help the cause of the Revolution and to bear arms for their country (for details see No. 212).

While the Quakers professed religious toleration in Pennsylvania, they had suffered persecution under the established Church of England, and they practiced vigorous dissent against the Church. Although the original charter of Charles II to William Penn, after the Restoration, made provision for the Church of England in the province, it was not until 1695, thirteen years after Penn's arrival, that the first Anglican church in the province could be organized (see Christ Church No. 205). Even then, under Quaker supremacy Christ Church was the only Anglican church in Philadelphia for the next sixty-six years.

During the colonial period George Keith caused a difference in the Society of Friends known as the Keithian controversy. Keith founded the town of Freehold, New Jersey, where he lived for some years while acting as surveyor-general for East Jersey. He was a Scottish Presbyterian, educated for the ministry, who had become a convinced Quaker (as compared with a birthright Quaker). He had toured Holland and Germany with George Fox and William Penn, and had come to America in 1684, two years after Penn. In the course of time, Keith's theology deviated from Quakerism, and as he aroused many enthusiastic followers, he antagonized even more Friends, both in America and England. When he proposed the introduction of the sacraments, it was too much for the Friends, and in the London Yearly Meeting of 1694 he was disowned. Keith then recognized his true calling, and was ordained an Anglican priest. In 1702 he returned to America as the first minister of the Society for the Propagation of the Gospel in Foreign Parts, and he toured the colonies for two years, preaching teaching, and organizing Anglican churches. Back at Freehold he converted many members of his old Friends Meeting and organized them as St. Peter's Church (No. 147). Keith's influence was felt in a number of the congregations in this collection, among which another example of his disrupting Quakers is found in the account of Trinity Church, Oxford, in Pennsylvania (No. 209). There the Keithian controversy had brought together Quakers who had separated from three different meetings. When Keith returned to England in 1696, the property was conveyed to the Church of England, and Anglican services were held in the log meeting houses until the present church was built in 1711.

In the nineteenth century a second controversy of a much more serious nature developed into a schism, and the Society of Friends in America separated into two distinct factions in 1827-28. The difference grew out of the preaching of Elias Hicks. His unorthodox views concerning Christ and the Scriptures were extremely liberal, and they were carried to even further extremes by some of his followers. In general the liberal faction was composed of country Quakers, while the orthodox faction was of city Quakers, such as those in and immediately around Philadelphia. When the various meetings divided, one faction retained the meeting house, the books, and the funds, and the other had to begin anew; in many cases the withdrawing faction built another meeting house, and the schism penetrated even to the burying ground. Every meeting house of this collection in New York was kept by the liberal faction. In the burying ground of the Jericho Friends Meeting House, Hicksville, Long Island, are the graves of Elias Hicks (1748-1830) and his wife Jemima. The Friends continued in their separate ways for more than a century. In 1945, New England Yearly Meeting was reestablished as a United Yearly Meeting for all Friends in that region. In Philadelphia there were two Yearly Meetings, Arch Street Yearly Meeting being the orthodox, and Race Street Yearly Meeting the liberal faction. After some years during which individual meetings here and there got together and carried on as united meetings, in 1955 the two factions finally united completely. Since that time there has been only one Philadelphia Yearly Meeting, and also the Baltimore and the New York Yearly Meetings continue on the united basis.

The work of the Friends is well known in the fields of education, slavery and individual freedom, racial problems, welfare, world service, and peace; and the membership of the Society of Friends continues to grow, as its influence is felt all over the world.

7. Mennonites

One colonial Mennonite meeting house survives in America. It was built in Germantown, Pennsylvania, where the Mennonites made their first settlement. These Germans were among the first in Europe to take advantage of the offer of land in Penn's province. The Frankfort Land Company obtained a grant of 6,000 acres north of the Schuylkill and northwest of Philadelphia. In 1683 a party of Mennonites from Crefeld, Germany, under the leadership of Francis Daniel Pastorius, agent for the company, arrived and settled Germantown. There a community log church was built, and the Mennonites held their services in it until they could build the present stone meeting house which stands on Germantown Avenue (No. 213).

Mennonites are a religious sect that originated in Zurich and was derived from the Anabaptists. The name is for Menno Simons (1492-1559), a religious leader and reformer of the Netherlands. He left the Roman Church in the early years of the Reformation, when there were many conflicting religious views and severe persecution. The original group at Zurich left the state Church and came together on the tenet that only believers should be baptized. They developed no hierarchy, but the members of the community elected "exhorters" as their leaders, among whom were elders to administer baptism and the Lord's Supper. They acknowledged no authority outside of the Bible and the enlightened conscience, and their aim from the first has been to live their lives in their own way. In Europe they were considered to be subversive, both by Protestants and the Roman Church; and in Zurich, where many of them were executed by drowning, the reformer Zwingli commented that drowning was an appropriate end for them. The Swiss Mennonites separated into two factions, the Uplanders and the Lowlanders. The Uplanders became known as Amish, from their leader Jacob Ammon; they differed from other Mennonites in minor respects, such as their belief that excommunication dissolved a marriage, and in wearing beards but no mustaches and having hooks on clothes but no buttons, because of an ancient tax on mustaches and buttons.

The Mennonites and the Amish in Pennsylvania still dress as they did in Europe, and by the peculiarity of their dress they can be distinguished. They adhere also not only to their ancient faith, but to the various forms in which it is practiced in their simple and austere lives. These are the people who are known as Pennsylvania Dutch. Immigrations subsequent to the first at Germantown brought Mennonites into Bucks, Berks, and Northampton counties, but the largest number came into Lancaster County and it became their thriving center. From Lancaster, where there is still a busy Mennonite farmers' market, the city of Philadelphia was supplied with produce, and the famous Conestoga wagon was designed and used for the transportation of it. In that county the Mennonites have turned the soil into the richest farmland in the United States; but times have changed since they came to Penn's province to escape economic depression and religious persecution in Europe — federal laws and regulations do not permit them to lead their own lives and farm in their own way, and some of them have left the United States to escape such federal controls. Although there is only one colonial meeting house, the Mennonites have more than two hundred active churches in the United States.

8. Dunkards

In Germantown, not far from the Mennonite Meeting House, stands another colonial house of worship which has much in common with it: Each is the sole survivor of its denomination from the colonial period. Each was built by the first congregation of the denomination in America. Both were built by Germans, and both churches are sects of German Baptists.

This First Church of the Brethren (No. 214), which stands on Germantown Avenue, was built by a congregation that was organized in Germantown in 1723. This is the mother church in America of the Church of the Brethren. These German Baptists are known as Dunkards (or Dunkers), a name derived from the German word *tunken*, to immerse. The Brethren were organized as a separate church in Germany, in 1708, but there they were persecuted, and they fled to Holland. From that country, as did so many other persecuted Protestant groups, they came to America between 1719 and 1729, long after the Mennonites. They settled first in Germantown and then in Berks, Montgomery, and Lancaster counties, to the northwest and west of Philadelphia.

A feature of the religious practice of the Dunkards is triune baptism, which is administered after the believer has reached the age of discretion. With the believer in a kneeling position, three immersions by bending forward are made, in the name of the Trinity. The Dunkards perform the rituals of the washing of feet and the Love Feast, (the agape, the breaking of bread in Christian fellowship in the manner of the Disciples).

Again like the Mennonites, the presence of only one colonial house of worship is no indication of the present flourishing condition of the Church, for the Church of the Brethren has more than a thousand active churches in the country.

9. Seventh Day German Baptists

At Ephrata, Pennsylvania, is the Cloister, the relic of the first Protestant monastery in America. In 1735 it was founded as a monastic community by Johann Konrad Beissel (1696-1768), who organized it as the Society of the Solitary. He was a native of the German Palatinate, a graduate of the University of Heidelberg, a Pietist, evidently a member of the German Reformed Church, and a mystic.

When he came to America in 1720, Beissel remained in Germantown for a year, where he became interested in the Church of the Brethren, which settled there at the same time, as outlined above. He became a pastor of their Dunkard church at Conestoga, and there he began to deviate from the Church of the Brethren on the question of the Sabbath day. The Brethren are First Day Baptists, celebrating Sunday as the Lord's day, as do most Christian churches, but Beissel came to the view that the seventh day is the Lord's day, as declared in Genesis 2:1, and should be observed as such, as it always has been by the Jews. This difference and the mysticism in his nature caused Beissel to leave his congregation and to go to the bank of the Cocalico Creek to live as a hermit. Sympathizers followed him, and as the company grew he organized the Society of the Solitary. Three years later, in 1738, he gave the community the Christian name of Ephrata, which was the ancient name of Bethlehem in Palestine.

The community had brothers and sisters, in their respective monastic buildings, and married families forming a village. The community had about three hundred members at its height. They were active in a number of industries in the community, in addition to composing, singing, writing, and printing music. After the Revolution the community declined, and finally it was dissolved. The property is now open to the public, under the care of the Pennsylvania Historical and Museum Commission. The Saal, in which meetings for worship were held, and the Sister House are still standing (for details see No. 248).

10. Baptists

The German Baptist congregations mentioned above built the only colonial Baptist meeting houses still standing in Pennsylvania. In Delaware there is one colonial Baptist meeting house, and in New Jersey there are two.

It was noted earlier that Welsh Quakers settled on a large tract west of Philadelphia. Part of the 40,000 acres purchased from William Penn by the Welsh was laid out in what is now Delaware. There the Welsh settlers were not all Quakers, for a congregation of them built the Welsh Tract Baptist Church (No. 21) at Cooch's Bridge. These Baptists came to America long after the purchase of the Welsh Tract in 1681. In 1701 the congregation of sixteen people was formed in Wales and emigrated to

America. In 1703 they organized the Welsh Tract Baptist Meeting, and in 1706 they built the first Baptist meeting house in what is now Delaware. This congregation of Primitive Baptists was the mother church from which churches were organized at Wilmington, Kenton, Cow March, and Mispillion, but none of their colonial houses of worship survive.

Of the two Baptist meeting houses in New Jersey, the oldest is Ye Old Yellow Meeting House at Imlaystown, built in 1737 (No. 145). The other is the Old School Baptist Church at Hopewell, built in 1747 (No. 141).

11. Moravians

There are three colonial Moravian houses of worship in America — one in Pennsylvania, one in New Jersey, and one in North Carolina — but this number is not in proportion to the importance of the Moravian Church in the colonial history of the United States.

In the section on Georgia in Chapter 2, it was noted that the Moravians established a settlement at Savannah in 1736, and that they influenced John Wesley in his search for faith and the founding of Methodism. It was noted also that, because of their work in England and the British colonies, Parliament recognized the Brethren as "an ancient Protestant Episcopal Church." They were aware in England of the ancient origin in Bohemia of this Episcopal Church, for Richard II had married Anne of Bohemia (1366-1394). She was in England during the last years of the life of John Wycliffe (c. 1320-1384), who was the spearhead of the Lollard movement for reform in the Church of England, and Wycliffe's writings were sent to Bohemia. There they served as the spark with which John Huss (c. 1374-1415) of Bohemia kindled the flame; and the flame of his preaching survived that which ended his life at the martyr's stake, to the extent that almost the entire nation of Bohemia became his followers. The death of Huss was followed by a long period of religious strife, the Hussite wars.

In eastern Bohemia, in 1457, with the Archbishop-elect of Prague, John Rockyana, supporting them, a group of Hussites organized their community as *Unitas Fratrum (Jednota Bratrska)*, the Church or Communion of Brethren, or the Unity of Brethren, for a time known as the Bohemian Brethren, and in its later phase as the Moravian Church. In 1467, Bishop Stephen consecrated three priests of the Unity as bishops, thereby endowing the Church with Apostolic succession and making it the first fully organized Protestant Church, other than the Eastern Churches that were separated from Rome. Bishop Stephen was burned at the stake, and many of the Brethren suffered persecution, but the Unity grew; chapels and schools were built, and by the time that Martin Luther launched the Reformation, there were at least 200,000 members in Bohemia. In 1501, Bishop Luke of Prague edited the first Protestant hymnal; in the following year he issued a catechism, which was distributed in

Switzerland and Germany, and it influenced Luther. Fifty of the sixty books published in Bohemia between 1505 and 1510 were from the press of the Unity, and the Kralitz Bible, published by the end of the century in Bohemian language, is still in use there.

In 1609, when Rudolph II signed the famous "Letter of Majesty," satisfying claims of Bohemian Protestants — the Brethren, the Lutherans, and the Reformed — and granting them control of the University of Prague, half of the Protestants in Bohemia, and more than half in Moravia, were Brethren. At this peak of their power in Bohemia, the Thirty Years' War between Catholics and Protestants broke out in 1618, and the Unity of Brethren was almost exterminated. At the Battle of White Hill, in 1620, the Bohemian Protestants were badly defeated, and the Brethren were killed in battle, were executed, or were driven into exile. Their lands were confiscated, and Roman Catholicism was completely restored in the country. The Brethren in Poland merged into the Reformed Church of Poland. Many of the Brethren fled to Saxony and others to England, and thereafter the Unity of Brethren was dormant for more than a century. It was the recollection of their near extinction that convinced the Brethren in Georgia, at a later date, to abandon their settlement rather than to bear arms again.

During the long dormant period, the "Hidden Seed" were worshiping secretly in Moravia, and Johann Amos Comenius (1592-1672), their last Bohemian bishop, was nurturing the dormant seedbed. It was Comenius who introduced the teaching of languages by pictures of things, with the words for them in the two languages in parallel columns, and he is known as the "Father of Modern Education." He prophesied that the Unity would be reborn, and he wrote a historical work, *Ratio Disciplinae Unitatis Fratrum*, which became useful much later when the Unity was revived. Comenius went to England in 1641, at the invitation of Parliament to take part in reforming the educational system of the country, but the Puritan Rebellion was brewing, and political unrest thwarted the project. He then went across to Sweden, and there the great minister, Count Axel Oxenstjerna (who was then fostering the colony of New Sweden on the Delaware), arranged a pension for Comenius, and a commission to furnish a plan for the school system of Sweden based on his principles. His papers were lost when the town of Lissa was burned by the Poles, and he died a little later in Amsterdam — that haven for Protestants and Jews through which flowed so many lines of inheritance to America.

The rebirth of the *Unitas Fratrum* took place in Germany. The "Hidden Seed" in Moravia began to germinate in 1722, when Christian David returned from a journey and reported to the Neisser family that he had found a Lutheran nobleman who would receive religious exiles. Augustin and Jacob Neisser and their families, led by David, found their way across the border into Saxony and to Berthelsdorf. This estate had been bought recently by Nicholaus Ludwig, Count von Zinzendorf (1700-1760), who had just reached his majority.

Zinzendorf was a Lutheran, of a southern Austrian family that had become Protestant in the Reformation, and had moved to Germany near Nuremberg. His grandmother, Baroness von Gersdorf, who raised him, was in touch with the Pietist leaders. Zinzendorf was sent to study at the famous Orphan House and Missionary Training School at Halle in Saxony, which was founded in 1695 by August Hermann Francke. There his godfather was Philip Jacob Spener, also the founder of Pietism and co-founder, with Francke, of the University of Halle. Also at Halle was Henry Melchior Muhlenberg, and the two were to found churches in Pennsylvania at almost the same time — Zinzendorf the Moravian Community of Bethlehem, in 1741 (No. 244), and Muhlenberg the Augustus Lutheran Church at Trappe, in 1742 (No. 231). Zinzendorf was offered a position at the Orphanage by Francke, but he went on to the University of Wittenberg and then returned to his estate in Saxony to devote his life to the Moravians, who had settled there.

In one corner of his estate the refugees had built a settlement which they called Herrnhut, meaning both "Under the care of the Lord" and "Standing Guard for the Lord." Among the refugees, who had fled here from many different places, there were Moravians, Lutherans, and various sectarians, and amidst considerable dissention Zinzendorf worked to bring them into accord. The Moravians had the definite purpose of reviving the Unitas Fratrum, and in 1727, after he had dismissed the lawless and arranged for some sectarians to emigrate to Pennsylvania, Zinzendorf drafted a "Brotherly Agreement," which then was signed by the men and women at Herrnhut. In the library of Zittau, a copy of the *Ratio Disciplinae Unitatis Fratrum* of Comenius revealed how faithfully the Moravians had retained the traditions of the ancient Unity, and it substantiated the articles in the Brotherly Agreement. On August 13, 1727, the pastor of the Berthelsdorf Lutheran Church, from whom they had been estranged, invited the Brethren to a celebration of the Lord's Supper, and that Communion marked the date that is taken to be the birthday of the Renewed Church.

With Count Zinzendorf often presiding at meetings, the congregation grew and its fame spread. Then persecution against Herrnhut began. In his concern for their future, Zinzendorf sought a haven for the Brethren abroad, and he welcomed the invitation from the trustees of the new colony of Georgia. Two bishops of the Brethren were found to hold the Episcopate — Daniel Ernst Jablonski, Court Preacher at Berlin and a grandson of Bishop Comenius, and Christian Sitkovius, Superintendent of the United Reformed and Brethren's Congregation of Poland. In order to enable the Brethren to ordain their own ministers in America, David Nitschmann, the carpenter and an elder at Herrnhut, was consecrated, in 1735, as the first bishop of the Renewed Unity of Brethren; Count Zinzendorf was consecrated soon after. With an Episcopal-Presbyterian polity that was both democratic and representative, their orders of the ministry were maintained — bishops, presbyters (elders), and deacons — and the Unity was now an independent Apostolic Church. It was in 1749 that the Act of Parliament, recognizing the work of the Brethren in England and the British colonies, referred to "an Ancient Protestant Episcopal Church."

Soon after his consecration, in 1735, Bishop Nitschmann sailed for Georgia with a company of thirty-six Brethren. It was on that voyage that they met John Wesley, and began the long relationship which had a profound effect on Wesley and the founding of Methodism. The Moravian mission to the Indians of Georgia was their third foreign mission — the first was to the Negro slaves of the West Indies in 1732, and the second to the Eskimos of Greenland in 1733. The Brethren were the first Protestant body to make the evangelization of the heathen a duty of the Church, rather than an instrument of colonial policy, and for that reason their missionary work had a broad influence. (It was the fear of the Jesuits in Japan, as instruments of Spanish colonial policy, that caused the Tokugawa shogun to outlaw Christianity in 1614, and in 1637 to close the door to all foreigners, until the arrival of Commodore Matthew Perry in 1854.) The influence, through the Brethren, of the Orphanage at Halle was felt at Savannah in the founding of the Bethesda Orphanage by George Whitefield, when he saw the conditions in the colony.

In 1736, Bishop David Nitschmann ordained Anthony Seifferth as a deacon in the Moravian Church, to serve the congregation at Savannah. As the Church of England had no bishop in America during the colonial period, this was the first Episcopal ordination to be performed in the colonies.

In 1740 the Brethren left Georgia, rather than become involved in war against the Spanish in Florida. Under the leadership of Peter Bohler, they accompanied George Whitefield to Pennsylvania. There they joined the Moravians at Philadelphia who had come direct from Germany, and who were followed in the course of time by many more. They founded the settlements of Nazareth, Lititz, and Bethlehem. At Lititz they worked for Whitefield on the construction of a building that he planned to use for a Negro school; Whitefield dropped his plans, and the building today is Whitefield House, a home for Moravian missionaries. From Lititz they moved to land that Bishop Nitschmann had acquired at the confluence of the Lehigh River and Monocacy Creek, on the bank opposite the site of Allentown, and there they founded the Moravian Community of Bethlehem. Count Zinzendorf was present at the Christmas Eve service, in 1741, which gave the Community the name "Bethlehem." A cloister was built which was similar in some respects to that at Ephrata, and the Gemein Saal (Common Hall) was used for worship until they built the adjoining chapel (No. 244). The Brethren conducted a mission for the Indians at Bethlehem, and they maintained friendly relations also with all Christian denominations. Their faith in practice blended in well with that of the Quakers. With the purpose of establishing a center for Indian missions again in the South, in 1752 Bishop August Gottlieb Spangenberg led a party from Bethlehem to North Carolina. There the Moravians established the settlement of Bethabara (No. 201), and went on to establish Bethania and Salem (now Winston-Salem). Also from Bethlehem they settled the Moravian Church in New Jersey (No. 156), near Sharptown, but the Moravian congregation there has vanished, and the property belongs to the Zion Episcopal Church. There are two active Provinces of the Moravian Church in America, North and South.

Particularly because of persecution in Europe, the evangelical policy of the Moravian Church, as directed by Zinzendorf, emphasized foreign missions and ecumenical work. The Church has administered to the Brethren in Diaspora, as the Jews have to their communities dispersed over the world. It has not worked deliberately to gain new members, but to spread the faith in Christian brotherhood. The place of the Moravian Church in American history is not to be measured by statistics, but by the profound influence which it has had in fellowship with other denominations.

12. Methodists

Methodism was the last of the Protestant denominations to take root in the colonies, and in Georgia the Wesleys and the Moravians had acted the prelude to its founding. Charles Wesley (1707-1788) returned to England in 1736, after about six months' stay in Savannah, and John Wesley (1703-1791) landed at Deal on February 1, 1738, after two years and four months on his only mission in America. On that day he wrote in his Journal: "I left my native country in order to teach the Georgia Indians the nature of Christianity, but what have I learned myself in the meantime? Why (what I least of all suspected), that I who went to America to convert others was never myself converted to God." On February 7 John Wesley wrote in his Journal that it was "A day much to be remembered," for "I met Peter Bohler, Schulius Richter, and Wensel Neiser, just landed from Germany." Before Bohler went on to join the Brethren in Georgia, and then to go with them and George Whitefield to Pennsylvania, he saw much of the Wesleys in England and they both were converted. Charles instructed Bohler in English, and he in turn instructed the brothers in salvation by faith. Ten days after their first meeting, John and Bohler were at Oxford when John became discouraged by his own lack of "an inner peace, a vivid consciousness of salvation," which he saw in Bohler. He considered giving up preaching, but Bohler dissuaded him. When asked what he should preach, Bohler replied, "Preach faith till you have it, and then because you have it, you will preach faith." On May 1 John arrived back in London, and that evening he wrote: "The little society began, which after met in Fetter Lane. Our fundamental rules were as follows: In obedience to the command of God by St. James and by advice of Peter Bohler, it is agreed by us, . . ." and eleven rules follow. Those rules formed the pattern on which the Methodist Society was formed at a later date. In that same month, first Charles and then John were converted.

In Georgia, John had been told about the Moravian community of a thousand Brethren at Herrnhut, on the Bohemian border of Saxony, and on August 1 he arrived there for a visit of about a month. Back in London, people began to come to John and ask him to pray with them and give his counsel, and he agreed to meet with them each Thursday night at the Foundry, a building which he had acquired for residence and chapel. From those prayer meetings, in 1739, the first Methodist Society was formed, and many more were to follow in England, Scotland, and Ireland, as well as in America. Both Wesleys were ordained Anglicans; John had been sent to Georgia as a missionary of the Society for the Propagation of the Gospel in Foreign Parts, and in Savannah he had served as rector of Christ Church, but soon after their conversion both Wesleys were barred from preaching in Anglican churches because of their radical views. The Moravians continued active in England, but during the next year disputes arose in the meetings at Fetter Lane, and the Moravians excluded John Wesley. He withdrew with about eighteen members of the society, and he began "field preaching," declaring that the world was his parish. For the rest of his life he traveled all over Britain, preaching on the average fifteen sermons a week, for a total of an estimated forty thousand in the course of his ministry.

George Whitefield (1714-1770) followed the same practice of itinerant preaching in the open, and circuit riding, and he preached to throngs of thousands, averaging about forty hours of preaching a week until his death. With his great ability as an orator, he reached into the conscience of his listeners and moved their spirit, and the "enthusiasm" (as it was called) stirred the spiritual revival, the Great Awakening. The origin of the Awakening was to be found in Pietism, which had inspired Germany after the Thirty Years' War (1618-1648). Whitefield went to Georgia at the request of John Wesley there, and between 1738 and 1770 he made seven journeys to America. In the course of preaching throughout the colonies from Georgia to Maine, he not only opened the way for Methodism, but he affected every denomination. The ecumenical character of his preaching was such that historians find it difficult to define the "New Lights," who are considered variously to have been converts of Whitefield, Methodists, Calvinistic Methodists, or Presbyterians of the Gilbert and William Tennent school, who were ardent followers of Whitefield. When John Wesley introduced a divergence from Calvinistic doctrine, Whitefield withdrew from the connection, though he remained friendly with Wesley and is considered to have been a founder of Methodism. He remained a priest of the Church of England the rest of his life, and he preached in many of the Anglican churches in America, but he frequently was in trouble with their ministry and was excluded from some of their pulpits. Whitefield was a preacher, going anywhere and preaching to anybody in God's name, and he left organization to others.

Methodism was introduced into America in New York and Baltimore, but Philadelphia is the birthplace of American Methodism. It had its origin there in the preaching of Whitefield, and the versatile Benjamin Franklin had a part in it. He heard Whitefield preach at Market and Second Streets and estimated that, in the open, he could be heard by a throng of thirty thousand. Franklin was convinced that the astonishing newspaper accounts of crowds of 25,000 in the fields, listening to Whitefield, were substantially accurate. He was aware of the Wesleyan movement, for his partner in Charleston, Lewis Timothy, printed Charles Wesley's first hymns, and in Philadelphia Franklin published Whitefield's sermons. He realized that people of all denominations were eager to hear the great evangelist, and when some of the local pulpits were closed to him, Franklin took part in buying land and erecting a large building, "for the use of any preacher of any religious persuasion who might desire to say something to the people of Philadelphia; the design in building not being to accommodate any particular sect, but the inhabitants in general . . ."

The "New Building" was used by Whitefield for a decade, and Gilbert Tennent preached there. In the nineteenth century, Methodists rented one end of it for a church. The building does not survive, but its site on Fourth Street, appropriately near Old St. George's Church (No. 208), is marked by a bronze tablet which reads: "On this site stood the 'New Building' erected in 1740 for George Whitefield and for a Charity School — subsequently used until 1812 by the School, Academy, College (1735) and University of Pennsylvania (1779) successively."

A trustee of Whitefield's building was Edward Evans, a convert who became one of the first Methodist preachers in America. In 1767, when Captain Thomas Webb came to Philadelphia, a nucleus of Methodists were meeting in a sail loft on Dock Creek (now Dock Street). Webb had been licensed to preach by John Wesley, and he proceeded to organize the group into the Society which became St. George's, one year after the organization of the John Street Society in New York. The Society in Philadelphia had grown to a membership of about one hundred by 1769, when they were joined by two missionaries sent by Wesley — Joseph Pilmoor and Richard Boardman. Pilmoor remained in Philadelphia and preached in good weather on the common (now Franklin Park) two blocks away from 8 Loxley Court (now Leather Place), where the Society then had a room. He began at once to look for a building adequate for the growing Society, and he was fortunate in being able to acquire an unfinished church building. The structure was begun by a German Reformed congregation that ran out of funds, and after the Methodists had acquired it they completed it as the present St. George's Church.

In 1771, Francis Asbury (1745-1816) arrived in Philadelphia from England, and at St. George's Chapel (as it then was called) preached his first sermon in America. This founder of the Methodist Church in America, who was to become its first bishop, followed the Wesley method of itineration and preached widely in the colonies. In the course of traveling over a quarter of a million miles, he preached about 16,500 times in America. In 1773, two years after his arrival, the first Conference of American Methodism was held at St. George's, with Asbury present. In that Conference, the authority of Wesley was recognized in America, and the doctrine and discipline of the Methodists, as contained in the English Minutes, were recognized to be the sole rule of their conduct in America. While there was no thought at that time of establishing a separate American organization, this first Conference took the first step in founding the Methodist Church. Methodism had developed as a sect in the Church of England, and the Methodists still took Communion in Episcopal churches. In Philadelphia it was their practice to worship at St. George's Chapel, and to go the few blocks to St. Paul's Church (No. 207) for the sermon and Communion. It will be noted, in the account of St. Paul's, that the church had been built to accommodate an Anglican priest who had been at Christ Church, but who was not continued there because he was an enthusiastic follower of Whitefield. St. Paul's, therefore, represented the transition from the Church of England to the independent Methodist Episcopal Church.

The next step toward organizing the Methodist Church was taken at Barratt's Chapel in Delaware (No. 24). There on Sunday, November 14, 1784, Asbury met with Thomas Coke and Richard Whatcoat. Asbury was surprised to see Whatcoat take the cup and assist in the administration of the sacrament. After the service he learned that Wesley had taken the step of ordaining Methodist preachers, in order for them to administer the sacraments to their own people in America, and later in Britain. On September 2, after the custom of the early apostolic church of Alexandria, where the presbyters exercised the right of ordaining a bishop from their own number, Wesley, Dr. Coke, and James Creighton (an ordained presbyter of the Church of England) had ordained Thomas Vasey and Richard Whatcoat as deacons; the next day the two men had been ordained elders. Coke had been consecrated Superintendent of the Methodist Societies in America. The preachers at Barratt's Chapel discussed the plan which Wesley had given to Coke, for organizing an independent Methodist Episcopal Church, and they agreed to call a general conference at Baltimore to be held the following month. In his Journal, Asbury wrote: "Friday, December 24, we rode to Baltimore, where we met a few preachers. It was agreed to form ourselves into an Episcopal Church and to have superintendents, elders and deacons."

The historic "Christmas Conference" was held on December 27, at Lovely Lane Chapel in Baltimore (unfortunately the chapel with the romantic name does not survive). Coke and Asbury presided, with sixty of eighty-three preachers present. Coke read the proposal from Wesley, and the Conference proceeded to separate the Methodist Societies in America from the Church of England, under the name of the Methodist Episcopal Church. Coke and Asbury were elected to the superintendency of the Church. After having been ordained deacon on December 25, and elder on December 26, Asbury was then consecrated as Superintendent on December 27. Assisting in the consecration of Asbury was Philip Otterbein, pastor of the Evangelical United Brethren Church of Baltimore (see Section 2 above, and Otterbein Church, No. 62).

Asbury promptly assumed the title of bishop, to the astonishment of Wesley in England. After the separation, for the first time some of the Methodist chapels were called churches. Not only was St. George's known thereafter as a church, but Bishop Asbury declared it to be "the Cathedral of Methodism." The Bishop's name was given to the Asbury Methodist Church in Wilmington, Delaware (No. 15), which he dedicated in 1789. He was present also, in 1785, at the raising of the log Rehoboth Church in West Virginia (No. 345). It is the westernmost of the colonial houses of worship in this collection, and one of the four which are Methodist.

13. Shakers

At Mount Lebanon, New York, on the western slope of the Berkshire Hills near the Massachusetts line, the Shakers had a thriving community. It was one of more than a hundred communistic societies that have been started in America. Like the Cloister at Ephrata, Pennsylvania, the Society at Mount Lebanon has been dissolved and the members have died, but there stands the only colonial Shaker house of worship in America.

The movement started in England in 1747, during a Quaker revival. As a variant of the name Quaker, the members first were called Shaking Quakers, a term derived from the physical movements of members during their meetings for worship. Their group worship involved marching around the common hall in twos or threes, with a choir of several members standing in the middle and singing hymns. As they marched, they wrestled with evil, and the more difficult the struggle, the more violent became the contortions. This manifestation is comparable to those of a number of other sects, such as the Netherland Dancers, the French Convulsionnaires, the Welsh Jumpers, and the Holy Rollers in the southern United States. The sect was organized as the United Society of Believers in Christ's Second Appearing, or the Millennial Church. The members preferred to be called "Alethians," from the Greek word for truth, but the name "Shakers" has endured.

The original group, led by James and Ann Wardley in Manchester, were influenced by the doctrines of the Camisards, French Protestants of Cévennes who waged war, from 1702 to 1705 and for years after, against the cruel persecutions following the Revocation of the Edict of Nantes. It had been prophesized that their deliverance from persecution and the fall of Babylon (Roman Catholicism) would be in 1689, and the English Revolution which dethroned King James for his adherence to Roman Catholicism had afforded some corroboration. During this long period the peasants were without ministers, who had been martyred or exiled, and in their misery they looked to prophesy for relief. Except for faith in revelations and prophesy, one finds little in common between the Camisards and the Shakers. To that extent, however, this last of the religious groups to enter the states before the Republic was related to the first, the French Huguenots.

Ann Lee (1736-1784), the daughter of a Manchester blacksmith, joined the group in 1758. She urged the members to fight sin more vigorously, and she was jailed frequently for dancing, shouting, profaning the Sabbath, and for blasphemy. After one such term in jail for a fortnight, she reported a revelation that salvation depended on celibacy and full confession before witnesses of all sins committed under the influence of the lusts of generation. After that revelation, she was chosen by the Society as "Mother in spiritual things," and she was called Mother Ann, although she referred to herself as "Ann, the Word." The Believers accepted Mother Ann as the reincarnation of Christ and the fulfilment of the prophesy of His Second Appearing.

In 1774, in obedience to a command received in another revelation, Mother Ann took a small band of disciples to New York City, where they spent two years. In 1776, John Hocknell, the disciple who had financed the trip, bought land up the Hudson at Niskayuna, in the Township of Watervliet near Albany, and the Shakers settled there. Mother Ann died at that community in 1784. She was succeeded first by James Whitaker, whom she had raised (probably as a relation) and brought to New York. He served for three years, and was succeeded in turn by Joseph Meacham (1742-1796), a former Baptist minister from Enfield, Connecticut, who had the gift of revelation second only to that of Mother Ann.

In 1787, three years after the death of Mother Ann, the inhabitants of New

Lebanon (now Mount Lebanon) organized the New Lebanon Society under Meacham's leadership. As the community at Watervliet had not been organized formally, the one at New Lebanon was the first Shaker society to be organized fully in America. When the Watervliet Society was organized soon after, the two formed a bishopric. A society was governed by a board of elders.

During the period of the Republic, the Shakers spread out and established communities in Massachusetts, Connecticut, New Hampshire, and Maine; and others were established in western New York, Ohio, Kentucky, and Indiana. As late as 1894 the Mount Lebanon Society established a community at Narcoossee, Florida. At Hancock, west of Pittsfield, Massachusetts, a Shaker society was founded. The neighboring communities of Mount Lebanon and Hancock both developed a number of industries and handicrafts, and they built many structures for shops and warehouses, in addition to farm buildings and living quarters. They raised and marketed pharmaceutical herbs, and they manufactured furniture which has become famous among antiquarians and is being copied by local craftsmen. Their many buildings were solidly built, and they are of interesting architecture. The only colonial Shaker house of worship to survive is the first meeting house at Mount Lebanon, erected in 1785 as the first building of that community (for details see No. 189).

By 1930 the membership of the Believers had dwindled until at Mount Lebanon there were only a few surviving. Sisters Emma Neale and Amelia Calver, anticipating that they were "going out," proposed that the property be sold for a school. In 1932, after the last Shaker meeting had been held, the Lebanon School was opened. In 1938 it was reorganized as the Darrow School, named for George Darrow, who owned the farm on which the community had been settled. Their first meeting house is now the house of the head master of the school. In 1947 there were only seven Shakers at Mount Lebanon, six women and one man, and they moved to the Shaker community at Hancock. There the community has vanished. The Hancock property, including all of its many buildings, was acquired and restored by Shaker Community, Inc., and in 1961 it was opened to the public. Shakers continue active elsewhere, as in their community at Sabbathday Lake, Maine.

14. Anglicans

The Church of England followed the earlier denominations into each of the Mid-Atlantic colonies — it was not first in any of them. Of the 140 colonial houses of worship in the Mid-Atlantic, 25 were built by Anglicans, 9 of which are in New York, 6 in Pennsylvania, and 5 each are in New Jersey and Delaware.

In New York the English period began in 1664, when the English took control of New Netherland from the Dutch. Like the Dutch, they permitted freedom of worship by all but Roman Catholics. Beginning in 1693, the Anglican clergymen were supported from public funds, and a few years later the Church was established by law as the official religion. In 1777, after the Declaration of Independence, the constitution of New York separated church and state and permitted "free exercise and enjoyment of religious profession and worship, without discrimination or preference."

In New York City stands one of the most interesting and beautiful of the colonial houses of worship, St. Paul's Chapel (No. 168). It was built as a chapel of ease to Trinity Church, which stands a few blocks south, on Broadway at Wall Street. Its architecture is outstanding, and it is of historical interest, among other reasons, because it was the official church of the royal government in New York, and of the first President of the United States after his inauguration in New York, when the government of the new Republic was located there; and the first commencement of King's College (Columbia), which was chartered in 1754, was held in the chapel.

In Westchester County stands St. Paul's Church (No. 177). It is of particular historical interest as a shrine commemorating the establishment of the principle of freedom of the press. St. George's Church, Schenectady (No. 190), is of historical interest because it was located in the Mohawk Valley, where the fur trade was thriving, and where the Indians and the French were constantly threatening the frontier.

In New Jersey the Church of England entered late, and it never became the established church. When the English took possession of New Netherland from the Dutch in 1664, the Dutch and the Swedes were well established in the territory. The assembly had the power, under the Concessions and Agreements of that year, to appoint ministers and to provide their maintenance from public funds, but it was not exercised. Instead, the assembly granted land for churches of any denomination, 200 acres to each, and it was this liberal invitation that brought in the many New England congregations, and settlers of various denominations from Europe, as noted earlier. It was not until the 1680's that the first Anglican priest, Alexander Innes (died, 1713), settled in New Jersey. George Keith, the first missionary of the Society for the Propagation of the Gospel in Foreign Parts, visited Innes in Monmouth County in 1702. As Quakers had become proprietors of both West and East Jersey, they were prominent among the inhabitants, and their influence in the government was one of the reasons why the Church of England was retarded in its penetration of New Jersey. Keith's comments on the work of Innes in this field are of interest, as follows: "Mr. Innes being in priests order often preached among them, and by preaching and conferences frequently with the Quakers and other sorts of people, as also by his pious conversation, has done much good among them and has been very instrumental to . . . bring them over to the church."

With Keith on his voyage to America in 1702, was John Talbot (1645-1727), who was serving as chaplain of their ship, H.M.S. *Centurion*. Talbot had been in Virginia, where he had a parish in 1692, and he was interested in the missionary field in America. On the voyage, Keith inspired him so much that, when the *Centurion* arrived in Boston, he resigned and became Keith's assistant by appointment from the Society. The two traveled and worked together from New Hampshire to Philadelphia, preaching, baptizing, and converting many Dissenters. Keith was particularly effective in converting Quakers, and at Freehold, New Jersey, where he had lived and served as an active member of the Society of Friends, he now converted a number of the Friends of his former Meeting, and, with the aid of Talbot, organized St. Peter's Church (No. 147). Keith went from Freehold to Shrewsbury, where he organized Christ Church (No. 148). The labors of Keith and Talbot were so effective that Anglican congregations became active in various parts of New Jersey, and the S.P.G. was overwhelmed with requests for ministers.

In 1704, Lord Cornbury, governor of New York and New Jersey, granted incorporation for "St. Anne's Church in Burlington," which name was in honor of his cousin, the Queen. Passage was delayed, however, and when the royal charter finally was passed, in 1709, it was for "St. Mary's Church in Burlington." That church, which was located in the capital of West Jersey, became the mother parish of New Jersey. Talbot laid the foundation stone in 1703, on the day of the Feast of the Annunciation of the Blessed Virgin, whose name the church bears. Five months later, Keith preached the first sermon in the church. Talbot was settled as rector of St. Mary's by the Society, in 1705, and while Keith went on to complete his two year mission in America and return to England, Talbot remained at St. Mary's and served the parish for about twenty-five years. In the course of his work in the colony, he became known as the "Apostle of New Jersey."

Christ Church, New Brunswick (No. 138), is historically interesting on several counts. It was organized as a direct result of George Whitefield's preaching in New Brunswick on his second tour of America. The pastors of the two churches in town — Theodore Jacobus Frelinghuysen at the Dutch Reformed Church, and Gilbert Tennent at the Presbyterian Church — intensified their preaching of austere Calvinism. As there was no other alternative, the Episcopalians built this church of their own. Samuel Seabury, who was to become the first American bishop of the Episcopal Church, was made rector of Christ Church in 1754. He was appointed as being particularly capable of meeting the challenge of the new College of New Jersey, which the Presbyterians had begun in Elizabeth in 1747 and then moved to Newark. He left Christ Church in 1758, before the Dutch Reformed Church had founded Queen's College (now Rutgers University) in New Brunswick. Christ Church was the scene of the meeting that was the first step to the General Convention at Philadelphia and the organization of the Protestant Episcopal Church in America (see Christ Church, Philadelphia, No. 205). It was the first interstate meeting in definite anticipation of a national organization. Through correspondence, Abraham Beach, the rector, was instrumental in initiating the meeting, and it was held in his church on May 11, 1784. A meeting had been held by several ministers of Maryland in 1780, at the Emmanuel Church at Chestertown (No. 73), at which the name "Protestant Episcopal Church" had first been proposed. On the historical occasion at New Brunswick, there were two meetings, first the members of the Corporation for the Relief of Widows, etc., and then a larger meeting of clergymen and laymen from Pennsylvania, New Jersey, and New York. Seabury was then in England seeking consecration as the first American bishop. The meeting sought measures for "the Union and Prosperity of the Episcopal

Churches in the States of America." As a result of that meeting, a second was held in New York, in October, 1784, which was called "A Convention of Clergymen and Lay Deputies of the Protestant Episcopal Church in the United States of America." Clergymen from nine states attended and drafted terms for the General Convention, and a committee was appointed to draft a constitution.

Christ Church, Philadelphia, is associated with many historical events, but none were of more immediate interest to the Church than the General Convention of 1789, in which the Protestant Episcopal Church in America was organized, by the adoption of the constitution and the amended Book of Common Prayer. The Convention held its opening sessions in Christ Church; in order to provide more room for the many delegates, the later session was moved to Independence Hall, and the constitution of the Church appropriately was approved in the room where the Constitution of the United States had been drafted.

In Delaware the first Anglican parish was Immanuel Church (No. 16), which was founded at New Castle in 1689. That was the year in which King James II was deposed for adherence to Roman Catholicism, and William and Mary succeeded him, launching a wave of intensive Anglican activity in the colonies. The church is located on the green of that historically interesting and unspoiled colonial town, which was settled by the Swedes, captured by the Dutch, and then taken over by the British. The close affinity between the Swedes and the English led to the merger of the Swedish churches into the Episcopal Church after the Revolution, and the Dutch Calvinists merged into the Presbyterian Church, which became so important in New Castle, as noted earlier. Of these strong religious bodies, no one dominated the Delaware territory. Among the Swedes, Finns, Dutch, English, Welsh, and Germans inhabiting Delaware, there were six church denominations during the colonial period. One of the six was Roman Catholic. Their first chapel was built in 1772, on the bank of Coffee Run, and although its name was St. Mary's, it was known as the Coffee Run Church. No colonial church of the Roman Catholics survives in Delaware.

7

BRICK

There are no two houses of worship in this collection exactly alike, and each can be recognized, even though they fall into only a few categories. It has been noted that, by coincidence, the three regions of the colonies — the South, New England, and the Mid-Atlantic — afford the framework for grouping the buildings, both by the three principal church polities and by the three principal building materials. While the material was determined largely by geography and geology, the style of the building was determined by the denomination. As we look over the whole collection, we find that in the South, where the Church of England became established in all the colonies, brick was by far the principal building material; in New England, where Congregationalism predominated, wood was generally used; and in the Mid-Atlantic, where Presbyterianism was predominant among the heterogeneous religious bodies, stone was the prevalent material (see Appendix III). While these generalities are interesting, they are not exclusive, and all three building materials are found in all three regions.

In the South, brick was used in 100 of the 126 houses of worship, compared to the 14 of stone, 11 of wood, and 1 of tapia. Of that total, 42 are in Virginia, 38 in Maryland, and 15 in South Carolina. In North Carolina 3 of the 4 buildings are of brick, and in Georgia 2 of 3. Brick had been used extensively in the English churches, and it is natural that the Anglicans brought the technique to the southern colonies. The colonial settlements were mainly in and around ports and tidewater plantations, and in a hot climate with high humidity, brick churches were durable, as compared to wood and its susceptibility to decay, termites, and fire. In England, with its damp, ocean climate, wood was not a practical material and timber was scarce. Clay was available in all the ports here, where the product of rock erosion had been deposited by flowing water. Brick clay was readily available in the Atlantic coastal region from Georgia to the Hudson, and brick-making was one of the earliest industries undertaken by the colonists.

The presence of brick churches in or near the colonial ports — Savannah, Beaufort, Charleston, Brunswick, Bath, Edenton, Norfolk, Baltimore, New Castle, Philadelphia, Burlington, Newport, Boston — would seem to verify the frequent statement that they were built of brick brought in as ballast from England. The repetition of the statement has established a legend that is widely known. Actually there is no evidence that brick was ever imported other than in occasional small quantities. In ships returning from exporting the huge tobacco crops of Virginia and Maryland, amounting to as much as 100,000 hogsheads annually around 1770, manifests reveal that some brick was brought in, but the quantities were too small for building houses, and it probably was special brick or tile. Slate, glass, lead for glazing, and flagstone were imported in the early colonial years, but not common brick. The legend apparently comes from misinterpretation of the church records. English brick was used extensively in Virginia and Holland brick in New Netherland. In some parish minutes of orders for building a church, English brick or Holland brick was specified, referring to brick of a certain standard size, English brick being larger in thickness than Holland brick. In many cases, following the specification of, say English brick, the minutes would say who was to supply the brick or where it was to be burned.

Like the two standard sizes of brick known as English and Holland there were also two standard bonds of brickwork, English bond and Flemish bond. Historically the use of Flemish bond in England and the English colonies reflects the bringing to England of craftsmen from the guilds of Flanders by Queen Elizabeth I, to stimulate the arts and crafts in England.

English bond is the pattern of brickwork in which courses of stretchers, or long sides, alternate with courses of headers, or ends. This ancient English bond was used in the ruined tower of the Jamestown Church (No. 293), and it is found also in the ruined tower of St. George's Church, built in the vanished town of Dorchester, South Carolina (No. 280). It is found in Virginia in the churches of Yeocomico (No. 331); St. Peter's, New Kent (No. 314); Lower Chapel, Middlesex (No. 326); and in the Wren Building of William and Mary College, Williamsburg, in which there is a chapel (No. 295). In Georgia, English bond is in the Jerusalem Church (No. 28).

Flemish bond is the pattern of brickwork in which stretchers and headers alternate in every course. This bond was used so generally during the colonial period that it practically is a hallmark of a colonial church. The headers in Flemish bond often have blackened or glazed ends in the exposed face of the wall, and the effect is a pleasing decorative pattern. The blackened ends are those that were exposed to the kiln fire. Glazed ends were deliberately made so; they vary in color from black through bister to dark cherry. On the south side of the James River, the clay produces a soft brick which does not glaze well, and the Flemish bond in that area is found to have black but not glazed headers, as at Old Brick Church, Isle of Wight (No. 297).

Dark headers were used for making patterns other than Flemish bond. At the church in Wethersfield, Connecticut (No. 6), and in Pennsylvania at Gloria Dei, Philadelphia (No. 202), and Trinity, Oxford (No. 209), the dark headers form diaper patterns. They were used also to record the building's date, as at the Friends meeting houses in New Jersey, Rancocas (No. 162), Salem (No. 154), and Woodstown (No. 155).

A third bond, which is in general use today but was not used in colonial churches, is the stretcher bond, in which no headers appear, and the stretchers are laid with the ends over the middle of the brick below. Where such brickwork is found in a colonial church, obviously it was inserted after the colonial period, during repairs or alteration. A number of excellent repair jobs and some restorations have been done with new Flemish bond brick (for example see Old Trinity, Dorchester County, Md., No. 78).

It has been assumed in the past that Flemish bond was introduced into Virginia about the end of the seventeenth century, but there is now considerable evidence that it came in much earlier. The Adam Thoroughgood house near Norfolk (see Donation Church, No. 306), built before 1640 and the oldest residence in Virginia, has three walls in English bond, but the front wall, which evidently is original, is in Flemish bond. The evidence is of particular interest concerning the age of the Old Brick Church, Isle of Wight (No. 297), which has Flemish bond and is generally believed to have been built in 1632.

The first structures of the first colonists at Jamestown were made of immediately available materials. Captain John Smith described the first church at Jamestown as being made of inverted tree crotches, carrying frameworks on which sod was placed, and the first four churches at Jamestown were of wood. The fourth building, which was new in 1636, contained all three materials, being built of frame on a foundation of cobblestone and brick. Footings evidently of that church have been excavated within the walls of the fifth church, which was built of brick in 1639, and of which only the tower survives (No. 293).

This fifth church at Jamestown was built in the first of three styles of brick churches in Virginia, where forty-two of the fifty-two churches are of brick (Appendix III). This earliest style was the buttressed rectangular building. By far the most prevalent style was the second, the plain rectangular church, and the third style was the cruciform church with apse.

In the style of the buttressed, rectangular brick church, three early churches were built in Virginia, and they were in a class by themeslves. The first was the Old Brick Church, Isle of Wight, built in 1632 and the oldest Protestant church in America (for details see No. 297). The second was the Jamestown Brick Church mentioned above. The third was built in 1681, in the middle of the present churchyard, as the second Bruton Church (for details see No. 294). These three buildings were in the medieval Gothic style of English country churches. Of the three, the church in Isle of Wight County is intact, and in it we see a number of features that are unique among all the surviving colonial churches — the Gothic windows with lancet arches are of double casements, separated by a mullion (evidently St. Mary's Church, Maryland, now vanished, had this feature); the rear gable is corbie, or crow-stepped, a Jacobean feature found in abundance in the Netherlands whence it came to England; and the tower has a rudimentary pediment over the front entrance, which is of Renaissance influence. After the early colonists in Virginia had built these few churches, modeled after those familiar to them in the home country, they dropped the style completely for the duration of the colonial period. The fashion in architecture known as the Gothic Revival did not begin in America until after 1800, the first church of the style being St. Mary's Church, Baltimore, built in 1807; and it did not win enough popularity to replace the current Greek Revival style until after the third Trinity Church, New York, designed by Richard Upjohn, was built in 1839-46.

The plain, rectangular brick church was the lowest in cost, and yet in the simplicity of design and the proper proportions — usually with the length about twice the width, and the width about or just under twice the height — a lovely effect was achieved, which grows on one favorably. The oldest of this rectangular style of colonial church is Merchants Hope Church, Prince George County, built in 1657 (No. 299). In a number of cases, the plain rectangular church had a tower added at a later date, when the parish had grown and the means were available.

Of the cruciform style, there are seven churches in the collection that were designed originally as such and are still in the form of a Latin cross — Bruton Parish Church (No. 294), which was built in 1711 and is the oldest of the cruciform churches; St. Paul's, Norfolk (No. 304); St. John's, Hampton (No. 310); Mattapony (No. 320); Abingdon (No. 318); Vauter's (No. 327); and Farnham (No. 328). Then there are three churches in the form of a Greek cross — Christ Church, Lancaster (No. 329); St. Paul's, King George (No. 332); and Aquia (No. 334). Of these three, Christ Church, Lancaster, is one of the finest examples of the colonial brick church, and it is preserved in its original state.

Several of the churches are of a style intermediate between the rectangular and the cruciform. Some of them have had a wing added, making an L or a T form. Others have been altered to an L or a T by the removal of a wing or two from a cruciform building; and in a few cases only a rectangle, or one member, of a cruciform building remains. One such church is St. George's, Accomac, known as the Pongoteague Church, on the Eastern Shore of Virginia (No. 309); it was built as a cruciform church with a semicircular apse, which gave it the name of the "Ace of Clubs Church"; now it is a rectangular building in which only the transepts survive. In the case of Old St. Mary's, Burlington, New Jersey (No. 159), the original was a rectangular building, which now is the nave of a cruciform church.

Several of the brick churches, and the one tapia church, were built with pillared porticos in the Greek style. As the Greeks were pagans and their temples were erected to pagan gods, it would seem inappropriate to have a Greek entrance to a Christian church; but the Greeks prepared the minds of the Mediterranian world for Christianity and the Romans adopted it, and the Christian church and cathedral architecture evolved from the Greek through the Roman temple. Greek porticos were rare among colonial churches, for the fashion in architecture known as the Greek Revival did not begin in America until soon after 1800 — the Baltimore Cathedral was designed in that style by Benjamin Henry Latrobe in 1805. St. Paul's Chapel, New York City (No. 168), was built in 1764, with a design based on the many London churches, in anticipation of the Greek Revival; the chapel and the Ionic pillars were built in stone, the predominating material in the Mid-Atlantic. King's Chapel, Boston (No. 95), was built earlier, in 1749; and even though the building is of stone, the Ionic pillars are of wood, the predominating material in New England. In Charleston, St. Michael's Church (No. 274) was built in 1752, with a portico of brick Doric columns. These three large and fashionable churches in large port cities were built with elegance of design, and the pillared portico in each case found its origin in London churches. It is a coincidence that the pillars in each were made of the predominant material of the region. The elegant brick church of the port city of Philadelphia, Christ Church (No. 205), features a great Palladian window (a design which became popular in the Classic Revival) in the end of the building facing the street, but there is no portico. In South Carolina there are three country churches with pillared porticos — the Sheldon Church near Beaufort (No. 288), built about 1745, and St. James, Santee (No. 282), built in 1768, both of which have brick columns; and Old White Church on St. Helena Island, near Beaufort (No. 287), was built of tapia, a type of Spanish masonry which in South Carolina was made of oyster shells and mortar made with lime burned from oyster shells. The fort built by the Spanish in the sixteenth century, after the Huguenots had been there, was made of tapia, and the ruins can be seen near Beaufort. Locally it is called "tabby." The brick columns and their bases and capitals were made of curved and molded bricks. The projecting top edge of the water table, where the thicker foundation wall projects out beyond the face of the upper wall, was covered with quarter-round brick. Special shapes were molded for cornices, window and door arches, pediments, pilasters, and other such ornamentation.

Many of the doorways were designed with classic pediments supported by pilasters. In some cases the enframements were made of stone, as at Christ Church, Lancaster (No. 329), Aquia (No. 334), and Pohick (No. 335); in others, however, they were made in special molded brick to give the required effect, as at Ware Church (No. 317), Upper Church, King and Queen (No. 319), Mattapony (No. 320), and St. John's, King William (No. 321). A special mullion brick was required for the double casement windows of the Old Brick Church, Isle of Wight (No. 297); and it was a mullion brick, excavated in 1938 at the site of St. Mary's Church, St. Mary's City (both extinct), that gave the clue that the design of the church was similar to that of the Old Brick Church.

Another special type of brick was used in window and door arches — water-rubbed brick. In order to produce a brick of a wedge shape with a certain angle, to form the prescribed curvature of an arch, bricks were rubbed together with sand by hand under water, and ground down to the required shape. The result was a brick with a lighter rose color than that in the walls around it. Such water-rubbed brick is found in the arches at Hungars Church on the Eastern Shore of Virginia (No. 308), Ware (No. 317), Christ Church, Middlesex (No. 325), Lamb's Creek (No. 333), and Falls Church (No. 337), all in Virginia.

Several of the brick churches have a Jacobean curvilinear gable. It is found on the tower end of St. Michael's, Charleston (No. 274), and on both ends of St. Stephen's Church at St. Stephens, South Carolina (No. 284), where the massive roof was inspired by St. Michael's design. At St. Peter's Church, New Kent, Virginia (No. 314), in the course of a restoration in this century, evidence of original curvilinear gables was discovered, and they were restored. The second Bruton church at Williamsburg, which was replaced by the present building, also had Jacobean curvilinear gables.

Inscribed bricks are found at many of the churches. The one bearing the date "1632" at Old Brick Church, Isle of Wight (No. 297) is historically so precious that it is cased and bolted to the altar behind the cross. Such caution may arise from the fact that the brick inscribed with the date "1734" was stolen from the wall above the entrance of St. Thomas' Church, Bath, North Carolina (No. 198); it was located later in a prominent museum and restored to its place. In a number of buildings, a dated brick appears high on a wall, indicating that the walls were completed at that time, and in other cases bricks are inscribed with names or initials of the builders.

Brick tile, usually of medium sized square blocks, was used in many churches for flooring. In later alterations, wooden flooring was often laid over the brick tile, but in most cases the aisle was left with the tile exposed, while in practically all cases the pews rested on flooring a step up from the aisle. In other churches the aisle was paved with flagstone, which in some cases was imported from Europe (see Merchant's Hope Church, No. 299).

The roofs of the brick churches are interesting. In the early years the brick churches in the South were roofed with cypress shingle, and there are cases of it lasting as long as a century. Many of them were reroofed in slate, fireproof but more expensive, as it was imported; for the city churches, which generally were better able to afford it, slate usually was bought in England. The roof designs varied considerably. In addition to the plain gabled roof with a straight pitch, there was the swag roof, in which the slope eased up near the eaves, as at Merchant's Hope Church (it was on one of the roof timbers of this church that the date "1657" was found inscribed, see No. 299), and at Yeocomico Church (No. 331). The hip roof was used infrequently, an example being at St. Paul's Church, King George (No. 332). On the First Presbyterian Church, Wilmington, Delaware (No. 14), is a gambrel roof, a style which is called "Dutch Colonial"; another of the same type is at the Donegal Church, Pennsylvania (No. 251), which also was closely related to the Dutch influence of New Castle, Delaware. St. Barnabas Church, in Maryland, built in 1774, has a hip roof of the Mansard type (No. 51). The plain bonnet roof, or truncated gable, is found on the Lower Chapel, Middlesex (No. 326), Old Presbyterian Church, New Castle (No. 17), and the Welsh Tract Baptist Church, Delaware (No. 21).

Most of the brick churches were frankly built of brick, but in some cases stucco was applied later. St. Michael's, Charleston (No. 274), however, was designed and built originally with all the brickwork roughcast, or plastered. The effect produced is that of a stone church, which was the intention of the designer. Stone, used so extensively in London churches, gave a substantial elegance that was fashionable, and it was simulated not only on brick but also on wood (as in the case of the wooden columns at King's Chapel, Boston (No. 95). In some cases plaster or stucco was applied later in the course of repairs, alteration, or restoration, for protection if not for the design effect. In South Carolina, Goose Creek Church (No. 275) and St. Andrew's (No. 279) have been stuccoed, with the corners of the walls grooved to simulate stone quoins; Strawberry Chapel (No. 278) and Christ Church (No. 281) have plain stucco with no quoins; at Beaufort, St. Helena's brick walls have been stuccoed (No. 286); and in Charleston the original walls of the Unitarian Church (No. 289) have been stuccoed in a Gothic remodeling that one would never recognize as having been a colonial church. In Virginia, Trinity Church, Portsmouth (No. 305), was stuccoed in the course of enlargement, but Grace Church, Yorktown (No. 313), which appears to be stuccoed brick, is built of marl. Further north the Asbury Methodist Episcopal Church at Wilmington, Delaware (No. 15), was stuccoed in the course of extensive alterations, and at Burlington, New Jersey, Old St. Mary's Church (No. 159) was covered with stucco when it was remodeled. In Baltimore, however, the brickwork of the Otterbein Church (No. 62) was stuccoed, and later the stucco was meticulously removed to expose the original brick.

In addition to the legend of churches built of brick imported from England, there is another concerning colonial churches in America that might be called "the Wren myth." All over New England there are church spires which are said to have been designed by Sir Christopher Wren. While his influence on American colonial church design was great — through his many magnificent London churches, his pupils and their work, and the books with drawings which were published — Wren did not draw a design for an American church. The nearest connection with a Wren design is the Wren Building of the College of William and Mary in Williamsburg. The plan was adapted for the purpose in Virginia from a design of Wren, and it was said to resemble his plan for Chelsea Hospital. Therefore the closest connection with Wren was not a design for a church, and the building has no spire, though it does contain the chapel of a college that was founded by the Church of England, which is the reason for its inclusion here.

In New England, where there are only five brick houses of worship of the total seventy-nine, three of them are in Massachusetts. The two in Boston, Old South Meeting House (No. 94) and Old North Church (No. 96), are historically interesting and, because of their association with the Revolution, probably are the best known in the collection. The third is Holden Chapel (No. 97), the third oldest building in Harvard Yard at Cambridge. The small chapel is nestled among tall brick buildings, and it is not widely known by the public; in fact, as it has been replaced by another chapel in the Yard, it is not well-known even among Harvard men.

In Connecticut the one brick church is the First Church of Christ, Wethersfield (No. 6). Like the two Boston buildings mentioned above, the one in Wethersfield has a fine brick tower, and in this case the front wall is decorated with a diapered pattern.

The one remaining brick building in New England is Touro Synagogue, Newport, Rhode Island (see Chapter 5 and No. 271). This brick building is the only colonial synagogue in America. The design was drawn by Peter Harrison of Newport, a prosperous importer who made architectural designs as an amateur. In addition to

Touro Synagogue, built of brick, he designed King's Chapel, Boston, in stone (No. 95), and Christ Church, Cambridge, in wood (No. 98), and he became known as "the prince of Colonial amateur architects." As they were Sephardic Jews at Newport, Touro Synagogue was designed in the Spanish-Portuguese style, with an interior following the layout of the mother synagogue in Amsterdam, Holland.

The smallest brick house of worship in the collection is about the size of a child's playhouse. It has the disproportionate name of Appoquinimink Friends Meeting House, and it is located at Odessa, New Castle County, Delaware (No. 19).

8

WOOD

Soon after the Pilgrims landed at Plymouth, in 1620, they built a large meeting house of wood on the hill by the harbor, and on its flat roof they mounted six cannon. The one building then served the first settlement in New England as town hall, church, and fort.

Timber was plentiful, and the pioneers had the skills to utilize it. On the New England coast, brick clay was not as plentiful as it was from New Jersey south. Glaciers had moved the eroded clay into the sea, giving to Long Island rich garden soil, as they did for West Jersey, leaving behind scarred outcroppings of stone. The working of stone was time-consuming, laborious, and costly, and it required skills that were scarce or not available among the pioneers. Wood, therefore, continued to be the principal building material in New England throughout the colonial period. As a result, of the seventy-nine New England buildings in this collection, seventy-two are of wood, five are of brick, and only two are of stone.

Visitors to Pioneers' Village, Salem, Massachusetts, see replicas of the earliest types of huts and houses built by the Pilgrims and Puritans. A particularly interesting exhibit there shows the technique for sawing plank from logs, by which the log is laid over a pit and sawed by two men, the "sawyer" standing on the log and the "pitman" in the pit — a technique which was the origin of two family names. It will be noted that none of those early houses were built with horizontal logs. The romance surrounding pioneers such as Daniel Boone, who moved across the mountains into Tennessee and Kentucky, has built up a legend about the log cabin, but the English settlers on the Atlantic coast did not use that type of construction. The two surviving colonial churches of the log cabin type are in the mountains — the Mill Creek Church (No. 342) was built in the Blue Ridge Mountains of Virginia in 1770, and Rehoboth Church (No. 345) was built in the mountains of West Virginia in 1785. The log cabin was not an English type of construction, but it had been used in Sweden for ages, and the Swedes introduced it into New Sweden on the Delaware, after their first colony was planted there in 1638. There seems to be no authentic record of the log cabin having been used for church construction in Connecticut, for example, during the seventeenth century, and wherever it was used in New England, it seems to have been at a later time.

Meanwhile, the New Englanders were building fine meeting houses of oak timbers and spruce or fir siding that are still standing. The oldest frame house of worship in America is the Old Ship Meeting House at Hingham, Massachusetts (No. 87), built in 1681. In that little harbor, north of Plymouth and south of Boston, the settlers organized the Congregational First Parish in 1635, and began then to build their first meeting house, the twelfth in the colony. The present venerable meeting house, their second, has features of construction that are particularly interesting. The timbers supporting the roof, which are open to view in the auditorium, are curved like the frame of a ship, and there is a widow's walk beneath the spire, with a compass rose on its ceiling under the base of the spire.

The second frame house of worship in America is the Third Haven Friends Meeting House (No. 76), on the Eastern Shore of Maryland, built in 1682. This frame structure seems out of place in the Mid-Atlantic region, amidst the many brick churches on the Eastern Shore; and an enlargement of the building, made by moving one wall back and carrying the roof out to it at a different angle from that of the opposite roof, gives the building a New England salt-box appearance.

The New England frame meeting house was built in two styles — the earlier style was the plain-gabled, rectangular frame structure of one or two stories; and the other was a structure built more as a church, with a frame tower and steeple. In some cases, the building was converted from one style to the other, by the addition of a tower and steeple long after the raising of the original frame. The church steeple was not popular in the early years of New England. The Pilgrims came to America as Dissenters and Separatists from the Church of England, and their purpose was to avoid all suggestions of the Established Church from which they had freed themselves. The Puritans who followed them were also Dissenters, but they were reluctant Separatists, until the Puritan Rebellion, and then they sought to destroy the Church and the Crown. The early meeting houses, therefore, were plain; the churchlike buildings appeared later, and even they avoided completely the Gothic style of church so prevalent in England, and which made an early but brief showing in Virginia.

One of the finest examples of the plain style is the Sandown Meeting House in New Hampshire (No. 119). Its beauty of mass, line, detail, and craftsmanship, and its interior furnishings, come to us in their original state. Another fine example of the same style is the Rocky Hill Meeting House at Amesbury, Massachusetts (No. 113). Some of the meeting houses of the plain-gable style were severely plain outside, looking like nothing more than a farmhouse, but inside having all the conventional furnishings — high pulpit with stairway, sounding board, box pews, and gallery — done with skilled craftsmanship that produced a beautiful result (see, for example, the Alna Meeting House in Maine, No. 37).

Friends meeting houses, of course, remained during the colonial period in the category of the plain building, and never assumed any features of a church. Old Newport Friends Meeting House, Rhode Island (No. 266), built in 1699, is the oldest in New England, but it is not used as a meeting house now, and its furnishings have been changed. The plainest Friends meeting house in New England is the one on Conanicut Island, above Jamestown, Rhode Island (No. 273). The smallest frame meeting house in the collection is the Seaville Friends Meeting House, Cape May County, New Jersey (No. 149), which was made of bog cedar and in damp weather gives off a pleasant cedar aroma. It has the local name of the "Old Cedar Meeting House."

Another severely plain frame meeting house was built by the sect of Six Principle Baptists — the Elder Ballou Meeting House in Providence County, Rhode Island (No. 264). This primitive structure, built about 1740, measures only thirty by twenty-five feet, and it is furnished with six long benches between side aisles, with a railing down the middle to separate the men and the women. There is a gallery, which also is furnished with plain benches equipped with a back rail. The one concession to conventional finishing is the plaster on the walls, which probably was added at a later date.

The oldest church building of the Seventh Day Baptists in America is the Sabbath Day Meeting House at Newport (No. 268). The second and present building was erected in 1729, but one would not recognize it as a frame building. In 1884 it was purchased by the Newport Historical Society, moved to its present lot, and in 1915 it was moved to join with the building of the Society, where it now stands encased in brick.

In the second style of the frame meeting house, the present First Church of Christ, Farmington, Connecticut (No. 7), is one of the loveliest in New England. It was built in 1771 as the third meeting house of the parish. The designer and builder was Captain Judah Woodruff, who also built ten of the finest houses in Farmington. The design is similar to that of the frame First Congregational Church in Brooklyn, Connecticut (No. 3), which was built the year before, and of the brick First Church of Christ in Wethersfield (No. 6). The beautiful steeple resembles that of the brick Old South Meeting House, Boston (No. 94), but it is more airy and graceful, as it rises 150 feet above the ground. The perspective of height is accentuated by the use of graduated widths in the clapboards, narrowing toward the top of the walls.

The principal ornamentation conceded to these frame meeting houses is found in the steeples. There the combination of tower, belfry, lantern, and spire provides the opportunity for imaginative design, particularly in the treatment of the transition from the square tower to the octagonal spire. In this area, the frame meeting houses of New England went so far as to emulate the designs of the fine London churches. In the steeple of the magnificent First Baptist Church, Providence (No. 260), we see the ultimate in this style. The design for the steeple was made by James Gibbs, a pupil of Sir Christopher Wren; it was one of several designs he made for his St. Martin-in-the-Fields, London, which were not used, and it appeared as Plate No. 30 in his *Book of Architecture, Designs, and Ornaments* (1728). The body of the building is similar to that of Marybone Chapel, London, and the whole building reflects the Wren influence. The designer of the building was an amateur architect, Joseph Brown, professor of philosophy at what was then Rhode Island College and now is Brown University.

In this mother church of the Baptist churches in America, we see the closest connection between New England church design and Christopher Wren. Just as any frame church in New England with a tall white steeple has become to be known as a "Colonial church," regardless of when it was built, so they have become to be "designed by Wren," regardless of who actually designed them. The "Wren myth" in New England is based on his well-deserved influence, but no design of his was made for or used in this region. It was noted in the previous chapter on brick, that the only design by Wren used in America was adapted for the Wren Building at William and Mary College, Williamsburg, which had been made for Chelsea Hospital, London. It was used in Virginia for a college, it had no steeple, it was not painted white, and it was made of brick. It is included in this collection only because the College was founded by the Church of England, and the building contains the colonial college chapel (No. 295).

Another persistent myth is the "white colonial church." In the colonial period, white lead pigment had not been developed to its present purity, and paint had some color. A variety of colors were used, even on the same building, and some of them would seem gaudy today. For example, the Hampton Congregational Church in Connecticut (No. 5), built in 1754, was repainted in 1805, and even at that late date the colors were as follows: red on the roof and rear wall, stone-yellow on the front side and two ends, white on the window frames, and chocolate on the doors and baseboards. Stone color was quite fashionable on painted frame churches, particularly on flush siding where stone could be simulated; stone gray often was specified, and a gray with a warm lavender hue was used at times.

Against severe opposition from the Puritans, the Church of England came late into New England. The first Anglican parish in Rhode Island, Trinity Church, Newport (No. 267), was organized in 1688. That was the year of the English Revolution against the Roman Catholic King James II, and two years after King's Chapel was organized in Boston, the first in New England (No. 95). The present frame building, which was begun in 1725 as the second building of Trinity, is a fine design in the Wren tradition. The architect was Richard Munday, another amateur, who ranked after Peter Harrison and Joseph Brown, and Trinity represents his best work. In frame he achieved a church that is comparable with Old North Church, Boston (No. 96), built of brick in 1723, two years before Trinity.

A warden and member of the vestry of Trinity, Newport, was Godfrey Malbone, a wealthy international trader and shipowner, and a colorful personality who entertained buccaneers at his home in Newport (see No. 267). He owned a large tract of land in Connecticut, and when his son and namesake returned from Oxford, he sent the son to Brooklyn to manage the estate. There the chip-off-the-old-block built an Anglican church of his own, rather than pay the tax assessed for building a new Congregational church in Brooklyn (No. 3). He named it Trinity, for his father's church in Newport, but it has generally been called the Malbone Church. This square building has a hip roof, which was rare for a frame colonial house of worship.

The oldest Anglican church building in New England is St. Paul's Church, Wickford, Rhode Island, known as Old Narragansett Church (No. 265). The parish, the next in Rhode Island after Trinity Newport, was organized soon after the founding of the Society for the Propagation of the Gospel at London in 1701, and the church was built in 1707. It stood on Congdon Hill in Kingston, about five miles from its present site, but the highway on which it stood did not prosper after the Revolution, and the church was moved. The versatility of the frame church was demonstrated, in 1800, when the building was moved here to the seashore beside Narragansett Bay. A number of these frame churches were moved, another example being the Congregational Church at Park Hill, New Hampshire (No. 126); that building was moved from one hilltop to another at a cost of £2,388 and one barrel of rum.

Versatility of the frame church is demonstrated further in the number that have been enlarged. The First Parish Church, Kennebunk, Maine (No. 32), for example, was built in 1733 and enlarged in 1803, by cutting it in two, moving the rear half back twenty-eight feet, and joining the halves. The steeple was built at that time. In fact, it has been so easy to enlarge, alter, add to, and remodel colonial frame houses of worship, that it is difficult to distinguish the colonial from the later parts. Much of the enlargement of old churches and building of new ones took place during the spiritual revival about 1840.

Not only white frame steeples, but a number of Greek porticos have been added to colonial meeting houses since the colonial period. At Longmeadow, Massachusetts, for example, the present second building, which was erected in 1767, was moved from the green to its present location facing it, in 1874; and at that time the building was enlarged, and the present front and spire were added (see No. 106). Its pillared portico is a feature that was not used in any of the frame meeting houses in the colonial period; wherever it appears on a frame building, it is the result of the Greek Revival which began after 1800. For example, the Old Congregational Church of Enfield, Connecticut (No. 9), became the Town Hall after the congregation had built a new church, and a Greek portico was added at that time, 1848.

Frame steeples have been often the victims of hurricanes. The most famous is that of Old North Church, Boston (No. 96). The original steeple, in which the lantern signal was hung for Paul Revere, was built in 1740 and was blown down by a hurricane in 1804. It was rebuilt from a design by Charles Bulfinch, a prominent architect of the time, which was similar to the original design. Then on the last day of August, 1954, hurricane Carol toppled the steeple again; an amateur photographer made a picture of it as it was about to fall from the tower. A nationwide campaign raised the necessary funds, and again the steeple was rebuilt; but this time it was firmly anchored to the tower. Another example is the Westminster Congregational Church in Connecticut. There the belfry and bell were blown down in the great hurricane of 1938; for five years the bell rested in the vestibule, until another belfry was built, as shown in the photograph (No. 2). At Old South Church, Newburyport, Massachusetts, when it was found that the steeple had been weakened by storms, it was torn down, and the tower was finished with a belfry but no steeple, as show in the photograph (No. 112).

The frame building of St. Paul's Church, Woodbury, Connecticut (No. 11), has been altered, and the front no longer resembles its colonial design. St. Paul's Parish, however, is worthy of special interest in the history of the Episcopal Church, for Samuel Seabury was elected, at a meeting in 1783 at the Glebe House, to go to England and seek consecration as Bishop of Connecticut, the first bishop in America. The Glebe House, which was built about 1690, still stands and is open to the public. After a frustrating year in England, Seabury finally was consecrated in Aberdeen, Scotland, in 1784. The present building of St. Paul's Church had no connection with the historic conference in the Glebe House, for it was erected in 1785, the year after Seabury's consecration.

During the nineteenth century, a large number of white-steepled frame churches were built, and there is considerable variety of design and beauty among them. They are particularly plentiful in the Connecticut Valley and western New England. As architecture still was a budding profession in America, design was left to the builder in most cases. To aid the builder, Asher Benjamin, one of the few architects in America at the time, published *The Country Builder's Assistant* in 1797. It contains many designs for churches, with a variety of steeples, and many frame churches in western New England are witnesses to the thorough use of the book. They are not colonial buildings, however, and it requires close observation and some research to determine which of the white-steepled frame churches or town halls were colonial meeting houses of worship.

9

STONE

Among the many stone buildings in this collection there is great variety. They may be divided into two styles, the plain-gabled and the steepled. These two groups may be divided again into two, the small and the large, making four general types, as follows:

The first type of stone house of worship is the small, rectangular plain-gabled, one-story, country building (some that were built in the wilderness by early settlers are now in towns or cities); in this type two good examples are the Norriton Presbyterian Meeting House (No. 230) and the Chichester Friends Meeting House (No. 217), both in Pennsylvania. The second type is the larger rectangular, plain-gabled, country house of worship with two tiers of windows; two good examples are the Buckingham Friends Meeting House (No. 241) and the Silver Spring Presbyterian Church (No. 257), also in Pennsylvania. The third type is the fine country church with a tower and belfry or steeple, such as St. Paul's Church, Eastchester, New York (No. 177). And the fourth type is the elegant city church, such as St. Paul's Chapel, New York City (No. 168), which compares favorably with the stone churches of London.

The use of stone for building houses of worship in colonial times was determined more by geology than by religious denomination or nationality. The style of architecture was influenced both by the denomination and the congregation's country of origin, but stone was used as a building material by the various religious groups, generally because of local availability. Among the stone houses of worship, ranging in style from the simple, austere Friends meeting house to the magnificent Anglican city church, we find them built by Dutchmen, Swedes, Germans, Englishmen, Irishmen, Scots, and Welshmen. Of a total of 345 buildings in the collection, 85 are in stone. In the Mid-Atlantic, 69 of the buildings are in stone; in the South there are 14, and in New England there are only 2 (Appendix III).

In the Appalachian Range, the stratified upheavals of limestone provided building material for churches from the Blue Ridge Mountains of Virginia into the Alleghenies and on north through the Catskills to the Adirondacks. In the regions close to the mountains the limestone varies in color from light gray to a bluish gray. Further from the mountains toward the coast, sedimentary deposits of sandstone (or freestone) were made, which in the Mid-Atlantic region varies in color from warm rose to rich brown. Granite, a third type of stone, which is plentiful in New England, was used in only one of these colonial churches, King's Chapel, Boston, which was built of dressed Quincy granite (No. 95).

The southernmost limestone church is the Timber Ridge Presbyterian Church in Rockbridge County, Virginia, west of the Blue Ridge; it is of particular historical interest as the boyhood church of Sam Houston (see No. 344). Further north, the Augusta Church at Fort Defiance, Augusta County, was built of the same light gray limestone; the architecture of the building is interesting, with its bonnet gables on the portico and the wings, as well as on the main building (No. 343). It was in the limestone that the great caverns of the Shenandoah Valley were formed. At the nothern end of the Blue Ridge, two more limestone buildings are found. The Goose Creek Friends Meeting House, at Lincoln, is now a residence, with ivy covering so much of the walls that only a patch of stone is visible (No. 341). In Frederick County, the Hopewell Friends Meeting House is an impressive two-story building with four chimneys at the corners. The walls are laid in light bluish gray stones of various sizes but with a smooth face (No. 340).

Continuing north into Maryland, the German Reformed Church at Hagerstown is in gray limestone (No. 66). In the Cumberland Valley of Pennsylvania, we find two limestone churches. The First Presbyterian Church at Carlisle (No. 256) was begun in 1757, and we know the date only because of a letter in which it was mentioned that hauling of stone for the new church was to begin the next day. The walls are of blocks of bluish limestone, decorated with courses of white marble in an unusual pattern. The blocks of stone are of diminished size toward the top of the walls, to heighten the perspective. The stone tower was added in 1873. Eleven miles down the valley toward the Susquehanna is the Silver Spring Presbyterian Church (No. 257), a two-story, plain-gabled limestone building. Crossing the Susquehanna and passing through Harrisburg we come to the suburban town of Paxtang, where stands the Paxton Presbyterian Church (No. 258), built of a bright limestone.

Following the same geological formation into upper New York, between the Catskills and the Adirondacks in the Schoharie and Mohawk valleys, there are five limestone churches. St. George's Church, Schenectady (No. 190), was built in 1759 as part of the stockaded fort, for this was Indian country, and the Schenectady massacre of 1690 had destroyed most of the settlement. The Fort Herkimer Reformed Dutch Church (No. 194) was begun as a church, but when the walls had reached the height of the specified one story, it was decided to make it a fort for defense against raids, and a second story was added; the two levels constructed at different times are distinguished by two colors of stone. At Schoharie the Reformed High Dutch Church also became a palisaded fort, and it is known both as the Old Stone Church and the

Old Stone Fort (No. 195). The other two limestone churches are on the Mohawk — the Palatine Church (No. 192), and the Dutch Reformed Church at Stone Arabia (No. 191).

In the northwestern tip of New York, the French Castle was built of stone in 1726, and it was fortified as Fort Niagara after having been established as a trading post in New France (No. 197). Work on the building did not begin until two vessels had been built on Lake Ontario to carry the stone from the eastern end of the lake, where La Salle had established Fort Frontenac (the present Kingston). The French Castle is the only building in the collection that was constructed of Canadian stone, and in it was furnished a Jesuit chapel, which distinguishes the building as the only French Roman Catholic house of worship in the collection.

Brown sandstone is easily sawn, and brown blocks resembling large bricks were used abundantly in New Jersey churches. A good example is the First Presbyterian Church, Newark (No. 132). The lime used in the mortar came from clam shells that had been piled for centuries on Indian middens beside Newark Bay. Another example of small, bricklike stone is found at Christ Church, New Brunswick (No. 138), where the present tower was part of the original structure of 1743, and all of the old stone from the main body of the church was used in the reconstruction of that part in 1852. Larger blocks of dressed brown sandstone were used also in some churches, a good example being the Old Stone Church at Easthaven, Connecticut (No. 10).

Compared to the sawn blocks, brown sandstone was used more generally in irregular shapes and sizes. The masonry was usually laid up in rough courses, and although the stones might be shaped to some extent, they were not cut into blocks. Excellent examples of this type of masonry are to be found in New Jersey in the Fairfield Presbyterian Church, New England Crossroads (No. 150); the Deerfield Stone Church (No. 152); the Mount Laurel Friends Meeting House (No. 161); and the Arney's Mount Friends Meeting House (No. 164). In Pennsylvania the following five buildings were constructed in the same type of masonry, by five different religious denominations: the Swedish St. James' Church, Kingsessing (No. 203); the Mennonite Meeting House, Germantown (No. 213); the Friends Meeting House, Frankford (No. 215); the Anglican Old St. David's of Radnor (No. 222); the Presbyterian Church, Newtown (No. 239); and the St. Peter's Lutheran Church, Middletown (No. 259).

In a number of buildings the stonework is in more than one type of stone. In the walls of the Church of the Sacred Heart, on Little Conewago Creek in Pennsylvania, the two types of brown sandstone were used — the dressed stone in the front wall presenting a smooth face, and field stone or run-of-the-quarry in the side walls (No. 254). In the Falckner's Swamp Lutheran Church at New Hanover, Pennsylvania, there is a variation in the combination of the two types — on the corners and between the windows there are pilasters of dressed sandstone, set in contrast against the walls made of stones in various sizes and shapes (No. 232).

Two of the Friends meeting houses in Pennsylvania reveal different building dates by a difference in color of the stone, or by combining two different types of stone.

At the Old Haverford Friends Meeting House in Oakmont, the stone in the southern half of the building, erected in 1697, has a slightly different color from that in the northern half, which was added in 1800 (No. 219). The contrast is even greater at Plymouth Meeting Friends Meeting House, where the original building (the end toward the burying ground) was erected in limestone, and the other half of the present building was added later in brown sandstone.

Mixtures of limestone and brown sandstone are found in a number of buildings. In the Hudson Valley, where both were available, the mixture was used in the Lutheran Old Stone Church at Red Hook (No. 188), where the stone can be seen only in the back wall, for the others are stuccoed. Further down the Hudson, the brown sandstone becomes predominant in the mixture, as at the Creek Friends Meeting House (No. 186); the Sleepy Hollow Dutch Reformed Church at Scarborough (No. 178); St. Paul's Church, Eastchester, Westchester County (No. 177); and St. Andrew's Church on Staten Island (No. 169). One other building with the mixture of the same two stones is the Gunpowder Friends Meeting House at Cockeysville, Maryland (No. 60).

A distinctive feature of the brown sandstone churches of New Jersey and Pennsylvania is the pleasing contrast created by the use of white mortar. It appears in most of the houses mentioned above, in which brown stone of irregular size was used, and it is a prominent feature of the Norriton Presbyterian Church, for the building is quite small (No. 230). There are two different methods of finishing the mortar, which are distinctive features of the stone buildings. The Exeter Friends Meeting House is a good example of fine troweling, in which the mortar is held to a line of equal width at the junction of the stones; this meeting house is also of historical interest in its association with the Lincoln family and Daniel Boone and his family (No. 247). In the walls of the Newtown Square Friends Meeting House (No. 220), and the Church of the Brethren in Germantown (No. 214), where the shapes are less uniform and more small stones are used, pointing was more difficult, and the mortar spreads irregularly and occupies a greater proportion of the wall surface. The extreme is found at the Old Sadsbury Friends Meeting House, near Christiana, Pennsylvania (No. 250), where instead of pointing, mortar was spread promiscuously over the wall surface. A quaint idea was carried out in the mortar of the Warrington Friends Meeting House in York County, Pennsylvania (No. 253); on the northern corner of the building the mortar between the stones, from the eaves down to the foundation, spells PRAYER.

A logical step in the course of repairing and maintaining stone walls is to give them a complete coat of rough cast, parget, plaster, or stucco, and the step has been taken with a number of buildings pictured in this collection. For example, the old stone building that was the original structure of the Evangelical Lutheran Church in Frederick, Maryland, is now a rear wing of a larger building, and has been so completely covered with stucco that it is hardly recognizable as a stone building (No. 64). In Pennsylvania, St. Peter's in the Great Valley is a fine example of a stuccoed stone church (No. 223). The stucco on the stone walls of the Donegal Presbyterian Church (No. 251) and Old Trappe Church (No. 231) is smooth and covers them completely, as it does on the Merion Friends Meeting House (No. 229) and St. Paul's Chapel at Bally (No. 246). On the walls of Neshaminy Presbyterian Church (No. 238), it is not thick enough to hide the contours of the stone, and at Old Kennett Friends Meeting House (No. 225), the coating appears to be little more than a heavy whitewash.

Among the larger country churches will be found a number of interesting roof styles. The bonnet gable, used on a number of brick churches, as noted earlier, is found also on many of the stone buildings. Old Swedes, Wilmington, Delaware, was built originally in 1698, with both ends of the ridge truncated to form bonnet gables; when the tower was added in 1802, one of the gables was eliminated (No. 13). The Sleepy Hollow Dutch Reformed Church, built in 1699 in the Hudson Valley, has a gambrel roof in the Dutch Colonial style (No. 178). The Palatine Church in the Mohawk Valley, has a gambrel roof with a swag at the eaves and a good cornice (No. 192). The Donegal Presbyterian Church, near the Susquehanna River in Pennsylvania, also has a gambrel roof (No. 251). The Old Trappe Church, in Pennsylvania, has a unique combination of gambrel and hip roof, which at one end covers a semi-octagonal apse (No. 231).

An outside stairway, for access to the gallery, was a feature of several stone churches. Stairways of that style are to be seen at Old Swedes, Wilmington, Delaware (No. 13), and Old St. David's of Radnor, Pennsylvania (No. 222). The Tinicum Presbyterian Church in Bucks County (No. 240), and the Church of the Brethren in Germantown (214) both had outside stairways, but they were eliminated in later alterations.

Grace Church in Yorktown, Virginia, is unique in the type of stone used in its construction. The walls were built with blocks of marl, a relatively soft stone which was cut from the bluff overlooking the York River, and which is composed of clay and lime of sea shells. The building was burned in 1815, and the heat is believed to have hardened the walls to the consistency of concrete.

Another unique masonry, mentioned in the chapter on brick, is tapia. It is neither brick nor stone, but is concrete composed of oyster shells and mortar, in which the lime was burned from oyster shells. This Spanish type of masonry was used in the Spanish Fort near Beaufort, South Carolina, and in the construction of the Old White Church, on St. Helena Island near Beaufort (No. 287). Tapia is known locally as "tabby."

10

THEIR NAMES

The names given to the colonial houses of worship reveal some of their history, and they tell something of the geography, and the character and customs of the people of the early congregations.

In accordance with common practice in the Church of England and the Church of Rome, some of the churches in South Carolina, Virginia, and Maryland were given saints' names during the colonial period. In many parishes that had saints' names, however, the churches were given homely names that had some local association. The early Anglican parishes in Virginia usually were named for the county or a land grant; and if there were more than one church in the parish, they were designated by their location, as the upper and the lower churches of that parish. For example, the Chuckatuck Church of Virginia was in Chuckatuck Parish, on Chuckatuck Creek, a tidal arm of the James River. Chuckatuck Parish was laid out as the West Parish, when the East Parish was on the opposite side of the Nansemond River, another tidal arm of the James which gave its name to the county. The East Parish was absorbed later into Suffolk Parish, when it became the Lower Parish of Suffolk. It was not until 1828 that the Chuckatuck Church was named St. John's Church, at a time when it was fashionable to rename colonial churches with saints' names. In the East Parish, which became the Lower Parish of Suffolk, the Bennett's Creek Church was given the name "Glebe Church" when it became one of the few Anglican churches in Virginia that was exempted from the law requiring all glebe lands to be sold after the Revolution. Swedish churches were named Trinity, and Lutheran churches used that name and also saints' names in some cases, but the Dissenters avoided such names, on the ground that they were Anglican and Roman.

The names of the vast majority of early colonial houses of worship were associated with the locality. Gunpowder, Aquia, Blackwater, Herring Creek, Lamb's Creek, Wye, Fork, Falls, Silver Spring, and Fishkill were all associated with water —

springs, streams, or rivers. The waters in some cases had been named for people, Lamb's Creek for example. Silver Spring originally was Silver's Spring, named for John Silver, the pioneer landowner there. St. Jones' Church in Delaware was so called because of its location on St. Jones' Creek; and the creek, in turn, was named not for a saint, but for one Robert Jones, the name of the "said Jones" appearing in a land patent as "sd Jones his Creeke" and "sd Jones his Line of Marked Trees."

Topography and the character of the terrain gave the names to houses of worship such as Spring Hill, Green Hill, Chestnut Hill, Arney's Mount, Mount Laurel, Longmeadow, Falckner's Swamp, and Crum Elbow.

Land grants and plantations gave the names to other houses of worship, such as Welsh Tract, Merchant's Hope, Nottingham, Doughoregan, Westover, and My Lady's Manor.

Priest Neale's Mass House was so called to avoid the Maryland laws against Roman Catholics and their public worship.

Vauter's, Saters', and Elder Ballou are houses of worship named for early settlers and prominent members of the congregation. Bird and Otterbein were leaders of new sects, whose congregations worshipped in the churches bearing their names.

Caroline, Charlotte, and Prince George are churches named for members of the royal family of the mother country.

Many Indian names identify early churches, such as Yeocomico, Saponey, Mattapony, Manokin, Mashpee, and Kiokee.

Some names are associated with the Old Testament, such as Zion, Rehoboth, Immanuel, Bethabara, and Congregation Jeshuat Israel. Others are identified with the New Testament and Christian faith, such as Trinity, Christ, All Faith, and All Hallows.

Many are identified only by the name of the town, and in some cases the town has disappeared. In New England, where the town and the Congregational church were united under the law, the meeting house usually carried the name of the town, while the religious society was a Church of Christ.

Many of these buildings carried humble and affectionate names — Old Swedes, the Old Yellow Meeting House, the Old Brick Church, the Old Cedar Meeting House, the Old Stone Church, Old Lighter Knot, Old Ship, and the Wayside Church.

Here they are, nearly three and a half hundred of them, marking our colonial heritage. In wilderness and in a state of ruin, hidden in the countryside, in hamlets and towns, and in cities amidst teeming millions of people, throughout the Atlantic region of the country these houses of worship stand in simplicity, dignity, and beauty, bearing witness to the birth of a nation and reminding us of the pioneers and settlers of the colonies and the founders of the Republic — the many in one. As it says in the parish seal at the Old Ship Meeting House, Hingham: "Let the Work of our Fathers Stand."

PHOTOGRAPHS
AND MAPS

CONNECTICUT

		Denomination	Material
1	Abington Congregational Church (1751) Abington, Windham County	Congregational	Wood
2	Westminster Congregational Church (1769) Westminster, Windham County	Congregational	Wood
3	First Congregational Church (1770) Brooklyn, Windham County	Congregational	Wood
4	Old Trinity Church (1770) Brooklyn, Windham County	Anglican	Wood
5	Hampton Congregational Church (1754) Hampton, Windham County	Congregational	Wood
6	First Church of Christ (1761) Wethersfield, Hartford County	Congregational	Brick
7	First Church of Christ (1771) Farmington, Hartford County	Congregational	Wood
8	Kensington Congregational Church (1774) Kensington, Hartford County	Congregational	Wood
9	Old Congregational Church (1775) Enfield, Hartford County	Congregational	Wood
10	First Congregational Church (1772) East Haven, New Haven County	Congregational	Stone
11	St. Paul's Church (1785) Woodbury, Litchfield County	Anglican	Wood
12	Christ Church (c. 1786) Middle Haddam, Middlesex County	Anglican	Wood

SUMMARY

Congregational	9	Brick	1
Anglican	3	Wood	10
		Stone	1
Buildings	12		12

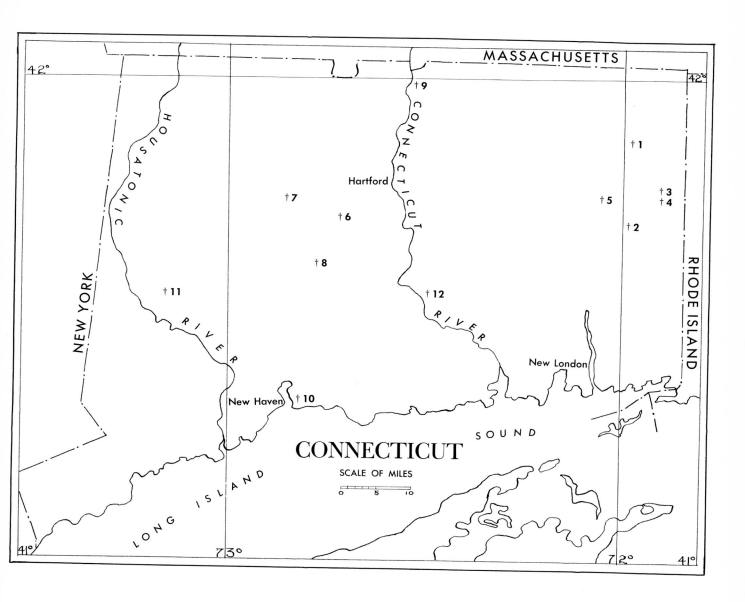

MASSACHUSETTS

42°   42°

† 9

HOUSATONIC

NEW YORK

CONNECTICUT

† 1

Hartford

† 7

† 5

† 3
† 4

† 6

† 2

RHODE ISLAND

RIVER

† 8

† 11

† 12

RIVER

New London

New Haven   † 10

SOUND

CONNECTICUT

LONG ISLAND

SCALE OF MILES

0   5   10

41°   73°   72°   41°

1

Abington Congregational Church (1751)

Abington, Windham County, Connecticut

The meeting house of Pomfret became inadequate for the growing parish, and in 1749 the General Assembly granted a petition by dividing the parish into two societies. Abington became the new parish, formed from the western portion of Pomfret. The new Society met the same year, and voted to build a meeting house of the same dimensions as that at Pomfret. In 1751 a building committee of five was appointed, and construction of the meeting house was begun. In 1753 the church was finished with the installation of pews and pulpit. The build-

ing was without a steeple until 1802, when one was added during general repairs. In 1834 a move to build a new meeting house caused a serious controversy. The opposing factions finally compromised by making major alterations in the colonial structure. The steeple of 1802 and all the original windows were removed. The interior was stripped of galleries and finish, and a new ceiling was installed below the former level. The walls were furred, lathed, and plastered, and the east windows were eliminated. At the western, or front, end of the building the present belfry was erected, pilasters and new fenestration were installed, and new cornices were substituted. For those who demanded a new meeting house, the alterations provided the appearance of a church of 1834, and all of the colonial features were lost.

4

Old Trinity Church (1770)
Malbone Church

Brooklyn, Windham County, Connecticut

Two men in Brooklyn represented the conflicting forces in the late colonial period that were leading inevitably to the War of Independence and the founding of the United States — Godfrey Malbone, Anglican and Tory, and Israel Putnam, Nonconformist and officer in the French and Indian War and in the Revolution. They clashed over the issue of building a new Congregational meeting house in Brooklyn, as we have seen in the preceding account (No. 3), but in his scorn for Nonconformists, Godfrey Malbone made an exception of Israel Putnam. The Godfrey Malbone who moved to Brooklyn in 1766, with his Southern wife and twenty-one Negroes, was born in Newport, Rhode Island. He and his father, bearing the same name, were brought up in the faith of the Established National Church, the Church of England, and they had no patience for Nonconformists. The father was born in Virginia, where the Church of England was the established church; in Newport he was a warden of Trinity Church

(No. 267) and a merchant of great wealth made in international trade and privateering. In 1740 the father bought from Governor Belcher of Connecticut 1,200 acres in Pomfret (now Brooklyn) for £10,500; the tract included part of Wiltshire Manor, the rest of which became the farm of Israel Putnam, and all of Kingswood Manor. The two had formed the manor of Mortlake, originally granted to an officer of Cromwell's army as a refuge for Irish Dissenters, but not used for that purpose, probably because of the Restoration. Increasing antagonism to England and the hazards of his bold operations caused severe financial losses in the Malbone fortune. Both he and his son were educated at Oxford. Because of the financial reverses, when the son returned from Oxford the father sent him to Brooklyn to manage the estate.

In 1766, the year of Godfrey Malbone's arrival in Brooklyn, the Congregationalists proposed to build a new meeting house, but they compromised by making repairs. In 1768 another meeting considered the move to build, and then Malbone strongly opposed the move, as he would be taxed about £200 — more than one-eighth the cost. He said that the move was a vain effort of the Non-Cons (Nonconformists) to build "a newer, a larger, and a yellower meeting house" than the one

for their meeting house under construction; but Malbone's church was completed and dedicated at the opening service April 12, 1771, and the Congregational meeting house was not completed until that summer. Malbone's petition to the General Assembly for relief from paying tax for the Congregational meeting house was granted by an exception to him, who bore a substantial part of the cost of his church, but not to all his parishioners. He named the new church Trinity after the one in Newport.

This interesting building in a beautiful setting is practically unchanged. The narrow white pine clapboards are original, as are the window frames and most of the glass, but the blinds are an inappropriate addition. This is the only colonial church in Connecticut with a hip roof. The old pulpit was rebuilt as the two desks in their present location; the sounding board was removed and the present altar is not original, but the old box pews are unchanged.

The first rector, the Reverend Richard Mosley, L.L.B., came from England as chaplain in H.M.S. *Salisbury*, and served as curate *pro tempore* until a permanent rector could be found. In May, 1772, a year after the church was opened, the Reverend Daniel Fogg, a graduate of Harvard College, who was rector of St. Thomas' Church at Bath, North Carolina (No. 198), became the first permanent rector. He lived with the Malbones many years, then at age fifty married Deborah, a niece of Colonel Malbone, and they built a house of their own. Even though a Loyalist he continued to serve as rector in Brooklyn for forty-three years, until his death in 1815. He is well known as one of the ten clergymen who met at St. Paul's Church in Woodbury (No. 11) in 1783, and sent Samuel Seabury to England and Scotland to be consecrated as the first American bishop and the first Bishop of Connecticut. Fogg's letters to Samuel Parker of Boston, who was unable to attend, give us our only account of that historic meeting. Colonel Daniel Putnam, son of General Israel Putnam, married the daughter of Colonel Godfrey Malbone; thus the two estates again were joined, and in the Trinity burying ground are found the graves of many Malbones and Putnams. One service is now held in Old Trinity Church each year on All Saints' Day, and it is attended by members of both families from near and far. As the parish had outgrown the church, in 1865 New Trinity Church was built in Brooklyn, in order to save the interesting and historic Malbone Church.

recently erected by the old Society in Pomfret. He was conveyed to the meeting on a sledge drawn by twelve oxen, whose horns were decorated with brilliant streamers, and he and his chair were carried into the meeting house by his "blacks," for he did not care to enter there by his own power. When he saw that the move to build would be approved, he started immediately to organize an Episcopal parish in Brooklyn; and in November, 1769, with the heads of nineteen families, Trinity Parish was founded. As a lay reader Malbone conducted services in his house, or in that of another member of the parish, until a church could be built. He contributed most of the funds raised in Brooklyn, and other members subscribed small amounts of money or their labor. He appealed to the Society for the Propagation of the Gospel, but it had ceased to contribute to building in the colonies where the opposition to England was growing, although it did contribute toward the support of a minister for a while before the Revolution. By letters to friends in Boston, Newport, and New York, he raised additional funds, and soon after the church was finished it was paid for — a remarkable accomplishment. He drew the design for the church and had the timbers cut and hauled. In June, 1770, the frame was raised, on land given by Azariah Adams. In March of that year the First Society voted the tax to be paid by December 1

5

Hampton Congregational Church (1754)

Hampton, Windham County, Connecticut

Settlement of the present Hampton began in 1708. The Society had seventeen members when it was organized in 1723 and on the same day, June 5, the first minister, William Billings, was ordained. It is not known just when the first meeting house was built. In 1717 there was a petition to the General Assembly concerning taxes for a meeting house and support of the minister, and it may have been begun then, but we know that it was ready for the ordination in 1723. It was still unfinished in 1726, at which time crops and funds were short.

The second and present meeting house was built in 1754, replacing the first structure. The available records start with 1793. In 1794 the bell was installed, and the next year it was turned to swing north-south, in order to be heard by the majority of the parish. The job of turning the frame was ordered to be let at vendue, meaning to the lowest bidder. In 1805 the exterior was repainted, and it is interesting that at this late date a variety of colors was used. In the colonial period it was common practice to use colors other than white, and then in the nineteenth century the use of all-white became fashionable. On this occasion, red was used on the roof and the rear wall, stone-yellow on the front and ends, white on the window frames, and chocolate on the doors and baseboards. In 1840 the building was moved to its present position, turned with the gable end, instead of a long side, facing the road. In this building, as with many other colonial churches during the spiritual revival that swept through New England at the time, many alterations were made, and the Greek Revival style was introduced. The portico, the three entrance doors, and the interior doors are all of that style. The windows were changed, and none of the original structure is seen inside the building.

6

First Church of Christ (1761)
Wethersfield, Hartford County, Connecticut

The settlement of Wethersfield, begun in 1634, was one of the earliest in Connecticut. The location was chosen on the fertile plain of the west bank of the Connecticut River, and during the colonial life of the town, cargoes of local commodities, including onions, were loaded for foreign markets at wharves not far from the present church. The Congregationalists built a meeting house immediately, and in 1647 (the earliest reference to the building now available), a vote was recorded for "underdaubing and clapboarding"

the structure. In his *History of Ancient Wethersfield*, Vol. I, p. 221, Henry R. Stiles assumes that the daub inferred a log building; but there is no record of log structures in Connecticut in the seventeenth century, and the building probably was of wattle and daub, a construction used by the earliest settlers following the practice in England. We refer to this building as the first meeting house, as it is not known whether it was preceded by another as is assumed by some historians. In 1686 the cornerstone of the second building was laid; and the block of red sandstone bearing the date and the initials "I. G.," probably those of Isaac Griswold, a Wethersfield mason of that time, is in the present building. All affairs of the meeting house prior to 1722 were voted upon in town meeting. After that year all such acts were those of the First Society, until 1816, when the First Ecclesiastical Society was formed.

In 1760 a building committee was chosen to erect the third and present meting house. The cornerstone was laid in 1761. The meeting house was completed and occupied in 1764, and it was considered the finest in New England outside of Boston. The new bell, ordered in 1784, was cast with the building date and the name of the man who superintended the construction without pay: "John Chester 1761." The taxes voted in 1760 to pay for the building became burdensome, and payment was accepted in onions at three pence per rope. So many parishioners paid in kind that the meeting house was said to have been built of onions. The brick was made by Colonel Elizur Goodrich, a veteran of the French wars and a member of the building committee. The brickwork is laid with a diaper pattern.

Extensive alterations were made in 1838, when the original pews, seats in the gallery, and the pulpit were replaced. The front gallery was moved back eight feet, the floor was raised two-and-one-half feet, and the front door was raised fifteen inches. The alterations of 1882, however, destroyed even more of the colonial design. The entire interior finish was removed and remodeled, and the small-paned windows of clear glass were replaced with the present tall windows and stained glass. After conveying its property to the church, in 1923 the Society was dissolved, and in 1929 the church was incorporated.

George Washington attended services here May 20, 1781, on the occasion of a conference with Rochambeau at the Webb house across the street.

7

First Church of Christ (1771)

Farmington, Hartford County, Connecticut

The third and present building of the Congregational Church in Farmington is one of the
loveliest of the eighteenth-century meeting houses
in New England, and it is the masterpiece of its
designer and builder, Judah Woodruff, who built
ten of the finest houses in Farmington. In 1640,
only twenty years after settlement of the Plymouth
Colony, some families from Hartford made the
first settlement here on the rich land of the Tunxis

River valley, and five years later they gave it the
name Farmington. The earliest meetings were held
in homes, until a meeting house could be built.
A record of 1650 states that the first meeting
house stood on "Meeting House Green," near the
site of the second and the present buildings. In
1707 a town meeting voted to build a new meeting house; in 1708 the First Ecclesiastical Society
was formed, and it took over all church affairs;
and in 1709 it voted to build, levied a tax, and
elected a building committee of three. In 1714
the second building was finally completed. It had
a pyramid roof, from the peak of which a drummer on a platform summoned the parish to wor-

ship, until a bell was installed in 1731.

Work on the third and present meeting house began in 1771, after it had been proposed in 1766, agreed that it was necessary in 1767, reported favorably by the committee in 1768, and voted upon by the Society in 1769 when the gathering of materials began. The oak timbers undoubtedly were cut near by, but the other lumber was brought from Maine. The old structure was demolished after completion of the new. The hazards experienced in raising such a building at the time were recorded in awards made to one man who was injured and to the widow of another who was killed. The designer and builder, Captain Judah Woodruff, who was an officer in the French and Indian War and in the Revolution, was born in Farmington in 1720, a descendant of Matthew Woodruff, one of the eighty-four proprietors of the town. The building is similar in design to the Wethersfield Meeting House (No. 6), and it resembles the one built at the same time in Brooklyn (No. 3). The spire resembles that of Old South Meeting House in Boston (No. 94), but it is more

airy and graceful, as it rises 150 feet above the ground. The perspective of height is accentuated by the use of graduated widths in the clapboards, narrowing toward the top of the walls. The original clapboards remain on the tower, the ends, and the rear wall of the building. The window frames are original, but the sash in those in the body of the building was installed in 1836. The porch and main entrance, in the middle of the west side, are later installations of the Greek Revival style, but the two doorways in the tower are original, as is the floor of the building. In 1836 the interior was altered; the seats were built from the old box pews, and the pulpit and sounding board were replaced by a new pulpit. In 1901 the back, or east, side was extended to house the organ. A new reading desk was built then in memory of Dr. Noah Porter, who was pastor from 1806 until his death in 1866. He was the father of the Reverend Noah Porter, eleventh president of Yale, and Miss Sarah Porter, who in 1844 founded a finishing school for girls, Miss Porter's School, now known nationally as Farmington.

8

Kensington Congregational Church (1774)

Kensington, Hartford County, Connecticut

Originally the settlement here was known as Great Swamp in Farmington. In 1705 it was set off by Farmington as a separate Society; in 1707 the new Society was organized, and in 1710 the name Kensington was chosen for the town. The first meeting house probably was begun in 1711, in the section now called Christian Lane. On December 10, 1712, the Second Church of Farmington was organized with ten members, and William Burnham was ordained as the first minister. The installation of pulpit, pews, and seats was completed in 1716. Galleries were added in 1720, but there was no steeple or bell, and parishioners were summoned by drum.

In 1733, after four years of controversy over the site, it was reported that the second meeting house was built. In 1754, fifty people left to form a new parish in New Britain, leaving 174 in Ken-sington Parish. In 1772 Kensington was divided into two societies, the east society becoming Worthington, and the west society retaining the name Kensington. Both societies built new meeting houses, sharing materials from the second building.

The third and present meeting house of Kensington was dedicated December 1, 1774, but as it was not completed it is assumed that it was begun that year. The structure was plain, with no porch or steeple. There were entrances on three sides and galleries on two. The exterior was painted a dull yellow, but eighteen years went by before the interior was painted and the building was completely finished. In 1837 repairs were made; the pulpit was moved from the north wall to the end, slips replaced the box pews, and a belfry was built. In 1868 the door in the middle of the east side, originally the main entrance, was closed up. By 1884 so little of the original structure was visible that the meeting house was rededicated, on February 28, by the Reverend Noah Porter, president of Yale College (see Farmington, No. 7). The addition at the north end was built in 1902 for social activities.

9

Old Congregational Church (1774)
Town Hall

Enfield, Hartford County, Connecticut

The Enfield area was known in early colonial times as Fresh Water Plantation. In 1681 the area was incorporated as the town of Enfield, then in Massachusetts. The town grant instructed the inhabitants to adopt measures as soon as possible "for the maintenance of Christian ordinance and for the support of an able, orthodox ministry." Orthodox meant Congregational, not Church of England. Two years later, in 1683, the first Ecclesiastical Society of Enfield was organized, and between sixty and seventy acres were provided for a place of worship and to support the ministry. Three parcels were leased for church income, and, in 1699, farm land was given to the first settled minister, Nathaniel Collins, and his heirs, as a payment for his services. The first small wooden meeting house stood by the Enfield Street Cemetery. The second was built in 1706 on the west side of Enfield Street, where a stone marks the location (and gives the building date as 1704 in error). An inscription on the stone informs us that "In this Meeting House on July 8, 1741, during the revival known as 'The Great Awakening,' Jonathan Edwards preached his celebrated sermon 'Sinners in the Hands of an Angry God.' " The second building was in use when, in 1750, under petition, the town of Enfield became part of Connecticut. The second meeting house was used until the third was completed.

The third meeting house was begun in 1774. It was completed and opened for use on the first day of 1775, when the Revolution was fomenting. In April the news of the battle at Lexington reached the tavern in Enfield while a prayer meeting was in progress in the church. Thomas Abbey left the tavern and marched around the meeting house beating a drum until the meeting broke up; he gathered seventy-five volunteers and left the next morning to join the Revolution, returning to Enfield after his service with a commission of captain. In 1848 this third meeting house was sold to the town for use as the Town Hall. It was moved to the west side of Enfield Street, where it still serves in that capacity. At the time of the move the portico in Greek Revival style was added. The Society dedicated their new and present meeting house February 14, 1849.

First Congregational Church (1772)
Old Stone Church

High and Main Streets, East Haven,
New Haven County, Connecticut

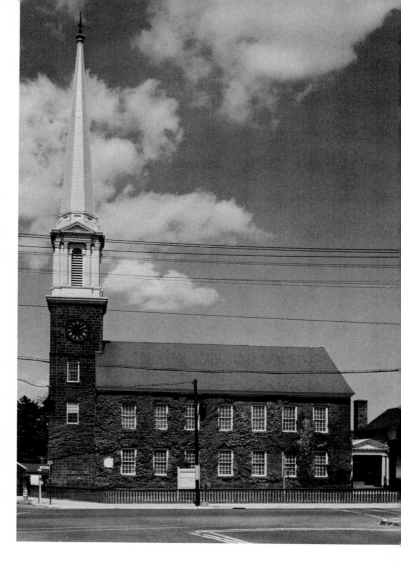

This third building of the First Congregational Church in East Haven, built in 1772, was the first stone house of worship in Connecticut, and it is the only stone colonial church-building in the state. It was an ambitious and expensive undertaking. The red sandstone was plentiful in local quarries, and shell-lime mortar was used, but workmen skilled in stonework were scarce. It took two years to complete the masonry, and the whole building was not completed until 1796, a generation after it was begun. The long period of building was added to another generation of controversy over the site.

The first settlement was made here in 1644. For many years the community worshipped in New Haven, but the trip across the Quinnipiac River was arduous and often dangerous, and in 1679 New Haven agreed that East Haven might worship separately. In 1706 the town voted to build a meeting house that was sixteen by twenty feet. This small building housed services in 1709 for the organization of the church Society, and in 1711 for the ordination of the first minister, Samuel Hemingway. In 1714 the Society voted to build a meeting house of adequate size; it was begun in 1718 and occupied the following year. It was a plain-gable, rude building with no tower or steeple; it was used for fifty-three years. In several meetings from 1746 to 1772 it was agreed to build a new meeting house, but the north and south factions of the parish could not agree on a site, until they finally achieved a judicial selection, in 1772, through the judges of the County Court. The site at Thompson's Corner was a compromise location convenient to both factions. In that year it was voted to build a stone meeting house sixty feet long, and work began in the summer on this third and present building. The length was then increased to seventy feet. When the masonry was completed in 1774, there was a tower but no spire. Although the structure was not finished, it was decided to occupy it, and the old meeting house was pulled down. There were galleries but no seats, and the Society undertook to build two seats around the galleries for the singers and others. " . . . the Singers that Carries the tenor should Set att the east end of the front gallery

the treble the north end of the east gallery the bass the South end of the west gallery." During the period of the Revolution the funds were depleted, and progress was slow. By 1780 the steeple was built, for then it was voted to shingle it. Finally, in 1796, the meeting house was finished. In the following year a hurricane partly deroofed the building, and in repairing the steeple a bell was installed to replace the function of the drummer. In 1850 the remodeling was so thorough that there remains to view, of the original structure, only the stone walls. The doors on the south side and in the tower were filled up, as were the windows on the east end and behind the pulpit on the north side. The upper tier of windows was lowered, two doors were placed in the sides of the tower, the pulpit was installed at the east end; and the walls, which originally carried plaster on the stone, were furred out, lathed, and plastered. So extensive was all this work that the church was rededicated on October 16, 1850.

11

St. Paul's Church (1785)

Woodbury, Litchfield County, Connecticut

St. Paul's Parish, Woodbury, is called the birthplace of American Episcopacy. It was in the Glebe House of the parish that, on March 25, 1783, ten clergymen of the fourteen in Connecticut met and elected Samuel Seabury to go to Great Britain for consecration as the first American Episcopal bishop. English law required an oath of loyalty to the king and to Parliament, which could not be taken by a bishop of the independent colonies. The meeting at Woodbury instructed Seabury, if he failed in England, to seek consecration in Scotland. There the Episcopal bishops had maintained apostolic succession, but they were "Non-Jurors" since the deposition of James II, when they had remained loyal to the Stuart line. While they continued as devout members of the Anglican Communion, they were independent of loyalty to the king and Parliament in mattters of the Church. After a frustrating year in England,

during which the Bishop of London and the Archbishop of Canterbury tried to find a legal basis for his consecration in England, Seabury proceeded to Scotland. At Aberdeen, on Sunday, November 14, 1784, Samuel Seabury was consecrated Bishop of Connecticut by the Primus, who was Bishop of Aberdeen, by the Bishop of Ross and Moray, and by the Bishop Coadjutor of Aberdeen. On the next day, November 15, a Concordat was signed by Seabury at Aberdeen, which eventually led to the Communion Office, in the Book of Common Prayer of the Protestant Episcopal Church of America, being based on the Scottish Book of Common Prayer, while the rest was based on the English Book of Common Prayer. A copy of this historical document may be seen in the Glebe House at Woodbury, which is open to visitors.

From 1740, when the first Anglican church was built in this region of a Congregationalist colony, until 1771, the Anglican communicants were ministered to by visiting missionaries sent from London by the Society for the Propagation of the Gospel in Foreign Parts. In 1771 the S.P.G. sent to this parish the first resident minister, the Reverend John Rutgers Marshall. For eighteen years he served as rector of St. Paul's Parish, until 1789, the year in which the United States began to function under its first President; the jurisdiction in America of the S.P.G., the Bishop of London, and the Church of England came to a close; and the Protestant Episcopal Church of America was organized. Upon the arrival of the Reverend Mr. Marshall in 1771, the Glebe House was provided as his rectory, and he was one of those who met there in the conclave mentioned above. During the final years of the Revolutionary period, he suffered abuse by the Congregationalists for his loyalty to the king, but he never ceased to be loyal to his sovereign, his parish, and the Christian work. He was the moving spirit in the building of St. Paul's Church, begun in 1785. He succeeded in obtaining consent from the First Congregational Society for the erection of an Episcopal church, and in raising the necessary funds for the building.

Before the building of the present church, St. Paul's Parish was permitted to worship in the old meeting house of the First Congregational Society, which had been replaced by a new meeting house, and which was used as a town hall, known as the "Old Town House," a building which is no longer standing. When the last frame of St. Paul's Church was raised on August 5, 1785, the comment was recorded: "Nobody much hurt." The plain rectangular structure had a tower built out at the front end, surmounted by a belfry, lantern, and spire, and having doors in the end and south side, as well as a window at the upper level and two circular windows at the ridge level. Mr. Marshall donated the window glass, which was brought over from England, and the members of the committee which held the title of the Glebe House sold that property and applied the funds to the cost of the building. The first meeting in the new church was held November 28, 1787. During the nineteenth century many alterations were made. The body of the building was brought out almost to the face of the tower to make vestibules, thereby adding one set of windows on the sides. The design of the steeple was altered in 1814, and the present building does not have the original tall spire. The original pulpit and the box pews have been replaced. In 1822 the church was dedicated by the Bishop of Connecticut, the Right Reverend Thomas C. Brownell, and on that occasion it was named St. Paul's Church, Woodbury.

12

Christ Church (c. 1786)

Middle Haddam, Middlesex County, Connecticut

The first settlement of Middle Haddam Landing, on the Connecticut River, was made in 1710. Sixty years later a beginning was made for an Episcopal parish by the Reverend Matthew Graves. He traveled out of New London as a missionary of the Society for the Propagation of the Gospel in Foreign Parts. In 1771 an Episcopal church was formed, but, after meetings were held for a few years, it was dissolved. The building erected in 1772, which stood about three miles from the village, in Young Street, was pulled down. The incident that closed this church was typical of the situation faced by the Church of England during the period of the Revolution. The Reverend Matthew Graves was warned not to read "offensive" parts of the Liturgy, but he could not be loyal to the Crown and the Church and change the service. Consequently, on the following Sunday, when he started the prayer for the king, the bell was rung as a signal, and he was seized by men in the congregation and thrown to the floor. Women rushed to his defense, and he was permitted to escape. The door was locked, and the church was not used for services until independence had been won and peace with England had been restored. On April 25, 1785, the

Parish of Christ Church in Middle Haddam was reorganized.

"The present building was erected in 1786 or '87, was thirty-six by forty-seven feet, and it belonged to the cure of Dr. Abraham Jarvis, of Middletown, until 1791." The early records are lost, and this statement of Dr. David D. Field, in "A Centennial Address" containing historical sketches of Chatham and surrounding parishes, is our authority for the beginning of the present building. The Dr. Jarvis referred to, afterwards became Bishop of the Diocese of Connecticut. The land was bought from Samuel Taylor, of Chatham, on September 19, 1786. Building started at once, but it was not completed until the time of the dedication on September 11, 1828. Reflecting the pattern of life in that homespun era, a member of the parish on the distaff side made enough cloth to pay for the lumber to build her pew. In 1840 the present tower and belfry were added, and the bell was installed. It was inevitable that the design of the additions of that year were in the Greek Revival style. In 1856, and again in 1867, repairs involved many changes. The window sash was removed and single mullion was installed to hold the present stained glass. The only remaining original window, with semicircular head, is in the west side of the tower, where it was installed at the time that the tower was built. The old cornice can be seen inside the tower, but the exposed cornice is later and larger.

DELAWARE

		Denomination	Material
13	Old Swedes (1698) Wilmington, New Castle County	Swedish Lutheran	Stone
14	First Presbyterian Church (1740) Wilmington, New Castle County	Presbyterian	Brick
15	Asbury Methodist Church (1789) Wilmington, New Castle County	Methodist	Brick
16	Immanuel Church (1703) New Castle, New Castle County	Anglican	Brick
17	Old Presbyterian Church (1707) New Castle, New Castle County	Presbyterian	Brick
18	Old Drawyers (1773) Odessa, New Castle County	Presbyterian	Brick
19	Appoquinimink Friends Meeting House (1785) Odessa, New Castle County	Friends	Brick
20	Hockessin Friends Meeting House (1738) Hockessin, New Castle County	Friends	Stone
21	Welsh Tract Baptist Church (1746) Cooch's Bridge, New Castle County	Baptist	Brick
22	Old St. Anne's Church (1768) Middletown, New Castle County	Anglican	Brick
23	Christ Church (1734) Dover, Kent County	Anglican	Brick
24	Barratt's Chapel (1780) Frederica, Kent County	Methodist	Brick
25	Prince George's Chapel (1757) Dagsboro, Sussex County	Anglican	Wood
26	Blackwater Presbyterian Church (1767) Sussex County	Presbyterian	Wood
27	Christ Church, Broad Creek (1771) Sussex County	Anglican	Wood

SUMMARY

Swedish Lutheran	1	Brick	10
Presbyterian	4	Wood	3
Methodist	2	Stone	2
Anglican	5		
Friends	2		
Baptist	1		
Buildings	15		15

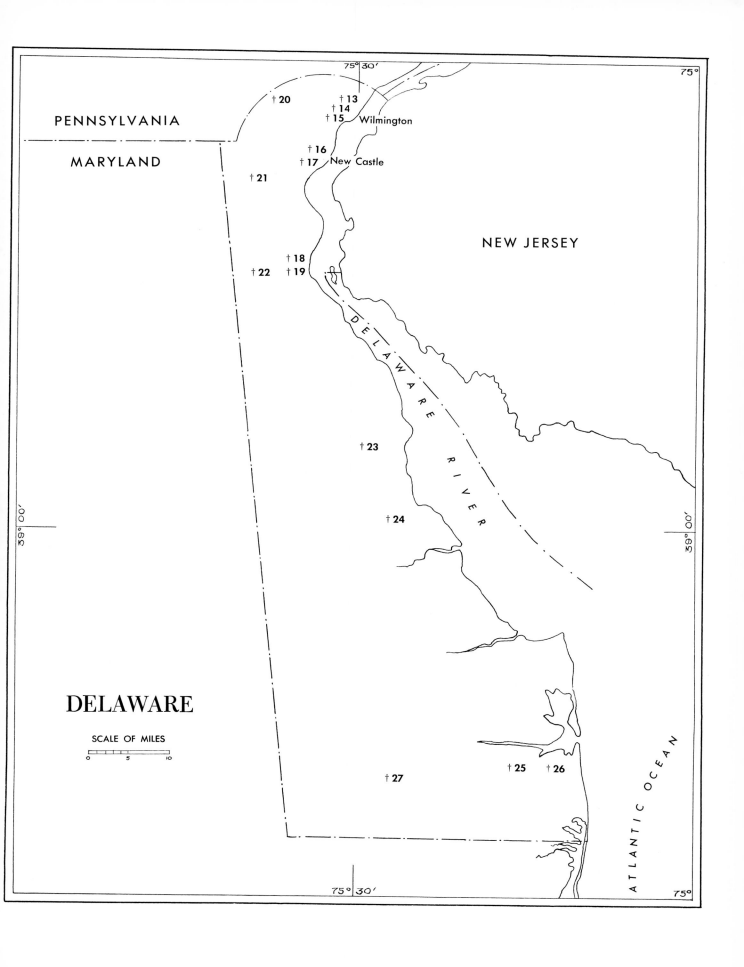

PENNSYLVANIA

MARYLAND

† 20

† 13
† 14
† 15 Wilmington

† 16
† 17 New Castle

† 21

† 18
† 22 † 19

NEW JERSEY

DELAWARE RIVER

† 23

† 24

DELAWARE

SCALE OF MILES

0   5   10

† 25   † 26

† 27

ATLANTIC OCEAN

75° 30'

75°

39° 00'

39° 00'

75° 30'

75°

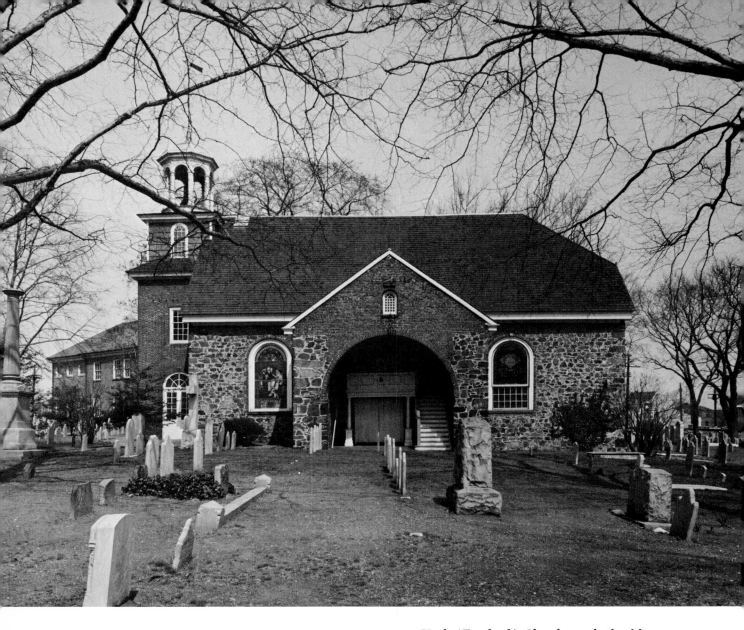

13

Old Swedes (1698)
Heliga Trefaldighets Kyrka,
or Holy Trinity Church

Wilmington, New Castle County, Delaware

In 1638 the Swedes made the first settlement in their New Sweden, at the site of the present Wilmington. The first Swedish Lutheran services were held in Fort Christina, named for the young Queen of Sweden. The first Swedish Lutheran priest in America, Reorus Torkillus, came from Sweden in the second expedition, 1639-40. The first church of this congregation was built at Christina in 1641-42. In 1666-67 the first Crane Hook (*Tranhook*) Church was built of logs, on a site that is marked by a monument near the Marine Terminal. Two parishes were organized in 1672, with Crane Hook as the lower parish and the upper parish at Wicaco (see Gloria Dei Church, Philadelphia, No. 202).

Eric Björck (1668-1740) came from Sweden in 1697 and took charge of the Crane Hook Church as pastor. Immediately he began preparing for building the present stone church, on a site nearer the center of Christina. The foundation stones were laid in May of 1698. The mason, Joseph Richardson, failed to complete his contract, and the work was finished by Joseph Yard and his three sons, of Philadelphia. The carpentry was undertaken by John Smart and John Britt, of Philadelphia. The glazier came from Holland to do his part

of the work; the glass generally was imported in the early colonial times. The building was consecrated on Trinity Sunday, June 4, 1699. It was a plain rectangular structure, with hooded gable ends, a shingle roof, and a floor of square brick tiles. The arched south porch was added in 1750, and in 1774 the gallery was built, with chairs outside on the south porch. The tower and belfry were built of brick in 1802. The building was allowed to fall into disrepair, and in 1830 it was abandoned for a new building at Fifth and King Streets. In 1842, however, Old Swedes was reopened after some repairs and alterations. In 1899 the church was fully restored for the Bicentennial celebration, and it has continued to be used in its original design. It has the box pews, the brick tile flooring in the aisle, the black walnut, high pulpit of 1698, and an octagonal sounding board, as well as the outside stairway, which is a distinctive feature of the building.

Ten Swedish pastors served here, and oil portraits of many of them hang in the vestry. One of the pastors, Israel Acrelius, wrote a history of New Sweden. The Swedish mission in America ended in 1789, when the Republic began and the Church of England was organized. The last pastor was Lawrence Girelius, who served until 1791, and the church became Episcopalian. In the church and around it were buried a number of the pastors and many parishioners who were prominent in the affairs of the colony. It is estimated that 15,000 burials were made in Old Swedes Cemetery, which originally extended beneath the present embankment of the Pennsylvania Railroad.

14

First Presbyterian Church (1740)
The Colonial Dames House

Park Drive and West Street,
Wilmington, New Castle County, Delaware

In a grove of trees overlooking the Brandy-wine River, stands the original Presbyterian Meeting House of Wilmington. It is of brick laid in Flemish bond. Its gambrel roof shows the Dutch Colonial influence. In the pattern of the wall facing the river appears the date 1740, the year in which it was built at its former site on Market Street near Tenth. When the congregation built a new church, and the last service was held in this building in 1878, the old meeting house was rented to the Historical Society of Delaware. In 1917 the building was moved to its present site, and it became the headquarters of the Colonial Dames of Delaware.

15

Asbury Methodist Church (1789)

Walnut and Third Streets,
Wilmington, New Castle County, Delaware

This church was organized in 1769, after Captain Thomas Webb had preached the first Methodist sermon under trees growing where King and Eighth Streets now cross. The cornerstone was laid in the summer of 1789, and in October the brick building was dedicated by Bishop Francis Asbury, first American bishop of the Methodist Church. He recorded in his journal: " . . . thus far we come after twenty years' labor in this place." The structure has been altered considerably, and little remains of the original features of this first Methodist church in Wilmington. The original interior was divided by a four-foot partition to separate the sexes, and the men and women entered by separate gates and doors. To the right and left of the pulpit were the "Amen corners" for the elders of the congregation. At the turn of the twentieth century the exterior brick walls were stuccoed.

16

Immanuel Church (1703)

New Castle, New Castle County, Delaware

Organized in 1689 as the Emanuel Church (now Immanuel), this congregation became the first Anglican parish in Delaware. Begun in 1703 and completed in 1706, the church stands on the Green near the site of the old log fort of 1672. It is built of brick in Anglican style, cruciform and oriented with chancel to the east. The stucco that covers the brickwork of the building and the wall surrounding the churchyard was applied some years later. In 1820-22 the tower and spire were added, and the altar and chancel were moved to the west end. Gifts from Queen Anne, which no longer exist, included a pulpit, altar cloths, and a box of glass. In 1710 the Governor of Pennsylvania, Colonel Charles Gookin, presented a silver flagon made in New York by Simeon Saumaine; it is shown with the church silver annually on the "Day in Old New Castle." Many men prominent in the founding of the country were buried here, including George Read, a signer of the Declaration of Independence and the Constitution.

17

Old Presbyterian Church (1707)

**Second Street, New Castle,
New Castle County, Delaware**

The Presbyterian congregation in New Castle probably grew from the early Calvinistic group that held services from 1651 when Fort Casimir was erected. The first church was a wooden building which the Dutch erected in 1657. The present church replaced it in 1707. Francis Makemie, a founder of the first American presbytery at Philadelphia the previous year, assisted the congregation in getting this church built. In 1854 a brownstone church was built next door, and the old building was used as a Sunday school. In 1950 the old building was restored to its colonial style, and the large brownstone building was removed. The restoration was part of the larger plan for restoring and maintaining the many beautiful colonial buildings in New Castle. The restoration of the old church is in keeping with the architectural style in this region at the end of the seventeenth century, and it has recaptured the charm and essential simplicity of the original design. It was a commendable project in the trend to preserve these landmarks in the colonial history of the country.

Gilbert Tennent, the eldest son of William Tennent (see Neshaminy Presbyterian Church, No. 238), preached here after being licensed in 1725. He was called to settle as pastor, but he left to become ordained at New Brunswick, New Jersey in 1726. With George Whitefield he took part later in the Great Awakening. New Castle was the port of immigration for many Scotch-Irish Presbyterians from Northern Ireland, and this church became the mother church for many others in the colonies. From here pioneers explored up the Susquehanna River and settled Donegal Church in Pennsylvania (No. 251). From there they pushed into the Cumberland Valley, where they settled several churches, and thence south into the Shenandoah Valley of Virginia, where we find more of their churches.

18

Old Drawyers Presbyterian Church (1773)
First Presbyterian Church in St. George's Hundred

Odessa, New Castle County, Delaware

This congregation was organized in 1708 as the Church of Appoquinimy, after services had been started in 1700 by the Reverend John Wilson, pastor of the Presbyterian Church in New Castle. The present building was erected in 1773 on Drawyers Creek, which flows into Delaware Bay. The plans were drawn by Robert May and Company of London, designers of a number of notable houses in and around Odessa and Philadelphia. The original wooden building of 1711, on the same site, was replaced by the present church. The brick was burned locally by a parishioner and laid in Flemish bond. The building is unaltered, but the box pews and pulpit were remodeled in 1833. Friends of Old Drawyers, mostly descendants of the early founders, maintain the church. They celebrate all-day services on Old Drawyers Sunday, the first Sunday in June, known also as Clover Sunday.

19

Appoquinimink Friends Meeting House (1785)

Odessa, New Castle County, Delaware

About five miles out of Odessa, Friends built George's Creek Meeting House in 1703. The name was changed later to Hickory Grove Friends Meeting. Still later, the meeting was moved to Cantwell's Bridge, now Odessa. Here, in 1785, the present small brick meeting house was built and presented by David Wilson. This house was not used for services between 1875 and 1939, when meeting for worship was resumed. The present Appoquinimink Preparative Meeting, named for the creek that flows near by, is of the Wilmington Monthly Meeting, Concord Quarterly Meeting, Philadelphia Yearly Meeting. This is the smallest brick house of worship in the collection.

20

Hockessin Friends Meeting House (1738)

Hockessin, New Castle County, Delaware

The year after the privilege of holding meetings for worship was granted by the Newark Preparative Meeting, this meeting house was built in 1738. Meetings had been held in a private home since 1730. The building is of brown fieldstone, now covered with stucco. In 1745 the house was enlarged. It rests on the knoll of a high hill near the Pennsylvania line and commands a superb view of the beautiful Hockessin Valley. The carriage block and the sheds remain. Hockessin is now a Monthly Meeting in Western Quarterly Meeting of Philadelphia Yearly Meeting.

21

Welsh Tract Baptist Church (1746)

Cooch's Bridge, New Castle County, Delaware

In 1701 sixteen people formed the original congregation in Wales and emigrated to America. They spent two years in Pennsylvania and then, in 1703, settled on land granted by William Penn. In that year they organized the Welsh Tract Baptist Meeting. The forty thousand acres have been known since as the Welsh Tract. The church was built at the foot of Iron Hill, which height gave the Welsh name of Pencader (Head Seat) Hundred to this section. The original church, built of logs in 1706, three years after they had acquired the tract, was the first Baptist church in Delaware.

The present quaint brick structure was built on the same site in 1746. It is situated two and a quarter miles south of Newark. The brick is laid in Flemish bond. The date appears in the tablet above the two doors. In the skirmish of Cooch's Bridge on September 3, 1777, when Cornwallis met Washington's troops on his advance to Philadelphia, a cannon ball passed through the building; the patches in the brickwork can still be seen. From this mother church of Primative Baptists sprang churches at Wilmington, Kenton, Cow March, and Mispillion (no colonial buildings surviving).

22

Old St. Anne's Church (1768)

**One mile south of Middletown,
New Castle County, Delaware**

The church was organized by 1704, under the name of Appoquinimy, a mission to which Queen Anne gave an embroidered cover which is still treasured. In 1705 the original log chapel was built on the Queen's Road, below Appoquinimink Creek. The present church succeeded it in 1768. The simple lines of the building are ornamented only with a cove cornice carried across the gable end below the shingle line. There are the original box pews and, behind the altar, a large Palladian window. The entrance porch was a later addition. There is a unique silver breaker made by Joannes Nys of Philadelphia, between 1700 and 1723. Annual services are held the third Sunday in June; regular services are held in St. Anne's in Middletown, built in 1872. St. Anne's oak, which stands in the churchyard, is more than three centuries old. The ivy was brought from England.

23

Christ Church (1734)
St. Jones' Church

Dover, Kent County, Delaware

The original congregation was organized as an Anglican mission in 1703, by the Society for the Propagation of the Gospel in Foreign Parts. Built in 1734, the present church replaced the log structure of 1706. It is located two miles south of Dover, on the Bay Road and on the east side of St. Jones' Creek. The name St. Jones' seems to have originated in the patent of land granted to Robert Jones in 1671, in which the said Jones is recorded as "sd Jones his Creeke," and "sd Jones his Line of Marked Trees." The name Christ Church first appears on the records in 1767. The original entrance was in the south wall, which was customary in the colonial churches, and the floor was of brick laid on the ground. Abandoned during the Revolution, it was restored to use in 1785. In 1850 it was reconditioned, and the high box pews were removed. The tower, chancel, wooden flooring, and porch were added later.

24

Barratt's Chapel (1780)

Frederica, Kent County, Delaware

The chapel was built in 1780 by Philip Barratt, who gave the land, and Waitman Sipple, his father-in-law, both of whom were among the many members of the Church of England on the Peninsula who were converted to Methodism by Francis Asbury and other followers of John Wesley. For the first sixty-five years the ground was the only floor. The half-brick niches in the outside wall were for putlogs used in scaffolding. In 1784, at a meeting here between the Reverend Thomas Coke, who bore a message from John Wesley, and the Reverend Francis Asbury, the first General Conference of American Methodism was appointed, and plans were made which resulted in the "Christmas Conference" in Baltimore and the organization of the Methodist Episcopal Church in America. In the interior photograph the pulpit-bench used by Asbury and Coke is shown, but the rest of the interior is of a later date. At the General Conference in Baltimore on Christmas Eve of 1784, a month after the meeting at Barratt's Chapel, Asbury and Coke were elected the first superintendents of the Church in America, and, against the opposition of John Wesley, both assumed the title of bishop. The Christmas Conference was held in Lovely Lane Chapel, which had been completed in 1775. It stood at German Street near South Street, on a site now occupied by the Merchant's Club of Baltimore, where a bronze tablet tells of the historic event.

25

Prince George's Chapel (1757)

Dagsboro, Sussex County, Delaware

This Anglican chapel was organized, probably in 1706, under the Maryland Act of 1692 that made the Church of England in the province the Established Church. The first building was of logs. The second was built of frame in 1738, the year of the birth of the English prince who became King George III, and the chapel was named for him. This third chapel was built in 1757, under the Maryland Assembly's Act of 1755, on Pepper's Branch, at Blackfoot Town, now Dagsboro. Until the boundary dispute was settled in 1767, at which time this area became a part of Delaware, this building served as a chapel of ease in St. Martin's Parish, Worcester County, Maryland (No. 86). The original pine interior survives and has never been painted. The shingles were applied to the exterior walls during repairs in 1929. In 1780 a transept and sanctuary were added by General John Dagworthy, veteran of three wars, who is buried under the chancel. Every Decoration Day, a group of Negroes lay flowers on the graves of their slave ancestors, who attended services here with their masters.

26

Blackwater Presbyterian Church (1767)

One mile west of Clarksville, Sussex County, Delaware, near the head of Blackwater Creek

This church was organized in 1667 when William Tunnell resigned from Prince George's Chapel to join the first session. The Tunnell family is still associated with this church and holds an annual reunion here. The first pastor was Charles Tennent, one of the four sons of William Tennent, all of whom were Presbyterian preachers (see No. 238). The church was built in 1767. One of the outside walls still has the original matched boards. The others were covered with clapboard in the repairs of 1893. The original brick floor is covered with wooden flooring, and little remains of the original interior furnishings. This site was in Maryland until the settlement of the long boundary dispute awarded it to Delaware in 1767, and the church still is associated closely with Old Buckingham Church in Berlin, Maryland.

27

Christ Church, Broad Creek (1771)

Three miles east of Laurel on Chipman's Pond, Sussex County, Delaware

Christ Church, Broad Creek Hundred, was built in 1771 by Robert Houston, who was also a shipbuilder. It was an Episcopal chapel of ease in

Stepney Parish, Somerset County, Maryland, and it continued to serve in that capacity even for some years after settlement of the boundary dispute between Maryland and Pennsylvania had included this territory in Delaware (see No. 80). The heart-of-pine interior has not been painted and is in excellent condition. As the church is situated in a pine grove, from which it was built, and from which fat pine knots were used for lighting fires, it has been known as "Old Lightwood," "Light'ard," and "Lighterknot." The old high pulpit and box pews survive.

GEORGIA

		Denomination	Material
28	Jerusalem Church (1767) Ebenezer, Effingham County	German Lutheran	Brick
29	Kiokee Church (1772) Appling, Columbia County	Baptist	Brick
30	Midway Church (1792) Midway, Liberty County	Congregational	Wood

SUMMARY

German Lutheran	1	Brick	2
Baptist	1	Wood	1
Congregational	1		
Buildings	3		3

28

Jerusalem Church (1767)

Ebenezer, Effingham County, Georgia

The method of settling the Georgia colony is well illustrated in the Jerusalem Church. After inviting the debtors, the oppressed, and the persecuted of Europe to his newly chartered colony, James Oglethorpe crossed the Atlantic to the Savannah River in 1733, and began the settlement of Savannah. In the following year, 1734, a group of seventy-eight Salzburgers, Lutherans who had been persecuted as Protestants in the Austrian duchy of Salzburg, emigrated through Bavaria to Georgia. In the group were two pastors, John Martin Balzius and Israel Christian Gronau, who,

as it is inscribed on their tomb here, for their faith in the doctrines of God's word, as taught in the Augsburg Confession, were banished from their homes in Austria. A guarantee had been given to the group by trustees of the colony covering passage, fifty acres of land to each person, and supplies until they could raise a crop. They landed at Savannah, went up the river about twenty miles, and made a settlement which they called Ebenezer ("Stone of Help"). Two years later, because of malaria and the poor soil, they moved to a ridge near the river and established New Ebenezer, where the church now stands. It is indicative of the hardships suffered by these pioneers that the first house built in the new town was an orphanage, one of the first built for the purpose in America. The orphanage served also as a house of worship until a frame church was built in 1744.

That first building of Jerusalem Church was succeeded by the present brick structure of 1767. The brick was burned locally and laid in English bond, alternate courses of headers and stretchers. Funds for the building were provided by friends in Germany. On top of the cupola, which houses two bells brought over from Germany, the Lutherans placed a metal swan, an emblem in the coat-of-arms of Martin Luther found on the spires of many Lutheran churches in Germany. The parish sided with the Revolution, but Ebenezer was captured by the British in 1779 and used as a camp for American prisoners of war. Jerusalem Church was used first as a hospital and then as a stable. In 1783, General Anthony Wayne recaptured Ebenezer, and the Lutherans returned to restore their homes and church. It was just before the present church was built when John Bartram of Philadelphia and Botanist to the King, visited Ebenezer on September 21, 1765. He noted in his journal that white mulberry trees were growing, and that silk raised here and sold in Savannah was the principal cash crop; he also noted that much of the land about Ebenezer was poor, and this fact led to the eventual decline of the town. Today only the church remains of a once thriving community. The church is still active, and it has been in continuous use since it was built. The congregation is mostly from neighboring farms. The Georgia Salzburger Society, composed of descendants of the founders, meets here for services each March 12.

29

Kiokee Church (1772)

**Three miles from Appling,
Columbia County, Georgia**

Kiokee (pronounced locally Kī-ó-kee) was organized as an Anabaptist congregation in 1772 by Daniel Marshall, a "New Light" evangelist who became a Baptist missionary. He had established churches in North Carolina before he came here, and he was one of several preachers responsible for spreading "Separate" Baptist influence in the South. The church was built the same year, of brick laid in Flemish bond, with a very high water table. Large rough stones serve as steps to doors on the north side and the west end. The interior is severe, with hand-hewn pews and a slave gallery. Marshall was arrested in the church, while leading the congregation in prayer, for violating the Act of 1758, which made the Church of England the Established Church in Georgia. He won over the officers, however, and was allowed to continue as the pastor of Kiokee until his death in 1784. Appropriately, he is buried in front of the Courthouse in Appling, where he was tried. The spring and pool below the church are still used for baptising.

30

Midway Church (1792)

Midway, Liberty County, Georgia

It is not a coincidence that the frame building of Midway Church, standing alone in the country-side of Georgia, resembles many others of the colonial period in New England, nor that it stands near the town of Dorchester. A group of 140 Puritans from Dorchester, Dorsetshire, England, under the leadership of the Reverend John White, founded a church in Plymouth in March, 1630 and immediately sailed to Massachusetts, where they settled the town of Dorchester, overlooking the site of the city of Boston. These forthright Puritans expressed their intentions "to do some-

thing for their country, a little for the Indians, somewhat for the fishermen, and a good deal for themselves." This Dorchester Company of Adventurers was the parent of the Massachusetts Bay Company, the body that governed the colony. In 1695, under the leadership of Joseph Lord, a group from that congregation organized a church at Charlestown, Massachusetts, and moved to South Carolina, where they settled another Dorchester on the Ashley River above Charleston. As the climate on the river was unhealthy, the inhabitants moved out, and today there remains only the ruin of the Episcopal church (No. 274). On May 16, 1752, thirty-eight families moved to Georgia and settled St. John's Parish, one of the parishes into which Georgia originally was divided, now forming Liberty County. They were the sixth and last large group to settle in this last of the British Colonies. They brought with them the name Dorchester for their settlement of plantations, and after some time it was used, surviving today in the name of the post office and railway station, about a mile east of the church. They settled on land between the Medway and Newport rivers, at the headwaters some ten miles from the sea islands. In his *History of the Midway Congregational Church, Liberty County Georgia,* James Stacy says: "It seems that at first no name was given either to the church or community. They were known simply as 'settlers on Medway and Newport,' and their house of worship only known as the 'Meeting House.' As the river was named Medway, and the district soon became familiarly known as the 'Midway District,' the church and community were sometimes called by the one and sometimes by the other." The church was located on the highway built by James Oglethorp, the founder of Georgia, about midway between its two ends at Savannah and Darien, and that position has been thought by some to be the origin of the name. St. John's Parish included Sunbury, a seaport nine miles away that rivaled Savannah, and the Midway Church was attended by some residents of that town. By 1776 St. John's Parish contained about a third of the wealth of Georgia, and here also was concentrated the revolutionary spirit that prevailed in Boston, which in both areas prepared for the founding of the United States. With its inherited Puritanism, the church was Congregational with Presbyterian inclinations.

In 1754, two years after their arrival, the congregation built the first house of worship, a temporary structure to serve until a larger one could be built. The second building was burned in 1778 by the British, who had captured the port of Sunbury. In 1784 when Dr. Abiel Holmes, father of Oliver Wendell Holmes, was called as minister, a third, and again temporary, building was erected. In 1785 it was enlarged by twelve feet on the east side, and a shelter for Negroes was built on the south side. Six years later, in 1790, and after the parsonage had been built in 1789, it was decided to build the fourth and present house of worship, and it was erected and completed in 1792 (one of the two exceptions to our arbitrary limit of the year 1789). The design was based on that of the second building. Cypress was used, and it has withstood time and weather. Alterations in 1849 changed the interior arrangement and moved the pulpit, galleries, and some doors to their present positions. During the Civil War the town suffered, and most of the houses were burned, but the church was spared. The cavalry of General Hugh Judson Kilpatrick occupied the churchyard, and later Sherman's army used it as a corral for horses and cattle. In the parish were many people distinguished in the affairs of Georgia, the Revolution, and the United States. They included two signers of the Declaration of Independence, Dr. Lyman Hall and Button Gwinnett. General Daniel Stewart, a hero of the Indian wars, lies buried among other prominent people in the churchyard; President Theodore Roosevelt was his great-grandson. The last pastor of the church was Dr. I. S. K. Axson, a grandfather of the first Mrs. Woodrow Wilson. After the Civil War the town declined. From 1867 to 1887 the church was used by Negroes, but now the property is owned and maintained by a committee of descendants of the early parishioners. There are no regular services, but an annual reunion of descendants is gathered. Only the church and the stones in the graveyard stand as witness to the history of these people of Dorchester.

MAINE

		Denomination	*Material*
31	First Congregational Church (1730) Kittery Point, York County	Congregational	Wood
32	First Parish Church (1773) Kennebunk, York County	Congregational	Wood
33	Old Meeting House (1757) Harpswell Center, Cumberland County	Congregational	Wood
34	Nequasset Meeting House (1757) Woolwich, Segadahoc County	Congregational	Wood
35	German Meting House (c. 1770) Waldoboro, Lincoln County	German Lutheran	Wood
36	Walpole Meeting House (1772) Walpole, Lincoln County	Presbyterian	Wood
37	Alna Meeting House (1789) Alna, Lincoln County	Congregational	Wood

SUMMARY

Congregational	5	Wood	7
German Lutheran	1		
Presbyterian	1		
Buildings	7		7

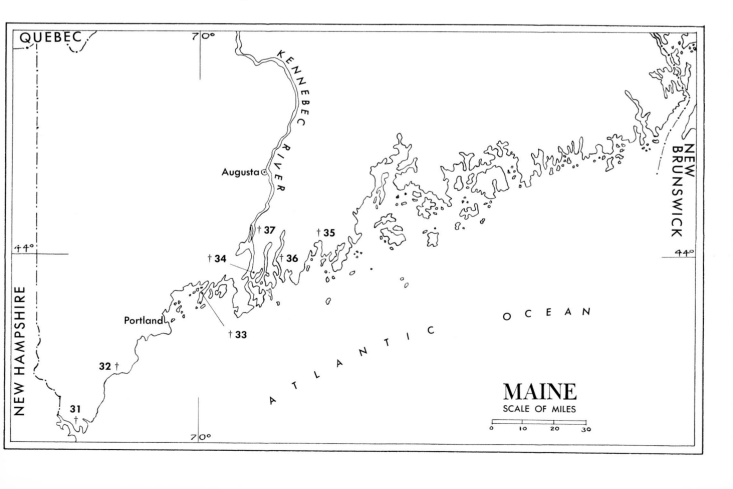

31

First Congregational Church (1730)

Kittery Point, York County, Maine

The first church organized in Maine was at York, the second at Wells, and the third at Kittery (a later name for the ancient territory of Piscataqua). The territory of Kittery was divided in successive stages into Berwick, Eliot, South Berwick, and the present Kittery. The second church organized within the ancient limits of Piscataqua was on Kittery Point. The first evidence of a minister being settled here is in the Kittery Town Records, where it is noted that in 1699 the Reverend John Newmarch was living at Kittery Point and had land granted him as minister of the town. He was hired as a preacher from year to year, until 1714, when the church was organized on November 4 by eighteen males and twenty-five females, and he was ordained. Assisting at the occasion were the churches of Portsmouth, York, Wells, Berwick, and New Castle. The Reverend John Newmarch preached here until 1750, sixty

years after his settlement; he was succeeded by Doctor Benjamin Stevens, who served for the next forty years, the two together spanning a century. The church declined after the latter's death; there were few male members; they dismissed the next minister and the next, and for years there was none.

The original meeting house was replaced in 1730 by the present building. In 1874 the building was remodeled, and the pulpit and steps on either side are of the later date, but the central portion of the building is the original. Across the street from the church is the Pepperell house. Sir William Pepperell was one of the church's original members and the town's outstanding citizen. He served in the militia as an officer, as a member of the Governor's Council, and as Chief Justice of the Court of Common Pleas. For commanding the force of New Englanders that captured the French fortress of Louisburg, Nova Scotia, in 1745, he was created a baronet the following year — the only native of New England to be honored by the British in that way. The service pieces given to the church by Lady Pepperell are still used.

32

First Parish Church (1773)

Kennebunk, York County, Maine

The second church to be organized in Maine was in Wells, and the residents in the growing village of Kennebunk were required by law to attend church at Wells. For seven years their petition for a separate parish was refused in the town meeting of Wells; the residents of Kennebunk then appealed their case to the General Court of Massachusetts and won. As a result, the Second Congregational Society was organized in 1750. The church of the Second Society was located at Kennebunk Landing until 1773; it then was moved to Kennebunk Village, where a meeting house, the present church, was built the same year.

A number of alterations have been made to bring the building to its present state. By 1803 the parish required a much larger building, and fortunately it was voted that year to enlarge the present building instead of replacing it. The church was cut in two, the rear half was moved back twenty-eight feet, and walls were built joining the two halves. The entrance on the south side was made at that time, and the tower and steeple were built. When the steeple was completed in 1804, a bell was installed that was one of the many cast in the famous foundry of Paul Revere & Sons, Boston. In 1838 the interior of the church was divided into two floors by the extension of the gallery level; the upper floor became the church auditorium, and the ground floor was devoted to service rooms. At that time the old box pews were replaced with slip pews. The church is now Unitarian.

33

Old Meeting House (1757)
Town Hall

Harpswell Center, Cumberland County, Maine

Here, on a narrow neck overlooking Casco Bay, the first meeting house of the settlement was built by Congregationalists in 1757. This old building has been kept in its original condition, even though for many years it has been used as the town hall. The original seats remain on the sides and in the gallery, but the center pews have been removed. The high pulpit and sounding board remain in their original positions, and even the original plaster is in good condition. Across the road from this old meeting house is the present church, the spire of which is seen in this photograph taken from the burying ground.

34

Nequasset Meeting House (1757)

Woolwich, Sagadahoc County, Maine

This meeting house, built in 1757, on the east bank of the Kennebec River, across from Bath, is the oldest meeting house east of the Kennebec. Josiah Winship was the first pastor; he was ordained by the Congregationalists here in 1765. The meeting house has a gallery at the entrance end. The pews are of the modern style.

The Kennebec might have shared with the James River the honor of harboring the first permanent settlement of Englishmen in America. In 1607, the year in which the landing was made at Jamestown, Sir John Popham, an English judge who took an active part in the colonization of Virginia by procuring patents for the London and Plymouth companies, sent an expedition to the Kennebec under the leadership of his brother George, but it failed to establish a settlement. The first Protestant clergyman in the territory that is now the State of Maine was the Reverend Richard Seymour, a member of the unsuccessful Popham Colony. Judge Popham had presided at the trial of Sir Walter Raleigh, in London, whose settlement on Roanoke Island, Virginia, long before the permanent one of 1607, also had been a failure.

35

German Meeting House (c. 1770)

Waldoboro, Lincoln County, Maine

The German Meeting House at Waldoboro marks the northeastern extremity of our collection. The German Lutherans who arrived here in 1748 named their settlement for General Samuel Waldo, proprietor of the Waldo Patent, which covered many thousands of acres. The proprietor had given a glowing picture of the land to his prospective settlers; an inscription on one of the stones in the graveyard reads: "This town was settled in 1748 by Germans who migrated to this place with the promise and expectation of finding a prosperous city, instead of which they found nothing but a wilderness." The Lutheran congregation in this new settlement was without a minister for twenty years, but the members met regularly for services on the Sabbath.

The present meeting house was built about 1770, on the east bank of the Medomak River. There were two meeting houses in the township in 1773, when the "westerly meeting house" was designated as the place for the first town meeting of that year. The one referred to was a log meeting house situated at "Meeting House Cove," which had been dedicated in 1763, but it had become inadequate, and the present structure had been built a few years later. Waldo had not given deeds to lots for church and school use on the eastern side, as he had on the western side of the river, and after a time this present meeting house, which was situated near the ferry crossing, became the subject of title difficulties. By 1795 claims to land on the other side had been settled, and deeds had been renewed, including land for church and school. In the winter of that year, when the river was frozen, the meeting house was moved to the western side and located on its present site. The building is painted yellow with white trim. The interior is natural wood, and it still contains the old box pews, a high pulpit, sounding board, and gallery. A glass case contains a collection of old German books and mementos of the early settlers. Services are held here once a year.

36

Walpole Meeting House (1772)
Old Presbyterian Church

South Bristol, Lincoln County, Maine

To the left of the road that follows the Damariscotta River south toward Christmas Cove stands the Old Walpole Meeting House, alone among woods on a low plateau. On the first survey of the region, in 1729, the name given to the township was Walpole. In 1767 the inhabitants voted to name the township Bristol, for the town in England whence many of them had come, but the name Walpole was given to the church when it was built in 1772.

There were many Scots in the township, and after meetings had been held for some years in private homes with visiting preachers, the Church was organized as Presbyterian. The first pastor was the Reverend Alexander McLain, a Scottish Presbyterian, who was born on the Isle of Skye and graduated from the University of Aberdeen; he came here from New Jersey, where there were a number of Presbyterian churches. His rugged character is revealed in his choice of a residence located seven miles from the church; he was in attendance regularly and on time regardless of weather. His parsonage burned in 1796, but his devoted parishioners rebuilt it, and it still stands. He served the parish from 1772, when the church was built, to 1800, when he resigned. During the last four years of his service he had an associate pastor, the Reverend Willis Riddle, who was

elected to succeed Mr. McLain. When that change was made, the polity of the Church also was changed from Presbyterian to Congregational.

From the outside, the meeting house looks like a private dwelling, but inside it is designed and furnished as a church in the style of the period, and it is practically unchanged. There are three entrances, galleries on three sides, a high pulpit reached by a curved stairway, a sounding board, and box pews. The galleries also are furnished with box pews, with the singers' bench in the front. The deacons' seat before the pulpit faces the congregation. Until recently there was no provision for heat, and in winter the congregation followed the usual custom of carrying foot warmers to church. The church possesses a pewter communion service made by Thomas Cary of London in 1687. In 1822 the church had ceased being active, and it was closed. For the Centennial in 1872 the meeting house was repaired and painted. Only occasional services are held during the summer.

156

The meeting house is strongly built, with hand-hewn beams twelve by fourteen inches. The design is the two-story, plain rectangular style, and the interior is furnished with the conventional features for a meeting house of the period; it is similar to the Walpole Meeting House. The building stands practically unchanged. In a high pulpit, with the reading level at a fixed height from the pulpit floor, a problem was presented by preachers who were short in stature. The problem was solved in various ways at different churches; at Alna there is a series of sliding shelves that come out at different heights for the preacher to select for his comfort. There has been no settled pastor at Alna Church for many years, but visiting pastors preach on Sunday afternoons in July and August, and there is good attendance of summer visitors. The town of Alna maintains the building.

37

Alna Meeting House (1789)

Alna, Lincoln County, Maine

About eight miles north of Wiscasset is Alna, and out in the open country on a high hill stands the Alna Meeting House, which was built in 1789. A third parish after that at Wiscasset had been established in the northern part of Pownalborough. It became the town of New Milford, which later became Alna. The building was erected under the direction of Joseph Carleton. The first preacher, Jonathan Scott, officiated until the congregation was organized. The Congregational Society was formally organized on September 27, 1796. The Reverend Jonathan Ward then became pastor. He was born in Plymouth, New Hampshire, was a graduate of Dartmouth College, and he served as pastor of the Alna Church until 1818.

MARYLAND

		Denomination	Material
38	St. Francis Xavier Church (1767) St. Mary's County	Roman Catholic	Wood
39	St. Ignatius Church (1785) St. Inigoes, St. Mary's County	Roman Catholic	Brick
40	St. George's Church (1750) Valley Lee, St. Mary's County	Anglican	Brick
41	St. Andrew's Church (1765) St. Mary's County	Anglican	Brick
42	Christ Church (1736) Chaptico, St. Mary's County	Anglican	Brick
43	All Faith Church (1765) Huntersville, St. Mary's County	Anglican	Brick
44	Durham Church (1732) Charles County	Anglican	Brick
45	Christ Church (1750) Wayside, Charles County	Anglican	Brick
46	St. Thomas' Manor (1741) Charles County	Roman Catholic	Brick
47	Christ Church (1698) Accokeek, Prince George's County	Anglican	Brick
48	St. John's Church (1723) Broad Creek, Prince George's County	Anglican	Brick
49	St. Paul's Church (1733) Baden, Prince George's County	Anglican	Brick
50	St. Thomas' Church (1733) Croom, Prince George's County	Anglican	Brick
51	St. Barnabas Church (1774) Leeland, Prince George's County	Anglican	Brick
52	Christ Church (1772) Calvert County	Anglican	Brick
53	Middleham Chapel (1748) Lusby, Calvert County	Anglican	Brick
54	St. James' Church (1762) Herring Creek, Anne Arundel County	Anglican	Brick
55	All Hallows Church (c. 1727) Anne Arundel County	Anglican	Brick
56	Doughoregan Manor (1727) Howard County	Roman Catholic	Brick
57	Sater Baptist Church (1742) Baltimore County	Baptist	Brick
58	St. Thomas' Church, Garrison Forest (1743) Baltimore County	Anglican	Brick
59	St. James' Church, My Lady's Manor (1750) Baltimore County	Anglican	Brick
60	Gunpowder Friends Meeting House (1773) Baltimore County	Friends	Stone

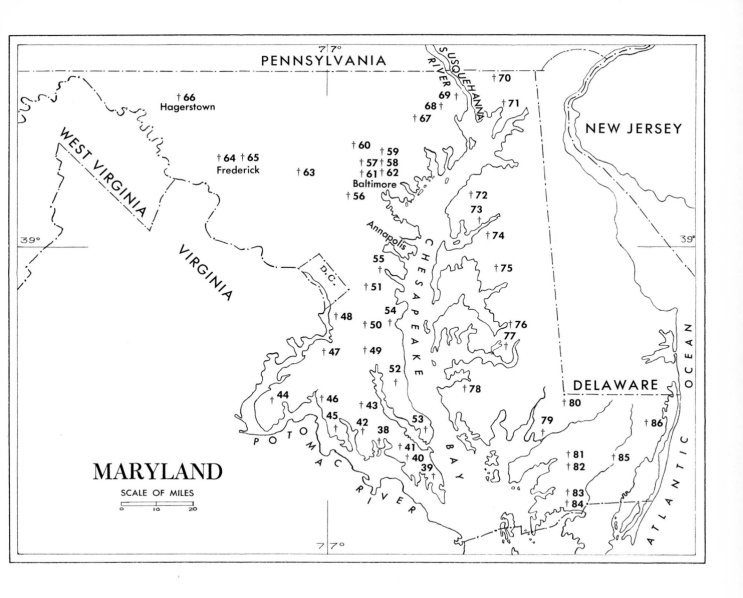

MARYLAND

SCALE OF MILES

	Denomination	Material
61 Patapsco Friends Meeting House (1781) Baltimore, Baltimore County	Friends	Brick
62 Otterbein Church (1785) Baltimore, Baltimore County	United Brethren in Christ	Brick
63 Holy Trinity Church (1771) Eldersburg, Carroll County	Anglican	Stone
64 Old Stone Church (1752) Frederick, Frederick County	German Lutheran	Stone
65 Trinity Chapel (1763) Frederick, Frederick County	German Reformed	Stone
66 German Reformed Church (1774) Hagerstown, Washington County	German Reformed	Stone
67 Little Falls Friends Meeting House (1773) Fallston, Harford County	Friends	Stone
68 Priest Neale's Mass House (1764) Harford County	Roman Catholic	Stone

		Denomination	Material
69	Deer Creek Friends Meeting House (1784) Darlington, Harford County	Friends	Stone
70	East Nottingham Friends Meeting House (1724) Calvert, Cecil County	Friends	Brick
71	St. Mary's Church (1742) North East, Cecil County	Anglican	Brick
72	St. Paul's Church (1713) Kent County	Anglican	Brick
73	Emmanuel Church (1768) Chestertown, Kent County	Anglican	Brick
74	Old St. Luke's Church (1730) Church Hill, Queen Anne's County	Anglican	Brick
75	Wye Church (1717) Talbot County	Anglican	Brick
76	Third Haven Friends Meeting House (1682) Easton, Talbot County	Friends	Wood
77	Old White Marsh Church (c. 1685) Talbot County	Anglican	Brick
78	Old Trinity Church (c. 1675) Church Creek, Dorchester County	Anglican	Brick
79	Old Green Hill Church (1733) Wicomico County	Anglican	Brick
80	Spring Hill Church (1771) Hebron, Wicomico County	Anglican	Wood
81	Manokin Presbyterian Church (1765) Princess Anne, Somerset County	Presbyterian	Brick
82	St. Andrew's Church (1770) Princess Anne, Somerset County	Anglican	Brick
83	Rehoboth Church (1706) Rehoboth, Somerset County	Presbyterian	Brick
84	Coventry Parish Church (1784) Rehoboth, Somerset County	Anglican	Brick
85	All Hallows Church (1784) Snow Hill, Worcester County	Anglican	Brick
86	St. Martin's Church (1755) Worcester County	Anglican	Brick

SUMMARY

Roman Catholic	5		Brick	38
Anglican	31		Wood	3
Baptist	1		Stone	8
Friends	6			
United Brethren in Christ	1			
German Lutheran	1			
German Reformed	2			
Presbyterian	2			
Buildings	49			49

38

St. Francis Xavier Church (1767)

St. Mary's County, Maryland

Newton Manor was a large tract of land at Breton Bay, overlooking the Potomac River. In 1668, Jesuits acquired a part of the land. On it they built a chapel near the present site and dedicated it to St. Francis Xavier. In 1677 a school that had been founded at St. Mary's City, the first settlement in Maryland, was moved here. The present church was built in 1767 by Father Ashley. The building has undergone repairs and alterations, and the choir loft and slave gallery have been removed. The bell is inscribed, "1691 S. T. Joannes Arden." The parish house, seen in the background, was built in 1740.

39

St. Ignatius Church (1785)

St. Inigoes, St. Mary's County, Maryland

The manor of Little Bretton, on a bay of the Potomac River, was granted to William Bretton in 1637. He and his wife, Temperance, gave the site of this church to the Jesuits, who had obtained title to St. Inigoes Manor in 1630. This grant of 3,000 acres was made to the priests by Governor Leonard Calvert, not for religious purposes, but in recognition of the contributions in men and money made by the Society of Jesus in England to Lord Baltimore's province. After the priests had been excluded from St. Mary's City, in 1705, they transferred their residence and mission to St. Inigoes. The original chapel here was the third in the province built for use by the Jesuits, following the Indian hut at St. Mary's City, which was the first used as a chapel by Father White, the "Apostle of Maryland." The original brick chapel here was still standing in 1700. The second here was built in 1745. The third and present church was begun in 1785, by Father James Walton, and dedicated in 1788. It is of brick laid in Flemish bond, but the glazed headers do not show through the yellow paint that now covers the walls. Inside are the original box pews. The frame entrance and shingled pediment were added in 1823, according to a tablet over the door.

40

St. George's Church (1750) Poplar Hill Church

Valley Lee, St. Mary's County, Maryland

An Anglican congregation was organized here in 1639, and in 1642 they built on this site the Poplar Hill Church to serve the inhabitants of St. George's Hundred and Poplar Hill Hundred. The present St. George's Church was built in 1750 on the same site, and it is said that brick from the original building was used. It was in William and Mary Parish, one of the thirty established in 1692. The brick is laid in Flemish bond; in recent years it has been painted white. The tower is a post-colonial addition. A difference in brick reveals that the circular window over the doorway replaced a rectangular window similar to the others. The old pulpit and gallery, together with the doors of the box pews, have been removed. The white colonial building, standing overshadowed by St. George's Oak in a wooded countryside, is a memorial of one of the earliest Protestant congregations in Maryland.

41

St. Andrew's Church (1765)

near Leonardstown, St. Mary's County, Maryland

St. Andrew's Parish was laid off from All Faith Parish (No. 43) and William and Mary Parish (No. 40) in 1744. The original place of worship was the chapel called Four Mile Run Church of Sandy Bottom, which had been serving

as a chapel of ease to All Faith Church. Built about 1703, that chapel stood until the present St. Andrew's Church was built. In 1764 St. Andrew's Parish was organized with the election of a vestry. A move was then made to build a church, and the site selected was "Waldrums Old Fields." The present building was begun in 1765 and completed in 1767. Only minor changes have been made since, and the building remains a unique combination of colonial and classic design. The brick building has twin square towers, with two semicircular niches in each, one above the other. The corners of the towers have brick quoins. Between the towers a portico gives cover for the arched entrance and two segmental arched windows. There is a Palladian window over the entrance, and inside are a stone floor, box pews, and a slave gallery. The silver chalice and paten of 1757 are still used. A governor who died in office (1791-1792), George Plater, is buried here.

42

Christ Church, Chaptico (1763)
Chaptico Church
Chaptico, St. Mary's County, Maryland

Chaptico was a baronial manor of the Calverts. The first parish antedated 1692, but in that year King and Queen Parish was laid out, one of thirty created by the royal government of Maryland in establishing the Church of England. Christ Church was built in King and Queen Parish, adjoining St. Andrew's Parish (No. 41). In 1694 a report to the council, dated July 30, said that the church was "going forward to be built." The present Christ Church was built in 1736 by Philip Key, high sheriff of Maryland. The old brick, laid in Flemish bond with glazed headers, can be distinguished even through the red paint which now covers the walls. The tower was added in 1913; it rises above an arched porch similar to that of St. Peter's, New Kent County, Virginia (No. 314). During the War of 1812, the British stabled their horses in the church and destroyed the tile floor. The church was consecrated twice, first as Chaptico Church in 1817, and second as Christ Church in 1840. It generally is called Christ Church, Chaptico.

43

All Faith Church (1765)
Huntersville, St. Mary's County, Maryland

All Faith Parish was organized in 1692, as a parish of the Church of England under the Act of that year. It was then in Calvert County, but as it lay west of the Patuxent River it later was in St. Mary's County. All Faith Church was built in 1765. It replaced a log church of the same name built on this site some years before 1692, possibly before 1675. The belfry is a later addition, and the interior has been modernized with open pews. Fluted Ionic columns support the barrel-vaulted ceiling. This church had a chapel of ease, the Four Mile Run Church, which served as the first parish church of St. Andrew's (No. 41).

44

Durham Church (1732)
near Ironsides, Charles County, Maryland

Durham Parish was laid out in 1692, one of the thirty created that year, when the royal government of Maryland established the Church of England, and services in the parish have been continuous since that time. It was one of the eight original parishes in the Diocese of Washington. The present Durham Church was built in 1732, replacing the original log church of 1692 on the same site. It was remodeled in 1791, when the walls were heightened, the upper tier of windows was added, and the building was all restored. In 1843 the old pews were replaced and the galleries on the south and east walls were removed. Maryland's most famous general, William Smallwood, of the American Revolution, is buried here; he was a member of the vestry from 1775 to 1791. George Washington visited the church in June, 1771.

45

Christ Church, Wayside (1750)
Wayside Church
Wayside, Charles County, Maryland

William and Mary Parish was one of the thirty laid out in 1692, when the Church of England was established by the new royal government in Maryland. There is some evidence that the first church building was standing in 1691, before the Establishment. We do not know just when the present church was built; it was enlarged and repaired by Act of Assembly in 1750, and, as it is not clear how much of the original building was used, we give that date for the present building. Occupied by Union soldiers in the Civil War, it was partly burned, and in 1869 it was rebuilt with part of the original walls incorporated. The belfry and windows obviously are of this later period.

46

St. Thomas' Manor House (1741)
St. Ignatius Church

Charles County, Maryland

At Chapel Point on the Potomac River is situated St. Thomas' Manor. Here the colonial house of worship is the manor house, built in 1741, rather than St. Ignatius Church, built in 1798 adjacent to it. This situation reflects the relationship between Lord Baltimore (Roman Catholic proprietary of Maryland), the Crown, and the Established Church of England. Roman Catholics were permitted to worship privately in their own way, but houses of public worship were required to be Anglican. The land here was acquired in 1649 by Father Phillip Fisher, who managed the property of the Maryland mission of the Society of Jesus, and the claim was made in the name of Thomas Copley in the capacity of bringing in settlers. In 1662 the Jesuits occupied the property fully and established a mission with pastoral residence and chapel. Father George Hunter built the present manor house and a small private chapel attached. When St. Ignatius Church was built, the little chapel was incorporated as the sacristy, thereby serving both literally and figuratively to link the private residence and the church during the period of transition. The substantial manor house is of brick with stone quoins. The brick in both the manor house and the church is laid in Flemish bond. The church was built by Father Charles Sewall. A tablet in the gable gives the name of "L. Pearson, Bricklayer."

47

Christ Church, Accokeek (1698)

Accokeek, Prince George's County, Maryland

The brick church at Accokeek was built originally in 1698, but the parish did not prosper. In its early days the parish went through a period of revolt when the rector married in Maryland after leaving a wife in England. The church was neglected for a long period after the disestablishment of the Church of England, and in 1856 the building was burned. It was reconstructed on the old brick foundations and parts of the original walls, and in 1857 it was reconsecrated. The brickwork up to the water table has the appearance of ancient brick, but the windows, belfry, cornice, and entrance are in the style of the period when the church was reconstructed.

48

St. John's Church (1723)

Broad Creek, near Piscataway, Prince George's County, Maryland

Piscataway Parish was one of the thirty Anglican parishes established in Maryland in 1692. It was known for a short time as King George's Parish and then as St. John's Parish. Two churches preceded the present one here, both built before the establishment of the parish. The present St. John's Church was built in 1723 of pink brick at a cost of 16,000 pounds of tobacco. The interior and the colored glass date from 1820, but a pew is preserved which is said to have been occupied by George Washington; Mt. Vernon is directly across the Potomac River.

49

St. Paul's Church (1733)

Baden, Prince George's County, Maryland

The parish was established as St. Paul's Parish by the Act of 1692, and a frame church was built that same year. The present church replaced it on the same site in 1733. The walls of the rectangular building were laid in Flemish bond. The transepts were added soon after, making the church cruciform, and the brick of the chancel was then laid in running bond. The windows are original, but the roof is modern. The sundial was installed above the entrance in 1753; the baptismal font dates from 1754. There is a window memorial to Thomas John Claggett. He was born near by, was ordained in London, and served here as rector from 1780 to 1786. He was consecrated Bishop of Maryland in 1792, the first bishop to be consecrated in the United States. He was buried at Croom, the Claggett estate near by (No. 50), and later his body was transferred to Washington, where it now rests in the National Cathedral at Mount St. Alban, in the vault beneath Bethlehem Chapel.

50

St. Thomas' Church (1733)

Croom, Prince George's County, Maryland

In 1733, while he was rector of St. Paul's Parish, Baden (No. 49), the Reverend John Eversfield directed the building of a chapel of ease known as Page's Chapel. It was then a plain, rectangular, brick structure. In 1851 St. Thomas' Parish was created from the northern part of St. Paul's Parish, and in that year the chapel was remodeled to become St. Thomas' Church; the colonial features were changed by Gothic alterations and additions. As it stands today — a red brick church in a grove of oaks in the countryside — it reveals little of its colonial history. Thomas John Claggett, first Bishop of Maryland, and the first consecrated in America, was rector of St. Paul's and in charge of Page's Chapel from 1780 to 1786. The tower was added as a memorial to him in 1888. Croom was the Claggett family estate here, and when he died at Croom in 1816, Bishop Claggett was buried here, before his body was moved at a later date to rest in the crypt of the National Cathedral in Washington.

51

St. Barnabas Church (1774)

Leeland, Prince George's County, Maryland

By Act of Assembly in 1705, Queen Anne's Parish was formed out of St. Paul's Parish, Patuxent River (see St. Paul's, Baden, No. 49). A brick church was begun in 1708 to replace a wooden chapel. This brick church was torn down in 1772, and in 1774 the present brick building was begun. That was in the first year of the ministry of the Reverend Jonathan Boucher, who was a close personal friend of George Washington. He was an outspoken Tory, who preached fiery sermons with a brace of pistols on the pulpit cushion, " . . . having given notice that if any man or men were so lost to all sense of decency as to drag me out of my pulpit, I should think myself justified before God in repelling violence." Finally he was restrained from mounting the pulpit, and he and his American wife sailed for England on the last ship out of Annapolis before the Revolution began. The building is of the early Georgian style and is one of the few with a hipped roof. The design is plain, and there is no ornamentation. The brick is laid in Flemish bond. The contract named Christopher Lowndes as builder.

52

Christ Church (1772)

near Port Republic, Calvert County, Maryland

Calvert County, named for Cecil Calvert, second Lord Baltimore and first proprietary of Maryland, was established in 1654. In 1672, as a result of preaching by George Fox, founder of the Society of Friends, there was a religious awakening in the region, and the first Anglican church was erected here on land given by Francis Malden out of his tract called "Prevent Danger." Christ Church Parish was one of the thirty Anglican parishes established in 1692. Two brick parish churches followed in succession: one was erected in 1732, and the second and present one in 1772. In 1881 and again in 1906 the building was remodeled. The stucco on the walls of brick, the buttresses, and the bracketed cornices are additions which conceal the building's colonial character. Middleham Chapel (No. 53) was built as a chapel of ease in Christ Church Parish.

53

Middleham Chapel (1748)

near Lusby, Calvert County, Maryland

Situated in the country near the head of Helen Creek, Middleham Chapel was built in 1748 as a chapel of ease in Christ Church Parish (No. 52). It replaced a building that was outgrown and in a ruined condition. The date, 1748, appears in the brickwork of the gable end. The bell is dated 1699. The petition to the assembly for the erection of the Anglican chapel called for a levy of 80,000 pounds of tobacco to pay the cost. No regular services are held in this cruciform brick chapel standing in a hickory grove of the countryside.

54

St. James' Church (1762)
Herring Creek Church

Anne Arundel County, Maryland

Anne Arundel, for whom the county was named, was the wife of Cecil Calvert, second Lord Baltimore and proprietary of Maryland. St. James' Parish was one of the thirty Anglican parishes laid out in 1692, and it was established formally in 1694. Evidently this site was used as a place of worship long before, for the gravestones of Christopher Birckhead and his wife are dated 1666 and 1665 respectively, the latter being the oldest known in Maryland. A bell was given to the early church in 1706, and in 1724 Queen Anne gave a silver alms basin. It is recorded that an early rector, the Reverend Henry Hall, having many Quakers living in his parish who refused to pay tithes as required by law, went to their meeting house and threatened to horse-whip them all unless they complied with the law.

The present brick church was begun in 1762, after John Weems had submitted to the vestry the low bid of £1,400 sterling. The contract was given public notice as follows: "Likewise Mr. John Weems has undertaking the building of a breek church in the sd Parrish according to the draft of the plan that was this day layd before the vestry, and is to build the sd church att fourteen hundred pounds cur without any further charges to the said Parrish in any shape whatever, in case the vestry git ann act of Assembly for what tob. will be wanting of the sum that is to build said church; for as they hant tob. enufe in hand for finniching of sd. church." Weems finished the church in 1765; he was probably a cousin of Mason Locke Weems, known as Parson Weems, who was born near Herring Bay to the east of the church (see All Hallows Church, No. 55). The brick walls of the simple rectangular building are laid in all-header bond, and the wide windows and doorway are arched.

55

All Hallows Church (c. 1727)
South River Church

Anne Arundel County, Maryland

Before All Hallows Parish was laid out in 1692, when thirty parishes were established in Maryland, South River Church was active here. Since that time it often is referred to as All Hallows Church, South River. The earliest legible gravestone is dated 1686. This region, originally Providence County, was settled by Puritans who left the Established Church in Virginia, and there was some Puritanical resistance here to the establishment of a church hierarchy.

The present church was built about 1727, the year that appears on its bell. The double windows have segmental arches, a style that was adopted temporarily between 1720 and 1740. After the Revolution the church was for some time without a rector. Dr. William Smith was active trying to reactivate the Episcopal churches, and a relative of his, Mason Locke Weems, became rector. Typical of the Episcopal churches of the period, accustomed to tax support by law as they were, voluntary contributions at All Hallows were small, and the rector had to teach and sell books to make a living. When Weems was not reappointed rector in 1792, he became an itinerant book salesman in clerical garb. He became famous as Parson Weems for his stories, tracts, and biographies. The best known of his compositions is the story of George Washington and the cherry tree, in his *Life of Washington*. In 1940 a fire destroyed the interior and roof of the church, and one now sees the building as it was restored. The photograph, however, was made before the fire.

56

Doughoregan Manor (1727)

near Ellicott City, Howard County, Maryland

This beautiful country home was built in 1727 by Charles Carroll, grandfather of Charles Carroll of Carollton, a signer of the Declaration of Independence, and it is still in the Carroll family. The building has a 300-foot façade. The ell at the right end of the building is the private chapel, considered the finest of its kind built in colonial times. As Roman Catholic churches were not permitted as places of public worship in early Maryland, private homes and chapels were used for Roman Catholic worship. The house in which Charles Carroll, the Signer, was born, for another example, was the first place used for Roman Catholic worship in Annapolis.

57

Sater Baptist Church (1742)

Baltimore County, Maryland

In wooded country off of Falls Road, near Baltimore, stands this first Baptist church in Maryland. It was begun by Henry Sater in 1742 and completed in 1743. This building and St. Thomas' Church (No. 58) were completed within four days of each other, and ever since, the congregation of each has believed that its building was the earlier. The original congregation held to the General Baptist, or Arminian, doctrine; in 1754 a group seceded as Particular, or Calvinistic, Baptists and built their own church on Winter's Run.

58

St. Thomas' Church (1743)
Garrison Forest Church

Greenspring Valley, Baltimore County, Maryland

In 1692 the new royal governor in Maryland, Francis Nicholson, ordered three forts built on the frontier for defense against the Indians, one of them in the Garrison Forest a few miles from the present church site. There was trouble with the Indians at the time, and the inhabitants of the forest had a long trip to their parish church, St. Paul's in Baltimore Town. In 1741 the vestry of St. Paul's voted funds to build a chapel of ease for the inhabitants of the forest, and in 1742 it was authorized by Act of Assembly. The brick building was erected in 1743 as the Garrison Forest Church. In 1745, after the death of the Reverend Benedict Bourdillon, rector of St. Paul's, the chapel was made an independent parish church with the name of St. Thomas' Church, and the Reverend Thomas Craddock was inducted as the first rector. The original rectangular building forms the nave of the present cruciform structure; the transepts were added for more room. Trinity Chapel was built in 1771 as a chapel of ease in this parish, in the forks of the Patapsco River near Eldersburg (see No. 63). Hounds of the Greenspring Valley Hunt are blessed at this church.

59

St. James' Church (1750)
The Manor Church

My Lady's Manor, Baltimore County, Maryland

St. James' Church was built in St. John's Parish as a chapel of ease to serve the inhabitants of Gunpowder Hundred. St. John's, or Gunpowder, Parish was one of the thirty laid out when the Church of England was established in Maryland in 1692; the parish church was at Joppa Town on the Gunpowder River, a port of entry for Baltimore Town. The present Episcopal parish was established in 1770, after the chapel had been built. In a corner of My Lady's Manor, the building was begun in 1750, and it is still called the Manor Church. It was completed in 1755. Four years later the rectangular church had to be enlarged to accommodate the growing parish; the Established Church was the only one that welcomed immigrants regardless of denomination. The enlargement was made, between 1759 and 1762, by using the existing building as a transept and adding a nave to the middle, thus bringing it to its present T form. The tower was added much later, but bricks from the old vestry were used in its construction. The church contains the old box pews, but the pulpit is modern. The Maryland point-to-point four-mile race is held annually on My Lady's Manor course, and a tilting tournament, for lady riders only, also is held annually on the church grounds.

60

Gunpowder Friends Meeting House (1773)

near Cockeysville, Baltimore County, Maryland

This old meeting house, built in 1773, is in its original condition. The cedar roof was burned and replaced in 1886, but the doors, windows, benches, and the high stone wall around the burying ground are original. Quakers do not always mark their graves, and most of the burying ground is bare lawn, but in recent years some markers have been placed. The two doors, two aisles, and two facing fireplaces accommodate the separate men's and women's meetings for business. The second floor was laid out for living quarters; it is not certain whether this was to accommodate visitors from a distance or a resident caretaker. Quakers have meetings here several times a year. The Meeting derived its name from that of the Gunpowder River.

61

Patapsco Friends Meeting House (1781)

Baltimore, Baltimore County, Maryland

The Patapsco River, from which the meeting of Friends took its name, is the river and the arm of the Chesapeake Bay on which Baltimore is located. A tablet on the wall beside the door of the meeting house informs the visitor that "Baltimore's earliest meeting was Patapsco Friends Meeting. 6th mo. 12th 1681 is the earliest record of this meeting. Removed to Asquith and Fayette Streets Baltimore Town, 2nd mo. 22nd 1781." That is this location, and this plain, rectangular brick building was erected here a century after the earliest record of the Quakers in Baltimore. In 1920 the property was acquired by the city for use as a playground. At that time the remains of about three hundred bodies were moved from the burying ground to other cemeteries. The building is now used for storing playground equipment.

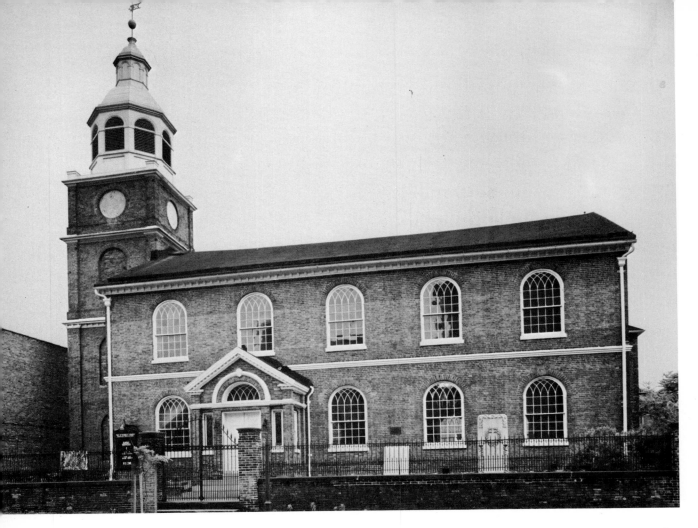

62

Otterbein Church (1785)
Evangelical United Brethren Church

**West Conway Street, Baltimore,
Baltimore County, Maryland**

A German Evangelical Reformed congregation gathered here in 1771. In 1774 it was organized with the Reverend Philip William Otterbein (1726-1813) as the first pastor. He was born in Germany and had come to America in 1752 as a missionary to the Germans of Pennsylvania. In his native Dillenburg, Nassau, Germany, the system of class-meetings was the basis on which he developed the secession that grew to be the United Brethren in Christ (the "New Reformed Church"). Otterbein was a Pietist, of the reform movement which started in the Lutheran Church of Germany, spread through the Dutch Reformed Church of Holland, and was influential in various

of these colonial churches in America. For five years before taking this ministry he had been working with Reformed congregations in the Frederick, Maryland area. The church was built in 1785. Not only is it named for Otterbein, but it is the mother church of the United Brethren in Christ, a new Church founded by him and Martin Boehm, a former Mennonite, in 1789. In that year two bells cast in Bremen, Germany, were presented to the Otterbein Church. In 1800 the first annual conference of the new group was held at Frederick, and the two founders were elected bishops, but Bishop Otterbein continued to serve as a Reformed minister. In 1946 the United Brethren in Christ united with the Evangelical United Brethren Church and adopted the latter name.

The building stands practically in its original condition. The brick walls were stuccoed for a time, but fortunately the plaster has been removed. The entrance through the tower has been blocked by a commercial building, and now the entrance is through the side doorway.

63

Holy Trinity Church (1771)

Eldersburg, Carroll County, Maryland

In the forks of the Patapsco River, to the west of Baltimore Town, near Eldersburg, Holy Trinity Chapel was built in 1771. It was a chapel of ease of St. Thomas' Church, Garrison Forest (No. 58). St. Thomas' had been a chapel of ease in the Parish of St. Paul's Church in Baltimore Town, a large parish which included this back country bordering the town.

This stone building was finished in 1773, and seats were put in. The Revolution followed in a few years, and like so many Anglican churches during and after the war, Trinity Chapel suffered from neglect. In 1806 permission was granted for the use of the chapel by Baptists, and Methodists used it also during the years following. In 1819 the building no longer was being used for services of any denomination, but had become a shelter for livestock. The vestry of St. Thomas' Church then ordered an investigation, being aware of the responsibility of the mother church for its Episcopal flock, and fearing that other denominations had "swept away the church in that neighborhood." There were no Episcopalian services, however, for another two decades, and by 1843 the building was dilapidated — the doors, windows, and roof were gone, and the floor had been ripped up. In that year the Diocesan Convention created a new parish and constituted this building as Trinity Church. The building was restored, and the church flourished for the rest of the century. It then fell again into neglect, and by the 1930's the building was in a state of ruin.

64

Old Stone Church (1752)
Evangelical Lutheran Church

Church Street, Frederick,
Frederick County, Maryland

This congregation was organized in 1738. A log church was built on the Monocacy River in 1743, and in 1746 another was built on the site of the present parsonage. In 1747 the constitution was adopted. It had been drafted by Henry Melchior Muhlenburg, who had come from Germany as a Lutheran missionary of the Augsburg Confession; he served practically as the overseer of all Lutheran churches from northern New York to Maryland, and he became known as the Patriarch of the American Lutheran Church (see Trappe Church, Pennsylvania, No. 231).

In 1752 the stone church was begun. The French and Indian War interrupted construction, and it was not completed until 1762. In 1825 it was rebuilt and enlarged as it appears today. In 1854 the large Gothic Revival church was built onto the Old Stone Church, and as a rear wing the latter serves for church functions.

65

Trinity Chapel (1763)

**West Church Street, Frederick,
Frederick County, Maryland**

The land for this church site was given to the German Reformed congregation by Daniel Dulany in 1745. The first church erected here, in 1747, was a log structure. In 1763 a church was built, with a steeple sixty feet in height, of which the congregation was justly proud. Of that building only the tower remains. In 1807 the present wood spire was built on the tower. In 1880 the church building, with the exception of the tower, was taken down and the present building was erected. The old foundations were used, with the result that the building has two cornerstones. They can be misleading; the one on the side in the original foundation bearing the date 1763 is valid for the tower, and the one on the front with the date 1881 refers only to the present body of the building and not to the tower. In 1881 the German Reformed Church merged with the Evangelical Reformed Church. On May 21, 1882, Trinity Chapel was dedicated; it was re-dedicated three generations later, January 8, 1953, when the lecture room had been restored to its colonial design, and additional space had been arranged to accommodate the entire Sunday school. Trinity Chapel continues to be used for Sunday school, Lenten services, weddings, and other special gatherings for its mother church, the Evangelical Reformed Church, which stands across the street.

66

German Reformed Church (1774)
Zion Reformed Church

**Potomac and Church Streets, Hagerstown,
Washington County, Maryland**

With thirty-nine members, the congregation
was organized in 1770. They built the German
Reformed Church in 1774; the cornerstone was
laid August 10 of that year. Jonathan Hager,
founder of Hagerstown and co-founder of the
church, was accidentally killed in his saw mill in
1775, while dressing lumber for use in the construction of this building, and was buried here.

The stone walls of the building are original. The
tower carries the rebuilding date of 1867; the appearance of the building was changed considerably
by the alterations made at that time. Early deeds
referred also to "The German Calvinist Church."
In 1855 the congregation divided over the continued use of the German language, and the name
Zion Reformed Church came into use about that
time. In 1934 the name became Zion Evangelical
and Reformed Church after the merger with the
Evangelical Synod. In 1957 the denomination
merged with the Congregational Christian
Churches to become the United Church of Christ,
but the name of this Church has not changed,
and Zion Reformed Church is the name generally
used.

67

Little Falls Friends Meeting House (1773)

Fallston, Harford County, Maryland

The first Friends meeting house here was a log building erected in 1738 with the help of Seneca Indians. After it was completed, the Indians attended services here. In 1773 the stone meeting house was built, replacing the log house. In 1843 this building was restored, and in the gable there are stones giving the two years.

68

Priest Neale's Mass House (1764)

near Poole, Harford County, Maryland

A Jesuit mission was established here in 1747; there are stones in the graveyard dating from 1750. Because of restrictions against building Roman Catholic churches for public worship, this land was acquired by the Jesuits for private use. Thomas Shea deeded the tract known as "Paradice" to Father Bennett Neale, who is believed to have built the house at that time. It is on a hill overlooking the valley of Deer Creek and is surrounded by rolling farm land. The crossing is known as Priest's Ford and Priest's Ford Bridge. The large hall was used as a chapel. About 1800 the property was bought from the Jesuits, and it has been used as a residence by the same family ever since. The old chapel is now a living room.

69

Deer Creek Friends Meeting House (1784)

Darlington, Harford County, Maryland

Bush River Meeting was settled before 1722, and this meeting evidently developed from it. As early as 1736 a Meeting for Worship was held in a private home here. This early meeting was under the care of Nottingham Monthly Meeting. As we see in connection with East Nottingham Friends Meeting House (No. 70), there was a question for a long time as to whether this region on the south bank of the Susquehanna, into which Deer Creek flows, was in Maryland or Pennsylvania, and jurisdiction in the Society of Friends depended on whether the meeting came under Baltimore Yearly Meeting or Philadelphia Yearly Meeting. In 1754 a Preparative Meeting was set up, and in 1759 it became a Monthly Meeting. The house where meetings had been held burned down, and it was replaced immediately, in 1784, with this stone meeting house. This building was restored in 1888. From it developed Fawn Grove Meeting in Pennsylvania, and both belong to Baltimore Yearly Meeting.

70

East Nottingham Friends Meeting House (1724)
Brick Meeting House

near Calvert, Cecil County, Maryland

In 1701 the first Friends Meeting here was organized on one of the controversial Nottingham Lots. For many decades this region on the south side of the Susquehanna River was in dispute between Lord Baltimore and William Penn. George Talbot held a grant known as Susquehanna Manor, and on this land William Penn had laid out thirty-seven lots of 500 acres each known as the Nottingham Lots. In 1765, when Mason and Dixon's line was run and the long dispute was settled, the land, including that of this Meeting, was restored to Maryland; it was determined, thereby, that the Meeting would belong to Baltimore Yearly Meeting.

The brick end of the house is the older. Replacing a log building of 1709, it was built in 1724. The other end was added in stone in 1751, when a fire caused repairs to be made to the woodwork in the older structure. The meeting house was used for a hospital in 1778, by a detachment of General William Smallwood's Continentals, and some of them are buried here. On April 11, 1781, Lafayette's army camped near by on the march to Yorktown. A number of Quakers from this Brick Meeting House Society fought in the Revolution and were read out of meeting. Quarterly Meetings are held.

71

St. Mary's Church (1742)

North East, Cecil County, Maryland

North Elk Parish, now St. Mary Anne's Parish, was laid out by Act of Assembly in 1706. The church stands in the town of North East, on Northeast Creek, which flows into Northeast River, which in turn empties into the northeast corner of Chesapeake Bay. In colonial days many of the congregation came to church by boat. Susquehannock Indian graves and markers dating from the early seventeenth century establish this as one of the oldest burying grounds in Maryland. The earliest church record is of a marriage in 1709.

The present brick church was built in 1742, evidently replacing the first building on the same site. The ceiling is barrel vaulted. Queen Anne presented a Bible and prayer book. In the mid-1800's changes were made in the interior; the old pulpit and box pews were replaced, and the altar was enlarged. The present brick tower replaced the original wooden tower in 1904. It was a gift of Robert Brookings, founder of the Brookings Institution, and was given as a memorial to his father, Richard, whose body rests here.

72

St. Paul's Church (1713)

near Fairlee, Kent County, Maryland

St. Paul's Parish was one of the thirty laid out in 1692, when the new royal government established the Church of England in Maryland; it covered all of lower Kent County. The first vestry was elected January 30, 1693, at "their majesties order" — King William and Queen Mary. There was a church on the present site at the time of the Establishment in 1692, and it may have been standing for some years before. The foundation of that first building has been discovered in digging for a grave.

The present church was built in 1713, replacing the original building. This fine example of a country brick church originally was cruciform, with a round apse at the east end; the south transept has been removed, however, and the remaining building has the form of an inverted T. The walls on the north side and of the apse are laid in Flemish bond with glazed headers; in the south wall, in which the alteration was made, the headers are not glazed. In 1714, thirty-four pews were installed. They were rented, or 1,000 pounds of tobacco bought one outright; one of the pews has been used by one family for more than ten generations. The building cost 140,000 pounds of tobacco. The vestry house standing near by was built in 1776 at a cost of 20,000 pounds of tobacco; the year appears in the brickwork of the gable. The great oaks in the churchyard had been standing for more than a century when the first white settlers came here.

73

Emmanuel Church (1768)

Chestertown, Kent County, Maryland

This brick church was built in 1768 as a chapel of ease in St. Paul's Parish; later it was made a parish church and became known as Emmanuel. As it stands today the colonial building is almost hidden; the rear wall of the building shows the original brick wall surrounded by the remodeling and extensions made in the late 1800's. The old church is known principally as a landmark in the history of the Episcopal Church. The rector, Dr. William Smith, was concerned with reviving the Church after the Revolution, and with the problem of ordination of ministers. In 1780 he called a convention here, at which the name "Protestant Episcopal Church" was proposed to replace the name "Church of England," and this was adopted officially in Maryland. The title was adopted officially for the entire Church, together with the constitution and revised Book of Common Prayer, in the convention of 1789 at Christ Church, Philadelphia (No. 205). Washington College at Chestertown was founded in 1782 by Dr. Smith, who served as its first president.

74

Old St. Luke's Church (1730)

Church Hill, Queen Anne's County, Maryland

The first church here was a wooden chapel of ease in St. Paul's Parish known as the Up River Chapel. Services were conducted by the rectors from Old Chester, St. Paul's Church in Chester, and Old Wye Church. In 1728 a separate parish was created, by Act of Assembly, from St. Paul's Parish. Two years later, in 1730, the present brick church was built. In the photograph the break in the gambrel roof is hidden by trees. The old building is of brick laid in Flemish bond, and it is distinguishable from the later additions. After being abandoned for some years, it was restored partially in 1842 and completely in 1881; a tower was added, and the small colonial window panes were replaced with stained glass. The settlement was known as Collin's Mill until St. Luke's was built and was called the Church on the Hill. The town then became Church Hill.

75

Wye Church (1717)
St. Luke's, Wye

near Wye Mills, Talbot County, Maryland

Old Wye Church stands beneath a giant oak
near the head of the Wye River, an arm of Chesa-
peake Bay, on the Eastern Shore of Maryland.
When the Church of England was established in
Maryland in 1692, Wye was a chapel of ease in
St. Paul's Parish. The parish church, St. Paul's,
then located at Hibernia, was known as Chester
Church; it had two other chapels in addition to
Wye — Up River Chapel (No. 74), and Tuckahoe
Chapel. The rector of St. Paul's was kept busy in

a parish that included all of the present Queen
Anne's and Caroline counties and more than the
present Talbot County. In 1709, for example, on
one Sunday he would hold services at Up River
Chapel in the morning and at St. Paul's in the
afternoon, and on the next he would be at Tuckahoe in the morning and at Wye in the afternoon.
Wye Chapel functioned as such until 1858, when
it was made a separate parish. Four years previously, in 1854, Old Wye had been consecrated
under the name of St. Luke's, Wye.

In 1698 the vestry proposed to build a new
chapel, but it was not until 1717 that the present
brick building was begun. It was finished and
opened for worship in October, 1721. The work
evidently was satisfactory, for the builder, William

Elbert, became a warden. During the post-Revolutionary period, and again during the nineteenth century, the chapel went through long phases of disuse and misuse; repairs and alterations were made at various times. In the Established Church, the sheriff had made collections of tithes in the form of tobacco and had turned them over to the vestry for expenditure; in 1794, for the first time in the disestablished Parish of St. Paul, a plate was passed in church for collections, and, as in all Episcopal churches of the period, voluntary collections were meager at first. In 1840 the vestry decided not to spend more money on repairs to the old building, and they built a new frame chapel in Queenstown. A year after Wye Church became independent the Civil War started. The

church was active after the war until about 1910, but then the building began to deteriorate again, as it was used only occasionally. In 1947 a thorough restoration, of the Williamsburg type, was undertaken through the generosity of Arthur A. Houghton, Jr., of Wye Plantation; it was completed in 1949. The old brick building was restored to its beautiful colonial condition; the vestry house, built oirginally in 1763, was rebuilt after the foundation had been discovered; and the church was refurnished with original and contemporary pieces and reproductions. Now as it stands under the giant oak, which was old when the brick chapel was built, Old Wye is enjoyed as a page of colonial history by thousands of visitors every year.

76

Third Haven Friends Meeting House (1682)

Easton, Talbot County, Maryland

At the head of the Third Haven River (from Tred Avon, a Welsh name meaning "Town on the River"), stands the oldest Friends meeting house and the second oldest frame house of worship in America (see Old Ship Meeting House, Hingham, Mass., No. 87). The first meeting of Quakers in Maryland was held in 1656. Third Haven Meeting was active before 1676, and the records are continuous from that year to the present time. George Fox, English founder of the Society of Friends, visited the Quakers of this vicinity in 1672. As early as 1679 there were at least two meeting houses in the region — one at Betty's Cove, the other at Tuckahoe. In December, 1682, after a visit with Lord Baltimore, William Penn attended a general meeting of Quakers on the Choptank River. In that same year, 1682, it was decided to locate a new meeting house at the present site; there is no evidence in the minutes that there was a previous meeting house here, nor that the present building was erected before 1684. Originally the building was symmetrical; in 1797, in order to enlarge it, a wall was moved back and the roof was extended, and the alteration gave the building a saltbox shape, familiar in New England but not in Maryland. In winter meetings are held in a modern brick meeting house on the grounds near by, and during the summer in this ancient Quaker meeting house.

77

Old White Marsh Church (c. 1685)
St. Peter's Church

Talbot County, Maryland

St. Peters' was one of the thirty Anglican parishes established by the Act of 1692. The damaged records show that the parish had a rector in 1690. Out in the open country near Hambleton, one finds this ruin of the brick parish church, which was built about 1685. The church was abandoned during the Civil War; in 1896 it was damaged by fire, and it was never restored. In the brick floor near the altar is a slab marking the graves of Daniel Maynadier, a Huguenot refugee from France after the Revocation of the Edict of Nantes (16....-1747, Rector 1711-1745), and his wife Hannah Martin. She had a harrowing experience that has been related in the family to this day. On the night that she was buried, grave robbers opened her grave to steal a precious ring. As they had difficulty in removing it from her finger, they cut off her finger. The shock revived her; she arose from the grave, made her way back to the house, and lived for several more years. Robert Morris, father of Robert Morris, the financier of the Revolution, died in 1750 and lies buried here.

78

Old Trinity Church (c. 1675)
Dorchester Parish Church

Church Creek, Dorchester County, Maryland

The Dorchester Parish Church at Church Creek, near Cambridge on the Eastern Shore of Maryland, was built between 1670 and 1680 and is one of the oldest churches in America. It antedates by more than a decade the establishment in Maryland of the Anglican Church in 1692. A tributary of Fishing Creek flows by the green lawn a few steps from the church, and the congregation can look out on it. Ezekiel Fogg wrote of ministering in Little Choptank as early as 1674, and this

building was erected in his time. The Little Choptank River, which gave its name to the region, is an arm of the Chesapeake Bay extending to within a few miles west of the church. The building has undergone two major alterations, one in 1850 when it was repaired and altered in many respects, the other from 1953-60 when it was restored completely to its original design of the seventeenth century. In 1850 the cruciform was altered to a T-form by the removal of the north transept, and three buttresses were added to support the north wall. The windows were altered to lancet style; the box pews, high pulpit, and sounding board were eliminated. The church then was given the name Trinity. The restoration of 1953-60 was a thorough project of the Williamsburg Res-

toration type, involving research into history and architecture, and requiring the skills of various artisans to duplicate the original design and materials. The restoration, costing about a quarter of a million dollars, was the project of Colonel Edgar William Garbisch and his wife Bernice as a memorial to her parents, Walter Percy Chrysler, automobile manufacturer, and his wife Della.

The building was restored in rectangular form by the removal of the remaining south wing. The round apse was retained, as shown in one of the photographs. The nave is only thirty-eight by twenty feet, and the sanctuary has a radius of six feet. Of the fifteen high box-pews, four are roundabouts facing the high, triple-deck pulpit and sounding board. The wooden floor was removed,

and the original large brick-tile floor was discovered. The Gothic-style lancet windows, clearly post-colonial, were restored to the colonial arched type. The brick, laid in Flemish bond, was given a pattern in lines parallel to the roof in the gable over the entrance at the west end.

When the restoration was celebrated in 1960, the forty-four families who are members of the church, and who filled most of the pews, were joined by a thousand visitors on the lawn around the church and on boats on the creek. All visitors are interested in the millstone, to the left of the round apse in the photograph, marking the grave of the miller, and the many stones dating from nearly three centuries ago, when this colonial Anglican church was new.

79

Old Green Hill Church (1733)
St. Bartholomew's Church

**on the Wicomico River,
Wicomico County, Maryland**

Stepney Parish was one of the thirty Anglican parishes established in 1692; it then was part of old Somerset County. No other trace remains of the town of Green Hill, a port of entry founded here on the Wicomico River in 1706. There were two chapels of ease in Stepney Parish: Christ Church, Broad Creek, Delaware (No. 27) and Spring Hill Church (No. 80). The first parish church, built before 1698, stood near the mouth of Haste's Creek and fifty yards from the site of the present building. The present Green Hill Church was built in 1733, on lot No. 16, in Green Hill Town, which had been sold to the Church in 1731. The building date appears in the brick of the gable end toward the river. The structure has not been altered inside or out. The original brick walls in Flemish bond, the box pews, the brick floor, the inside brick walls painted white, the high pulpit, and the clerk's desk all survive. The building was restored to good condition and, in 1887, consecrated as St. Bartholomew's Church.

80

Spring Hill Church (1771)
St. Paul's Church

Hebron, Wicomico County, Maryland

Stepney Parish was one of thirty parishes established by the Church of England in Maryland by the Act of 1692. The parish church was Green Hill Church (No. 79). Spring Hill was one of two chapels of ease in Stepney Parish, which was then in old Somerset County (see Christ Church, Broad Creek, Delaware, No. 27). The present building was erected from 1771-1773. Entries in an account book of Stepney Parish were made for payments to John Hobbs for work on the building in each of those three years. It replaced a chapel which had been built here before 1725. In 1827 Spring Hill Parish was formed from Stepney, and St. Paul's became the parish church. The woodwork, the altar, and the pews are original.

81

Manokin Presbyterian Church (1765)

Princess Anne, Somerset County, Maryland

Presbyterian meetings have been held in this area since 1672. This congregation was organized about 1686 by the Reverend Thomas Wilson. He was associated with Francis Makemie in establishing Presbyterianism in the Province of Maryland (see Rehoboth Church, No. 83). The present church was built in 1765, replacing a church that is believed to have been here as early as 1690. The Victorian-style tower was built in 1888. Only the brick walls in Flemish bond, now painted red, remain of the original building.

82

St. Andrew's Church (1770)

Princess Anne, Somerset County, Maryland

The Parish Church of Somerset stood about ten miles southwest of Princess Anne, on the bank of the Manokin River near Chesapeake Bay, at a point between the present estates of Almodington and Elmwood. The present brick house of worship in Princess Anne was built, in 1770, as a chapel of ease in Somerset Parish. The land had been bought three years earlier from Robert Gaddis. The building cost 1,400 pounds of tobacco, then equivalent to £800 sterling. The parish was one of the thirty into which Maryland was divided in 1692. The chapel here succeeded the King's Mill Chapel, which stood at King's Creek on two acres of land bought from Whittington King. When that building became unfit for use, the present chapel was built to replace it. The Parish Church of Somerset downstream became inundated, and it now is a submerged ruin under the waters of the Manokin River; the chapel in Princess Anne was made the Somerset Parish Church. It did not have another name until 1845, when the building was consecrated in the name of St. Andrew.

The simple rectangular building of 1770 remained unchanged until 1859, when the tower was built, the gift of a vestryman, William W. Johnston. It originally had a higher open belfry, but in 1893 the tower was reduced in height and the present spire was erected. Many of the interior furnishings were changed in 1865; the original pulpit, desk, and communion table were replaced, and the nave was rearranged with new pews on the sides of the present broad center aisle. In 1897 the east end of the building was rebuilt; the chancel was deepened, and the present high altar of marble was installed. The memorial windows of stained glass, beautiful in themselves, are modern departures from the colonial character of the old church. After a parish house had been built, the room attached to the church for a church school was refurnished, in 1935, as a chapel. In that same year, there was published a history of the parish, *Old Somerset on Eastern Shore, Maryland: A Study in Foundations and Founders*, by the Reverend Clayton Torrence, the rector of St. Andrew's Church.

83

Rehoboth Church (1706)
Makemie's Church

Rehoboth, Somerset County, Maryland

The Reverend Francis Makemie, of Scottish descent and born in Ireland, founded this church in 1683. He was sent here in that year from the Presbytery of Laggan, Ireland, at the request of Colonel William Stevens, of the Governor's Council. At Stevens' Rehoboth plantation on the Pocomoke River there was a community of many Presbyterians. The name, "Rehoboth," meaning "open spaces," was taken from Genesis 26:22, "and he called the name of it Rehoboth; and he said, For now the Lord hath made room for us, and we shall be fruitful in the land." As the congregation was organized by Presbyterians rather than by Calvinists of the Reformed or Congregational churches, it is considered to be the first Presbyterian church in America.

The first church building is believed to have stood beside the Pocomoke River, and to have been built of cypress. The present building was erected in, or immediately after, 1706, the year in which Makemie served as moderator in the formation of the first presbytery in America, the Presbytery of Philadelphia. Because of the law in Maryland against a church owning property, it was built on his own land, and it was called Makemie's Church. Upon his death the property was willed to the congregation. (Ten miles south of Rehoboth, in Accomac County, Eastern Shore of Virginia, a granite statue marks his grave.) The design of the brick building is similar to that of the church in Ireland (now Northern Ireland) where Makemie was ordained. Originally it had doors in the south wall and a pulpit to the north, in the Scottish style; later alterations made windows of the doors, opened an entrance at the west end, and, to conserve heat, installed a lower ceiling under the original high-arched ceiling. The old pulpit in which Makemie preached has been replaced, but the old box pews are still in use.

84

Coventry Parish Church (1784)
Rehoboth Episcopal Church

Rehoboth, Somerset County, Maryland

This is the ruin of the second Coventry Parish Church, built in 1784. (A bronze tablet on the wall gives the date 1740, evidently in error.) The first Coventry Parish Church building, erected before 1697, stood adjoining the present site and immediately behind the ruin. The foundations of the first building were discovered in 1933, and their corners are marked; it was erected before 1697. The vestry of Coventry Parish recorded a protest against the preaching of the Reverend George McNish in "a Meeting house lately erected very nigh to the church at Rehoboth." McNish was a Presbyterian minister who had accompanied the Reverend Francis Makemie to Rehoboth from London, where the latter had gone to arouse interest in the Presbyterian Church in America. The Episcopal church stood on the Rehoboth plantation near Makemie's Church (No. 83).

This second church building was used until 1900, after which time it was allowed to fall into ruins. In 1928 the walls were capped and an altar was built in the roofless rectangle.

85

All Hallows Church (1748)

Snow Hill, Worcester County, Maryland

Snow Hill Parish was one of the thirty Anglican parishes established by the Act of 1692. In 1713 it was referred to as All Hallows Parish, and it has had that name ever since 1724. Originally the parish was in old Somerset County; in 1742 this parish was divided off as Worcester County, and in 1744 the northern part of the county was set off as All Hallows Parish. The parish church has always been located at Snow Hill, on the Pocomoke River. The first church was built, about 1697 to 1700, in the western part of the town, between the present site and the river. The parish had a chapel of ease, dating from some time before 1703, at the site of the present St. Martin's Church (No. 86).

In 1748 building began. The old pews and interior woodwork were replaced in the 1870's, and the present altar, the reredos, the gallery, and the ceiling were installed in the 1890's, but the exterior is original. The Bible, dated "London 1701," shown in the vestibule, was a gift from Queen Anne; it was first used in the present building when it was completed in 1756.

86

St. Martin's Church (1755)

Worcester County, Maryland

As early as 1703 in Snow Hill Parish, later called All Hallows Parish (No. 85), there was a chapel of ease located here in the South Branch (then known as "Chapell Branch") of the St. Martin's River. In 1744 the northern part of All Hallows Parish was set off as Worcester Parish, and St. Martin's Chapel became the parish church when Worcester Parish was organized in 1753. St. Martin's, in turn, had a chapel of ease in a region that was in Maryland until the settlement of the long border dispute awarded it to Delaware (see Prince George's Chapel, Dagsboro, Delaware, No. 25).

The present St. Martin's Church, replacing the former chapel on the same site, was built at the same time as All Hallows, Snow Hill. It was begun in 1755 and finished in 1759. The brick is laid in Flemish bond, and there is a cove cornice beneath the low-pitched roof. The box pews, gallery, and chancel were installed in 1763, and the building, which is almost square, and its furnishings are substantially unchanged. Services were held throughout the difficult period of the Revolution, even though the rector, the Reverend John Bowie, in 1776 was taken to Annapolis and imprisoned as a royalist. In the 1800's, however, the church was neglected and it became dilapidated. Today it stands restored but alone in a pine wood, a reminder of a colonial period of activity and growth in Maryland.

MASSACHUSETTS

		Denomination	Material
87	Old Ship Meeting House (1681) Hingham, Plymouth County	Congregational	Wood
88	First Parish Meeting House (1747) Cohasset, Norfolk County	Congregational	Wood
89	South Hingham Meeting House (1742) South Hingham, Plymouth County	Congregational	Wood
90	Pembroke Friends Meeting House (1706) Pembroke, Plymouth County	Friends	Wood
91	West Parish Meeting House (1717) West Barnstable, Barnstable County	Congregational	Wood
92	Old Indian Church (1717) Mashpee, Barnstable County	Congregational	Wood
93	Old North Vestry (c. 1732) Nantucket, Nantucket County	Presbyterian	Wood
94	Old South Meeting House (1729) Boston, Suffolk County	Congregational	Brick
95	King's Chapel (1749) Boston, Suffolk County	Anglican	Stone
96	Old North Church (1723) Boston, Suffolk County	Anglican	Brick
97	Holden Chapel (1742) Cambridge, Middlesex County	Congregational	Brick
98	Christ Church (1760) Cambridge, Middlesex County	Anglican	Wood
99	Old Meeting House (1732) Burlington, Middlesex County	Congregational	Wood
100	First Parish Meeting House (1755) Groton, Middlesex County	Congregational	Wood
101	First Church (1762) Dedham, Norfolk County	Congregational	Wood
102	Clapboardtrees Meeting House (1730) Westwood, Norfolk County	Congregational	Wood
103	First Congregational Church (1766) Shrewsbury, Worcester County	Congregational	Wood
104	Chestnut Hill Meeting House (1769) Millville, Worcester County	Congregational	Wood
105	Congregational Church (1784) Phillipston, Worcester County	Congregational	Wood
106	Longmeadow Meeting House (1767) Longmeadow, Hampden County	Congregational	Wood
107	Southampton Congregational Church (1786) Southampton, Hampshire County	Congregational	Wood
108	Old Parish Congregational Church (1760) Sheffield, Berkshire County	Congregational	Wood

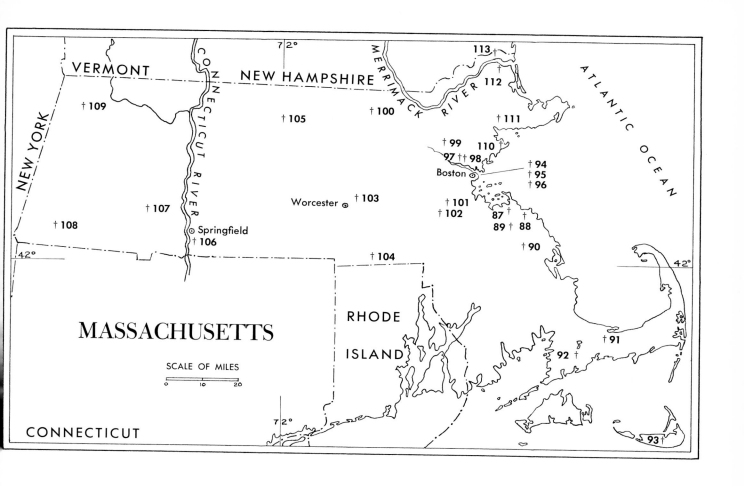

	Denomination	Material
109 East Hoosac Friends Meeting House (1786) Adams, Berkshire County	Friends	Wood
110 St. Michael's Church (1714) Marblehead, Essex County	Anglican	Wood
111 Second Congregational Church North Beverly, Essex County	Congregational	Wood
112 Old South Church (1714) Newburyport, Essex County	Presbyterian	Wood
113 Rocky Hill Meeting House (1785) Amesbury, Essex County	Congregational	Wood

SUMMARY

Congregational	19	Brick	3
Friends	2	Wood	23
Presbyterian	2	Stone	1
Anglican	4		
Buildings	27		27

87

Old Ship Meeting House (1681)
First Parish Meeting House

Main Street, Hingham, Plymouth County, Massachusetts

Here in Hingham, on the South Shore of Boston, within a short distance of the site of the Pilgrims' landing at Plymouth, stands the oldest frame house of worship in America, built in 1681. The parish was organized and the first meeting house was begun in 1635 (the twelfth to be built in Massachusetts), under the first pastor, Peter Hobart. He was a graduate of Oxford, and had come that same year from Hingham, England, to Bare Cove, where fellow townsmen had settled; in September they changed the name of the settlement to Hingham. The congregation was Congregational with Presbyterian influence, and it was to become Unitarian.

Peter Hobart was succeeded as pastor, in 1678, by John Norton, a graduate of Harvard College. In the latter's ministry, Old Ship, the second and present meeting house, was built. The frame was raised the twenty-sixth, twenty-seventh, and twenty-eighth days of July, 1681, and the building was opened for public worship January 8, 1682. The cost to the town was £430. The name, "Old Ship," is suggested by the curved timbers and knees used in the supporting roof structure by ship's carpenters, and by the captain's walk in "the turret" and the compass rose beneath the spire and, again, beneath the sounding board over the pulpit. The west gallery was added in 1730; in 1755 the east gallery, the high pulpit, and the box pews were installed. In 1731 a ceiling was built below the beams and trusses. The meeting house had a narrow escape from destruction in 1791; it was voted to tear it down and replace it with a new building, but fortunately the plan was not carried out. In 1869 alterations were

made that included removal of the old pulpit and the box pews. In 1930 a thorough restoration was undertaken, through the generosity of Eben Howard Gay, a descendant of the third pastor, Ebenezer Gay. The ceiling was removed, and the ship-like timbers supporting the roof again were exposed. The original pulpit was found, and thirty-two of the eighty pew doors were located and restored, many of them having been kept by descendants of the original pew holders. The pews are marked where services were attended by General Benjamin Lincoln, who received the sword of General Cornwallis at Yorktown, and Samuel Lincoln, an ancestor of Abraham Lincoln, who had come to Hingham in 1637, and who, together with many other people prominent in colonial times, lies buried in the Old Ship graveyard. This Congregational church was involved from the first in the Unitarian movement that swept New England after the Revolution. Dr. Ebenezer Gay became known as the first American Unitarian, and his successor, Henry Ware, was called from Old Ship to be Hollis Professor of Divinity at Harvard, where the movement originated. His appointment precipitated the Great Debate of the Unitarian Controversy, and the American Unitarian Society was founded, in 1825, as a result. The First Parish in Hingham, as it is officially called, continues to be Congregational in polity, though Unitarian by affiliation.

88

First Parish Meeting House (1747)

**The Green, Cohasset, Norfolk County,
Massachusetts**

The Cohasset area was discovered by Captain John Smith in 1614, after some years in Virginia but six years before the arrival of the Pilgrims at Plymouth. In his *Generall Historie*, Smith described a fight with the Indians here. Cohasset was a part of Hingham (see Old Ship, No. 87). The first meeting house was built about 1713, on "The Plain." This was then the Second Parish of Hingham. The first pastor was Nehmiah Hobart, a grandson of the Reverend Peter Hobart,

first pastor at Hingham; he was a Harvard classmate of Ebenezer Gay, who became the third pastor at Hingham. Cohasset was incorporated as a town in 1770, and the parish became the First Parish of Cohasset. The second, and present, meeting house was built in 1747. Before the building was finished a new pastor was installed, the Reverend John Brown, another Harvard graduate; he encouraged the congregation to fight for liberty, and he served as chaplain to a Colonial regiment. Originally the building had a belfry on the roof. The steeple was built to replace it, and the front entrance was made through the tower. The meeting house contains a gallery and two flights of stairs. The fine pulpit is supposed to have been copied, in 1755, from the one in Old Ship Meeting House, Hingham (No. 87).

89

South Hingham Meeting House (1742)

South Hingham, Plymouth County, Massachusetts

Originally the Congregationalists of South Hingham were members of the first parish in Hingham. Cohasset was set off as the second parish, and in 1745 South Hingham was set off as the third. In 1746 Daniel Shute was ordained pastor of this Third Church of Christ, Hingham, and he served as such until 1800. When Cohasset was incorporated as a town, South Hingham became the Second Congregational Parish. It was separated from the Hingham parish only after a long controversy between Dr. Daniel Shute, an ardent Whig, and Dr. Ebenezer Gay, a moderate Tory who opposed separation. In the course of the controversy Dr. Gay wrote to Dr. Shute the following words which had been engraved on the wall of a new meeting house: "Build not for faction nor a Party, but for promoting Faith and Repentance in communion with all that love our Lord Jesus Christ in sincerity."

Three years before the separation a meeting house had been built, in 1742, on Glad Tidings Plain. Typical for its time, the building had an entrance on the south side and another to the galleries on the west side. The pulpit and sounding board were on the north side, and there were box pews. The repairs of 1756 changed it little. In 1792 the west porch was added, and a tower was built on the east end. From 1829-1830 the south and west entrances were abandoned; the tower was widened, and its two doors became the main entrance. The box pews were replaced, and the pulpit was moved to the west end. Other changes were made in 1869, and today the meeting house no longer resembles the original colonial structure. Like the church in Hingham, this one is now Unitarian.

90

Pembroke Friends Meeting House (1706)

North Pembroke, Plymouth County, Massachusetts

There is evidence of the Society of Friends being active in the Pembroke region before 1660. Their official records began in 1676, but they have been lost. The first meeting house of the Society was built in 1678 at Scituate, on the coast north of Pembroke and south of Boston. The first preacher was Edward Wanton, who, as a member of the King's Guard in Boston, had witnessed the execution of Quakers, and who was so impressed with their faith that he had been converted. He moved to Scituate in the Plymouth Colony, where Quakers were not severely persecuted as they were under the Puritans in Boston, and there he drew many people to the faith of the Friends, as did his son Michael after him.

When the congregation outgrew the first meeting house, a second was built on the land of Edward Wanton. In 1706 it was moved to the present location in North Pembroke. Tradition gives two versions of the move: one that it was hauled by oxen on the ice of the river, the other that it was carried on large flat boats called gundalows that were used on the river for carrying hay and wood. The building is given this date of 1706 in the absence of any record of the year in which it was built. The general austerity of the interior, with plain benches on bare floor, is in the Quaker tradition. The rope handrail to the gallery and the treatment of the hand-hewn uprights in the corners, with carving at the top, reflect the proximity to the ocean and the tradition that the building was erected by shipbuilders.

The Society flourished for two hundred years, but it declined in the present century, and meetings were discontinued. In 1928 the building was restored by descendants of the early members, with donations also from various other denominations and faiths, and it is now in the care of the Pembroke Friends Meeting House Association. Meetings for worship are held on one First Day in July, August, and September, under the sponsorship of Friends Meetings from Cambridge, Lynn, New Bedford, Providence, and other localities.

91

West Parish Meeting House (1717)

West Barnstable, Barnstable County, Massachusetts

This congregation was established in Barnstable by the founders of Congregationalism in England under the Reverend Henry Jacob. He passed slowly from Puritanism to Separatism, and he founded an open-minded and tolerant Congregationalism that came to prevail in the Plymouth Colony, as compared to the narrower spirit of Puritan Congregationalism in the Massachusetts Bay Colony. The Baptist Church derived from the Congregationalism of the Plymouth Colony (see First Baptist Church, Providence, No. 260). In 1616 Jacob organized a church in Southwark, across the Thames from London, which has been referred to as the mother church of the denomination. In that country of the Established Church of England, Jacob's successor, John Lothrop, was imprisoned for three years and then was banished. In 1634 he sailed to Boston with thirty-four members of his church and went to Scituate. In 1639 he and most of his group moved to Barnstable. Here they built the first meeting house, on Lothrop's Hill. A second building was erected in 1681.

The present meeting house was built in the West Parish of Barnstable and dedicated in 1717. In 1852 the colonial structure was remodeled drastically. At that time it was of the style of the meeting house in Cohasset (No. 88), but the remodeled building revealed little of its colonial design. The frame was retained, cut in half and lengthened, new clapboards and roof were applied, and a new steeple was built. The new windows were "in the modern style." In recent years

the building again needed repairs, and in 1947 a campaign was started to restore the historic structure to its colonial design. In 1953 the work was undertaken, sponsored by the West Parish Memorial Foundation, and a thorough and beautiful restoration has been accomplished. The added length was removed, and the building resumed its original dimensions. Markings in the framing gave clues to locations and measurements, and with the aid of old records, the high pulpit, sounding board, pews, galleries, and stairs were all restored in their original places. Some of the original material, used in the remodeling of the tower and other features in 1852, was now used again in its original place. Even some of the window frames and paneling that had been auctioned in 1852 for local use, were recovered or copied. The West Parish Meeting House now stands as an authoritative New England meeting house of the First Period, and it houses a congregation that was derived directly from one of the oldest of that denomination in the world.

92

Old Indian Church (1717)

Mashpee, Barnstable County, Massachusetts

The first Indian church at Mashpee was established by Richard Bourne, a Congregational missionary, in 1658. The original frame building was erected at Bryant's Neck, North Mashpee, in 1676. It had only one center door. In 1717 it was moved to this site, on Falmouth Road between North and South Mashpee, and was remodeled. Two doors were installed, with steps made from a halved millstone. In 1923 the building was completely restored, and the early features were retained; it was rededicated that year. There are box pews, an arched ceiling, and an organ gallery. There is an old burying ground. The original church was Congregational, but according to the records of the Reverend William Apes, a Pequot Indian preacher, the Wampanoag Indians native to this section did not always enjoy the privileges of that Church; through the influence of "Blind Joseph Amos," another Indian preacher, the Indians became Baptists under a special act of the legislature (see West Parish Meeting House, West Barnstable, No. 91). At first they were under a neighboring Baptist church, but later they became independent. In summer the church is open to visitors, and services are held.

93

Old North Vestry (c. 1732)

Nantucket, Massachusetts

There is a tradition, evidently unfounded, that the building on Nantucket Island called the Old North Vestry was built originally in 1711 as a Friends meeting house at Maxcy's Pond and moved here. We know that in 1765 the structure was moved to the site of the present church on Beacon Hill, and was finished as the North Shore Meeting House. While it is not certain, there is evidence that originally it was the Presbyterian Meeting House, which was new in 1732. A tower was added in 1795. In 1834 the present North Church was built, and the old structure, after the tower had been removed, was set back and made the Vestry. It is now used by the Sunday school and for parish affairs of the adjoining North Church, the First Congregational Church.

94

Old South Meeting House (1729)
Third Church, Congregational

Washington and Milk Streets,
Boston, Suffolk County, Massachusetts

In 1662 the General Synod of Massachusetts was convened to discuss the question of church membership being required for citizenship. Twenty-nine members of the First Church of Boston disagreed with the requirement; they seceded and formed the Third Church, known as Old South. The feud between the two continued for some years, and it ended only when the two Congregational groups found themselves allied in opposition to the introduction of the Church of England into Boston. The first meeting house was built in 1699, a two-story cedar building with a steeple. The site was that of the last residence of Governor John Winthrop, "Governor's Green." Benjamin Franklin was born January 6, 1706, across Milk Street from the meeting house, and on that day he was taken over to be baptized. The pastor, Samuel Willard, forced Judge Samuel Sewall (1652-1730), who had presided at the witchcraft trials in Salem, to make a public confession of his error in the meeting house.

In 1729 work began on the present brick meeting house, which replaced the first. It was designed by Robert Twelves and built by Joshua Blanchard; the latter also built Faneuil Hall, which, like Old South, was a hotbed of revolution. Both were danger signals to Pitt and Burke in Parliament at London. In addition to services for worship in the meeting house, there were meetings in opposition to the English Church, English taxes, and English government. The Boston Tea Party, for example, on December 4, 1773, started from an angry meeting of about seven thousand people in and around the meeting house, in which Samuel Adams and Josiah Quincy inflamed the crowd to action against the tea tax. The British took revenge on the meeting house; during their military occupation of Boston in the Revolution, General Burgoyne had the pews ripped out, except one that was used as a pigsty, and the auditorium served as a riding ring for the Queen's Light Dragoons. The pews were restored after the Revolution, but in 1876 they were removed again when the building ceased to function as a church. Because of the increased land value, the property was offered for sale at that time; it was bought by the women of Massachusetts, who preserved

it as a historical landmark. The fabric of the building — its brick laid in Flemish bond, its doors, windows, and two tiers of galleries (the upper gallery was used by Negro slaves) — are all original. The pulpit is a replica of the one that rang out in social and political protest. The congregation now worships at Copley Square in the New Old South Third Church.

95

King's Chapel (1749)

Boston, Suffolk County, Massachusetts

During its colonial history, King's Chapel was the first Episcopal church in New England, and it became the first Unitarian church in America. After the arrival of the Reverend Robert Ratcliffe in Boston — the first Anglican priest commissioned to officiate in New England — the parish was organized May 15, 1686. The Puritans, who had three Established Congregational churches in Boston, had left England as Dissenters from the Church of England, and they refused to permit the use of their meeting houses for Anglican worship. With their permission, the first services were held in the library of the town house. Then Governor Edmund Andros ordered the congregation of Old South Church (No. 94) to permit the use of their meeting house for Anglican worship until a church could be built. The result was about two years of joint use of Old South under conditions of considerable hostility, the Congregationalists and the Anglicans holding services consecutively on a Sunday. Meanwhile, the Congregationalists would not sell a plot of land for an Anglican church site, and the Governor again intervened by ordering a corner of the burying ground to be made available. The building of the first church was begun in 1688. The congregation, who had been meeting without any name, called the new church Queen's Chapel for a time and then changed the name to King's Chapel. It was enlarged in 1710, but by 1741 the congregation had outgrown the building which had been doubled in size, and plans for a larger one were started.

In 1749 the cornerstone of the present building was laid. The designer was Peter Harrison, who had come from Yorkshire to Newport, Rhode Island. Starting as an amateur, he became the first of American architects and the most distinguished one of his time; he also designed Christ Church, Cambridge (No. 98), and Touro Synagogue, New-

port, Rhode Island (No. 271). The original design, now lost, called for a spire on the tower, but funds were short, and to this day the spire has not been built. The walls are of Quincy granite, and the exterior of dressed stone is plain. The interior, however, which is from that of James Gibbs at St. Martin-in-the-Fields, London, is one of the finest in America.

As this church was the Chapel Royal while Massachusetts was under the rule of a British governor, it accumulated a wealth of interior decorations, silver service, and fabrics, and, with uniformed officers of various British regiments present in the congregation, the splendor did not escape the notice of the Puritans of Boston. After the Continental troops under George Washington had driven the British forces from Boston in 1776, the rector of King's Chapel and eighteen other clergymen, together with about thirty families of the congregation and many others who were still loyal to the Crown, sailed to Halifax in a ship of the British fleet. For a time the church was called simply the "Stone Chapel," and then the old name was resumed. Old South Meeting House being in need of repair at the time, its congregation was invited to worship at King's Chapel; this kindness put an end to the old feud between the two congregations. The pillared portico was installed at the tower entrance about 1790, and was not part of the original design; the massive columns, associated with the heavy granite tower, surprisingly are made of wood painted gray. It was in 1785 that, under the rectorship of the Reverend James Freeman, King's Chapel became openly Unitarian. In 1814 the bell cracked, and in 1816 a new one was cast by Paul Revere at the Canton, Massachusetts foundry. This bell, which still rings here, was number 161 of the nearly four hundred cast by the Revere company.

96

Old North Church (1723)
Christ Church

Boston, Suffolk County, Massachusetts

Old North Church is the oldest church still standing in Boston. It was built on Copp's Hill in 1723. Donations for the building were made by many of the congregation of King's Chapel, its mother church, which was no longer large enough for its parish. The Reverend Timothy Cutler, former Congregational minister and rector of Yale College, had been ordained in the Church of England, and he became the first rector, serving for many years. William Price, cabinetmaker and dealer in books and engravings, drew the design. The spire, rising to 195 feet, was built in 1740; it was blown down in 1804 and was rebuilt to a height of 175 feet, from a design by Charles Bulfinch that was similar to the original. The peal of eight bells was made by Abel Rudhall, of Glouces-

ter, England, in 1744, and was rung by Paul Revere as a boy. When Longfellow wrote "one if by land, two if by sea," in his poem, "Paul Revere's Ride," he referred to signal lanterns to be hung in the tower of Old North Church. A statue of Paul Revere on horseback stands in the park behind the church. In 1912 the building was restored to its colonial condition. The box pews were restored with much of their original materials, and their doors were marked with the names of the original holders. The son of Paul

Revere bought one of the pews, and it has continued to be held in his family. The apse was restored to its original plan with a large window. In the celebration service, upon completion of the restoration and the removal of "improvements," Bishop William Lawrence preached from the original text of the first rector, Timothy Cutler, written 189 years before. In 1954 the steeple was blown down again by a hurricane, and again it has been restored, by popular subscription from all over the country.

97

Holden Chapel (1742)

Cambridge, Middlesex County, Massachusetts

Built in 1742, Holden Chapel is the third oldest building in Harvard Yard. It is sixteen years older than Christ Church, Cambridge (No. 98). This gem of Georgian architecture was the gift of the widow of Samuel Holden, a wealthy merchant of London. His will provided that if his estate exceeded £60,000 the surplus be distributed, at the discretion of his wife and children, in charitable uses, "such as promoting true Religion, I mean Sobriety, Righteousnes, and Godliness, without regard to any party or denomination, either here

or in New England." Holden had been a member of Parliament, a governor of the Bank of England, and a leader of the Dissenters. He had been sympathetic with the Dissenters in Massachusetts, and in 1741, when the northern part of Worcester was made a township, it was given the name of Holden in his honor. The chapel served the College in its capacity as such for twenty years, and since then, according to Samuel F. Batchelder in his *Bits of Harvard History*, it has been used as "senate-chamber, court-house, barracks, carpenter-shop, engine-shop, dissecting theatre, recitation building, museum, lecture-hall, clubhouse, laboratory, general auditorium — everything *but* a chapel." Harvard College was Congregational during the time when the building served as its chapel.

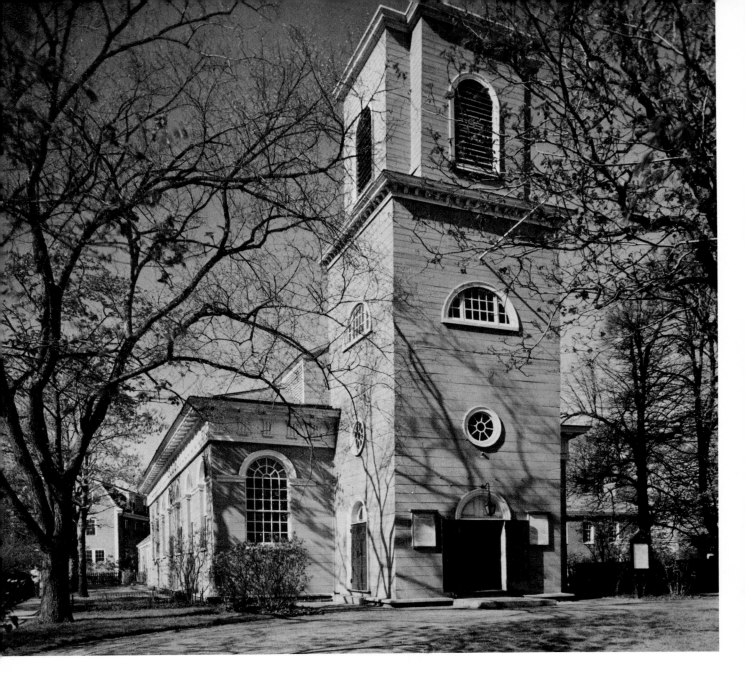

98

Christ Church (1760)

Cambridge, Middlesex County, Massachusetts

Christ Church was built in 1760, partly with the contribution of two years' salary by its first rector, East Apthorp. He was one of eighteen children of Charles and Grizel Apthorp, all devout members of King's Chapel. He had gone from Boston Latin School to Cambridge, England, had been ordained there and made a fellow of Jesus College, and had returned as a missionary of the Society for the Propagation of the Gospel in Foreign Parts to found this church, against the active opposition of the Puritans. The architect was Peter Harrison, who also designed King's Chapel, Boston (No. 95) and Touro Synagogue, Newport, Rhode Island (No. 271). Although it is in wood instead of stone, the simple design of the exterior resembles King's Chapel, even to the flat tower with belfry but no spire. Inside there are no side galleries as there are in King's Chapel. The organ loft is original, but most of the interior resulted from various alterations.

During the Revolution, with strong feeling against everything English, the church was closed, and the parish did not recover fully for a long time after the war. Following the Battle of Lexington in 1775, the building was used to shelter some of the troops of the growing revolutionary army. It was opened for services on Sunday, December 31, 1775, at which Colonel Palfrey read the prayers, and General George Washington and his wife Martha attended. It was opened again for the funeral of a British officer, who had been held in Cambridge among the captives taken at Fort Ticonderoga; a mob from the town then entered the church and wrecked its interior. The

mark of a musket bullet remains in the wall beside the entrance. In 1857 the building was enlarged by the addition of two bays between the chancel and the nave. In 1853 the forty-four box pews were replaced, and in the 1880's the building was decorated along the lines of Victorian taste; the chancel was enlarged at that time to accommodate the choir, which was transferred from the loft. The Old Town Burying Ground, 1636, lies between Christ Church and the First Parish Church, and there in common ground lie the remains of Anglicans and Congregationalists who were severely divided during their colonial lives.

99

Old Meeting House (1732)
Church of Christ

Burlington, Middlesex County, Massachusetts

When this meeting house was built, in 1732, this section known as Sawshin, or Shushan, was part of Woburn. In 1799 it was incorporated as the town of Burlington. As it was some distance to the Congregational meeting house in Woburn, this one was built, and three years later, in 1735, this Second Parish of Woburn was organized. The pastor in 1799 was the Reverend John Marrett, a direct descendant in the fifth generation of Henry Dunster, the first president of Harvard College. The building was repaired and painted that year, and the diamond panes were replaced with square glass.

Originally the building was plain, with no tower or ornamentation. It was used in that form until 1846, and then commenced a series of alterations and remodelings. The first changes to be made that year were so drastic that, before the work began, the pastor preached a "Farewell to the pews — the galleries, where singers sang, Deacon's Seat, Sounding Board, Pulpit, House of God in thy present form." The length of the building was increased by ten feet; a steeple was built and a bell was installed, and a porch was added. After the work was completed in 1846, the meeting house was dedicated for the first time. The new form satisfied the congregation until 1888; then the steeple was removed, a new tower and porch were built, and the interior was entirely changed, from single auditorium with gallery to multiple rooms for the accommodation of various parish functions. Upon its reopening in 1888 the meeting house was rededicated. This meeting house stood among scenes of the American Revolution. On the green in front of the building, troops assembled, and they attended church bearing arms. Here gunfire was heard during the long siege of Boston by the Continental Army. The congregation remained Trinitarian while many of the Congregational churches in the Boston area were becoming Unitarian.

100

First Parish Meeting House (1755)

Groton, Middlesex County, Massachusetts

Groton is one of the old towns in the Boston area; it was settled and incorporated in 1655. The Reverend John Miller was the first pastor of the Congregational Church in Groton; he came here in 1662. During the war with the Indians known as King Philip's War, 1675-1676, Groton was destroyed and abandoned. Within two decades after being rebuilt, the town again was raided by Indians during Queen Anne's War, and a number of the inhabitants were killed. The present meet-ing house was erected in 1755. As the Congregational Church was established by law in Massachusetts, town meetings were held in this meeting house until 1859. Here also sat the Court of General Sessions of the Peace and the Court of Common Pleas for Middlesex County from 1776 to 1787. During the Revolution men of Groton were active in the army. Many of them fought in the Battle of Bunker Hill, June 17, 1775. In 1839 the building was turned to face the Common, and it was remodeled extensively; the Greek Revival portico is of that date. Practically none of the original interior survives. In 1826 this church became Unitarian, and the Congregational-ists of the parish who remained Trinitarian were forced to build a meeting house elsewhere.

101

First Church in Dedham (1762)
Church of Christ in Dedham

Dedham, Norfolk County, Massachusetts

By order of the General Court of the Bay Colony, a plantation was laid out in 1636, about two miles from the Charles River. The petition requested that the name be "Contentment," but the General Court ordered that the new plantation be "Dedham." The first recorded meeting of the inhabitants was held on August 18, 1636. The Church of Christ in Dedham was gathered on November 8, 1638. After the South, or Tiot, Parish had been laid off in 1730, the remainder of Dedham became known as the First Parish in Dedham, and the church as the First Church in Dedham. The parish, instead of the town, then began to support the church, a point that became important nearly a century later. In 1638 work was begun "to contrive the Fabricke of a Meetinghouse." The roof of the first building was thatched. As was customary in all towns where the Congregational Church was established by law, town meetings were held in the meeting house on week days and religious services on Sundays. Meetings in this first building were summoned by the beating of a drum. The choice of pews was in the order of magnitude of the tax paid. The second meeting house was built in 1673, and it served for nearly a century.

In 1762 the third and present building was erected on the site of the second, as soon as that building had been pulled down. There were entrances through the tower at the north end, which carried a steeple and bell, and through porches on the east and south sides. This form was kept until after a schism had occurred in the church. In 1818 a pastor was called by the parish, and the action did not win the concurrence of the majority of the church. A suit of replevin was brought by the deacons of the First Church in Dedham against the deacon of the non-concurring majority to recover the church property. With Daniel Webster representing the defendants, the case was tried by jury in 1820, and the plaintiffs won the "Dedham Decision." The case established the interest of the parish in the property of the church. The non-concurring group then broke away and formed the Allin Congregational Church, which stands across the street from the Church Green. The old meeting house was then remodeled extensively. The tower and steeple were removed from the north end, the roof was turned to run east and west, the east end was extended, and the present tower and steeple were built at the east end facing the Church Green. The old square pews were removed after the Civil War. The church is now Unitarian.

102

Clapboardtrees Meeting House (1730)
First Baptist Church

Westwood, Norfolk County, Massachusetts

The towns of Westwood and Norwood originally were parts of Dedham, and their inhabitants went five or six miles to attend church and town meetings at the Church of Christ in Dedham (No. 101). The Westwood section was known then as Clapboardtrees Parish. About 1729 both communities petitioned to be set off as a separate parish, and the Court acted favorably by creating the Second Parish of Dedham, including both. The two could not agree on a place for a meeting house, and both built their own. The present Clapboardtrees Meeting House was begun in 1730. The Court acted on this division of the Second Parish by returning the Clapboardtrees Parish to the First Parish of Dedham, and allowing Norwood to continue as the Second Parish. The people of West Dedham, as it was called for many years, continued to worship in the Clapboardtrees Meeting House instead of the First Parish Church; the Court then relented by setting off the present Westwood as the Third Parish of Dedham. The town of Westwood was not incorporated until 1897.

All went well in this Third Parish until 1809. By then the old Clapboardtrees Meeting House was in need of repair, and in the course of considering whether and where to build a new one, the parish divided into two factions. One faction erected a new building on a hill near the site of the old one, and they became Unitarian, as did the mother church in Dedham. The old meeting house was sold at auction; the other faction bought it and moved it in sections by ox-cart to its present site on Church Square. As the law forbade more than one church of a denomination in a parish, this group organized the First Baptist Church of Dedham and Medfield, and services were held in the two towns on alternate Sundays.

In 1824 the church was incorporated as the First Baptist Society of Dedham, and when the town of Westwood was incorporated, in 1897, it became the First Baptist Society of Westwood.

An unusual feature of the structure is that the clapboards run in width from one and one-half inches at the base of the walls to four and one-half inches at the eaves. Usually the scale was reversed in order to give an added perspective of height. In 1834 the church was enlarged, and it is believed that the rear gallery section, the vestibule, and the belfry were added at that time. The building was moved a second time, by a few feet, to accommodate a new road, and it now stands on a narrow triangle where the streets restrict any further expansion.

103

First Congregational Church (1766)

Shrewsbury, Worcester County, Massachusetts

Not until 1717 was the original grant made to forty families for settling Shrewsbury. It provided that an orthodox minister (Congregational) be settled within three years. The first meeting house in the new settlement was built in 1721. "Setting up" the meeting house was accomplished after two sawmills had been set up. It was located on Rocky Pine Plain, a little northeast of the present site. The parish was organized in 1723, when the first minister, Job Cushing, was installed. He had been born in Hingham, where his grandfather had come from England in 1638, three years after Peter Hobart (see Old Ship Meeting House, Hingham, No. 87), and he had been graduated from Harvard College in the Class of 1714.

When the congregation outgrew the old meeting house, they pulled it down in 1766 and built the present one near by. In accordance with custom, the town had provided a barrel of rum from Boston, and after raising the frame all who had taken part joined in a supper. The first sermon preached in the new building, July 17, 1766, was from Genesis 28:17 — "this is none other but the house of God, and this is the gate of Heaven." The Reverend Joseph Sumner, the pastor, had been graduated from Yale College in 1759. He and his wife lived for thirty-four years in the Artemus Ward House, which he had bought. Ward was the outstanding citizen of Shrewsbury and a devout member of this church — soldier, general in the Revolution and the first general to be commissioned in the Colonial Army, merchant, lawyer, representative in the General Court, and chief justice. His house was given by a descendant to Harvard College, and it is now open to the public.

The architect of this second building was Daniel Hemingway, a well-known church builder. In 1807 the tower and steeple were added. In 1834 the high pulpit and box pews were replaced, the building was turned, a vestry was built on the basement floor, and the south and east porches were removed. In the hurricane of 1938 the steeple was blown down, but it was rebuilt promptly on the ground and raised into place.

104

Chestnut Hill Meeting House (1769)

Millville, Worcester County, Massachusetts

The location of the Chestnut Hill Meeting House was in Mendon, settled in 1662. In 1845, after a rousing meeting in the present meeting house, the inhabitants seceded from Mendon to form the town of Blackstone, and in 1916 the small village of Millville was incorporated. The congregation was organized in 1768 as the Third Parish in Mendon, Congregational. The meeting house was built in 1769. It had a short life as a church. The first and only settled minister left after a few years, as a result of a dispute over wood supply and stipend. The pastor of the First Church in Mendon conducted services on Sunday afternoons until about the time of the Civil War. The building was repaired for the Centennial in 1869, and since then the property has been in the care of a corporation as a historical landmark and for occasional services.

The building is a typical square meeting house practically in its original form. There is a high pulpit with stairway, a sounding board, deacons' seats, white box pews with batten doors, a drop-leaf communion table on the chancel rail, and three galleries — the choir was in the center gallery and unmarried boys and girls were in separate galleries on the two sides. The window behind the pulpit contains several panes of the original glass.

105

Congregational Church (1784)

Phillipston, Worcester County, Massachusetts

This building was begun in the fall of 1784, and in January, 1785, the "pew ground" was auctioned. The location was in the town of Templeton, a part of the grant known as "Narragansett Number Six" which had been settled in 1751. In 1786, when the town was incorporated as Gerry, the Honorable Elbridge Gerry wanted to do something for this town which was taking his name, and he gave the glass for the church, which was still unfinished. It is possible that some of his window panes still survive. Gerry became governor of Massachusetts in 1810, and Vice President of the United States in the administration of James Madison in 1812. He is probably best known for the political practice which still carries his name, "gerrymandering." The town was ashamed of Gerry's political reputation and, in 1814, petitioned to have the name changed to Phillipston, in honor of the lieutenant governor of the Commonwealth, William Phillips, who served as deacon of Old South Church in Boston (No. 94).

The church was supported by taxation, and town meetings were held in the meeting house for over a century. Ballot boxes were stovepipe hats placed on the communion table. During a period of prosperity, in 1838, the church was moved fifty feet north to its present position. Here sloping ground permitted construction of a basement floor for Sunday school and town meetings. The front was extended fifteen feet, and the porch and spire were added. At the rear the old pews with doors are two steps above the aisle. In the gallery are the old high-back benches. The interior lighting is still by oil lamps.

106

Longmeadow Meeting House (1767)
First Church of Christ

First Church of Christ
Longmeadow, Hampden County, Massachusetts

The "long meddowe" on the Connecticut River was purchased from the Indians in 1636, and the town was settled in 1644 by families from Springfield. In 1709 those in the lower part of the town moved to the present higher location to be above flood water from the river. The first meeting house was built by the Congregationalists in 1714. The second and present one was built in 1767, and it served for sixty years without alteration. In 1828 the pulpit was moved, galleries were built on three sides, and modern pews replaced the box pews. In 1874 the building was moved from its location on the Green to its present site beside and facing it, and the meeting house was then enlarged. The side walls were kept intact while the rear end was moved back and the building was extended; the interior was remodeled completely, and the present front and steeple were added at that time. The Paul Revere bell was cracked in ringing in celebration of peace concluded with Great Britain in 1815, and it had to be recast. The old parsonage beside the church, known as Storrs Parsonage, is now the home of the Longmeadow Historical Society.

107

Southampton Congregational Church (1786)

Southampton, Hampshire County, Massachusetts

The community of Southampton was settled in 1732, and the town was incorporated in 1775. The Reverend Jonathan Judd came here to a wilderness as a young man, and he served this congregation for sixty years. In 1743 he organized the parish, and he saw the building of the first and second meeting houses. He made his home a refuge and stronghold against Indian attack during various times of trouble, including the French and Indian War, and his own sons and others of the parish fought in three wars. At his funeral service held in this church, the sermon was preached by the Reverend Enoch Hale of Westhampton, brother of the Revolutionary spy, Nathan Hale, and grandfather of the clergyman and author, Edward Everett Hale.

In 1785 the town voted to start preparing for setting up the second and present meeting house the following year, 1786. The building was dedicated in September, 1788. It was a plain, rectangular frame meeting house, but it has been altered considerably since that time. The steeple and porch were added in 1822. Originally the building faced north, but in 1840 it was turned to face east. The box pews were replaced then, and the pew doors were used in the present wainscoting. The meeting house was used both for town meetings and church services until 1831, when the town was divided into parishes and a town hall was erected. About 1846 a floor was added to make an upper story for a parish hall.

108

Old Parish Congregational Church (1760)

Sheffield, Berkshire County, Massachusetts

On the Housatonic River among the Berkshire Hills, the town of Sheffield was settled in 1726 and incorporated in 1733. As the Act of Incorporation required that a meeting house be built within three years, the First Congregational Church was organized in 1735 and the meeting house was built, the first in the region of western Massachusetts. It was located on Sheffield Plain, to the north of the present meeting house. In accordance with custom the town voted "three barrels of good Beare for raising of the meeting house," and "twenty gallons of Rumb for the rais-

ing of the meeting house or for the town's use, and twenty pounds of sugar to go with the rumb." It was voted also that any capable person who did not attend the raising was to be fined ten shillings per day; there is no record of a fine. In 1743 it was voted that John Ashley, a selectman, should have liberty to build a pew at the back on the women's side, provided that he did not raise its floor above the floor of the meeting house. His father, Captain John Ashley, had come here in 1722 as one of a committee to buy land in the wilderness from the Indians for the settlement of the Housatonic Townships, and to lay out and grant lots in the township of Sheffield, which originally included Great Barrington. The son had been graduated from Yale College in the Class of 1730, had been admitted to the Bar of Hampshire County, which included this region, and had made the survey of the township of Sheffield for its incorporation. He was active in parish and town affairs and became an outstanding citizen. He was active in three campaigns and was promoted to the rank of colonel in the Massachusetts Bay Militia. In the French and Indian War he led his Sheffield company to relieve Stockbridge. In 1787 he was the colonel in command of the Sheffield force which went out in sleighs to the plain northwest of Sheffield and defeated a band of insurgents in the Shays' Rebellion. In 1761 Berkshire County was set off from Hampshire, and Ashley was appointed Judge of the Court of Common Pleas. At Sheffield he built a home in 1735, the year that the church was organized, and it is now owned by a corporation that maintains it as a historical landmark, the oldest house in western New England.

The first minister was Jonathan Hubbard, a graduate of Yale College. He was ordained as pastor in 1735, by a council of ministers and deacons from Springfield, Northampton, and Sunderland in Massachusetts, and Enfield and Litchfield in Connecticut. Among them was the Reverend Jonathan Edwards, pastor of the church in Northampton, great theologian and preacher, whose influence was then stimulating a spiritual revival which swept through the colonies and became known as the Great Awakening. Edwards was to leave the Northampton church and to become pastor of the church in Stockbridge, another town within the original Housatonic Townships, twelve miles north of Sheffield, where he served as a missionary to the Stockbridge Indians. The Reverend Jonathan Hubbard was the only pastor of the first meeting house in Sheffield, and he lived until after the second had been built.

The second and present meeting house was built in 1760, the year before Berkshire County was established. It was originally a plain-gable structure which contained a "Broad alley" and a high pulpit. The pews were built at various times. In 1819, during the ministry of the fourth pastor, the Reverend James Bradford, alterations were made in the building. It was moved back from the highway a few rods to its present position, the structure was enlarged, the steeple and bell were added, and new clapboards replaced those on the front end and sides. The clapboards on the back end, with beaded edges attached by hand-wrought nails, are original, and they reveal where a window in that wall has been closed off. Town meetings were held in the meeting house from the time the first was built until 1846.

109

East Hoosac Friends Meeting House (1786)

Adams, Berkshire County, Massachusetts

In 1744 a Meeting for Worship was established by Saratoga Monthly Meeting. In the following year East Hoosac Preparative Meeting was set up. It became the East Hoosac Monthly Meeting in 1778, with independent status as part of New York Yearly Meeting. After 1800 many members migrated into western New York State, and no meetings are held now.

The meeting house was built in 1786, and it was used for more than sixty-four years. The date appears on the chimney. The interior was divided by a movable partition, in accordance with Quaker custom, for separate men's and women's business meetings, the women being given the side with the fireplace. In meetings for worship the partition was removed. The building stands on a hill overlooking the Hoosic River valley at the foot of Mt. Greylock in the Berkshires.

110

St. Michael's Church (1714)

Marblehead, Essex County, Massachusetts

In 1629 Marblehead was settled, as a plantation of Salem, by fishermen from Cornwall and the Channel Islands of Jersey and Guernsey. In a colony where Puritan Congregationalism was established by law, the Church of England entered late in the pioneering period, but Marblehead was the fourth town where the Anglican Church was organized in New England, following Boston, Newbury, and Newport. The people of this port town lived by fishing and selling the catch in Boston, and the subscription list for building St. Michael's Church was found in the early records of King's Chapel at Boston, where a number of that parish had subscribed. The date of organization is not known, but as early as 1707 subscriptions were made. The list of "Benefactors" was headed by General Francis Nicholson, who, while lieutenant-governor of New York in

1710, was in command of the forces sent against Port Royal in Acadia, which resulted in Great Britain taking Nova Scotia from the French. Crews for naval vessels for all such expeditions throughout the colonial period were recruited among the seagoing men of Marblehead. After New York, Nicholson served in the governments of Maryland and Virginia, and while he was governor of South Carolina, about 1724, a letter from the church in Marblehead reminded him that they were waiting for him to give the church a name. The name "St. Michael's Church" appears first in the reports of the Reverend Alexander Malcolm, who became the fourth rector in 1740.

The first rector, the Reverend William Shaw, arrived from England in 1715, the year after the church was built, with credentials from the Bishop of London, who was over all the Anglican churches in America. The second rector came also from England in 1718, the Reverend David Masson; he served until 1727, when he became rector of St. Peter's Church, New Kent, Virginia, where he officiated at the wedding of George and Martha Washington, and where we find his name spelled "Mossom" (see No. 314).

The building was erected in 1714. It was square, with seven gables and a ceiling arched in the form of a Greek cross. The high wineglass pulpit stood in the center of the north side, with sounding board overhead and reading desk in front. The chancel was in the center of the east side; behind the altar was a reredos and royal coat of arms brought from England. The original pews were square with high backs. In 1728 the building was extended by fifteen feet on the north side. Under the present roof, which was installed to cover the extension, can be seen the original roof structure. The brass chandelier was installed in 1732. In 1771 the west door was closed off, and the porch was built at the south door. In 1883 the square pews were replaced with slip pews, the chancel was moved to the north end, and the pulpit was moved to the west and the desk to the east side of the church. During the great fire of Marblehead in 1877 the roof caught fire, but the building was saved by an act of heroism. In 1888 the paper was removed from the walls and they were frescoed; the windows became lancet in form; and the small diamond panes were replaced with stained glass. The present chapel and parish house were built in 1893 to replace the earlier structure. The old English bell, which cracked while proclaiming the Declaration of Independence, was recast by Paul Revere in 1818.

During the Revolution the parish was in a dilemma. The Reverend Joshua Weeks, who had been sent by the parish to London for ordination and had become the sixth rector in 1763, remained loyal to the Crown. After the vestry had closed the church, about 1778, when the Provincial Congress had forbidden the use of the Liturgy, services were held for a time in private homes; but when it became evident that he could not remain in Marblehead during the Revolution, Weeks went to Nova Scotia with other loyalists. In the parish there were a number of men active in the war. William R. Lee, for example, was a major in the Marblehead regiment, and Samuel R. Trevett commanded a company of artillery at the Battle of Bunker Hill. Marblehead fishermen organized the crossing of the Delaware River on the night before the Battle of Trenton, and under the command of Captain Blackler, a member of St. Michael's Parish, they rowed the boat that carried General George Washington across. The church was reopened in 1780, and when Bishop Samuel Seabury, the first American bishop, came to St. Michael's in 1787, a group of 120 persons was presented for confirmation. It is interesting to note that in the 1820's, when the Second Congregational Society of Marblehead became Unitarian,

an attempt was made by the orthodox Congregationalists, who retained their Puritan faith, to seize St. Michael's Church for their own use. They petitioned to have the charter repealed and a new one issued declaring it to be a Congregational meeting house. The petition was denied, and St. Michael's continues as an active Episcopal church.

111

Second Congregational Church (1714)
North Beverly, Essex County, Massachusetts

The colonial building of the Second Congregational Church in North Beverly stands on Conant Street, named for Roger Conant, who was one of the "Old Planters" to whom the 1,000-acre grant of this section was allotted. Situated on the coast north of Salem, the community here attended church in Salem for many years. In 1626, only six years after the landing of the Pilgrims at Plymouth, Bass River was settled here, and in 1668 the settlement was incorporated as the town of Beverly. In 1713 the General Court of Massachusetts, in response to a petition from the inhabitants,

established the Upper Parish, in the Precinct of Salem and Beverly, now North Beverly, and at that time the Second Church was organized. During the following year the meeting house was built.

The raising of the frame took place on June 8, 1714, with all the community either taking part or witnessing the major event. Joseph Green, the pastor from Salem Village (now Danvers) asked God's blessing on the undertaking. In 1715 the first minister, John Chipman, was called as pastor and teacher. He served the parish for sixty years. The original building, which is now the church auditorium (to the left in the photograph), has undergone several alterations and additions. In 1837 a major renovation involved moving the building a few feet to the north, turning its axis, replacing the foundation timbers, and building a frame entrance in Greek Revival style on the west end. A schism developed in the congregation, as the theology departed from the strict Calvinism of the Puritans and moved toward Unitarianism, and some members who withdrew organized the Fourth Congregational Society. In 1865 the division was ended, and the members of the new Society took over the old meeting house and repaired it. In 1897 another renovation gave the building Victorian features, such as stained glass, oak furniture, and stenciled walls.

In 1929 the restoration was begun, which has returned the old part of the building to its colonial style, and has added the beautiful entrance on the south side and the parish house as the east wing. The Phillips Chancel at the west end was developed in 1929. In 1954, on the occasion of celebrating the 240th anniversary of the raising of the original frame, the building pro-

gram was half completed. On December 23, 1956, the finished building was dedicated. At the west end, the Greek Revival entrance was eliminated, and a section was added to the length of the building to enclose the chancel. The walls of the old building are now plastered inside, but a section of the original wall on the north side, shown in the interior photograph, has been exposed with panel doors. In this section one sees a timber hewn as a scroll arch, which had been closed up many years before.

112

Old South Church (1756)
First Presbyterian Meeting House
Newburyport, Essex County, Massachusetts

Newbury, including what is now Newburyport, was settled in 1635. Newburyport is situated at the mouth of the Merrimack River, and the white tower of Old South may be seen from the river, rising above the buildings near the waterfront. From its origin the church has been associated with the Reverend George Whitefield, the English evangelist and preacher to multitudes, who, with the Reverend Jonathan Edwards of Massachusetts, created the revival known as the Great Awakening, which swept through the American colonies between 1740 and 1743. Whitefield was ordained in the Church of England, but his Calvinistic theology offended that Church and he preached to all denominations. He swayed many listeners to change their views, and the converts became known as the "New Lights," while those who retained orthodox views were the "Old Lights."

In 1740, when he was only twenty-six years old, Whitefield visited Newburyport on one of his many trips to America. Delayed here by a blinding snowstorm, his preaching inspired a group to form their own church. These New Lights were mostly from the First and Third Presbyterian Churches of Newbury. In 1742 they built a small chapel, which they used until it was outgrown. The first pastor was the Reverend Jonathan Parsons, who had been proposed by Whitefield. In 1746 the present church was organized, and from the beginning it was Presbyterian, although that polity was not adopted formally until 1802.

In 1756 the old chapel was torn down and the present church was built. The tower and a spire were completed two years later. In recent years a hurricane weakened the spire; it was

removed to prevent it being blown down, and the tower is now finished without a spire. In 1770, on his seventh trip to America, Whitefield came to his final rest here. After preaching all over Great Britain and in all the principal towns of the American colonies to millions of people, averaging about forty hours a week of preaching, he was now limiting himself to preaching only once a weekday and thrice on Sunday. Planning to preach on that day at Old South, he died at Newburyport on September 30. At his request he was buried before the pulpit in this church. In 1829 his body was moved to a crypt beneath the pulpit, where thousands of people from all over the country have reviewed the remains; in recent years the tomb has been sealed. At the same time other changes were made in the building — the box pews were replaced, the vestibule was added, the ceiling was lowered, and the galleries were built. The bell was cast by Paul Revere.

On September 17, 1775, Benedict Arnold and men of his Quebec Expedition worshiped here. Many members of this church took part in the Revolution. On the Sunday following the Battle of Lexington, a company of sixty volunteers was enrolled in the aisle following the sermon preached by the pastor, the Reverend Jonathan Parsons. His son, Major General Samuel Holden Parsons, was a trusted friend of General George Washington. In 1789, when Washington visited Newburyport, the Presbytery of the Eastward went from Old South to greet him.

113

Rocky Hill Meeting House (1785)

Amesbury, Essex County, Massachusetts

The two finest examples of the colonial Congregational meeting house, both preserved in their original condition, are the Sandown Meeting House in New Hampshire (No. 119), and the Rocky Hill Meeting House at Amesbury. About 1644, Amesbury was settled as a part of Salisbury, and in 1654 the two towns, both named for towns in Wiltshire, England, agreed to function independently. The Congregational Society of Salisbury set off the West Parish Society in Amesbury, and that congregation built the present fine meeting house in 1785, a duplicate of the original building of 1716. It has a full two-story auditorium, a high pulpit with straight stairway, a sounding board mounted above a cornice and a plain architrave on two pilasters, a reading desk in the deacons' pew before the pulpit, box pews of unpainted pine, and galleries on three sides. The round pine pillars supporting the galleries and the pilasters behind the pulpit have a marbleized finish. The date of the building appears in the gable above the entrance portico. Town meetings of Salisbury were held here until 1886, when the west part of old Salisbury was added to Amesbury. In 1942 the West Parish Society of Salisbury presented the building and their funds as endowment to the Society for the Preservation of New England Antiquities.

NEW HAMPSHIRE

		Denomination	Material
114	Dover Friends Meeting House (1768) Dover, Strafford County	Friends	Wood
115	Newington Meeting House (1712) Newington, Rockingham County	Congregational	Wood
116	Community Congregational Church (1756) Greenland, Rockingham County	Congregational	Wood
117	Salem Town Hall (1738) Salem, Rockingham County	Congregational	Wood
118	Danville Meeting House (1760) Danville, Rockingham County	Congregational	Wood
119	Sandown Meeting House (1773) Sandown, Rockingham County	Congregational	Wood
120	Hampstead Town Hall (1745) Hampstead, Rockingham County	Congregational	Wood
121	Congregational Church (1772) Chester, Rockingham County	Congregational	Wood
122	East Derry Parish Church (1769) Derry, Rockingham County	Presbyterian	Wood
123	Bird Meeting House (1746) Nashua, Hillsboro County	Presbyterian	Wood
124	Congregational Meeting House (1771) Amherst, Hillsboro County	Congregational	Wood
125	Old Meeting House (1775) Jaffrey, Cheshire County	Congregational	Wood
126	Congregational Church (1762) Park Hill, Cheshire County	Congregational	Wood
127	Washington Town Hall (1786) Washington, Sullivan County	Congregational	Wood
128	Union Church (1773) West Claremont, Sullivan County	Anglican	Wood
129	First Church (1789) Hopkinton, Merrimack County	Congregational	Wood
130	Old Town House (1786) Henniker, Merrimack County	Congregational	Wood

SUMMARY

Congregational	13	Wood	17
Presbyterian	2		
Anglican	1		
Friends	1		
Buildings	17		17

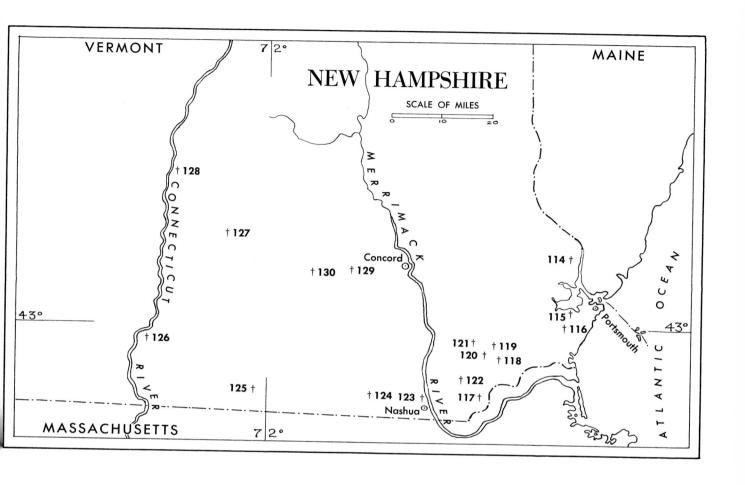

VERMONT

MAINE

NEW HAMPSHIRE

SCALE OF MILES

0   10   20

† 128

† 127

† 130   † 129

Concord

114 †

43°

115 †
† 116

Portsmouth

43°

ATLANTIC OCEAN

† 126

121 †   † 119
120 †   † 118

125 †

† 122

† 124 123 †   117 †

Nashua

MASSACHUSETTS

CONNECTICUT RIVER

MERRIMACK RIVER

7 2°

7 2°

114

Dover Friends Meeting House (1768)

**Central Avenue, Dover, Strafford County,
New Hampshire**

Quakers came to the Dover region at a very early date. Dover Monthly Meeting was established in 1680. The present records of the Meeting began in 1702. There was an early meeting house at Dover Point, which stood until the present one was built, and then it was taken down.

The Friends Meeting House, on what is now Central Avenue in Dover, was built in 1768. It is a two-story building, with the upper windows at the gallery level. In the usual Quaker style, there are two entrance doors into the auditorium, which was divided for business meetings by a movable partition, the women's meeting on the left and the men's on the right. Like all Quaker meeting houses, the inside finish and furnishing is plain. The latest innovation was the installation of oil lamps hanging in the room, which is now used for the Quarterly Meeting; meetings for worship have been discontinued, and the benches have been removed from the gallery.

The father and mother and the maternal grandparents of John Greenleaf Whittier, the well-known Quaker poet, were married in this meeting house. He attended meeting here when he visited his grandmother at the Hussey farm, where his mother, Abigail Hussey, had been born.

115

Newington Meeting House (1712)

Newington, Rockingham County, New Hampshire

Although the village of Newington is located across the Great Bay from the present city of Dover, it was settled about 1670 as a part of Dover. The present meeting house was built in 1712, and in the following year Newington was set off from Dover as a separate parish. This is the oldest Congregational meeting house in the country still in use by that denomination. The first pastor settled here was Joseph Adams, the uncle of President John Adams. Born in 1689 at Braintree, Massachusetts, he was graduated from Harvard College in 1710 and was ordained here in

1715. He died in 1783, after serving the parish for sixty-eight years, and was buried in the graveyard of the church.

The inhabitants of Newington suffered in the Indian wars. The region had been bought by the first settlers from an Indian chief known as "Ould Robin Hood." When his son, "Hope Hood," came into his inheritance, he took exception to his father's deal and led raids against the settlers. In 1689 he practically wiped out the settlement on the Cochico River a few miles away, and in 1690 he attacked Fox Point, two miles northwest of the present village of Newington, killing fourteen and capturing six persons. In the pursuit of the Indians and their captives, Hope Hood was killed. Across the bridge at Dover Point are the sites of the First and Second Congregational meeting houses, built in 1633 and 1654 respectively, which were fortified garrisons surrounded by palisades during these Indian troubles.

The original design of this building provided a private door at one end, to admit directly to his pew a prominent parishioner, Colonel John Downing. The main entrance was on the side opposite the pulpit. The structure was then one story in height, but since that time it has been heightened to make a two-story auditorium. The windows have been altered and the tower has been added, but the old box pews are still in place. Near-by stands the Old Parsonage, built in 1710, a fine example of the New England saltbox design with a large central chimney.

116

Community Congregational Church (1756)

Greenland, Rockingham County, New Hampshire

After it was incorporated in 1703, the town of Greenland, situated just east of Great Bay, remained a part of Portsmouth, or Strawberry Bank as it was still called. The inhabitants had to travel five or six miles to attend the North Congregational Church at Portsmouth. Because of the danger from Indians and the rigors of winter, they petitioned Governor Joseph Dudley, in 1705, for "a minister and schoolmaster among themselves." The town then had 320 inhabitants. In the following year, 1706, Greenland became the second parish to be separated from "the Bank." The Congregational church then was organized with twenty-nine charter members, and under the law the inhabitants of the town constituted the parish. In 1707 the first pastor, William Allen, a graduate of Harvard College in 1703, was ordained. He served the parish until his death in 1760, at age eighty-four, when he was laid to rest in the burying ground here. Samuel McClintock, who had been called in 1756 to assist the aging pastor, succeeded him after his death. McClintock had been graduated from Princeton in 1751, and he received the degree of Doctor of Divinity from that college. During the French and Indian War and the Revolution, he showed the Presbyterian influence of Princeton by serving as a chaplain of the army and a fighting parson in battle, where he prayed for the soldiers and their cause and loaded muskets. There is a painting of the Battle of Bunker Hill, by John Trumbull, showing McClintock with a musket in the thick of it. He served the parish until his death in 1804, when he also was buried in the Greenland cemetery. He and his wife, Mary, had fifteen children, of whom three sons died in the Revolution. With this spirit prevalent in the state when the Constitution of the United States was being established, New Hampshire cast the deciding vote for ratification.

McClintock came to this parish in 1756, when the second and present meeting house was being finished, after the frame had been raised on June 14. Until then a smaller frame building had been in use since the founding of the church Society. The new meeting house, measuring sixty by forty-two feet, was erected under the direction of a building committee of eight. The original design included windows in two tiers and a tower, belfry, and steeple projected from the end of the building. During the early years, singers occupied the gallery behind the pulpit, and a bass violin accompanied the singing. To meet the needs of a growing congregation, the building was remodeled in 1834. The two tiers of windows were joined to make one tier of tall windows, the pulpit was moved from between the narthex doors to the rear of the church facing those doors, and the pews were reversed. The ceiling was lowered almost six feet, but its height is still twenty-six feet above the floor. The tower now rises from the ridge above the main entrance in the east end. The present pews and pulpit were installed in 1881. Since 1949, when Sion M. Lynam became pastor, the colored glass, dating from the period of alterations, has been replaced with the small panes of clear glass in the colonial style.

The present Community Congregational Church represents a merger between the local Methodist and Congregational churches. The second church building of the former Methodist Church now is used as a parish house for the united congregation.

Salem Town Hall (1738)

Salem, Rockingham County, New Hampshire

The town of Salem was settled in the valley of the Spiket River, near the present boundary between Massachusetts and New Hampshire. This region was in Massachusetts, and was claimed by both colonies until 1741, when the king in council settled the boundary on the Merrimac River. Originally this was a part of Haverhill; in 1725 it was laid off and incorporated with the Methuen and Dracut district. It was difficult for the inhabitants to journey to any of those settlements to attend church, and after repeated petitions it was granted, in 1737, that Salem might have its own church and meeting house. In June of 1738 the town appointed a committee for building a meeting house. The timbers were sawn at Henry Sanders' mill during the summer. According to the historical address of 1959, by Howard S. Willis, Chairman of the Board of Selectmen of Salem, to the Historical Societies of New Hampshire, Inc., the frame was raised in November of 1738, in the presence of the entire parish membership. The building measured forty-eight by thirty-eight feet, with a twenty-two-foot post. For many years the meeting house, a plain rectangular building, was unfinished. The inside timbers were exposed, rough benches served as seats, and the windows were open until 1749, when sash and glass were installed. At a later time a pulpit was placed at the north wall; it was not until 1764 that box pews were installed to fill the house.

On January 16, 1740, a little more than a year after the raising of the frame, the Congregational Church was organized here as the Second Church in Methuen, and Abner Bailey was chosen as pastor. Two weeks later he was "set apart to the pastoral office by laying on of the hands of the Presbytery," as it was expressed by Robert F. Lawrence, in his *New Hampshire Churches*. In 1741, the year in which the boundary dispute was settled — with the line running through Methuen and placing this town in New Hampshire — the proprietors gave the parish about six acres for a burying ground and a drill ground for the militia. In 1750, Governor Benning Wentworth, commander-in-chief of the Province of New Hampshire under George II, granted a town charter to the North Parish in Methuen under the name of Salem. The first meeting of the new town

was held in this building on May 30 of that year. Bailey continued as pastor until 1776, when an agreeable settlement was made with the town.

Following the Revolution, the Congregational parish declined. A Methodist church was built near by, and it was thought that the old church would die. In 1835 it was voted, at a town meeting, that religious denominations had equal rights in the Congregational meeting house, "according to their poll and estate." In 1838, a century after it was raised, the building was moved to its present position beside the old burying ground. The town then voted to repair it and make some alterations, including a room for selectmen and a floor for a second story. There was a delay in carrying out the alterations, until 1851. By that time the Congregational Society had gained new life; in 1840 they had ordained a new pastor, Jonas Fisk, and had built a new church. This left the old meeting house for town and community use, and the alterations were then made for those purposes. The lower floor is known as the Town Hall, and the upper floor as Salem Hall, where community functions are held by the various town organizations.

118

Danville Meeting House (1760)

Danville, Rockingham County, New Hampshire

In the back country about eight miles north of the Merrimack River is the little village of Danville. The Danville Meeting House was built by the Congregational community in 1760. Also in that year the town was incorporated as Hawke, in honor of the British admiral. Not until 1836 was the name changed to Danville. The old cemetery dates from 1740. The first minister, the Reverend John Page, died of smallpox in the epidemic of 1780 while caring for others, and he was buried in the old cemetery. The two-story structure is severely plain, and at a glance it could be mistaken for a private dwelling. The exterior, with its graduated, scarf-jointed clapboards, is original. There is a window over the pulpit. The colonial interior was stripped of furnishings in 1870, when the auditorium was converted to a dance hall. In 1936, through the generosity of Lester A. Colby, the building was restored; most of the old pews, with spindles topping their partitions, have been replaced and the rest have been copied. The Old Meeting House Association owns the property, and an annual service of homecoming is held the last Sunday in August.

119

Sandown Meeting House (1773)

Sandown, Rockingham County, New Hampshire

The town of Kingston was settled in 1736. In 1756 Sandown was set off from it and incorporated as a separate town. There was a protracted disagreement over the location of the meeting house, which was finally settled by locating it at the center of Sandown township. This does not mean that it is on a village street, for it stands removed from the town on a low hill amidst fields and woods, and it is a joy for the traveler to discover.

The building, which is practically in its original condition, is the finest colonial meeting house in New Hampshire and one of the finest in America. It was begun in 1773 and finished in 1774, the two dates appearing on two of the three doorways. The style is typical of the Congregational meeting house of colonial New England. The two-and-a-half-story structure is almost square, forty-four by fifty feet. The high wineglass pulpit with stairway, the canopy above it serving as a sounding board, the deacons' pew before the pulpit, the slave gallery, and the box pews are all beautifully executed within the restrictions of the plain style. This building is outstanding also for the

proportions in the design and the detail, and for the craftsmanship that went into the construction. The doorways, for example, have pilasters surmounted by dentilated pediments. The double doors of the front entrance have ten panels each and the side doors eight. They are paneled with oak outside to withstand the weather and pine inside to match the interior. The wall clapboards are scarf-jointed. The thirty-eight windows each have twenty-eight panes of glass. The hand-wrought iron hardware is interesting and beautiful: the butterfly hinges on the pulpit door, the H hinges on the box pew doors, the strap hinges on the outside doors. The interior finish is in natural wood, except the wainscoting on the gallery front and the pulpit which are stained cherry, and the columns and pilasters which have been marbleized.

The Congregational Society was dissolved in 1834 and services were discontinued, but town meetings were held in the meeting house until 1729. The property is maintained by the town and the Sandown Old Meeting House Historical Association.

120

Hampstead Town Hall (1745)

**Hampstead, Rockingham County,
New Hampshire**

The township of Hampstead is bounded on the north by Sandown and Danville, and on the west by Derry, in each of which there is a colonial meeting house (see Nos. 119, 118, 122). The town was settled in 1721 and called Timber Lane. It was part of Haverhill and Amesbury, Massachusetts, until 1741, and the congregation here was in the North Parish of Haverhill. The town was granted a charter of incorporation by Governor Benning Wentworth in 1749, and renamed Hampstead for the town in England five miles north of London.

In the hamlet of Hampstead, on a broad, wooded hill, work began in 1745 to build the meeting house. The date appears in the pediment over the main doorway of the building, which still stands. When the building was enclosed with sawn

planks and the roof was on, rude benches were installed for seats. In this primitive state, the building was used for the following half century, both for church services and town meetings. Although it was proposed frequently in town meeting to finish the building, the community was poor, and there were never funds to do so during the rest of the colonial period. In 1752, Henry True, a graduate of Harvard College in 1750, was ordained pastor, and this Congregational church was organized with sixty-eight members. He had to endure the austere structure during all of his ministry of thirty years, until his death in 1782. For the next decade the parish was without a minister. In 1792, John Kelly was ordained, to begin a ministry of forty years, and in that year the building was finished in its present style. The walls were covered with clapboard, and the tower was built at the west end, surmounted by a belfry and steeple modeled after the design at Old Ship Meeting House, Hingham, Massachusetts (No. 87). The Revere bell was given by Thomas Huse in 1809. The builders in this phase were Colonel Thomas Reed and Abner Rogers, who received two pews in part payment.

In 1837 the last sermon was preached by the Congregational minister in this meeting house, and the congregation transferred to the new church which they had built in the valley. The old meeting house here on the hill was left to be used by other denominations, but no other church was organized here. In 1852 the building was converted by the town for use exclusively as a town hall. The pulpit and pews were removed, and a second floor was built at the gallery level to provide town offices. It has served ever since as the Hampstead Town Hall.

Congregational Church (1772)

Chester, Rockingham County, New Hampshire

Situated in a farming community, the small village of Chester includes a number of colonial houses and a colonial Congregational church on the village Green. The town was settled in the tract known as the "Chestnut Country," by families from Portsmouth, Newbury, Haverhill, and Hampton. They received their grant from the governor of Massachusetts in 1720. The proprietors of Chester adopted plans for the first meeting house on October 7, 1729, and the building was completed in 1731. The first settled minister of Chester, Moses Hale, was ordained as pastor on October 20 of that year, and the church was organized. During the ministry of Hale in the established Congregational parish-town, many Scotch-Irish settlers moved in. These Presbyterians were resented by the early settlers, for they wanted their own minister, and they did not want to pay taxes for the support of a Congregational minister. After serving for a short time, Hale had to retire on account of illness, and at that time the Presbyterians acted. They objected to paying for the support of his successor, and instead they supported John Wilson whom they had ordained in their Church. In 1736 Ebenezer Flagg was ordained by the Congregationalists, and in 1739 an act of the legislature excused the Presbyterians from contributing to his support. In that same year the Presbyterians built a church of their own, which later was demolished to make way for their post-colonial building. Flagg befriended Wilson, and the two denominations lived in harmony thereafter.

On March 28, 1772, the Congregational parish voted to build a new meeting house. The method of raising the money to pay for the new structure is recorded as follows: "Voted, that there shall be a Committee to Sell Said pews within a convenient time, Sold for Bords, Shingle, timber, Labour, or any article that is wanting for Said meeting house, at cash price." Five men were then named to sell the pews and erect the building. On October 16 it was "Voted, to build a steple and porch to the New meeting house, agreeable to the Plan" and "Voted, to Set the New meeting house upon Land that the Revd. mr. Flagg gave for that youse." The deed for the land, which Flagg previously had bought from Sir John Wentworth, governor of New Hampshire, is recorded in that year. In front of the pulpit was the pew called the elders' seat, and in front of that was the deacons' pew, both facing the congregation. From that point to about the middle of the church there were long plain benches, the common or free seats. The rest were box pews with seats on three sides. The seats in the pews turned up to accommodate standing for prayers, and in his *History of Old Chester*, Benjamin Chase says, "At the close of a prayer there was quite a refreshing clatter by the falling of these seats."

In 1839 most of the alterations were made that changed the colonial structure to its present state. The building was turned on its axis to face in the present direction, the spire was cut away, and the entire interior was remodeled and refurnished.

East Derry Parish Church, Presbyterian (1769)
First Church in Derry, Congregational

Derry, Rockingham County, New Hampshire

The Scotch-Irish Presbyterians who settled the Londonderry section were from the town of that name on the north shore of Northern Ireland. Their Puritan ancestors had left Scotland under pressure from the English Crown and Church, and after years of conflict with the Church of England and the Roman Catholic Church in Ireland, a company of sixteen families emigrated here. On the day after they had landed, in 1720, James McGregor, a Scotch Presbyterian, stood on the east shore of what now is called Beaver Pond and preached to the little company the first sermon in this section. The company then gave McGregor a formal call to be their pastor. As there was no presbytery in New England at the time, they conformed to the procedure of the Independents, the minister receiving the people as his charge and they him as their pastor. Thus the first Presbyterian church in New England was organized. The congregation grew rapidly, and when McGregor died, in 1729, there were 375 communicants in the church.

The extensive township here originally was called Nutfield, but when it was granted to the settlers in 1722, they changed the name to that of their home port, Londonderry. As the habitations grew, the township was divided into separate towns. In 1740 it was divided into two parishes, East Parish and West Parish. In the following year, the western part was incorporated as Windham, in 1751 the northwestern part as Derryfield (now Manchester), and in 1827 the eastern part as Derry. Using the water power of Beaver Brook, industries were developed in Derry, the major one being the manufacture of linen, and Derry linen became a famous brand. It is recorded in *New Hampshire*, "The American Guide Series," that a Derry weaver named Montgomery wove linen for George Washington and his officers during the Revolution, for which he was awarded payment by Congress in the amount of £40 and a diamond ring. Linen is still the major industry in the homeland of the settlers.

In 1721 the first meeting house was built, near the site of the present one. It served until 1769, when the present building was erected. The undertakers of the contract were Deacon Daniel Reynolds and Joseph Morrison. Originally this was a plain, rectangular building measuring sixty-five by forty-five feet. The church was furnished in Presbyterian style, with the high pulpit on the north wall, and before it a pew for the two deacons facing the congregation, behind which was the larger pew for the many elders. As the congregation continued to grow, it became necessary to enlarge the building. In 1824 this was accomplished by cutting the building in two and moving the rear portion back twenty-four feet. At the same time the tower and steeple were added. The fine design of the steeple probably was influenced by the books of architectural designs by Palladio and Inigo Jones. In 1845 the interior was altered drastically. An upper floor was built to provide a church auditorium, and on the ground floor rooms were made for sessions of the elders, a vestry, a town hall, and a parish library. The old pulpit, with its semicircular front, was replaced, but the original was kept in the store room. The main entrance is now at the rear of the building, and not through the tower doors as is usually the case.

During the Great Awakening, which aroused the churches in all the colonies after 1739, George Whitefield, the leading light of the revival, spoke in Londonderry. West Parish participated in the general revival, but, according to Robert F. Lawrence, in his *New Hampshire Churches*, the East Parish here gave the new movement no countenance whatever. Subsequently the discipline and faith in this parish declined. When Jonathan Brown was ordained as pastor here, by the Londonderry Presbytery in 1795, a large and vigorous minority opposed his settlement, and they withdrew to form a Congregational Church and Society. The Society was incorporated as the Third Parish of Londonderry. In 1804 the opposition to Brown was renewed, and he resigned. Five years later, the First Parish (Presbyterian) and the Third Parish (Congregational) appointed a joint committee to seek a basis for union. The articles of agreement which they drafted were adopted, and the two parishes were reunited and incorporated as the First Parish in Londonderry. With the parishes reunited, the two churches then appointed a joint committee to seek union. The articles proposed by the committee, including a creed and a covenant, were adopted, and the long period of division was ended. The united church was essentially Congregational, and a few mem-

bers of the old Presbyterian church refused to unite, but they caused no difficulty. The church has continued active in that form to the present time, but it now has a later name: the First Church in Derry. A granite stone marks the site of the house of a prominent resident of the parish, Matthew Thornton (1714-1803). He was a signer of the Declaration of Independence, and from 1776 to 1782 he served as a justice of the State Supreme Court. His parents had brought him here from Northern Ireland among the first settlers.

We find that the Scotch-Irish immigrants in Pennsylvania also brought from the old country the name for their Derry Presbyterian Church, a congregation which settled the present town of Hershey (see No. 258).

revival that was called the Great Awakening (see Old South Church, Newburyport, Mass., No. 112), and as such he was a "New Light." At Dunstable, as Nashua was then called, Jonathan Lovewell and a few others of the New Lights in the local church took action to modernize it. In the winter of 1746 they began the building of a new meeting house. It was a plain, rectangular frame building. On August 31, 1747, the Reverend Samuel Bird received a call to serve as pastor of the new church, and soon afterward he was ordained in the new meeting house. The Old Lights of the congregation objected so strongly to his Calvinistic theology and Presbyterian preaching that they refused to contribute to his support; they organized a conservative church and began to worship again in the old meeting house. Mr. Bird probably did not serve longer than a year. On October 16, 1751, he was installed as the minister of the First Church, New Haven, Connecticut. The Bird Meeting House was put to other uses. When the photograph was made, the building was being used as the polishing shop of the American Shearer Company.

124

Congregational Meeting House (1771)

Amherst, Hillsboro County, New Hampshire

The village of Amherst, clustered about the long common, contains many colonial buildings of interest, including the Congregational Church with a white spire rising above the rest of the town. After the King Philip's War (1675-1676) several townships known as the Narragansetts were granted by the General Court of Massachusetts in recognition of services rendered in the war. The one that became known as Souhegan West No. 3 was settled in 1735. When the petition to incorporate was granted, in 1760, the town was given its name in honor of General Jeffery Amherst, who had just been made governor-general of British North America, following his successful campaign which established British dominion in Canada.

The first meeting house was built in 1735, and the church was organized in 1741, when the Reverend Daniel Wilkins became the first minister. The building, located near the village on the Plain at Upper Flanders, served as town house and church until the present building was erected, and then as the first county courthouse until it burned down in 1788.

123

Bird Meeting House (1746)

Nashua, Hillsboro County, New Hampshire

On the bank of Salmon Brook in Nashua, behind a large factory on Main Street, of which it is a part, stands the Bird Meeting House. It was built during the Great Awakening as a house of worship for the ministry of one man, and it was never used as such under the ministry of any other.

The Reverend Samuel Bird was born in 1724 at Dorchester, Massachusetts, a community with a long history of Congregationalism with Presbyterian leanings (see Midway Church, Ga., No. 30). He was a follower of George Whitefield, whose Calvinistic preaching aroused the spiritual

In 1770 the town voted to build a new meeting house on the Training Field on the Plain, and in 1771 the present building was begun on a site a little to the southeast of its present location. It was dedicated January 19, 1774. During the following few years separate parishes were established in neighboring towns. In 1828 the town and church were separated, and in 1832, when the town offered the meeting house for sale, the First Congregational Church and Society was organized to buy the property. The terms of sale were unusual, for the town retained ownership of the basement for town meetings and the

steeple, clock, and bell for public use. The building was then moved from the common to its present site and alterations were made. In 1872 the interior was remodeled again, and in 1874, 1902, and 1932 other features were changed. In 1932 the First Congregational Church and Society was abolished and merged with the Congregational Church, which then was incorporated. In 1950 extensive renovations were made in the interior, and while it has not been restored fully to its colonial style, some of the old pews and paneling and part of the old gallery are retained. In the lower tier the old windows still have small panes.

125

Old Meeting House (1775)

Jaffrey, Cheshire County, New Hampshire

The town of Jaffrey is on a hill surmounted by the white meeting house, which faces toward Mt. Monadnock across the valley. The town originally was part of the Masonian Grant of 1629, which extended to Maine; in 1746 Benning Wentworth, governor of New Hampshire, purchased this part of the grant from John Mason, a descendant of the original owner. In 1773 the town was incorporated by an act granted by Governor John Wentworth, nephew of his predecessor. George Jaffrey for whom the town was named,

was one of the proprietors of the Masonian Grant; he served the Province of New Hampshire as Chief Justice of the Supreme Court, a member of the Governor's Council, and treasurer. The Jaffrey grant of 1746 stipulated the building of a meeting house within six years, but there was none when the town was incorporated in 1773.

In 1774 the town voted to build a meeting house on the common, and the frame was raised on June 16 and 17, 1775. There were men returning from the raising who claimed that they heard gunfire from the Battle of Bunker Hill seventy miles away — at least the story fixes the date of the meeting house. The original entrance on the south side is the one used today. In 1823 the tower and spire were built at the west end of the plain rectangular structure, and the Paul Revere bell was installed; it cracked later and had to be recast. The arrangement of the interior was typical of the Congregational meeting house of the day — high pulpit with two stairways under a round-arched window; sounding board; elders' pew before the pulpit and a slip pew for the deacons; three galleries, one of which was for the choir; and box pews with banister backs and hinged seats. Between the pulpit and the pews, which were sold at auction, were the free seats.

Only the Congregational Church, established by law, had the use of the meeting house in its early days. In 1819 the Toleration Act was passed, and thereafter the several denominations in Jaffrey were entitled to use it. The arrangement was not satisfactory, and the growing community built other churches. Even the Congregationalists built a brick church at the Center in 1831, and after 1844 only town meetings were held in the old meeting house. The pulpit and pews were destroyed, and the building became dilapidated until 1870, when it was remodeled as a town hall and high school. In 1872 John Conant gave a sum to start a repair fund. In 1926 the Jaffrey Village Improvement Association remodeled the interior.

126

Congregational Church (1762)

Park Hill, Cheshire County, New Hampshire

Near the town of Westmoreland, a colonial Congregational church stands on the summit of Park Hill, which formerly was called Federal Hill in memory of the men of Westmoreland who served in the American Revolution. Park Hill, overlooking the Connecticut Valley, is the oldest part of Westmoreland, which was "No. 2" of the townships granted in 1735 by the Massachusetts Colony. It was known as Great Meadows until it was granted by New Hampshire in 1752, and then it was incorporated as Westmoreland.

The church was built in 1762 on another hill to the north beside the old cemetery. It reached its present location in two moves; the first in 1779 to about a hundred feet south of the present site, the second in 1827 to its final resting place on the summit of the hill. The first move between hills was a critical affair. The building was stalled in the valley, and the men were about to abandon it, when a barrel of rum was promised; the men's

spirits revived and they completed the job without further interruption, at a total cost of £2,388 and one barrel of rum.

The structure that was moved was smaller than the present one, and it had no steeple. After the final move in 1827, twenty feet were added on the front; the porch and fine steeple were built to a design by General Simeon Cobb, whose descendants still occupy the interesting old Cobb House standing near the church. A Paul Revere bell was hung in the belfry of the new steeple. Of the nearly four hundred bells cast by the foundry of Paul Revere & Son, this was No. 366, and like approximately forty-seven of the total, this one cracked in 1847 and was recast. In 1853 the gallery was removed and a second floor was installed; the auditorium was then on the upper floor. Town meetings were held in the church vestry until a town hall was built in the 1850's.

127

Washington Town Hall (1786)

Washington, Sullivan County, New Hampshire

The hamlet of Washington, consisting of a long green at a fork in the road, lined by a number of colonial buildings, is one of the highest towns in New Hampshire. Situated on a broad, high hill, it commands a view across the valley to Mt. Monadnock. On the north side of the common stands the town hall, which was built originally as the meeting house for both church and town use. Beside the town hall stands the Washington Central School, a post-colonial building, and beside the school is the Washington Congregational Church, founded in 1780, and this building erected in 1840 — all three appear in the photograph. The township was granted first by

the Massachusetts Colony as Monadnock No. 8. In 1752 a New Hampshire charter was granted, and in 1768 the town was granted by the Masonian proprietors to Colonel Reuben Kidder as sole proprietor. He settled the town under the name of Camden, in honor of Lord Camden, a friend of Governor John Wentworth. In 1785 the town voted to build the meeting house, and in the autumn of 1786 timbers were prepared. Over the door of the town hall a sign reads, "Washington Incorporated 1776. This Building Erected 1789." The name and both dates have great significance for the United States, as the Declaration of Independence was signed in the year of the town's incorporation, and George Washington was inaugurated in 1789, the year in which the meeting house was completed. When the name was changed from Camden, this was thought to be the first town to honor Washington, but it was second to Washington, North Carolina.

The early settlers, most of whom came from Massachusetts, were given 150 acres each as an inducement. In 1780 the inhabitants installed George Leslie as their first pastor. He had come from Ireland as an infant and had been graduated from Harvard College. He held services in John Safford's barn. The first winter was so cold that twenty-seven cattle died in the settlement, including Leslie's only cow, and his family was without salt until spring had thawed the road and opened access to the nearest source of supply. The congregation came to church services on oxsleds. The frame of the meeting house probably was raised in the spring of 1787. A committee was appointed in that year to see that the frame was boarded and that it was "done workmanlike." In 1789 the interior was finished by two joiners, Church Tabor and Joseph Tabor. The Society was organized in that year, and the first two deacons were appointed. Part of the cost of the building was raised by the sale of pews, the terms of which required each purchaser to pay down two pounds of flax per pound sterling on his note. The meeting house originally was a plain rectangular building, with a gallery and standard furnishings of a Congregational church, but there was no steeple. The tower and steeple evidently were added early in the nineteenth century, for the design is in the style of Asher Benjamin and probably was taken from his *The Country Builder's Assistant* (1797), which was a source for church designs through the Connecticut Valley in that period. After the Congregational Society had built their present church, in 1840, the meeting house remained for use only as a town house.

128

Union Church (1773)

West Claremont, Sullivan County, New Hampshire

Claremont, the largest township in New Hampshire, has never been incorporated. When the town was granted by Governor Benning Wentworth in 1764, it was named for the country place of Lord Clive in England. West Claremont is the part of the township on the Connecticut River that was called the West Part; the cemetery across the road from the Union Church is called the West Part Burying Ground. The name "Union" reflects the fact that the church was planned by Anglicans and Congregationalists together, but the Congregationalists withdrew before the building was finished.

This oldest Anglican church in New Hampshire was built in 1773. The plans were presented by Governor John Wentworth; he also promised to provide nails and glass, but the Revolution was brewing and he had to flee to Halifax before the materials were procured in England. The parish was organized in 1771 by the Reverend Samuel Peters, of Hebron, Connecticut, a missionary of the Society for the Propagation of the Gospel. Ranna Cossitt, another missionary of the S. P. G., who had conducted services here and in other churches of the region, became the first rector. There were many Tories in Claremont, and the feeling against them during the Revolution delayed the finishing of the church until 1789, and led to physical violence. Until the church was finished, services were held during the summers only, with a desk instead of a pulpit. At the height of the feeling against England, members of the church and others in the Valley were taken into custody, dragged through mud, and placed in jail or in private homes. One of them wrote in a letter that the Reverend Mr. Cossitt had suffered the most insults as a member of the S. P. G., which the rebels said propagated loyalty to the king in the name of religion. With his life in danger, the rector was forced to leave Claremont in 1785. At the close of the war, however, there were more members of Union Church than at the beginning.

The belfry was added in 1801. In 1820 the building was extended twenty-five feet at the east end, the organ was transferred from the gallery to the chancel, and the gallery was removed. The old box pews remain, to remind one of the church's colonial origin.

129

First Church (1789)

Hopkinton, Merrimack County, New Hampshire

The town that was incorporated as Hopkinton, in 1765, was settled in 1735 by pioneers from Hopkinton, Massachusetts. Indian raids and massacres retarded growth of the town, until after the end of the French and Indian War in 1763. The first meeting house, a simple frame structure, was built in 1751 on the common, where a stone now marks the site, across the road from the present church. Six years later, in 1757, the Congregational Society was organized. George H. Moses, in *A Sketch of Henniker*, relates that James Scales, a graduate of Harvard College in 1733, was the first settler in that town, though his residence was temporary (see No. 130). He left Hopkinton and went about nine miles west to that tract, where he owned land. He built a log house, but after six months he returned to Hopkinton, where he was ordained as the first minister in 1757, when the Society was organized. He served here until 1770. The Scales parsonage of 1760 still stands on Putney Hill. The hill bears the name of the first settler here, and it was the site of Putney's Fort, built in 1744, which housed the early public meetings.

During the years between 1787 and 1789, the town took a number of votes in a protracted controversy over the site for a proposed new meeting house. In Putney Hill, the east end, and in the west end of the township, all wanted the meeting house for their convenience. During the controversy, a youth forced the issue by setting fire to the first building. In her *Colonial Meeting Houses of New Hampshire*, Eva A. Spears gives an account of the ordination of a new minister in the subsequent interval when the parish was without a meeting house. Out-of-doors in front of Major Babson's tavern, with a platform serving as an altar, the minister was ordained. On the question of a building site, a town meeting called in the tavern had to be adjourned to a barnyard for more room, and there it failed to reach a decision. The town then submitted the question to the arbitration of the selectmen of Washington, Gilmanton, and Linesborough. After careful study of the situation and the proposed sites, they decided that the site of the burned building was the best. The present building was erected on that site the same year, 1789. Within four months after work had begun, and before it was finished, the meeting house was in use. In 1811 a belfry was built and the Paul Revere bell was installed, which is still in use after having had two large cracks welded.

In 1829 the Congregational Society bought the meeting house and moved it from the common across the road to its present site. It then was remodeled in its present style.

130

Old Town House (1786)

Henniker, Merrimack County, New Hampshire

Here among the hills, on the boiling Contoo-kook River, the township was settled that became known as Henniker. Originally this part of a large tract was designated as "No. 6," and it continued under that name until long after the town was settled. "No. 6" was granted in 1732 to veterans of the ill-fated expedition against Quebec. In 1752 it was granted again, by the Masonian proprietors, to a group of Scotch-Irish applicants in Londonderry, New Hampshire; as the veterans had done nothing to settle here, they were granted another town instead, Waterford, Maine. The first person to build and live here was James Scales, who came from Hopkinton and spent six months in a cabin that he built. He then returned to Hopkinton and became the first pastor of the church there (see No. 129). Also from Hopkinton came James Peters, in 1760, the only one of the new proprietors to come here, and he built a house as the first permanent resident. In

1763 other settlers came here from Marlborough, Massachusetts, and they named the town New Marlborough. In 1768 the proprietors petitioned for a town charter; it was granted by Governor John Wentworth with only one condition, that the name of the town be changed to honor his good friend, John Henniker, a London merchant who dealt in leather and furs from Russia, and who became the first colonial secretary of Nova Scotia and the first Baron Henniker. The residents are proud to live in the only Henniker in the world.

The town started its search for a Congregational minister before the charter was granted, and in 1768 Jacob Rice began his ministry here. He accepted the call on condition that his salary rise and fall with the price of silver, thus revealing a canny awareness of inflation. In 1770, two years after his settlement, the first meeting house was begun. It was a log structure, which was occupied for worship even before the roof was built. It was in use for church and town meetings only for a decade, and on the "dark day" in 1780 the log meeting house was burned. There followed a protracted controversy over a site for a new building. In 1783 the town voted to build, but nothing was done for the next three years.

Early in 1786 the town voted to build the second meeting house, and in August the frame was let as a job ready for raising. The raising occupied three days, and some idea of the magnitude of the occasion may be gained from the bills paid. To Gideon Adams went £1–4s. for sugar, to Sam Kimball £5–15s. for beef, and to Dr. Hunter £12–5s. for ninety-three gallons and a quarter of rum and three barrels. No further work was done on the frame until the following March — and little wonder! In November, 1787, the first meeting was held in the new building, to choose a Grand and a Petit Jury. There were no pews, and rough boards on blocks were used as benches. In 1788 the town voted to sell the pew ground, and a committee was appointed to mark off the pews, with a three-foot "alley."

This second meeting house, which still stands, is unusual in that it has porches at both ends, and within each, stairs lead to the upper level. Originally there were galleries at the ends of the building, which were connected by another on one side. In the galleries the first step was furnished with benches, which at a later time were occupied by singers, and the upper step had pews like those on the floor. The box pews had hinged seats that turned up during prayers, when the congregation stood. The pews were screened with turned spindles in two tiers around the partitions. There was a center aisle and two side aisles, all between blocks of pews. The high pulpit and sounding board were in the middle of the north side. Before the pulpit were the seats for the two deacons, a narrow slip. Behind the deacons' pew, at a higher level and with their back to the pulpit, were the pews for the ruling elders; these pews were larger and nearly square. In 1801 the town voted "to see that the Meeting House was underpined with hewn stones, handsomely and decently."

In the *History of Henniker*, by Leander W. Cogswell, there is an account of a schism which developed in the congregation and persisted for many years. It came to a head in 1801. In that year, Moses Sawyer was settled as pastor, after years of controversy during which Rice had been dismissed. Sawyer immediately formed the Calvinistic Congregational Society of Henniker and separated his congregation from the town. This move in Henniker anticipated by many years the statewide disestablishment of the Congregational Church. It was not until 1819 that the Legislature of New Hampshire passed the Toleration Act, which separated towns from churches of all denominations, relieving them of taxes for the support of ministers and churches. This new Society and the Church ordained Sawyer in 1802, and the town voted that they might use the meeting house on the Sabbath, if the town did not need it. In 1804 the congregation built a new church. Soon after Sawyer had been dismissed in 1826, on an agreeable settlement, the old members who had objected to his Calvinistic beliefs, formed the Congregational Society of Henniker, and in 1827 they ordained Jacob Scales. Services were held alternately in the present old meeting house and in the new church, until 1833 when the new church was burned. In 1834 the present Congregational church was built, and since that time the old meeting house has been used only as a town house. At the time of its Centennial, in 1887, the building was remodeled. All church furnishings were removed, the galleries were taken down, and an upper floor was installed to serve as an auditorium with a stage. The lower floor was used for town offices. Now that Henniker has another town hall, this colonial building is used by the American Legion and many other organizations for community affairs.

was closed (see Neshaminy Presbyterian Church, Pa., No. 238), steps were taken to form a broader college incorporating its interests, which were New School. In 1746 a charter was granted for a college in New Jersey, and in 1748 a second charter was granted to the trustees of the "College of New Jersey." The new College opened in Elizabeth in 1747 (see First Presbyterian Church, Elizabeth, No. 133), under the administration of the Reverend Jonathan Dickinson. When he died after four months of the life of the College, his successor was the Reverend Aaron Burr (father of the Vice President of the United States), the seventh pastor of this church in Newark, and the College was moved to Newark. Here the first commencement was held, and Burr organized and developed the College and curriculum. In 1752 the College was moved to Princeton.

133

First Presbyterian Church (1784)

**Broad Street, Elizabeth, Union County,
New Jersey**

On Broad Street in Elizabeth stands a fine
example of Georgian-colonial architecture, the
First Presbyterian Church. Like the church at
Newark (No. 132), the congregation originally
was Independent, that is, Congregational, and
here also the polity became fully Presbyterian at
about the same time, 1717-18. It is an old congregation, being only a year younger than that in
Newark. The land in Elizabeth Town was bought
from the Indians, and the first church was built
of wood in 1664. The first settled minister was
the Reverend Jeremiah Peck, 1668-78. In 1724
the second building was erected. In it the first
meeting of the Synod of New York was held in

1745, with the Reverend Jonathan Dickinson as
moderator. It was in another building on the
parish grounds that the first classes were held
during the summer of 1747 in the College of New
Jersey, which was to become Princeton University. Among the students were Alexander Hamilton and Aaron Burr. When Dickinson died that
same year, his successor was Aaron Burr, Sr., seventh pastor of the church at Newark, and the
College was moved there. During the Revolution,
in 1780, the second building was burned by Tory
refugees.

The third building was begun in 1784 on the
same site; it was completed in 1789. This building also has suffered from storm and fire. In 1899
the spire was blown down in a storm; it was rebuilt in 1902. On June 25, 1946, the interior of
the church was destroyed by fire, and the walls
were left standing in ruins. While there may be
no connection, the fire was one of a series that
burned churches and hotels in various parts of
the country after World War II. On December
14, 1947, a ceremony was held at the beginning
of the long task of restoration, with the presidents
of Princeton and Rutgers universities as the principal speakers. In colonial days Rutgers College
maintained a covenant with the Dutch Reformed
Church, and its presidents still are members of
that Church. A fund of a quarter of a million dollars was contributed by people of various denominations, and reproductions of specific features,
such as the pulpit, lectern, two crystal chandeliers,
and baptismal font, were subjects of private gifts.
The restored interior followed as closely as possible the design of the original church, even to
box pews with doors, and it recalls the pre-Revo-
lutionary days when it served as a town meeting
house as well as church, and the later period
when the New Jersey General Assembly met here.

134

First Presbyterian Congregation of Connecticut Farms (1783)

Union, Union County, New Jersey

Connecticut Farms was settled in the summer of 1667, when the Reverend Abraham Pierson and a company of families came here from Branford, Connecticut. The town became Union, which is situated adjacent to Elizabeth. Mr. Pierson became the first pastor of the church in Newark (No. 132), and the rest of the settlers traveled the five miles every Sunday to the church in Elizabeth Town (No. 133). About 1730 the congregation organized a separate society. The first pastor, the Reverend Simon Horton was installed in 1734. He had been graduated from Yale in 1731 and was a Congregationalist, but at the age of twenty-three he became pastor of this church, which was Presbyterian in polity. Their first church, a frame structure, was built about 1730 and before 1734. There are no records of that early period; it is believed that the records were destroyed when the town, the church, and the parsonage were burned by the British on June 23, 1780, as they returned to Staten Island after the battle at Springfield three miles away.

At the time of the battles at Springfield and Connecticut Farms, there was no pastor of the church here. The Reverend James Caldwell, pastor of the First Presbyterian Church in Elizabeth Town, had moved his family to Connecticut Farms for greater safety when his church was burned, and had taken up residence in the parsonage. In addition to being a pastor, Mr. Caldwell was chaplain of Colonel Dayton's New Jersey regiment and Deputy Quarter-Master General. It is said that a visitor to his office, upon seeing the letters D.Q.M.G. following his name on a sign, said that it must mean "Devilish Queer Minister of the Gospel." On June 23 he played a courageous part in the battle at Springfield (see No. 135). While he was there, a lone redcoat crossed the garden of the parsonage at Connecticut Farms, fired a musket through a window, and killed Mrs. Caldwell. When he returned from the battle, Caldwell found the town, the church, and the parsonage in ruins and his children motherless. The tragedy served to renew the spirit and effort in the Revolution. Hessian soldiers killed in the fighting here lie buried in the churchyard.

In 1783 the church was rebuilt on the same site. The red sandstone is typical of the churches of the period in this region. It lent itself to being dressed to the shape of large brick, and the variations in shade made it possible to lay up a wall in a pattern, such as one sees in this building. The gable ends are of wood. In 1847 the building was repaired, and it has undergone alterations at various periods to meet the needs and fashions of the times. In 1789, the year in which the Republic began under its first President, the congregation voted to abolish the custom of men and women sitting on opposite sides of the church during services. The custom was quite prevalent in New England as well as in this region, but under the new Republic families here could sit together in church.

135

Springfield Meeting House (1791)
First Presbyterian Church

Springfield, Union County, New Jersey

The original building of the First Presbyterian Church of Springfield was erected in 1746. Additional wooded land, which provided the parsonage with firewood for many years, was given to the parish for the payment of "one pint of spring water when demanded on the premises." Less than two decades later, in 1761, the second meeting house was completed. In 1778 the meeting house became a depot for military stores, and church services thereafter were held in the attic of the parsonage.

As the Revolution developed, Springfield became strategic in the effort of the British to drive Washington out of New Jersey. The Battle of Springfield was fought on June 23, 1780, and much of the fighting was waged in the village around the meeting house. The chaplain of Colonel Dayton's New Jersey regiment, the Reverend James Caldwell, who was pastor of the First Presbyterian Church at Elizabeth which had been burned recently by the British (see No. 133), was in the midst of the battle. When he saw that the troops were short of gunwadding, he rushed into the church and carried out armfuls of Watts' hymnals; tossing them to the soldiers he said, "Now put Watts into them, boys!" Even though the Continentals, supplemented by farmers from the countryside, were greatly outnumbered, the British force was driven to retreat, but not until after the village and the church had been burned. A monument commemorates the initiative of the "fighting parson," whom the Tories called the "high priest of the Revolution." On the lawn before the present meeting house stands a statue of a militiaman with the inscription "Of what avail the plow or sail or land or life if Freedom fail!"

In the course of their retreat to Staten Island, the British burned the town of Connecticut Farms, the church, and the parsonage and killed Hannah, the wife of the Reverend James Caldwell (see No. 134).

In 1791 the meeting house was rebuilt on the old foundations (one of the two exceptions to our arbitrary limit of the year 1789). Its colonial style is along the lines of its predecessor. The walls are covered with hand-split shakes, and the nails and hardware are hand-wrought. About 1880 some minor alterations were made in the interior, but the building is still practically in its original condition, a reminder of critical times in the founding of the nation.

136

Plainfield Friends Meeting House (1788)

Watchung Avenue, Plainfield, Union County, New Jersey

The first organization meeting of Quakers in this section of the Province of East Jersey was held in Amboy, now Perth Amboy, in 1686. In 1704 the Meeting was transferred to Woodbridge, but it was discontinued as a result of the Keithian controversy, which was causing some difficulty among Quakers in both England and America. A member of that Meeting, John Laing, obtained permission to hold a meeting at his home in Piscataway Township, near the boundary of present Plainfield. He bequeathed land to the Society, and in 1731 a meeting house was built on it, three and one-half miles from the present meeting house. That building served for over fifty years, and then in Eleventh month of 1787 the Friends voted to find a suitable place to build a new meeting house in Plainfield. The present building was erected in 1788, and the first Monthly Meeting was held in it the 20th of Eighth month in that year.

Materials from the old building were used in constructing the new. In the horse sheds, converted to office and rooms for classes and storage in recent years, may be seen some of the earlier timbers. Edward Fitz Randolph, a member of the building committee and a carpenter in the construction, served as guide to General Washington to a high point in the Watchung Mountains, now called Washington Rock, where he and his staff could observe movements of the enemy on the plain. In 1873 fire damaged one end of the building, but the rest of the shingled walls and structure is substantially the original. In 1836 the Society sold adjacent land for a railroad right of way, and ever since 1837 trains have been interfering with meditation and speaking in the meeting house. The Library of Congress has designated it as a Historic American Building.

137

Randolph Friends Meeting House (1758)
Mendham Friends Meeting House

near Dover, Morris County, New Jersey

Out in the country a few miles south of Dover and toward Littleton, stands a small, square frame meeting house painted white. In 1758 it was built in the township of Mendham, and was known as Mendham Friends Meeting during its colonial life. It also was referred to occasionally as Mill Brook, the name of the near-by village and stream. In 1805 the northern part of the township was set off, and the new township was named Randolph, in honor of Hartshorn Fitz Randolph, one of the founders of this Meeting. For three-quarters of a century it was the only place of worship in the township. Near the meeting house there are abandoned iron-ore pits which once fed the Dover furnaces and made mining an important industry of New Jersey.

The Meeting was established in 1740, when Woodbridge (replaced later by Rahway as a result of the Keithian controversy) Monthly Meeting granted liberty for Friends in Morris County to hold meetings at the house of William Schooley. As the Friends increased in number, the original grant of four meetings a year was increased to

weekly meetings and, in 1756, to week-day meetings as well. In that year a Preparative Meeting was allowed to meet every three months. Two years later these Friends were allowed to build on Robert Schooley's land. The committee to select the site, to plan the present building, and to promote subscriptions, included Hartshorn Fitz Randolph. Within two months a fund of £75 was subscribed and building was begun. The overall dimensions are twenty-five by twenty-six feet. The structure is pegged, even in the floor boards, where one would expect to find nails. This small building contains a gallery and a partition for dividing the men's and women's business meetings. Known as the "shutters," this partition consists of two long panels on the floor, with a door between, and swinging battened panels hinged to the overhead beams which can be unlatched and lowered to meet the floor panels and divide the room, or raised to open the one large room for meetings for worship. For heat in winter there is a trap in the floor covering a two-foot pit, in which flagstones held burning charcoal; the individual footwarmers could be stoked from this central supply. Some of the benches are plain and some have backs. The interior of the meeting house has never been painted.

In 1786 the Meeting was still a part of Philadelphia Yearly Meeting. In 1835 it was joined to Shrewsbury Quarter to strengthen the latter, and it then became a part of New York Yearly Meeting. In 1864, after an active life of about one hundred and twenty-four years, the Meeting was laid down. The records then went to Plainfield (see No. 136). In 1954, however, the meeting house was reopened for a Meeting for Worship to be held First-days during the summer months; it proved to be lasting, and meetings have been held regularly ever since. In 1956 the Dover Monthly Meeting was established, and it became part of All Friends Quarterly Meeting, New York Yearly Meeting.

138

Christ Church (1743)

Church and Neilson Streets, New Brunswick, Middlesex County, New Jersey

On the corner of Church and Neilson Streets in New Brunswick stands Christ Church, where occurred an important event in the history of the Episcopal Church in America. The Dutch Re-

ing the recent accomplishment of independence from England. Sixteen clergymen and laymen from New York, New Jersey, and Pennsylvania attended, and from this meeting issued the call which resulted in the first general convention and the subsequent adoption of the Book of Common Prayer and the Constitution of the new Church (see Christ Church, Philadelphia, No. 205).

139

Zion Lutheran Church (1750)

Oldwick, Hunterdon County, New Jersey

In 1732 German Lutherans from the Rhine Palatinate came to New Jersey and settled in the Mahwah district near the New York border, at Oldwick, at Long Valley, and at New Brunswick. In 1750 these northern New Jersey Lutherans united and built the present stone church in Oldwick. It is the only colonial German Lutheran church still standing in New Jersey, and it continues with an active congregation. The building has undergone a series of remodelings, in 1831, 1854, and 1883, and it has lost much of its original colonial character.

formed Church was the first in New Brunswick, being active here as early as 1717. A generation later, in 1742, Christ Church Parish was organized through the efforts of William Skinner, the missionary in Perth Amboy for the Society for the Propagation of the Faith in Foreign Parts. The church was an unintended result of the second visit of George Whitefield to America and his vigorous revival preaching in New Brunswick. The pastors of the two churches in town, Theodore Jacobus Frelinghuysen of the Dutch Reformed Church and Gilbert Tennent of the Presbyterian Church, were encouraged to intensify their preaching of austere Calvinism. As there was no other church to attend, the Episcopalians in town took the occasion to build a church of their own. The first church of the parish was built of stone in 1743. In 1852 the body of the building was taken down, and all of the stone was used in the present building. The tower of 1743 was retained and made a part of the present church.

The Reverend Samuel Seabury, who was to become the first American bishop (see St. Paul's Church, Woodbury, Conn. No. 11), was rector here from 1754 to 1757. At a meeting of the corporation for the relief of widows and children of clergymen held in this church May 11, 1784, a major step was taken to promote the organization of the Episcopal Church in America, follow-

140

St. Thomas' Church (1769)

Alexandria, Hunterdon County, New Jersey

About 1723, in frontier country of Hunterdon County east of the Delaware River, a colonial Anglican parish was gathered as St. Thomas', Kingwood. It was known by that name until about 1815, when it was given the name Alexandria from the township in which it is located. There is neither a town nor post office of Alexandria, and the town of Kingwood lies many miles to the south. The church is about two miles west of Pittstown and about eight miles northwest of Flemington.

John Talbot, the "Apostle of New Jersey," visited the community about 1723, and it is assumed, according to Nelson Burr in his *The Anglican Church of New Jersey,* that the parish was organized and the first church was built about that time. Talbot (1645-1727) had come to America with George Keith in 1702, and was serving as a missionary of the Society for the Propagation of the Gospel in Foreign Parts. He had founded St. Mary's Church, Burlington (No. 159), the mother church of the Anglican Communion in New Jersey.

The first church was built of logs. It was located on the Pittstown Road at Everittstown, about three miles west of the present site. Mortises and other marks on the timbers of the present

building indicate that they came from that first structure. The church was one among many stations of the northwest frontier mission, which were visited by traveling missionaries of the Society. In 1760 Andrew Morton, a missionary of the Society, took charge here. In 1752 John Stevens, who became a member of the Governor's Council and president of the board of East Jersey Proprietors, and who owned a large tract of land in Hunterdon County, took part in establishing an annual sum for the Amwell (Lambertville) and Kingwood churches.

Morton was succeeded by William Frazer, who was licensed by the Bishop of London December 21, 1767, and assigned to Kingwood, Amwell, and Musconetcong. He found the log church here unfit for services, and he undertook at once to have the present stone church built. The land was given by Lewis Stevens, a part of his Cornwall Plantation. His memorial stone is in the floor of the church before the chancel. The stone walls were erected in the summer of 1769, but the building was not completed and finished for many years, and in 1772 it could be used only during the summer months. During the Revolution the church was closed; the patriots persecuted Frazer, but he conducted services privately and remained here until his death in 1795. After the Revolution he reopened the church, but the congregation was small and services were intermittent. The building was neglected, but the church was kept alive by a few faithful members. About

1822 there was a revival, and the building was repaired, after the appointment of Daniel Higbee as missionary. With the encouragement of visiting missionaries from other churches, St. Thomas' had forty years of activity, but by 1875 the building again was unfit for use. In 1875-76 the church was completely repaired through the generosity of Frederick A. Potts, and since that time St. Thomas' has been active under the care of near-by parishes. At the west end, a rectangular window above the present arched window has been blocked up, and rectangular frames have been fitted into the arched apertures of the smaller lower windows. There is a large arched window in the east end behind the altar. The old glass survives in the window sash. At present St. Thomas', Alexandria, is a mission church in the care of Calvary Episcopal Church, Flemington, and services are held during July, August, and September.

141

Old School Baptist Church (1747)

Hopewell, Mercer County, New Jersey

This church was organized in 1715. Meetings were held in various homes until this first meeting house was built in 1747. It was constructed of brown stone. In 1822 it was enlarged by extending the front. The new front wall was built of brick, and brick covers the side walls. The rear wall has stucco on the original stone. The site was given by John Hart, a signer of the Declaration of Independence. The meeting house was used as a hospital during the Revolution.

142

Stony Brook Friends Meeting House (1726)

Princeton, Mercer County, New Jersey

The old Quaker meeting house stands alone at the end of a wooded lane called Quaker Road, about a mile south of Princeton. In 1710 the Meeting was indulged by Chesterfield Monthly Meeting, which owns the property. In 1726 it was established. The meeting house is of two periods; the end near the drive was built in 1726 and the rest in 1760. The two-story building has fireplaces at both ends. Until 1757 this was the only house of worship in the Princeton area, and it was attended by most of the town's residents. Many of the early settlers and prominent inhabitants of the town lie buried in the unmarked graves of this Quaker burying ground, including Richard Stockton, a signer of the Declaration of Independence. Immediately north of the meeting house the Battle of Princeton began on, as the Quakers record it, First month 3rd, 1777. Regular meetings are held, and on special occasions descendants of early members come from distant places to attend.

placed with a new one. The front part of the present church is of that date; the remainder of the building is the product of remodeling done in the 1800's. From the time the building was erected, town meetings were held here during the colonial years. Located on the Great Highway, the town and the church saw many famous travelers, as well as the passing and repassing of the armies during the Revolution. In 1810 a school that became the Lawrenceville School, a preparatory school for boys, was founded by the church during the ministry of the Reverend Isaac Van Arsdale Brown.

143

Presbyterian Church of Lawrenceville (1764)
Maidenhead Presbyterian Church

Lawrenceville, Lawrence Township, Mercer County, New Jersey

In 1798 the early colonial town of Maidenhead was incorporated. Situated on the Great Highway between Philadelphia and New York, it had served as a post on that road during the colonial period. In 1816 the name was changed to Lawrenceville in honor of Captain James Lawrence. When his command, the *Chesapeake*, was being captured by the British of the *Shannon* off Boston, on June 1, 1813, his dying words gave the United States Navy a rallying cry for all time: "Don't give up the ship!"

The earliest record of a Presbyterian house of worship here is found in a deed of 1698, "for the erection of a meeting house, and for burying-ground and school house. . . ." The date of the organization of the church here is not certain, but it is assumed to be that year, 1698. Neither is the exact location of that early plot of land quite certain, but the present site was deeded in 1710. It is believed that there was a meeting house on the site in that year. The church secured a regular pastor in 1715, and the first definite record of the meeting house here is in 1716.

In 1764, as the building had become outgrown by the congregation, it was razed and re-

144

Trenton Friends Meeting House (1739)

East Hanover and Montgomery Streets, Trenton, Mercer County, New Jersey

Early meetings at Trent Town were allowed by Chesterfield Monthly Meeting in 1734. This first brick meeting house in Trenton was built in 1739, enlarged in 1872, and again remodeled in 1896. It was occupied by the British during the Revolution. Among other settlers buried here is George Clymer, a signer of the Declaration of Independence. Regular meetings are still held.

145

Ye Olde Yellow Meeting House (1737)

Imlaystown, Monmouth County, New Jersey

In the early 1700's a 2,000-acre tract of land, situated at the confluence of the Buck Hole Creek and Doctor's Creek at Imlaystown, belonged to Richard Slater. He gave the land on which the Baptists built Ye Olde Yellow Meeting House in 1737. The two-story building stands among great oaks in the countryside near the town. It is still painted yellow with blue shutters, and it is preserved in its colonial state. There are three en-trances, each with a steppingstone of half a mill-stone. Inside are the old white, high-backed benches and a gallery at the rear. The congrega-tion now uses a newer church in Imlaystown. On the last Sunday in July descendants of early mem-bers gather at the old meeting house for all-day services and picnic lunch. Captain James Law-rence, for whom Lawrenceville was named (see No. 143), was descended from a member of this church.

It is of interest to note that the word *Ye* in the name is pronounced *the*. The letter *Y* was the nearest in early movable type to the thorn, a rune of Anglo-Saxon script for the sound "th."

146

Tennent Church (1751)
The Scots Church, Old Freehold
Church, First Presbyterian Church
in Freehold

Tennent, Monmouth County, New Jersey

Tennent is a hamlet of a few houses less than four miles from Freehold. At the western edge of the Monmouth Battlefield is White Hill, on which stands the Old Tennent Church. The congregation of Scottish Covenanters, organized in 1692, was the earliest Presbyterian congregation in New Jersey and one of the earliest in the country. Their first meeting house was built about five miles north of the present site. On White Hill this Presbyterian church was founded in 1731, and a frame meeting house was erected in that year. It is said that, in 1746, the Reverend David Brainerd, the missionary who had been ordained at Old First, Newark (see No. 132), administered Communion to his Indian converts at the communion table which is still in use. King George II granted a royal charter to the church in 1749. As the meeting house was found to be too small for the congregation in 1751, it was replaced by the present building. It stands relatively unchanged since that date.

In 1733, two years after the church was built, the Reverend William Tennent, Jr. became pastor. He served until his death in 1777 and was buried beneath the church floor. He was one of the four sons of William Tennent, Sr., pastor of Neshaminy Presbyterian Church in Pennsylvania (No. 238), and he attended the Log College (forerunner of Princeton University), which had been founded there by his father to educate his four sons and other youths for the ministry. A second son, the Reverend John Tennent, also served as pastor of the Freehold Church; the other two sons, Charles and Gilbert, became ministers and served churches in Delaware (see Nos. 17 and 26). In 1859 the church was renamed in honor of this outstanding Presbyterian family. They were New Side Presbyterians, influenced by the Pietists and George Whitefield, who preached here in 1740.

Some months after the death of the pastor, William Tennent, Jr., who had supported the American cause from the earliest days of the Revolution, the Battle of Monmouth was fought here on Sunday, June 28, 1778. General Washington's army of about fifteen thousand intercepted General Clinton's force of similar size, which was escorting a wagon train of loot on the Shrewsbury Road, on its way to Sandy Hook to embark. The battle was indecisive, as the British decamped during the night and reached their embarkation, but they left behind many more dead than did the Americans, and greatly encouraged the army of soldiers who had come from the bitter winter quarters at Valley Forge. Lieutenant Colonel Monckton, a British officer who was killed in the middle of the battle, lies buried in the cemetery with a monument marking his grave; there lie also the remains of many others who died in the battle. The meeting house was used as a hospital after the battle, and bloodstains still show on the old benches. The building was torn by bullets, and the holes were left as they were, until they had to be repaired to save the building. The Reverend John Woodhull, who succeeded the late William Tennent, Jr., as pastor in 1778, had served as a chaplain in Washington's army, and is said to have taken part in the Battle of Monmouth.

147

St. Peter's Church (c. 1770)

Freehold, Monmouth County, New Jersey

The earliest meetings of this parish were in Topanemus, four miles north and in the township of Freehold. There a community of Quakers built a meeting house in 1683. Prominent in the history of the Meeting was George Keith (c. 1639-1716). He was a Scottish Presbyterian educated for the ministry, who had been converted to Quakerism, had toured Holland and Germany with George Fox and William Penn, and had come to America in 1684. In East Jersey, after William Penn had founded the Province of West Jersey in 1676, Keith was surveyor-general. He founded the town of Freehold and lived here for some years. He alienated the Quakers, in both America and England, on points of theology, and upon his return to London he was disowned by the Yearly Meeting of 1694. In 1700 he became an Anglican priest. In 1701 the Society for the Propagation of the Gospel in Foreign Parts was chartered in London, and from 1702 to 1704 he served in America as a missionary of the Society. In that capacity he was influential in founding or expanding a number of churches (see for example Christ Church, Shrewsbury, No. 148).

In 1702, upon the return of George Keith to Topanemus, together with John Talbot who worked with him, some of the Quakers of the Meeting were converted to the Church of England, and St. Peter's Church was founded. That was also the year in which East and West Jersey

reunited as one Crown colony. By 1709 so many of the Friends had become Anglicans that the Friends meeting house was willed to the church by the owner, Thomas Boels, a parishioner who died that year, and it became the first church of St. Peter's. Keith and Talbot went from here to Burlington, where St. Mary's Church was founded (see No. 159).

About 1770 St. Peter's Church moved from Topanemus to Freehold and erected the present building on Throckmorton Street. At the time of the Battle of Monmouth, in 1778, the interior of the church had not been finished, but the church was used to shelter the wounded during and after the battle. The framework of the larger part of the nave is that of the original building. During the nineteenth century alterations were made, including the arrangement of doors and the introduction of lancet windows of a style sometimes referred to as "carpenter Gothic." Some of the original handmade shingles cover the walls, and some of the pews evidently have been reconstructed from the original box pews.

148

Christ Church (1769)

Shrewsbury, Monmouth County, New Jersey

Shrewsbury was settled by Congregationalists in 1664. It was difficult for the Church of England to enter New Jersey against the strong opposition of the Dutch Reformed Church, the Independents or Congregationalists, and the Presbyterians. In 1698 the Anglican Church made a beginning in the colony, at what is now Perth Amboy, near Shrewsbury, but it never became the Established Church in New Jersey as it did in all the colonies of the South.

In Shrewsbury, as well as in the Freehold area (see No. 147), the Reverend George Keith was active as the first missionary of the Society for the Propagation of the Gospel. In 1702, the year in which Keith returned from England to America, and the year following the founding of the S.P.G. in London, the parish here was begun with the baptism of twenty-four people. Among them was William Leeds, who eventually willed his large estate to the Church. The first building was erected between 1703 and 1705. The communion service, which is still used in Christ Church, was presented by Queen Anne in 1708. The Society was a special interest of hers, and she presented articles to each new Anglican church formed in America. In 1738 the building was small for the congregation, and it was replaced with a larger one. The church was granted a royal charter by King George II. The parish still possesses a John Baskett Bible of 1717, and also a Prayer Book of 1760, which was presented in 1767 by the Honorable William Franklin, son of Benjamin Franklin, while he was serving as the last royal governor of New Jersey.

The third and present church was built in 1769. The exterior is substantially in its original condition. Two changes have been made in the interior — the chancel was added in 1844, and the entrance through the tower was installed in 1874. The Reverend Samuel Cook, rector at the beginning of the Revolution, expressed Tory sympathies and was forced to leave. However, the British crown on the spire has survived, although it and the ball below it bear the marks of bullets fired by patriots.

149

Seaville Friends Meeting House (1727)
Old Cedar Meeting House

Seaville, Cape May County, New Jersey

The Cape May — or Seaville as it is now called — Meeting of Friends was established in 1702. It was at one time part of Great Egg Harbor Monthly Meeting, now discontinued. The minute book of the Monthly Meeting records that the present meeting house was built in 1727, and before that date meetings were held in the homes of members. The meeting house is said to have been built of fossil cedar dug from swamps, and at times it has the odor of cedar. It has the distinction of being the smallest frame meeting house in the country. There are no members; the meeting house is under the care of Salem Quarterly Meeting. Meetings for worship are held in Sixth through Eighth months at 10:30 A.M.

150

Fairfield Presbyterian Church (1780)
Old Stone Church

**New England Cross Roads,
Cumberland County, New Jersey**

We have seen that Connecticut Farms, near Elizabeth, was settled by families from Connecticut (see No. 134). In this southwest section of the colony, families from Fairfield County, Connecticut, were among the early settlers. They established at Cohansey the first Puritan Church in West Jersey, under the ministry of the Reverend Thomas Bridge (1692-1697). Five miles south of Bridgeton we come to New England Cross Roads, and here we find the Fairfield Presbyterian Church, named for the town and county in Connecticut.

The congregation was organized in 1680. A century later it was incorporated by an act of the legislature, in 1783, during the administration of the first governor of the State of New Jersey. The first church was built of logs. It stood beside Cohansey Creek, about a mile west of the present site. The second building, erected between 1713 and 1715, was a shingled frame structure of New England style. The present stone building was completed in 1780. It was used by the congregation until 1850, when they transferred to their present church in Fairton.

ing house between 1680 and 1685, and they built it in 1686. In 1694 the Preparative Meeting was established. In 1770 Greenwich Monthly Meeting was formed jointly by Greenwich and Alloways Creek (No. 153). The old meeting house burned down, and the present brick meeting house was built in 1771. An extension was added on the southeastern end at some later date. The county court was held here until the Revolutionary War began, and then the county seat was moved from Greenwich to Bridgeton. In 1893 the Monthly Meeting was laid down, and in 1903 the Meeting for Worship was discontinued. The property belongs to Haddonfield and Salem Quarterly Meetings.

151

Greenwich Friends Meeting House (1771)

Greenwich, Cumberland County, New Jersey

West of Cohansey Creek from New England Cross Roads (see No. 150), and about seven miles southwest of Bridgeton, we come to the village of Greenwich, named for a town in Fairfield County, Connecticut. Quakers were early settlers in this section; here they provided land for a meet-

152

Deerfield Stone Church (1771)
Deerfield Presbyterian Church

Deerfield, Cumberland County, New Jersey

Deerfield was settled in 1725 by families from the near-by towns of Fairfield and Greenwich and Scotch-Irish immigrants. Those who came here from Connecticut were Calvinistic in their religion, and those from Northern Ireland were Presbyterians in the old country. The town, originally called Deerfield Street, according to tradition was named for Deerfield in Massachusetts, which was well known to pioneers for its Indian massacre. The first house of worship was a log church built in 1732, according to tradition (the earliest records of the parish date from

1737). The first settled pastor was Andrew Hunter, who was installed in 1746. Enoch Green, who was installed as pastor in 1767, also tutored students in Latin for entrance to Princeton University. He became a chaplain in Washington's army and died of camp fever contracted at Valley Forge. In 1777 John Brainerd was installed. He served as pastor of the First Presbyterian Church, Newark (No. 132), where his brother David Brainerd was ordained and went forth to become famous as a missionary among the Indians. John succeeded his brother in that field, after David died of tuberculosis in 1747, at the age of twenty-nine. David had been a follower of George Whitefield, and both Brainerds were New Side Presbyterians. In addition to Whitefield, famous Presbyterians who preached here were Gilbert Tennent and Samuel Blair.

The present stone church was erected in 1711. There have been three renovations: in 1858 the recess was installed in the front of the building; in 1907 the gallery was removed, and graves of pastors buried in the aisle were moved to the churchyard; and in 1947 a stone floor with radiant heat was installed, and the windows were reglazed to simulate the original New Jersey glass.

The Christian Education Building was erected in 1878.

153

Alloways Creek Friends Meeting House (1754)

Hancock's Bridge, Salem County, New Jersey

The village of Hancock's Bridge is situated on Alloways Creek near its mouth at the Delaware River. The earliest meetings of Friends were held in 1678 at the home of John Penn. They were continued there until a meeting house was built in 1684 on the north side of the creek. Members had some difficulty in crossing the creek, and in 1710 a second meeting house was built on the south side. In 1754 the third and present meeting house was built in the village of Hancock's Bridge. In 1784 an addition was built. Since the spring of 1939, when the one lady died who had been attending each First-day, the meeting house has not been opened regularly each week. Meetings are held Second and Fourth Sundays, May through September, at 2 P.M. The property is in charge of Salem Quarterly Meeting.

154

Salem Friends Meeting House (1772)

**East Broadway at Walnut Street, Salem,
Salem County, New Jersey**

The Salem Meeting of Friends is an active and strong Meeting. Meetings were held in the homes of Friends as early as 1675. In the following year, 1676, Preparative and Monthly Meetings were established. In 1676 the land on which Salem was situated was in dispute between two Quakers, John Fenwick and Edward Byllinge. The settlement of the dispute and the disposition of the land led to William Penn and four other proprietors becoming masters of the Province of West Jersey. The Quarterly Meeting was established with Burlington in 1682. In 1686 Salem and Newton Meetings separated from Burlington and formed a Quarterly Meeting. From 1684 Half-Yearly Meetings were held alternately at

Salem and Burlington. Travel between the two became so great that, in 1681, the King's Highway was surveyed and work was begun to connect them. In that year Samuel and Ann Nicholson deeded their log house and plot of land on Wharf Street (now West Broadway) for the use of Salem Monthly Meeting. In 1683 the house was enlarged. In 1700 a brick meeting house was built on the same lot near the Salem Oak. In 1772 the present meeting house was built to replace the older one, which was outgrown. It is situated on what is now East Broadway opposite Walnut Street. It is a beautiful example of the Friends brick meeting house of the period, and it has been kept in good condition. Regular meetings are held each First-day at 10:30 A.M.

In February, 1778, Anthony Wayne brought a force to this section foraging for supplies to feed Washington's army at Valley Forge. When he was successful in driving a herd of about one hundred and fifty cattle to the relief of the army, Salem beef became famous.

155

Woodstown Friends Meeting House (1784)

Woodstown, Salem County, New Jersey

Woodstown was begun when a Quaker, Jackanias Wood, built the first house here in the early 1700's. Meetings for worship were held in the homes of Friends from 1715 to 1719, when the first meeting house was built. About 1725 the Meeting was organized. In 1794 the Monthly Meeting was established as a division of Salem Monthly Meeting. The present meeting house was begun in 1784 and finished in 1785. In 1849 additions were built. Regular meetings are held; like Salem, Woodstown is an active and strong meeting.

156

Moravian Church (1786) *Zion Episcopal Church*

near Sharptown, Salem County, New Jersey

About three miles north of Sharptown on the King's Highway, the great road surveyed in 1681 to connect Salem and Burlington, the old Moravian Church stands on Oliphant's Hill. The Moravian Church is the oldest Protestant denomination (see Chapter VI), having originated before Martin Luther and the Reformation. Several churches of the denomination branched out from Bethlehem, Pennsylvania (see No. 244). The Moravians here built their first church of logs, in 1747, near the present site, and on August 31, 1749, Bishop A. G. Spangenberg dedicated the building. In June of 1786 they began to build the present brick church to replace the old structure. It was dedicated on July 5, 1789, by Bishop J. Ettwein. By 1836 it was no longer active, and the property was conveyed to the Protestant Episcopal Church on October 15 of that year; by that denomination it was called Zion Episcopal Church. Now it is not used by Episcopalians, and only memorial services are held. The two-story, plain interior has no altar, but a facing chair and high-backed pews. A glass case holds an old Bible and relics of the past history of the church.

157

Trinity Church (1784)
Old Swedes

Swedesboro, Gloucester County, New Jersey

Continuing north from the Moravian Church on the King's Highway, built in 1681 by order of the provincial legislature of West Jersey, we come to the church of another denomination. Here in Swedesboro, on a hill above Raccoon Creek, its white spire rising above the town, stands Old Swedes Church. Like the one built by the Swedes in their original settlement at Christina, New Sweden (Wilmington, Delaware No. 13), it was given the name Trinity.

The Swedish Lutherans, who had come here to the town of Raccoon and made it their own, actually were settling in Swedish territory. They entered New Jersey soon after 1638, when they had established a fort and trading post across the Delaware at Christina. In 1640 they bought from the Indians a vast tract of land on the New Jersey side, extending from Cape May to Raccoon Creek; small trading posts were established, for the trappers who worked the streams flowing into the Delaware River, but they grew slowly. The Dutch of New Amsterdam (New York) took over the Swedish forts on the Delaware in 1655, and in

1664 the British took over the Dutch domain, including all of New Jersey. Different names were given to the creek here by these various inhabitants — the Indians called it Naraticon, the Dutch made it Naraticon's Kil, the Swedes called it Araratcung, which became abbreviated to Ratcung, and the British named it Raccoon. The isolated pocket of Swedes here submitted peacefully to British rule. During the Revolution, particularly before the British evacuated Philadelphia in 1778, the town, the countryside, and the people suffered from "plundering, marauding, imprisoning, and burning of houses," but the church was spared.

The congregation was founded here before 1700. At first its members attended Trinity Church at Christina (Wilmington). In the records of that church they are referred to as the people "on the other side of the river." Obviously they could not endure for many years the long and hazardous journey to attend church, and in 1703 they built their first church, a modest log structure. They had contributed to the building of the church at Christina, with the understanding that the mother church would contribute to the building of theirs; when the time came, however, Trinity Church, Christina, subscribed nothing and actively opposed the project. The present building was erected in 1784, after the War of the Revolution had ended. The pastor took an active part in the work by building ovens for drying rain-dampened brick; in a gable can be seen the difference between bricks that had been dried and those laid damp. Only a few years after the church was finished, the Republic of the United States began, and the Swedish mission in America came to an end. For a short time Trinity Church had a German Lutheran minister, but in 1789 it became a part of the Protestant Episcopal Church. The silver communion service of 1730 is still in use.

158

Woodbury Friends Meeting House (1715)

Woodbury, Gloucester County, New Jersey

Continuing north from Old Swedes at Swedesboro on the King's Highway, we come to Woodbury, the county seat of Gloucester County. Here on Broad Street, a part of the King's Highway, stands the Woodbury Friends Meeting House. The town is named for John Wood, in whose house the early meetings were held, beginning in 1696. He deeded land for a meeting house which was built in that year, situated near Woodbury Creek on the side toward the Delaware River. After the King's Highway was built the present site was bought, and the brick meeting house was built here in 1715. In 1785 a large extension was built on the east end (the right in the photograph), which doubled the size of the building; the dividing line is visible in the wall. There are school rooms on the second floor, and a room and open attic on the third, where the old hand-hewn beams can be seen.

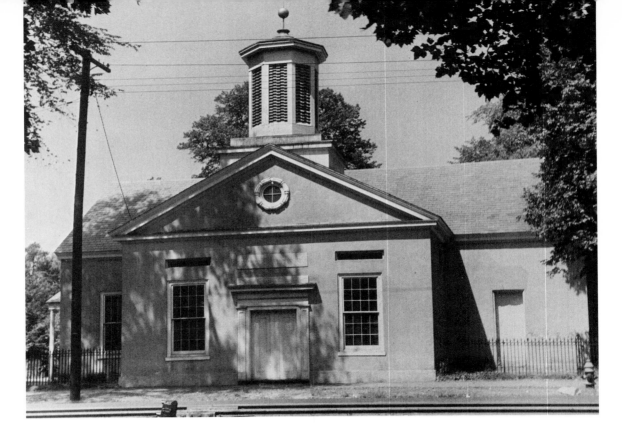

159

Old St. Mary's Church (1703)

Burlington, Burlington County, New Jersey

As we have seen at St. Peter's Church, Freehold (No. 147), George Keith and John Talbot, two clergymen of the Church of England, came from London to America in 1702, and served as missionaries of the Society for the Propagation of the Gospel in Foreign Parts. For the purpose of founding Anglican churches in America and providing ministers for them, particularly in those colonies where the churches of Dissenters and Separatists were established and growing, a charter had been granted the year before, founding the Society. Keith and Talbot, therefore, were among the first missionaries of the Society, and both became highly successful in their work. Together they left Freehold, after founding the church there, and went to Burlington, where they founded St. Mary's Church on All Saints' Day, November 1, 1702, in the Burlington Town Hall. The Town of Burlington had been settled by Quakers in 1677, and in 1702 the Friends were well established (see No. 160). The provinces of East Jersey and West Jersey were reunited in that year, but Burlington, which had

been serving as the capital of West Jersey, continued to share the honor with Perth Amboy, and there was a need for an Anglican parish in the capital of the royal colony. George Keith went on from Burlington to cover the field all the way into Virginia, while John Talbot remained here and became the first rector of St. Mary's Church, in November of 1705. For a while he was pastor of all New Jersey except Monmouth County, where he had helped to found St. Peter's Church, and he became known as "the Apostle of New Jersey." For twenty years he wrote to London and advocated the establishment of an American Episcopate, which was accomplished finally in 1787, after the Revolution, by the consecration of Samuel Seabury as Bishop of Connecticut.

In 1703, on March 25, the Feast of the Annunciation, the cornerstone of the present building was laid, and the church was dedicated to St. Mary the Virgin. In August the building was sufficiently advanced to be used for services. During the following year an attempt was made by Lord Cornbury, a member of the parish who had been serving as governor of West Jersey, to name the Church "St. Anne's," in honor of his cousin, "Good Queen Anne," who took such an active interest in the American churches, and who gave to this church lead, glass, and silver chalice and paten which are still in use. The name "St. Mary's" remained, however, both for its association with the date of the foundation stone and with St. Mary's Church at Bridlington, Yorkshire, the home of some of the founders of the town.

The building originally was rectangular, but the original part now forms the nave of a cruciform structure. In 1769 the first of a series of alterations was made; the building was extended on the west, a gallery was added, and a bell with the date was installed. Like the Liberty Bell, this bell was cast in England by Lester and Pack. In 1811 an apsidal chancel was added. In 1834 the building was enlarged to its present size and given the form of a Latin cross. The brick then was rough cast, to resemble freestone or granite. The New St. Mary's Church was completed on the same grounds in 1854, under the rectorship of George Washington Doane, who at the same time was the second Bishop of New Jersey and used St. Mary's Church as the cathedral. The plan was drawn by Richard Upjohn, who designed Trinity Church in New York, and who led the Gothic Revival in America. The old church is used for Sunday school and occasional services. In the old churchyard lie the remains of John Talbot; Bishop Doane; William H. Odenheimer, third Bishop of New Jersey and former rector; and Wallace John Gardner, sixth Bishop of New Jersey, in addition to forty-eight priests and deacons; Elias Boudinot, ninth president of the Continental Congress, who signed the treaty of peace with Great Britain in 1783; and William Bradford, attorney general in President Washington's administration.

160

Burlington Friends Meeting House (1784)

Burlington, Burlington County, New Jersey

After following the King's Highway up the Delaware River from the south, we come to its origin at Burlington. The towns of Burlington and Salem were founded in the course of the settlement of claims, negotiated by William Penn, that led to the formation of the Province of West Jersey. The Province of New Jersey had been granted to his brother James; and when William had negotiated satisfactorily the claims in dispute, which involved the land on which Salem was to be located, and new land purchased from the Indians for the site of Burlington, he was made

one of the five proprietors of the new province. He drafted its constitution, entitled "Concessions," on the lines of the laws of England, but he made history when he placed at the head of the list of human rights the new principle of perfect religious freedom.

Burlington was settled by Quakers in 1677, when two companies arrived on the *Kent,* one from London and the other from Yorkshire. The Indian Chief Ockanickon died in that year, and a rough stone marks his grave near the present meeting house. The new settlement was first named New Beverly, and later it became Bridlington (for the Quakers' home in Yorkshire), which name evolved to the present form. In 1678 a second company of Quakers arrived in the *Shield,* and the community grew rapidly as a Quaker town. In 1681, after the Province of West Jersey had been formed, Burlington became the capital and the port of entry. From 1702, after the reunion of East and West Jersey, Burlington served, with Perth Amboy, as one of the two capitals of

the royal province, and the legislature met at both alternately, under the provincial and then the state governments, until 1790.

The Monthly Meeting was set up in 1678, the year after the original landing. The first meeting house was built in 1682, the year in which William Penn first came to America. In 1696 an addition was built. In 1784 the present brick meeting house was built on the site of the first; the bricks of the first went into the building of their first school, now the Y.W.C.A. The Yearly Meeting, established in 1681, was held here until the Quakers had become established in Philadelphia; it was then held in both alternately until 1760, when it was transferred permanently to Philadelphia. The 250th anniversary of Philadelphia Yearly Meeting was commemorated at Burlington in 1931, where William Penn had attended it in his time. Regular meetings are held at Burlington.

161

Mount Laurel (Evesham) Friends Meeting House (1760)

Burlington County, New Jersey

About three miles south of Moorestown, Mount Laurel rises to an elevation of 450 feet, the highest hill in the region. It looks down upon villages which, like Moorestown, were early Quaker settlements on this rich level land of West Jersey. The old stone meeting house stands alone on Mount Laurel Road. In 1694 the earliest meetings in Evesham Township were held in the home of William Evans. The names "Evesham" and

"Mount Laurel" are used in connection with the different meetings. The Evesham Monthly Meeting was set off from Haddonfield Monthly Meeting in 1760, and the older part of the present meeting house was built in that year. In 1798 the building was enlarged, and that date appears on the west end. Meetings are held on First-day from Fifth month 1st to Tenth month 1st. The vocal ministry is borne mostly by visitors. Haddonfield and Salem Quarterly Meeting is held at Mount Laurel in Sixth month. The 200th anniversary was commemorated in a historical meeting held Sixth month 16th, 1960.

162

Rancocas Friends Meeting House (1772)

Rancocas, Burlington County, New Jersey

In 1681, the year in which the Yearly Meeting was established at Burlington, the first meetings here were held in the home of Thomas Harding. The first meeting house was built in 1720, the year in which John Woolman, a prominent Friend and author, was born at the town which was still called "Ancocas." He went to school there, and lived on the family farm until he moved to Mount Holly in 1740. The present brick meeting house replaced the first in 1772, the year of Woolman's death. The date appears in the brick pattern of a gable. Meetings for worship have been held ever since 1681. The Burlington Monthly Meeting is held here regularly. Burlington Quarterly Meeting is held here in alternation with other locations. They all are in Philadelphia Yearly Meeting.

163

Mount Holly Friends Meeting House (1775)

Mount Holly, Burlington County, New Jersey

Mount Holly was settled partly on land purchased in 1676 from Edward Byllynge and the trustees of West Jersey, of whom William Penn was one. The town was settled by Quakers. As early as 1687 meetings were held in private homes. The present brick meeting house, on Main and Garden Streets, was built in 1775; the Mount Holly Monthly Meeting was established in 1776 by division of Burlington. In 1850 the meeting house was enlarged. During the Revolution, British troops used the meeting house as a commissary, and it is believed that the knife marks on the benches were made at that time. In November and December of 1779, Mount Holly was the temporary capital of New Jersey, and the legislature met in the meeting house. It was here that Governor William Livingston designated Thursday, December 9, 1779, as the first Thanksgiving Day for New Jersey under the new resolution of Congress. In 1796 the county seat was transferred from Burlington to Mount Holly. Regular meetings of Friends are held in this meeting house. In Mount Holly the red brick home of John Woolman (1720-1772), a distinguished member of the Religious Society of Friends, and a member of this Meeting, is preserved as the John Woolman Memorial. The building, which was built in 1783, is furnished in the style of his time; the library includes several editions of his well-known *Journal*, in which he expressed concern for brotherhood and social welfare.

164

Arney's Mount Friends Meeting House (1775)

Burlington County, New Jersey

Arney's Mount Meeting House stands alone in the country about five miles northeast of Mount Holly. Early meetings were held in 1743 in a school house; a meeting house of logs was built as early as 1771. The present building was erected in 1775 of bog-iron stone. Bog iron found in this section of New Jersey was the iron used in the colonial period; it went into guns and cannon balls for the Continental Army. The interior woodwork of the meeting house was burned twice, in 1800 and 1809. The Preparative Meeting was set up in 1776, and was laid down in 1870. Appointed meetings are held in the summer. Former members living in Pemberton joined Mount Holly Monthly Meeting. Several families living in the neighborhood now worship here twice a month on First-day mornings.

165

Old Springfield Friends Meeting House (1775)
Copany Friends Meeting House

Jacksonville, Burlington County, New Jersey

This old Friends meeting house has been popularly known as Copany, from Mattacopany, an Indian chief of the region. The Meeting was established in 1682. The first meeting house was built in 1698. The second and present building was erected of brick in 1775. During the Revolution it was used as a hospital after skirmishes had been fought in the neighborhood. The Preparative Meeting apparently was laid down in 1914. In 1959 the interior was reconstructed with rooms for a dwelling, and the house was occupied by an active Friend.

166

Friends Meeting House (1740)

Bordentown, Burlington County, New Jersey

On Farnsworth Avenue in Bordentown, tucked in between the Bordentown Banking Company and a row of other commercial buildings, one finds a small, plain brick building, covered with yellow stucco and ivy, and occupied by the Building and Loan Company. It is set back from the sidewalk a few paces, beneath evergreen trees on a small lawn. It was built in 1740 by Friends, the first house of worship in Bordentown.

167

Chesterfield Friends Meeting House (1773)

Crosswicks, Burlington County, New Jersey

Friends came here from England about 1677 and settled on the Crossweeksung (Divided Creek), where there was an Indian village. Early meetings were held in the home of Thomas Lambert. About 1680 the Meeting was settled by Friends of Trenton, and it was given the present name. The first meeting house was built of wood in 1693. The second was built of brick in 1707, at a location not far from the first.

The third and present meeting house was built in 1773, by which time the older one was not large enough. After consideration had been given to enlarging the old building, it was decided to build a new one, at a location near the burying ground and the site of the first meeting house. A committee was sent to study Buckingham Friends Meeting House in Pennsylvania (No. 241), and to learn its cost. That building was of stone, and it was decided to build the third meeting house of brick, using the brick from the second building, at a cost of about £750. This building is a fine example of Quaker meeting house architecture of the period, both exterior and interior. Another brick building on the grounds was built in 1784 and used as a school until recent years.

On June 23, 1778, a battle was fought here, when American troops tried to prevent a detachment of British troops from crossing Crosswicks Creek, on their march from Philadelphia to Monmouth (see Tennent Church, No. 146). Three cannon balls were fired through the meeting house — two went through the roof, and the third lodged in the north wall over a doorway, where it still can be seen. Hessian troops occupied the meeting house after the battle, and small round dents can be seen in the floor, where they bumped the muzzles of their muskets while cleaning them. By the wall surrounding the grounds is the great Crosswicks Oak, which is over seventeen feet in circumference; it was there when the first Quakers came to this country.

NEW YORK

		Denomination	*Material*
168	St. Paul's Chapel (1764) New York, Manhattan	Anglican	Stone
169	St. Andrew's Church (1709) Richmond, Staten Island	Anglican	Stone
170	Flushing Friends Meeting House (1694) Flushing, Queens County	Friends	Wood
171	Manhasset Friends Meeting House (c. 1750) Manhasset, Nassau County	Friends	Wood
172	Matinecock Friends Meeting House (1725) Oyster Bay, Nassau County	Friends	Wood
173	Jericho Friends Meeting House (1788) Hicksville, Nassau County	Friends	Wood
174	First Presbyterian Church (1784) Huntington, Suffolk County	Presbyterian	Wood
175	Caroline Church (1729) Setauket, Suffolk County	Anglican	Wood
176	Charlotte Church (1769) Oakdale, Suffolk County	Anglican	Wood
177	St. Paul's Church (1761) Eastchester, Westchester County	Anglican	Stone
178	Sleepy Hollow Dutch Reformed Church (1699) Scarborough, Westchester County	Dutch Reformed	Stone
179	St. Peter's Church (1767) Van Cortlandtville, Westchester County	Anglican	Wood
180	Chappaqua Friends Meeting House (1754) Chappaqua, Westchester County	Friends	Wood
181	Peach Lake Friends Meeting House (1762) North Salem, Westchester County	Friends	Wood
182	First Reformed Dutch Church (1731) Fishkill, Dutchess County	Dutch Reformed	Stone
183	Trinity Church (c. 1769) Fishkill, Dutchess County	Anglican	Wood
184	Oblong Friends Meeting House (1764) Quaker Hill, Dutchess County	Friends	Wood
185	Crum Elbow Friends Meeting House (1779) Dutchess County	Friends	Wood
186	Creek Friends Meeting House (1777) Clinton Corners, Dutchess County	Friends	Stone
187	Nine Partners Friends Meeting House (1780) Millbrook, Dutchess County	Friends	Brick
188	Old Stone Church (1730) Red Hook, Dutchess County	German Lutheran	Stone
189	Shaker Meeting House (1785) Mount Lebanon, Columbia County	Shaker	Wood

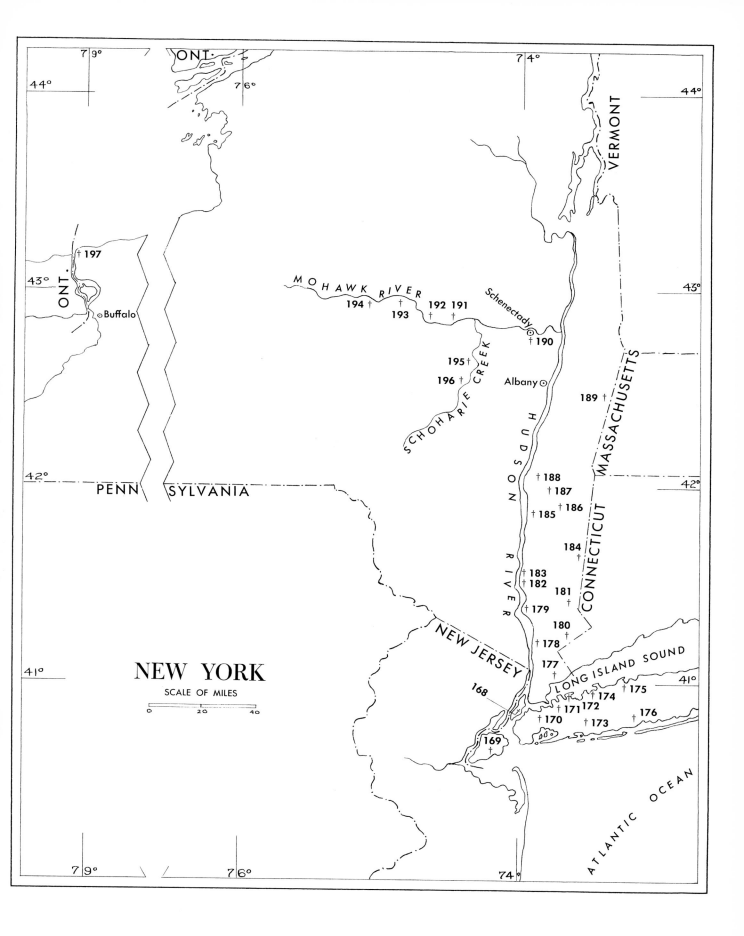

ONT.

79°

44°

76°

74°

44°

VERMONT

43°

† 197

ONT.

Buffalo

43°

MOHAWK RIVER

Schenectady

194 † † 192 191
   193 † †

† 190

SCHOHARIE CREEK

195 †

196 †

Albany

MASSACHUSETTS

189 †

42°

PENN SYLVANIA

HUDSON

RIVER

† 188

† 187

† 185 † 186

184 †

CONNECTICUT

42°

41°

NEW YORK

SCALE OF MILES

0   20   40

NEW JERSEY

† 183
† 182
      181 †
† 179

180 †

† 178

177 †

LONG ISLAND SOUND

41°

168

† 174 † 175

† 171 172
† 170 † 173   † 176

169 †

ATLANTIC OCEAN

79°

76°

74°

		Denomination	Material
190	St. George's Church (1759) Schenectady, Schenectady County	Anglican	Stone
191	Dutch Reformed Church (1788) Stone Arabia, Montgomery County	Dutch Reformed	Stone
192	Palatine Church (1770) Montgomery County	German Lutheran	Stone
193	Indian Castle (1769) Herkimer County	Anglican	Wood
194	Fort Herkimer Reformed Dutch Church (1730) Herkimer County	Dutch Reformed	Stone
195	Reformed High Dutch Church (1772) Schoharie, Schoharie County	Dutch Reformed	Stone
196	Reformed Dutch Church (1786) Middleburg, Schoharie County	Dutch Reformed	Brick
197	French Chapel (1726) Old Fort Niagara, Niagara County	Roman Catholic	Stone

SUMMARY

Anglican	9	Brick	2
Friends	10	Wood	15
Presbyterian	1	Stone	13
Dutch Reformed	6		
German Lutheran	2		
Roman Catholic	1		
Shaker	1		
Buildings	30		30

168

St. Paul's Chapel (1764)

Broadway and Vesey Street,
Borough of Manhattan, New York, New York

In the old part of New York City, on downtown Broadway, with a churchyard around it covering a city block, St. Paul's Chapel stands as the only colonial house of worship on Manhattan Island. It is one of the finest of all the English colonial church buildings in America, and it is the one most closely connected with the beginning of the new Republic of the United States. After the English had taken possession of Manhattan Island from the Dutch in 1664, New Amsterdam became New York, and, although the treaty granted toleration to the Dutch Church and all Protestant churches, the Dutch Reformed Church gave way to the Church of England as the official church. Anglican services began in a chapel built by the English within the fort and given the name King's Chapel, and they continued there until the first building of Trinity Church, which was begun in 1696, was opened for services in 1698. A royal charter to the Parish of Trinity Church was granted by King William III in 1697, the only church to be chartered in the city. The building was enlarged in 1737, but in 1776 it was destroyed in the Great Fire, which threatened the whole city, only four days after it had been occupied by the British under General Howe. Fortunately St. Paul's Chapel had been built near by a decade before,

and it could be used as the parish church until the present Trinity Church was built in 1841. The design was drawn by the English architect, Richard Upjohn, and the building was regarded so highly that it stimulated the Gothic Revival in American architecture.

In 1756, St. Paul's was established as a chapel of ease in Trinity Parish. The vestry of Trinity Parish, in April of 1763, authorized a committee to find a lot, and in November to build a new church on the ground at Division Street, now Fulton. The location is so near to Trinity Church that it is hard for us now to realize that the new location was in the suburbs of the city, beyond the wall, with open ground sloping down to the Hudson River. The foundation stone of St. Paul's Chapel was laid on May 14, 1764. The building was opened for worship and dedicated on October 30, 1766. It is a supreme example of Georgian architecture based on London churches. The architect was Thomas McBean, a Scot and a pupil of James Gibbs, who had been a pupil of Sir Christopher Wren. The Gibbs masterpiece in London, St. Martin-in-the-Fields, influenced the design of St. Paul's. The stone is local Manhattan micaschist, with quoins of brownstone. The woodwork is handcarved, and all the hardware is handwrought iron. The fourteen chandeliers are the original Waterford cut glass. Before the pulpit is the clerk's desk, and above it the sounding board is surmounted by the crest of the Prince of Wales with its plumes. Over the altar at the Broadway end is a "Glory" designed about 1788 by Pierre

Charles L'Enfant, French architect and major of engineers in the Continental Army, who afterwards laid out Washington, D. C.

St. Paul's was the church of the British government of the colony. The governor had a pew, and seats were allotted to the legislature and the council. In the early part of the Revolution St. Paul's was closed, but during the British occupation of the city it was the church of the officers; Lord Howe, Major André, and Sir Guy Carleton, a general and administrator, worshiped here among many other British officials. On April 30, 1789, after his inauguration as the first President of the United States, George Washington and his wife, together with a number of government officials, attended a special Service of Thanksgiving at St. Paul's. He continued to attend services here while the capital of the country remained in New York, and his pew on the north aisle is marked. On April 11, 1786, the first commencement of Columbia College was held here — in 1754 a charter had been granted to King's College, and in 1784 the name had been changed to Columbia. The distinguished people who are buried here or who served the colony, the state, and the country while members of this parish are too numerous to be noted here. The beautiful St. Paul's Chapel is a living memorial to the country's colonial history and the early days of the Republic.

169

St. Andrew's Church (1709)

Richmond, Staten Island, New York

Cocclestown was settled by the Dutch in the seventeenth century. It evidently was named for the abundance of oyster and clam shells from the waters of Fresh Kills near by. During the Revolution it became known generally as Richmond Town. In 1705 the Reverend Aeneas Mackenzie came here as a missionary of the Society for the Propagation of the Gospel in Foreign Parts. An early congregation of Huguenots in Richmond had a church. The Huguenot Church was similar to the Church of England in many ways, so much so that after the Revolution most of the Huguenots in America became Episcopalian, and Mr. Mackenzie was welcomed to preach in their church here on Sunday afternoons. After four years his congregation had grown to the point where the Anglicans could build a church of their own; it was begun in 1709 and completed in 1712. In 1713 Queen Anne gave the church a

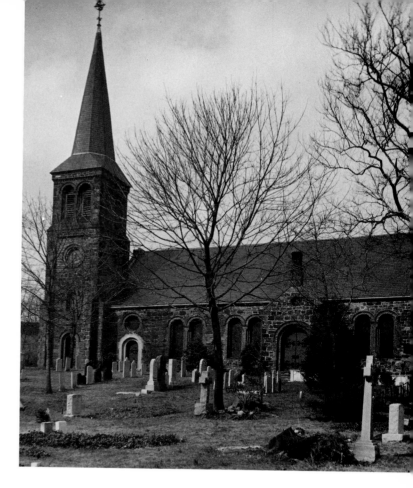

Bible, Prayer Books, a flagon, two chalices, a paten, a communion cover, and a bell; only the chalice and paten remain, and they are in the Metropolitan Museum of New York City.

The original building, forty by twenty-five feet in size, has been enlarged, remodeled, burned, and restored to such an extent that it is not recognizable now as a colonial building. The original stone walls were used in the remodeling of 1743, and they survived the successive alterations of 1770 and 1831, as well as the restorations after the fires of 1867 and 1872. The present size of forty by eighty feet dates from 1770. The steeple was blown down in a storm at one time and damaged by lightning at another, but it was restored after both events. Minor damage was done to the building in two skirmishes during the Revolution. In the second, on August 8, 1777, a raiding party of Americans reached Richmond from the north shore of Staten Island and drove British troops to seek cover in the church. A relief party of British soldiers forced the Americans to withdraw, but not until they had broken the windows of the church by firing on the soldiers inside. St. Andrew's continues as an active Episcopal parish in the Diocese of New York.

170

Flushing Friends Meeting House (1694)

**Flushing, Borough of Queens, New York,
New York**

In the Dutch town of Flushing on Long Island, across the arm of the Sound from Manhattan Island, Quakers were among the early settlers. Meetings for worship were held in 1657, and in 1662 they were regularly established at the house of John Bowne, which had been built the year before. It still stands, a few blocks from the meeting house on a street named for him. In the autumn of 1692 sufficient funds had been raised to buy a lot for a meeting house. During the following year lumber was cut and gathered, and in 1694 the meeting house was built and occupied. The first recorded meeting in the new building was the Quarterly Meeting of November of that year, even though the meeting house was not shingled, plastered, or floored. Further work was done in 1699, and the benches were probably installed at that time. In 1704 the building was shingled, plastered, and repaired.

By 1716 there was need for a larger building, and the records show a decision to build a new meeting house. This was taken by at least one authority to mean that the present meeting house was built between 1716 and 1719. However, John Cox, Jr., while chairman of the Committee on Records of the Religious Society of Friends, studied the records and the building, and he concluded that the alternative and more economical plan of extending the existing building was carried out, and that the present building is the result of that enlargement. In 1763 the gallery was removed, the whole auditorium then had two tiers of windows. The original Flushing Monthly Meeting was the first in the Province of New York. In 1795 the name was changed to New York Monthly Meeting; in 1805 the present active Flushing Monthly Meeting was set off from New York Monthly Meeting.

During the Revolution, Friends of Flushing, like those elsewhere, suffered for not fighting or contributing funds for the support of either army. Their meeting house was used for commissary storage, as a barracks, a prison, and a hospital. In 1783, after the war had ended, it was restored as a meeting house. The Friends have always been concerned with human rights; in this meeting house, in 1716, was held the first public meeting in New York on the abolition of slavery. Four Yearly Meetings dealt with the subject, and the address made by William Burling, at the Yearly Meeting of 1718 at Flushing Meeting House, was one of the first antislavery statements issued in the country.

171

Manhasset Friends Meeting House (c. 1750)

Manhasset, Nassau County, New York

Manhasset Bay is the second bay to the east of Flushing Bay on the North Shore of Long Island. At Manhasset a Meeting for Worship was established in 1704. The Preparative Meeting was established, at an unknown date, as a part of Westbury Monthly Meeting. This frame meeting house was built about 1750. Regular meetings are still held. Westbury Monthly Meeting and Westbury Quarterly Meeting are in New York Yearly Meeting.

172

Matinecock Friends Meeting House (1725)

Oyster Bay, Nassau County, New York

The Matinecock Meeting for Worship was established in 1671. Together with Jericho and Westbury, a Monthly Meeting was established by 1682. This frame meeting house was built in 1725, and regular meetings are still held here.

173

Jericho Friends Meeting House (1788)

near Hicksville, Nassau County, New York

The Jericho Friends Meeting House is located on the present Jericho Turnpike near the town of Hicksville. The name "Hicks" was a momentous one in the Religious Society of Friends. Elias Hicks and his wife Jemima lie buried in the burying ground near the meeting house. They both were influential Quakers. He died at eighty-two in 1830, three years after the Great Separation of 1827. His preaching caused a schism in the Society, and the various meetings divided into two branches, Hicksite and Orthodox. It is a coincidence that all the Meetings of New York in this collection became Hicksite; this means that the followers of Hicks were in the majority and retained the old buildings, while those who retained Orthodox views were forced to withdraw and find other places to meet. For a century and a quarter the division generally persisted. After some Meetings had united, the division finally was healed in 1955, when the two branches united as one New York Yearly Meeting.

The congregation of Friends was gathered here at an early date. The Meeting for Worship was established in 1671. The date of establishment of the Jericho Preparative Meeting is not known. The Monthly Meeting was established with Bethpage in 1789. The present meeting house was built in 1788, and meetings are held regularly.

174

First Presbyterian Church (1784)

Huntington, Suffolk County, New York

Returning to the North Shore of Long Island at Huntington Bay, we find the white shingled First Presbyterian Church in Huntington, on the corner of East Main Street and Sabbathday Path. In the eastern part of Long Island, Calvinism was evident in some of the earliest Puritan settlements; the congregation here was organized in 1665. The first building was erected in that year.

The second was built on the same site in 1715. During the Revolution the British used that building as a barracks. The bell was taken down by the British in 1777 and carried to New York on the frigate *Swan*. By order of Count Rumford, in 1782, the church was torn down, and the materials were used to build Fort Golgotha on Burying Ground Hill. Had it been an Anglican church it would have received better consideration. The third and present building was erected in 1784. Upon petition to Admiral Digby the bell was returned, in 1783, in damaged condition; it was recast and hung in the new church building, where it has been in use ever since.

175

Caroline Church (1729)

Setauket, Suffolk County, New York

Continuing east on the North Shore of Long Island, in Suffolk County, we come to Setauket, a small town on a hill above a snug harbor. As Suffolk County was settled by Puritan

Independents with Presbyterian leanings, it is not surprising that one of the first references to the Church of England was a protest, made in a town meeting of Brookhaven (later Setauket) in 1685, against the use of the Prayer Book by the "Minister of the town." (At Brookhaven now is the great laboratory for research on atoms for peace.) The next reference, in 1702, is to the work of the Reverend George Keith, a Scot educated as a

Presbyterian minister, who had turned Quaker and had been active among the Friends of Pennsylvania and New Jersey, had been ordained in the Church of England, and in this same year had returned to America as a missionary of the Society for the Propagation of the Gospel. He traveled from Boston to Charleston preaching and founding new churches, and he devoted some time to the work of the Church in Suffolk County.

The Anglican parish in Setauket was organized in 1723, when the Reverend James Wetmore was sent here by the S.P.G. He remained until 1725, and he was followed by a succession of ministers who were maintained by the Society until the Revolution. The building was erected in 1729 by shipbuilders of this little port. The knees bracing the roof timbers are reminiscent of Old Ship Meeting House in Hingham, Massachusetts (No. 87). At first it was called Christ Church, but in the second year, 1730, the name was changed to Caroline Church, in honor of George II's queen. She gave the silver communion service which is still in possession of the church. The gallery, which was added in 1744, is cambered like a ship's deck.

In this eastern part of Long Island the inhabitants were generally loyal during the Revolution, and here was an important source of provisions for the British Army. Patriots from Connecticut crossed the Sound to this North Shore and made foraging raids; bullet holes in the church belfry still can be seen as evidence of one of these raids. After the Revolution, Trinity Church in New York aided this church. In 1814 the Reverend Charles Seabury, son of Samuel Seabury,

first Episcopal bishop in America, became the rector of this church. The interior of the building was spoiled by the remodeling in 1844, 1888, and 1908, but in 1937 the Victorian and pseudo-Gothic features were removed, and the church was restored to its charming colonial simplicity.

176

Charlotte Church (1769)
St. John's Church

Oakdale, Suffolk County, New York

We now cross Long Island, from Caroline Church on the North Shore to Charlotte Church on the South Shore. These two churches and one at Huntington, which no longer has a colonial building, were the only Episcopal churches in Suffolk County during most of the colonial period, and one clergyman was usually in charge of all three. The church at Islip, a harbor town on Great South Bay, is situated just north of the town on the former Bourne estate in Oakdale. The church at Setauket was the mother church of the other two. The Charlotte Church was organized in 1765, and the building was erected in 1769. It was named for George III's queen. It acquired the name of St. John's at a later date. In 1843 the building was enlarged to its present size, but it is still a small church. At that time it was consecrated by Dr. Benjamin Tredwell Onderdonk, Bishop of New York. The church is in charge of a vicar, and on Sundays there is a service of Evening Prayers at 3:00 P.M.

177

St. Paul's Church (1761)

Eastchester, Westchester County, New York

The village of Eastchester was settled in 1665, the year after the British captured New Amsterdam from the Dutch. It was located on the Boston Post Road, upon marshy land beside the Hutchinson River. The leader who planted the company of settlers was Thomas Pell; his name was given to Pell's Point and to the town of Pelham. He came from Fairfield, Connecticut, and the first church here was Presbyterian, like that at New England Cross Roads, New Jersey, which also was settled by a man from Fairfield (see No.

150). The first meeting house was erected in 1692, a wooden building located near the present site. In 1702, soon after the Act was passed establishing the Church of England in New York, this congregation changed from Presbyterian to Anglican.

The present stone building was begun in 1761. By 1765 it was still in an unfinished state when funds were exhausted, and it was not until 1788 that it was completed for worship with a high pulpit and forty box pews. At the beginning of the Revolution, because it was forbidden to use the Book of Common Prayer with its prayers for the English sovereign, the church was closed by its rector, the Reverend Samuel Seabury, who was to become the first American bishop (see

St. Paul's, Woodbury, Conn., No. 11). The building was put to various uses thereafter. It stood on the village green, which was used as an election place and as a training ground in both the French and Indian War and the Revolution. During the Revolution the church was used as a barracks and hospital for Hessian soldiers, after the Battle of Pell's Point; ninety of them died the first night in the church and were buried in the cemetery. In 1775 the church bell, which, like the Liberty Bell, was cast in England by Lester and Pack, was buried to hide it from the British, and it is still in use. In 1787 the building was reopened and used as a courthouse; Aaron Burr pleaded court cases here. In the following year the building resumed its service as a church. Pew holders at the end of the war included the families of Van Cortlandt, Rhinelander, Pinckney, Morgan, Drake, and Roosevelt. In the 1850's the interior was modernized, and the high pulpit and box pews were replaced. On December 15, 1952, St. Paul's Church was formally dedicated as a National Historic Site, a shrine of the Bill of Rights and the freedom of the press, commemorating a courageous act of John Peter Zenger. He was a printer from the German Palatinate and editor of the *Weekly Journal*, who was arrested for his accurate reporting of an election held on the green in 1773. It involved a petty tyrant, William Cosby, who was the royal governor of New York. Zenger spent nine months in jail, but was vindicated at his trial. In closing his address to the jury, the attorney for the defense, Andrew Hamilton from Philadelphia (vestryman of Christ Church, see No. 205, and architect of Independence Hall), spoke of the right, in nature and in law, "of opposing and exposing the tyranny of arbitrary power in these parts of the world, at least by speaking and writing the truth."

178

Sleepy Hollow Dutch Reformed Church (1699)

Scarborough, Westchester County, New York

At North Tarrytown, in the little village of Scarborough, is the Sleepy Hollow Dutch Reformed Church. It was the family church of the Philipse family on their manor of Philipsburgh. The Philipsburgh Manor was one of the four most important patroonships granted by the Dutch West India Company, with Van Cortlandt Manor

(see No. 179), Livingston Manor (see No. 188), and Rensselaerswyck Manor. The stone church was built by Frederick Philipse and his wife Catherine Van Cortlandt in 1699. It has been altered and remodeled so many times that only the stone walls are original. The church had pews for the family and a gallery for servants and slaves. The Sleepy Hollow Cemetery behind the church was made famous by Washington Irving in his *The Legend of Sleepy Hollow*. The grave of the real Katrina Van Tassel of the story is in the cemetery, as is that of Washington Irving. At the turn of the last century in this region were the homes of many wealthy families. Among the graves of other famous people in the Sleepy Hollow Cemetery are those of Andrew Carnegie and his wife.

179

St. Peter's Church (1767)

Van Cortlandtville, Westchester County, New York

Van Cortlandtville is a small town adjacent to and just south of Peekskill. The Van Cortlandt Manor was one of the four most important patroonships in the Hudson Valley granted by the Dutch West India Company, the others being Philipsburgh Manor (see No. 178), Livingston Manor (see No. 188), and Rensselaerswyck Manor. The

little family church here, like the Sleepy Hollow Dutch Reformed Church (No. 178), was built by the Van Cortlandts on their manor for the use of the family and their tenants. A marked difference between the two is the denomination. The church here was built in 1767, several generations after New York City had been acquired from the Dutch by the English, and it has been Episcopalian from the beginning. Lieutenant-Governor Pierre Van Cortlandt, who was a founder of the parish, became a warden in 1793. The pew to the right of the pulpit was for the lord of the manor and his family. The present pew, a replica of the original, was made during a restoration. The stairs and the gallery (which is built in three stages for benches), are original. George Washington attended services here during his stay at the Upper Van Cortlandt Manor House, after the Battle of White Plains. The building is in care of the rector of St. Peter's Church in Peekskill, and it is opened for occasional services during the year.

180

Chappaqua Friends Meeting House (1754)

Chappaqua, Westchester County, New York

The old Chappaqua Friends Meeting House stands in the town of New Castle, about a mile north of Chappaqua. The congregation of Friends was established as a Meeting for Worship at the house of Abel Weeks in 1745, and as a Monthly Meeting in 1785. The present frame meeting house was built in 1754, and enlarged in 1778. After the Battle of White Plains, wounded soldiers of Washington's army were treated in the meeting house, and some of those who died were buried here. Regular meetings are held.

181

Peach Lake Friends Meeting House (1762)

North Salem, Westchester County, New York

The old meeting house is situated on the east side of Peach Lake, in the town of North Salem. The congregation of Friends was established as a Meeting for Worship in 1760. The present frame meeting house was built in 1762. Only an annual Meeting for Worship is held, in Eighth month, appointed day.

182

First Reformed Dutch Church (1731)
Old Dutch Church

Fishkill, Dutchess County, New York

This old town of Viskil was located by Dutch settlers on the Albany Post Road, which followed the east bank of the Hudson River and was an extension of Broadway from New Amsterdam. In the early 1700's the Dutch congregation held services in private houses and barns. In 1716 the present church was organized.

In 1731 the church was built, a square structure with a hip roof surmounted by a cupola and bell. It was unusually large for the time and place, but by 1786 it was necessary to provide even a larger church for the growing congregation. In that year the present building was given its basic dimensions and style. The exterior has been changed very little. The white-stuccoed stone walls, making a vivid contrast with the red brick quoins framing the doors and windows, are a yard or more in thickness. The wooden beam structure has mortice-and-tenon joints and is pegged. The main pillars are over eighty feet in height, and at the top, where they support the tower, they are eighteen inches square. Portholes in the upper structure, closed to the weather, provided for de-

fense by musket or small cannon. The interior has been remodeled four times — in 1806, 1820, 1854, and 1882. The slave gallery was occupied by Negro slaves for services during the entire colonial period. The old high wineglass pulpit and curved stairway leading to it, as well as other colonial furnishings, have been replaced; the earliest pulpit furniture is in the parlor of Washington's Headquarters in Newburgh.

During the seven months from August, 1776, to February, 1777, the church served as the capitol of the State of New York, while the New York Provincial Convention drafted and adopted a constitution that changed the province to a state. Among the leaders who met here were John Jay, Philip Livingston, Robert Morris, Robert R. Livingston, Pierre Van Cortlandt (see No. 179), and Robert Van Rensselaer.

During the Revolution the church, with its sturdy stone walls, was used as a prison for captured British soldiers or Tories. The most famous person to be imprisoned here was Enoch Crosby, who acted as a spy and led recruits for the British Army to be captured and imprisoned with him. He was given a mock trial by General Israel Putnam and permitted to escape, by leaping from a window of this building into a tree. In *The Spy*, by James Fenimore Cooper, Crosby appears as Harvey Birch.

Trinity Church (c. 1769)

Fishkill, Dutchess County, New York

The Anglican Trinity Church Parish was organized in 1756, much later than the Dutch Reformed Church in this town that had been settled by the Dutch. The Reverend Samuel Seabury, who arrived that year on horseback, in his work as a missionary of the Society for the Propagation of the Gospel, organized the parish. He was the father of the Reverend Samuel Seabury who was to become the first American Episcopal bishop (see St. Paul's Church, Woodbury, Conn., No. 11).

The church building was erected about 1769. It was occupied for a short time by the New York Provincial Convention, which moved here from White Plains after the evacuation before the British Army in 1776. Because of the unfinished condition of the building, the Convention moved to the Old Dutch Church in town (No. 182). When the prayer for the king was forbidden during the Revolution, the first rector, the Reverend John Beardsley, closed this church and the one at Poughkeepsie, which was also in his care; in 1777 the Committee of Safety banished him and sent him with his family and goods down the Hudson by sloop to New York. The building was used as a military hospital by Washington's army until 1783. In 1788 the vestry received from the government £350 as compensation, and used it for repairs and finishing the church. In 1789 the building was distinguished by the State of New York in convention signing the ratification of the Constitution of the United States. The exterior of the building is original, except that the steeple became unsafe and was removed in 1803. The interior was entirely remodeled between 1860 and 1870.

Oblong Friends Meeting House (1764)

Quaker Hill, near Pawling, Dutchess County, New York

For more than half a century an oblong strip of land was in dispute between New York and Connecticut. In 1731 the dispute was settled by awarding to New York the disputed Oblong and to Connecticut the strip of land on Long Island Sound extending down into Westchester County, New York, which now includes Stamford and Greenwich. Meanwhile the Quakers from New England and Long Island, who had moved into the Oblong, had purchased it from the Wappinger Indians and had settled Quaker Hill.

A Preparative Meeting was established here in 1742, the first in Dutchess County, and the Monthly Meeting in 1744. The present meeting house was built in 1764, replacing the original structure of 1742. Three sides are shingled, and the fourth is covered with the old clapboards. In 1767 the Meeting here went on record that "it is inconsistent with Christianity to buy and sell our fellow men for slaves." Slavery, which was prevalent all over the colonies, was then abolished in the Oblong. A further proposal was made that the freed men be paid for their past services, but Quakers are well known for being canny, and a committee reported that "the Negroes appear to be satisfied without further settlement."

In 1778 Washington camped his army below Quaker Hill at Fredericksburgh, now a part of Patterson, and the meeting house was used as a hospital. Because the Quakers take no part in war, the record does not mention this episode in their history. The position of the Friends here, on a no-man's-land between rival factions of New York and Connecticut, was similar to their position between the two sides at war in this region during the Revolution.

Disunion, following the Hicksite schism and the Separation of 1828, scattered the members. There have been no regular meetings since 1885, but an annual meeting of descendants of the original settlers is held here. They come principally from the neighboring communities of Chappaqua and Poughkeepsie. This obscure section has been brought to the attention of the public in recent years by the proximity of the farms and residences of Thomas E. Dewey, ex-governor of New York and Presidential candidate, and Lowell Thomas, radio commentator, traveler, and author.

185

Crum Elbow Friends Meeting House (1779)

near East Park, Dutchess County, New York

The Crum Elbow Friends Meeting House is out in the country about four miles from the little village of East Park. Its quaint name comes from the Dutch name for a sharp bend in the Hudson River, "Krom Elleboge," meaning "Crooked Elbow," or more freely "Elbow Bend." Crum Elbow Creek flows into the Hudson near the bend.

A Meeting for Worship was established in 1778. It was established as a Preparative Meeting in 1797. A century later, in 1899, it was discontinued. The meeting house was built in 1779. In the roof can be seen a dividing line; the smaller eastern section is the original, and when it was found to be inadequate soon after it was built, the western section was added. The building is in the care of the Crum Elbow Rural Cemetery Association and is open to all Friends. An annual meeting is held, usually in Ninth month.

In recent years this rural section of the Hudson Valley has received public attention, because of its proximity to the Hyde Park home of President Franklin Delano Roosevelt and his wife Eleanor.

186

Creek Friends Meeting House (1777)
Clinton Corners, Dutchess County, New York

The small village of Clinton Corners is situated about three miles east of Crum Elbow Friends Meeting House, about midway across Dutchess County. Here the Creek Meeting was established as a Meeting for Worship in 1771, as a Preparative Meeting allowed by Nine Partners Meeting (see No. 187) in 1776, and as a Monthly Meeting in 1782. The present stone meeting house was built in 1777. Regular meetings have been discontinued long since, and only appointed meetings are held. Currently it is Creek Executive Meeting within New York Yearly Meeting.

187

Nine Partners Friends Meeting House (1780)
Millbrook, Dutchess County, New York

The name "Nine Partners Tract" was given to the land granted to nine men as partners. It covered most of Dutchess County. The partners divided the tract into various patents, and Quakers settled on land sold without restrictions, in fee simple. Nine Partners Meeting was established as a Meeting for Worship in 1742, as a Preparative Meeting in 1744, and as a Monthly Meeting in 1769. The present brick meeting house was built in 1780, replacing a log structure which burned. The site of the Nine Partners School is

near by; it was opened by the Friends in 1796. It flourished until the Hicksites withdrew in the Separation of 1828 and established a rival school under Jacob and Deborah Willetts. He was the author of popular arithmetic and geography text books and the modern version of the jingle "Thirty days has September." Nine Partners Half-Yearly Meeting is held here in Eleventh month of the odd years. There are appointed meetings and an annual meeting in the summer. The regular Meeting is now part of the Lyall Memorial Federated Church and comprises about forty-eight friends.

188

Old Stone Church (1730)
Evangelical Lutheran Church of
St. Peter the Apostle

Red Hook, Dutchess County, New York

A community of German Lutherans settled on Livingston Manor, one of the four great Dutch patroonships on the Hudson River granted by the Dutch West India Company. They were Palatines who migrated to New York from the Palatinate of the Rhineland in 1710, after spending a year in London in the reign of Queen Anne. They

worked on Livingston Manor in the production of naval stores, under contract with the English government to pay their expenses and passage; but the industry proved to be less economical than production from southern pine, and they were released from their contract. In the course of farming on the leasehold system, by which they were required to pay uneconomic rents without land ownership, the Palatines became discouraged, and most of them eventually migrated up the Hudson to the Mohawk and Schoharie valleys.

In 1729 a group of the Germans applied to Gilbert Livingston for land at Kirchehoek, near the German church which was then standing here, and he donated the site of the present church for its use forever. This stone building was erected in 1730. The oldest gravestone in the cemetery is that of Carl Neher, who died January 25, 1733; he was one of those who worked on the building. In 1824 the building was enlarged. The tower and the walls at both ends and the side toward the road were stuccoed and painted yellow. In the photograph the rear wall is seen with the original stone exposed. After the German congregation had moved to the Mohawk, where we find other churches of theirs, the settlement here declined, and the Old Stone Church was left to stand alone in wooded country.

189

Shaker Meeting House (1785)

Mount Lebanon, Columbia County, New York

This first Shaker meeting house in America was built in 1785 at New Lebanon (since 1861 called Mount Lebanon), New York, on the western slope of the Berkshires near Massachusetts, under the direction of Father James Whitaker. Two years later, in 1787, the community was organized as the New Lebanon Society, the first Shaker community to be organized in America. The sect had originated in 1647 at Manchester, England, during a Quaker revival, and the variant was called Shaking Quakers. In Manchester, Ann Lee founded the formal organization called officially "The United Society of Believers in Christ's Second Appearing." In 1774 Mother Ann responded to a revelation by bringing a group of eight

Believers to America. After two years in New York City they moved to Watervliet, near Albany, and settled on a farm. Before that community had been organized formally, however, Joseph Meacham, a former Baptist pastor and one of Mother Ann's original disciples, organized the community at Mount Lebanon, about thirty miles southeast of Watervliet. When Mother Ann died in 1784, she was succeeded first by James Whitaker and then by Joseph Meacham. The New Lebanon Society grew to become a Christian commune consisting of eight families of celibate men and women, including the North Family (the last to survive), South Family, Center Family, and Church Family.

The meeting house, the first building to be erected in the community, was located with the Church Family; it was the only one of their buildings painted white. The settlement was made on the Darrow farm, and this first structure of their community was built on the site of George Darrow's house. In 1823 the building was moved a few rods to make way for a larger meeting house. It was enlarged and heightened for use in drying seeds, which were packaged and sold as one of the many Shaker industries. This first meeting house is now the residence of the head master of the Darrow School, a preparatory school for boys. The second meeting house was used as the school gymnasium until 1959, and in 1962 it was opened as the Heyniger Memorial Library. A school was proposed by Sister Emma Neale and Sister Amelia Calver, who saw that the Shakers, with their vows of celibacy and a declining rate of converts, were "going out." After the property had been bought from the Shakers and the last meeting had been held in the meeting house, in 1932 the Lebanon School was opened; in 1938 it was reorganized as the Darrow School. In 1947 there were six women and one man, members of the North Family, remaining at Mount Lebanon; they moved that year to the Shaker Community a few miles east in Hancock, Massachusetts. Today there are no Shakers at Mount Lebanon or at Hancock. In 1960 a corporation was formed, Shaker Community, Inc., and the Shaker Community of Hancock, comprising seventeen buildings and 972 acres, has been acquired and made available to the public as a Shaker village museum. A post-colonial meeting house of 1798 has been moved there from another Shaker community at Shirley, Massachusetts, where the colony ceased activity in 1908 and the state acquired the property.

All Shaker meeting houses were similar in design. Their meetings were unlike any other religious service. They were held in a large room that was bare of furniture, except benches around the walls, like a ball room. The meeting was devoted to marching and singing. An elder opened the meeting with a sermon, and at the command, "Go forth and march!" a group of singers formed in the middle of the room and sang hymns, while the rest marched around them, marking time with their hands. The faster the step, the harder they were wrestling with evil, and their twisting motions gave rise to the name of Shaker. The meeting room here at Mount Lebanon occupied the entire first floor. The thirty-four-foot pine beams in the ceiling are still exposed. Modernization of the house has been accomplished with a minimum of change in its unique character.

190

St. George's Church (1759)

**North Ferry Street, Schenectady,
Schenectady County, New York**

As the site of the settlement was at the end of the portage from the Hudson to the Mohawk River, the Mohawk Indians called it *Schenectady,* meaning "at the end of the pine plains." Having left the Hudson Valley and come to the Mohawk Valley, we find here a colonial Anglican church. The settlement was made by the Dutch about 1662, as a trading post for furs from the Indians, and they founded a Dutch Reformed Church in 1670. In the Indian massacre of 1690, most of the settlement was destroyed; sixty inhabitants were killed, including the first resident Dutch pastor, Petrus Thessehenmaecker, and twenty-seven were taken captive to Canada. The first Anglican service in the settlement was held in 1695 by the Reverend John Miller. In 1710 an Anglican congregation was gathered; the Reverend Thomas Barclay of Albany preached here infrequently. The present parish was organized in 1735. The

first resident clergyman was the Reverend William Andrews (1770-73).

In 1759 the building was begun. It is located on North Ferry Street, on land that was part of the stockade that extended down to the ferry on the Mohawk River. The stockade had a blockhouse and a cannon. The church building was completed in 1766. Services were suspended during the Revolution and the building was used as a barracks. Services were resumed in 1798. The west end, except the tower, is part of the original building. In the 1840's it was enlarged by the addition of transepts, and in 1881 the recess in the chancel was built. The tower, originally of wood, was rebuilt of stone in 1870. The box pews are retained. This is the oldest house of worship in the Mohawk Valley.

Sir William Johnson contributed to the building of the church and worshipped here. In 1755, only four years before the building was begun, he had been created a baronet for his victory at Lake George in the French and Indian War. He was a prominent and colorful figure during this period of history in the Mohawk Valley from here to Fort Niagara (see No. 197). In trading with the Indians he had developed such fast friends among them that the Mohawks had made him a sachem, and Governor Clinton made him superintendent of the Six Nations (Iroquois). In later life he retired to his estate, which had been granted by the king in recognition of his services, located on the site of Johnstown, and he was active colonizing that tract of 100,000 acres until his death in 1774. (See Indian Castle Church, No. 193).

191

Dutch Reformed Church (1788)
Stone Arabia Reformed Church

Stone Arabia, Montgomery County, New York

On a hill above the north bank of the Mohawk River near Palatine Bridge, the small village of Stone Arabia commands a sweeping view of the valley. It was settled by Germans from the Palatinate on land that they acquired in 1723.

Most of the Palatines came to America in three major migrations — in 1708, 1710, and 1722. Many of them settled first in the Hudson Valley as tenants on the vast manors, such as Livingston Manor (see Old Stone Church, Red Hook, No. 188), and then left under the pressure of the land-tenure system and came to make permanent settlements in the Mohawk and Schoharie valleys. They brought with them the Protestant faiths of both the Lutheran and the Reformed Churches. At Stone Arabia they built both the present Dutch Reformed Church and the Lutheran Church standing near by (built in 1792 to replace their original log building, which was destroyed in the raid of 1780). The Dutch Reformed Church in

general included both Dutch and German congregations, and both are found among these colonial churches of the Mohawk and Schoharie valleys, but the congregation of this church was German. The present name is the Stone Arabia Reformed Church.

The first church of this congregation was a frame building. It was destroyed during the Revolution in the raid of 1880, when Sir John Johnson, son of Sir William Johnson (see St. George's Church, Schenectady, No. 190), led a force of British troops and Indians on a devastating expedition through the Mohawk and Schoharie valleys. In front of the church is a monument to Colonel John Brown, the leader of the force of

patriots which tried in vain to halt the raid in the Battle of Stone Arabia on October 19; he lies buried in the church cemetery.

In 1788 the present building was begun. The stone is a local light-gray sandstone. The origin of the name "Arabia" is obscure; in some of the early records it is "Raby." The building was a fine colonial structure for its time and place, but it has undergone a series of alterations. In 1820 the entrance was shifted from the east side to the south end. At a later date the windows were rebuilt in their present rectangular style. The colonial character of the interior has been lost in the process of remodeling. The church is active, with services every Sunday.

192

Palatine Church (1770)

near Nelliston, Montgomery County, New York

Upon the rolling plateau north of the Mohawk River, a few miles west of Stone Arabia and north of Nelliston, stands the Palatine Church. It was built in 1770, of limestone, by Evangelical Lutheran Palatines. A tablet in the east wall gives the date in German: "Erbaut im Jahr Christi —1770 Den 18th Aug." Beneath the tablet can be seen the arch of the former doorway which has been blocked up. The principal founders were the Nellis, Reber, and Hess families. During the Revolution the families were divided; some went to Canada and joined the loyal forces, including members of the Nellis family, who settled there after the war. In the raid of 1780, when Sir John Johnson and a force of British soldiers and Indians swept through the Mohawk Valley, one of the Nellises (a lieutenant in Butler's Rangers of the British force) saved his home church from an attack by Indians with flaming arrows, and, unlike the two at Stone Arabia, it survived the war. The church is still used for reunions of the scattered descendants of these early settlers. In 1870, at the time of the church's Centennial, the interior was remodeled, and the original high pulpit, sounding board, balcony, and pews were all replaced.

193

Indian Castle Church (1769)

Herkimer County, New York

Off the main road that follows the south bank of the Mohawk River, between Fort Plain and Mohawk, stands the Indian Castle Church. It is the only relic of all the Mohawk castles, a series of Indian settlements and strongholds that dotted the valley. On a hill overlooking Nowadaga Creek (meaning "place of the mud turtles"), this site was the location of the Upper Castle of the Mohawk Bear Clan from 1700 to 1775. Sir William Johnson (see St. George's Church, Schenectady, No. 190) built Fort Hendrick here in 1756, and named it for his good friend and ally, the Mohawk chief "King" Hendrick, who had been killed fighting with him the year before at Lake George, in the French and Indian War.

Sir William Johnson had this present Anglican church built in 1769, and gave it to the Indians. The builder was Daniel Muller. Originally the entrance was on the east side, and there was an open Georgian cupola. The present tower and the entrance were installed in the nineteenth century.

Joseph Brant and his sister Molly were Indians who were connected with this church, and with Sir William Johnson and his son Sir John they figured prominently in the history of the region. Joseph Brant was sent as a youth by Sir William to be educated at Lebanon, Connecticut, in Moor's Indian charity school, which was the origin of Dartmouth College. He became a devout churchman as well as chief of the Mohawks and a fearless warrior. Remaining loyal to the English, he fought in the French and Indian War, and as a colonel in the Revolution he led the Six Nations (Iroquois) on the British side. He took part in the raids of destruction and death throughout this region, in the campaign directed by Sir John Johnson. After the wars Brant settled here at the Upper Castle and worked for the Church of England as a missionary, both here and in Canada. It was here, in 1787, that he translated the Prayer Book and the Gospel of St. Mark into the Mohawk language.

After the death of Lady Johnson, Sir William had, among others, two Indians as mistresses — one the niece of King Hendrick, the other Molly, the sister of Joseph Brant. He became enamored of Molly here at Fort Hendrick, and she presided

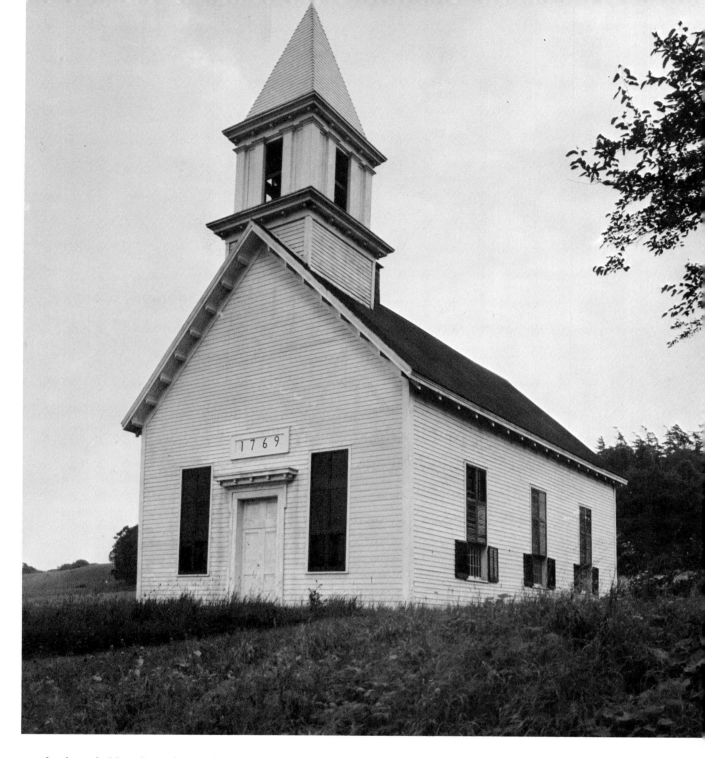

over his household and was known by his friends as "the Brown Lady Johnson." After Johnson's death Molly remained loyal to the English. She informed her brother Joseph, who was at Fort Stanwix (near the present Rome), of the plans of General Nicholas Herkimer to go to the relief of Fort Stanwix, and thereby she made possible the ambush of Tories and Indians that trapped the patriots in the Battle of Oriskany on August 6, 1777. In 1779 the Indians were removed from this Upper Castle, and the land became the property of white settlers. Sir John Johnson arranged to have a reservation for the Mohawks established in Canada. Brantford, Ontario, became the headquarters of the Six Nations (Iroquois), and the city was named in honor of Joseph Brant.

194

Fort Herkimer Reformed Dutch Church (1730)

Mohawk, Herkimer County, New York

The Mohawk Valley was an active area in the wars and raids of the frontier that extended all the way to Fort Niagara (see No. 197). A little more than nine miles from the Indian Castle Church, up the south bank of the Mohawk River, and near the town of Mohawk, stands a fortified church which was built by German Palatines both for worship and defense, and which was used effectively in both capacities.

In 1730 an acre was deeded for the present church site, and work was begun on building the "Reformed Protestant Church of German Flatts." This present building replaced the log structure of 1723. When construction had been carried to the level of the sills of the upper windows, the necessity for taking security measures against the French and Indians halted work on the church. The one-story stone structure with a temporary

roof then became a part of the stockaded Fort Herkimer. In 1767 the original church building was completed by Johan Herkimer, father of General Nicholas Herkimer and twelve other children, who had started a trading post here in 1722. The date of completion is inscribed on a stone above the original entrance on the north side, "J.H.E.1767" (Johan Herkimer *erbaut* 1767). It safely withstood the Tory-Indian raid of 1778, in which the rest of the neighborhood was devastated. Adam Helmer was the hero of the occasion when he ran the twenty-two miles to Fort Herkimer, with a warning of the approaching raiders in time for the inhabitants to enter the fort for safety. When the building was completed it had a steep roof and a conical steeple. In 1812 the church was enlarged; the walls were raised eight feet, a gallery was installed, and the entrance vestibule at the west end replaced the old entrance, which is now filled in. The stone walls in the older first story are darker than the upper walls which were added, revealing the two distinct functions and periods in the history of the building.

195

Old Stone Church (1772)
Reformed High Dutch Church
Old Stone Fort, Lower Fort

Schoharie, Schoharie County, New York

The Schoharie (Indian for "bridge of drift-wood") Creek rises in the Catskill Mountains and flows north into the Mohawk River at a point between Schenectady and the colonial churches that we have just seen. The valley and the town of Schoharie were settled partly by Dutchmen of the Reformed faith, but mostly by German Palatines of both the Lutheran and Reformed faiths who came to America in the great migrations of 1708, 1710, and 1722. Many of the Palatines had settled on the east side of the Hudson River on the vast Livingston Manor, as at Red Hook (see No. 188), and had been forced to move by the failure of the naval-stores enterprise, the low productivity of the rocky soil, and the land-tenure system; they established several settlements in the Mohawk Valley, as we have seen, and in the

Schoharie Valley seven settlements, each bearing the name of its founder. The first preachers at Schoharie were Joshua Kocherthal, a Lutheran, and Johann Friederich Heager, a member of the Church of England who was the pastor of a Reformed congregation that emigrated from the Palatinate in 1709. In those early years on this frontier there was no separation of the Lutheran and Reformed denominations, and the visiting minister of whatever denomination gathered the community for worship. The Lutherans organized St. Paul's Church at Schoharie in 1714, and in 1743 they built the Lutheran parsonage which still stands, but no colonial church building of theirs survives here. The Reformed Dutch congregation here organized a church about 1720.

The Old Stone Church was the third built by the congregation. Records of the early days are meager, but it is evident that they built their first church of logs in 1724, two years after the third migration from the Palatinate. The church was located on a site not far from the present building. It was intended only for temporary use, but it served for a decade. In 1734 the second church, a frame structure, was built a few rods northeast of the present building; it was a square structure with a hip roof and a graceful belfry.

In 1772 the third and present building was erected by the High Dutch Church of Foxendorf. The parish was fifteen miles in extent, and the parishioners hauled in a variety of sandstone and limestone for the building; many of the stones have the names of the contributors engraved on them. Galleries were built on three walls; there were a high pulpit with a curved stairway, a sounding board, box pews on both sides of the pulpit for deacons and elders, and the tower with a graceful belfry and spire. In 1830 the belfry and spire were removed, and the weathercock, which was brought from Holland in 1752 for the second building, is now in the museum in the present building.

By 1772, when this building was erected, the community was divided into Lutheran and Dutch Reformed faiths, both High Dutch and Low Dutch, and the German and Dutch languages were being used, while English was coming into use. Divisions in faith and language, however, were overcome by common necessity for defense of the inhabitants of this frontier outpost. There was a long period of continuous threat, first from the French and the Indians and then the British and the Indians, and the Old Stone Church served as

the Old Stone Fort from 1777 to 1785. On the Schoharie Creek three forts were established: farthest upstream there was the Upper Fort near Fultonham, at Middleburg there was the Middle Fort, and here the church became the Lower Fort. In 1778, six years after it was built, the church was enclosed by a stockade covering half an acre. Block houses were built at the northeast and southwest corners, and a small cannon was mounted on each. A lean-to was built inside and against the palisade for each family of the community who might need to seek protection there. Two loopholes for cannon, which are still to be seen, were then opened in the front wall on both sides of the entrance, and the church furnishings, pulpit and pews, were removed. In 1779, the year after his church had been converted to a fort, the Reverend Johannes Schuyler, pastor for thirty-one years, died and was buried beneath the pulpit.

On October 17, 1780, the town of Schoharie was attacked by a force of about eight hundred British Tories and Indians led by Sir John Johnson and the Mohawk chief, Joseph Brant. They had burned Middleburg in the morning, and they burned Schoharie in the afternoon. An Indian attack on the Stone Fort was broken and driven back by sharpshooters stationed on the tower. Johnson's force to the west of the fort fired two cannon balls from a swivel gun into the roof of the building, but it was not captured. Colonel U. Veeder sent a report that day to General Robert Van Rensselaer saying that "The enemy have burnt the whole Schohary . . ." A tall monument stands in front of the church commemorating another episode in the Revolution; it marks the grave of David Williams, one of the three men who, on September 23, 1780, captured Major John André bearing treasonable papers written by General Benedict Arnold in an attempt to surrender the military post of West Point to the enemy.

In 1785 the Lower Fort was restored and refurnished for use as a church. Church services continued here until 1844, when the Reformed High Dutch Society built their present brick church in the village. In 1857 the Society sold the Old Stone Church to the State of New York, and then the galleries were removed and the second floor was built. The building was used by the New York National Guard until 1873, when it was given to Schoharie County, and since 1889 it has been occupied by the Schoharie County Historical Society and its museum.

196

Reformed Dutch Church (1786)

Middleburg, Schoharie County, New York

In the autumn of 1713 a large group of German Palatines under the leadership of Johann Conrad Weiser, Sr., came to the Schoharie Valley and started here the settlement of Weiser's Dorf, the first of seven Palatine settlements in the region. The name Middleburg was adopted at the end of the century. This group left the Rhine Palatinate in 1708, spent more than a year in London through the hospitality of Queen Anne and the English government, and came to New York in 1710 as a part of the second of three great migrations of Palatines. They spent two years working on Livingston Manor on the east side of the Hudson River, at East Camp and West Camp, producing pine tar for the British Navy to repay their passage. The trees did not produce as well as the southern pines, however, and when the British government released them from their contract, in 1712, they moved to Schenectady and in 1713 to the Schoharie. Conrad Weiser kept a diary in which he recorded the difficulties experienced by the group and the hard life they led in this new frontier settlement. During the first several years they were without government or a preacher. His son, John Conrad Weiser, Jr., moved to the Schoharie in the fall of 1712 as the adopted son of a Mohawk chief, and he became the famous Indian interpreter in Pennsylvania (see Nos. 231, 248, 256).

About 1732, after two decades in the life of the new settlement, the Reformed Dutch Church in Weiser's Dorf was organized, the third of three mother churches in the Schoharie Valley, after the two in Schoharie (see No. 195). During the Revolution their first church, a frame building, was burned with the town in the raid of October 17, 1780, led by Sir John Johnson and the Mohawk chief, Joseph Brant. In 1786 the present building was erected. It is of brick on stone foundations. An unusual feature of the plan places the tower directly above the pulpit.

197

French Chapel (1726)
French Castle, Old Fort Niagara

Youngstown, Niagara County, New York

The Jesuit Chapel in the French Castle of Old Fort Niagara is the only French Roman Catholic place of worship in this collection. The northwest tip of New York was on the border of the vast territory explored and claimed by the French that extended from Quebec to Louisiana by way of the St. Lawrence, the Great Lakes, and the Mississippi. English America was Protestant, and in the long process of development during the colonial period, a major factor was the pressure on the colonies maintained by the Spanish Catholics on the south and the French Catholics on the north and west, involving the French and Indian War. In the thirteen states there is no Spanish church from the colonial period, and this one relic of French occupancy and worship was a turning point in the struggle between the French and the English. The presence of the French on this side of Lake Ontario and the Niagara River was resisted by the English with increasing strength. In 1759, after a long siege, Fort Niagara was captured by Sir William Johnson; it was held by the English until the United States took it over in 1796. In the War of 1812 the British recaptured it, but it was restored to the United States in 1815 by the Treaty of Ghent. Thus the fort has flown the flags of three nations in succession, and all three are flown there together today.

The first fort was a crude house of wood surrounded by a palisade. It was erected here in 1679 and named Fort Conty (Conti) by René Robert Cavelier de La Salle, the great explorer whose ambition it was to extend the French empire through the wilderness of North America. Operating under letters patent from King Louis XIV, he had explored from Quebec up the St. Lawrence, across Lake Ontario, and to this point at the mouth of the Niagara River overlooking both the river and the lake. His Fort Conty, es-

tablishing the Niagara frontier and opening the gateway to the West, became one in a system of sixty forts built by the French over a period of years. The first fort was destroyed by fire; it was replaced by another on the same site in 1687, named Fort Denonville in honor of its builder, the Marquis de Jacques Dené de Brisay Denonville, the royal governor of New France.

In 1726 the present stone building was begun with the name Fort Niagara. Work did not begin, however, until two barques had been built on Lake Ontario at the opposite end, where La Salle had established Fort Frontenac, the site of the present Kingston; the vessels were used to carry the stone for the building, and for policing the Indians on the lake engaged in competitive trade with the English at Oswego. The stone building was designed and built by Gaspard Chassegros de Lery, the chief engineer in Canada for King Louis XV. It was conceived by the Marquis de Vaudreuil, then royal governor of New France, as a fortification against the Iroquois and the English as well as a trading post, but it was intended only for trading during the Peace. The Iroquois were the Five Nations, then actually six since the Tuscaroras had joined in 1715, following the massacre in Bath, North Carolina (see St. Thomas' Church, Bath, No. 198). They gave the French permission to build a "House of Peace," but they were not told that the entire third floor

was to be a gun deck and the dormer windows in the roof gun ports. There were accommodations for a hundred soldiers and officers.

The main room on entering the castle was the trading room, where Indians from a vast area brought beaver pelts during the many years when this was one of the most important trading posts in North America. A room on the second floor was furnished as a Jesuit chapel — one of the first Christian churches on the frontier — and in it the Jesuit priests held services for troops, traders, and trappers. When the English took over, they built an Anglican chapel in front of the castle near the present flagpoles; they stripped the French Chapel of its furnishings and plastered over the holy-water font in the stone doorpost. A thorough restoration of the chapel and castle in 1927-34 was made in accordance with the plans of de Lery, which had been found in the Colonial Archives of the French War Department. In the course of the work, the holy-water font was discovered. The hand-carved furnishings are reproductions as far as there was information on the originals. The statue on the left is of St. Joseph, and on the right is St. Francis Xavier, the patron saint of the Jesuit mission among the Hurons. The restored chapel has been consecrated as a place of worship. The fort and castle are now open to the public under the administration of the Old Fort Niagara Association.

NORTH CAROLINA

		Denomination	Material
198	St. Thomas' Church (1734) Bath, Beaufort County	Anglican	Brick
199	St. Paul's Church (1736) Edenton, Chowan County	Anglican	Brick
200	St. Philip's Church (1740) Brunswick, Brunswick County	Anglican	Brick
201	Moravian Church (1788) Bethabara, Forsyth County	Moravian	Stone

SUMMARY

Anglican	3	Brick	3
Moravian	1	Stone	1
Buildings	4		4

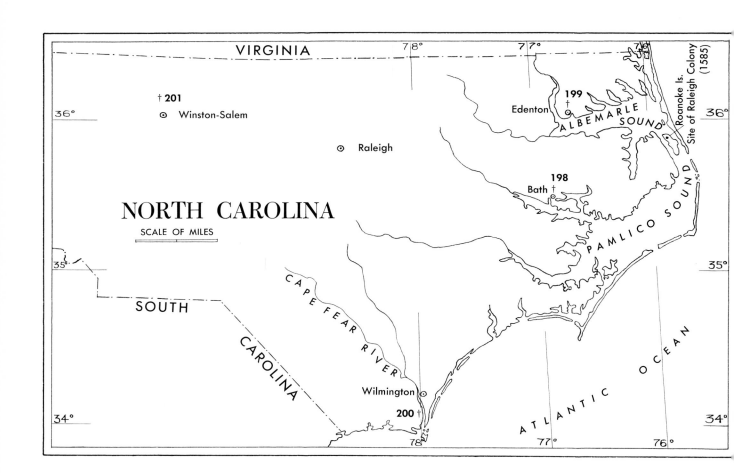

198

St. Thomas' Church (1734)

Bath, Beaufort County, North Carolina

Old Bath County was named for the Earl of Bath, one of the Lords Proprietors. The town of Pamticoe (Pamticough or Pamlico), was settled on Old Town Creek on the peninsula formed by Bath Creek and Back Creek. The present Pamlico River is an arm of Pamlico Sound. The town was incorporated as the Town of Bath in 1705, the county seat and the oldest town in North Carolina. It was no coincidence that the Parish of Pamticoe, which became the Parish of St. Thomas, was organized with a vestry in 1701, the year in which the Society for the Propagation of the Gospel in Foreign Parts was chartered in London. Thomas Bray, an English clergyman, was appointed by the Bishop of London as his commissary to establish the Anglican Church in Maryland, and he served there from 1699 through 1700. He founded a large number of parish libraries throughout England and America; among them the one established at Bath in 1700, the first public library in North Carolina, led directly to the found-

ing of this parish the following year. The reports and recommendations of Bray to the Bishop of London brought about the founding of the Society for the Propagation of the Gospel, while his libraries led to the founding of the Society for the Promotion of Christian Knowledge (1699). In 1702 Queen Anne, who as princess had been active for some years encouraging the establishment of Anglican churches in the colonies, began her reign. In the following year, in accordance with her consistent practice of making donations to each new church, Queen Anne gave the Bible which was newly published in England in 1703, and which is still in use at the church. The bell is also known as the Queen Anne bell; there is a tradition that she gave it in 1710 and it was recast in London in 1732, the date which it bears. Another charity of hers was Queen Anne's Bounty, a trust established by her in 1703, to augment the income of poor parishes. There was resistance by the Dissenters in the Province of North Carolina against establishing the Church of England, but in 1711 the rebellion led by Thomas Carey while he served as deputy governor was resolved by the Church of England being made the Established Church in North Carolina.

In 1711 the Tuscarora Indians, who inhabited this region, waged war on the whites for encroaching on their territory. In that year they massacred a large number of people at Bath, and about sixty of those killed were buried beneath the brick tile floor of the first church building to protect the bodies from desecration. After they were defeated finally in 1713, the Tuscaroras migrated to northern New York, where they became the sixth nation of the Iroquois (see Old Fort Niagara, No. 197), and took part in the Revolution, some on the British side and some on the American (see churches in the Mohawk and Schoharie valleys).

Charles Eden, the governor of North Carolina from 1714 until his death in 1722, maintained a mansion in this parish at Bath. Edward Teach, the pirate "Blackbeard," also had a house at Bath and made it his headquarters until 1718, when he was killed in an attack on his ship. The two were in collusion, and there were stories of the pirate ship being unloaded at night and goods being carried from the dock into the governor's house.

The second and present building, which was erected in 1734 on the site of the first, is the oldest church still standing in North Carolina. In 1735 King George II gave the silver candlesticks that are used on the altar. The present pews stand on a board floor a step above the original brick floor beneath which the victims of the massacre were buried, and in the aisle the old brick is exposed. The church had a brick tower, but it was destroyed by a storm in 1905, and the marks remain in the end wall where it was attached. The brick in that wall above the height of the side walls is smaller and obviously of a later date than that of the side walls laid in Flemish bond. A brick above the doorway carries the inscription, "Bath 1705 — Church 1734." Some years ago the brick disappeared, but it was located in the Metropolitan Museum in New York and returned to its place in the wall.

199

St. Paul's Church (1736)
Edenton, Chowan County, North Carolina

Chowan Parish (later St. Paul's) was organized in 1701, the first religious body and the first corporation in the Province of North Carolina. It was situated on Albemarle Sound between Pembroke Creek and Queen Anne's Creek. The parish records have survived. Known as Queen Anne's Town until 1722, this was the first permanent settlement in North Carolina, although Bath was the first to be incorporated. When Governor Charles Eden died in 1722, and was buried in St. Paul's churchyard, the town was named for him, and it served as the capital of the Province of North Carolina when the legislative assembly met here occasionally.

The first church of the parish, a wooden structure built in 1701-02, was the first in North Carolina. It was located on the Sound, about a mile from the present site. The way of the Church was difficult in those pioneering days. In 1711 an Anglican clergyman, John Urmston, wrote that "the Vestry met at an ordinary where rum was the chief business . . . the church had neither floor nor seats . . . all the Hoggs and Cattle flee thither for shade in the Summer and Warmth in the Winter." The present building was begun in 1736, when the vestry spent £100 for a part of the brick needed, and "£8,7 shillings, 6 pence for 25 Bushels of shells for lime and mortar." After an interval of nine years "Ye roof was righted" in 1745, but the first service for worship was not held in the church until April 10, 1760, and the interior woodwork was not finished until 1774. Although the plan is typical of the medieval parish church, with the main entrance through the tower and another on the south side, the style and decoration of the building is Georgian. The interior has a nave and aisles, and box pews. The building was restored after the fire of 1949.

Services were not permitted in this Anglican church during the Revolution. Dr. Daniel Earl served as rector from 1757 until his death in 1790, adhering to the Church of England throughout the Revolution while fostering revolutionary activities. He presided over a mass meeting on August 22, 1774, protesting the Boston Port Act. Fifteen days before the Declaration of Independence was signed in 1776, the vestry of St. Paul's signed the following declaration:

THE TEST

"We the subscribers professing our Allegiance to the King and acknowledging the constitutional Executive power of government do solemnly profess, testify, and declare that we do absolutely believe that neither the Parliament of Great Britain nor any member or constituent branch thereof have a right to impose taxes upon the colonies, to regulate the internal policy thereof, and that all attempts by fraud or force to establish and exercise such claims and powers are violations of the peace and security of the people and ought to be resisted to the utmost, and that the people of this province singly and collectively are bound by the acts and resolutions of the Continental and Provincial Congress because in both they are freely represented by persons chosen by themselves, and we do solemnly and sincerely promise and engage under the sanction of virtue, Honor and sacred love of Liberty and our country to maintain and support all and every the Acts, Resolutions, and regulations of the said Constitutional and Provincial Congress to the utmost of our power and ability. In testimony whereof we have hereto set our hands this 19th of June 1776.

Signed: Reded Hoskins, David Rice, Aaron Hill, Pelatiah Walton, William Hinton, William Roberts, Thomas Bonner, William Boyd, Thomas Benburg, Jacob Hunter, John Beasley, William Bennett."

200

St. Philip's Church (1740)

Brunswick, Brunswick County, North Carolina

The town of Brunswick, of which the church is one of the few remaining traces, was founded in 1725 on the south bank of the Cape Fear River. Orton Plantation, begun the same year near the site of the church, is still in operation. Four years later, in 1729, North Carolina became a royal province. In 1735 Brunswick was made the capital of the province, when Governor Gabriel Johnston established the seat of government here. St. Philip's Church, as the official church of the royal

governor, became the Chapel Royal. After the Revolution, Brunswick was abandoned. The neighboring swamps and their fever mosquitoes made the site untenable, and the inhabitants retreated to the higher land on the north bank of the Cape Fear River, where they joined the town now known as Wilmington.

The brick church was begun in 1740, but it was not completed until 1765; meanwhile the congregation used a shed for services. It was a beautiful little building for its time. An unusual feature was the height of the four arched windows in each of the two side walls, seven by fifteen feet; the brick walls were thirty-three inches thick at the base. The slender arched windows of the chancel were flanked by doorways. Within the church the governor had a pew raised above the level of the others. Two of the royal governors served in Brunswick and were buried in the churchyard, Arthur Dobbs (1754-65) and William Tryon (1765-71). Alfred Moore, Justice of the Supreme Court of the United States (1799-1805) also was buried here.

John Bartram of Philadelphia, botanist to the king, corresponded with both royal governors on botanical subjects, and on a journey down the Atlantic Coast, in 1765, he recorded in his *Journal* a visit with Governor Tryon in Brunswick on August 8. Beside the church, on the river bank, stood Fort Anderson. It was bombarded during the Civil War, when the Union fleet was blockading Wilmington, and the church has been in ruins ever since. Today the entire site is wooded; trees grow among the ruined walls of the church and the gravestones, and they cover the breastworks of the fort. These few relics are the only signs that remain to remind us of this once thriving capital of the Royal Province of North Carolina. One other relic, the altar rail from this church, is in use at St. Philip's Church at Southport, a few miles to the south on Cape Fear.

201

Moravian Church (1788)

Bethabara, Forsyth County, North Carolina

The Moravians came to North Carolina by a devious route as they wove their way through American colonial history. As members of the old-

est Protestant denomination in the world, some of the Brethren, followers of John Huss (the "Reformer before the Reformation"), fled Bohemia and Moravia under persecution, settled on the estate of Count von Zinzendorf in Saxony, migrated from there to Georgia, moved from Georgia in 1740 to found the Moravian settlement of Bethlehem, Pennsylvania (see No. 244), and from there a company of families, led by Bishop August Gottlieb Spangenberg, migrated in 1752 to settle in North Carolina. They went first to Edenton to confer with representatives of the governor, and after enduring many hardships in the wilderness they took up a grant of a large tract of land in the three forks of the Yadkin River. The country reminded them of Wachau, the former estate of the Zinzendorf family in southern Austria, and they gave the name "Wachau" to their tract. The name was Anglicized as "Wachovia," and the names "Wachovia" and "Zinzendorf" appear today in Winston-Salem on commercial establishments. The town of Bethabara ("House of Passage") was founded in 1753, the first to be settled in the Wachovia Tract. It became known as "Old Town" when the "New Town" of Bethania (Bethany is synonymous with Bethabara) was settled (until recently also called Housertown).

The present stone church was built in 1788. It replaced the original frame Gemein Haus ("Common House"), which stood just to the west of the present site. The building is typical of the Pennsylvania stone structures of the period. Bethabara was a frontier settlement in Indian country, and during its early years the church was within a stockade. The foundations of the fort, which can be seen in the churchyard, carry a plate with the date 1756, which was three years after the first settlement. The church here was their principal place of worship until the Home Moravian Church at Salem (the old part of Winston-Salem), begun in 1798, was dedicated in 1800. In 1749 the British Parliament had recognized the Moravian Brethren as "an ancient Protestant Episcopal Church," and in the Province of North Carolina theirs was the only denomination that enjoyed full freedom and recognition by the Church of England; the only requirement was that they read the English service a few times a year, to accommodate visitors unacquainted with the German language. During the Revolution some of the Moravians in North Carolina bore arms, but most of them helped the cause of the patriots by furnishing supplies.

PENNSYLVANIA

		Denomination	*Material*
202	Gloria Dei Church (1697) Philadelphia, Philadelphia County	Swedish Lutheran	Brick
203	St. James' Church, Kingsessing (1760) Philadelphia, Philadelphia County	Swedish Lutheran	Stone
204	Christ Church, Upper Merion (1760) Montgomery County	Swedish Lutheran	Stone
205	Christ Church (1727) Philadelphia, Philadelphia County	Anglican	Brick
206	St. Peter's Church (1758) Philadelphia, Philadelphia County	Anglican	Brick
207	St. Paul's Church (1760) Philadelphia, Philadelphia County	Anglican	Brick
208	St. George's Church (1763) Philadelphia, Philadelphia County	Methodist	Brick
209	Trinity Church, Oxford (1711) Lawndale, Philadelphia County	Anglican	Brick
210	St. Mary's Church (1763) Philadelphia, Philadelphia County	Roman Catholic	Brick
211	Pine Street Presbyterian Church (1766) Philadelphia, Philadelphia County	Presbyterian	Brick
212	Free Quakers Meeting House (1783) Philadelphia, Philadelphia County	Friends	Brick
213	Mennonite Meeting House (1770) Germantown, Philadelphia County	Mennonite	Stone
214	Church of the Brethren (1770) Germantown, Philadelphia County	Dunkard	Stone
215	Frankford Friends Meeting House (1775) Frankford, Philadelphia County	Friends	Stone
216	Chester Friends Meeting House (1736) Chester, Delaware County	Friends	Brick
217	Chichester Friends Meeting House (1769) Upper Chichester, Delaware County	Friends	Stone
218	Concord Friends Meeting House (1728) Concordville, Delaware County	Friends	Brick
219	Old Haverford Friends Meeting House (1697) Oakmont, Delaware County	Friends	Stone
220	Newtown Square Friends Meeting House (1711) Newtown Square, Delaware County	Friends	Stone
221	Radnor Friends Meeting House (1718) Ithan, Delaware County	Friends	Stone
222	St. David's Church (1715) Radnor, Delaware County	Anglican	Stone
223	St. Peter's Church in the Great Valley (1744) Chester County	Anglican	Stone

		Denomination	Material
224	New Garden Friends Meeting House (1743) New Garden, Chester County	Friends	Brick
225	Old Kennett Friends Meeting House (1710) Hamorton, Chester County	Friends	Stone
226	Birmingham Friends Meeting House (1763) Chester County	Friends	Stone
227	Marshallton Friends Meeting House (1764) Chester County	Friends	Stone
228	East Caln Friends Meeting House (1726) Chester County	Friends	Stone
229	Merion Friends Meeting House (1695) Montgomery County	Friends	Stone
230	Norriton Presbyterian Meeting House (1698) Montgomery County	Presbyterian	Stone
231	Old Trappe Church (1743) Montgomery County	German Lutheran	Stone
232	Falckner's Swamp Lutheran Church (1767) Montgomery County	German Lutheran	Stone
233	Plymouth Meeting Friends Meeting House (c. 1710) Plymouth Meeting, Montgomery County	Friends	Stone
234	Abington Friends Meeting House (1699) Jenkintown, Montgomery County	Friends	Stone
235	Bristol Friends Meeting House (1709) Bristol, Bucks County	Friends	Stone
236	Fallsington Friends Meeting House (1789) Fallsington, Bucks County	Friends	Stone
237	Wrightstown Friends Meeting House (1787) Wrightstown, Bucks County	Friends	Stone
238	Neshaminy Presbyterian Church (1743) Bucks County	Presbyterian	Stone
239	Newtown Presbyterian Church (1769) Newtown, Bucks County	Presbyterian	Stone
240	Tinicum Presbyterian Church (1768) Ottsville, Bucks County	Presbyterian	Stone
241	Buckingham Friends Meeting House (1768) Buckingham Township, Bucks County	Friends	Stone
242	Makefield Friends Meeting House (1752) Dolington, Bucks County	Friends	Stone
243	Plumstead Friends Meeting House (1752) Danboro, Bucks County	Friends	Stone
244	Old Chapel (1751) Bethlehem, Northampton County	Moravian	Stone
245	First Reformed Church (1775) Easton, Northampton County	German Reformed	Stone
246	St. Paul's Chapel (1743) Bally, Berks County	Roman Catholic	Stone
247	Exeter Friends Meeting House (1758) Berks County	Friends	Stone

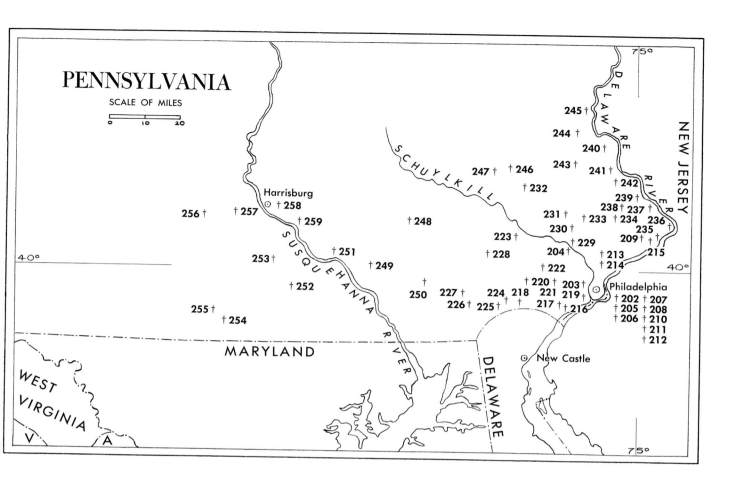

PENNSYLVANIA

SCALE OF MILES

0   10   20

245 †

244 †

240 †

247 †   † 246   243 †   241 †

† 242

† 232   239 †

238 † 237 †

256 †   † 257   231 †   † 233 † 234   236

Harrisburg ⊙ † 258   230 †   235

† 259   † 209 † †

† 248   223 †   204 †   † 229   † 213

† 228   † 214   † 215

† 251   † 222

253 †   † 249   † 220 †   203 †

† 252   250   227 †   224 218   221   219 †   Philadelphia ⊙

226 †   225 † † †   217 † † 216   † 202 † 207

255 †   † 205 † 208

† 254   † 206 † 210

MARYLAND   ⊙ New Castle   † 211

† 212

WEST

VIRGINIA

V   A

NEW JERSEY

DELAWARE RIVER

SCHUYLKILL

SUSQUEHANNA RIVER

DELAWARE

40°

40°

75°

75°

		Denomination	Material
248	The Saal (1741) Ephrata, Lancaster County	Seventh-Day German Baptist	Wood
249	Holy Trinity Church (1761) Lancaster, Lancaster County	German Lutheran	Brick
250	Old Sadsbury Friends Meeting House (1777) Christiana, Lancaster County	Friends	Stone
251	Donegal Presbyterian Church (c. 1740) Lancaster County	Presbyterian	Stone
252	York Friends Meeting House (1765) York, York County	Friends	Brick
253	Warrington Friends Meeting House (1769) York County	Friends	Stone
254	Church of the Sacred Heart (1785) Conewago, Adams County	Roman Catholic	Stone
255	Great Conewago Presbyterian Church (1787) Hunterstown, Adams County	Presbyterian	Stone
256	First Presbyterian Church (1757) Carlisle, Cumberland County	Presbyterian	Stone
257	Silver Spring Presbyterian Church (1783) Cumberland County	Presbyterian	Stone
258	Paxton Presbyterian Church (1740) Paxtang, Dauphin County	Presbyterian	Stone
259	St. Peter's Church (1767) Middletown, Dauphin County	German Lutheran	Stone

SUMMARY

Swedish Lutheran	3		Brick	14
Anglican	6		Wood	1
Methodist	1		Stone	43
Roman Catholic	3			
Presbyterian	10			
Friends	26			
Mennonite	1			
Dunkard	1			
German Lutheran	4			
Moravian	1			
German Reformed	1			
Seventh-Day German Baptist	1			
Buildings	58			58

Gloria Dei Church (1697)
Old Swedes'

**Delaware Avenue near Christian Street,
Philadelphia, Pennsylvania**

Gloria Dei was the first Christian congregation organized in the section now covered by Philadelphia. After the Swedes had made their first settlement in Delaware, they moved up the Delaware River and made the first settlement in what is now Pennsylvania on Tinicum Island, where the present Essington is located. There, after John Printz had made it his capital of New Sweden, they built a small house of worship in 1639, but their town of Prinzhof was burned twice, and it faded into history. This area was organized as the upper parish in 1672, when Cranehook (Wilmington) became the lower par-

ish. In 1677 Jacob Fabritius, a clergyman of the Church of Sweden, the Evangelical Lutheran Church, and the first minister of the congregation at the present location, obtained the use of a log blockhouse in Wicaco (Wycacoa) for a church. The Swedish settlement of Wicaco became a part of Philadelphia; the blockhouse stood on the site of the present church, which is located at Delaware Avenue and Christian Street. In 1669 the congregation held its first services here.

The present building was begun September of 1697, the year before the first stone was laid for Old Swedes' in Wilmington (see No. 13). The foundation is of stone, and the walls are of brick laid in Flemish bond, with glazed headers and diapering. The steep pitch of the roof, the square belfry, and the small spire are characteristic of Swedish architecture. At the dedication of the church on July 2, 1700, Eric Björck, the pastor, said: "Through God's blessing we have completed a great work, and have built a church superior to any in this country, so that the English themselves, who now govern this province and are beyond measure richer than we are, wonder at what we have done." The earliest record of a musical recital in Pennsylvania was that played in this church by the Hermits of the Wissahickon, a group of mystics. The occasion was the ordination of Justus Falckner in 1703, when the little orchestra used the viol, oboe, kettledrum, and trumpet. In 1704 the walls of the church were buttressed by the addition of a sacristy on the north end and a vestibule at the entrance on the south end. The tower and spire were built some years after the body of the building, and the interior, including the gallery and pulpit, is in good taste.

In 1710 permission was granted for the church to be used for services of the Church of England. In appreciation for this cooperation, the Anglicans ended their services by singing a hymn in Swedish. The use of the Swedish language gradually died out; after the commencement of the Republic the Swedish pastors in America were withdrawn, and in 1789 Gloria Dei was taken into the newly-formed Protestant Episcopal Church. On March 31, 1942, the Department of the Interior designated Gloria Dei Church as a National Historic Site, being a splendid example of the cultural and religious aspects of Swedish colonization in the United States. The designation was made at the recommendation of President Franklin D. Roosevelt, at a time when the United States had been involved for three months in World War II. Two other Swedish churches were built in the Philadelphia area as outgrowths of Gloria Dei: St. James' Church, Kingsessing (No. 203), and Christ Church, Upper Merion (No. 204).

203

St. James' Church, Kingsessing (1760)
Woodland Avenue, Philadelphia, Pennsylvania

By 1760 Old Swedes' Church (Gloria Dei, No. 202) had become crowded, and in that year the cornerstone was laid for the first child of that mother church, St. James' Church in Kingsessing. At that time the Kingsessing section was outside Philadelphia to the west, but now it is part of the city. The church was opened for the first services of the Swedish Lutheran congregation in 1762; the year appears on a stone brought from

England for the occasion and placed in the gable wall. About 1854 the transepts were added, making the building cruciform, and a number of alterations have been made since. Like the other Swedish churches, this congregation gradually changed from the use of Swedish to English, and after the Revolution the church became Episcopalian. In the churchyard, among many early settlers, are soldiers of Washington's army who were killed in the Battle of the Brandywine.

204

Christ Church, Upper Merion (1760) Old Swedes

Bridgeport, Montgomery County, Pennsylvania

From the congregations at Wicaco, where they built Gloria Dei (No. 202) in what is now South Philadelphia, and at Kingsessing, where they built St. James' (No. 203) in what is now West Philadelphia, the Swedes moved further up the Schuylkill River to the Upper Merion section, and established a Swedish settlement on land obtained from the Indians by purchase or treaty. For some years they attended services at

St. James' or Gloria Dei, traveling by canoe on the Schuylkill. As their congregation grew it became more convenient to hold services in private houses, and then in a schoolhouse that had been built in 1735, with lay readers, or occasionally with the minister from Gloria Dei officiating. In 1758 the present Christ Church was organized, a member of the Swedish Lutheran denomination.

The present building was erected in 1760, as a rectangular stone church. It was dedicated on June 25, 1760, on which occasion the sermon was preached by Charles Magnus Wrangel, a clergyman who had been sent here the previous year by the Archbishop of Sweden. The building assumed its cruciform style when the transepts, the chancel, and the tower were added in 1837. In 1861 the windows were given their Gothic style and stained glass was installed. As was the case in the older Swedish congregations, English gradually replaced the Swedish language with the influx of Welsh settlers, and following the Revolution, after many years of close co-operation with the Church of England, the church became Episcopalian. In 1843 the union with the other Swedish churches was dissolved, and this church became independent.

205

Christic Church (1727)

**Second Street near Market, Philadelphia,
Pennsylvania**

Christ Church, the first Anglican church in the province, was gathered by laymen and organized in 1695, under a provision of the original charter of Charles II to William Penn. For the next sixty-six years it was the only Episcopal church in Philadelphia. No church is more intimately connected with the founding of both the United States of America and the Protestant Episcopal Church of America. Governors and officials of the State of Pennsylvania and the United States, worshiped here.

A deed of 1695 covered most of the present site, and the first church was built of logs within a year. In 1711 the building was enlarged and rebuilt, to the extent that it is referred to as "the second church." An adjoining lot was purchased in 1725, and in 1727 work was begun on the present beautiful building. The design was drawn by a vestryman, Dr. John Kearsley, a physician

and amateur architect, who served also on the committee for building the State House (Independence Hall). On the same committee was the architect of that building, Andrew Hamilton, who also was a vestryman of Christ Church, and the able lawyer who defended Peter Zenger to establish the principle of freedom of the press (see St. Paul's, Eastchester, N. Y., No. 177). In 1737 the building was completed, except the tower, which was added in 1754. The organ dates from 1765 and the pulpit from 1769. During the 1800's several alterations were made; it was lengthened two or three times, but the building is essentially the original structure. In 1834 the high-backed box pews were replaced with lower ones, and the galleries were set back of the pillars. At that time pew No. 58, which had been held by George and Martha Washington from 1790 to 1797, was placed in the National Museum in Washington. In 1881 the present pews were installed.

Among the many treasures of the church are the communion silver, which was given by Queen Anne about 1708, and the bells. The first bell dates from 1702; the peal of eight bells was brought from London, in 1754, and placed in the tower, which had been finished the year before. They were bought with funds raised by the "Philadelphia Steeple Lottery," which was run by Benjamin Franklin. These bells and the Liberty Bell were cast in England by Lester and Pack, and they pealed with the Liberty Bell to proclaim the Declaration of Independence. Henry Wadsworth Longfellow visited Philadelphia for the Centennial in 1876, and in his poem, "Evangeline," the closing scene includes these lines:

Distant and soft on her ear fell the chimes from the belfry of Christ Church,
While, intermingled with these, across the meadows were wafted
Sounds of psalms, that were sung by the Swedes in their Church at Wicaco.

Among the scores of distinguished people who were baptized at the historic baptismal font, which dates from 1695 and has served for most of the life of Christ Church, was William White, who was to become a rector of the parish. He served as chaplain to the Continental Congress, as the first Bishop of Pennsylvania, and as the Presiding Bishop of the Protestant Episcopal Church of America, from 1795 until his death in 1836, when he was buried before the chancel rail. He was the prime mover in organizing the Episcopal Church, after the Revolution had put an end to the jurisdiction of the Church of England and the Bishop of London over the American churches. His pamphlet of 1782, "The Case of the Episcopal Churches in the United States Considered," led to a series of conventions, in which most of his proposals were adopted. He was the architect of the constitution of the new Church, which was adopted at the final convention in 1789 (some months after the inauguration of George Washington as the first President of the United States); and, in the course of his presiding over the convention, it was largely due to the tact and diplomacy of Bishop White that the convention was able to succeed in the organization of the new Church. The constitution was presented at the first session of the convention, which was held in Christ Church from July 28 to August 8. In order to have more room, the convention adjourned to Independence Hall for the session in October. With Bishop White presiding (in the hall where the Declaration of Independence had been adopted, the Articles of Confederation had been ratified, and the Constitution of the United States had been drafted) the convention adopted the constitution of the Protestant Episcopal Church and an amended Book of Common Prayer. Christ Church has among its treasures the Edward VI Prayer Book in which amendments were written by Bishop White.

Another rector of Christ Church was Robert Blackwell, chaplain of the American Army at Valley Forge. Among the many prominent people who attended services here were General Lafayette, as a guest of the Washingtons, and President John Adams, who used the same pew during his administration. Other pew holders included Robert Morris, treasurer of the Revolution; Francis Hopkinson, signer of the Declaration of Independence and designer of the national flag; his son, Judge Joseph Hopkinson, author of the hymn "Hail Columbia"; and Betsy Ross, who made the first flag. On July 20, 1775, the Continental Congress attended services in a body. In the two cemeteries of Christ Church many prominent people were buried. Seven of them were signers of the Declaration — Benjamin Franklin, Joseph Hewes, Stephen Hopkins, Robert Morris, George Ross, Benjamin Rush, and James Wilson. The funeral of Benjamin Franklin was attended by 20,000 people, and he was buried in the corner of Christ Church Burial Ground at Fifth and Arch Streets. John Penn, a grandson of William Penn and a governor of Pennsylvania, who had signed the church charter in 1765, was buried near the pulpit.

Because of its intimate association with the founders of the nation, Christ Church was designated a national shrine, in 1952, by an Act of Congress.

St. Peter's Church (1758)

Third and Pine Streets, Philadelphia, Pennsylvania

The cornerstone of St. Peter's Church was laid September 21, 1758. As Christ Church had been the only Anglican church in Philadelphia since its founding in 1695, St. Peter's was built in this fast growing section of the city as a chapel of ease to Christ Church (No. 205). It was opened for services in 1761, with the two churches, known as the United Churches of Christ Church and St. Peter's Church, sharing one rector and vestry. The land was given by Thomas and Richard Penn, sons of William Penn, who were members of the Church of England even though their father was the most prominent of Quakers, and who were Proprietaries of the Province of Pennsylvania. The last of the building debt was paid off in 1771.

The design probably was drawn by Samuel Rhodes. The master architect in charge of building the church was Robert Smith, assisted by Dr. John Kearsley, vestryman and designer of Christ Church. The interior of St. Peter's is the original. The wineglass pulpit, sounding board, desk, and chancel rail were installed in 1764. The organ loft over the chancel was added in 1789. The tower and steeple with the chimes were not in the original plan but were added in 1842. They replaced the original cupola, which contained two bells; before the British occupied the city in 1777, the bells were carted secretly at night through their lines, together with the chimes of Christ Church and the Liberty Bell, and at Allentown were hidden beneath the floor of Zion Reformed Church. The bells of St. Peter's and the Liberty Bell were cast in England by Lester and Pack. The interior has a most unusual arrangement: the pulpit is at one end of the center aisle,

against the tower, and the chancel and altar are at the other end, before a Palladian window; the congregation may shift to the opposite benches in the box pews, or sit with their backs to part of the service.

In 1775 Jacob Duché became the rector of Christ Church and St. Peter's. He called a special meeting of the vestry at his house on July 4, 1776, after the Declaration of Independence, and

it was voted to omit the prayers for the king in the services at the two churches. He was appointed the first chaplain to Congress, but after three months he resigned. He had thought that the Declaration was a bluff, and in a letter to George Washington, whom he urged to desert his cause, he revealed that he was a loyalist. The feeling against him ran high, and in 1777 he sailed for England. After the Constitution of the United States had been adopted, and with Washington's kind forgiveness, he returned to Philadelphia, where he died in 1798 and was buried in the churchyard of St. Peter's. Thomas Coombe, who had charge of both churches after the departure of Duché, remained loyal to the Crown, and after the occupation of the city by the British had ended, he also returned to England. William White (see Christ Church, No. 205) was loyal to the American cause from the first; he moved back into Philadelphia after the occupation and became rector of the two churches. George Washington, on his first Sunday in Philadelphia, September 25, 1774, attended Quaker meeting in the morning and St. Peter's in the afternoon. During the winter of 1781-82, after the victory at Yorktown, when they lived near the church on Third Street below Willing's Alley, the Washingtons used pew No. 36 (now No. 41), which belonged to Samuel Powel, mayor of Philadelphia.

In the churchyard there are graves of many patriots and distinguished citizens, including William Shippen, who was killed in the Battle of Princeton; Captain Gustavus Conyngham, the naval hero who captured many English ships in waters around the British Isles in 1777; Stephen Decatur, naval hero of the War of 1812; Nicholas Biddle, president of the United States Bank; and Charles Willson Peale, famous portrait painter.

Since 1832 St. Peter's has been united with Christ Church only in the administration of a home for aged gentlewomen, Christ Church Hospital, where hangs one of the bells from the original cupola of this church.

207

St. Paul's Church (1760)

South Third Street and Willing's Alley, Philadelphia, Pennsylvania

St. Paul's Church served as a transition from the Church of England to the Methodist Church in America. George Whitefield preached many times in Philadelphia from 1739 to 1770. He was the great evangelist and friend of John Wesley, who prepared the way for Methodism in America, and who, with Jonathan Edwards in New England, aroused America to the Great Awakening. William McClenachan a priest of the Church of England (who had neglected his frontier mission in the Kennebec, Maine region to practice medicine in Boston), during a visit to Philadelphia preached at Christ Church. He was received enthusiastically and was invited to become an

assistant in that church, but he had Calvinistic leanings, and his wife was such a vigorous supporter of George Whitefield (who continued to be a priest of the Church of England for the rest of his life) that the Bishop of London received objections and did not permit the appointment. In a meeting at the State House (Independence Hall) the faction in the dispute that leaned toward Calvinism took steps to build a new Anglican church, and St. Paul's was the result, with McClenachan instituted as the first rector. Meanwhile the Methodists were gathering a congregation with the spirit stimulated by Whitefield.

The building of St. Paul's was begun in 1760; it was ready for use on Christmas Day, 1761. According to the Methodists, who were still affiliated with the Church of England, the design was more in accord with Wesley's church conceptions than was tolerated in other Anglican churches. In 1769 the Methodists acquired the neighboring building that became St. George's Church (No. 208), and in finishing it they copied the pulpit and chancel in St. Paul's. Until 1784, when the Methodist Church became a separate denomination, the congregation walked the few blocks from their services in St. George's to St. Paul's for the sermon and Communion; here worshiped such founders of Methodism as Joseph Pilmoor, Richard Boardman, and Francis Asbury. St. Paul's continued as an Episcopal church. When the British occupied the city, and the rector, William Stringer, preached from the text Ezekiel 20:38, "I will purge out the rebels from among you," many of the men were at Valley Forge, and the reaction was such that Stringer was forced to resign.

Alterations made in 1830-32, to accommodate the Sunday school, destroyed the colonial features of the interior. The high-back pews and sounding board were removed; the two wooden angels from the ends of the choir loft were transferred to St. Peter's Church (No. 206). The exterior walls were stuccoed, but the front wall has been uncovered to reveal the original brick.

Stephen Girard, banker, financier, and founder of Girard College, was married in the church in 1777. In the burial ground, among the graves of many early residents of the city, is that of Daniel Hall, who was a partner of Benjamin Franklin in the printing business for eighteen years. The building is now used by the Philadelphia Protestant Episcopal City Mission. Here at Willing's Alley is the site of the Friends Alms House, where Evangeline, in the poem of that name by Henry Wadsworth Longfellow, finally found Gabriel.

344

208

St. George's Church (1763)

Fourth Street between Race and Vine
Philadelphia, Pennsylvania

St. George's Church is the oldest Methodist house of worship in the world. Here many steps were taken to found Methodism in America. Near the church, at 62 North Fourth Street, a bronze tablet marks the site of the first house of worship to be used by Methodists in Philadelphia: "On this site stood the 'New Building' erected in 1740 for George Whitefield and for a Charity School — subsequently used until 1812 by the School, Academy, College (1753) and University of Pennsylvania (1779) successively." Benjamin Franklin, a nonsectarian, took part in raising funds for building this great hall (measuring 100 by 70 feet), after hearing Whitefield preach effectively to throngs of thousands of people, of any and all denominations, in the streets and on the common (now Franklin Park). For a decade the hall was used by Whitefield, a founder of Methodism in America, and by Gilbert Tennent, a Presbyterian preacher of the New Lights and a follower of Whitefield (see Neshaminy Church, No. 238). In 1750, Franklin, who served as trustee both for the property and the Academy, arranged for the Academy to buy the hall and to start there the forerunner of the University of Pennsylvania.

Whitefield preached all over colonial America and converted thousands, but he organized no societies. He parted from John Wesley on theological grounds, and he left organization to him and his Methodist missionaries, or to Presbyterians, Congregationalists, or any other denomination. Whitefield was more ecumenical than denominational, but in Philadelphia his preaching led directly to the organization of a Methodist Society. Edward Evans, who was converted in 1739 or 1740 by Whitefield, on the first of the evangelist's many visits in Philadelphia, became a trustee of the "New Building" and one of the first Methodist preachers in America. (John Wesley designated them as preachers, not priests or ministers.) Under the leadership of James Emerson, the nucleus of Methodists who were to form a Society met for a time in a sail loft on Dock Creek (now Dock Street). In 1767 Captain Thomas Webb, who had been licensed by John Wesley to preach, came to Philadelphia and organized the group into the Society which became St. George's. The Society moved from the sail loft to a room at 8 Loxley Court (now Leather Place), a building formerly used as a "pot" or public house. In 1769 the Society had grown to a hundred members, when they were joined by the two missionaries sent by Wesley — Joseph Pilmoor and Richard Boardman. Pilmoor remained in Philadelphia, preaching on the common (Franklin Park, two blocks away) in good weather and otherwise in their room.

As they approached winter and the room could not hold half their members, the Methodists sought to build a chapel, but their means were limited. Then a windfall came. A congregation had begun a building in 1763, to be a German Reformed Church with the name "Georg Kirche," in honor of the reigning king of England. Their funds ran out, and, with the principals in debtors' prison, the unfinished shell was sold to the Society for £700. On November 24, 1769, the day after the purchase, the unfinished building was dedicated by Pilmoor, who preached to a congregation of about two thousand. The purchase price did not include the grounds, and the ground rent was paid until 1802, when it finally was "extinguished." For some years the Methodists referred to "our preaching house" and "our meeting house," and then they named it "St. George's Church" for the patron saint of England. Heretofore they had established chapels; this was the first Methodist house of worship in the world to to be called a church, and with its seating capacity of over a thousand, it was referred to later, by Bishop Asbury, as "the Cathedral of Methodism."

Until after the Revolution the congregation used slat-backed benches on the dirt floor, and then only the east end was covered with a rough plank floor. The first three Conferences of American Methodism were held on the dirt floor of this unplastered, unpainted building. In 1784 the walls were plastered; in 1790 the floor was completed and more comfortable seats were installed. The pulpit, sounding board, and chancel, and their arrangement in the finished church, were copied from St. Paul's Church, which had been built in the neighborhood on South Third Street in 1760 (see No. 207). Until the Methodist Episcopal Church was organized as a separate denomination, in 1784, the congregation of St. George's had gone to St. Paul's for the sermon and Communion, but then the relationship ended. In 1845 the high pulpit was removed, and the present pulpit is a replica standing in the original location. In 1792 the galleries were built on three sides, and Asbury noted that they were filled when he preached there soon after. In 1836 the basement was excavated and accommodations were provided for Sunday school and Class (a division in a Methodist church) purposes. In this church Francis Asbury preached his first sermon in America in 1771, the First Conference of American Methodism was held in 1773, and in 1789 John Dickins organized the Book Business, now the Publishing House.

The Benjamin Franklin Bridge over the Delaware River was planned originally for the approach to go from Franklin Park directly above St. George's Church, but to save this historic landmark the position of the bridge was moved fourteen feet. Fourth Street was lowered to pass under the approach, and there is now a high retaining wall in front of the church.

209

Trinity Church, Oxford (1711)

**Oxford Avenue and Disston Street, Lawndale,
Philadelphia County, Pennsylvania**

About 1692, as a result of the Keithian controversy (see St. Peter's Church, Freehold, N. J., No. 147) a group of Keithian Quakers who separated from their meetings — Poetquesink (now Byberry), Lower Dublin (now Abington, see No. 234), and Oxford (now Frankford, see No. 215) — built and used a log meeting house on this site. By 1696 George Keith had returned to England, and these members who had withdrawn from the Society of Friends had joined other demoninations; the property was then conveyed to the Church of England, and Anglican services were held in that building until the present one was built.

The present church was built in 1711, the original part being the west (near) end with the main door. The old meeting house near by evidently was used by the "Oxford Church" as a school, then as a stable, and finally was demolished. This original brick wall is laid in Flemish bond, with glazed headers used in a diaper pattern. Brick was made from the clay beds on which Philadelphia stands. (Brickmaking was one of Philadelphia's earliest industries.) The north wing was built in 1833 and the east end in 1839. The tower, in the angle between the east end and the covered porch on the south wall, is also a modern addition. The interior was made cruciform when the vestry was converted to a recess chancel and the wall was removed between the east end and the old tower. Church Road was built to enable one rector to serve both this church and St. Thomas', Whitemarsh, nine miles away. Trinity Church afforded one of the many examples of active cooperation between the Swedish Lutheran Church and the Church of England. Andrew Rudman was one of the first three priests who came from Sweden when the Swedish mission in America began in 1697. While he was pastor of Gloria Dei (No. 202), he served also as the minister of this church. The distance between the two was eight or nine miles, which he undertook to walk, but, according to Nelson Burr in his "The Early History of the Swedes and the Episcopal Church in America," he "found this beyond his strength and was compelled to buy a horse."

St. Mary's Church (1763)

224 South Fourth Street, Philadelphia, Pennsylvania

There is evidence of Mass being read publicly in Philadelphia as early as 1707 by a missionary dressed as a Quaker. The first Roman Catholic house of worship in Philadelphia was St. Joseph's Chapel, and St. Mary's was built as its first mission. St. Joseph's was founded by Joseph Greaton, a Jesuit missionary who came to Philadelphia as early as 1729. He came from Maryland by way of Conewago, where he is believed to have held the first services in the first Roman Catholic house of worship in Pennsylvania (see Church of the Sacred Heart, No. 254). Because of the laws against Roman Catholics and their having public houses of worship, Father Greaton came to Philadelphia disguised in the common dress of a Quaker, and in 1733 he bought a plot in the seclusion of Willing's Alley, on which he built a Mass house, a residence in which a room was furnished as St. Joseph's Chapel.

The issue of religious liberty in Pennsylvania was decided on that chapel. William Penn's Charter of Privileges stated: "Because no People can be truly happy tho' under the greatest Enjoyment of Civil Liberties, if abridged in the Freedom of their Consciences as to their religious Profession and Worship . . . I hereby grant and declare, That no persons inhabiting in this Province . . . shall be in any Case molested . . . because of his or their conscientious Persuasion or Practice. . . ." This triumph of religious freedom, won for Pennsylvania and the nation in 1734 is recorded on a tablet at St. Joseph's Church, which was dedicated on May 21 and 22, 1956, and which reads as follows:

"When in 1733 St. Joseph's Roman Catholic Church was founded and dedicated to the guardian of the Holy Family it was the only place in the entire English speaking world where public celebration of the Holy Sacrifice of the Mass was permitted by law.

In 1734 the Provincial Council of Pennsylvania defending the liberty of worship granted by William Penn to this colony successfully withstood the demand of the Governor of the Province that this church be outlawed and such liberty suppressed.

Thus was established permanently in our nation the principle of religious freedom which was later embodied into the Constitution of the United States of America."

Although it had been enlarged, by 1763 St. Joseph's Chapel was too small for the congregation, and St. Mary's Church was built in that year, only half a block away. The two were

Pine Street Presbyterian Church (1766)

Fourth and Pine Streets, Philadelphia, Pennsylvania

In 1761 the Third Presbyterian congregation in Philadelphia was organized by members of the Market Street Church, or First Presbyterian, and others, for the purpose of building the Pine Street Presbyterian Church. Robert Smith was chosen as architect, and the building was begun in 1766. Funds ran out the following year, and a lottery was conducted which supplied about £2500 to finish the building. The original building had a single story with two tiers of windows, including a Palladian window over the entrance. In 1837 it was converted to two stories by lifting the roof, building up the original walls, and covering the whole structure with a new roof. The old roof and gable ends can be seen in the loft. The brick walls, now covered with stucco, rest on a stone foundation that rises about five feet above the ground.

One of the original trustees was Dr. William Shippen, Jr., the first professor of medicine in America and director general of all hospitals during the Revolution; another was John Tittermary, ropemaker to the Continental Army. George Duffield became pastor in 1771. Sixty-seven of the one hundred and ten men who signed the call to him served in the Revolution. He actively inspired the War of Independence and supported the cause of the patriots during the war. In addressing the militia and members of Congress he urged a declaration of independence four months before the official declaration. Dr. Duffield was made chaplain of all the Philadelphia Militia and later served with William White, rector of Christ Church (No. 205), as a chaplain of the Continental Congress. The church was used as a hospital by the British during their occupation of the city, and the pews were destroyed. It served later as a stable for the dragoons. The British offered a reward of £50 for the capture of Duffield, and they showed no respect for a Presbyterian church. After the war the building was dilapidated and the congregation was without a church. Dr. Duffield returned and restored the church, gathered the congregation, and served again as its pastor, until he died of yellow fever in 1790. He was buried in the center aisle of the church. President Adams was a member of the church, as was the mother of Dr. Benjamin Rush, a signer of the Declaration of Independence, who attended services here.

affiliated until 1821, when St. Mary's was set off as a separate parish. In 1838 the present St. Joseph's Church replaced the historic colonial building of St. Joseph's Chapel. St. Mary's was dedicated in 1788. It has been enlarged and remodeled. In 1782 alterations were made, and in 1810 the west end was extended twenty feet and the north side twenty feet to make the present form of the building. The interior has been remodeled completely. In 1886 the stained glass windows were installed.

The Continental Congress attended services officially at St. Mary's at least four times. The Mass of Thanksgiving for the ending of the Revolution, celebrated on November 4, 1781, was attended by the Congress, by French troops under Rochambeau and Dillon and troops from the armies of Washington, Wayne, and Stephen Moylan, which were then in Philadelphia. Moylan, who served as aide-de-camp and secretary to Washington during the siege of Boston and later commanded all the cavalry forces, was a member of this parish and was buried here. In the churchyard is the tomb of Commodore John Barry, who became known as the Father of the United States Navy. He was in command of the *Lexington* when, on April 17, 1776, it became the first commissioned American ship to capture a British vessel.

At the beginning of the Republic, Baltimore was over all Roman Catholic churches in the United States. In 1808 Pope Pius VII erected Philadelphia as an episcopal see separate from the Diocese of Baltimore. In 1810, when Michael Egan was consecrated bishop, he made St. Mary's his cathedral church for the short period until his death in 1814.

212

Free Quakers Meeting House (1783)

Fifth and Arch Streets, Philadelphia, Pennsylvania

The Free Quakers Meeting House, situated across the street from Benjamin Franklin's grave in Christ Church Burial Ground, was erected in 1783. The tablet in the north gable reads: "By General Subscription for the FREE QUAKERS Erected in the Year of our Lord 1783 of the Empire 8." The Free Quakers became known as "Fighting Quarkers," for they held themselves free to help the cause of the Revolution and to bear arms for their country. The sect was organized by patriots who had left or had been read out of their respective meetings, and it attained a membership of about four hundred. Their leader was Samuel Wetherill, Jr., who served as preacher and clerk of the Meeting, and whose great-grandfather had been among the original Quaker settlers in New Jersey. The group included such patriots as Timothy Matlack, colonel in the army and member of the Committee of Public Safety; William Crispen, commissary in Washington's army; Colonel Clement Biddle, quartermaster general under General Gates; Christopher Marshall, well-known patriot and member of the Committee of Safety, whose diary of Philadelphia during the Revolution is a vaulable historical document; Elizabeth Griscom (Betsy Ross), who had been read out of meeting for her aid to the Revolution; and Lydia Darragh, who also had been an active patriot. (It was Lydia Darragh who was the heroine of a legend which related that, in her house in Philadelphia in 1777, she overheard General Howe and his staff planning to attack Washington and his army outside of Philadelphia at Whitemarsh, and that she walked there in the cold of winter to warn him.) The reference of the Free Quakers to the "Empire" reflects the uncertainty, in the period between the Declaration of Independence and the foundation of the Republic, as to what form of government the new nation would adopt. After the Revolution the members here became less active; some returned to their former meetings, and some joined other denominations. John Price Wetherill, son of Samuel, was an old man when he found himself alone, and the sect ceased to be active. The spirit of the Fighting Quakers revived in the Civil War, however, and a number of Quakers took part. For many years the annual meetings of the defunct Society have been reunions of the Wetherill family, in which they vote the proceeds of the accumulated funds to charitable causes.

This was the only building in a wide area that was not demolished to make way for the Mall and Independence Hall National Park during the last few years. The land on which the meeting house was built and the building were purchased by the Commonwealth of Pennsylvania, under a plan to widen Fifth Stret, to move the meeting house back fifty feet, and to restore the interior of the building, which has been used for some years by commercial firms, to its original colonial design — a joint project of the federal, state, and city governments.

213

Mennonite Meeting House (1770)

Germantown Avenue above Washington Lane, Germantown, Philadelphia County, Pennsylvania

William Penn offered freedom from religious persecution and economic opportunities in his province. Among those who took advantage of the offer were Germans who migrated to Pennsylvania in large groups. Most of these "Pennsylvania Dutch" were Mennonites, whose sect was derived from the Anabaptists and named for Menno Simons, a Dutch priest (1492-1559). In

1683 a large group of Mennonites emigrated from Crefeld, Germany, under the leadership of Francis Daniel Pastorius, agent for the Frankfurt Land Company, took up a grant of 6,000 acres northwest of Philadelphia, and founded Germantown. In 1688 William Rittenhouse, who built in the Wissahickon Valley near by the first paper mill in America, was chosen by the Mennonites as their first minister. In 1689 William Rittenhouse drew Lot No. 9, and on it, in 1691, the "Little Log Church" was built, a community church which was attended by Mennonites. A section of the lot that included the site of the present meeting house and burial ground was given by Rittenhouse, part in 1702 and the rest a little later. In 1708 the first Mennonite meeting house in America was built on this site, and Rittenhouse died in the same year.

The present stone meeting house was built in 1770, replacing the earlier structure on the same site. The small single room is austere in its plain design and furnishing. During the Battle of Germantown, October 4, 1777, patriots firing on the British troops from behind the church walls killed Brigadier General Agnew, and the building was damaged to some extent.

214

Church of the Brethren (1770)

Germantown Avenue and Montana Street, Germantown, Philadelphia County, Pennsylvania

The Church of the Brethren in Germantown is the first and mother church of the sect in America. The German Baptist Brethren was founded in Germany in 1708, but it is American. From the time of their organization the members were per-

secuted in Germany, and they fled to Holland. Thence they emigrated to Pennsylvania between 1719 and 1729. The first group to arrive in America settled in Germantown in 1719, and there they organized the present Church in 1723. The German Brethren are called also "Dunkards" or "Dunkers," from the German word *tunken,* to immerse; their trine baptism, performed after a person has reached the age of discretion, consists in three immersions made in the name of the Trinity.

In 1770 the present church was built. Until the stone structure was finished, services were held in a wooden building. In 1896 the church was remodeled by the addition of the rear wing. It was enlarged further in 1815. An outside stairway formerly led through a doorway to the gallery; the stairway was removed, and a round window is now in the place of the doorway. Otherwise there has been practically no change in the front part of the building.

In 1742 the first American quarto edition of the Bible was published by Christopher Sauer, an active member of this church. His son Christopher, who also was a printer and publisher of the Bible, became a bishop of the Church of the Brethren in 1753. At the time of the Battle of Germantown, October 4, 1777, the third edition of the Bible was in production, and printed sheets were drying in the church loft while others were being printed with the limited type in the print shop. British soldiers used the papers in the church for bedding on the cold ground after the battle, and the edition was ruined except for the completed copies that had been sold. The church possesses a copy of the Bible that Sauer, after retrieving the soiled pages, bound and gave to his children. Six soldiers killed in the battle were buried in the churchyard.

215

Frankford Friends Meeting House (1775)

Unity and Waln Streets, Frankford, Philadelphia County, Pennsylvania

This meeting house was built in 1775, when Frankford was still a small settlement in the country. Frankford Meeting was derived from Oxford Meeting (see Trinity Church, Oxford, No. 209). There was a close association in the early years between Abington (No. 234), Byberry, and Oxford Meetings. In 1805 the name here was changed from Oxford to Frankford Preparative Meeting. The first meetings were held in 1682. The year taken for the establishment of Frankford Meeting is 1683, when Tacony Monthly Meeting was established by Philadelphia Quarterly Meeting and it was held at the home of Sarah Seary, near Frankford and Oxford (now Lawndale). A meeting house of logs was built, but it had not been in use for many years when the controversy was started by the preaching and the proposals of George Keith, which led to his being disowned by the Yearly Meeting in America in 1692 (in London in 1694) and resulted in a schism in the Society of Friends. Oxford Meeting came to an end when its members withdrew, some to join other denominations and others to support Frankford Meeting. Frankford continues active, with meetings held regularly. It is an Indulged Meeting under Green Street Monthly Meeting (which includes Germantown and Fair Hill Meetings) and Philadelphia Quarter.

352

216

Chester Friends Meeting House (1736)

Market Street near Market Square, Chester, Delaware County, Pennsylvania

The first recorded meeting of Friends in Pennsylvania was held in 1675 at Upland (now Chester), in the home of Robert Wade. The first Monthly Meeting was held in 1681. William Edmundson was active in establishing it. In 1682 "the meeting was settled to be in the Court House." The first meeting house was built a decade later, in 1693, on Edgemont Avenue between Second and Third Streets (no longer standing).

The present brick meeting house was built in 1736. At the time of the Separation, in 1829, the Hicksites kept this building and the Orthodox Friends built another. After using it for a century the Hicksites, then Race Street Friends, closed the building in 1928 and reunited with the Or-

thodox, or Arch Street Friends. For a time the building served as the Full Gospel Tabernacle of a Pentacostal denomination. Then it became a center for Negroes, the Robert Wade Neighborhood House. Redevelopment plans of the City of Chester recently called for a near-by housing development to include the Robert Wade Neighborhood House and the demolition of this colonial building.

217

Chichester Friends Meeting House (1769)

Upper Chichester Township, Delaware County, Pennsylvania

The old Township of Chichester included the site of the present industrial town of Marcus Hook, on the bank of the Delaware River below Chester. Near Marcus Hook, back in the country on Meeting House Road, stands Chichester Friends Meeting House. Meetings for worship were held in the township as early as 1682. Concord Quarter was established in 1683, and in 1684 Chichester Monthly Meeting was established.

The first meeting house was built about 1686. It was followed by a second which burned in 1768. The third and present building was erected in 1769. Chichester Meeting was laid down about 1908. Appointed meetings are arranged through Concord Monthly Meeting (No. 218), successor to Chichester.

218

Concord Friends Meeting House (1728)

Concordville, Delaware County, Pennsylvania

The first meetings for worship were held in the township in 1685, at the house of Nicholas Newlin. Concord Quarter had been established in 1684. Concord Preparative Meeting was established in 1700. The first meeting house was built in 1695 on land leased by the trustees for "one peppercorn yearly forever." The eastern (right) end of the present building was built in 1728. In 1788 the meeting house was burned and rebuilt at once, on a larger scale in both length and height, using the old walls and extending them to the west (left). Concord continues as an active Meeting.

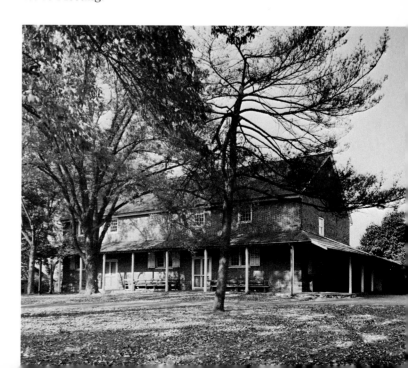

219

Old Haverford Friends Meeting House (1697)

Eagle Road, Oakmont, Delaware County, Pennsylvania

In 1684, the first Monthly Meeting of record in this section was held. It was called Haverford and later Radnor Monthly Meeting. It grew to comprise three particular meetings, covering all of the Welsh Tract southwest of the Schuylkill, which met in turn at Merion (No. 229), Haverford (this Meeting), and Radnor (No. 221). In 1684 meetings were held in the home of John Bevan, who said that they planned to emigrate to Pennsylvania because his wife thought "it might be a good place to train up children among sober people." When he returned to his native Wales, about 1704, he wrote, "The aim intended by my wife was in good measure answered." In 1688 Haverford Preparatory Meeting was estab-

lished, and a log meeting house was built. In 1697 a second meeting house was built, which became the southern part of the present building when the northern part was added in 1800. The 1930 addition is a room for the First-day School. Another addition was built in 1949 by the hands of members and neighbors. William Penn visited this Meeting, and in 1699 it was visited also by Thomas Story, a prominent Quaker minister and friend of Penn.

220

Newtown Square Friends Meeting House (1711)

Newtown Square, Delaware County, Pennsylvania

In 1692 permission was granted by Chester Quarterly Meeting for a Meeting for Worship to be held here in the home of William Lewis. In 1696 the Meeting was settled under Radnor

Monthly Meeting. In 1711 the meeting house was built, and in 1791 it was enlarged and remodeled. In 1939 Goshen Monthly Meeting was divided into Goshen, Willistown, and Newtown Square Monthly Meetings, and the Meeting here continues active under Concord Quarter. The 250th anniversary of this meeting house was commemorated by the Friends Historical Association in 1961.

221

Radnor Friends Meeting House (1718)

Ithan, Delaware County, Pennsylvania

The early settlers here were Welsh Quakers, who bought from the Proprietary in England a tract of 40,000 acres. The portion of the tract on the southwest side of the Schuylkill was settled as three townships: Merion, Haverford, and Radnor. Located now on the Philadelphia Main Line, at the corner of Sproul and Conestoga Roads, this Radnor Friends Meeting House was built in 1718. The first meeting at Radnor was held in 1684 at the home of William Shaver. Meetings were held also in the homes of Hugh Roberts, an intimate friend of William Penn, and John Bevan, until the first meeting house was built in 1693. The Radnor Monthly Meeting, which included and met alternately with Merion (No. 229) and Haverford (No. 219), was organized in 1684. The Preparative Meeting was organized in 1698, the year in which the Yearly Meeting made provision for such. The meeting house was used for two years by soldiers during the Revolution, and some were buried in the graveyard. Officers from Camp Field, an outpost of Valley Forge, used the meeting house for headquarters in 1778. For a time no meetings were held, but in 1937 Radnor United Monthly Meeting was organized, and regular meetings have been held since.

222

St. David's Church (1715)

Radnor, Delaware County, Pennsylvania

St. Peter's Church in the Great Valley (No. 223) and St. David's were served by one minister and functioned as one in the parish for about fifty years. The parish was founded as a mission, in this section of the Welsh Barony where Welsh was the common language, by Evan Evans, a Welshman who was sent to Philadelphia as a missionary of the Society for the Propagation of the Gospel. From 1700 to 1718 he served as rector of Christ Church, Philadelphia (No. 205) and wrote: "But Montgomery and Radnor next to my own beloved Philadelphia had the most considerable share in my Labours, where I preached in Welsh once a fortnight for four years, till the Arrival of Mr. Nicholas Minister of Chester in 1704." This statement confirms 1700 as the founding date of the parish. The first house of worship in the parish was a log cabin, built about 1700. Tradition relates that it was located in Berwyn, and that it burned in 1710 or 1711.

After the fire, the inhabitants of the lower or southeastern end of the parish built this small stone church and give it the name of St. David,

the patron saint of Wales. The cornerstone was laid May 9, 1715, but the building was not finished for many years. About fifteen families did the work, and then only in the winter when they were not farming. The dirt floor was used until 1765, when a floor finally was laid. "Pew ground" was sold to parishioners for building their own pews, and other pews were rented by the vestry to parishioners. In 1771 galleries were built on three sides; the subscriber heading the list was Anthony Wayne, father of the famous general whose name was given to the neighboring town. In 1790 and 1830 additional alterations were made. An interesting feature of the exterior is the covered stone stairway leading to the gallery.

William Currie, a Scot, had three churches in his Anglican mission — St. Peter's, St. David's, and St. James', Perkiomen (not in this collection). After the Declaration of Independence in 1776, when he was ordered by the vestry to omit the prayers for the king, Currie remained loyal and resigned; he continued to administer to the congregation until 1785, although during the Revolution church services were held infrequently, and the building here was used in turn by both armies. The lead of the window sashes holding the small diamond panes was melted for bullets by the Continental Army. After the Battle of the Brandywine, sixteen soldiers were buried west of the gallery steps. The grave of General Anthony Wayne is marked by a monument in the churchyard. While returning from commanding the forces opposing the Indians on the frontier of Ohio and Kentucky, he died at Erie in 1796 and was buried by the blockhouse there; in 1809 his remains were brought to his home church. In May, 1876, while in Philadelphia for the Centennial, Henry Wadsworth Longfellow visited the church and afterwards wrote the fine memorial poem, "Old St. David's at Radnor."

223

St. Peter's Church in the Great Valley (1744)

near Paoli, Chester County, Pennsylvania

In the Chester Valley, known as the Great Valley, on Church Road between Swedesford Road and Yellowsprings Road, St. Peter's Church is located in open country. The Anglican parish was organized by colonists in the Welsh Barony about 1700. In the lower parish St. David's Church (No. 222) was established at Radnor,

and for nearly fifty years the two shared the same minister. According to tradition a log chapel was built about 1700 near Berwyn, which served for about ten years and then burned. When St. David's was built, in 1715, a second log church was constructed in the upper parish by the people of Tredyffrin (Town in the Valley), East Whiteland, and Charlestown.

Built in 1744, the present stuccoed stone structure replaced the second log church near its site. The new church was dedicated in 1745. The original design was similar to that of St. David's. "Pewing" the congregation was accomplished in 1749, when the members took "pew ground" and built their own pews. In 1752 the "gallory" was finished. The long body of the church is the original building. At one end is a two-story ell built in 1856, and the wing, built in 1901, is the parish house. In 1944, on the 200th anniversary of the building, the restoration of the interior to its colonial design was dedicated.

By 1750, three languages were being spoken in the church — Welsh, English, and German. Welsh was the common language at first, and the first clergyman, Evan Evans, founded the parish while serving as rector of Christ Church, Phila-

delphia (No. 205). English was spoken by the Scottish parson from Glasgow, William Currie, who was minister of the parish from 1737 until 1776. In June of 1750 an entry was made in the *Journal* of Heinrich Melchior Muhlenberg, the German Lutheran who became known as the Patriarch of the Lutheran Church in America (see Old Trappe Church, No. 231), as follows: ". . . I made a trip of 17 miles to the neighborhood where a great many of our German people are indentured to English people as domestic servants. The English church was opened for me and as I had promised I preached an English sermon and afterwards a German sermon. The English people were very attentive and much moved, and they desired that I should come frequently. . . . There was weeping among the Germans, as is usually the case when they have been deprived of the Word of God for a long time. The English were amazed at our singing and almost went into raptures over it, for some of the people had fine musical voices and knew how to sing in harmony."

William Currie resigned in 1776, when he was not permitted to continue the prayers for the king, and in 1785 he ceased all ministrations to the three churches of his parish (St. James', Perkiomen being the third). In 1786, under an act of the General Asembly of Pennsylvania of 1783, St. Peter's was incorporated and granted a charter.

224

New Garden Friends Meeting House (1743)

New Garden Township, Chester County, Pennsylvania

New Garden Friends Meeting House is located near the Delaware border in open country about one and a half miles south of Toughkenamon and U. S. Route 1. In 1713 meetings were allowed by Chester Quarterly Meeting. They were held here at the residence of John Miller, under the care of Kennett Preparative Meeting. A log meeting house was in use in 1715, when a Preparative Meeting was established. Three years later the New Garden Monthly Meeting was set off from Kennett Monthly Meeting. It is under Western Quarterly Meeting, which was organized in 1758.

The present meeting house was built in 1743. That original building became the south end of the present meeting house when the north end was added in 1790. The original brick can be distinguished from that of the later addition, as it is laid in Flemish bond with glazed headers. The porte-cochere was a more recent addition. The large wooden carriage shed, provided with most Friends' meeting houses, still stands. Regular meetings are held, and there is a thriving First-day School.

225

Old Kennett Friends Meeting House (1710)

Hamorton, Chester County, Pennsylvania

In this neighborhood, four miles from Kennett Square, meetings were allowed in private houses in 1707. In 1710 the present meeting house was built. It was enlarged in 1719 and again in 1731. Kennett Monthly Meeting was started as Newark Monthly Meeting at New Castle, Delaware, about 1686. It was held later at Newark, Center, and New Garden. It was held here first in 1721. The name became Kennett Monthly Meeting in 1760. Located only three miles from Brandywine Creek, the first skirmish of the Battle of the Brandywine took place here on September 11, 1777, between American sharpshooters, sheltered behind the meeting-house walls and gravestones, and the advancing Hessians. While war raged outside, Quaker calm prevailed at the meeting in progress inside.

Kennett is under Western Quarterly Meeting. In 1959 a new meeting house was built, in the colonial style of Quaker architecture. On Fifth month 21st, 1960, the 250th anniversary of the old meeting house was celebrated by the spring meeting of the Friends Historical Association held here at both meeting houses and at Longwood Gardens, the beautiful estate here built by Pierre Samuel du Pont. This section was known as the Long Woods until the time of the Civil War; here was located a station of the "Underground Railroad," where Kennett Friends assisted slaves in their flight from the South. Meetings are held in the old meeting house during the summer.

226

Birmingham Friends Meeting House (1763)

Birmingham Township, Chester County, Pennsylvania

On a hill in rolling country, the Birmingham Meeting House looks out over the beautiful Brandywine Valley. A few miles away was Chads (now Chadds) Ford, where Washington's army planned to prevent the British Army, advancing on Philadelphia, from crossing the Brandywine Creek. A mile and a half nearer and upstream from it is Brinton's Ford, and another mile upstream is Jones' Ford, both of which figured in the Battle of the Brandywine. The American Army was in ignorance, however, of a crossing above the Forks, but the British were better informed and they used it.

In this pioneering territory where the Lenni-Lenape Indians (or Delawares) lived, the Quakers, who maintained good relations with the Indians under the policy of William Penn, held their first meeting in 1690. The meetings were held at the home of William Brinton, one of the first settlers in what is now Birmingham Township. In 1704 the Meeting was allowed. In 1727 Birmingham Preparative Meeting, and in 1815 Birmingham Monthly Meeting, were established. They are now in Concord Quarter (see Concord Friends Meeting House, No. 212). The first meeting house was built probably in 1721, on the Great Birmingham Road; it was constructed of cedar logs. In 1763 the stone meeting house was built which forms the west end of the present building; the east end was added in 1818. Regular meetings are held.

In anticipation of the battle, in September, 1777, the American commissaries took over the meeting house for use as a hospital. On First-day 7th, Quakers coming to meeting found the house occupied by American soldiers. They took benches outside and tried to hold their meeting, but it was found impossible to hold Quaker meeting amidst comments from the soldiers. Four days later the Battle of the Brandywine was fought. Generals Howe, Cornwallis, and Knyphausen moving toward Philadelphia were opposed by the American Army on the east side of the Brandywine. Howe unexpectedly flanked the American forces by crossing the Brandywine at the Forks above Buffington's Ford, and, passing unseen within a mile and a half of the American force, engaged them around the Birmingham Meeting House. As Henry Seidel Canby points out, in an account of the battle in his book *The Brandywine,* the Americans were surprised and defeated because of misinformation on the fords and lack of information on the flanking movement. The countryside was populated with Quakers, and he concludes that it was due to their strict policy of not aiding any army in any way that Washington's men were not informed, and the maneuver was incredibly successful.

Several companies of American light infantry fired on the British from the cover of the graveyard wall. After the battle, Howe took the meeting house for a hospital. Many soldiers from both sides were buried in the graveyard. In 1825 General Lafayette brought his son here and had a large and warm reception at the old meeting house. The graveyard is named Lafayette Cemetery, and in it is a fifty-foot stone monument to Lafayette and Pulaski.

227

Marshallton Friends Meeting House (1764)

Marshallton, Chester County, Pennsylvania

Marshallton is three and a half miles west of West Chester. The first meeting house was built in 1735. It was replaced in 1764 by the present stone meeting house. The Meeting was laid down about 1910, but in 1933 it was reopened under a concern of a member of the Yearly Meeting Extension Committee. It is now active as a part of Bradford Monthly Meeting, Caln Quarter.

The meeting house stands across the road from the stone house of Humphrey Marshall (1722-1801), for whom the town was named. He was a distinguished Quaker and botanist, and a cousin of John Bartram, botanist to the king (whose work contributed much to our knowledge of American plants and trees, and whose house and gardens in Philadelphia are visited by the public). He was the son of Abraham Marshall, who was an interested member of Bradford Meeting when it was organized.

228

East Caln Friends Meeting House (1726)

Chester County, Pennsylvania

On a high wooded hill, East Caln Friends Meeting House is located on the King's Highway about two and a half miles west of Downingtown. In 1716 the Preparative Meeting was established under Concord Monthly Meeting and Chester Quarterly Meeting. In 1726 the present stone meeting house was built, replacing an earlier one of wood probably located down the hill. In 1800 Caln Quarterly Meeting was established, and in the following year this meeting house was enlarged. In 1913 other alterations were made. After the Separation of 1827, the meeting house was used by both branches of Friends, which accounts for there being two burial grounds. By 1910 meetings had been discontinued. In 1955 the two branches of Friends reunited, and now regular First-day Meeting for Worship is held during the summer, and Caln Quarterly Meeting is held here each Eighth month.

There was also a West Caln Friends Meeting House just west of Wagontown, a small stone building that was standing in 1756, which we included originally in this collection. In recent years, however, the building had not been in use;

it was allowed to fall into ruins, and there is no plan to restore it. Accordingly, the word "East" has been dropped from the name of the present Meeting.

229

Merion Friends Meeting House (1695)

Lower Merion Township, Montgomery County, Pennsylvania

On Philadelphia's Main Line, at Montgomery Avenue and Meeting House Lane, stands Merion Friends Meeting House, the oldest in Pennsylvania and one of the three oldest in America. Families from Wales acquired from William Penn, the proprietor of Pennsylvania, a large area of land on the southwest side of the Schuylkill that became known as the Welsh Tract, and settled it as the three townships of Merion, Haverford, and Radnor. As Penn was a Quaker, it is logical that the early settlers of Merion were also Quakers. The original group arrived on the ship *Lyon* in August of 1682. The heads of the families in that group were Edward ap Rees, William ab Edward, and Robert ap David (the "ap," or "ab" as it is misspelled in one case on the old records, being the Welsh for "son of"). They gave their new township the name Meirion (now Merion) for their home county in northern Wales,

Meirionydd (Merionethshire), which in turn had received its name from that of a prince who had ruled the region a millenium before.

Merion Preparative Meeting was established soon after their arrival in 1682. In April of 1684, the first Monthly Meeeting was held. For some years it was held "in course" at Schuylkill (a Meeting which existed at what is now Market and 32d Streets), Merion, Haverford (No. 219), and Radnor (No. 221). That early Schuylkill Meeting does not exist now; the others are in Radnor Monthly Meeting, Philadelphia Quarter.

The oldest grave in the burial ground here is that of Catherine Reese, who died Eighth month 23d, 1682, the month of their arrival. Upon arrival these Friends worshiped in the open and beneath a tent, until a log house was built about two hundred feet east of the present site. In 1695 the present stone meeting house was begun. It is now a cruciform building, and it is believed to be the only such Friends meeting house in the world. It was not the plan of the Quakers to make it so, but it grew into this form through the addition of the north or front section during the period between 1711 and 1713. In his booklet *Merion Meeting House*, Samuel J. Bunting, Jr. has analyzed the old records concerning the dates of the original building and the alterations. In 1829 the building was repaired, and the stone walls unfortunately were covered with stucco. A stone then was set in a wall with the inscription "BUILT 1695 REPAIRED 1829."

William Penn attended meetings here. Dr. Thomas Wynne, Penn's physician on the ship *Welcome*, which brought him to America, was one of the early members of this Meeting. At the home of Hugh Roberts was held the first meeting of Friends of Merion of which there is any record, and his good friend William Penn often stopped there. Roberts presented the Meeting with a sundial, which was set beside Montgomery Pike for the benefit of travelers as well as the congregation, but it was made of lead and was melted for bullets during the Revolution. Both armies, whichever was in command of the region at the time, confiscated goods and money for war purposes, contrary to the policy and wishes of the Friends. The Meeting today is active, with regular meetings, a First-day school, and a Boy Scout troop. The Preparative Meeting is held on one First-day of each month, when it convenes at the rise of the Meeting for Worship. At the 250th anniversary of the building celebrated here in 1945, the historical address was given by the late Justice Owen J. Roberts, who had recently retired from the Supreme Court of the United States.

230

Norriton Presbyterian Meeting House (1698)

Montgomery County, Pennsylvania

On the old Germantown and Perkiomen Turnpike, at the twentieth milepost, where the present Trooper Road crosses, stands the Norriton Presbyterian Meeting House. The building and the graveyards are the earliest evidence of Presbyterian activity in Pennsylvania. The first settlers were Hollanders who came here between 1660 and 1670. According to tradition (unfortunately the early church records are lost), soon after their arrival they built a log house of worship, which was of the Dutch Reformed Church. The deed to the graveyard is dated 1678, and there had been burials here for twenty years when the present church was built in 1698. At that time there were many Scotch-Irish settlers in the congregation, and their religion, like that of the Hollanders, was Calvinistic or Presbyterian. At a later time a number of German families were in the congregation, and names of all these people were recorded in the graveyard.

In 1704 William Penn sold to his son William all the lands comprising the Township of Norriton, and in that year Isaac Norris and William Trent bought the tract. In 1712 Norris acquired Trent's interest and developed the Norriton Plantation and Mill Tract which became Norristown, five miles from the church. Matthias Rittenhouse, a Mennonite (see No. 213) and father of David, famous watchmaker, mathematician, and astronomer, bought the land with the meeting house on it. In 1737 he gave the church a clear title to the plot on which the meeting house stands. Benjamin Franklin visited him and David at their house on the adjoining grounds. Of that house only the foundation and cornerstone, dated 1749, remain in the present house, but the boxwood on the grounds was brought from France by Franklin and presented to David. In 1730 the Presbyterians organized the Norriton and Providence Church, later called the Lower Providence Church, and by legal succession it became the owner of the church property here.

Three alterations in the building have been made — in 1735, about 1775, and in 1884. In the work of 1774-75 the old hip roof was removed and the style was changed to the present plain-gable roof. In 1844 the old pulpit with curved stairway and sounding board was removed, and the straight board benches with high backs were replaced. The two small windows on the north or rear side, which lighted the original high pulpit, are still there. In the course of repairing the foundations of the building at that time, gravestones were used, and some of the oldest markers were destroyed. During the Revolution, Washington's army passed here on the way to Valley Forge, and the church was used for shelter against the cold. The building was used also as a hospital. After the war the Pennsylvania Legislature voted to permit a lottery for raising funds to repair damage to the building suffered during the war.

231

Old Trappe Church (1743)
New Providence Church
Augustus Lutheran Church

Trappe, Montgomery County, Pennsylvania

Old Trappe Church, on the old Philadelphia-Reading Turnpike at Trappe, is the oldest Lutheran Church building in America. It is a historic shrine to its builder and the founder of the Lutheran Church in America, Heinrich (Henry) Melchior Muhlenberg (1711-1787). He came here in 1742 as a missionary of the Orphan House and Missionary Training School of Halle, Germany. That institution, *Franck'sche Stiftungen*, bears the name of its founder, August Hermann Francke (1663-1727), whose son persuaded Muhlenberg to accept the call here. Halle was a center of Pietism, a theological movement originated in the Lutheran Church of Germany by Philip Jacob Spener; Francke and Spener were founders of the University of Halle. These Pietists sought to reform intellectual Lutheranism and to revitalize Christian living through a change in heart and a return to Luther's principles. It was a movement that grew until it became known as the second Reformation. It influenced the founding of the Moravian Church by Count von Zinzendorf, godson of Spener and a student at the Orphan House (see Moravian Chapel, Bethlehem, No. 244), and of the Methodist Church through John Wesley (see St. George's Church, Philadelphia, No. 208), and it prepared the way for the Great Awakening, the revival inspired in America by George Whitefield, who was the greatest single influence in the religious life of the colonies. Muhlenberg was one of four Pietists who were pioneers in the religious life of America; beside Zinzendorf, there were Guilliem Bertholf at the First Reformed Dutch Church, Hackensack, New Jersey (No. 131), and Michael Schlatter at the First Reformed Church, Easton, Pennsylvania (No. 245). As a Pietist, Muhlenberg had little sympathy with orthodox Lutherans of the old school, but he was friendly with the Reformed congregations, the Tennents of the New Side Presbyterian churches (see Neshaminy Church, No. 238), and George Whitefield. As he traveled, visited, preached, and taught among the Lutherans and other congregations from northern New York to Maryland, Muhlenberg became known as the Patriarch of the Lutheran Church in America.

The congregation here in the wilderness of the Perkiomen Valley had been active since 1730. It was poor in material things but rich in spirit and determination. Muhlenberg preached his third sermon in America in a barn at Trappe, and the congregation continued to use the barn until they could build the present stone church. Work on the building began in 1743, the year after his arrival. Evidently Muhlenberg designed the building; in one of his reports to Halle, he attached a copy of the plan for a stone church that they were using to raise funds for building. The specifications were for a building "54 *Schuh lang bei* 39 *Schuh breit*," and there was to be provided an ample supply of "*Rom und Brandwein*" for the builders. Half of the estimated cost of £200 was raised at once, and the German minister at the Court of St. James in London raised additional funds for the cause. The church was built as the New Providence Church, but the name of the

confession of faith, rather than that of the church, was inscribed on the tablet in the wall. In translation the Latin inscription reads: "Under the guidance of Christ, Heinrich Melchior Muhlenberg together with the elders, I. N. Grosman, F. Marsteler, A. Heilman, I. Mueller, H. Hass, and G. Kebner, erected from the very ground this building dedicated to the denomination adhering to the Augsburg Confession, A.D. 1743." Muhlenberg later named it the Augustus Lutheran Church, in honor of August Hermann Francke. After two years the building was completed, and it was dedicated in September of 1745. Services were held here regularly for more than a century. In 1852 the congregation built a larger church near by, and Old Trappe Church was saved as a historic shrine and for occasional weddings and services.

There are many interesting features of the building. Very few changes have been made — the stone floor has been covered with board flooring, the stone walls have been stuccoed, and the original window sash has been replaced, but essentially the building is in its colonial condition. The bonnet roof is unusual, and particularly in its treatment to accommodate the octagonal apse and sanctuary. The interior woodwork is in Jacobean style. There are galleries on three sides; the northeast loft was built in 1751 for the new organ imported from Europe, one of the earliest in a Pennsylvania country church. Singing in harmony was a feature of the Lutheran service, as was noted when Muhlenberg preached at St. Peter's in the Great Valley (No. 223). The high-backed box pews were in natural wood. Those beneath the organ loft were for the elders; those beneath the western gallery, with doors and locks, were for the more prosperous members, and others had open ends, a few of which remained unchanged when doors were added at a later date. As was customary in most colonial houses of worship, the sexes were separated; here the women sat on the northeast side and the men opposite. Servants and boys used plain benches in the gallery under the supervision of the sexton. The high pulpit is of paneled walnut. The white painted altar stands before the pulpit on a hexagonal pedestal.

In January of 1733, the month in which it was voted to build this church, a school was opened, with Muhlenberg as teacher. Here the Lutherans began bringing education to the people, as the other denominations did throughout the colonies; Muhlenberg College, an Evangelical

Lutheran institution at Allentown, was named for him. Beside the church are the graves of Heinrich Melchior Muhlenberg and his wife. In 1745, two years after the church was built, he had married Anna Maria Weiser, daughter of John Conrad Weiser, Jr., the famous Indian interpreter, whose home at Womelsdorf near Reading (which town he founded) is now Conrad Weiser Park. Johann Conrad Weiser, Sr., founded Middleburg, Schoharie County, New York (see No. 196). Of their eleven children, four sons became clergymen. Also buried here is one of the four, Peter Gabriel Muhlenberg, who was educated in his father's school and was confirmed here. He was pastor of a church in Woodstock, Virginia, when, in 1775, he preached his famous sermon on the text from Eccles. 3:1-8, "To every thing there is a season, and a time to every purpose under the heaven . . . a time of war, and a time of peace." Removing his clerical robe, he stood in the uniform of a

Continental soldier, and gathering new recruits he went into active service in the Revolution. He became a major general and won such respect from the German Hessian troops of the British Army that they called him "Teufel (Devil) Pete." Washington's army passed Augustus Church on the march from Brandywine to Germantown; on September 23, 1777, General Armstrong's regiment camped in the churchyard, and he used the schoolhouse and church as his headquarters. After the Battle of Germantown, October 4, 1777, the church was used as a hospital, and General Washington visited his men here on October 5.

Another son, Frederick Augustus Muhlenberg, a Lutheran minister, was the first Speaker of the House of Representatives. He was the first functioning head of the United States Government, when he presided over the House in New York for the month preceding the inauguration of George Washington as the first President.

232

Falckner's Swamp Lutheran Church (1767)
New Hanover Lutheran Church

Hanover Township, Montgomery County, Pennsylvania

Daniel Falckner, an early settler, was a Lutheran minister as well as a land agent. A tract of some 22,000 acres, which he sold, was known as Falckner's Swamp, and the name was given to the church which he organized in or before 1700.

This is the earliest German Lutheran congregation in America. Two log structures were followed by the present gray-and-brown stone church, which was built in 1767. It was remodeled in 1867, and the two dates are engraved on a white stone in the wall above the main entrance. Just beneath the white stone is one of the original stones in the wall inscribed, "ADAM WARDMAN . JACOB EBLI MATIAS . REICHERT . ALSBUERN — 1767." Engraved in a top stone of the side wall under the eaves is a name probably of the master mason: "M. M. Michael *Stoffet* AO 1767."

233

Plymouth Meeting Friends Meeting House (c. 1710)

Plymouth Meeting, Montgomery County, Pennsylvania

The earliest meetings for worship were held in 1680. This meeting house was built in 1710, or about that time — there is no record of the exact date. It was constructed in two sections at different times and of different materials; the older section is of limestone, and the newer of brown sandstone. The older end of the building is near the old part of the burial ground. One end was built for school facilities. In 1867 the building burned, but it was rebuilt the same year incorporating the old walls. Later changes have not altered its appearance appreciably.

234   *(See photo on following page)*

Abington Friends Meeting House (1699)

Jenkintown, Montgomery County, Pennsylvania

Richard Wall arrived in Philadelphia in 1682, with a certificate from Friends in Stoke Orchard, Gloucestershire, England, and he was accepted in Philadelphia Monthly Meeting. In the following year, 1683, a Monthly Meeting was organized at the home of Sarah Seary, near Frankford (see Nos. 209 and 215), which recorded the same year that a Meeting was settled near Cheltenham at the home of Richard Wall. The Meeting was called variously Oxford, Dublin, and Cheltenham, before it was removed to Abington Township. The Monthly Meeting was held in rotation at Oxford (see Trinity Church, No. 209), Byberry, and at Richard Wall's. The Wall House, a mile away on

Church Road, is maintained by Cheltenham Township as a memorial to the early settlers of this region.

In 1697 a bequest of John Barnes gave to the Meeting 120 acres of land in Abington Township. A stone meeting house was built on the land in 1699, and the Meeting was moved here from the homes of Friends. Germantown Preparative Meeting became a part of Abington Monthly Meeting, and Abington Road, now Washington Lane, connected the two meeting houses. In 1786 Abington Quarterly Meeting was established by division of Philadelphia Quarterly Meeting. Establishment of Abington Quarter required an enlargement of the meeting house; reconstruction

was started in 1786 and was completed in 1787. In the walls of the northeast (right) part of the present building were incorporated the walls of the original building. The old walls were raised to enclose the present galleries and were extended. In 1797 the western end was rebuilt. The original walls are in the northern two-thirds of the eastern half of the present building. In 1863 the old hoods over the doorways were replaced with the present long porch and shed, to accommodate the large congregation in bad weather. The addition on the western end was completed in 1929.

In 1815 Germantown and Frankford Preparative Meetings, which had been parts of Abington Monthly Meeting, together formed the new Frankford Monthly Meeting. In 1688, during its association with Abington, Germantown Meeting had issued the first public protest against slavery. After the Separation of 1827, the Orthodox Friends left this meeting house to the Liberals, who were in the majority. In 1836 they built a meeting house of their own near by, and it is still in use. The formation of the General Meeting of Friends of Philadelphia in 1946, in which Abington Quarter had a part, contributed to the final reconciliation and reunion, in 1955, as the Philadelphia Yearly Meeting of the Religious Society of Friends.

Bristol Friends Meeting House (1709)

Wood and Market Streets, Bristol, Bucks County, Pennsylvania

Meetings of Friends were held in Bristol as early as 1709. Starting in 1714 meetings for worship were held each First-day. The founders were Samuel and Edward Carpenter, owners of the Bristol Mills estate, who gave land for the meeting house, burying ground, and pasture. In 1709 the present meeting house was built. The old stone walls are now covered with stucco. Samuel Carpenter is buried here, in the burying ground on Wood Street. The building is in its original design, and there have been no alterations. The inside walls are whitewashed, and the plain benches are unpainted. The house was used as a hospital during the Revolution. Regular meetings are held. Bristol Monthly Meeting is in Bucks Quarter with Makefield (No. 242), Wrightstown (No. 237), Buckingham (No. 241), and Fallsington (No. 236), among others which are not colonial buildings.

236

Fallsington Friends Meeting House (1789)

Fallsington, Bucks County, Pennsylvania

Meetings for worship were held here as early as 1680 in private homes. Members attended Monthly Meeting across the Delaware River at Burlington (No. 160), until Falls Monthly Meeting was established here in 1683. The first meeting house was built in 1690. The present stone meeting house was built in 1789. William Penn gave the land to the original Meeting. He worshipped here in 1700-1701, while in residence at Pennsbury Manor, his favorite home which he planned and built on the Delaware a few miles away. (From 1938-40 the plantation, with the manor house and its various buildings, was reconstructed in a thorough restoration, and it is open to the public.)

For some years before 1955, when the two branches of the Society of Friends reunited after the long Separation, this Meeting anticipated the reconciliation by functioning as a United Monthly Meeting, formed by the joining of Arch Street Meeting, Race Street Meeting, and the Primitive Meeting of Friends (sole survivor of a group organized in 1861). Falls Monthly Meeting is in Bucks Quarter with four others that have colonial meeting houses (see Bristol, No. 235; Wrightstown, No. 237; Buckingham, No. 241; Makefield, No. 242).

237

Wrightstown Friends Meeting House (1787)

Wrightstown, Bucks County, Pennsylvania

The first meetings were held here in 1686, under Neshaminy Monthly Meeting, at the house of the first settler, John Chapman. As an Indulged Meeting under Middletown (Langhorne), it continued until 1724, when it was made a Preparative Meeting under Buckingham Monthly Meeting (No. 241). The first meeting of Wrightstown Monthly Meeting was in 1734. It is in Bucks Quarter. Built in 1787, this stone meeting house replaced the first one which was built of logs in 1721. The old stones are now covered with stucco.

A monument near the meeting house marks the starting point of the famous "Walking Purchase," in which territory from this point north was stepped off to be conveyed by the Indians.

William Penn had made the walk in person with the Indians in 1683, a leisurely walk of a day and a half. When Indians protested the infiltration of settlers north of that limit, a second "Walk" was arranged in September of 1737. It was a fraud perpetrated as a land grab. Again the time was a day and a half, and the Indians expected it to cover about forty miles, but three hardy men were entered in a race for a prize of cash and land. They ran until exhausted — one dropped on the trail and died after a few days, another collapsed and survived only a few years, and the third covered sixty miles and lived until he was ninety. The line was drawn from that point to the Delaware River in a northeasterly direction, instead of due east as agreed. The Delaware Indians protested strongly for a long time, but the dominant Six Nations (Iroquois) persuaded them to submit in the treaty of 1742. The episode illustrates the contrast between the relationships with the Indians maintained by William Penn, Friend, and some of his successors.

238

Neshaminy Presbyterian Church (1743)
Warwick Presbyterian Church
Log College Church

**near Harstville, Warwick Township, Bucks
County, Pennsylvania**

Neshaminy Presbyterian Church is located
on Bristol Road and the bank of the Western
Branch, or Little Neshaminy Creek. This region,
known as the Forks of the Neshaminy, was settled
about 1700, when the land was obtained from
William Penn. Many of the original congregation
were Scotch-Irish. William Tennent, a cousin of
James Logan, secretary of the province under
William Penn, was the first minister of record.
He came to America from Northern Ireland in
1716, when he was a priest of the Church of
England. He joined the Presbyterian Synod of
Philadelphia in 1718, and after serving as pastor
at Bedford, New York, and Bensalem and Smithfield in Bucks County, was called to Neshaminy
in 1726. In that year he organized the present
church.

The first building was erected immediately
in 1726-27, on a plot now occupied by the burying ground. It was forty by thirty feet, with a
front of dressed stone, and rooftile brought from
England, pieces of which have been excavated.
In 1741 the congregation became divided between the Old Light and the New Light theolo-
gies. The New Lights were inspired by the
preaching of the great evangelist George Whitefield, who was a founder of Methodism in America (see St. George's Church, Philadelphia, No.
208), and who preached here and at many Presbyterian churches (see Old South Church, Newburyport, Mass., No. 112). Tennent and other
followers of Whitefield withdrew from the church
and two years later, in 1743, built the present
stone church. The two factions were reunited in
1758, and the old church was pulled down. When
the present building was enlarged to its present
size in 1775, the original walls were incorporated.
In 1842 it was remodeled in its present style, and
details introduced at that time, such as the stained
glass and lancet windows, are not colonial.

In October of 1727, as soon as his first
church building was completed, William Tennent
founded a school to train his four sons for the
ministry. Nine students were added, making an
original enrollment of thirteen; they boarded at
farms or lived in the Tennent household. A log
house of about twenty by twenty feet was built,

374

and it became famous as the Log College, the first institution of higher learning affiliated with the Presbyterian Church. All four sons became Presbyterian preachers, and they all preached in colonial churches that still stand — Gilbert, the eldest son, at Old Presbyterian Church, New Castle, Delaware (No. 17); John, the third son, at the Tennent Church, Freehold, New Jersey (No. 146); William, Jr., the second son, at Freehold, where he succeeded John; and Charles, the fourth son, at Blackwater Presbyterian Church in Delaware (No. 26). The Log College was closed in 1747, when its successor was opened, the College of New Jersey at Elizabeth Town, New Jersey, which became Princeton University (see Nos. 133, 132). All of the thirteen original students became pioneers of Presbyterianism in America, and a number of them founded educational institutions. Fifty-one colleges that stemmed from the Log College are listed on a monument at the site of the building in the neighborhood of the church (see Chapter VI, Section 5, Presbyterians).

239

Newtown Presbyterian Church (1769)
Newtown, Bucks County, Pennsylvania

In 1734 the Presbytery of Philadelphia granted to the people of Newtown that William Tennent, Pastor of Neshaminy Presbyterian Church (No. 238), might preach to them on one Lord's Day each month. The original records of the organization of the church have been lost. The deed to the original church site is dated 1744, and it is not clear whether there was a church building during the previous decade. The first church was built of logs half a mile west of Newtown, on Swamp Road. It was used until the present church was built in 1769, and then was sold and moved to a farm near the chain bridge over Neshaminy Creek, where it was used as a wagon house.

The present stone church, built in 1769, had a high pulpit on the north and entrances on the south, a brick floor, fifty-nine high box pews, a gallery on the south side, and dressed stone in the south and east walls and rough stone in the others. A lottery helped raise funds to finish the building. Following the Battle of Trenton, December 26, 1776, General Washington housed his Hessian prisoners here, while he occupied a brownstone house near by and wrote letters to Congress concerning the battle. In 1842 alterations moved the pulpit to an alcove in the west end and installed galleries on the east and north sides, and two entrances on the east facing the highway. The box pews have been replaced. The congregation uses a church built in town in 1934. At least one service is held in the old church each year.

It had a hip roof, an outside stone stairway leading to the gallery, and two tiers of tall rectangular windows. For a few years, starting in 1785, the congregation shared a third of the time of the pastor of the Deep Run Church. By 1843 the congregation had diminished to such an extent that it could not support a minister, and a half interest in the property was deeded to the Reformed and the Lutheran congregations. The building was then drastically remodeled by its new owners. The roof was changed to a plain gable, the outside stairway was removed, and the interior was changed. The families of the congregation gradually migrated westward, first to middle and western Pennsylvania and later to Ohio, and the old church has been idle for many years.

241

Buckingham Friends Meeting House (1768)

Buckingham Township, Bucks County, Pennsylvania

Most of the early settlers in this region were Friends. Located at the present Lahaska, the Buckingham Meeting and the township, as well as the county, were named for Buckinghamshire in England, the abbreviation for which is Bucks. A Meeting for Worship was allowed by Bucks Quarterly Meeting in 1701. Meetings were held in private houses until the first meeting house was built of logs in 1706. In 1720, when the Monthly Meeting was established, the log building was enlarged. In 1731 a second meeting house was built of stone near by. It was completely destroyed by fire during a meeting in 1768, and it was rebuilt the same year. The building stands on top of a hill on Old York Road, which connected it in the early days with Abington Meeting (No. 234). It is one of the finest Georgian-Colonial Quaker meeting houses, both as to size and detail inside and out. The gabled hoods over the doorways, the arched windows of the lower tier, and the cove cornice are distinguishing features of this style. The interior has the original wooden benches, including facing benches for the elders, a gallery, and wooden "shutters" for dividing the meeting house for business meetings of the men and the women. The natural woodwork has never been painted, and it has taken on a beautiful sheen during the years of loving care.

240

Tinicum Presbyterian Church (1768) Red Hill Church

Ottsville, Bucks County, Pennsylvania

Ottsville, formerly in Nockamixon Township, now is in Tinicum Township. Tinicum congregation was organized about the year 1738, under the instrumentality of James Campbell, a licentiate of Scotland, who was ordained for the congregation and continued for about twelve or thirteen years. The congregation was composed of about fifty-five families, chiefly from Northern Ireland, and it maintained close relations with the Newtown Presbyterian Church (No. 239). The first church, called the "Old House," was located at the Stewart Burying Ground on the Robert Stewart plantation, now known as Bunker Hill Cemetery, in Tinicum Township, two and one half miles northeast of Ottsville; the building long since has disappeared. In 1749 the majority of the congregation removed to Red Hill. As a result of the dissension over the move, which he strongly disapproved, Mr. Campbell resigned and went to the Carolinas in 1750. The land was deeded in 1762, long after the church was built.

The present stone church was built in 1768. This second building was tall and nearly square.

242

Makefield Friends Meeting House (1752)

Dolington, Bucks County, Pennsylvania

Makefield Meeting was established in 1750, when meetings were held twice monthly in the homes of Benjamin Taylor and Benjamin Gilbert. By 1752 this meeting house was "so far finished as to be fit to meet in." It is of stone, now stuccoed. The house was enlarged in 1764 and repaired extensively in 1861. This was an Indulged Meeting of Falls Monthly Meeting until 1790, when a Preparative Meeting was allowed. In 1820 Makefield Monthly Meeting was established. It is in Bucks Quarter. Regular meetings are held.

243

Plumstead Friends Meeting House (1752)

Danboro, Bucks County, Pennsylvania

The earliest meeting of Friends in this section near Gardenville was held about 1727. A Meeting was settled in 1730. This stone meeting house was built in 1752. A century and a quarter later, instead of being enlarged, as was usually the case, the building was reduced in size, and signs of the old longer foundation can still be seen. The stone walls are now covered with stucco. The meeting house was used as a hospital in the Revolution, and some of the soldiers were buried near by. In the burying ground is the grave also of Joseph Smith, inventor of the iron

plow. This is an Indulged Meeting under Buckingham Monthly Meeting, Bucks Quarter, with a large annual meeting held each summer on a First-day afternoon in Eighth month.

244

Old Chapel (1751)
Moravian Community

Bethlehem, Northampton County, Pennsylvania

The Moravian Church originated in the time of John Huss of Bohemia, the "Reformer before the Reformation," who was an advocate of the reforms of John Wycliffe and died at the stake in 1457, three centuries before the chapel was built here. The Brethren of the *Unitas Fratrum* (Church of the Brethren) were persecuted and driven from Bohemia and Moravia. Some of them settled in Germany on the estate of Count Nikolaus Ludwig von Zinzendorf, a Pietist (see Trappe Church, No. 231), who joined the Brethren and sponsored their settlements in America, coming in person to take part in the founding of the Moravian community named Bethlehem. Moravians came from Georgia to Pennsylvania. In Savannah they had been associated with John Wesley and George Whitefield, founders of Methodism (see St. George's Church, Philadelphia, No. 208). In 1740, rather than becoming involved in war when Georgia took up arms against Florida, they abandoned their settlement and five years of work, and led by Peter Bohler they came to Philadelphia. Whitefield, who maintained an orphanage at Savannah, had acquired 5,000 acres at the forks of the Delaware, where he planned to establish a revival headquarters. He employed the Moravians to clear land and build a school for Negroes and other buildings, in the section that is now Upper Nazareth Township, about six miles northeast of Bethlehem. Before they had completed the stone building for the school, the Moravians and Whitefield disagreed, and he abandoned his plans. In 1755 the Brethren finished the house, which they called Ephrata and today is known as the Whitefield House.

In 1741, as soon as their work at Nazareth had stopped, Bishop David Nitschmann acquired for the Brethren 500 acres at the confluence of the Lehigh River and Monocacy Creek, and here the Moravian community of Bethlehem was

founded. It became the headquarters of their missionary work among the Indians and of Moravian affairs in America. In December of that year Count von Zinzendorf arrived here and was present at the Christmas Eve ceremony at which the community was given its name. Their new log house was shared by cattle, and one of the Brethren recorded the ceremony as follows:

"Because of the day, and in memory of the Birth of our dear Savior, we went into the stable in the tenth hour and sang with feeling, so that our hearts melted:

Nicht Jerusalem (Not Jerusalem,
Sondern Bethlehem But Bethlehem —
Aus dir Kommet From thee comes
Was mir Frommet." That which benefits me.)

Thus with a carol the new community was christened Bethlehem, and ever since that night, sacred music of a high order has been an important part of the Moravian culture. In the following year they held a *Singstunde*. In 1744 they organized a *Collegium Musicum* and conducted it until 1820, when it was reorganized as the Philharmonic Society, an instrumental and oratorio group. When the number of choral members had diminished, in 1882 Dr. J. Frederick Wolle, organist and choir leader of this church, organized the Bethlehem Choral Union, and from it grew, still under his leadership, the Bethlehem Bach Festival. For two days in May the music of Johann Sebastian Bach, including always the *B Minor Mass*, is played and sung. In 1905 the Bach Festival was held in the church here, and since 1912 it has been held across the river a few blocks away, in the Memorial Chapel of Lehigh University. The Moravians here published a number of Bach's works before they were published in Europe. In the Old Moravian Burying Ground on the hill above the Old Chapel, where burials were begun in 1742, all men are equal in the eyes of God, and the gravestones all lie flat on the ground. Here on the hill, in 1754, the Easter sunrise service was accompanied by a trombone choir, and ever since the tradition has been continued, here and at other Moravian churches.

The *Gemein Haus* (Common House) was built of logs in 1741, the year in which the community was settled, to house married families. With clapboard covered walls, it stands on the west side of a horseshoe of buildings in the Moravian group, the oldest building in Bethlehem

(at the right in the photograph). The present Old Chapel, a rectangular stone building extending northward from the end of the *Gemein Haus*, was built in 1751. Lying across it in the photograph can be seen the shadow of the Central Moravian Church which stands across the street; it was built by the Brethren in their spare time between 1803 and 1806, and at that time it was large enough to hold the entire population of Bethlehem.

Here the relationship with the Indians was so peaceful that, during the French and Indian War, Bethlehem was a refuge for white settlers, and the Indians supplied them with venison. In the Moravian center stands a building which was moved here from the Indian village of Nain, near Bethlehem, a mission where the Brethren had converted the Indians to Christianity. Education also was a mission of the Moravians, and here is the Moravian College and Theological Seminary, which originated in 1807 at Nazareth, in Nazareth Hall, a house that had been built for Count von Zinzendorf before he returned finally to Europe; the College was moved to Bethlehem in 1858. In 1752, the year after the Old Chapel was built, a company of Brethren under the leadership of Bishop August Gottlieb Spangenberg set out from Bethlehem for North Carolina, where they founded the Moravian community of Bethabara (No. 201).

245

First Reformed Church (1775)
First United Church of Christ
(Evangelical and Reformed)

Easton, Northampton County, Pennsylvania

In the town of Easton, where the Lehigh River flows into the Delaware, there stands the only colonial building of a German Reformed Church in Pennsylvania. The congregation was founded in 1745, and for the following decade they worshiped in a log structure on Mammy Morgan's Hill, south of the town overlooking the Forks of the Delaware. In 1746, Michael Schlatter (1716-1790), a Swiss, was sent to America by the Dutch Reformed Synod of Holland to visit colonists of the Reformed faith. He was a Pietist, of the faith that had begun in Germany and spread into Holland, developing into the "second Ref-

ormation" (see also Bertholf, No. 131; Muhlenberg, No. 231; von Zinzendorf, No. 244). In the course of traveling 8,000 miles on horseback through Pennsylvania, Maryland, and Virginia, he visited forty-seven congregations. He was in Easton in June of 1747, where he found and reported that there was no minister. He presented to this congregation, as a gift of the Synod of Holland, a Bible that had been printed in 1747, the year of his visit, and together with the pewter communion service dated 1746 it is a prized possession of the church.

In 1750 Thomas Penn ordered the land here surveyed for a town, and two years later a plan was made for the town, which he named Easton, for Easton-Weston, the estate of his father-in-law, Lord Pomfret, in Northamptonshire, England.

Schlatter was active in developing both schools and churches. With money from the Schlatter Fund, raised by subscription from churches in Europe through the Synod of Holland, a second log building was erected in 1755, which was used for public worship and as a charity school. There was a close relationship between the Dutch Reformed and the German Reformed churches in America, as we have seen in the Schoharie Valley of New York, and through the activities of Schlatter, the first records of the existence of this congregation are in the annals of the Dutch Reformed Church in Holland. Not until 1793, at Lancaster, Pennsylvania, did the German Reformed Church in the United States become independent of the Dutch Reformed Church of Holland. This second building was erected in town, on present church property, at the corner of Church and Sitgreaves Streets. The building was used for two decades, and then the present church was built. In 1778 a stone building was erected as a schoolhouse on the site of the log house; it is called the Historical Building, and is used as the church office and study.

In 1775 (a little more than a month after Paul Revere's famous ride) the cornerstone was laid in the present stone church. In November of 1776 the building was dedicated (four months after the Declaration of Independence). The land on which it rests was granted by the heirs of William Penn, and the deed conveying title is an indenture, which hangs in a frame on the wall beside the pulpit. In 1777, the year following the dedication, an important treaty with the Six Nations was negotiated and signed in the church. Teedyuscung, Chief of the Delawares, led the other war chiefs of the Six Nations in the council here. George Taylor and George Walton had been commissioned by the young Congress in Philadelphia to treat with the powerful Confederacy, and if possible to win them over from the British. Thomas Paine was among the colonists present. In the following year, 1778, the treaty concluded in this council was broken with the massacre at Forty Fort, in the Wyoming Valley near Scranton. The Wyoming massacre was fomented by Tories and Indians in the struggle between Connecticut and Pennsylvania for settlement of the valley, known as the Pennamite-Yankee War. The church building was used as a hospital during the Revolution, and wounded soldiers of Washington's army were brought here from several battles fought in New York, New Jersey, and Pennsylvania.

The original building was a plain, rectangular stone structure of two stories in height, with circular windows in the two gable ends. In 1832 a number of alterations and additions were made. The ceiling was lowered, and the circular windows were removed; the tower and steeple were built; the main entrance on the south side was replaced by a window, and the door of the north end in the tower became the main entrance; and the exterior stone walls were covered with stucco. A new pulpit was installed at the south wall, and the three galleries and the seating of the box pews were shifted to face it. In 1885 remodeling was done, some of which was out of keeping with the style of the building. New pews replaced the box pews, the four windows in the south end were closed up, stained glass was installed in the remaining windows, a porch was built at the main entrance, and stairways were built from the vestibule to the galleries.

In 1951 a restoration was begun, which had been the wish of the pastor, George A. Creitz, for fifteen years. It was a costly project, but the money was raised, and the restoration was accomplished with beautiful results. It was found to be impractical to return to the original design of 1775, and instead the building was restored to that of 1832, which was still colonial in character. The stained glass, except that in the narthex, was replaced with clear glass; the interior was painted white, including the pews, which had been given a dark color; and the ends of the slip pews were modified to resemble the box-pew style. On June 8, 1952, exactly a year after the restoration had begun, the church was rededicated.

Chapel of St. Paul (1743)
Church of the Blessed Sacrament

Bally, Washington Township, Berks County, Pennsylvania

Goshenhoppen was the original name of the hamlet of Germans where the Chapel of St. Paul was built. Later it became Churchville, and finally, when a post office was established here in 1883, it was given the present name in honor of Father Augustin Bally, a beloved Jesuit priest from Antwerp, Belgium, who had administered here to the Roman Catholics of this section from 1837 to 1881.

The first Catholic missionary here was Theodore Schneider, S. J., who served from 1741 to 1764. The Chapel of St. Paul was built under his leadership in 1743. It was the third Roman Catholic chapel in Pennsylvania, after that at Conewago (No. 254) and St. Joseph's at Philadelphia (see St. Mary's Church, No. 210). He received wholehearted assistance from the German inhabitants, regardless of their former church affiliations. Among them were Mennonites and Herrnhuters (Moravians, so called for Herrnhut, Saxony, their settlement on Count von Zinzendorf's estate), and they all gathered stone and building materials and assisted in the erection of the chapel. The original building was fifty-five by thirty-two feet, and it was described as a magnificent chapel. In 1743, Father Schneider founded what is said to be the first Roman Catholic parish school in America. The work of Father Schneider took him also to New York, where he administered to the few Catholics living there. Because Catholics were forbidden and the governor of New York had placed a price on his head, he traveled as a doctor rather than as a Jesuit priest.

In 1827 the present Church of the Blessed Sacrament was built, and the walls of the old chapel were incorporated in the sacristy of the larger church. The old chapel altar is still in use, and before it the founder, Father Schneider, lies buried; on his tombstone it is recorded that there was missionary activity here in 1716. The original bell still hangs in the cupola of the chapel, and the old vestments are still here. There is also a painting of "The Last Supper" dated 1767, which was presented to Father Schneider by the ex-prince-elector of Saxony.

247

Exeter Friends Meeting House (1758)

Exeter Township, Berks County, Pennsylvania

On a country road in a farming region that is still as rural as it was when Daniel Boone and the ancestors of Abraham Lincoln lived here, stands the Exeter Friends Meeting House. It is located half a mile east of Stonersville and two and a half miles from Baumstown. The section here was in Oley Township. As early as 1721, meetings for worship were held in the home of George Boone, Daniel's grandfather, a log house which he had just built in 1720. The site is marked by stones from the chimney. The house that he built of stone in 1733 is still in use as a private dwelling.

In 1726 a small log meeting house was built. When Oley Monthly Meeting was established in 1737, a larger meeting house was built. The name of the Monthly Meeting was changed to Exeter in 1742, after the township had been divided. The present stone meeting house was built in 1758, and it remains in its original design, unchanged inside or out. The building was used continuous-

ly until the Monthly Meeting was laid down in 1899. In recent years Exeter Monthly Meeting has been reestablished, and meetings are held regularly in this colonial building.

Nearby is the birthplace of Daniel Boone (1734-1820). It is a brownstone farmhouse which was built by his Quaker father, Squire Boone, in the early 1730's and enlarged in 1779. The property was acquired and restored by the Pennsylvania Historical Commission, and in 1938 it was dedicated as Daniel Boone Park. In 1751 Daniel moved with his father to the Yadkin Valley in North Carolina, but many of the Boones remained here. In the burying ground, twelve Boones were buried between 1823 and 1863, for which period the records are available. There are no gravestones, and one end of the yard is higher than the rest of the ground, where a second tier of graves has been laid. Within the same period there were burials of six Lincolns. In the neighborhood is the brownstone house built in 1733 by Mordacai Lincoln, a great-great-grandfather of Abraham, who came here in 1720 (see also Old Ship Meeting House, Hingham, Mass., No. 87). The name Mordacai [sic] appears in a number of the burial records, both in the Lincoln and the Lee families.

248

The Saal (1741)
The Cloister

Ephrata, Lancaster County, Pennsylvania

Ephrata was founded as a monastic community in 1735, the first Protestant monastery in America. In that year Johann Konrad Beissel (1696-1768) organized the Society of the Solitary, a secessionist group from the Church of the Brethren (German Baptists known as "Dunkards"). The community at first was called the *Kloster* (Cloister), and by nickname "Dunkerstown." In 1738 Beissel gave his Christian commune the name Ephrata, as ancient Bethlehem in Palestine had been called, and it became the Seventh Day Baptist Society of Ephrata. Beissel was a native of the German Palatinate and a

graduate of the University of Heidelberg. He was a mystic, a Pietist, and evidently a member of the German Reformed Church. In 1720 he came to America and settled for a year in Germantown, where was located the mother church for the Church of the Brethren (see No. 214). He was pastor of the Dunkard congregation at Conestoga when his difference with the Church, on the question of the Sabbath day, became firm. In 1732 he left his congregation of First Day Baptists and came here to Cocalico (Snake Den) Creek, where he and Emanuel Eckerlin shared a hut and lived as hermits. Sympathizers followed him, and when the Society was formed and buildings were erected, the community grew until it reached a peak of about three hundred. Beissel, who took the monastic name of Father Friedsam Gottrecht ("Peaceable Godright"), was head of the order until his death in 1768, when he was

buried here. He was succeeded by the prior, Peter Miller (Brother Jaebez).

The "Berghaus," one of the first to be built, soon became too small, and another house, named "Kedar" (a son of Ishmael), was built in 1735 on "Zion Hill," above the meadowland where the present buildings stand (Zion was the Temple hill in the City of David, Jerusalem). One principal room was used for worship, and smaller rooms were provided for the brethren on the lower floor and the sisters on the second floor. This building also was soon outgrown and replaced.

The Saal was built in 1741. It was the chapel, the house of worship for the whole community. Originally it had two stories, but two more were added later. The sisters used the upper floors, where rooms or cells were furnished like those in the adjoining Saron. The architecture was unique in America. The roof, which is typical of many towns in Germany, has a very steep pitch and a number of low dormer windows with long pent roofs instead of gables. The walls were filled with stone between the timbers, and plastered with clay mixed with straw and then with white plaster. The ceiling of the main room is of wide boards. The room is furnished with plain tables and benches and a plain lectern. Also on the ground floor is a dining room and a kitchen with a large fireplace. Religious services were held on the seventh day, their Sabbath, followed on the first day by the rites of the washing of feet and the Lord's Supper — the agape or love feast, always held in the evening. The ritual was similar to that in the Church of the Brethren.

Attached to the Saal (to the left in the photograph) is the Saron (or Sharon, a plain or level country) which is called the "Sister House." It is a large frame building, which was occupied by the Sisterhood of the Spiritual Virgins, or Roses of Sharon. In it they had a chapel for midnight services. The Brother House, Bethany (or Bethania, a town near Jerusalem), was a similar large building; it was torn down after 1900. Other buildings that survive include Beissel's house; the almonry, a stone house where food, money, and clothing were distributed to the needy; the farm cottage; the barn of stone and frame; the pastor's house; and Ephrata Academy, a frame building of the 1830's.

Music was an important part of their religious life, and a singing school was started in 1742 by Beissel, who was a composer as well as conductor and violinist. He introduced here the first new system of harmony in America. In a room of Saron the sisters recorded over two thousand pieces of music by hand before the printing shop was installed by the brethren. A book of about five hundred songs, most of them composed by Beissel, copied in illuminated manuscript form, is in the music division of the Library of Congress. Among the industries of the Society were spinning and weaving linens and carpets and the making of pottery and baskets. There was a grist mill, an oil mill, a fulling mill, and a paper mill which supplied the printing shop, for which they also manufactured the type and ink. Benjamin Franklin printed a number of books for Beissel, starting even before the Cloister was founded, the first of which was *Divine Melodies of Love and Praise.* Christopher Sauer, of Germantown, also printed a number of books for the Society, the first of which was also the first book to be printed in German type in America — their great hymn book, *Zionitischer Weyrauth's-Hugel* (Zion's Hill of Incense), dedicated to "All the Solitary Turtle Doves that Coo in the Wilderness." (For the Sauer Bible see the Church of the Brethren, Germantown, where he was a member, No. 214.) In 1745 ten books and tracts were published at the Cloister, on a press which had been imported from Germany. The most ambitious publication of the Cloister appeared in 1748, *Der Blutige Schau-Platz oder Martyrer-Spiegel* (The Martyr's Mirror), a book of about fifteen hundred quarto pages which was three years in the making by the brethren. In 1786 Brothers Lamech and Agrippa wrote a history of the Society,

Chronicon Ephratense. In 1795 the presses left the possession of the Cloister, and one of them went to the Historical Society of Pennsylvania in Philadelphia, but it is now at the Cloister on indefinite loan.

John Conrad Weiser, Jr. (1696-1760), joined the order as Brother Enoch (Dedicated). He was the founder of Reading, northeast of Ephrata, and the Lutheran Church there. His home, northwest of Reading, is now Conrad Weiser Park. As a youth he came with his father from the Palatinate to New York, and his father founded Weiser's Dorf, now Middleburg, in the Schoharie Valley (see No. 196). He was adopted by a Mohawk chief, and, after coming to Pennsylvania in 1729, he became the great Indian interpreter who helped James Logan and William Penn establish good relations with the Indians. He served, for example, as interpreter for Benjamin Franklin and the commission in negotiating the important Indian treaty of 1753 at Carlisle (see No. 256). His daughter, Anna Maria, married Henry Melchior Muhlenberg, the "Patriarch of the Lutheran Church in America" (see Old Trappe Church, No. 231).

It was against the principles of the Society to fight in wars, but the Cloister was opened to the wounded soldiers from the Battle of the Brandywine. A number of the soldiers were buried on Zion Hill, and several buildings had to be burned to prevent the spread of typhus. After the Revolution the community declined, and in 1934 the Society was formally dissolved. In 1941 the property came under the care of the Pennsylvania Historical and Museum Commission, which restored the buildings and opened them to the public.

249

Holy Trinity Church (1761)
Evangelical Lutheran Church of the
Holy Trinity

Lancaster, Lancaster County, Pennsylvania

The earliest Lutherans settled in Lancaster County in 1710. The Lutheran Church here had its beginning with the baptism of children in 1729. Trinity Church was organized and the town of Lancaster was incorporated in 1730. Four years later the congregation began to build the first church, and in 1738 they dedicated it. The stone building had a steeple with bells. Before 1744 a pipe organ was installed. A church school

was established which, in 1748, became a community school. Heinrich Melchior Muhlenberg, D. D., the "Patriarch of the Lutheran Church in America," aided the development of this church; he was in complete charge in 1747-48, and he was supply at various times between 1745 and 1769 (see Trappe Church, No. 231). His son Gotthilf Henry Ernst Muhlenberg, one of several who became Lutheran ministers, served as pastor here from 1780 until his death in 1815. He was even better known as a botanist who published two learned books on American plants. His stone house stands a few blocks away at 33 North Duke Street.

In 1761 the cornerstone was laid for the present building. The design was based on that of Christ Church, Philadelphia (No. 205). The church was consecrated in 1766; by that time the membership had reached a thousand. In 1771 a new organ built by David Taunenburg of Lititz, Pennsylvania, was installed. The tower was begun in 1785 and completed in 1794; it houses a London bell of 1768 and a set of chimes. The interior is the result of later alterations; in 1893 there was a renovation, and in 1922 another. When Congress was forced to leave Philadelphia in 1777, during the British occupation, and met in Lancaster, many of the members worshiped here. The German language continued in use until 1825, when English was adopted for the services. Zion Church was established in 1827 by those who insisted on retaining the German language.

A number of chapels, churches, and schools originated in this Church. Among them, the best known is Franklin and Marshall College here in Lancaster. It is the result of the merger in 1853 of Franklin College, established in Lancaster in 1787 and named for Benjamin Franklin, and Marshall College, founded at Mercersburg in 1836 and named for John Marshall, Chief Justice of the United States Supreme Court. Franklin headed the list of subscribers to found the college that bears his name, and original supporters of the college included four signers of the Declaration of Independence — Benjamin Rush, Thomas McKean, George Clymer, and Robert Morris — in addition to Thomas Mifflin, a signer of the Constitution of the United States. James Buchanan served as the first president of the board of trustees. General Thomas Mifflin, who succeeded Franklin as president of the Supreme Executive Council of Pennsylvania and served as the first governor of the state, is buried beside the church.

250

Old Sadsbury Friends Meeting House (1777)

Christiana, Lancaster County, Pennsylvania

The first meeting of Friends in the Christiana section was held in 1724. The first meeting house was built of logs the next year. Sadsbury Monthly Meeting was established in 1737. In 1747 the second meeting house was built. After it was destroyed by fire in 1777, the present stone meeting house was built. It stands two miles north of Sadsbury. It is unique with its square shape and the four stone chimneys exactly on the corners. In 1902 the Meeting moved into a new meeting house built in Christiana, and Old Sadsbury Meet-ing House has been idle since. The property still belongs to Sadsbury Monthly Meeting, and the trustees permit its use on occasion.

251

Donegal Presbyterian Church (c. 1740)

East Donegal Township, Lancaster County, Pennsylvania

Presbyterians from Northern Ireland, fleeing persecution in the old country, were settling along the eastern shore of the Susquehanna River before 1720. The tide of immigration had reached as far as the valley of the Chiquesalunga Creek when the Donegal Church was gathered there in the 1720's. The Presbyterians on Conestoga Creek

had business with New Castle in 1721, according to a reference to them in the minutes of the Presbytery of New Castle. In the same year, the Presbyterians of the settlement here at Chicken's Longus (Chiquesalunga) sent Andrew Galbreath to New Castle with a petition to the Presbytery to supply them with a preacher; in response George Gillespie was appointed to preach to them, which appointment he fulfilled. This Presbyterian settlement became famous as the Donegal congregation, and it was recorded by that name in 1723. The first pastor, who was settled here in 1727, was James Anderson. He was born in Scotland in 1678, arrived in America in 1709, settled at New Castle, and was in New York when called to the Donegal Church in 1726. The Donegal Presbytery was organized by the Synod of Philadelphia, with five ministers and eight churches, and held its first meeting here October 11, 1732.

A log church served the congregation in its early years. It is believed that the present church was built after a patent was granted by Thomas Penn to the elders in 1740, for the land that they had occupied for nearly twenty years. In 1786 a charter was granted for selling the land, and this is the earliest of the documents of the church to survive. In 1851 some land was sold, and the proceeds were used to repair and remodel the church and to build the present schoolhouse. Even though dates for the founding of the church and the remodeling appear in the church, they are not certain. The pillars, pulpit, pews, and brick pavement in the aisles were removed; board flooring and a vestibule were installed; the south and west entrances were closed, and one was added at the east end; square windows replaced the original arched ones, and the ouside stone walls were stuc-

coed. The gambrel roof is the only original feature retained.

Members of Donegal Church fought in several wars, as did most of the Presbyterians from Northern Ireland. There are several versions of a tradition that the congregation gathered around the huge white oak by the church and pledged allegiance to the cause of the colonies, and it became known as the "Witness Tree." From this church a company of soldiers marched to the Battle of the Brandywine. The old church is located about two and a third miles out of the present Maytown. The movement of pioneers from Donegal Church and this region continued up the Susquehanna and into the Cumberland Valley. There a number of Presbyterian churches of the Donegal Presbytery were founded, including that at Carlisle (No. 256) and Silver Spring (No. 257). From there these Scotch-Irish Presbyterians continued their migration, through the Cumberland Valley and south into the Shenandoah Valley beyond the Blue Ridge Mountains of Virginia. There they settled the Augusta Church (No. 343) and the Timber Ridge Church (No. 344), and called on the Donegal Presbytery for supply.

252

York Friends Meeting House (1765)

**Philadelphia Street and Park Alley, York,
York County, Pennsylvania**

The Friends of York were organized in 1754 as an Indulged Meeting of Warrington Monthly Meeting. This Meeting became a Preparative Meeting in 1767 and a Monthly Meeting in 1786. It is in Baltimore Yearly Meeting.

The meeting house was built in 1765, and it has been in continuous use ever since. The eastern section was added in 1766, and in 1776 the west end was enlarged. The brick is laid in English bond, and the wood trim is painted gray. In the burial ground beside the meeting house, many of the graves are unmarked.

253

Warrington Friends Meeting House (1769)

between Wellsville and Rossville, York County, Pennsylvania

Friends settled in this northwestern part of York County as early as 1735. The first settlers came from Chester County, Pennsylvania, and New Castle County, Delaware. In that decade they established a school here, and until 1885 their log schoolhouse stood about three hundred yards from the present site of the meeting house. A number of Irish Quakers came to Warrington between 1748 and 1773. A log meeting house was built in 1745. In 1747 the Warrington Pre-

parative Meeting was organized, and the first Monthly Meeting was held here the same year.

The present meeting house was built in 1769. In 1782 an addition was built to enlarge the meeting house. Benjamin Walker was appointed overseer of the construction, and he was occupied "hauling sleeper," "the summer beam," and "35 bushels of lime from the Pigeon Hills," soaking the oak shingles, and purchasing shutters at four shillings and doors at ten shillings. The walls are covered with Virginia creeper. At the northern corner of the building, the mortar between the stones spells the word "Prayer," reading down from the cornice to the foundation. The interior is the original, with hand-hewn beams, wide board floors and wainscoting fastened with hand-wrought nails, two fireplaces, and pegged benches, some with backs and others without. Migration westward to open new lands drained the congregation, and for nearly a century after 1856 meetings were held only twice a year. As new birthright Friends moved in, and convinced Friends increased the number in the congregation, weekly meetings were resumed in 1946. Warrington Meeting is a part of Baltimore Yearly Meeting.

254

Church of the Sacred Heart (1785)

Conewago, Adams County, Pennsylvania

Conewago (Co-ne-wā-go) is the oldest Roman Catholic community in Pennsylvania. Jesuit missionaries were here soon after 1700, ministering to the Indians, and by 1720 they had an established place of worship. The present Conewago consists of the church and the farm of the old Jesuit mission. It is located in the country, on a high bank of Little Conewago Creek, a branch of Great Conewago which flows into the Susquehanna River; in neither Conewago, however, does one find "the Rapids" implied in the Indian name. The Jesuits came into Pennsylvania from their mission at Bohemia in Maryland, at a time when the border region was still in dispute between Maryland and Pennsylvania. Germans started settling in this region as early as 1727. Joseph Greaton was the first Jesuit priest to hold services here. According to tradition, he came through Conewago on his way to Philadelphia, where, disguised in the common dress of a Quaker, he founded St. Joseph's Chapel (see St. Mary's Church, No. 210). Services were conducted for a time in the large stone Mass house that still stands as a part of this group; it was built before 1734. A log chapel was built in 1740, adjoining the house and serving as a private chapel, as was the custom in Maryland to avoid the law against Roman Catholics building public houses of worship. In 1753 the chapel was enlarged. In 1763 James Pellentz became the first resident pastor.

On the site of the 1740 chapel, the church was begun in 1785 and completed in 1787. Father Pellentz dedicated it to the Sacred Heart, the first church in America to be so designated. He lived here until 1800, and then he was buried near the sanctuary where there is a tablet in the wall. In 1850 the church was enlarged and made cruciform by the addition of transepts and the apse at the eastern end. At that time the interior was decorated with murals, by Franz Stecher, on the theme of the love of Christ. The church as it now stands was finished in 1871 by the addition of the spire.

Great Conewago Presbyterian Church (1787)

Hunterstown, Adams County, Pennsylvania

Scotch-Irish Presbyterians from Northern Ireland settled on the Great Conewago Creek between 1738 and 1740. During those years this congregation was organized, and it appears on the minutes of the Presbytery of Donegal in 1740 (see No. 251). The first church building was erected of unhewn logs, between 1743 and 1749. The present stone building was erected in 1787, the sixth year of the pastorate of Joseph Henderson, whose name appears together with the date in the circular stone in the gable end. In the middle of the nineteenth century the building was remodeled; the side doors were closed and the door at the end became the one entrance, and the old goblet-shaped pulpit and sounding board were replaced. The old pulpit, which had been preserved, was burned by rebels during the Civil War, at the time of the Battle of Gettysburg, and the building was used as a hospital. Bloodstains remained on the seats and floors until the church was repaired in 1874. The church is now in the Presbytery of Carlisle. It is situated in open, rolling country near the crossroads hamlet of Hunterstown.

First Presbyterian Church (1757)

Carlisle, Cumberland County, Pennsylvania

The pioneering movement of Scotch-Irish Presbyterians continued up the Susquehanna from the Donegal Church region (see No. 251) and, in 1734, crossed the river from the northeast bank into the Cumberland Valley. Under the Donegal Presbytery they founded churches in the valley at five springs — Silver Spring (No. 257), Meeting House Springs (Carlisle), Big Spring (Newville), Middle Spring, and Falling Spring (Chambersburg). They were spaced at eleven-mile intervals, as a result of a church rule giving jurisdiction to each church over an area with a radius of five and a half miles. The present church in Carlisle is the second building, succeeding the one built at Meeting House Springs in West Pennsborough Township, about two miles to the northwest. This church and Silver Spring Church were referred to as the Upper and Lower Pennsborough churches respectively.

Alexander Craighead was the first Presbyterian minister to enter the Cumberland Valley. In October of 1734 the Donegal Presbytery ordered him to preach to the "people over the river for two or three Sabbaths in November." In 1736 the Donegal minutes first mentioned "the people

on the Conodoguinet" Creek. Samuel Thomson, arriving from Northern Ireland in 1737, was made a minister in the Donegal Presbytery, and promptly was ordered to supply this church. In 1738 he was called and in 1739 installed as pastor to both the Upper and Lower churches; Craighead presided at the ordination. The first reference to a meeting house at Pennsborough was entered in 1737, by which the date is established for the log building that served as the first house of worship at Meeting House Springs, on a hill overlooking Conodoguinet Creek. The old graveyard is still there, but there is no trace of the building. The land was granted to the church by the Penns, the proprietaries, in 1749.

The first settler in Carlisle was a French trader, James Le Tort, who set up a trading post at the spring on the stream that bears his name. The town was laid out in 1751, and named for the seat of Cumberland County in England. The growth of the town called for a church more convenient to the congregation, and a letter dated June 30, 1757, records the beginning of the present building in these words: "Tomorrow we begin to haul stones for the meeting house on the north side of the Square." In 1760 a lottery helped to pay the cost of the building. The walls are of blue limestone, decorated with courses of white marble in an interesting design. The blocks of stone are diminished in size toward the top of the walls, to heighten the perspective. The tower was added in 1873.

The congregation suffered the prevailing division between Old Lights and New Lights; for a time they worshiped separately, but they were reunited. Like the Presbyterians throughout the colonies, the congregation here was early and vigorous in supporting the cause of independence; on May 23, 1776, they drafted a declaration of their own. In this predominantly Presbyterian community Dickinson College was founded in 1783 by Dr. Benjamin Bush (see Pine Street Presbyterian Church, Philadelphia, No. 211), a famous colonial physician and a signer of the Declaration of Independence. Carlisle was a frontier town, and it was here, in 1753, two years after the town was laid out, that Benjamin Franklin and other members of a commission, concluded a treaty with the Six Nations and five tribes from the Ohio country. It was far-reaching in its importance for the future of the province, and it launched Franklin on his career of diplomacy. The Indian interpreter during the negotiations was the famous John Conrad Weiser, Jr.,

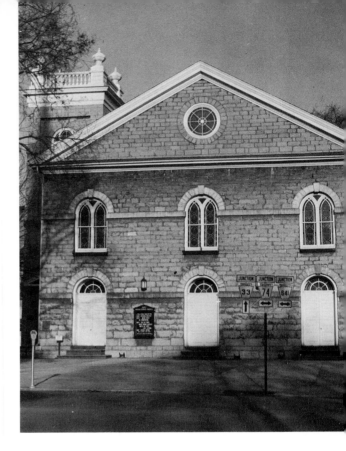

whose daughter married Henry Melchior Muhlenberg (see Old Trappe Church, No. 231), and who became a member of the Society at the Ephrata Cloister (No. 248). It was here also that the Carlisle Indian School was founded in 1879, which became famous throughout the country.

257

Silver Spring Presbyterian Church (1783)

Cumberland County, Pennsylvania

James Silver, who settled here in 1724, owned 532 acres. His name was given to the spring, and originally it and the church were designated as Silver's Spring. This was one of the five springs in the Cumberland Valley at which the Scotch-Irish pioneers built Presbyterian churches. John Hoge came here in 1724, and the place of his residence became known as Hogestown. The first gathering of the congregation in 1734 was probably at the home of Silver or Hoge. In 1735 they built their first house of worship, a log cabin. The land of this region was conveyed to the Penns in a grant by 233 Indian chiefs on August 11, 1736, and the church acquired its plot from the Penns. When the stone church was built, the log structure was sold for a barn, and it was moved a second time for the same use on the Hoover farm near Hogestown.

The church here and that at Meeting House Springs, eleven miles away, were founded by the Donegal Presbytery (see No. 251). These two churches in Pennsborough Township, the Lower Church here and the Upper Church at Carlisle, were closely related in their early years, and in the beginning they shared the same pastor (see No. 256).

In 1782 Samuel Waugh was called to be pastor of the Silver Spring Church. In the following year, 1783, the present stone church was begun under his direction, and in the same year he married Miss Alice Hoge. He was active until his death in 1807, when he was buried here. In 1866 the church was remodeled. The "Study House," which had been erected at the rear of the church, was torn down, and the stones were used in the remodeling of the main building. The original cornerstone is now over the main entrance. The ceiling was changed, the pulpit recess was enlarged, and stained-glass windows were installed.

In 1928 the church was restored to its colonial design of 1783, in memory of Henry McCormick and his wife Annie Criswell McCormick. The address at the rededication service May 23, 1929, was made by the Reverend Walter J. Hogue (modern spelling), pastor of the First Presbyterian Church in York, a descendant of early members of the congregation, including John and Gwendolyn Hoge, who gave a pewter communion set and a pulpit in 1747. The restored interior has a wineglass pulpit, box pews, and galleries around three sides. This constructive project was carried out before the restoration of Williamsburg had brought public attention to the value in preserving the colonial heritage of the country.

The movement of Scotch-Irish Presbyterian pioneers did not stop here. Many families continued to migrate through the Cumberland Valley and south into the Shenandoah, the Valley of Virginia, and there they founded the Presbyterian churches of Augusta (No. 343) and Timber Ridge (No. 344). Others moved north from the Susquehanna to settle Harrisburg and the Presbyterian church at Paxtang (No. 258).

258

Paxton Presbyterian Church (1740)

Paxtang, Dauphin County, Pennsylvania

The present city of Harrisburg, the capital of Pennsylvania, lies on the east bank of the Susquehanna River. The Indians called the section around the site *Peshtank* or *Peixtan,* meaning swampy, and the name has evolved as Paxtang. At the large Indian village of Paxtang, three miles east of the site of the present city, John Harris settled about 1712 and established a trading post with the Indians and a ferry on the river. John Harris, Jr., was born in 1727, at the settlement then known as Harris' Ferry. In 1785 he laid out the town that he called Harrisburg, and beside selling land from the extensive family holding, he continued to operate the ferry, which was on an important route to the western frontier.

Some of the Scotch-Irish Presbyterians who had come from Northern Ireland to New Castle, Delaware, and had formed Donegal Church on the Susquehanna (No. 251), migrated upstream and settled here, where they established the Paxton Church, the mother church of Harrisburg Presbyterianism. There were Paxtons among the families in this migration, which moved also south into the Shenandoah Valley, and there, in the congregation of the Timber Ridge Presbyterian Church (No. 344), the mother of Sam Houston was a Paxton. The similarity of this family name and that of the town is a coincidence. Preaching began as early as 1715, when George Gillespie preached here. It is also traditional that David Evans preached here in 1720 and Adam Boyd in 1725. In 1726, James Anderson became the first regular preacher.

In 1732 the frontier Presbyterian churches were organized as the Donegal Presbytery, and among them at that time the churches of Paxton and Derry (eight miles east of Paxtang, where the congregation developed as the present town of Hershey) were organized officially. The first item of business in the first meeting of the new Presbytery was a call for William Bertram to serve as pastor of the Paxton and Derry congregations; the call was approved, and he was installed. Four years later the two congregations decided on independence, and Bertram remained with Derry. In 1738, John Elder was ordained and installed as pastor of the Paxton Church. He was a courageous leader in this frontier region, and he became known as the "Fighting Parson." He served until 1791 and died the following year. During his ministry the Great Awakening took place, a spiritual revival which divided the Presbyterian churches into "Old Side" and "New Side" (and their congregations into "Old Lights" and "New Lights"). In 1745 John Roan came here and, drawing from the congregation of both Paxton and Derry, organized two New Side congregations and built two meeting houses. The one at Paxtang stood two miles east of Paxton Church. After Bertram's death in 1746, Paxton and Derry, having lost members, united again, and Elder served both churches until 1791. The controversy was settled in 1758, but Roan continued to serve the two New Side churches until 1775, and thereafter the members returned to Paxton and Derry. In 1874 these two separated once more.

When Bertram began his ministry in 1732, services were held here in a log meeeting house which had been built about 1716, on a site just south of the present church where there is a stone

marker. In the grove north of the present church stands the Scout Lodge, which was built in 1950 as a replica of the log meeting house, through the generosity of Dr. J. Loomis Christian. In 1740, during Elder's ministry, the stone meeting house was built. That was during the schism which reduced the congregation and the income, and for many years the interior was without flooring or pews. Puncheons resting on the dirt floor served as benches, and it was not until 1789 that the laying of flooring was undertaken. In 1808 the rafters were enclosed with a pine ceiling. In 1847 the interior was refinished. In 1887 alterations were made, and new pews and a chestnut pulpit were installed. The porch on the eastern end was built during the present century. In 1931, with a gift from Mary Boyd McCormick, wife of Henry B. McCormick, and with contributions from many others, the church interior was restored to its original colonial style. Mary Boyd was descended from William Boyd, who came from Northern Ireland to Pennsylvania, in 1732, and served in the Provincial Council, and her grandfather and father were prominent members of this church. Henry B. McCormick was the son of Henry and Annie Criswell McCormick, in whose memory Silver Spring Church was restored in 1928 (see No. 257).

The pewter communion set has been in use here ever since 1734. In the graveyard were buried pioneers and early settlers, including John Harris, Jr., and four of the six commissioners who laid out Harrisburg with him in 1785. In addition to ministers, elders, legislators, statesmen, and people of the farms and the town, the many generations of Paxtonians buried here include soldiers of all the wars — French and Indian, Revolutionary, Mexican, Civil, and World Wars.

At Hershey, made famous by one man and his chocolate, the only colonial Presbyterian structure remaining is the Old Session House, a clapboard-covered log house built in 1732, the year that Bertram became pastor of the two churches. It served as the pastor's study and an academy, and to preserve the historic landmark it has been enclosed in glass. The original Derry Meeting House, built of logs in 1724, was replaced by a frame building, which in turn gave way to the present stone Derry Presbyterian Church in 1884. We find the name Derry imported from the old country by Scotch-Irish immigrants also in New Hampshire (see No. 122).

St. Peter's Church (1767)

Middletown, Dauphin County, Pennsylvania

The main highway between Lancaster and Harrisburg runs through Middleburg at the Square, and one block north of the Square stands Old St. Peter's Church, a Lutheran landmark of colonial history. There is evidence that there was a Lutheran congregation here in 1764, for then the lot on which the church stands was presented by George and Hannah Fisher to Peter Woltz, George Frey, and Detrick Schob in trust for the Lutheran congregation, at a rental of one grain of wheat per annum. In the same year King George III granted through John Penn, lieutenant-governor of the Province of Pennsylvania, permission to raise funds for building a church.

The cornerstone of this brownstone building, bearing the name *Sant Peter's Kierch,* was laid July 13, 1767. The church was dedicated at the first service, on September 12, 1769, by Henry Melchoir Muhlenberg, the foremost missionary and "Patriarch of the Lutheran Church in America" (see Old Trappe Church, No. 231). His *Journal* records that the church was not entirely finished at that time. In 1813 the bell tower was built. In 1830 a wooden floor was laid over the brick floor, a new pulpit and new pews were installed, and wood stoves were provided for the building's first heating. The interior was remodeled in 1850 to its present style. In 1879 the last regular service was held on January 26, and on the following Sunday, February 2, the congregation marched from the old church to the new St. Peter's Lutheran Church at Spring and Union Streets. Since that time the old church has been used only for historic and special occasions.

RHODE ISLAND

		Denomination	*Material*
260	First Baptist Church (1774) Providence, Providence County	Baptist	Wood
261	Providence Friends Meeting House (1725) Providence, Providence County	Friends	Wood
262	Saylesville Friends Meeting House (1703) Saylesville, Providence County	Friends	Wood
263	Cranston Friends Meeting House (1729) Cranston, Providence County	Friends	Wood
264	Elder Ballou Meeting House (c. 1740) Cumberland, Providence County	Six Principle Baptist	Wood
265	St. Paul's Church (1707) Wickford, Washington County	Anglican	Wood
266	Old Newport Friends Meeting House (1699) Newport, Newport County	Friends	Wood
267	Trinity Church (1725) Newport, Newport County	Anglican	Wood
268	Sabbath Day Meeting House (1729) Newport, Newport County	Seventh Day Baptist	Wood
269	Dr. Hopkins' Meeting House (1729) Newport, Newport County	Congregational	Wood
270	Second Congregational Church (1733) Newport, Newport County	Congregational	Wood
271	Touro Synagogue (1759) Newport, Newport County	Jewish	Brick
272	Portsmouth Friends Meeting House (1700) Portsmouth, Portsmouth County	Friends	Wood
273	Conanicut Friends Meeting House (1786) Jamestown County	Friends	Wood

SUMMARY

Baptist	1	Brick	1
Six Principle Baptist	1	Wood	13
Seventh Day Baptist	1		
Friends	6		
Anglican	2		
Congregational	2		
Jewish	1		
Buildings	14		14

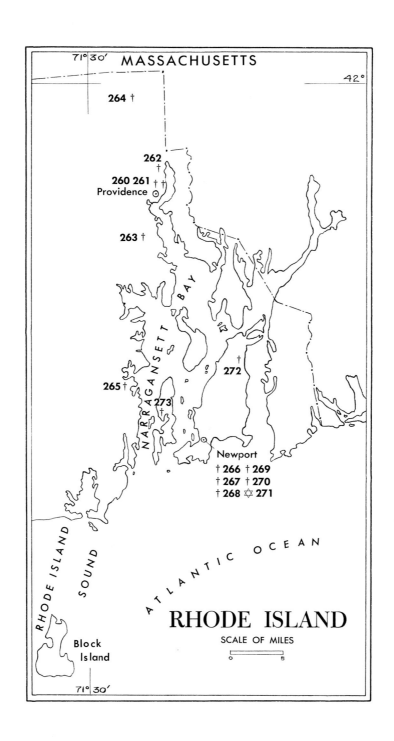

71° 30' MASSACHUSETTS

42°

264 †

262
†

260 261
Providence ⊙ † †

263 †

N A R R A G A N S E T T   B A Y

272 †

265 †

273
†

Newport
† 266 † 269
† 267 † 270
† 268 ✡ 271

R H O D E   I S L A N D   S O U N D

A T L A N T I C   O C E A N

RHODE ISLAND

SCALE OF MILES
0   5

Block
Island

71° 30'

First Baptist Church (1774)

Providence, Providence County, Rhode Island

Providence was founded in 1636 by Roger Williams, an exile from the Massachusetts Bay Colony. He was a Separatist with strong convictions, which he expressed as teacher in the church at Salem. When he insisted, among other points in opposition, that the civil authorities had no jurisdiction over the consciences of men, the Puritan officials at Boston, who had the combined authority of church and state, tried him and ordered him banished. The Plymouth Colony, where the Pilgrims differed with the Puritans, controlled the territory to their south, and they helped Williams to avoid being deported to England by escaping to that region. Upon arrival he named the place Providence in gratitude to God for His many mercies. Williams was the first to proclaim religious freedom as a basic principle in the colonies, and Rhode Island was the first colony to become identified with the principle.

In 1638 Williams and eleven others took steps to form a church of baptized believers. Ezekiel Holliman was deputed to baptize Williams, who then baptized Holliman and the others, and this group of twelve or more became the first Baptist church in America. Williams was the first pastor, but he became concerned with the loss of apostolic church organization, and after a few months he withdrew. He remained friendly with the church group, while maintaining the individual role of a seeker. He continued to live in Providence and to work for the new colony, which he served in several capacities, until his death in 1683.

For two generations the congregation worshiped in private homes or outdoors, and it was not until 1700 that they had a meeting house. The first structure was built in person by the sixth pastor, Pardon Tillinghast. In 1711 the property was deeded to the parish. It was located at the present North Main and Smith Streets. In 1726 the meeting house was replaced by a second on the same site.

The third and present meeting house was begun in 1774 and dedicated in May of 1775. It stands on a plot of one and a quarter acres about one-eighth of a mile south of the former site. The design was drawn by Joseph Brown, an amateur architect and student of mathematics, astronomy, and philosophy, who became a professor at Rhode

Island College (Brown University). As a guide he used the *Book of Architecture, Designs, and Ornaments*, by James Gibbs, a pupil of Sir Christopher Wren (see St. Michael's Church, Charleston, S. C., No. 274). The spire is from Plate No. 30, one of many unused designs made for St. Martin-in-the-Fields, in London, and the body of the building is quite similar to that of Marybone Chapel (St. Mary-le-bourne, i.e., on the bank of the Tyburn), both being in the Wren style. James Sumner, of Boston, was the "master-workman." The basement walls are of stone, and the rest of the building is of wood. The original exterior remains except ornaments and the spire, which have been renewed. A number of alterations have been made inside. In 1832 the box pews and high pulpit were replaced and the sounding board removed. In 1834 the original gallery for slaves, freedmen, and Indians was removed to make way for an organ. In 1884 the present platform and furniture, the recess for the baptistery, and the stained glass window were donated. The bell was cast originally in London with the inscription:

> For freedom of conscience the town was
>   first planted,
>   Persuasion, not force, was used by the
>   people:
> This church is the oldest, and has not re-
>   canted,
>   Enjoying and granting bell, temple and
>   steeple.

The last line emphasizes that only in the colonies, and not in England, could a nonconform-ist house of worship be called a church and have a steeple and bell. This bell cracked three times and was recast each time in this country. It now bears the date of the founding of the church and the name of its founder, Roger Williams, "its first pastor, and the first asserter of liberty of conscience." It also bears the inscription: "It was the first church in Rhode Island, and the first Baptist Church in America."

Rhode Island College, now Brown University, which had been founded in Warren in 1764, was moved to Providence in 1771. In 1775 the president of the college, the Reverend James Manning, accepted the call to preach to this congregation, and the prospectus published for the new building stated that the First Baptist Meeting House would be "For Publick Worship of Almighty God, and also for holding Commencement in." The meeting house has served in both capacities ever since.

261

Providence Friends Meeting House (1725)

77 Hope Street, Providence, Providence County, Rhode Island

Early meetings of Friends were held in Providence in 1666, only a decade after the first Quakers came to America and arrived in Boston. James Burnyeate was the leader for those earliest

meetings. In 1672, two years before land was sold to Quakers in West Jersey where they made their first settlements, George Fox, the founder of the Society of Friends, was in America preaching from Carolina to Providence, and he held meetings here. The conditions of freedom of conscience and individualism under which Roger Williams had founded Providence Plantation were congenial to the Quaker faith and philosophy. Friends settled here early and flourished until they ruled the colony.

Several meeting houses were built in Providence Plantation, as the colony originally was called. Friends in the town of Providence worshiped in the meeting house in Saylesville (No. 262) until the one shown here was built. This is the only one in the town of Providence that survived the colonial period. It was moved twice. In 1724 the meeting house was proposed, and in 1725 it was built on Stamper's Hill near the foot of Olney Street. Twenty years later it was moved to a site on North Main Street between Meeting and South Court Streets. In 1784 an addition was built. In 1844 the old building was moved to the present location, where it is a two-family residence, and a small meeting house was built which still stands at the former site.

262

Saylesville Friends Meeting House (1703)

Saylesville, Lincoln Township, Providence County, Rhode Island

The ell is the original structure of the Saylesville Friends Meeting House. It was erected in 1703, as a one-story plain building. It was the first of four Quaker meeting houses built in the town of Providence, and the Friends of Providence attended meeting here until they built the one shown in No. 261. The two-story addition was built in 1745, making the ell with the old structure. The building was repaired in 1929.

This Meeting for Worship originally was under Greenwich Monthly Meeting. In 1718 Providence Monthly Meeting was set off from Greenwich, and this Meeting was included. In 1731 the name of that Providence Monthly Meeting was changed to Smithfield Monthly Meeting, without change in the constituents. This Meeting for Worship then was known as the Lower Smithfield Meeting, and Woonsocket Meeting was the Upper Smithfield Meeting. In 1783 the present Providence Monthly Meeting was set off from

Smithfield Monthly Meeting, including the Lower Smithfield Meeting. In 1871 the town of Lincoln was set off from the town of Smithfield and was incorporated, including the Lower Smithfield Meeting. When the village in which it is situated was named Saylesville, for the Sayles family, the Meeting here was given the same name. This means that the business of this Meeting until 1718 was conducted through Greenwich Monthly Meeting, from 1718 to 1783 through Smithfield Monthly Meeting, and from 1783 to the present through Providence Monthly Meeting.

263

Cranston Friends Meeting House (1729)

**229 Wilbur Avenue, Cranston,
Providence County, Rhode Island**

For many years Cranston was the center of the religious life of Quakers living south of Providence. Meetings were held here in 1705, in the home of Roger Burlingham. The meeting house was built in 1729 by the Meshanticut Meeting. It was repaired in 1785, 1807, and 1817. Twenty feet were added to the length in 1819. The membership then began to decline in Cranston, and by 1861 there were so few remaining that they united with those in the town of Coventry. In 1866 the meeting house was sold to Baptists, and it was moved to its present site. Quakers continued to use it occasionally for privileged meetings until 1874. It was used as a church until 1879, when the Oaklawn Baptist Church was built on the roadside in front of the meeting house.

Elder Ballou Meeting House (c. 1740)
Cumberland, Providence County, Rhode Island

The wilderness of this section was first settled in 1713 by a few people including the Ballou family. James Ballou was an ancestor of James A. Garfield, the twentieth President of the United States, and of Adin Ballou, who preached his first sermon in this meeting house at the age of eighteen. The Six Principle Baptist Church was organized in Rhode Island about 1723, as a separate sect. They denied Calvinism, while maintaining faith in free will and universal salvation. The first elder of this Society in Cumberland was Joseph Cook.

The meeting house was built about 1740. It is the most primitive of the meeting houses in New England not built by Quakers. The plan is thirty by twenty-five feet. There are six long benches between two side aisles, with a rail down the middle to separate the men and women. The benches are unusually uncomfortable because of a rail which protrudes from the back. On the north side is the pulpit, a platform above a few steps, with a board front surmounted by a plain board for a desk, and furnished with a plain bench; it is lighted by a window higher than the others. Before the pulpit is the deacons' or elders' pew, to the front of which is hinged a board for Communion. There is a gallery furnished with crude benches, which have only a back railing. The framing is of oak. The interior walls were plastered, probably at a later date. Elder Abner Ballou served the Society as elder from 1775 until his death in 1806, and the meeting house was named for him. After his time the Society declined, and there have been no services here in many years.

At Wyoming, Rhode Island, where the sect was organized, there is a Six Principle Baptist Church, but we have been unable to find evidence that the present building is colonial.

265

St. Paul's Church (1707)
Old Narragansett Church

Wickford, Washington County, Rhode Island

Narragansett Parish, or St. Paul's, is the second Anglican parish to be founded in Rhode Island, after Trinity, Newport. It was organized soon after the Society for the Propagation of the Gospel had been founded in London in 1701, and it received aid from the Society until the colonies became independent. Queen Anne presented to the new parish silver communion vessels and a baptismal bowl — in 1851 the latter was made into a large paten — and they are still used on occasion.

The church was built in 1707, on Congdon Hill in Kingston, about five miles south of the present town of Wickford, where it was on a busy highway between Boston and New York. The church thrived until 1774, when the feeling against England was such that the church was closed to stop the prayers being said for the king. During the war American soldiers used the empty

building for a barracks. After the war, in 1784, the church was reopened, but it did not thrive. The Venerable Society, as it was sometimes called, had to end its support, and the community did not grow as had been expected when the church was built. In 1799 it was decided to move the building to Wickford, and in 1800 the move was made. The building was repaired, a bell was installed, and in May the church was consecrated for the first time. After two more generations, the congregation, in 1847, built a new church in Wickford, and the Old Narragansett Church again was deserted. It was allowed to become dilapidated, but in 1870 it was repaired again. More recently the church has been restored to its colonial style, and it is used for services in summer. It stands among trees, facing across a small green to the waters of Narragansett Bay — a beautiful landmark of colonial history.

266

Old Newport Friends Meeting House (1699)

30 Marlborough Street, Newport, Newport County, Rhode Island

Quakers settled early in the colony known as Providence Plantations, which had been founded by Roger Williams, in 1636, on the principles of liberty and individualism. In 1657 Robert Fowler and eleven associates came to Newport in the ship *Woodhouse*. Beginning in that year, meetings in Newport were held in the home of William Coddington, on Marlborough Street near Duke Street. Before coming to Newport, Coddington had spent a year at Portsmouth (see No. 272). The Society of Friends thrived to the point that Quakers ruled the colony. William Coddington was the first governor of Portsmouth and of Newport, and then of Portsmouth and Newport, and under the charter of 1663 he was governor of Rhode Island for two terms and William Coddington, 2d, for one term. The first General Meeting of Friends in America was held in Newport about 1661, and George Fox, the founder of the Society of Friends in England, attended meetings and preached here during his visit to America in 1672. He stimulated the organization of Friends in the colony. Monthly, Quarterly, and Yearly Meetings were established, and Newport, Portsmouth (No. 267), and Jamestown (No. 268) formed the Quarterly Meeting.

Although he had founded the colony on the principle of freedom of conscience, Roger Williams as a "seeker" did not let the theology of others go unquestioned. He put Quakerism to the test during the visit of Fox, and his account of his disputation on the theology of Quakers was printed in a pamphlet bearing the revealing title: "George Fox digg'd out of his Burrowes, or an offer of disputation on fourteen proposals made this last summer, 1672 (so call'd) unto G. Fox then present on Rode Island in New England, by R. W. As also how (G. Fox slily departing) the Disputation went on being managed three dayes at Newport on Rode Island, and one day at Providence, between John Stubs, John Burnet, and William Edmundson on the one part, and R. W. on the other. In which many quotations out of G. Fox & Ed. Burrowes Book in folio are alleged: with an appendix of some scores of G. F., his simple lame answers to his opposites in that book, quoted and replyed to by R. W. of Providence in N. E."

The first meeting house at Newport was built in 1672, on the east side of Farewell Street near Marlborough Street, and opposite the Coddington burying ground. This second meeting house was begun in 1699 and finished in 1700. The master builder was John Jones, and in several places on timbers under the shingles were found the inscription, "John Jones, the King's own, in the year of our Lord 1700." In 1705 the first building was torn down, and some of the lumber was used in the present building. The auditorium is almost square, forty-six by forty-five feet. Because of the curved timbers supporting the hip roof, it was called "Old Ship Room." A wooden tower rises above the peak of the roof. Two decks of galleries were installed. In 1808 a women's section was added at one end of the building, and in 1857 an addition was made at the other end. In 1922 another meeting house was built in Newport, and Newport Monthly Meeting continues active under the Ohio Yearly Meeting. In 1926 this old building became a museum. It has been used since as a community recreation hall.

267

Trinity Church (1725)

141 Spring Street, Newport, Newport County, Rhode Island

The first Anglican parish in Rhode Island was organized at Newport, in 1688, by Sir Francis Nicholson. He was serving in New York as deputy of Sir Edmund Andros, governor of the Dominion of New England, the territory of which had been extended that year to include New York and New Jersey, and which had its capital in Boston. In 1699 a group of Anglicans here sent a petition to England for a clergyman, but no action was taken until the Society for the Propagation of the Gospel was organized in 1701. This parish was the first to apply to the Society for aid and the first to receive it, and Trinity Church was the largest beneficiary of the Society in New England. The

first church was built in 1702, and James Honeyman was appointed as the first rector by the Lord Bishop of London. Queen Anne presented to the new church a bell, which has been recast.

The second and present building was begun in 1725 and completed in 1726. It faced a long green that sloped gently down to the harbor, but it is now surrounded by buildings. The architect evidently was Richard Munday, an amateur who was the first in Rhode Island, and who ranked third in New England after Peter Harrison (see Touro Synagogue, No. 271) and Joseph Brown (see First Baptist Church, Providence, No. 260). The design is quite similar to that of Old North Church, Boston, built two years before, but carried out all in frame rather than in brick and wood. It is believed that the designs of both were derived from some design by Christopher Wren for a London church, but the conjecture arises from similarity to several such churches, and it seems to have been a matter of influence rather than of copying any one exactly. The two are the only colonial churches to use square columns, and the use of superimposed orders is rare. The columns of the lower order here, supporting the gallery, are paneled, and those of the upper order, supporting the vaulted ceiling, are fluted.

In 1762 the church was enlarged by dividing the body and moving the back section. During the Revolution, after the British had occupied Newport, when the Continental troops re-entered the city they destroyed the royal coat of arms which had hung on the church wall. Otherwise the interior remains substantially as it was. There is a three-deck pulpit; the lower desk was for announcements by the clerk, the middle one for reading the lessons, and the one at the top for the sermon. The organ was presented in 1733 by George Berkeley, Lord Bishop of Cloyne, who had been received warmly by the rector and congregation in 1729, when his ship on a voyage to Bermuda was driven by a storm to seek refuge in the harbor. He had offered the organ to the church at Berkeley, Massachusetts, but they had rejected it as "an instrument of the devil for trapping men's souls."

A colorful warden of the church was Godfrey Malbone, an ardent Anglican and Tory, and a wealthy merchant and operator of vessels engaged in commerce and privateering. There were stories of lavish parties given, after successful voyages, for buccaneers at his home in Newport. The hazards of his bold operations and the increasing antagonism to England and Tories caused severe financial losses to the Malbone fortune. Two of his new ships sailed from Newport and were lost, his property in Newport was destroyed by mobs, and his new residence, designed by Peter Harrison and one of the finest in the colonies, was burned during a large dinner party. When servants reported that the house was on fire, Malbone declared that he might lose his house but he would not lose his dinner, and the party was moved to the lawn, where they dined while the house burned to the ground. Because of the financial losses, when his son, Godfrey Malbone, Jr., returned from Oxford, where they both were educated, he sent the young man to manage his large land holding at Brooklyn, Connecticut. There the son built another Trinity Church, which has been called the Malbone Church (No. 4).

268

Sabbath Day Meeting House (1729)

82 Touro Street, Newport, Newport County, Rhode Island

The first congregation of the Sabbatarian sect, or Seventh Day Baptist Church, was organized at Newport in 1671 by Stephen Mumford. It was one of the several groups resulting from the insistence of Baptists on freedom in affairs of religion. The seventh day was the Sabbath in the Old Testament, and it is observed as such not only by Jews but by some Christian churches (see Ephrata Cloister, No. 243).

The second and present meeting house was built of wood in 1729, under the supervision of Jonathan Sabin and Henry Collins, a founder of the Redwood Library (designed by Peter Harrison). It replaced an earlier building on the same site. It is the oldest church of the Seventh Day Baptists still standing in America. The design is supposed to have been drawn by Richard Munday, the designer of Trinity Church (No. 267), and the plane marks reveal that the two buildings had the same workmen. By 1835 the Sabbatarians had died out in Newport, and the church thereafter was used by various groups. In 1884 the Newport Historical Society bought the wooden structure and moved it from Barney Street to Touro Street. In 1915 the building was moved to the back of the lot and incorporated with the building of the Society, and since then it has been a museum for the early Newport collection. The walls of the old frame meeting house were bricked over to preserve them, and the original structure

is enclosed. The clock, which was made for the church in 1731 by William Claggett, hangs on the front of the gallery in its original place facing the pulpit, and with its original works it still keeps time. The original box pews have been retained, but they have been moved to the sides of the room.

269

Dr. Hopkins' Meeting House (1729)
First Congregational Church

83 Mill Street, Newport, Newport County, Rhode Island

The Congregationalists organized the First Church in Newport about 1720. Their first meeting house stood on Tanner Street (now West Broadway). The second building of three, which became known as Dr. Hopkins' Meeting House, was erected in 1729. It was designed by Cotton Palmer of Taunton, Massachusetts. Originally the building had a steeple, but in the 1820's it was sawed loose and pulled down by a group of a hundred people including the pastor, and in its place pinacles were erected at the corners.

There was a schism in the congregation caused by Nathaniel Clapp, the first pastor, who considered his congregation unworthy of receiving Communion. When he had not served Communion for three years, but gave them figs saying, "A fig for you all," a group withdrew from the church. They formed the Second Congregational Society and, in 1733, built a meeting house on Clarke Street. The two Congregational groups reunited later and built a third meeting house, near this one on Mill Street. The original cornerstone from the meeting house here, bearing the

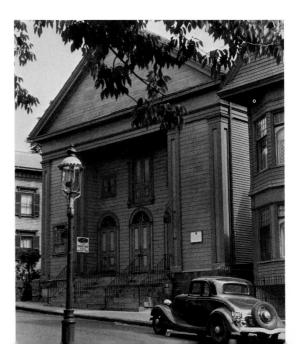

inscription "For Christ and Peace," is now in the basement of that new Congregational Church. The building on Clarke Street was taken over by Baptists (see No. 270), and the one here on Mill Street was used in 1835 by the first congregation of Unitarians in Newport. Later it was used by Episcopalians, and still later by Roman Catholics of the northern part of the city. In the photograph it is the Knights of Columbus Hall.

The meeting house got its name from Dr. Samuel Hopkins, who served here as pastor of the First Church from 1770 until his death in 1803. He had been graduated from Yale College in 1741 and studied divinity at Northampton, Massachusetts, under Jonathan Edwards, who, with George Whitefield, aroused America in the revival known as the Great Awakening. Hopkins maintained close relations with his teacher, and during his pastorate of twenty-six years (1743-1769) at the Sheffield North Parish Church (now Great Barrington, see No. 108), he was largely responsible for Edwards being called to serve as pastor of the Congregational Church at the neighboring town of Stockbridge (1751-1758). During that period in the Berkshires, Hopkins aroused opposition to his theology, and he was dismissed before coming to the church here. Through his work, study, and preaching he developed a theology which became known as the Hopkinsian theology, and he was considered to be as able a preacher as his more famous teacher. From 1776 to 1780, during the British occupation of Newport, he preached at Newburyport, Massachusetts, and at Canterbury (see No. 2) and Stamford, Connecticut, and then returned to the First Church here. Hopkins was the first Congregational minister in New England to take a firm position against slavery, although he had been a slave owner. The law of 1774 which prohibited the importation of Negro slaves into Rhode Island, and the law of 1784 which declared to be free all children born of slaves in Rhode Island, were largely the results of his persistent efforts against strong opposition.

270

Second Congregational Church (1733)
Second Baptist Church

15 Clarke Street, Newport, Newport County, Rhode Island

When the schism occurred in the First Congregational Society at the church on Mill Street (see Dr. Hopkins' Meeting House, No. 269), the

group that withdrew formed the Second Congregational Society, and built this meeting house on Clarke Street in 1733. Like the building on Mill Street, this one was designed by Cotton Palmer, and their original plans were quite similar; both had the main entrance on the long south side, which was common practice in the eighteenth century, and a tower and steeple.

Many changes have been made in this building. From 1758 to the Revolution, the pastor was Dr. Ezra Styles, who records in his diary that his was the first church to be equipped with "Dr. Franklin's lightning rods." The parsonage built for Dr. Styles still stands directly across the street from the church. During the British occupation of Newport the building was used as a barracks, and as the British had less regard for dissenting churches than for the Church of England, the pews, pulpit, and fixtures were destroyed.

As Rhode Island was founded by Baptists, Congregationalism was never as strong here as it was in the neighboring colonies of Massachusetts and Connecticut, where it was established by law. The Second Congregational Society reunited with the First Church, and they built a new meeting house not far from the old one on Mill Street. In 1847 the meeting house here was bought by the Second Baptist Church, which had been organized in 1656. They made major alterations and repairs to the building. The steeple was cut down to a stump, and the Greek Revival front and gingerbread trim were installed. It has been called the Central Baptist Church, and it is used by a congregation of United Baptists.

Touro Synagogue (1759)
Congregation Jeshuat Israel
(Salvation of Israel)

72 Touro Street, Newport, Newport County, Rhode Island

Touro Synagogue is the only colonial synagogue in the United States. The building was begun in 1759 and dedicated in 1763. In the Western Hemisphere it is antedated only by Mikveh Israel Synagogue in Curaçao (Dutch West Indies), consecrated in 1732, and by Zedek ve Shalom Synagogue in Paramaribo, Surinam (Dutch Guiana), dedicated in 1737. The congregation at Newport was the second to be gathered in the American colonies, after one in New York City. The first synagogue in the colonies was built in New York, but it no longer stands.

All the Jews who came to colonial America were Sephardic Jews (see Chapter V). The Sephardic Jews differed from those who went to Germany, Poland, and Russia, in that they enjoyed five hundred years of equality and freedom as allies of the Moors who conquered the Spanish kingdoms. That epoch of freedom came to an end in 1492, when Ferdinand and Isabella reconquered Granada, the last of the Spanish kingdoms held by the Moors, and relied on the Inquisition to Christianize the Moors and Jews or eliminate them. In the same year, Christopher Columbus concluded the agreement with their Catholic majesties, and sailed on the voyage that opened the New World. By a peculiar irony of history, the sovereigns who drove the Jews again from their homes or persecuted them, at the same time opened new lands to them. Many of the Jews went to England and to liberal Holland, where Amsterdam became their home base, and many went with the Dutch to settle in Brazil (until the Portuguese reconquered it from the Dutch), in Dutch Guiana, and in the Dutch West Indies. Most of those who came to America were prosperous merchants, and they established communities in the ports and trading centers of New York, Newport, Charleston, Savannah, Philadelphia, Baltimore, and Richmond. The Jews of the other colonies came to regard Newport as the mother community.

Those who remained in Spain and Portugal, and saved their lives by professing Christianity, were known as Marranos. Some of the community in Newport had been Marranos, who here were able to resume the open practice of Judaism, and many more came from Curaçao and other Dutch lands. After the colony had been founded by Roger Williams, in 1636, on the principle of liberty of conscience, the code of laws drafted in 1647 concluded, ". . . all men may walk as their consciences persuade them, every one in the name of his God. And let the saints of the Most High walk in this colony without molestation in the name of Jehovah their God, forever and ever." Such assurance was an open invitation to the Sephardic Jews, and within eleven years, by 1658, there were a few in Newport. In the yard here there is a monument with a bronze tablet bearing an inscription quoting in part from the Rhode Island Charter of 1663: "Dedicated to the principle that all and everye person and persons may from tyme to tyme and at all tymes hereafter freelye and fullye have and enjoye his and theire owne judgments and consciences in matters of Religious concernments." In 1677 the "Jews and their Nation Society or Friends" purchased a plot of land for a burial ground, located at the head of Jews' Street (now Bellevue Avenue). It became the subject of Henry Wadsworth Longfellow's poem "The Jewish Cemetery at Newport." In 1684 the protection promised in the code of laws and the charter was threatened, and it was tested by a petition of Simon Mendez and David Brown, of this community. The General Assembly declared, ". . . they may expect as good protection here as any strangers being not of our nation residing among us, in His Majesty's colony, ought to have, being obedient to His Majesty's laws."

With this renewed assurance, the community was augmented by new arrivals, particularly by a large group from Curaçao toward the end of the seventeenth century. From 1700 until the Revolution, the Jews of Newport were active in the development of trade, shipping, manufacturing, and the cultural life of Newport. They owned shops and stores, they introduced the manufacture of soap, Castile soap, and spermaceti candles; they manufactured potash and snuff, and they worked in foundries of iron and brass. They served in the French and Indian War and in the Revolution, and they supported fully the cause of the colonies. The Philosophical Society was succeeded by the Redwood Library as a center of culture in Newport, and in 1747 among the early members were Abraham Hart, Moses Lopez, and Jacob Rodriguez Rivera of this community.

During all this time their services of worship were held in private homes. Finally in 1759, on a lot on Griffin Street (now Touro Street), the cornerstone was laid, and Aaron Lopez and Rivera laid the first two stones of the foundation of the present brick building. The design was by Peter Harrison. Fiske Kimball, the late director of the Philadelphia Museum of Art and an authority on Colonial architecture, declared Harrison to be "the prince of Colonial amateur architects." Harrison, who was born in England in 1716, settled in Newport in 1740, where he prospered as an importer. His work in architecture was done without pay. He designed the Redwood Library (1748) and the Brick Market (1761) in Newport, in addition to King's Chapel, Boston (No. 95), and Christ Church, Cambridge (No. 98), both in Massachusetts, and the residence of Godfrey Malbone (see Trinity Church, No. 267). The synagogue

was four years in the building. On the first day of Hanukah, December 2, 5523 (1763), it was dedicated in a service performed by the rabbi, Dr. Isaac de Abraham Touro, and the Books of the Laws were deposited in the Ark. One of the scrolls, which is about four centuries old, was brought from Spain during the Inquisition.

The square building with an ell, of brick painted tan, has remained unchanged in the exterior or interior. The architecture is in the Spanish style of Sephardic synagogues of which the mother synagogue (1675) is in Amsterdam. The Ark is a beautiful Georgian cupboard drawn from a plate of Batty Langley's *Treasury of Designs* (1745), which Harrison used also for the altar piece in King's Chapel, Boston. According to Kimball, the scheme of the interior and the panel above the Ark, containing the Ten Commandments, were based on designs of William Kent,

the great English amateur, which were engraved in Isaac Ware's *Designs of Inigo Jones and Others* (1745), and other details were drawn from James Gibbs. "All of these," Kimball wrote, "were combined with rare sense of harmony and proportion." The Ark is in the wall at the east end of the building, and with that end facing due east, the building stands at an angle to Touro Street. The seats are along the north and south walls, at right angles to the Ark, and the "banco," or raised seat for the presiding officer, is at the middle of the north wall. The reading desk is in the center, and there is open space between it and the Ark. Five large candelabra hang from the ceiling, as does the lamp with the perpetual light before the Ark. Men use the ground floor; there are galleries for women on three sides, supported by twelve columns of superimposed orders, Corinthian over Ionic, which are said to represent the twelve tribes of Israel.

The Revolution and the British occupation of Newport dispersed the Jewish community, closed the synagogue, and dealt a blow to the city from which it has never recovered. The Reverend Isaac Touro went to Jamaica and died there. His widow returned with the two sons, Abraham and Judah, but even after the Revolution not enough Jews returned to hold regular services. During the visit of General George Washington to Newport in 1781, a town meeting was held here. In that year the General Assembly of Rhode Island convened its first session in the synagogue, and it continued to meet here until 1784. During that period the State Supreme Court held sessions here. In August of 1790, when President Washington was in Newport, testing public opinion and arousing interest in national government, he visited the synagogue. He was presented with an address on behalf of the congregation by Moses Seixas, who was Grand Master of the Freemasons in Rhode Island. Washington replied in a letter of August 21 addressed to the Hebrew congregation, in which he said: "The citizens of the United States of America have a right to applaud themselves for having given to mankind examples of an enlarged and liberal policy: a policy worthy of imitation. All possess alike liberty of conscience and immunities of citizenship."

A quorum of ten was required to hold services, and in the first half of the nineteenth century there still was not a quorum in the community. In 1822 Moses Lopez, the last of the old community, left Newport. In 1850 the synagogue was opened temporarily for services by descendants of the second, third, and fourth generations. In 1883 the community was reorganized, and the synagogue was reopened. Since that time the development has been continuous.

In the ell of the building is the oven, where unleavened bread was baked. Also in the ell hangs a Gilbert Stuart portrait of Abraham Touro (1774-1822), the eldest son of the Reverend Isaac Touro. In the Redwood Library, which was among the many beneficiaries of the subject's generosity, hangs a portrait, by an unknown artist, of Judah Touro (1775-1854), the second son. The latter was born on June 16, the eve of the Battle of Bunker Hill, and he and Amos Lawrence of Boston provided the funds for finishing the Bunker Hill Monument, which was dedicated in 1843. Although Judah lived and died in New Orleans, Newport and Touro Synagogue as well as Louisiana received a number of his benefactions. In accordance with his wish, his remains were brought here to be buried in the Jewish Cemetery. The city declared a public funeral, and it is said to have been the most impressive function in Newport since the funeral of Commodore Oliver Hazard Perry (Battle of Lake Erie).

In 1947 Touro Synagogue was rededicated as a National Historic Site by the National Park Service of the Department of the Interior. This was the fourth house of worship to be so designated, the others being San José Mission, near San Antonio, Texas; Gloria Dei (Old Swedes' Church), Philadelphia, Pennsylvania (No. 202); and St. Paul's Church, Eastchester, New York (No. 177). The bronze tablet on the south wall, which was unveiled upon that occasion, quotes from Washington's letter to the congregation in 1790, ". . . happily the Government of the United States . . . gives to bigotry no sanction, to persecution no assistance." Kimball wrote: "The little building, lovingly preserved, is well worthy of its status as a National Monument, one of the most perfect works of Colonial architecture."

272

Portsmouth Friends Meeting House (1700)

Portsmouth County, Rhode Island

Portsmouth was the first settlement on Aquidneck Island (Rhode Island). It was settled in 1638 by William Coddington, John Clarke and Anne Hutchinson, who purchased the island. Anne was a leader in the Antinomian dispute in Boston, where she was tried and banished for fomenting opposition to the authorities on questions of the law in religion. After a year in Portsmouth, where they were dissatisfied, Coddington and Clarke withdrew, in 1639, and moved from this northern end of the island eight miles to the other end, where they settled Newport. At the new settlement, the first meetings of Friends were held in Coddington's house (see Newport Friends Meeting House, No. 266).

In 1692 a stone residence was purchased here, on what has since been known as Quaker Hill. In it the first meeting of Friends in this community was held the following year. In 1699 the site was prepared for the present meeting house. In 1700 the stone house was sold and a new meeting house of frame and shingle was begun. The first record of its use is 1702. An addition built in 1705 was for the "convenience of the women's meeting." Business was conducted through the Rhode Island Monthly Meeting. In 1890 the structure was moved back thirty feet, and the interior was remodeled. The entrance vestibules formerly were separate, but they have been joined to form an additional room. The meeting house was used as a barracks by Hessian soldiers during the occupation of the island by the British during the Revolution. In 1784 a Friends Boarding School was founded here; it was moved to Providence in 1819, where it became the Moses Brown School. Portsmouth Monthly Meeting continues active under Ohio Yearly Meeting.

Conanicut Friends Meeting House (1786)

Conanicut Island, Jamestown County, Rhode Island

There were Friends on Conanicut Island before it was incorporated as a township in 1679, by the Assembly of Rhode Island, and named Jamestown in honor of King James. The island was named for Conanicus, chief of the Narragansett Indians. He was visited here in 1636 by Roger Williams, when Williams was seeking land for his group of refugees from Puritan Massachusetts. Two decades later, in 1656, the island was purchased from the Indians by a group of a hundred Friends. Until 1840 the Friends had the only religious organization at Jamestown.

In 1709 Newport Monthly Meeting granted permission for Friends at Jamestown to build a meeting house. The land was given by Ebenezer Slocum to the trustees of the Meeting by a deed dated September 10, 1710, and the deed mentions that a meeting house was then standing on the land. It was located on what is now Cemetery Lane, beside Cedar Cemetery (now the Old Burying Ground). In 1733 Newport Monthly Meeting recorded the desire of Jamestown Friends to build a new meeting house, and on June 27, 1734, it was authorized "to remove the old Meeting House at Jamestown to the place where is appointed to build the new Meeting House and to build an addition of 18 feet Cantew fashion with a Chimney at the end." The site was that of the third and present building as well as the second. The Quakers were driven off the island during the Revolution. In 1775 there was a naval engagement off the shore, and later the British landed at Jamestown in a raid, during which they plundered and burned houses and barns. Most of the Friends then left the island, and when the meeting house was abandoned, soldiers took possession.

The meeting house did not survive the war, and in 1786 the Newport Monthly Meeting recorded: "Friends of Jamestown aforesaid are at Liberty to build a house in the manner proposed (20 by 25 feet of one story) on the Lot where Friends Meeting House used to stand." That new building was the present simple meeting house, which stands amongst pines on the sloping hill overlooking Jamestown. For generations Jamestown has been the summer home of Friends from Philadelphia, and meetings are held only in summer. It is surprising to learn that, at the ocean end of the island, Fort Wetherill was named for a Philadelphia Quaker. But then in Philadelphia we find the Free Quakers Meeting House (No. 212), which was built by "Fighting Quakers" under the direction of Samuel Wetherill, Jr.

SOUTH CAROLINA

		Denomination	Material
274	St. Michael's Church (1752) Charleston, Charleston County	Anglican	Brick
275	Goose Creek Church (c. 1713) Berkeley County	Anglican	Brick
276	Pompion Hill Chapel (1763) Berkeley County	Anglican	Brick
277	Biggin Church (1761) Berkeley County	Anglican	Brick
278	Strawberry Chapel (1725) Berkeley County	Anglican	Brick
279	St. Andrew's Church (1706) Charleston County	Anglican	Brick
280	St. George's Church (1719) Dorchester County	Anglican	Brick
281	Christ Church (1724) Charleston County	Anglican	Brick
282	St. James' Church, Santee (1768) Charleston County	Anglican	Brick
283	Prince George's Church, Winyah (c. 1741) Georgetown, Georgetown County	Anglican	Brick
284	St. Stephen's Church (1767) St. Stephens, Berkeley County	Anglican	Brick
285	St. David's Church (1768) Cheraw, Chesterfield County	Anglican	Wood
286	St. Helena's Church (1724) Beaufort, Beaufort County	Anglican	Brick
287	Old White Church (1726) St. Helena Island, Beaufort County	Anglican	Tapia
288	Sheldon Church (c. 1745) Beaufort County	Anglican	Brick
289	Unitarian Church (1772) Charleston, Charleston County	Congregational	Brick
290	Ebenezer Church (1788) Fairfield County	Presbyterian	Brick

SUMMARY

Anglican	15	Brick	15
Congregational	1	Wood	1
Presbyterian	1	Tapia	1
Buildings	17		17

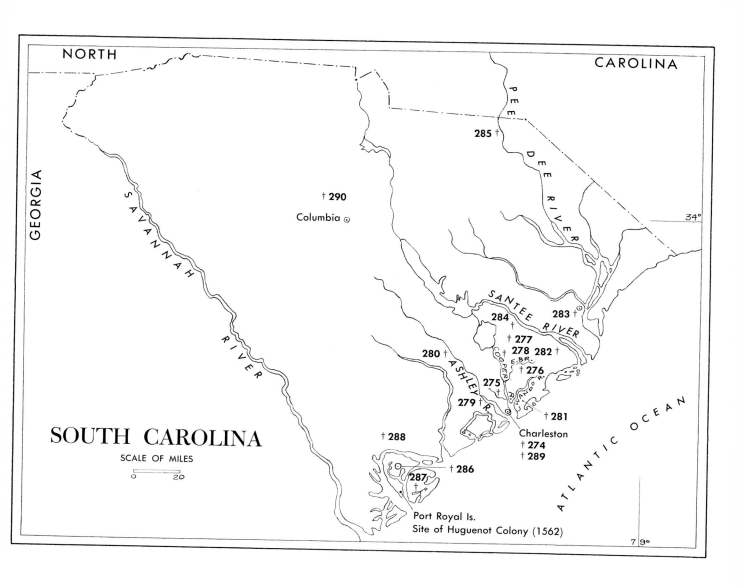

NORTH

CAROLINA

GEORGIA

PEE DEE RIVER

SAVANNAH RIVER

† 285

34°

† 290

Columbia ⊙

SANTEE RIVER

283 †

284

† 277

278 282 †

E.BR.

COOPER R.

† 276

280 †

ASHLEY R.

275
†

279 †

WANDO R.

† 281

† 288

SOUTH CAROLINA

SCALE OF MILES

0   20

Charleston
† 274
† 289

ATLANTIC OCEAN

† 286

287
†

Port Royal Is.
Site of Huguenot Colony (1562)

7 9°

274

St. Michael's Church (1752)

**Broad and Meeting Streets, Charleston,
Charleston County, South Carolina**

St. Philip's Church, built at Charles Town between 1682 and 1690, was the first in Carolina. St. Michael's Church was the second in the town, and it became the mother church from which sprang a number of others in the tidewater region. The original charter for the Province of Carolina was granted, in 1663, by Charles II to eight noble-

men, and it was confirmed by a second charter two years later. Following voyages of exploration along the coast in 1669, the province was established in 1670 with a settlement at the confluence of the Ashley and Cooper rivers. Anthony Ashley Cooper was one of the Lords Proprietors. His secretary, John Locke, devised a "Fundamental Constitution" for governing the province, which provided religious freedom from the beginning. "National religion of all the King's dominion" (the Church of England) was to be followed in Carolina, but freedom of worship was granted to "every church or profession" so long as its members believed in God and His public worship and bore witness to the truth. Should any gathering fail to meet these requirements it was to be "punished as other riots." The religious freedom provided in the constitution of Carolina was equalled only by that of Rhode Island, and Nonconformists flourished together with churchmen of the Established Church and Sephardic Jews (see Touro Synagogue, Newport, R. I., No. 272) in Carolina during the colonial period. There were Anglicans, Baptists, Congregationalists, Huguenots, Jews, Lutherans, Methodists, Presbyterians, Quakers, and Roman Catholics. It was the Dissenters who complained of the toleration of the Established Church in the early eighteenth century, that "at this last Election, Jews, Strangers, Sailors, Servants, Negroes and almost every French man in Craven and Berkeley County came down to elect, and their Votes were taken, and the persons by them voted for were returned to the Sheriff" (Elzas, 25).

As the Anglican Church became the Established Church in the province, the parishes were laid out by acts of the General Assembly, and funds for building were partly appropriated from the public purse. The first Church Act of 1704 was restrictive, barring all but Anglicans from the General Assembly, but in 1706 it was annulled and replaced by one that was satisfactory. This second Church Act made the Church of England the Established Church, and it established nine parishes in Tidewater South Carolina. In those nine parishes, seven colonial houses of worship survive — St. James' Parish, Goose Creek Church (No. 275); St. Thomas' Parish, Pompion Hill Chapel (No. 276); St. John's Church, Berkeley (No. 277), and Strawberry Chapel (No. 278); St. Andrew's Church (No. 279); Christ Church (No. 281); and St. James', Santee (No. 282).

In 1711 the second building of St. Philip's was begun, replacing the original building of black cypress with one of brick, but it was not completed until 1733. No colonial church of St. Philip's Parish survives. The parish continued to grow rapidly with the thriving port of Charles Town. In 1751 the town was divided into two parishes, when the Act of the General Assembly on June 14 established the new St. Michael's Parish, comprising all the town lying south of Broad Street, and ordered St. Michael's Church to be built on the site of the old church of St. Philip's. For a building committee the act designated nine commissioners, a number that reached fifteen through replacement of those who died or resigned before the building was finished, and it was an imposing roster of prominent men: Charles Pinckney, for example, served as attorney general of South Carolina, speaker of the assembly, and Chief Justice. Alexander Van Dussen, of St. James' Parish, Goose Creek, was the commanding colonel of a regiment with General Oglethorpe in the Florida Campaign (1739-1740), and served in the assembly and council. Edward Fenwick, a prosperous planter of John's Island, signed the petition against the Boston Port Bill (London, 1773), and he was well known for his racing stable maintained at Fenwick Hall. William Bull, Jr., of Sheldon Hall and Prince William's Church (No. 288), served as lieutenant governor for sixteen years (1759-1775), following his father's tenure of the same office for seventeen years. Benjamin Smith, a prosperous merchant, was speaker of the house, and though a member of St. Philip's was elected to the vestry of St. Michael's. Othniel Beale commanded the town militia and served as a member and president of the council. Gabriel Manigault, considered to be the richest man in America, served as treasurer of South Carolina. Robert Pringle, another prosperous merchant, served as a lay assistant judge. Thomas Middleton, of Oaks Plantation, commanded a regiment raised against the Cherokees in 1761. Jordon Roche was an Indian trader and a member of that assembly.

The comissioners began immediately in 1751 to make plans for the new church, and to gather materials on the site at Broad and Meeting Streets. On February 17, 1752, the cornerstone was laid by His Excellency the Governor, John Glen, attended by some members of His Majesty's Council and the assembly and the commissioners. In its report of the ceremony, the *Gazette* said: "This Church will be built on the Plan of one of Mr. Gibson's Designs . . ." As no architect named Gibson is known to have been practicing at the time, it has been suggested that the reporter referred

to James Gibbs, whose book of designs, *A Book of Architecture* (London, 1728), was available in America. It contains designs that had been rejected or used for his London churches, such as St. Mary-le-Strand and St. Martin-in-the-Fields. As St. Michael's tower lacks the identifying Gibbs' urns, and the building is less adorned than those of Gibbs, some authorities see the more direct influence of Christopher Wren, with whom Gibbs had studied. The commissioners evidently adopted a general design derived probably from both Gibbs and Wren, and they awarded the building contract to Samuel Cardy.

Materials were imported from England and Holland in slate, glass, iron, and sundry items. Lime was supplied by Isaac Lesesne and by Robert Rivers, on whose plantation there was an Indian midden of oyster shells. Brick was burned by James Withers and at the kilns of Zachariah Villepontoux, at Parnassus Plantation on Back River. The latter made both common and molded brick, including the curved brick for the Tuscan columns of the portico and the special types for cornice and molding. The brick columns, unusual in colonial churches, are comparable with those of St. James', Santee (No. 282), Prince William's, Sheldon (No. 288), and Old White Church (No. 287). The brick walls of St. Michael's, after the building was finished, were rough cast and painted. The builder found that beams would support the slate roof, and the support pillars that had been planned were omitted, giving an open auditorium. The rich wood carving of the interior was done by Henry Burnett. Progress with the building was impeded by several factors — lack of funds, diversion to the building of the new State House diagonally across the street corner, a hurricane that flooded the lower floor and spoiled much of the material, and the French and Indian War. It took eleven years, until December, 1762, to complete the building, and then the commissioners met as a building committee for the last time.

The bells of St. Michael have had a romantic history in the civil and religious life of Charleston. The story is told by Francis S. Rodgers in his book *The Bells of St. Michael's*, and it is the subject of a chapter of seventy-four pages in George W. Williams' definitive book *St. Michael's, Charleston, 1751-1951*. In the minutes of the first vestry meeting, in 1762, plans were recorded for a ring of eight bells, a clock, and an organ. In 1763 the ring of eight bells and the clock were ordered. Lester and Pack, in England, commenced work

at once to cast the bells. The firm was the founder also of the Liberty Bell and of bells for several of the colonial churches in this collection. Betsy Bramfield was born in Charleston on the day that the bells arrived, July 15, 1764, and they were rung for the first time at her baptism on September 21. The thirty-hour clock arrived the same year. The bells pealed with joy, tolled and rang muffled in mourning, struck the time, and sounded alarms for fire and war, besides summoning the parish to worship. St. Michael's Ringers were organized for change ringing, but the practice died out with the eighteenth century.

In 1782 the bells were taken by a British artillery officer as a prize of war and were sent on their second voyage to England, where they were purchased by the successors of Lester and Pack, William Mears and William Chapman. Two of the bells that had been cracked were recast with the mark "Chapman & Mears London faciunt, 1783," and the set was sold and shipped to Charleston in that year. There they were taken at once by the vestry and rehung in the steeple of St. Michael's, with rejoicing but without payment to the purchaser, even after years of appeal. In 1838 the two small bells were cracked and sent to England on the fourth crossing to be recast; they returned on the fifth crossing the same year. During the Civil War the great bell, or "Great Michael," remained in the belfry to sound alarms, while the other seven were sent to Columbia for safe keeping in a shed at the State House. When the city was burned by General William T. Sherman, February 17, 1865, the old State House and shed were burned and the bells were ruined. In the course of a long search after the war, five of the bells were discovered in the ruins, two having disappeared. The five were sent to Charleston, and, together with "Great Michael,"

which had cracked in the course of sounding alarms during the war, they made the sixth voyage of the Atlantic to England. There the complete set was recast by Mears & Stainbank, successors to Lester and Pack, using "the same trammels for making the moulds." On the seventh voyage the ring of eight bells crossed the Atlantic to Charleston, and on March 21, 1867, they chimed "Home Again" and "Auld Lang Syne" from the steeple of St. Michael's.

Robert Cooper, assistant minister at St. Philip's became the first rector of St. Michael's in 1761. He served until two days before the official Declaration of Independence, when he was dismissed for loyalty to the Crown. After the Revolution he returned to Charleston from England and served for two years as rector of St. Philip's. Originally the steeple of St. Michael's was surmounted by the figure of the saint holding a lightning rod as the spear transfixing Satan. It was a symbol both of the victory of the spirit over the power of evil and the survival of the building from the damage of tornado, hurricane, flood, earthquake, war, and the threat of drastic alteration. In 1865 a shell burst in the chancel and destroyed most of the fixtures, and in 1866 the chancel was rebuilt. The tornado of 1885 and the earthquake of 1886 damaged the building. In 1905 Tiffany renovated the chancel again. The hurricane of 1938 did severe damage, which was repaired. In 1818 the cross-aisle was eliminated to gain seats, and other alterations have been made, but in general the building is in its original condition.

At Christmas time in 1949, the steeple of St. Michael's was illuminated at night. The effect was so pleasing that it has been lighted nightly ever since, affording a landmark for ships at sea, as well as a monument of colonial history.

St. James' Church, Goose Creek (c. 1713)
Goose Creek Church

Berkeley County, South Carolina

The Goose Creek Church, which is just off a highway approaching Charleston from the northwest, probably is the best known of the colonial churches around the city. The building is the most interesting of the rural churches, and historically the congregation was the earliest settlement of Anglicans outside of the city. According to Samuel G. Stoney, a warden of St. James' and author of *Plantations of the Carolina Low Country*, a congregation of Barbadians was on Goose Creek in 1685, and these "Goose Creek Men" were the backbone of the party that established the Church of England in the province. The first missionary in South Carolina, and the third in America sent by the Society for the Propagation of the Gospel, Samuel Thomas, came to Goose Creek in 1702, the year after the Society was founded in London. Here he taught Negroes, and in 1703 he reported to the Society that twenty had learned to read and write, using the Bible as a text book. In 1706 the General Assembly passed an act that made the Church of England the Established Church in Carolina, and laid out nine parishes, St. James among them. The congregation here used a wooden building as a church for a number of years, until the present building was erected.

The year in which the present building was begun is not known for certain. Several dates from 1706 to 1714 have been given. The reign of George I began in 1714, and his royal arms still reside behind the pulpit, but it is assumed that the church was begun before his reign, probably about 1713. Queen Anne's War and the Yamasee War of 1715 slowed the work, but finally, in 1719, it was recorded in the journal of the vestry that the building was finished and given the name of St. James' Church. At the same time a pew was awarded to Arthur Middleton, who had promoted the building and given four acres for the parsonage. The building was erected under the first rector of the parish, Francis Le Jau, of Angers, France, who had served as a canon of the Cathedral Church of St. Paul in London.

The building is of brick, rough-cast and tinted pink. It survives substantially in its original design, and it is generally believed that the presence of the royal arms, which still form the reredos, saved the building from desecration during the Revolution. In the earthquake of 1886 the west end, with its main entrance, was completely destroyed, and it has been restored twice, the last time in 1955. The truncated gable of the jerkinhead roof is above this main entrance. The sculpture in the pediment of the doorway is the

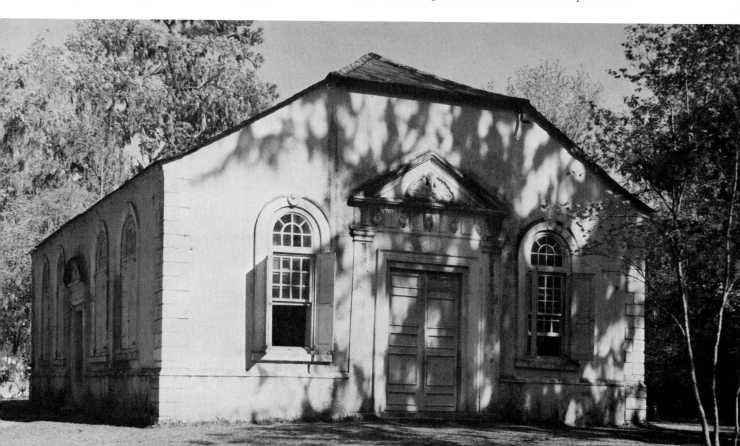

"Pelican in her Piety," the mother bird plucking her breast to care for her young, which was the emblem of the S.P.G. This is probably the fourth sculpture in that place; it was cast in cement from a model made by Stoney, who presented it to the church in memory of his father, whom he succeeded on the vestry. In the key blocks of the window arches are carved heads of cherubs. In addition to the main entrance, there are beautiful doorways on the north and south sides. The quoins add considerable distinction to the building of such small size.

The interior is one of the finest of all the small colonial churches in the country. The main door opens into a vestibule, in which there is a stairway to the gallery. There are box pews against the two side walls and two sections of box pews between, with two side aisles and a central aisle. The central aisle, which is paved with flagstone, runs from the door to the chancel rail, and centered at the end opposite the door, within the chancel, stands the pulpit beneath its sounding board. There is a curved stairway to the pulpit. Behind the pulpit is a shuttered window in a high arched frame. Corinthian pilasters on both sides of the arch support a classic order sur-

mounted by a broken pediment, in the center of which, at the key of the arch, rests the royal arms with the lion and the unicorn. The arched tablet at the right carries the Lord's Prayer and the Creed, the one at the left the Ten Commandments. The walls are white and the woodwork natural.

The vestry of Goose Creek Church was incorporated in 1778. As the Revolution brewed, there was trouble over prayers for the king. On a wall of the church there is a hatchment of Ralph Izard, of which name there was more than one in the parish. The story is told that on one occasion when the rector said the prayer for the king in the Liturgy, instead of responding, "We beseech thee to hear us," Izard cried out, "Good Lord, deliver us!" Soon after, as in many Anglican churches, services were discontinued for the duration of the war.

In 1844 St. Michael's Church paid for repairs to the Goose Creek Church. During the Civil War, the communion silver disappeared. With the growth of Charleston, the congregation here diminished during the years, and now there is only an annual service and an occasional wedding held in the church building.

In the early years of St. James' Parish, there was a chapel of ease located about seven miles below Strawberry ferry. It was a cruciform brick building standing on a glebe of one acre. The land had been presented by a Mr. Dutargue, evidently one of the many French Huguenots in the region. In his *Historical Account of the Protestant Episcopal Church in South Carolina* (1820), Frederick Dalcho records that a date inscribed on a brick appeared to be 1721, and that a road law noted the chapel in 1725. When his book appeared a century later, the chapel was in ruins. In connection with these churches and chapels on the rivers around Charleston, it is interesting that the General Assembly passed an act, in 1731, that gave free passage on all ferries to persons crossing to attend church.

A prominent vestryman of Goose Creek Church was Zachariah Villepontoux, the famous brick maker with kilns at his Parnassus Plantation on Back River. His brick was used in St. Michael's Church and Pompion Hill Chapel.

276

Pompion Hill Chapel (1763)
Parish of St. Thomas and St. Denis

Berkeley County, South Carolina

The first Anglican church outside of Charles Town was built in 1703 on Pompion Hill, a low rise of land on the east bank of the East Branch of the Cooper River, east of the city. It was a building thirty feet square made of cypress, and it served until the present brick chapel was built in 1763. It has been known locally as "Pumpkin (or Punkin) Hill Chapel." In 1706, three years after the first church was built, the Church of England became the Established Church in Carolina, and nine parishes were laid off, of which St. Thomas' Parish was one. At the same time, the lower part of the parish, which included Orange Quarter, a French Huguenot settlement, was divided as the distinct but not separate Parish of St. Denis, another of the nine. French Protestants had settled here about 1680, more than a century after their unsuccessful attempt to found a permanent settlement near Beaufort. The Orange settlement was augmented by the arrival of persecuted Huguenots after Louis XIV had revoked the Edict of Nantes in 1685, and in 1687 they built their first

church, which they named St. Denis for the patron saint of France. In 1707 a brick building was begun which became the Parish Church of St. Thomas and St. Denis, on the northwest side of the Wando River near Cain Hoy (named for ferryman Cain on the Cooper River). That building was destroyed by a forest fire in 1815, and in 1819 it was rebuilt. It was dilapidated when Harry F. Guggenheim acquired the property of his Cain Hoy Plantation, and he restored the church and the old vestry room, a separate building. As this second building of the parish church is not colonial, it is not included in the present collection.

It was unique to have two churches and two parishes in one. The reason for it was that, while the parish of about one hundred twenty families of Huguenots used the Liturgy of the Church of England, they spoke only the French language. Their Church of St. Denis, which was made the parish church, and which became known as the "Old Brick Church" or the "Wando Church," was responsible for the parochial duties only of that congregation. In the act of December 18, 1708, the General Assembly provided that when the language of the service should be changed to English, their church would become the chapel of ease in the Parish of St. Thomas and St. Denis. However, it worked out the other way around —

in 1747 an act declared Pompion Hill to be a "Parochial Chapel of Ease," and the provision for St. Denis to become a chapel was rescinded. In his *Historical Account of the Protestant Episcopal Church in South Carolina* (1820), Frederick Dalcho defines a "parochial" chapel of ease as one with the authority to perform baptism and burial.

In 1736 the vestry of the Parish of St. Thomas and St. Denis was incorporated. The purpose was to execute the trust of Richard Beresford. Land known as "Beresford's Bounty" was bought and a free school was established, which thrived for many years. In 1743 Alexander Garden arrived in the parish and became teacher of languages in the school (no relation to the Bishop's Commissary of the same name, or the one for whom the gardenia was named). In the same year he had been ordained, and the Society for the Propagation of the Gospel appointed him to take charge of the church, succeeding Thomas Hasell, who had served for thirty-five years.

In 1762 the cypress church at Pompion Hill was in ruinous condition, and it was decided to replace it with a brick church. In 1763 Garden wrote to the Society regarding the beginning of the present building, and in 1765 he wrote that it was nearly finished. The brick building, with a slate roof in the jerkin-head style, is in its original condition. On the north and south doors are carved the initials of Zachariah Villepontoux. His brick kilns at Parnassus Plantation on Back River supplied brick also for St. Michael's, Charleston (No. 274). Here and on St. Stephen's Church appears the name of William Axson with Masonic emblems. The floor is laid with brick and tile in a herringbone pattern. The tile and £50 were donated by Gabriel Manigault, treasurer of South Carolina and a commissioner for building St. Michael's. The chancel and pulpit are at opposite ends. High brown pews on the tile floor at the chancel end were used by slaves, and white pews on a raised wooden floor before the carved cedar pulpit were for the masters and their families.

Services were held only in the cool months, as the climate was unhealthy in summer. In 1768, the minister of the French colony, John James Tissot, and the French-speaking parishioners having died, the vestrymen were ordered by Act of Assembly to sell the lands and buildings of the French congregation and to apply the proceeds for the benefit of the poor of the whole parish. In 1784 an act ordered the sale of the two glebes. In recent years services have been held in both of the churches occasionally during the winter months.

St. John's Church (1761)
Biggin Church

near Monck's Corner, Berkeley County, South Carolina

Biggin Hill in Kent, England, evidently gave the name to the hill, the creek, and the church located here, although in the deed the church is said to be situated on Tipicop-Haw Hill. In the community were Huguenots who had settled at an early date, and until the Anglican church was built the inhabitants worshiped at a Huguenot church in the neighborhood. After the Anglican church was built, many Huguenots were in the congregation. The location, near three highways, was convenient to a large area.

St. John's Parish, Berkeley, was one of the nine laid off under the Act of 1706, which established the Anglican Church in the province. A minister was settled here in 1707, but the journals of the vestry before 1725 were burned, and those between 1725 and 1732 were lost. Sir John Colleton gave three acres for the church plot. He was one of the Lords Proprietors, and as a county nobleman of Wadboo Barony he was a landgrave, a designation used under the Fundamental Constitution of Carolina. According to Samuel G. Stoney, in *Plantations of the Carolina Low Country*, in 1712 Colleton sold 110 acres to the parish for the upper glebe, five miles from the church, and later his family sold land for the lower glebe, four miles above Strawberry. In 1710 the first church building was begun. In 1755 the building was destroyed by fire, the first of three to beset the church here.

In 1761 the second and present building was erected to replace the burned church, in accordance with the Act of 1756. During the five-year delay, brick and materials were gathered for the new church. It was laid out on a plain rectangle. There were doors in one end and in the middle of both sides. There were thirteen windows. The building served for two decades, and then, in 1681, it was burned by the British. Monck's Corner, four miles away, was a tactical point of importance, and British forces took a stand here. They used the church for storing supplies, and when they were forced to evacuate they set fire to the stores and the building.

After the Revolution the church was repaired. The communion silver had been brought over by Huguenots from La Rochelle, the city that had

been besieged by the forces of Cardinal Richelieu, when it was the last stronghold of the Huguenots in France. During the War of 1861-65, when federal troops were invading the region, Keating Simons Ball buried the silver under a barn on Comingtee Plantation. After the war the treasure could not be located. In 1947, with the aid of a land mine detector, it was discovered. Strawberry Chapel, a chapel of ease built when St. John's, Berkeley, was a large and flourishing parish, and where the Ball family have been faithful members to the present time, now has possession of the silver (see No. 278). The parish dwindled as the city of Charleston grew, and the church became neglected. Toward the end of the century a forest fire burned the building and left only the open brick walls. For years these walls were a source of brick for other uses in the neighborhood; in recent years the raids on the property have been stopped, and the remaining ruins are the only monument to a once thriving parish church. Near the walls can be seen the tomb of Sir John Colleton III, great-grandson of the Lord Proprietor of the Province of Carolina.

278

Strawberry Chapel (1725)

Berkeley County, South Carolina

The Province of Carolina originally was divided into three large counties, and the central one, Berkeley, contained Charles Town. When St. John's Parish was laid off under the Act of 1706, it covered such a large area that it was impractical for its inhabitants all to attend the parish church, known as the Biggin Church (see No. 277). James Child, a member of the parish, planned a new town to be founded on the east bank of the West Branch of the Cooper River, about eight miles south of the Biggin Church. Here a rise of land known as the Strawberry constituted the only practical ferry landing on that side of the river. The new town took the name of its founder and was called Childbury. The founder's plan and his several legacies provided a grove near the river for a college square, a lot for a free school and house for its master, an acre and a half for a church or chapel, and a sum of money for their support. Of these buildings planned, the school was built and was active for some time, and the chapel was built. In addition, the town achieved a tavern, fifteen houses, and five streets — Craven, Church, Ferry, Mulberry, and Bay — but it failed to grow, and today only the chapel remains. The name Childbury has disappeared, and the chapel carries the name of the river bluff. Protruding from the trunk of a large cypress by the river, there is a weathered board which once was nailed to the trunk of the tree to display the ferry tolls at Strawberry Landing. An act of 1731 provided that ferry service to churchgoers would be free.

With subscriptions from the parishioners, the chapel building was begun in 1725. When the building was completed, the Act of December 9 of that year provided for "founding and establishing a Parochial Chapel of Ease at Childbury to the Parish Church in St. John's Parish." It ordered "the Rector or Minister to preach there every fourth Sunday but not oftener." In connection with this chapel, Frederick Dalcho (1769-1836), a clergyman who served as assistant at St. Michael's, Charleston, in his *Historical Account of the Protestant Episcopal Church in South Carolina*, (1820), defined a "parochial" chapel as follows: "Chapels of Ease, according to the original meaning of the term, are not now known in this country. In England there is a distinction between a Chapel of Ease, and a Parochial Chapel of Ease. Chapels of Ease are founded for the convenience of the people in large parishes, in attending Public Worship, where they live at a distance from the Parish Church, to which, however, the Sacraments and Burials are restricted. Parochial Chapels of Ease possess the parochial rights of baptising and burying, but have neither Rectory nor Endowment. The Curate or Vicar of both, is dependent on the Parochial Minister. To preserve this parochial dependence, a reservation is made of repairing to the Parish Church, on the great festival days. This explains the Sections in several Acts of Assembly founding Chapels of Ease in South Carolina, wherein Christmas Day, Easter Day, and Whitsunday are exclusively reserved for the service of the Parish Church." Strawberry Chapel was for the convenience of the inhabitants in the Lower Beat of the large parish. In the upper part of the parish, twenty-five miles from the Biggin Church, the settlers had built a log house of worship at what has been called Chapel Hill since that time. In 1770 the assembly passed an act providing for the building of a chapel there, behind the Forty-five Mile House at Markeley's Old Field, but the building does not stand.

Strawberry Chapel stands today substantially as it was built, with the later addition of a vestry room off the side opposite the main entrance. The brick walls are covered with stucco. The roof, like that at Pompion Hill (No. 276), is in the jerkinhead style. There has been little change in the unpaved road, which winds through the woods of live oaks and semitropical growth past Wadboo Bridge and to the chapel. Because of the condition of the road, for burials in the chapel yard transport often was made by way of the river to Strawberry Landing. Among those buried here are members of the Ball family. It was Keating Simons Ball who had buried, in 1865, the communion silver of the parish church, which had been brought from La Rochelle, France, by Huguenots, to be rediscovered only in 1947 and taken into the possession of Strawberry Chapel. The photograph was made when we attended one of the occasional services here, with members of the Ball family. After the service the congregation had a basket lunch in the chapel yard. When our lunch was spread on the horizontal tombstone inscribed with the name Ball, we could appreciate Mrs. Ball's earlier remark; "When we go to Strawberry Chapel, we have lunch on grandfather." Among the prominent men who were associated with Strawberry Chapel, and whose names appear in the old vestry books, were Henry Laurens (1724-1792), who served as a member of the first provincial congress of South Carolina, and as president of the Continental Congress succeeding John Hancock, and who from 1780 was imprisoned in the Tower of London for fifteen months during the Revolution; General William Moultrie (1730-1805), who defended Charleston during the Revolution, and for whom the fort is named; Thomas Broughton, who served as lieutenant governor from 1735 to 1737, during the Royal Period; and Francis Marion, the Revolutionary general known as the "Swamp Fox."

279

St. Andrew's Church (1706)

Charleston County, South Carolina

St. Andrew's is the oldest church building of the Episcopal Establishment in South Carolina, having been begun in 1706, the year in which an act of the General Assembly established the Anglican Church and laid off nine parishes. The original Parish of St. Andrew covered a vast area — it was bounded by St. James' Parish, Goose Creek; the Atlantic Ocean; the Stono River; Colleton County; and Berkeley County. In 1717 the upper part of the parish was laid off to form St. George's Parish, Dorchester (No. 280). St. Andrew's is situated on the west side of the Ashley River, and as it is beside the road from Charleston to Middleton Place, one of the main tourist

attractions of the area, it is better known than the isolated churches in the Cooper River area east of the city.

The church was built as a rectangle of forty by twenty-five feet. The "supervisors" of the construction were John Fitch and Thomas Rose; their initials are inscribed on a red tile, together with the date 1706, at the end of the transept toward the Ashley River. In her book, *Architects of Charleston*, Beatrice St. Julien Ravanel gives accounts of both builders, and notes that Rose made brick. The transepts and choir were added in 1723, to provide more room for the growing congregation. The additions made the building cruciform, and brought the dimensions to fifty-two by forty feet. In the west end a gallery originally provided seats for people who had no pew; later it was used by "People of Colour." The original plan called for a steeple, but it was never built. The building was burned to the brick walls in 1764; with funds raised by popular subscription, it was restored promptly. In 1855 the interior was refinished in the style then in fashion.

In the early days of St. Andrew's Parish, missionaries from the Society for the Propagation of the Gospel worked among the Negroes, as they did at Goose Creek. With both Negro and white members from plantations on the Ashley and the large area in the parish, the congregation grew, and the church became fashionable. It went through the periods of difficulty during the Revolution and the early Republic, and it was in a state of decline in the first half of the present century. In 1949 the building was renovated, and thereafter St. Andrew's Church resumed the status of a fully active parish.

280

St. George's Church (1719)

Dorchester, Dorchester County, South Carolina

There was a continuity from the town and church at Dorchester, England, through those in Massachusetts, South Carolina, and Georgia. There is an outline of the history in connection with the Midway Church in Georgia (No. 30). In 1630 a group of Puritan Congregationalists, with Presbyterian leanings, left England and sailed for Massachusetts. In 1695 under the leadership of Joseph Lord, a group that had stemmed from the church at Dorchester, Massachusetts, formed a congregation at Charlestown, Massachusetts, and moved here to the Ashley River. On the east side of the river, about eighteen miles north of Charles Town, they settled the third town of Dorchester, and Lord remained as pastor for more than twenty years. About 1700 they built a brick meeting house, thirty feet square, situated about a mile out of Dorchester on the road to Charles Town. In 1752, when the mosquito was winning the competition for this territory, a large number of families of the Congregationalists moved to Georgia, where they settled the fourth Dorchester and founded the Midway Church.

When the Church of England was established in the province, in 1706, and nine new parishes were founded, this section was in the Parish of St. Andrew (No. 279). By Act of Assembly in 1717, the upper part of St. Andrew's Parish was laid off to form the new Parish of St. George, named for the patron saint of England. In 1719 building the Parish Church of St. George was begun, and the exterior of the building was finished the following year. The Society for the Propagation of the Gospel supplied the first missionary, Peter Tustian. The brick building was a substantial one of fifty by thirty feet, with the chancel in addition. A brick parsonage was built, and a glebe of 145 acres of land was provided. Noting the growth of the town, in 1723 an Act of Assembly was passed "for settling a Fair and Markets in the Town of Dorchester, in Berkeley County, being a Frontier in that part of the country." By 1733 the church building was in such a condition that an act was passed to build a new one, but in 1734 it was repaired and enlarged and pewed. Also in that year a free school was incorporated. The tower (which is the only remaining evidence of a once thriving town), and a steeple were added in 1753, and a ring of bells was installed.

The town covered about forty-eight acres, with surrounding farm land in addition. A town map of 1742 shows all the streets and houses. On the river bank there were shelters for trading with the Indians, who brought skins and fresh-water pearls to trade for beef. By 1789, when St. George's was incorporated, Dorchester had declined. In his *Historical Account of the Protestant Episcopal Church in South Carolina*, Frederick Dalcho reports that a lecture was appointed "to be preached annually on St. George's Day, by an Episcopal minister, at the Parish Church of St. George's, Dorchester," and that it had been delivered every year until within a few years of the publication of his book in 1820. He said also that the church building was then in a state of dilapidation; it had no altar, priest, or congregation, and the parish register and journals were lost, but there was a handsome service of communion plate. Over a period of years, as families moved away for reasons of health or income, Dorchester declined and died. Today it is only one of the many colonial ghost towns, where the ruin of the church is the only monument to recall the history of a thriving community. The brick tower here faces the Ashley River. Near by, on the river bank, is the ruin of Fort Dorchester, which was built, of tapia masonry, as an outpost for the defense of Charleston against the British in the Revolution. It is now in the custody of the Colonial Dames.

Christ Church (1724)

Charleston County, South Carolina

The Parish of Christ Church was one of the nine laid out under the Act of Assembly of 1706, which established the Church of England in the province. The foundations for the first building were laid the following year, 1707, at a location east of Charleston Harbor and near the Atlantic Ocean. The town of Mount Pleasant, west of the church, grew as a summer resort for the people of the Low Country to the north, where marshes and mosquitoes made it unhealthy in summer. In those parishes of the Cooper River area, church services were not held in summer, for the planters and their families sought relief in the pine highlands or near the coast.

The first church building was not finished for some time after 1707. The parish church suffered two fires, and many of the records were lost. The earliest record of church officers was in 1708, when the two wardens were elected, David Maybank and Henry Gill, and the first clergyman, Edward Marston, was called. In 1724 that building was accidently destroyed by fire. With a grant from the assembly and private contributions, the present church promptly was built of brick. The brick walls were roughcast, i.e., covered with stucco. The length of time required to finish the building is indicated in the record of 1729: "At a Vestry was ordered drawn on all yt Subscribed to ye rufcasting of ye Church." (Here we see the letter "y" used to replace the thorn, a rune for the sound "th"; "yt" is the clerk's shorthand for "that.")

When the building is free of debt and can be given to God, the consecration of a church is performed by a bishop, but in the colonies there were no American Episcopal bishops. In 1727 the new church here was dedicated, and Frederick Dalcho, in his *Historical Account of the Protestant Episcopal Church in South Carolina*, defines the occasion as follows: "Before the establishment of the Episcopate in America, our churches could not be consecrated. They could be set apart for Public Worship, and declared to be secluded from all secular uses. . . . The first church consecrated in South Carolina was St. Paul's, Colleton, January 10, 1818." The church here was consecrated, by Bishop W. B. W. Howe, on Sunday, December 27, 1874. The day was the Sunday nearest Christ-mas, and the church was consecrated in the name of Christ.

In 1782 this building was burned to the brick walls by the British. A house of one of the church officers was burned also, and with it were lost some of the parish books and journals and communion plate. The church was rebuilt within the old brick walls. In 1787 the church was incorporated. The wooden steeple rising from the center of the hip roof was built in 1835 and heightened in 1838. During the War Between the States, the building was used by troops and badly damaged. After the war it was repaired. In 1924 the church was completely restored by John F. Maybank, a descendant of the first senior warden. In the churchyard is an old vestry building. It was used for meetings and for sheltering the servants who looked after the horses or parishioners during services. The building was repaired and in recent years has been used for Sunday school.

282

St. James' Church, Santee (1768)
Wambaw Church

Charleston County, South Carolina

St. James' Parish, Santee, was one of the nine laid out under the Church Act of 1706. The Santee River drains the area to the east of the Cooper River. The parish originally covered the area on both sides of the Santee, extending from the coast inland to include the present Parish of St. Stephen (No. 284) and northeast to include the present Parish of Prince George, Winyah (No. 283). The lower parish was settled by French Huguenot refugees after the Revocation of the Edict of Nantes in 1685. The section was known as the French Settlement, or French Santee. When the upper parish was laid off and St. Stephen's Parish was founded, in 1754, that parish became known as the English Santee. On the other side of the Santee, Prince George's Parish, Winyah, was founded in 1721, when it was laid off from St. James', Santee.

The church of the Huguenots at James Town, a frame building on a brick foundation, was made the first Parish Church of St. James. It does not

survive. During the succeeding years, in efforts to suit the convenience of the inhabitants of the large parish, four other houses of worship were built. In 1714 an Act of Assembly ordered the erection of a parochial chapel of ease at Echaw, in Craven County. It did not prove to be useful and was abandoned. Chapels were ordered built in both the upper and lower parish. That in this lower parish was built in 1742, near the chapel of ease at Echaw. When St. Stephen's Parish was set off, this second chapel at Echaw was declared to be the Parish Church of St. James', Santee. The location in a corner of the parish was inconvenient for the majority of the parishioners. Upon application to the assembly, an act was passed in 1768 directing that a new church be built near the Wambaw Bridge to serve as the parish church of St. James', Santee, and the Echaw church was to become the chapel of ease. That building at Echaw does not survive. The situation of the present brick building, on the south side of Wambaw Creek, which flows easterly into the Santee, led to its being called the Wambaw Church.

The design of this building is graceful and interesting. It is unfortunate that the original design was altered to disorient the chancel and to place it at the north side instead of at the east end. To accomplish the change, the portico and apse are now on the sides instead of the ends, the chancel was moved away from the Palladian window, which was designed to light the communion table; the north aisle was blocked, and the long axis was lost. Possibly the original design might be restored some day. The Greek portico, with columns made of brick molded specially to form the design, is similar to that at the Sheldon Church (No. 288). At the occasional services here, the old folio Bible and Book of Common Prayer are brought out. They were donated by the Revolutionary heroine Rebecca Brewton Motte, widow of Jacob Motte of the French Huguenot family De la Motte. After he had died, leaving their plantation burdened with debt, the house was occupied by the British and fortified. Generals Francis Marion and Henry Lee besieged Fort Motte but hesitated to burn the building, out of consideration for Mrs. Motte, who was living in one of the farm houses. She encouraged them to fire it with an African bow and arrows which she provided, and when the fire forced the surrender of the garrison she gave a banquet for the officers of both sides. On credit, she bought land here on the Santee, developed a fortune, and paid off all of her late husband's debts. Another of the many prominent parishioners was Thomas Lynch, Jr., a signer of the Declaration of Independence.

283

Prince George's Church, Winyah (c. 1741)

Highmarket and Broad Streets, Georgetown, Georgetown County, South Carolina

An Act of Assembly in 1721 laid off from St. James' Parish, Santee, the section northeast of the Santee River and founded Prince George's Parish, Winyah (or Winyaw). The new parish was bounded by the Atlantic Ocean, the Santee River, the Cape Fear River, and extended "Westward as far as it shall be inhabited by his majesty's subjects." The first church was begun in 1726, a wooden building located at Brown's Ferry, twenty miles from Georgetown. In 1734 this parish in turn was divided, and the Parish of Prince Frederick was founded. The new parish included the parish church, and a church had to be built in the remaining Parish of Prince George. In 1767 another part of the Parish of Prince George was laid

off to form the Parish of All Saints, Waccamaw, extending from the sea to the Waccamaw River.

In 1735, after the first of these two divisions had taken place, the church was ordered to be built for Prince George's Parish. The land for the church was given by William Scriven, the first Baptist minister in Carolina. His son, Elisha Scriven, laid out the town of Georgetown, with its wide streets. In 1736 there was a subscription for the building fund, and in 1741 an Act of Assembly provided for paying part of the costs with duties levied on all imports of liquor in Georgetown for three years. The building has a semicircular apse. Its curvilinear gable in Jacobean style can be seen behind the tower. The interior was burned during the Revolution and repaired after the war. The tower was added in 1820. The gallery and organ were installed shortly before 1820. The communion silver, which is still in use, was donated in 1750 by a clergyman, Thomas Morritt.

284

St. Stephen's Church (1767)

St. Stephens, Berkeley County, South Carolina

In the Yamasee War of 1715, the area around St. Stephens was on the frontier, and a garrison was massacred here. By Act of Assembly in 1754, a portion of St. James' Parish, Santee (No. 282), was laid off to form St. Stephen's Parish. The lower part of the parish had been settled by French Huguenots, and it was known as French Settlement, or French Santee. After the division, this upper part became known as English Santee, although there were many French people in the section. The first house of worship in the new St. Stephen's Parish was a wooden building erected as a chapel of ease in the upper Parish of St. James', Santee.

In 1767 the present church was built to replace the old building. The chapel had become decayed, and it was inadequate to accommodate the growing congregation of planters, who were prospering with indigo. Eight years had elapsed since the vestry had first planned this church, in 1759, by ordering brick to be made equal to that of Zachariah Villepontoux, whose brick had gone

into St. Michael's, Charleston (No. 274). The brick made on the first trial was rejected in 1762, as was that resulting from the second, and it was only after the third run that the brick was finally approved that went into this building. The workmanship was of the same meticulous nature. Francis Villepontoux, a member of St. Stephen's and nephew of Zachariah, had worked on Pompion Hill Chapel (No. 276) and here undertook the brick work and most of the building operations. His name and that of A. Howard appear on the building as fellow supervisors. William Axson, who also took part in building Pompion Hill Chapel, was active here, and again, as a member of the Wambaw Lodge of Freemasons, inscribed his name on a brick above the Palladian window of the chancel, together with the insignia of a Master Mason and a Blue Lodge. The Jacobean curvilinear gables are bold in their execution. In order to carry a ceiling designed after that at St. Michael's, the whole roof was made too heavy to be in proportion, but the design of the building has created an effect that is interesting and pleasing. Another distinctive feature of the architecture is the use of Doric pilasters, of which there are six on each side and four on each end. A mahogany pulpit was donated to the church. A large gallery was installed at one end and forty-five pews on a tiled floor. The pewing of the church was not satisfactory to all, and on that account Philip Porcher of Oldfield advised his fellow commissioners for the building that he would cease to be a member, according to a letter quoted in one of the last entries in the vestry book. The journals of the vestry are lost. The communion silver dates from 1759. In 1932 regular services were resumed. Among the Huguenots in the parish was Gabriel Marion, who subscribed to the building fund and, in 1765, served as warden. His brother was General Francis Marion, who became famous as the "Swamp Fox" for his military operations during the Revolution.

285

St. David's Church (1768)

First and Church Streets, Cheraw, Chesterfield County, South Carolina

The Great Pee Dee River flows south from North Carolina and into the Atlantic Ocean at Georgetown. The inhabitants of the Pee Dee section near the present North Carolina border, then in old Craven County, were within the parishes of Prince George, Winyah (No. 283); or Prince Frederick, laid off from Prince George; or St. Marks, laid off from Prince Frederick. By 1768 there were enough inhabitants in this inland region to demand a parish church of their own, and in response to their application the General Assembly passed the Act of 1768 that established the Anglican Parish of St. David. It was named for the patron saint of Wales.

In the same year, 1768, the present church was erected on Cheraw Hill, on the west side of the Pee Dee River. The building of frame on brick foundation measured fifty-three by thirty by sixteen feet. It is in the New England colonial style, with arched windows and a cove ceiling. After five years it finally was completed in 1773, at a cost of £2,600. During the Revolution, in 1780, the British under Lord Cornwallis used the building as a hospital; fifty soldiers died of smallpox and were buried beside the church. During the Civil War there was a skirmish at the near-by bridge over the Pee Dee River, in which the Federal troops were led by Generals Benjamin Harrison and James Garfield, both of whom became

Presidents of the United States. In the early years of the Republic, when the young Episcopal Church was struggling to replace the Church of England, the building was used for a time by Baptists and then by Presbyterians. The Episcopal Church regained possession, and services of the Anglican Communion were resumed. In the graveyard is a stone inscribed, "Captain Mose Rogers, died Nov. 11, 1821. Commander of S.S. *Savannah*, First Steam Ship to cross the Atlantic. Crossed in 1819." Here lie soldiers of all the wars fought for the United States — the Revolution, the War of 1812, the Seminole War, the Mexican War, and the World Wars.

St. Helena's Church (1724)

Church Street, Beaufort, Beaufort County, South Carolina

Port Royal Island is surrounded by tidal rivers on the Atlantic coast. Beaufort is situated at the middle of the eastern side of the island on the Beaufort River. Just below Port Royal Island is Paris Island, on which was made the earliest settlement of European Protestants in North America. We have seen several parishes, on the Cooper River east of Charleston, where French Huguenots were early settlers. The first Huguenots came to America in 1562, under the leadership of Jean Ribaut, intending to establish a colony in New France. They sailed into the harbor, which they named Port Royal, and made a temporary settlement on Paris Island, where they built Charlesfort. That was twenty-three years before Walter Raleigh began his effort to colonize Virginia with the temporary settlement on Roanoke Island, North Carolina, in 1585, and twenty-six years before the Battle of the Armada, in 1588, which led to the treaty of peace and commerce between England and Spain, and the opening of North America to settlement by European Protestants. The settlement at Charlesfort lasted only a matter of months, but the temporary beachhead had prepared the way for the settlement of the Province of Carolina some years later.

By Act of Assembly in 1712, Granville County was made an Anglican parish with the name of St. Helena, and a church and parsonage were ordered to be built on Port Royal Island. The large parish was bounded by the Combahee River, St. Helena Sound, the Savannah River, and the Atlantic Ocean. The distance was too great for the inhabitants on Port Royal Island to benefit from the two parishes in Colleton County to the east. Anabaptists and Presbyterian clergymen had been in this section, but none were settled when the first Anglican minister, William Guy, came to the parish. Within the extensive parish lay lands of the Yamasee Indians, and in the uprising of 1715, known as the Yamasee War, there was considerable suffering and destruction in the parish. Guy and his congregation fled, and the church property was destroyed. Guy went to North Carolina and returned later to St. Andrew's Church (No. 279).

The present church was built in 1724. The brick walls, which meet in quoins, are covered with stucco and coursed to resemble masonry. The original dimensions were forty by thirty feet, with a chancel thirty feet square. In 1817 the building was repaired and altered, and in 1841 it was enlarged. It had a spire 118 feet high, which decayed and had to be removed in 1866; it was replaced by the present two-staged tower of wood, to which another spire was added in 1940. The main entrance is enframed with Doric pilasters and a fanlight. Most of the windows are arched. The chancel and altar are in a semicircular apse with a domed ceiling. The communion silver was given to the church by Captain John Bull, in memory of his wife, who was taken by the Yamasee Indians in the uprising of 1715. The vestry journal dates from 1726. The vestry of St. Helena's Church was incorporated in 1786. In 1861 the organ and furnishings were removed, and the church was used as a hospital. In the graveyard is the tomb of John Barnwell, who came here from Ireland in 1701. He became known as "Tuscarora Jack" after he had led the successful campaign to subdue the Tuscarora Indians in their uprising in North Carolina (see St. Thomas' Church, Bath, No. 198). In England, in 1719, he presented the cause of the colonists when South Carolina protested the abuses of the Lords Proprietors. Old White Church, St. Helena Island, was built, probably in 1726, as a chapel of ease in St. Helena Parish (see No. 287).

287

Old White Church (1726) St. Helena Island Church

Frogmore, St. Helena Island, Beaufort County, South Carolina

This island originally was part of St. Helena's Parish, which was laid out in 1712 (see No. 286). To accommodate the many families of planters on the island, this Anglican church was built, supposedly in 1726, as a chapel of ease to St. Helena's Church, Beaufort, which had been built two years before. The minutes of the vestry for 1734 record, "It is ordered that Mr. Jones go to St. Helena Island to perform divine service once in six weeks for six months." The building was sixty by forty feet originally; it was enlarged later, and the chapel became a distinct cure, or separate parish church. The structure is of tapia, or "tabby," a type of masonry made of oyster shells cemented with oystershell lime, and in this respect it is unique among the colonial churches. Water-rubbed brick went into the window arches to give them their curve. The tapia columns of the covered portico were similar to the columns of molded brick of the Sheldon Church (No. 288) and St. James', Santee (No. 282). The church was burned in a forest fire about 1865, and it has been in ruins ever since.

288

Prince William's Church (c. 1745)
Sheldon Church

Beaufort County, South Carolina

North of Beaufort and southwest of Poco-taligo lies Hoopsa Neck, where rich lands were lost by the Yamasee Indians. Here lived many prosperous planters, the Bull family among them. Stephen Bull's plantation was given the name Sheldon Hall, after the family home in Sheldon Parish, Warwickshire, England. This section was within St. Helena's Parish, of which the Anglican parish church was at Beaufort (see No. 286). Upon application of the growing congregation for a parish and church of their own, the assembly passed an Act of 1745 which laid off Prince William Parish from St. Helena's. The new parish was bounded by the waters of the Coosaw River, the Port Royal River, the Coosawhachee River, and the Combahee River. The parish was given the name of the Royal Duke of Cumberland, who had defeated Prince Charles in 1746, at the Battle of Culloden Moor in Nairnshire, Scotland. The leaden equestrian statue of Prince William, which stood in the churchyard, was melted into bullets during the Revolution.

The present building was begun soon after the parish was founded in 1745. The land was given by Elizabeth, widow of Landgrave (landed nobleman) Edmund Bellinger. William and Stephen Bull were commissioners for building the church and receiving money and subscriptions for the purpose. In 1753 the pews were sold, and the proceeds were used to finish and adorn the church. When finished, this was the finest church in South Carolina outside of Charles Town. The six pillars of the portico, made of curved brick, are similar to those at St. James' Church, Santee (No. 282). There are four half-round pilasters on each side and two on the rear end, and at the corners there are three-quarter-round pilasters.

There were both Whigs and Tories in the Bull family, but the Tories failed to save the church from being burned by the British. In 1779, when a British force that had attacked Charles Town came this way on its march to Savannah, it burned the church and Sheldon Hall. In 1826 the church was rebuilt in the old walls. Again in 1865 the building was burned to the walls, by General Sherman's 15th Corps, and the ruin remains standing among moss-hung live oaks and thicket. The date of Sherman's fire appears on a ruined wall of the chancel in glazed headers.

In 1748 a minister was appointed to preach here periodically. A decade passed before there was a settled rector of the parish, and then, in 1758, Robert Cooper was elected. After a year at this church, he went to St. Philip's Church, Charleston. Of the communion silver, two chalices are inscribed as the gift of Evans Palmer in 1753. The rest is inscribed as the gift of William

Bull. The father of that name served as lieutenant governor for seventeen years, and his son, who succeeded him in that office, served for sixteen years. Both were active in establishing the church here, and the son was one of the commissioners for building St. Michael's Church, Charleston. In the churchyard are tombs of John and Mary Bull. (His first wife was carried off by the Yamasee Indians.) An account has been recorded that gives a picture of plantation life and hospitality. Stephen Bull usually invited the gentry of the congregation to dine with him at Sheldon Hall after church services, and his overseer entertained the rest of the parishioners. On Sundays there were usually sixty or seventy carriages at the church.

289

Unitarian Church (1772)

4 Archdale Street, Charleston, South Carolina

The original brick building, which is incorporated in the present Unitarian Church, was erected as a daughter church of the Independent Congregational and Presbyterian Church on Meeting Street (now the Circular Congregational Church). Early records are lost, but according to tradition the land was given by Thomas Lamball, a parishioner. Construction of the building is believed to have begun in 1772; it was still in progress in 1774, and it was completed about the time of the beginning of the Revolution. During that war, while the British occupied Charles Town, the church was used to stable their horses, and there were barracks in the churchyard; at that time the alley behind the churchyard became known as "Bottle Alley," and the name has persisted.

The congregation and the fifteenth minister, Anthony Foster, became Unitarian in 1815. This schismatic group met for a time in the building of the Carolina Society. In 1817 the church became the first Unitarian church in the South. From 1852-54, at the time of the Gothic Revival in the United States, the church was repaired and, incorporating the original brick walls, remodeled in its present perpendicular Gothic style. The architect was Francis D. Lee, a parishioner, who based his plans on the Chapel of Henry VII in Westminster Abbey, including the rare interior of fan-tracery Gothic. Samuel Gilman, of Gloucester, Massachusetts, was the minister here for thirty-eight years (1819-57) preceding the War Between the States. Dr. Gilman is best

known as the author of the song, "Fair Harvard," and Harvard University, where Unitarianism originated, gave the Gilman Room in the tower as a memorial to him. He and his wife, Caroline, were buried in the churchyard. In 1943 the Gilman Lectures, given in the church, were inaugurated in his honor.

441

290

Ebenezer Church (1788)
Little River Church, or Brick Church

**near Jenkinsville, Fairfield County,
South Carolina**

Presbyterians migrated early from Scotland to Carolina. After the Battle of Bothwell Bridge, fought in 1679 between Royalists and Covenanters, many Scots were banished, and in 1684 a party of twenty-two sailed from Glasgow on the ship *Eaglesham and Eastward* for Carolina. We have seen that Puritan Congregationalists with Presbyterian leanings came in 1695 from Dorchester by way of Charlestown in Massachusetts to Charles Town and settled Dorchester in South Carolina (see No. 280). During the eighteenth century the Church of England was the Established Church and dominated the religious life of the Low Country. The Presbytery of James Island was formed in 1722, but many of the Scottish Presbyterians, with the strong pioneering initiative that motivated the movement westward throughout the Carolinas and Virginia, moved inland. Fairfield County is in the west-central part of South Carolina, and the Presbyterian church

here that survives the colonial period is the farthest inland of any of these colonial churches in the state.

In a wooded section on a country road, beside the Little River, stands the Brick Church. It was built in 1788 by a congregation of Associate and Reformed Presbyterians. The congregation had been formed before the Revolution, and its log church stood here before the brick church. The brick was made locally by the farming parishioners. The Synod of the Carolinas (A.R.P.) was organized at this church in 1803, and became the Associate Reformed Presbyterian Synod of the South. During the Civil War, Union soldiers ripped out the timbers and flooring to rebuild Kincaid's Bridge over Little River, which had been burned by the retreating Confederates; the incident is recorded in a note of apology written on the door frame and signed, "A Yankee." The church was not repaired until 1891, when the congregation was revived by the Reverend A. G. Kirkpatrick, and services were resumed. Articles of communion service of the early times are still in use, including a tray, a tankard, cup, and Irish linen. In the churchyard is a gravestone inscribed, "Rev. James Rogers a native of County Monaghan Ireland died 1830 aged 62. 40th year of his ministry."

VERMONT

	Denomination	Material
291 Rockingham Meeting House (1787) Rockingham, Windham County	Congregational	Wood
292 First Congregational Church (1787) Thetford Hill, Orange County	Congregational	Wood

SUMMARY

Congregational   2   Wood   2

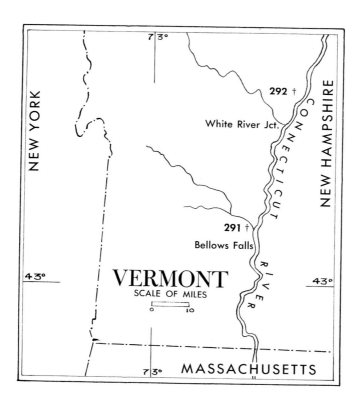

291

Rockingham Meeting House (1787)

Rockingham, Windham County, Vermont

On a knoll above the village of Rockingham stands the oldest meeting house in Vermont. It looks over the valley of the Williams River. The river, which flows into the Connecticut between Bellows Falls and Springfield, was named for the most famous citizen of Deerfield, Massachusetts — John Williams, minister of its Congregational church. He was captured by Indians in the great raid on Deerfield, in 1704 during Queen Anne's War, in which half the town was burned and forty-nine inhabitants were killed, and with other captives he was taken to Canada. He preached a sermon at the river's mouth, when the party of 240 Indians, with 112 captives, camped here on their return journey to Canada. The best account is Williams' own, *The Redeemed Captive*.

The first meeting house was built in 1772. This pioneering country, settled late in the colonial period, was still in dispute between New York and New Hampshire, whose Governor Benning Wentworth had issued grants for much of the land; its independence as a separate state was not asserted successfully until 1777. As in New Hampshire and Massachusetts, the Congregational Church was established, and church and state were one; the meeting house was both a town house and a house of worship.

At a town meeting in 1778, it was voted to build a larger meeting house to replace the old one on the same site. The present building was begun in that year, but it was not completely finished until 1800. It is recorded that General Fuller was the master builder. The structure is a fine example of the New England colonial meeting house, and it remains today practically in its original form. The stairway to the high pulpit originally was curved, and the pulpit was higher than it now is. There are a sounding board, the old box pews with high backs, and a gallery at the end, reached by a stairway in the two-story closed porch.

After 1839 the meeting house, which was still being used for all town meetings, was used only occasionally for worship, and there was no regular congregation. In the period between the Civil War and 1907, the building became dilapidated. In that year it was restored with voluntary contributions and town funds. Since then there has been an annual gathering here on a Sunday in August.

First Congregational Church (1787)

Thetford Hill, Orange County, Vermont

The town of Thetford is situated north of White River Junction, on the Ompompanoosuc River a few miles before its mouth at the Connecticut. The town was chartered by the Province of New Hampshire in 1761, before Vermont had become a state. In 1782 the boundary between this territory and New Hampshire was settled on the west bank of the Connecticut River, but New York continued to press claims in the territory until 1790. At a convention in Windsor in 1777, Vermont was asserted to be a separate state, but the state was not recognized by Congress until 1791, when it was admitted into the Union, and meanwhile it existed as an independent republic — a phase of its history that made its mark on the character of its inhabitants. In 1764 John Chamberlain began the first permanent settlement at Thetford. The congregation was organized in 1773 as the Church of Christ in Thetford. Clement Sumner was the first pastor, but he was a staunch Tory, and with the Revolution brewing he was forced to leave. Their first church building was erected of logs on the North Thetford road in 1780.

In 1787 the present church building was erected on the common. The site was decided by the County Court, as a compromise between factions in the two valleys beside the hill. To cover the cost of construction, the town levied a tax of two pence on each acre of land in the township. As the Rockingham Meeting House also was built in 1787, it can be said of the church on Thetford Hill that it is the oldest in Vermont in continuous service as a house of worship. Unlike the one at Rockingham, it is not in its original position or condition. In 1830, when the Society bought the building from the town, a number of changes were made to the plain rectangular building — it was moved to its present position on a near-by street; a tower, bell, and vestibule were added, and the box pews were removed. Further changes were made in 1858, when the old high pulpit was replaced by the present one in modern style on a platform, the pews were rebuilt, the ceiling was raised, and the elliptical arch, the cornice, and the chandeliers were added to the interior. In 1908 the platform was enlarged and panels were added.

Doctor Asa Burton (1752-1836) succeeded Sumner and served as pastor for fifty-seven years. He was a graduate of Dartmouth College, located on the New Hampshire side of the Connecticut and not many miles downstream from Thetford, where, as a boy, he had worked at clearing trees from the campus. In 1785, at Windsor, he preached an "Election Sermon" before the governor, the deputy-governor, the council, and the House of Representatives. In 1786 the sermon was printed at Windsor by George Hough and Alden Spooner, who, three years before, had acquired the first printing press used in North America north of Mexico. Stephen Daye had brought it from England in 1638 and set it up in Cambridge, Massachusetts. His first work on it was "The Freeman's Oath," printed in 1639. In the following year the press produced *The Bay Psalm Book*, the first book printed in English America. The press now is in the Museum of the Vermont Historical Society.

VIRGINIA

		Denomination	Material
293	Brick Church, Jamestown (1639) James City County	Anglican	Brick
294	Bruton Parish Church (1711) Williamsburg, York County	Anglican	Brick
295	Wren Chapel (1729) Williamsburg, James City County	Anglican	Brick
296	Hickory Neck Church (1774) Toano, James City County	Anglican	Brick
297	Old Brick Church (1632) Isle of Wight County	Anglican	Brick
298	Lower Southwark Church (1751) Surry County	Anglican	Brick
299	Merchant's Hope Church (1657) Prince George County	Anglican	Brick
300	Blandford Church (1735) Petersburg, Dinwiddie County	Anglican	Brick
301	Saponey Church (1728) Dinwiddie County	Anglican	Wood
302	Glebe Church (1738) Nansemond County	Anglican	Brick
303	Chuckatuck Church (1752) Nansemond County	Anglican	Brick
304	St. Paul's Church (1739) Norfolk, Norfolk County	Anglican	Brick
305	Trinity Church (1762) Portsmouth, Norfolk County	Anglican	Brick
306	Donation Church (1736) Princess Anne County	Anglican	Brick
307	Eastern Shore Chapel (1754) Princess Anne County	Anglican	Brick
308	Hungars Church (1742) Northampton County	Anglican	Brick
309	Pongoteague Church (1738) Pungoteague, Accomac County	Anglican	Brick
310	St. John's Church (1727) Hampton, Elizabeth City County	Anglican	Brick
311	Westover Church (1731) Charles City County	Anglican	Brick
312	St. John's Church (1741) Richmond, Henrico County	Anglican	Wood
313	Grace Church (1696) Yorktown, York County	Anglican	Stone
314	St. Peter's Church (1701) New Kent County	Anglican	Brick

446

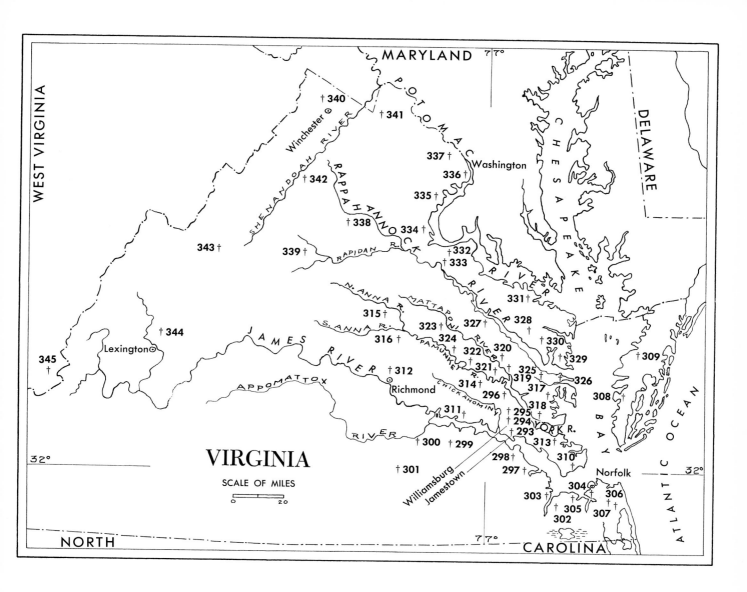

MARYLAND 77°

WEST VIRGINIA

† 340

Winchester ⊙

SHENANDOAH RIVER

† 341

POTOMAC

DELAWARE

337 †

Washington

336 †

335 †

† 342

RAPPAHANNOCK

334 †

† 338

† 332

CHESAPEAKE

339 †

RAPIDAN R.

† 333

RIVER

343 †

N. ANNA R.

MATTAPONI

331 †

328

RIVER

315 †

323 †

327 †

S. ANNA R.

† 344

316 †

324

320

330

329

Lexington ⊙

JAMES RIVER

322 †

PAMUNKEY R.

319

325

† 309

345 †

† 312

321

314

317

326

308

APPOMATTOX

Richmond ⊙

296

318

CHICKAHOMINY

295

ATLANTIC OCEAN

311

294

YORK R.

32°

RIVER

† 300

† 299

293

313 †

310

298 †

VIRGINIA

† 301

Williamsburg
Jamestown

297 †

Norfolk

32°

SCALE OF MILES

0   20

303 †

304

306

305

307

302

NORTH

77°

CAROLINA

		Denomination	Material
315	Fork Church (1735) Hanover County	Anglican	Brick
316	Slash Church (1729) Hanover County	Anglican	Wood
317	Ware Church (c. 1690) Gloucester County	Anglican	Brick
318	Abingdon Church (1754) Gloucester County	Anglican	Brick
319	Upper Church (c. 1725) King and Queen County	Anglican	Brick
320	Mattapony Church (1755) King and Queen County	Anglican	Brick
321	St. John's Church (1732) King William County	Anglican	Brick
322	Acquinton Church (c. 1760) King William County	Anglican	Brick
323	Mangohick Church (c. 1730) King William County	Anglican	Brick
324	Cat-Tail Church (1748) King William County	Anglican	Brick
325	Christ Church (1712) Middlesex County	Anglican	Brick
326	Lower Chapel (1717) Middlesex County	Anglican	Brick
327	Vauter's Church (c. 1719) Essex County	Anglican	Brick
328	North Farnum Church (c. 1737) Farnham, Richmond County	Anglican	Brick
329	Christ Church (1732) Lancaster County	Anglican	Brick
330	St. Mary's White Chapel (1740) Lancaster County	Anglican	Brick
331	Yeocomico Church (1706) Westmoreland County	Anglican	Brick
332	St. Paul's Church (c. 1766) King George County	Anglican	Brick
333	Lamb's Creek Church (1769) King George County	Anglican	Brick
334	Aquia Church (1757) Stafford County	Anglican	Brick
335	Pohick Church (1769) Fairfax County	Anglican	Brick
336	Christ Church (1767) Alexandria, Fairfax County	Anglican	Brick
337	Falls Church (1767) Falls Church, Fairfax County	Anglican	Brick
338	Little Fork Church (1776) Culpeper County	Anglican	Brick

		Denomination	*Material*
339	Hebron Lutheran Church (1740) Madison County	German Lutheran	Wood
340	Hopewell Friends Meeting House (1759) Frederick County	Friends	Stone
341	Goose Creek Friends Meeting House (1765) Lincoln, Loudon County	Friends	Stone
342	Mill Creek Church (1770) Hamburg, Page County	Baptist	Wood
343	Augusta Church (1747) Fort Defiance, Augusta County	Presbyterian	Stone
344	Timberidge Presbyterian Church (1756) Rockbridge County	Presbyterian	Stone

SUMMARY

Anglican	46	Brick	42
German Lutheran	1	Wood	5
Friends	2	Stone	5
Baptist	1		
Presbyterian	2		
Buildings	52		52

293

Brick Church, Jamestown (1639) Jamestown Church

Jamestown, James City County, Virginia

The ruined brick tower of the Jamestown Church is the only fabric that remains of the first permanent English settlement and the first Protestant parish in America, which were established here in 1607. Jamestown has disappeared from this wooded land among marshes on the north side of the James River, where the company in the *Susan Constant,* the *Godspeed,* and the *Discovery* had come to settle after their first landing on Cape Henry. Partly because it has disappeared, it has been difficult to recapture in the imagination the scene of the first town in this country, and the pageant of history marching through this capital city of the first colony. "James Towne," named for the reigning king, became the center of James City, one of the four borough

corporations by which the "plantation" was organized for government in 1618 — the others were Elizabeth City, Charles City, and Henrico — and James City County was one of the eight original shires into which Virginia was divided in 1634.

The settlers were Englishmen, who claimed the land for the Crown and the Church of England, and Captain John Smith, who was made the governor here in 1608, described the first service after landing as being held beneath an old sail, "till we built a homely thing like a barne, set upon crachets, covered with rafts, sedge and earth . . ." That first structure of 1607 is referred to as the cruck church, being made by one of the three medieval types of log construction being used in England — in the palisade type, logs stood on end to form walls; in the puncheon type, the vertical logs were hewn flat on the outside, and usually they were chinked with wattle and daub (there were no horizontal log cabins built in England, nor in America during the early colonial period); the cruck was the crotch of a tree, inverted and stood on the ground, like the letter A, and the roof lay against the two sides from the ground up to the ridge. It is interesting that today "modern" churches are being built in the style of this first Anglican church in America. In 1608 the whole settlement was burned by accident, and when its reed thatch caught fire, the church was destroyed.

The second church was built in 1610. The type of construction is not known, but it probably was of frame. It was a substantial building, measuring sixty by twenty-four feet, with two bells at the west end and casement windows. It became known as Lord Delaware's Church. In 1609, Thomas West, Lord de la Warr, was appointed governor and captain-general of Virginia for life. In 1610 he sailed for Jamestown just in time to intercept and turn back the colonists, who had abandoned their settlement in desperation and embarked for England after three years of frightful hardships. He restored order and rebuilt Jamestown, including the second church. It was in this church, in April of 1613, that the Reverend Richard Buck married Captain John Rolfe and Pocahontas, christened Rebecca, the daughter of Powhatan, the ruling Indian chief of the region. Their marriage united the two peoples in peace, and averted a bloody war that was about to be launched against the Indians. Sir Thomas Dale, who had worked for the conversion of Pocahontas, foresaw the far-reaching benefits of the marriage of an Englishman and an Indian princess, and ended his plan for a war of extermination.

The third church, built in 1617, became known as Argall's Church. Samuel Argall had been left as deputy, when Governor de la Warr returned to England in 1611; his rule was so tyrannical that the Governor embarked for Virginia in 1618, but died on the voyage. The building was smaller than the second, measuring fifty by twenty feet. It stood within the palisades of the fort, half a mile downstream from the site of the present brick tower. It was in Argall's Church, in 1619, the first year of the governorship of Sir George Yeardley, that the burgesses and councilors, later to become the House of Burgesses, met as the "General Assembly." This was the first English representative assembly to meet in America. Richard Buck, the rector mentioned above, attended as chaplain.

The fourth church is known to have been standing in 1636, on land adjoining that of the Reverend Thomas Hampton. It evidently was on the site of the Brick Church. The brick and cobblestone footings excavated within the walls of the latter church, in 1906, are identified as those of the fourth church, by Henry Chandler Forman, in his *The Architecture of the Old South* (1948). These first four churches were of wood.

The fifth building, the Brick Church, was begun in 1639 and finished in 1647. It was Gothic in design, with buttressed walls, and was similar to medieval Gothic country churches in England. It was one of only three such churches known to have been built in colonial Virginia — the others were the Old Brick Church (St. Luke's), Isle of Wight County, built in 1632 and still standing (No. 297), and the Second Bruton Church in Middle Plantation (Williamsburg), which was built in 1679 and was demolished (see No. 294). The buttressed walls were revealed in the footings of the ruin of this fifth building. While it may have had the corbie gable similar to that of the Isle of Wight church, it was only by assumption that that church was taken as the model for the reconstruction here, in 1907, for the Tricentennial celebration. At that time only the footings and the tower remained.

This fifth church served as the parish church of Jamestown and the official Anglican church of the Government of Virginia. The building was gutted by fire in Bacon's Rebellion of 1676. Nathaniel Bacon (1647-1676), in a revolution exactly a century before the War of Independence,

rebelled against taxation in Virginia without proper representation, and neglect of the inhabitants of the frontier. He marched against Governor Berkeley and burned the capital city of Jamestown, including the church. He died of malaria that same year, leaving the reactionary party in control to continue their exploitation. In 1680 the church building was completely restored.

The ruined tower has several features of architectural and historical interest, although the remnant usually is so covered with ivy that the brickwork is hardly visible. Over the circular-headed doorway, where there now is a gap connecting the doorway with the window opening above, there was a rudimentary pediment, like that at the Isle of Wight church. The mutilated belfry had Jacobean brick quoins. There were doors in the front and back of the tower at ground level. On the second level there was a window in front and a doorway in back, opening on a gallery. The plain arches over all these circular-headed openings were of one brick length in depth, constructed with stretchers and headers alternating, and the headers alternating glazed with common brick. George Carrington Mason, in his *Colonial Churches of Tidewater Virginia*, mentioned that all "these arches have brick imposts projecting into the opening, a primitive feature found in no other colonial churches in Virginia except the contemporary Old Brick Church in Isle of Wight." The third story, the belfry, was ventilated by slots, two in each of the three exposed walls. The wooden spire was burned after the restoration of 1680, and charred ends of timbers remained in the tower. The brickwork is laid in English bond, with a projecting band of two courses in Flemish bond around the main doorway. Glazed headers were used at random.

Malaria finally drove the inhabitants out of Jamestown, and in 1699 the seat of government was removed to Williamsburg. Thereafter the town and the church declined. In 1758 the church was without a congregation, and it was abandoned. The bricks were taken away for other uses, until only this tower remained. The silver communion vessels went to Bruton Parish in 1806 (see No. 294). In 1893 the site of Jamestown, with the brick tower and gravestones here as the only visible evidence of the historic town, was deeded to the Association for the Preservation of Virginia Antiquities. For the Tricentennial in 1907, the body of the church was rebuilt onto the ruined tower. Now the rebuilt structure is in ruins.

294

Bruton Parish Church (1711)
The Court Church, the Chapel Royal of Virginia

Williamsburg, York County, Virginia

Middle Plantation, which became Williamsburg, was laid out about 1632 (the year in which the Old Brick Church was built in Isle of Wight County, No. 297), seven miles from James-Town and midway between the James and the York rivers. Middle Plantation Parish was created the following year. Most of the parish was in York County (see Grace Church, Yorktown, No. 313), but part lay in James City County. Duke of Gloucester Street in Williamsburg is the boundary between the two, and Bruton Church stands on the York side. In 1658 Middle Plantation Parish and Harrop Parish were united to form Middletown Parish, and in 1674 Marston Parish was united with Middletown to form Bruton Parish. The upper church probably was Marston Church; the lower church, Middletown Church,

became the first Bruton Church in the year that the new parish was formed. The site of that first building is not known; it may have been within the present churchyard. The first rector of Bruton Parish (1674-1688) was a great-grandfather of Martha Washington, Rowland Jones. He was buried in the second church building; his grave was moved to the present church, on the north side of the chancel near the font.

The second Bruton Church was built on a site that is now in the middle of the present churchyard. That brick building, with five buttresses on each of the side walls, was of a medieval Gothic style of country churches in England; it was matched in colonial churches of America only by the Jamestown Church (No. 293) and the Old Brick Church in Isle of Wight County (No. 297). The vestry decided in 1677 not to repair the upper and lower churches, but to build this new church instead; the contract was let to Francis Page in 1681, and the building was completed in 1683. The land was given by Colonel John Page, who had come from Bruton Parish in Somerset, England, as had the Ludwell family here, and Governor Sir William Berkeley.

Page died in 1692, and his grave is in the churchyard at the site of that second church. The building was small but quite adequate for a country parish, until the College of William and Mary was established here (see No. 295) and the capital was moved here from Jamestown. With the arrival of the government in 1699, Bruton Church became the Chapel Royal for Colonial Virginia, the official Anglican church. All government officials subscribed to the Communion, and they were provided seats, in addition to those of the growing congregation of planters, tradespeople, and slaves.

In 1706 the second church had become outgrown and in bad repair, and the vestry ordered a new church to be built. It was not until 1711, however, that building began. In that year, James Blair, the rector, submitted for Governor Alexander Spotswood a plan for the building, cruciform in style and measuring seventy-five by twenty-eight feet, with two wings twenty-two feet in width. The Governor undertook the cost of erecting all but fifty-three feet of the building, and the vestry was to provide the rest. In 1715 the building was completed, and it has been in continuous use ever since, the oldest church in the South with that distinction. In 1752 the chancel was enlarged by twenty-five feet to accommodate an organ, and in 1754 the wall was built around the churchyard. In 1769 the church was completed as it now stands, with the addition of the tower. In its wooden belfry hangs the "Liberty Bell of Virginia," donated in 1761 and rung for the Declaration of Independence, the surrender of Cornwallis, and the signing of the peace treaty in 1783. The governor, his Council of State, and members of the House of Burgesses were seated in the transept. The gallery in the west end, which dates from 1715, was assigned to students of William and Mary during the colonial period, and the railing carries initials carved 200 years ago; it was reached by a covered outside stairway, which has been removed. The church has three sets of colonial communion silver, including the Jamestown Silver of 1616.

During the nineteenth century the interior was altered completely, and the colonial features were lost. It was partially restored from 1905-1907, under the leadership of the rector, Dr. W. A. R. Goodwin. It was he who proposed to John D. Rockefeller, Jr. the restoration of Williamsburg, and who took part in that unprecedented project. After that undertaking had started, Bruton Church was restored more completely in

1938, and today it is seen in its style of the eighteenth century. Goodwin's grave is under the aisle of the crossing.

The baptismal font is believed to have been brought from Jamestown when the church there was abandoned in 1758; George Washington stood as godfather for at least fourteen slaves who were baptised here. He also served as a vestryman for twelve years and missed only eight meetings during that time. Among other prominent patriots of the parish were George Mason, Thomas Jefferson, Patrick Henry, George Wythe, Edmund Pendleton, and Peyton Randolph. Their ideals of liberty, justice, and the rights of the individual, which went into the Declaration of Independence and the founding of the Republic, originated in the Christian principles fostered in this church. Even the disestablishment of the church itself was led by its members here, when George Mason and James Madison drafted the provision for religious toleration in the Declaration of Rights of 1776, and when Thomas Jefferson's Statute for Religious Freedom was introduced in the Capitol at Williamsburg in 1779. It is interesting to note, however, that even though the Episcopal Church in America was separated from the Church of England and from government, there never has been an interruption of their membership in the Anglican Communion for the Episcopal Churches in England, America, and all of the English-speaking countries of the world.

295

Wren Chapel (1729)
College of William and Mary
Williamsburg, James City County, Virginia

The College of William and Mary was chartered by King William and Queen Mary in 1693, as an Anglican college, "to the end that the Church of Virginia may be furnish'd with a Seminary of Ministers of the Gospel, and that the Youth may be piously educated in good Letters and Manners, and that the Christian Faith may be propagated amongst the Western Indians, to the Glory of Almighty God." This second oldest college in the country had the same primary purpose as the oldest, Harvard (1636): to educate ministers, but for the Church of England rather than for Congregationalism. The founder and first president of the College was James Blair (1656-1743), a Scottish churchman, who served as the

Bishop's Commissary in Virginia and rector of St. John's Church, Richmond (No. 312). Eight presidents of the College have been rectors of Bruton Parish Church (No. 294). As the Church of England was the Established Church in Virginia, the College was supported until the Revolution by taxation in both of the two tobacco colonies, Virginia and Maryland. The chair of divinity later was discontinued, and when James Madison, cousin of the fourth President of the United States, was president of the College, he said, ". . . it is now thought that Establishments in Favor of any particular Sect are incompatible with the Freedom of a Republic." The executors of the estate of the British scientist, Robert Boyle (1627-1691), divided the income from his estate, which had been willed for charitable purposes, between Harvard and William and Mary to educate Indian youths. Until the Revolution had ended payments from that source, there were Indian students at William and Mary, at times a dozen or more, but there is no record of any having entered the ministry, as had been hoped. Most of the prominent men in Virginia were alumni of the College, including Thomas Jefferson, James Monroe, and John Mar-

shall. George Washington was chancellor for eleven years (originally the Archbishop of Canterbury and the Bishop of London alternated as chancellor), and four of the first ten Presidents of the United States were associated with the College.

The Wren Building is the oldest academic building in use in America. The cornerstone was laid in 1695, two years after the College was chartered. It was named for the great London architect, Sir Christopher Wren. The first professor of mathematics on the faculty, the Reverend Hugh Jones, wrote in his "Present State of Virginia," in 1722: "The Building is beautiful and commodious, being first modelled by *Sir Christopher Wren*, adapted to the Nature of the Country by the *Gentlemen* there; and since it burned down, it has been rebuilt and nicely contrived, altered and adorned by the ingenious Direction of *Governor* Spotswood and is not altogether unlike Chelsea Hospital." Neither the commission of Queen Mary to Wren nor his original plan has survived, but this statement by Jones within a year of Wren's death is accepted as definite evidence that Wren was the architect for the original plan. We referred to the Wren myth and the

455

assumption that many of the colonial churches were designed by him. This chapel is the only house of worship in America built from a Wren design. The fire mentioned by Jones was in 1705. The building was burned again in 1859 and in 1862. In each case the wooden interior was burned, but the brick walls survived, and the walls today are substantially the original. The brickwork is in English bond, like that of the church tower at Jamestown (No. 293). Only three other colonial brick churches with English bond survive in Virginia — St. Peter's, New Kent (No. 314); Lower Chapel (No. 326), and Yeocomico (No. 331).

A copper plate found in the archives of the Bodlein Library at Oxford, England, which now is treasured in Williamsburg, shows the Wren Building from the back (west), with two symmetrical wings, as in our photograph. The plate was made between 1723 and 1747. The plan was intended eventually for a quadrangle, but the fourth side connecting the two wings was never built, although Thomas Jefferson drew a design for it about 1773. The north wing, to the left in the photograph, is the Great Hall, where the General Assembly of Virginia met while the Capitol was being built, and where the faculty and students dined in common in the eighteenth century. The south wing, to the right in the photograph, is the chapel. It was begun in 1729 and completed in 1732. Here the masters and students, as well as visitors, attended morning and evening prayers and special services. The dormer rooms on the top floor were used in the early days for students' sleeping quarters and later, when other buildings had been added to the College, for storage and various purposes. It was in this building that sliding sash in windows was first used in America. In 1928 the building was restored. The interior of the chapel has high paneling on the walls in the late Jacobean style. Today the chapel as well as the College is non-denominational, but in the photograph the altar is furnished in the style of the seventeenth century, when the Wren building was erected. Among the distinguished people to be buried beneath the floor were Governor Lord Botetourt; Sir John Randolph; Peyton Randolph, "The Tory"; and Bishop James Madison, president of the College from 1777 to 1812. George Wythe, the first signer of the Declaration of Independence, who lies buried at St. John's, Richmond (No. 312), was the first law professor in America and had among his students in the college here John Marshall, who became a statesman and Chief Justice of the Supreme Court. Wythe was a grandson of George Keith, who served in the colonies from 1702 to 1704 as a missionary of the Society for the Propagation of the Gospel.

296

Hickory Neck Church (1774)
Lower Church of Blisland Parish

Toano, James City County, Virginia

Blisland Parish, named for one in Cornwall, England, and often misspelled, was founded by 1653. In 1688 the boundary between Blisland Parish and the neighboring St. Peter's Parish, New Kent County (see No. 314), was in dispute. The Lower Church of the parish was built here in 1734-38. The vestry book of this parish is the only one to survive in colonial James City County. In 1774-76 a south transept was added to the building. During the Revolution the church was used as a hospital, and the British, French, and American troops encamped at various times in

the churchyard. For many years thereafter the building was used as a school. By 1825 it was in bad repair, and the trustees of Hickory Neck Academy, to make the building useful as a school, pulled down the old part and repaired the newer transept of 1774-76; this is the present church building. During the Civil War it was used at different times by both sides as a barracks, and following that war again it was used as a school. In 1907, the year of the Virginia Tricentennial celebrating the settlement at Jamestown, the building was returned to the parish, and it was then restored as a church. In 1953 it was reconsecrated as All Saints' Church, Hickory Neck, Blisland Parish.

297

Old Brick Church (1632)
St. Luke's Church

Isle of Wight County, Virginia

About twenty-two miles downstream from the site of Jamestown, south of the James River, stands the historic Old Brick Church. Its date has been the subject of considerable research, and it is not known with certainty. The traditional date of 1632 gives the building the distinction of being the oldest house of worship still standing in the original colonies. It is the oldest Protestant house of worship in America and the only colonial Gothic church still standing. (For comments on the date, see note at opening of the Bibliography.)

In 1619, only twelve years after the settlement of Jamestown, Sir Christopher Lawne settled at Lawne's Creek, on the James, and named his place Isle of Wight Plantation. The region here was part of James City Corporation, one of the

four borough corporations into which the colony was divided in 1618. It was named Warrosquyoake, for the local Indian tribe, and it became one of the original eight shires in the 1634 division of the colony. The same name (spelled more than a dozen different ways in the records) was given to the parish, which was made coextensive with the county in that year. By 1637 Isle of Wight had replaced Warrosquyoake as the name of the county. The area of the present county was established in 1752, when Southampton County was laid off to the south, and the name of the parish here was changed to Newport Parish. (Christopher Newport had been captain of the *Susan Constant* on her historic voyage, with the *Godspeed* and the *Discovery*, from England to Virginia in 1607; there was also the town of Newport, the capital of the Isle of Wight.) After the Indian massacre of 1622, Isle of Wight Plantation was abandoned, but Governor George Yeardley drove the Indians out during the following year. By 1634 the census gave a population

of 522 in the county. By order of the Virginia Assembly in March of 1623, this was one of the four places outside of Jamestown where the General Court of Virginia could convene, and as the "Lord Governour and Captain Generall" would attend both court and church, it was important to erect a suitable building. Furthermore, the Act of Assembly of February 1631-32 specified that "in all such places where churches are wanting, or decayed, the inhabitants are tyed to contribute towards the building of a church" or forfeit fifty pounds for failure to erect one by Christmas of 1632. It probably is more than coincidence, therefore, that this building was erected in 1632. The Brick Church was then in the Lower Parish (later called Newport Parish), which extended at that time from Lawne's Creek (see Lawne's Creek Parish, No. 298) to Chuckatuck Creek (see Chuckatuck Church, No. 303). During its long colonial history, this building was known as the Brick Church, or later as the Old Brick Church. Not until 1828, when a young deacon,

William G. H. Jones, used the name in a report to the Episcopal Convention, was this venerable and unique church called St. Luke's; it has never been given the name officially. A brick church was a rarity in those days, and when the one was built in Jamestown, in 1639 (see No. 293), it was called simply the Brick Church in Jamestown. Architecturally the two buildings had much in common, bringing to America the heritage of European culture represented in the medieval Gothic cathedrals and the country churches of England. With its brick buttresses, corbie or stepped gables, brick-mullioned double-lancet windows, brick quoins, rudimentary pediment, timber-trussed roof, and great window in the chancel, the Brick Church might have been moved from England of the sixteenth century to Virginia; it closely resembles Woodham Walter Church, Essex, built 1563-64, and similar churches in the country of Gloucestershire and Surrey. Only three such medieval Gothic, buttressed brick churches were built in colonial America, the third of which, the second church of Bruton Parish at Williamsburg, does not survive (see No. 294).

Finishing the church took many years, possibly twenty-five. Active in the parish during that process was Colonel Joseph Bridger of "White Marsh," member of the Council of State for Virginia to Charles II; he brought from England members of the Driver family to work on the church, and he superintended the work. In recognition of his active interest in the church, Colonel Bridger's remains were entombed beneath one of the inscribed stones in the floor of the chancel. The third story of the tower was added during the last quarter of the seventeenth century, and the initials "C.D. & T.D." were inscribed, probably by the second generation of the Driver family, Charles and Thomas. The original cypress shingle roof lasted a full century and was then replaced. During the eighteenth century the interior was modernized; a plaster compass-vault was installed, which covered the medieval tie-beam roof structure; the rood screen was eliminated; and the early furnishings were replaced. During the Revolution the church was threatened when Colonel Tarleton's British troops camped around it, but it escaped without damage. The vestry was dissolved in 1777, as Virginia gained independence from the Crown and the Church of England; in 1785 the Church of Virginia was disestablished. For the next forty years services were held only occasionally in the Old Brick Church, and the building was not maintained. Between 1821 and 1836 the church was used, but after a new church had been built in Smithfield the old one was used only as a summer chapel. In 1887 a storm caused the roof and part of the east gable to fall; the building seemed doomed to ruin, but the Reverend David Barr raised enough aid to repair it. In 1953 the foundations, walls, and roof were in danger of giving way, and this historic treasure again was threatened. The Old Brick Church then was declared a national shrine, and under the leadership of Henry Mason Day, descendant of one of the earliest settlers of the region, and with funds collected from aroused citizens all over the country, a major program of restoration was accomplished between 1953 and 1959. Research into the original structure, and the architecture in England of the style at the time when it was built, enabled the men working on the project to make the restoration in keeping with the original. The early windows, however, were made of thin, diamond-shaped panes; the stained glass, made in Munich and placed in the great window of the chancel during the restoration of 1887-1893, is still in place, and the side windows are of Tiffany glass. As stained glass was never used in American colonial churches, consideration is being given to moving the stained glass to the Gate House and replacing it with clear diamond panes; then the restoration will be complete. Today the Old Brick Church is a beautiful relic of the early years of the country and the founding of the nation.

298

Lower Southwark Church (1751)
Old Surry Church, Lawne's Creek Parish
Surry County, Virginia

Surry County lies on the south side of the James River, across from Jamestown, where the first settlement was made in 1607. It was named for Surrey, the county on the south side of the Thames River, across from London. In 1652 the county was laid off from James City County, one of the eight original shires, which was then confined to the north side of the river. Surry originally included the present Sussex County, extending southward toward the North Carolina line. Two Anglican parishes were formed in the part of Surry north of the Blackwater River to the James. Lawne's Creek Parish was founded in 1639. Lawne's Creek, named for Sir Christopher Lawne, who settled at its mouth on the James in 1619, is over the eastern boundary in Isle of Wight County. Southwark Parish was founded in 1647. The name was brought from Southwark Borough (the home of the mother church of Congregationalism, see West Barnstable, Mass., No. 91), on the south side of the Thames, which is connected with the City of London by the Southwark Bridge and London Bridge; here the location was similar in relation to the capital city. In 1738 these two parishes were united as Southwark Parish; Lawne's Creek Parish then ceased to exist, even though the name persisted for a time, and it has been applied in error to the present building. Situated as it was, across the river from the first settlement, Lawne's Creek Parish was among the oldest in the colony. Its first church was built before 1647 and probably before 1639, when the Brick Church at Jamestown was built. It was a brick building, located on a hill near Hog Island Creek, overlooking the

James. When it was abandoned, the bricks were taken away for other uses in the neighborhood. As Lawne's Creek Parish lay downstream from Southwark Parish, when the two were united, Lawne's Creek became the Lower Southwark Parish; the present building was the second Lower Southwark Church.

Although the exact date is not known, the first church in the original Southwark Parish was built about 1650. It stood a few miles southwest of Surry Courthouse. Marking the site of the second Southwark Church, three and a half miles west of Surry Courthouse, in the woods beside the road, stands a small monument made of brick from the walls and stone from the aisle paving. The church was erected there some time before 1673, when it was mentioned in a will. A third church built in the two parishes was the Cypress Church, a brick building begun in 1753, on the north side of Cypress Swamp and a mile west of Surry Courthouse. In 1919 the roof of that building fell in, and bricks from the walls were taken away thereafter for local uses. The present building was the fourth and last colonial church to be built in the two parishes. In addition to these churches, there were two Cabin Point chapels, built in 1680 and 1711, at the western boundary of Surry county, near Cabin Point in Prince Charles County. The first Benjamin Harrison, who

was born in Southwark Parish in 1645, was buried at Cabin Point Chapel (see Merchant's Hope Church, No. 299).

The present second Lower Southwark Church was begun in 1751, thirteen years after the merger of the two parishes in 1754. Even as a ruin, it is the only one to survive in the county. It was a beautiful rectangular church. There were four tall windows and an entrance on the side shown in the photograph, five windows on the opposite side, a high arched entrance in the west end, and a pair of high arches rising from the floor level in the east end. By 1857 the congregation had grown, and the Episcopalians built a new church near by, St. Andrew's Church. The congregation included the wealthy planters of the section, and Bishop Meade, in his *Old Churches, Ministers and Families of Virginia*, records that it was called the "silk stocking church." After the new church was built, Old Surry Church was used by other denominations. In 1868, during the difficult period of reconstruction following the Civil War, the church was burned by Negroes. Since that time it has stood in ruins, with trees rising between the walls and periwinkle blooming at their feet.

Near the ruin is Bacon's Castle, a residence built about 1650 and fortified in Bacon's Rebellion of 1676.

299

Merchant's Hope Church (1675)

Prince George County, Virginia

Merchant's Hope Church is one of the oldest colonial churches in the country. It stands amidst pines and oaks apart from any town, in a region that was settled soon after Jamestown. Prince George County is on the south side of the James River, upstream from Surry County. It was laid off from Charles City County in 1702. Charles City Corporation was one of the four areas organized in 1618, which became a county in 1634, covering both sides of the James; in the division of 1702, it was confined to the north side. This new county on the south side was named for the Danish consort of Queen Anne. Merchant's Hope Church, with God's Acre on which it stands, is

the only part of a vast, early colonial plantation that retains its romantic name. In 1634 the ship *Merchant's Hope* was sailing between England and Virginia, and it is assumed that its owners were among the company of men who, in 1635, received a grant of land here. The tract of 1,250 acres extended from the lands called Merchant's Hope, which had been granted previously to William Barker, mariner. Among these owners, beside Barker, there were John Sadler and Richard Quiney, merchants. Thomas Quiney, brother of Richard, in 1615 had married Judith, one of William Shakespeare's twin daughters. Other tracts were acquired by Barker; Sadler added to the holdings a portion of Martin's Brandon, another vast tract that had been granted to John Martin, a companion of Captain John Smith on his first voyage to America. When the heirs of Quiney and Sadler repatented Merchant's Hope in 1711, it comprised 2,208 acres. In 1720, Quiney's heirs conveyed a half of Merchant's Hope and Martin's Brandon plantations to Nathaniel Harrison, who bought the other half from the heirs of Sadler. Nathaniel was the grandson of Benjamin Harrison, of the long line of illustrious men of that name, who was born, in 1645, in Southwark Parish, Surry County, and was buried at the Cabin Point Chapel, which was associated with Merchant's Hope Church. Most of the property remained in the Harrison family until recent years, when the last of it was sold. Brandon is still one of the show places of Tidewater Virginia. The Harrison family, which produced a signer of the Declaration of Independence and two Presidents of the United States, was associated also with Southwark Parish (No. 298) and Westover Parish (No. 311). Westover, which is now on the north side of the river, for many years was on both sides, and Westover, Weyanoke, and Wallingford parishes shared one minister with Martin's Brandon Parish.

Long before 1643, when Bristol Parish was laid off from it, Martin's Brandon Parish had been flourishing. The early parish records are lost, but a small farm at Brandon called Church Pastures, where there is a grove with a few gravestones, probably is the site of the first parish church. Near this site is the grave of the wife of John Westrope, a merchant who willed to the church, in 1655, his great Bible and a fund of tobacco for repairing the church or building a new one, and for buying a communion cup. In that same year an Act of Assembly urged the founding of parishes, building of churches, and buying of glebes. The will was executed in 1658; the two articles mentioned were used by both churches until they were divided into separate parishes in 1857, and then the cup remained at Brandon Church and the Bible, a New Testament of 1639 with an Old Testament of 1640, went to Merchant's Hope.

The present church is located seven miles from Prince George. On a rafter of the roof, the date 1657 was inscribed, a year between the signing of the will and its execution, and in the absence of church records it is taken to be the year in which the new church was built, although the plain rectangular style generally is associated with a later period. In 1667 a plot of 200 acres for a glebe was granted to "the parish of Martyn's Brandon . . . between Captain Johnson's land and the 'Merchant's' ", midway between the sites of the two churches. The building is sixty by thirty feet, with brick walls twenty-two inches thick. The swag

roof is a distinctive feature of its architecture. Aisles from the two doors, on one side and the end, meet at the chancel and are paved with flagstone. A crown was found engraved on the lower side of one of the stones, and it is assumed that they were imported. On one side in the west end is a small vesting room, and on the other is the stairway to the gallery. Originally the curved ceiling was plastered, but later it was finished in wood. A high pulpit originally stood midway in the length of the building, and the upright that held the sounding board is still behind the ceiling. During the Civil War the original pulpit and chancel furniture were destroyed; the chancel rail and gate have been replaced by a curved walnut rail. The box pews were removed at the same time; they were replaced by modern pews.

Before the Civil War the parish enjoyed a prosperous period from 1837, when the rector of Brandon and Cabin Point (Southwark Parish in Surry County) took charge of Merchant's Hope, formed a vestry, and repaired the building. During this period a chapel was built for the slaves of two adjoining estates, and the rector worked diligently among the Negroes. In 1857 came the separation, when Brandon Church and Cabin Point became the new Parish of Martin's Brandon and Southwark, leaving Merchant's Hope independent. After the war, this church prospered for several decades and then declined. When N. P. Dunn wrote the article on Merchant's Hope Church in *Colonial Churches in the Original Colony of Virginia*, published in 1907 for the Tricentennial of the settlement of Jamestown, he said, "Unfortunately the church has been closed since last September . . . the tide of life swept out and left it stranded."

In 1957, to celebrate the 300th anniversary of the building, an organization was chartered by the state to insure its preservation, The Merchant's Hope Church Foundation, Incorporated. With money raised by general subscription and a grant from the Commonwealth Fund, the building was restored thoroughly in 1958. Four years later, the foundation still was soliciting funds for the restoration of the interior furnishings, for which drawings have been made. Services are held on the second and fourth Sundays from June through September and on special occasions, such as Garden Week and the Autumn Pilgrimage. There are no tombstones in the churchyard here, and the building stands alone among the oaks and pines to remind us of the early history of this country.

300

Blandford Church (1735)
Brick Church on Wells's Hill

Crater Road, Petersburg, Dinwiddie County, Virginia

Bristol Parish, which was established on both sides of the Appomattox River by Act of Assembly in 1643, was laid off from Martin's Brandon Parish (see Merchant's Hope Church, No. 299). It extended from the mouth of the Appomattox, at the James River, up to Peter's Point and the falls, where Petersburg now is located. Abraham Wood was one of the principal pioneers in this section, and Wood's Church was built in 1707, five miles from the point, on the north side of the river. He was commander of Fort Henry located here. Peter Jones succeeded him in command of the fort, and the Point probably was named for him. In the diary of his "Journey to the Land of Eden," Colonel William Byrd of Westover (see Westover Church, No. 311) noted in 1733: "When we got home, we laid the foundation of two large Cities. One at Shaco's, to be called Richmond, and the other at the point of Appomattuck, to be nam'd Petersburg." The Ferry Chapel was built on the south side of the river, across from Conjurer's Neck, between City Point and the falls. Three other chapels were built in the parish on the south side — on Namozine, Saponey, and Flat Creeks. Of these five houses of worship, only the chapel on Saponey Creek survives (see Saponey Church, No. 301). By Act of

Assembly of 1734, all of Bristol Parish north of the Appomattox was laid off in 1735, to form two new parishes in Chesterfield County.

In 1733, before that northern part of the parish was severed, the vestry of Bristol Parish "Ordered that a new Church be built of Brick on Wellses Hill for the Conveniency of this Parish Sixty foot long and twenty-five Wide in the Clear Eighteen foot pitch with Compass Sealing and Compass windows the Isle Eight foot wide Laid with portland stone or Bristol marble . . . etc." In 1734 agreements with the workmen were ordered to be made, and levies of 25,000 pounds of tobacco were laid that year toward building the church. There was a delay in starting the building, as parishioners over the river, who were to be cut off from the parish in 1735, objected to paying the tax for a church which would not be theirs.

The issue was decided by the governor at Williamsburg, and work on the present brick church began in 1735. It was completed in 1737, as specified in the builder's agreement, and the Ferry Chapel then was abandoned. There were now two houses of worship in the newly defined Bristol Parish — the present Brick Church and Saponey Chapel (later Church). As the parish was growing, it was necessary to build two more chapels of ease in the lower parish — one on Jones' Hole Creek, the other on Hatcher's Run — neither of which survives. These changes in the parish took place during the ministry of George Robertson, who served as rector from 1694 until his death late in 1739 or early 1740. In 1742 Bristol Parish again was divided to form Bath

Parish. Bristol retained the present Brick Church and the chapel on Jones' Hole Creek, while Saponey became the Bath Parish Church and Hatcher's Run its chapel of ease. The church here on Wells's Hill was in the Town of Blandford, which lay between the hill and the river. The town was one of the principal tobacco ports of Virginia until the time of the Revolution, after which Petersburg overshadowed it. The line of the incorporated town of Petersburg was run to include the church.

The addition of the long transept on the north side, which gave the building its T-shape, was ordered in 1752 and completed in 1764. In 1757 the brick wall was built around the churchyard. The basic design of the building remains unchanged since then. After the Revolution the parish struggled to maintain a minister, until the new St. Paul's Church was built in Petersburg, between 1802 and 1808. Thereafter, services were held alternately between the two for a time, and then Old Blandford Church was abandoned. The closing battles of the Civil War were fought around Petersburg and the church. Crater Road, which runs by the church, leads to the near-by site where a mine was exploded by federal troops in the Confederate defenses during the siege of Petersburg. The end of the war came soon after the siege, with Lee's surrender at Appomattox, about eighty miles to the west. The old church became dilapidated after the war, and about 1880 it was reroofed to save it from ruin. In 1901 the Petersburg Ladies Memorial Association restored the building as a memorial chapel, dedicated mainly to participants in the Confederacy.

Saponey Church (1728)
Dinwiddie County, Virginia

Alone in deep woods near the middle of the county, about five miles southwest of Dinwiddie, the county seat, and near the present town of Dewitt, stands the oldest house of worship in the county. On Saponey Creek, which took its name from the local tribe of Indians, it was built in 1728 as a chapel of ease in the Anglican Parish of Bristol. At that time the mother church of the parish was on the north side of the Appomattox River. In 1735, when the part of the parish north of the river was laid off, the Blandford Church (No. 300) was built as the parish church; the Ferry Chapel, which had been serving in this southern part of the parish, was abandoned; and Saponey Chapel became the only chapel of ease in the newly defined Bristol Parish. The population was growing rapidly, and in 1742 the parish again was divided, by laying off this western section to form Bath Parish. Saponey Chapel then became the Bath Parish Church.

Saponey is one of the few colonial frame houses of worship which survive in Virginia or elsewhere in the South. The plain-gabled building, with the eaves of the gable at the entrance end returned to form a pediment, has been kept in good repair, and it still is in use. Here again we find the trail of the second Colonel William Byrd of Westover; on his return journey after surveying the Virginia-North Carolina boundary, he recorded a meeting with the Saponey Indians here.

302

Glebe Church (1738)
Bennett's Creek Church

Driver, Nansemond County, Virginia

Nansemond County lies on the south side of the James River, west of Norfolk, and extends to the North Carolina line. It was a part of Elizabeth City Corporation, one of the four divisions of the colony in 1618 and one of the eight original shires of 1634. New Norfolk County was laid off in 1636, and was subdivided, in 1636, into Lower and Upper Norfolk. In 1646 the name of Upper Norfolk County was changed to Nansimum, which evolved through many spellings to its present form. At this early time Puritan ministers came to Virginia, in 1641, and they gained their strongest hold in Nansemond. During the time of the Rebellion in England (1649-1660), dissent from the Church of England was disloyalty, and in this corner of Virginia the Independents and the Anglicans were going through the struggle that became a factor also in the American Revolution, more than a century later.

In 1642 three Anglican parishes were established in the county — the South, the East, and the West parishes. They became known respectively as Upper, Lower, and Chicokatuck (later Chuckatuck) parishes. The Nansemond River, a tidal arm of the James, divides this section of the county, with the Lower Parish, in which the present church is located, on the east side and Chuckatuck Parish (No. 303) on the west. About 1725, as they could not support separate ministers, the two parishes were united to form Suffolk

Parish (before the town of Suffolk was founded, which now lies to the east in Norfolk County). For many years there was contention between the two churches ruled by one vestry.

One of the early settlers was Richard Bennett, who in 1635 acquired 2,000 acres on the Nansemond River. He became an outstanding citizen of the county and the colony, and a benefactor of the Lower Parish. He was a member of the Governor's Council, even though he was a Roundhead (Puritan). He also fell under the spell of George Fox, the founder of the Society of Friends in England, who preached with lasting effect in Nansemond during 1672. The Quakers became well established in the county; the Chuckatuck Friends Meeting recorded that they had four meeting houses in the county. Colonel William Byrd II of Westover (see Westover Church, No. 311), who was a member of the party that surveyed the Virginia-North Carolina boundary, recorded in 1728 that he had passed two Quaker meeting houses in the county.

Soon after the three parishes were established, the first church of this East, or Lower, Parish was built in 1643. The foundation of the building was discovered three centuries later, when a farmer broke a plow point on it, at a site about a hundred yards from the Nansemond River. The brick foundation, measuring forty by twenty feet, probably supported a wooden building. As this church was in ruinous condition, in 1737 the vestry of Suffolk Parish ordered a new brick church to be built on Jordon's Mill Hill, a location considered to be more convenient than the old one. Objections from the Chuckatuck side delayed the project. In 1738 the governor in council decided the issue and ordered the second church to be erected, thereby establishing the date of this present building. The council ordered also that no more vestrymen at Chuckatuck be elected until the number of those in Lower Parish was equal.

The present church, known as Bennett's Creek Church, was erected on high ground at the head of the west fork of Bennett's Creek. The mill pond on the creek disappeared in recent times. The plain, small structure measured forty-five by twenty-three feet inside. The brickwork is in Flemish bond with glazed headers. The building was oriented, with a main doorway in the west end and a doorway on the south side near the east end. There were only three windows in the north, two in the south, and one in the east, or chancel, wall. In 1759 an addition was built as a wing on the north side, with a gallery that was reached by an outside covered stairway. In 1777 the only other addition was made in the form of a private gallery for a new vestryman. After the disestablishment of the Church of England, in 1785, the church became inactive. The north wing was in ruins by 1812, and the whole building was dilapidated. In 1856 the north wing was torn down, the bricks were used to close the gap in the old wall and to build a vestry in the west end, a doorway was opened on the north side opposite the south door, a gallery was built in the east end, and the colonial orientation was reversed by moving the chancel to the west end. Soon after 1900 the present arrangement was made by opening a main entrance in the original chancel wall and making windows of the north and south doorways.

In 1758 the vestry of Suffolk Parish was dissolved temporarily by Act of Assembly, at the request of the people of Lower Parish. The vestry held in trust valuable lands and cash, donated by Richard Bennett, his son Richard, and Thomas Tilly, for the benefit of the poor in Lower Parish. The vestry of the united parish, with life tenure and the arbitrary power which it permits, had colonized the poor of Chuckatuck to benefit by the trust. In 1802 the legislature passed an act requiring all glebe lands to be sold and the proceeds to be turned over to the overseers of the poor, except those glebe lands which had been private donations that might be claimed by living heirs. The rector of Suffolk Parish, Jacob Keeling, carried a case through court and won the exemption for the glebe lands here in Lower Parish, which had been given by individuals. They are still held by the trustees of the parish, and the church has been known ever since as the Glebe Church. It has continued active in Lower Parish, served now by the rector of St. Paul's Church in Suffolk.

303

Chuckatuck Church (1752)
St. John's Church

Chuckatuck, Nansemond County, Virginia

Located on the west side of the Nansemond River, a tidal arm of the James River dividing the northern part of the county, Chuckatuck Parish originally was laid out, in 1642, as the West Parish, one of three established at that time in

the county. On the east side of the river East Parish was laid out, which became known as the Lower Parish (see Glebe Church, No. 302). About 1725 the two were united as Suffolk Parish, with one vestry and one minister, for they could not support separate ministers. In 1764 the assembly passed an act exempting parishioners from paying toll when crossing the ferry to attend church, but the vestry protested through a committee sent to the capital at Williamsburg, and thereafter the exemption was confined to the minister, who conducted services in both churches. The congregations had different interests on opposite sides of the river, and a number of difficulties arose between the two in the united parish.

In 1755 the present brick building was erected near the site of the original one. The foundation of the tower of the first building was discovered by a gravedigger, in the churchyard beside the present building. About 1700 a second church was built, in the southeast corner of the churchyard; it stood until the present third building was completed, and then it was pulled down. The vestry ordered this third building in 1751; the contract was awarded in 1752, and the building

was accepted by the vestry in 1755, although it was not finished until the following year, when the second building was removed. This third building, which runs northeast-southwest, with the chancel in the northeast end, was an exception to the prevailing principle of orientation. The brickwork is in Flemish bond with glazed headers; the date "1753" is in the top of the south wall near the east end, implying that the walls were completed then. The initials "A.H." and "E.H.," which appear with the date, according to tradition are those of Anthony Holladay, churchwarden, and his wife Esther, who had given the land for the site from their Holladay's Point plantation. Originally the building had the conventional arrangement of the main entrance in the west end and a second in the south wall. During the present century the south doorway was converted into a fourth window, matching the four on the north, and the two windows in the chancel end were replaced by one smaller window. The aisle of red flagstone was raised to the level of the wooden floor.

It was in 1758 that the vestry of the united parish was dissolved, on the complaint of the Glebe Church across the river that the poor of Chuckatuck had been permitted to benefit by funds left in trust for the poor of Lower Parish. It may be as a result of this action that, after the assembly had passed an act in 1775, requiring the poor to wear a badge with the name of the parish on the shoulder of the right sleeve or have the allowance stopped, only here in Suffolk Parish was it carried out. At the time of the Revolution the rector of the two churches, John Agnew, was forced to leave the parish because of his loyalty to the Crown. In 1778 a new minister was instituted, Henry John Burgess, and he was so popular that within six months the vestry noted that the church was crowded, and there was not room in the pews for all who attended regularly. It was not until 1845 that the Chuckatuck Church is referred to in the vestry book as St. John's Church. It is served now by the rector of St. Paul's Church in Suffolk.

304

St. Paul's Church (1739)
Borough Church, Elizabeth River Parish

North Church Street and East City Hall Avenue, Norfolk, Norfolk County, Virginia

On the south side of the mouth of the James River, there were two settlements soon after the founding of James Town, one at Sewell's Point and the other at Lynnhaven. At Sewell's point was built the first parish church in Elizabeth River Parish, 1640-41, and it served in that capacity until late in the seventeenth century. It was at Sewell's Point that the Jamestown Exposition of 1907 was held, commemorating the 300th anniversary of the first settlement. At Elizabeth River, eight miles away, a town was growing which became the present Norfolk. In recognition of the need there for a chapel of ease, one was granted by the governor and council, and in 1638 the Court of Norfolk County ordered that the work on the chapel be finished. It continued to drag, however, and it was not until 1641 that it finally was finished.

The site of the early chapel evidently was here where the present church stands. St. Paul's Church was built in 1739, and the churchyard had been a cemetery for a long time before, the earliest date of a tombstone being 1673. Ten years after the new church was built, the vestry ordered that the bricks and timbers of the old chapel be given to James Pasteur for building a schoolhouse. On a brick in the south wall of the present building is the date 1739 and below it the initials "S. B.," evidently for Samuel Boush, who gave the land and served as a vestryman. His son, Captain Samuel Boush, also served as vestryman and, in 1682, gave a chalice to the church. In that same year the town of Norfolk was founded. In 1736 Norfolk was incorporated as a borough by royal charter, and for many years this church was known as the Borough Church. This means that it had replaced the one at Sewell's Point as the parish church. In 1761 Elizabeth River Parish was divided, and St. Bride's (Berkeley) and Portsmouth (see Trinity Church, No. 305) were laid off from it.

The rector of the parish was Thomas Davis from 1773 to 1776, when the Revolution broke out and Norfolk was attacked. He was an ardent patriot — president of the Sons of Liberty and chairman of the town meeting in protest against the Stamp Act. On the question of the clergy's

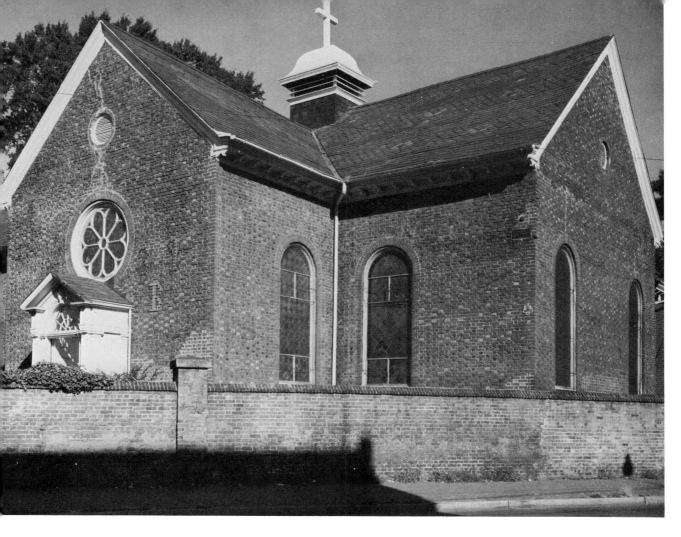

division of loyalties between the Crown and the colony, the following appears in the account of St. Paul's and Thomas Davis by Bishop Coadjutor Beverley Dandridge Tucker, in *Colonial Churches in the Original Colony of Virginia*, 1907: "Despite the statement of historians, a careful study of the records will show that the large majority of the clergymen of the Episcopal churches in Virginia at the breaking out of the war were true to the American cause, and that a bare handful were loyalists. The contrary is one of the flagrant mistakes of history which the facts contradict."

On the first day of 1776 a naval force under John Murray, Lord Dunmore, bombarded Norfolk, and a ball fired from the frigate *Liverpool* struck the south wall of the church, where it may be seen imbedded today. Most of the town, including the church, was burned by the Americans to prevent the British from occupying it. The church walls remained standing, but the interior and the old records were destroyed. After the war the building was partially restored, but

the congregation became divided and a faction built the First Christ Church. After 1800 the old church was used by a congregation of white Baptists, followed by another of Negro Baptists. In 1832 the Episcopal congregation was reorganized, and the church was repaired and consecrated in the name of St. Paul.

During the Civil War, when Norfolk was captured by federal troops and the church was taken by the military, the members of St. Paul's worshiped with the congregation at Christ Church. In 1863 the commanding general ordered the wardens of St. Paul's to provide religious services for his officers and men, and in 1865 the church was turned back to the congregation. In 1892 the building was repaired and restored completely to its early style. In 1901 the semidetached tower was built. The small rose windows are of this late period. An interesting relic in the possession of the church is the armchair, upholstered in leather, in which John Hancock sat when he signed the Declaration of Independence.

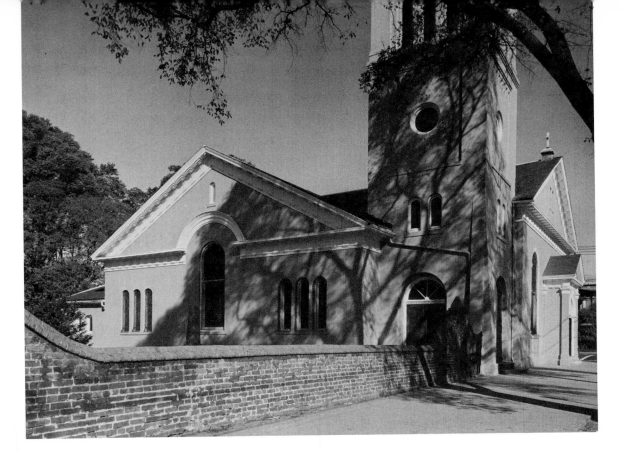

305

Trinity Church (1762)

**Court and High Streets, Portsmouth,
Norfolk County, Virginia**

In 1761 Portsmouth Parish was laid off from Elizabeth River Parish (see St. Paul's Church, Norfolk, No. 304). In the following year, 1762, Trinity Church was built. Colonel William Crawford had given the land at these four corners for public buildings, and this churchyard was the first burying ground in Portsmouth. In it were buried a number of men who were prominent in the Revolution, including Commodore James Barron (1768-1851), commander of the *Chesapeake;* Colonel Bernard Magnein, aide to General Lafayette; and John Bradfoot, the second rector here (1774-85) and a chaplain in the Continental Army.

The main body of the building contains the walls of the original rectangular church. The repairs and remodeling of 1829 and the additions of later years have hidden the original colonial character of the building; even the old brick is now covered with stucco. The bell, which cracked while ringing in celebration of the surrender of General Cornwallis at Yorktown in 1781, has been recast.

306

Donation Church (1736)
Lynnhaven Parish Church, Brick Church

Princess Anne County, Virginia

Lynnhaven Parish, which antedated Princess Anne County, was established early in the colony. At its northeast corner was Cape Henry, at the entrance to the Chesapeake Bay and the James River; there the first English settlers had come ashore, in 1607, and had claimed the land for Church and King, before sailing up the river and settling James Town. This historic section of Tidewater Virginia has the Atlantic Ocean on the east, Currituck Sound on the south, the Elizabeth River on the west, and on the north the Chesapeake Bay, into which flows the Lynnhaven River. Adam Thoroughgood (Thorowgood) settled here in 1634, when the region was established as Elizabeth City, one of the eight original shires. In 1643 Lynnhaven Parish was set off from Elizabeth River Parish (see St. Paul's Church, Norfolk, No. 304). It was in Lower Norfolk County when that new county was set off from Nansemond in 1649. Princess Anne County was set off from Lower Norfolk in 1691, and its boundaries coincided with those of Lynnhaven Parish. The parish was named for the river and bay, which are famous for Lynnhaven oysters; both were named for Lynn near the mouth of the Ouse River in Norfolk County, England.

The earliest church in Lynnhaven Parish was standing in 1639. It probably was a wooden building, and it had a brick foundation. It was situated on the Lynnhaven River at the present Church Point, at the northern shore where the early settlements were made. It was built on land of Adam Thoroughgood, who, with his family, was an active member of the church, and whose house of that time (he died in 1640) is now famous as the oldest residence in Virginia. The second building was a brick church, built in 1692. It was located about a mile from the Chesapeake, on the west bank of the Lynnhaven River near Little Creek, the boundary with Elizabeth River Parish. In 1724 the shingle roof was decayed and had to be replaced. At that time there were two chapels in addition to the church — the Eastern Shore Chapel (No. 307), about three miles from the bay, and the Upper Chapel, called

Pungo or Machipungo, about four miles southeast of Princess Anne Courthouse, which does not survive. There were also two reading places in the parish, one at Knott's Island in North Carolina on Currituck Sound, the other in the Black Water District. Fishermen at the bay shore reopened an old channel near the first church, from the river to the bay, in order to avoid a long trip around by way of the estuary. Storms opened the channel enough to divert the main current of the river; the ancient graveyard was inundated, and it now lies at the bottom of the Lynnhaven River at Church Point.

In 1736 the present church was built on Ferry Farm, further inland for greater convenience in the parish. In 1748 Robert Dickson (sometimes spelled Dixon) succeeded as minister of the parish, and he served until his death in 1776. He willed his land and slaves in trust to the vestry to establish a free school for orphan boys, and the Brick Church became known as Dickson's Donation and then as the Donation Church. The rectangular building measured sixty-

five by thirty by fifteen feet, with three bricks to the water table and two to the top in all walls. The builder was Peter Malbone. In the same year, the glebe house was repaired and enlarged. The glebe was the gift of the Thoroughgood family, and in the new church they were assigned a pew adjoining that of the magistrates and their wives, on the north side. Adam Thoroughgood was living in the parish in 1629, and he served as a representative in the House of Burgesses.

Puritans came early into Nansemond County and thence into Lynnhaven Parish. During the Revolution, Dissenters took every opportunity to attack the Church of England, even though the majority of the members of the county committee, for the cause of independence, were officers and vestrymen of this church. As late as 1801, Dissenters were trying to take over the church property, and even in 1813 the church was involved in a suit with the Dickson heirs in Scotland. The church weathered these difficult storms, and the building was repaired by order of its vestry in 1822; but after Emmanuel Church was built about 1850 at Kempsville, it was abandoned. In 1882 this building was gutted by a forest fire, and at the turn of the century the ruined walls stood with trees growing between them. In 1895, while this building was in ruins, the eastern half of the parish, including Eastern Shore Chapel, was set off as a separate parish. In 1916 the Donation Church was restored. It is now equipped in modern style, with a low pulpit and slip pews. The silver communion service, the pewter alms basin, and the baptismal font, all from the old Brick Church by the river, are in the possession of this church.

Cases of witchcraft in the American colonies were not confined to Salem, Massachusetts, where the last trial was held in 1692. There were several cases in Lynnhaven Parish from 1655 to 1698. Two miles north of the church there is Witch Duck on the Lynnhaven River, where Grace Sherwood was tried by water in 1698. She was examined by "a jury of Anciente and knowing women," who reported that she was not like them nor like any other women that they knew. In his account of Lynnhaven Parish in *Colonel Churches in the Original Colony of Virginia*, the Reverend C. B. Bryan, D.D., mentions these cases of witchcraft and adds: "The common tradition is that Grace Sherwood brought rosemary across the sea in an eggshell to Princess Anne, where the fragrant shrub still abounds."

307

Eastern Shore Chapel (1754)

Princess Anne County, Virginia

The present brick building of Eastern Shore Chapel was erected in 1754. It was the third building to be erected and the second on this site, as a chapel of ease in Lynnhaven Parish. The other two were frame structures. The land, which was donated by the heirs of William Cornick about 1690, was part of his Salisbury Plantation, patented in 1657. The location was about a mile south of Donation Church and two and a quarter miles west of the Atlantic coast, until the building was moved in 1962. This brick chapel was built during the ministry of Robert Dickson, who had succeeded Henry Barlow as minister of the parish in 1748. It was Dickson's legacy to the parish for a free school which led to the parish church being called the Donation Church (see No. 306).

The specifications of the colonial structure were thirty-five by twenty-five by eighteen feet, with three windows on the two sides, two at the east end, and one in the gallery; a roof of heart cypress shingles, and paint of sky blue throughout. Joseph Mitchell, of Norfolk, was the builder; he tried to finish it by Christmas, 1754, but it was March, 1755, when the finished building was received by the vestry. Victorian gables with slight returns and the vestry on the south side, giving an L shape, were features added at a later date. The chapel served in Lynnhaven Parish un-

472

til 1895, when the eastern half of the parish was set off as East Lynnhaven Parish. Recently the Jet Age overtook this colonial building, and it was moved about three miles to the northwest to make room for expansion of the Oceana Naval Air Base to accommodate jet planes. The present site is at London Bridge. After the move, construction was undertaken, in 1962, to enlarge the building by about thirty feet, thereby increasing the seating capacity from 210 to 450. The Eastern Shore Chapel now is a self-supporting church, although it retains its historic name of "Chapel." The photograph was made before the move of 1962.

308

Hungars Church (1742)

Northampton County, Virginia

On the Eastern Shore, the peninsula that lies across the Chesapeake Bay, separated from the rest of Virginia, the first settlement was made in 1614, only seven years after that at Jamestown. It was described in 1616 by John Rolfe, who married Pocahontas, as being on the coast near Cape Charles. The Indian name "Accomack," meaning "the other side place," was given to this region, and it became one of the eight original shires established in 1634. In 1643 the county was renamed Northampton and divided into two parishes; the Upper Parish, which became known as Nuswattocks Parish and soon after as Hungars Parish, and the Lower Parish. Probably in 1662, while the lower part of Northampton County retained that name, the upper part resumed the name Accomack. In 1670 the two parts of the county were reunited, but after three years they again were divided as they now are.

The first settlement was on the bay side of the peninsula. The first and third Lower churches were built near the shore, a few miles west of the present town of Eastville, in 1624 and 1663 respectively; the second Lower Church was built, possibly in 1641, at Fishing Point, a little further south, where the original settlement probably had been made. A few miles to the north of these sites, on the north side of Hungars Creek, the Nuswattocks Church, which became the first Hungars Church, was built in 1646. A few miles to the north of that site, at the head of Hungars Creek, a tidewater inlet lying between Church Neck and Hungars Neck, the second and the present third Hungars churches were built, in 1680 and 1742 respectively. The origin of the name Hungars is not clear, but in a census of 1625 a grant of land was recorded as being at Hunger's. In 1691 the two parishes of Northampton County, Upper and Lower, were reunited as Hungars Parish, which then became coextensive with the county, and Hungars Church became the Upper Church. The first building is believed to have been of frame, without brick even in the foundation. The second also was of frame, with oak timbers on locust blocks; the wall boards were flush, and the roof planks were lapped. A prominent member of the parish and a pewholder in this building was John Custis, Jr., son of the immigrant and ancestor of Martha Washington's first husband, Colonel Daniel Parke Custis.

A record concerning the assignment of pews implies that the present third building was completed in 1742. In 1752 the acre of land on which the building stands was deeded to the church. It adjoins the acre that had been given by William Spencer, on which the second building had stood. The deed describes the lot for the present building to be surrounded on three sides by sycamores, and so it is today. Traces of the kiln in which the brick was burned can be seen, as well as traces of the colonial highway that passed close by the churchyard. When it was completed, this rectangular building was the longest colonial church in Virginia, measuring ninety by forty feet. The brick was laid in Flemish bond. There was one main entrance in the west end, rather than two as at present, and there were doorways also in the middle of both the north and south sides. There has been no change in the number of windows — four on each side and two in the east end. There was a barrel ceiling. The chancel was hung with rich velvet trimmed with pure gold braid, a gift from Queen Anne to an earlier church here. The church had an organ that was one of the earliest in America, but it was not the first, as has been claimed — one had been installed in 1737 at Poplar Spring Church, Gloucester County.

The vestry book covering the years 1759 to 1782 is the only one to survive the colonial period. The current one commences in 1819. The interval between the two was the difficult period following the Revolution and disestablishment of the Episcopal Church, when the church here was abandoned. The rich furnishings were taken away and they disappeared, and the building was desecrated. In 1809 the lead from the organ pipes was used for weighting fishnets. Some time before 1840, the building was repaired and opened for services, which alternated weekly with Christ Church, Eastville. In 1850 the building was unsafe, and a fund was started to restore it. In 1851 the vestry resolved to take it down and build a new church on the same site. Fortunately for the preservation of the historic landmark, an alternative proposal, made by Thomas H. Stevenson, of Snow Hill, Maryland, was approved. He carried out the restoration, and he inscribed and signed a shingle in the roof, stating that he had done the work in 1851 and had "sunk a hundred dollars" in the process. He preserved all that he could of the original features, and his workmanship was excellent, the new brickwork being hardly distinguishable from the old. One of the gables had swayed out of line and had to be pulled down, with a weakened portion of the side walls; the new gable was erected with the length of the building reduced from ninety to seventy feet, and the two side doors were eliminated in the process. The barrel ceiling was replaced with a flat one. Although the arrangement of doors and windows was changed, the original casings and sash seem to have been retained, and the rubbed brick arches were preserved and installed in their new positions. Two aisles, which replaced the one center aisle, reduced the size of the pews but made more of them; the pulpit was moved from the side of the church to the chancel. The present altar canopy is not of colonial style. The only treasures of the parish to survive are a linen altar cloth, with the date "1749" done in eyelet needlework, and the communion silver given to "the Upper Church of Hungars Parish" in 1742, by John Custis of Arlington. A similar set, which he had given to the Lower Church in 1741, and a silver plate presented by Governor Francis Nicholson about 1692, are in use at Christ Church, Eastville.

Pongoteague Church (1738)
Ace of Clubs Church
St. George's Church

Pungoteague, Accomack County, Virginia

In Accomack, the upper county on the Eastern Shore of Virginia, as in the lower county, one colonial church survives, the Pongoteague Church. It was one of eight colonial churches built in the county. Settlement of the peninsula, which began in the lower county, Northampton, near Cape Charles, gradually penetrated northward, and the early churches here are of later dates than those in Northampton. In his *Colonial Churches of Tidewater Virginia*, George C. Mason brings to light two churches not revealed by previous historians — Nandue Church, built in 1653, and Occahannock Church, built in 1656, both in the southern part of the county on the bay side. In the upper part, above Pungoteague, there were Assawaman and Onancock churches, both of about 1680, Middle Church of 1723, Lower Church of 1773, and New Church of 1767.

The present Pongoteague Church stands at the head of the creek and near the town which bears the name Pungoteague, with different spelling. As early as 1663 there was a vestry, but the parish that became known as Accomack Parish was not established until 1667. In 1762, when St. George's Parish was laid off from Accomack Parish, this building became the parish church and was called St. George's Church. It has been assumed by several writers that it was built about 1656, but in his thorough research, Mason finds no evidence that it could have been built so early, or that the present building is the first. On the other hand, he finds documentary evidence that the present building was erected in 1738, replacing the first building, which probably was of wood. In that year there is a record of assignment of tobacco levied by the vestry for building of Pongoteague Church. This second building had an unusual and interesting design. It was cruciform, measuring sixty-nine feet east to west by fifty-four feet. There was a semicircular apse, capped by a semiconical roof against the east gable (see also Old Trinity Church, Md., No. 78). The main roof was of hipped gambrel style. The chancel and the nave were slightly longer than the transepts. The form gave the church the local name of the "Ace of Clubs Church."

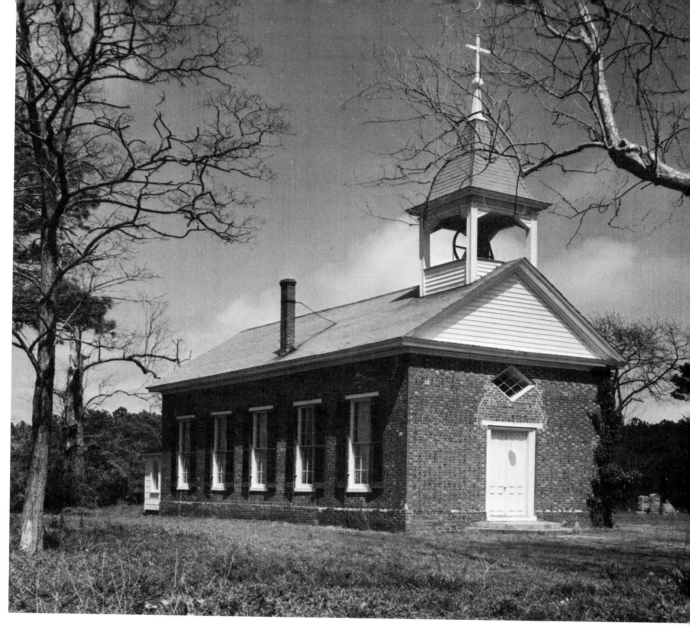

The curved apse had a large double window, and there was a single window on each side of the chancel and the transepts, and probably two on each side of the nave. There were doorways at the ends of the transepts and at the west end.

Unlike most of the colonial churches in Virginia, during the long period of difficulties for the Episcopal Church following the Revolution and disestablishment, the Pongoteague Church continued in service until the War of 1812. There was a revival on the Eastern Shore in 1819, when the building was repaired and restored in its original form. A sketch made by the rector at that time preserves its appearance for us, which was nothing like the remodeled rectangular structure that survives. In 1858 it was repaired again, but during the Civil War Federal troops used the building for a stable and ruined it. All the interior woodwork was ripped out, and bricks from one of the walls were used to build a cookhouse. About 1880 the ruin was remodeled in its present form. The nave and the apse were not worth saving; their brick was used to close the gaps at the crossing, making the present rectangular building of the transepts. In this form the building continues in active service as an Episcopal church. The communion silver, made in London in 1735, and inscribed, "This belongs to the Parish of Accomack," is still in use. Around the churchyard stand old sycamore trees, which were characteristic of colonial churchyards on the Eastern Shore.

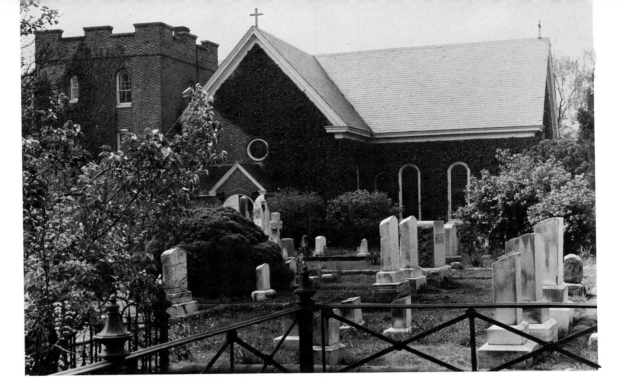

310

St. John's Church (1727)

**Queen and Court Streets, Hampton,
Elizabeth City County, Virginia**

Hampton is on the north side of the James River near its mouth. Elizabeth City County covers the point of the peninsula separating the James from the York River and the Chesapeake Bay. Originally it included the south side of the river to Cape Henry, where, after their historic voyage in 1607, the first English settlers had landed and claimed the land for the King and Church of England. They sailed then, in their three ships, up the Powhatan, which they called the James River, to make their settlement of James Town. On their way they touched here at the pleasant Indian village of Kecoughtan, consisting of eighteen houses. Captain John Smith reported many advantages in its situation, and it would have served the colonists better than the swampy area that they selected and later abandoned. During the next three years they visited the Indians here, and they were hospitably entertained, but in 1610, after one of their number had been killed by Indians, the Englishmen took possession of Kecoughtan and began the settlement that became Hampton, the oldest continuous settlement of English origin in America. In that year Elizabeth City Parish was founded, and it has continued as the oldest active parish of the An-

glican Church in America, next after James City Parish, which still survives in name only. In 1616 John Rolfe (1585-1622), who married Pocahontas, reported that there were twenty inhabitants here. In 1619 the name Kecoughtan was changed to Elizabeth City and applied to one of the four corporations which included all the settlements. The corporation, which became Elizabeth City County in 1634, was coextensive with the parish. The county became much smaller as Nansemond, Norfolk, and Warwick counties were laid off from it.

The spiritual welfare of the new colony during the formative years from 1610 to 1617 was in the charge of three ministers — Richard Buck at Jamestown, Alexander Whitaker at Henricus (Richmond), and William Mease, the first minister at Kecoughtan. Here the parishioners of Kecoughtan built one of the earliest Anglican churches in America. The probable site is north of the Hampton-Old Point Comfort road, in a clump of trees which was on the glebe land, later private property. Here in 1910 excavations discovered foundations of cobblestone and brick. The building was probably of frame, like its contemporary, Argall's Church in Jamestown (No. 293), which was built in 1617. While the first wooden church was still standing, about 1667 a second church was built at Pembroke Farm, a mile west of the present site of St. John's. In the churchyard there are tombstones dated as early as 1697. That building also was of wood, on a brick foundation. In his *Journal*, George Keith, the ex-Quaker who had just become an Anglican priest and the first missionary of the Society for the Propagation of the Gospel, and who was influential in many of the houses of worship in this collection, recorded that on Sunday, May 2, 1703, he "preached at Kicketan Church by James River." The site and the surrounding nine acres still belong to Elizabeth City Parish. In 1717 the borough lacked a church, and services of the Established Church of England were held in the courthouse. The demand for a new church grew, and it was granted that one should be built, but there was a controversy over the location.

In 1727, after the governor had decided that it should be located in the town of Hampton, which had been founded by an act of 1680, the third and present church was built. A court order directed certain men "to lay off an acre and a half of ground at the upper end of Queen street for the building of a church thereon." English brick was specified, meaning not imported brick but brick of English specifications. A contract was let to Henry Cary to furnish wood from the school grounds for burning the brick, and until the turn of the present century there was a pit in the churchyard, where it was said the bricks were made.

The cruciform building was neglected after the Revolution and was ransacked in the War of 1812. Through the inspiration of Bishop Moore, who held services in the ruin and the initiative of Mrs. Jane Barron Hope, daughter of Commodore James Barron, the building was restored; in 1830 it was consecrated by Bishop Moore and given the name of St. John's. In 1861, when Federal troops were approaching, the inhabitants set fire to their homes, and the church was burned out. The roof and the tower were destroyed, but the walls stood, and for several years the ruin was used by squatters to support their sheds for sheltering their cattle and themselves. The inhabitants slowly rebuilt their homes during that hard period of reconstruction in the South, meanwhile holding religious services at Old Point Comfort and in temporary quarters in Hampton. In 1869 the building again was restored, and the parish has prospered since that time. The present square brick tower was built, in 1901, onto a corner of the chancel, where it did not injure the original walls.

The church has a Breeches Bible dated 1599, and it came into possession of a silver chalice and paten that have been in use longer than any other English communion silver in America. They bear a London hallmark of 1617, and they were given in 1619, by an unknown donor, to the new church at Smith's Hundred, which later became Southampton Hundred and a part of Westover Parish (see No. 311). The settlement there was destroyed in the massacre of 1622, after which Governor Yeardley took the silver to James Town; later it was given to the church at Hampton, and here it has served Communion to many Indian students of the Hampton Normal School (now Hampton Institute). The only English church silver in the United States that is older is at St. Peter's Church, Perth Amboy, New Jersey, according to George C. Mason, in his *Colonial Churchs of Tidewater Virginia*. That church was founded in 1698, and the silver, made in London in 1611, was then imported. The vessels at Hampton, therefore, have been in use much longer in this country. Also in the parish is the oldest free school in the country — the Symms-Eaton Free School. It was founded by a bequest of Benjamin Symms and an endowment of Thomas Eaton in 1634, and it has been active ever since, presently as part of the public school system.

311

Westover Church (1731)

Charles City County, Virginia

Westover, one of the oldest and most interesting parishes in Virginia, is located upstream from Jamestown, on the north side of the James River. Charles City corporation was one of the four corporations set up by the Virginia Company, in 1618, to govern the Plantation. Charles City County was one of the eight original shires into which Virginia was divided in 1634 (after King James had ended the Plantation period by dissolving the Virginia Company, in 1624, and taking the colony under royal control). The vast area of this county lay on both sides of the James, from James City County on the east to Henrico County at the Appomattox River on the west.

On the Appomattox, in 1612, Charles City Hundred was settled and Bermuda Hundred was granted. To Bermuda Hundred, Governor Sir Thomas Dale soon added "West and Shirley" Hundred, on the north side of the James, which became a part of his New Bermudas. Wyanoke was a plantation developed from 2,200 acres that were given to Governor Sir George Yeardley, in 1617, by the Indian Chief Opechancanough. Smith's Hundred was established in 1618, the first large plantation in the colony, being a tract of 100,000 acres between Weyanoke and the Chickahominy River, north of the James. St. Mary's Church was established in Smith's Hundred by the will of Mrs. Mary (Ramsay) Robinson of London, which was proved in 1618; if a church building was erected, it was contemporary with Argall's Church at Jamestown (see No. 293). In 1619 a silver communion cup, bearing a hallmark of 1617, was presented to the church in Smith's Hundred. The settlement, then called Southampton Hundred, was wiped out in the Indian massacre of 1622, and the only relic of the church is the silver cup, which now is at St. John's Church, Hampton (No. 310), the oldest piece of English church silver in length of service in America. Westover plantation got its name from the West family. Thomas West, Lord Delaware (de la Warr), was governor of Virginia from 1609 until his death in 1618 (see Jamestown, No. 293). In 1619, the year after his death at sea on his return voyage to Virginia, a tract of land was granted to Francis West, his younger brother, who also was prominent in Virginia, for Henry West, his son and heir. Lord

Delaware had married Ceciley Sherley (or Shirley) and in West and Shirley Hundred the union of the two families was commemorated.

West and Shirley Hundred developed into Westover Parish, lying on both sides of the James and extending up to Henrico County. Weyanoke plantation developed likewise into Weyanoke Parish, on both sides of the James. On the south side, in 1655, Martin's Brandon Parish was laid off from Weyanoke, and Jordon's Parish was laid off from Westover Parish for a brief life before it was rejoined (see Merchant's Hope Church, No. 299). Wallingford Parish was established in the area of the vanished Smith's Hundred. In 1703, Prince George County was laid off on the south side, and Charles City County was confined to the north side. In 1720 an Act of Assembly gave Charles City County its present boundaries; it also dissolved Wallingford Parish and added to Westover the section west of the Chickahominy, dissolved Weyanoke Parish and added its section north of the James to Westover, and south of the James the sections of both Weyanoke and Westover parishes were added to Martin's Brandon Parish. In 1724, Wilmington Parish was dissolved,

and its section south of the Chickahominy was added to Westover Parish. From that time to the present, Westover Parish has been coextensive with the county.

The first church of Westover Parish stood within a few hundred yards up the James from the plantation house, nearly two miles from the present site. There the old churchyard contains tombstones that date from 1637; it was in that year that Captain Thomas Pawlett patented 2,000 acres that became known as Westover, and undoubtedly he was influential in having the church built on this part of his land, which he left to the church by his will. There are tombstones of the Bland, Byrd, and Harrison families. Theodorick Bland, who bought Westover from the heirs of Captain Pawlett in 1665, died in 1671 and was buried there. His sons sold Westover to the first William Byrd in 1688. He was born in London in 1650, came to Virginia in 1674, and died here in 1704, after serving as receiver-general of His Majesty's revenues for the colony, and as a member of the King's Council and the House of Burgesses. His son, the second William Byrd, was born at Westover in 1674 and died there in 1744. His monument is in the garden near the old churchyard. He succeeded his father as receiver of the colony's revenues, and for thirty-seven years was a member of the King's Council. He founded the city of Richmond, surveyed the Virginia-North Carolina boundary, and built the present beautiful brick mansion of Westover, which continued in the family, and the present brick church. His son, the third Colonel William Byrd (1728-1777), also served as a member of the Council of Virginia, and in 1756 as colonel of the 2d Virginia regiment in the French and Indian War. He married Eliza, daughter of John Carter of near-by Shirley plantation. Senator Harry F. Byrd, Admiral Richard E. Byrd, and Thomas B. Byrd of our time — the famous Tom, Dick, and Harry — were born in the eighth generation of the line from the first William Byrd.

Benjamin Harrison, of near-by Berkeley plantation, was buried in the old churchyard. He was the cousin of Benjamin Harrison of Brandon; the father of Benjamin, speaker of the House of Burgesses; grandfather of Benjamin, a signer of the Declaration of Independence, who was born at Berkeley about 1740; great-grandfather of William Henry Harrison, ninth President of the United States in 1841, who was born at Berkeley in 1773; great-great-grandfather of John Scott Harrison, congressman; and great-great-great-grandfather of Benjamin, twenty-third President of the United States in 1889. In the churchyard are the tombstones of Nathaniel Harrison and his wife, of Berkeley.

The last occupant of the glebe was Sewell Chapin, who came to Westover Church about 1793. Parson Chapin, as he was called, baptized John Tyler, tenth President of the United States and successor of William Henry Harrison. The Tyler homestead was Sherwood Forest, and there a portrait of Parson Chapin hung, until it was taken to Richmond for safekeeping during the Civil War and was burned with the city. Chapin died at Weyanoke, the residence of F. Lewis, and was buried under the chancel of the present church.

For many years, Westover was the county seat of Charles City County, and the courthouse as well as the church stood near the mansion. In 1731 that first church was replaced by the present building, located about a mile and a half from the mansion, on the north side of Herring Creek. As the section of the parish south of the James had been separated, it was not important to have the church on the river bank, and the new church was more convenient to the parish now confined to the north side. There was another reason for moving the church — the custom of the congregation staying for dinner at Westover had become so firmly established that Colonel Byrd was unable otherwise to end it. It is established by Byrd's journal for December 12, 1740, that the two buildings stood simultaneously for a while; and in the Byrd title book it was noted that, when the church was moved to Herring Creek, the land left by Pawlett was to be sold, and that that was done in 1731. The last grave at the old site is that of Miss Evelyn Byrd (1707-1737), daughter of the second William Byrd; and the first at the present site is dated 1748.

The rectangular building, of brick laid in Flemish bond, was designed in the conventional Georgian style. During the difficult times for the Episcopal Church in the early nineteenth century, the building was used as a barn, and in the Civil War, Federal troops used it for a stable. In the course of repairs, the colonial design was modified — the door on the south side was replaced by an additional arched window, in the east end a window was replaced by a door, and the high-backed box pews were replaced by modern pews. Westover continues as an active Episcopal parish church, and thousands of visitors come here annually, while touring historic Tidewater Virginia.

St. John's Church (1741)
Henrico Church, Richmond Church,
or Town Church

Richmond, Henrico County, Virginia

Captain John Smith was in a party of explorers under Captain Christopher Newport, which sailed up the James River, in 1607, and planted a cross on an island by the site of the present Richmond. Henrico Parish, one of the oldest parishes in America, was founded by the Church of England in 1611, four years after the first settlement and parish were founded at Jamestown, and one year after Elizabeth City Parish (see St. John's Church, Hampton, No. 310). The original Henrico Parish included the area of the present counties of Chesterfield and Powhatan on the south and Goochland and Henrico on the north side of the James. In 1611, when Sir Thomas Dale founded Henricopolis on the peninsula in the river, and named the settlement for Prince Henry, the eldest son of James I, he immediately built a church. A more substantial brick church was built soon after, near the site of the Dutch Gap canal. The first rector of Henrico Parish was Alexander Whittaker, the "Apostle of Virginia." He and Dale worked together for the conversion of Pocahontas, daughter of the sachem Powhatan, and he baptized her with the name Rebecca. After her marriage with John Rolfe, the famous couple lived on Rolfe's plantation at Henricopolis until he took her to England; a descendant of theirs was John Randolph (1775-1833), a member of the prominent family, who served in Congress during Jefferson's administration. Dale built a rectory on the glebe of 100 acres, on the south side of the river. At a much later time the glebe was located on the north side. In 1622 the Indian massacre swept away Henricopolis, as well as many other settlements, including Smith's Hundred (see Westover Church, No. 311). For the next century there are few records of the parish. An outstanding rector of the period was James Blair. He served the parish from 1685 to 1694, was appointed commissary of the Bishop in 1689, and resigned here to become the founder and first president of William and Mary College (1693) at Williamsburg, the capital (see No. 295). Henrico was diminished in area in 1727, when Goochland and Powhatan were cut off, and in 1735, when Dale Parish was founded in Chesterfield. In that year, David

Mossom was invited to preach here every fifth Sunday; he was rector of St. Peter's, New Kent (No. 314), where he married George Washington and Martha Custis, and he had been rector of St. Michael's, Marblehead, Massachusetts (No. 110). The oldest surviving vestry book begins in 1730. At that time the parish church was Curle's Church, located on the north side of the James a few miles below Richmond. There was also another church and a chapel in the parish of 400 families. A demand grew for a church in town, and after controversy over the site, it was decided to build it "on Indian Town, at Richmond."

The present church was built in 1741. The rector at the time was William Stith, a native Virginian who was educated at William and Mary and in England; he wrote a history of Virginia during his ministry here. The building operation was supervised by Richard Randolph of the famous Virginia family. In 1733 the second Colonel William Byrd of Westover, who owned large tracts of land on the James, had founded the town of Richmond. The two lots that he gave for the church cover half of the present burying ground. The rectangular frame building, measuring sixty by twenty-five feet, was oriented west to east, and over its west end was a cupola belfry. In 1772 the building was enlarged, when the nave was built as an addition on the north side, giving a T-form with the two ends of the original building as transepts. In the 1820's the nave was enlarged to its present size of forty-five feet wide by thirty-nine feet deep, two aisles were made to replace the one center aisle, and the arrangement of galleries was changed. The original belfry was removed from the west end, and the present tower and belfry were built. During the period of remodeling, the name of St. John's was given

to the church, and it is so called in the record of the convention of 1829 and the vestry book for that year. In 1905 a large chancel, an organ chamber, and a vestry room were built on the south side of the original building, completing the present form of a cross.

The original box pews, with their backs cut down, are still in the church. In one of them, to the left near the front, stood Patrick Henry when he made his famous address, in 1775, to the second Virginia Convention, ending with the words that inspired the Revolution: "Give me Liberty, or give me death!" Among the members of the Convention were other patriots, such as George Washington and Thomas Jefferson, and the church has been referred to as the "Birthplace of Liberty." In 1777 the records of that state were moved from Williamsburg, and in 1779 Richmond became the capital. In 1781, when the city was occupied and burned by the British forces under the command of Benedict Arnold, the church was used by their troops as a barracks. At the first convention of the reorganized Diocese of Virginia, which was held in 1785 at the Capitol, with services at the church here, Edmund Randolph (1753-1813), a vestryman, represented Henrico Parish. He was elected treasurer of the Diocese and filled that office for thirty years, and he worked for the Diocese of Virginia to join the Protestant Episcopal Church. In 1787 he became governor of Virginia; in 1789 Washington appointed him the first Attorney General of the United States; and in 1794 he succeeded Jefferson as Secretary of State. In the churchyard is the grave of George Wythe (1726-1806), the first signer of the Declaration of Independence, and the first professor of law in America, at William and Mary, where he was the teacher of John Marshall, who became Chief Justice of the Supreme Court. Wythe was the great-grandson of George Keith, the first missionary in America for the Society for the Propagation of the Gospel. The oldest grave in the churchyard is marked by the sarcophagus of Robert Rose, just outside the east doorway. He was the rector of St. Anne's Parish, Essex (see No. 327), and St. Anne's, Albermarle County. He died in 1751, when he had been called here for his counsel by the officials laying out the city. His brother, Charles Rose, was the earliest recorded rector of Yeocomico Church, Cople Parish (No. 331). The communion silver which had been presented, in 1722, to the Lower Chapel, Middlesex, found its way to Richmond after the chapel had been abandoned by Episcopalians; in 1846 it was purchased by the vestry of St. Paul's, and it is used occasionally.

313

Grace Church (1696)
York Church

Yorktown, York County, Virginia

On the peninsula between the York and the James rivers, Yorktown is situated near the mouth of the York where it flows into the Chesapeake Bay. The long, narrow strip of territory forming York County, along the south side of the river, was settled early, as it was in the region of the first settlement at Jamestown, and only twelve miles east of the second capital at Williamsburg. Three Anglican parishes were formed in the county. In the lower part was New Poquoson Parish, with the river of that name flowing through it (Old Poquoson referred to the original name of Elizabeth City, the next county extending to the point in the bay); in 1692 the name was changed to Charles Parish. In the upper county two parishes were established, Hampton and York. In 1630 plantations were settled around the Indian village of Kiskyache, and in 1642 a parish was established with the same name, spelled also Chisiack and Chescake, which was changed later to Hampton (distinct from the town of that name

to the south). York Parish was settled in 1632. The two parishes shared one minister, the first being Anthony Paton, 1639-40, and in time they became the united parish of York-Hampton.

A contract to build the first York Church was let in 1642. The church was built on Temple Farm (a few miles from Yorktown), and the plot became known as "Church Field." In the historic Moore House on Temple Farm, on October 18, 1781, the commissioners drafted the Articles of Capitulation under which the British Army of General Cornwallis surrendered, ending the Revolution. Yorktown was founded in 1691, as a port of entry for the county; a courthouse was built here, and the county seat was moved from the half-way house on the Williamsburg-York road, where the Hampton Church was located. In 1724, in his report to the Bishop of London, to whom all the Anglican priests in America reported, Francis Fontaine mentioned his two churches, one in Yorktown and the other eight miles away. In his parish, twenty miles long and four broad, there were 200 families with 60 communicants at Yorktown and 20 at Hampton Church.

The principal evidence that the present church was built in 1696 is the subscription of £20 for the purpose by Governor Francis Nicholson that year, provided that the church be built within two years. The year before, he had given three and a half acres for a free school. The church was built on a bluff, high above the water, commanding a broad view of the river and the bay. Originally the building was in the form of a T, with the nave oriented. The walls were built of marl, a soft stone taken from the river bluff, which is used in the manufacture of cement. The building was damaged by the British during the Revolution, when they used it as a magazine. In 1815, during the War of 1812, they burned the church. The fire hardened the marl into the solid blocks, which are covered with the stucco that we see on the walls today. In prehistoric times, vitrified forts were made by a similar technique, as in Nairnshire, Scotland, by firing the walls from trenches, inside and out. It was many years after the fire when the church finally was restored. The walls of the transepts were torn down, and the restored building consisted of the nave measuring sixty by thirty feet. The bell, inscribed "Yorktown 1725," was broken in the fire. The church suffered again during the Civil War, when a signal tower was built on it to take advantage of the view. The pieces of the bell were taken by Federal troops in 1865, but they were located in

Philadelphia, and after it had been recast in 1882, the bell was restored to the church.

After the Revolution the port declined, and the parish did not grow. The Hampton Church became neglected and was allowed to go to ruin. When York and Hampton churches united, the latter owned the communion silver of 1649, which is now in the possession of Grace Church. The present name was given to the old York-Hampton Church after the formation of the Republic. Among the prominent members of the parish were the Nelson family, of which three, father, son, and grandson, lie buried in the churchyard — Thomas Nelson (1677-1745), William Nelson (1711-72), and General Thomas Nelson (1738-89), a signer of the Declaration of Independence.

314

St. Peter's Church (1701)
The Brick Church

New Kent County, Virginia

Between the Chikahominy and the Pamunkey Rivers, thirty-three miles west of Williamsburg and twenty-two miles east of Richmond and situated deep in the woods, the Brick Church of St. Peter's Parish is well worth finding. It is one of the oldest churches in Virginia, and it is the "First Church of the First First-Lady." In this church on January 6, 1759, Martha (Dandridge) Custis and George Washington were married. Martha's parents were on the parish list before

she was born, in 1731, and in 1735 her father, Major John Dandridge, was chosen as a warden of the church. When she was eighteen, she married Colonel Daniel Parke Custis, another parishioner and vestryman of St. Peter's. After his death in 1757, she continued to live with her two children at their home, the "White House," situated on the Pamunkey River quite a few miles from the church, until she married Washington a year and a half later; they then went to live at Mt. Vernon. The marriage ceremony in the Brick Church was performed by the rector, the Reverend Doctor David Mossom, who had come to America in 1718, had been rector of St. Michael's, Marblehead, Massachusetts (No. 110) from 1718 to 1726, and he served as rector of St. Peter's here for forty years, 1727-1767.

The Act of 1656 required all counties to be laid out into parishes, and New Kent, which had been formed from York County two years earlier, became St. Peter's Parish. It was divided into Upper and Lower Parish, and in 1704 Upper Parish was laid off to form St. John's Parish. The remaining St. Peter's Parish then had two churches, an old frame building "commonly known as ye Broken back'd Church," and the new Brick Church, built in 1701 because of the condition of the old building and the inconvenience in reaching it. The design of this present Brick Church was drawn by Will Hughes, and the land was bought from Thomas Jackson, according to the first entry in the vestry book referring to this building, August 13, 1700. In 1703 the new brick building was opened for services and vestry meetings. The plain, low-pitched rectangular building, sixty by twenty-four feet, remained unchanged for twenty years. The brickwork is in English bond. In 1719 a brick wall was built around the churchyard, a copy of the one around the Capitol at Williamsburg, but it was removed later. In 1722 a belfry was built at the west end of the church to house a fine bell given to the parish that year. In 1740 the present steeple and vestry room were ordered built. In this tower, above the Norman-arched porch, is the vestry room, and the finial on the southeast corner of the tower is the chimney from the room. The room is reached now by an inside stairway, but in a Brady photograph of 1862, showing Major General E. V. Sumner and Union troops in the churchyard, a straight wooden stairway runs up through the porch. After the Revolution the congregation was scattered; the church was not used until 1820, when it was repaired and adopted by Presbyteri-

ans. In 1843 Episcopal services were revived, and the two denominations used the church jointly, with services alternating weekly and happily mingling the congregations, until 1856 when the Presbyterians built a church of their own. During the Civil War the church was stripped of its furnishings and used as a stable, and in the years following the parish was small, poor, and not very active in the church. In 1922 a group of people of various denominations took steps to save the historic building by forming the St. Peter's Church Restoration Association. The annual meeting is held in the church each third Sunday in September. In 1953, for the 250th anniversary of the completion of the building, it was restored to its original design. In the course of research for the restoration, the prototype of the design was discovered in a seventeenth century building near St. Peter's village in Kent, England. In charge of the restoration was the late George Carrington Mason, historiographer of the Diocese of Southern Virginia and a leading authority on colonial churches. During repairs he discovered, at the gable ends, signs of Jacobean curvilinear gables that had been removed, and these are the principal changes in the recent restoration. In the east end there was originally a large window like that at Christ Church, Middlesex (No. 325), ten feet wide by six feet high, but it has been filled in.

315

Fork Church (1735)

Hanover County, Virginia

The York River is formed by the confluence of the Mattaponi and the Pamunkey rivers, and the Pamunkey is formed by that of the North Anna and the South Anna rivers. The Annas form the Fork, which joins near the towns of Hanover and Ashland and gives the name to this section. The Fork Church is located in the country near Beaver Dam, eight miles north of Ashland. Hanover County was laid off from New Kent County in 1720, and St. Paul's Parish was the mother parish for the several Anglican parishes formed in the county. In 1726 St. Martin's Parish was laid off from St. Paul's and named for St. Martin-in-the-Fields, London, which was finished that year. In 1742, seven years after the present church was built, Louisa County was laid off from Hanover, and Fredericksville Parish was laid off from St. Martin's; when Fredericksville was divided in turn, at a later date, the part bordering St. Martin's was called Trinity Parish. There were two other churches in the western part of St. Martin's, one at Allen's Creek, the other at Hollowing Creek, but no trace of either survives. The Slash Church of St. Paul's Parish still stands (No. 316).

farm where there now is a graveyard in "Church Field," near Glebe Point. A petition to the court and council in 1680 requested permission to build another church in Ware Parish; although the date of construction is not known, the present building is supposed to be the result. William Byrd Lee, the rector in 1907, when he was author of the article on this church in *Colonial Churches of Virginia*, thought that it must have been built in 1690. Because of its architecture, others have placed the date as late as 1715, although similar buildings were erected in the seventeenth century. This church is outstanding in several respects — it is a classic example of the rectangular style, it was the largest (eighty by forty feet) and the most costly of its time, and the three doorways, on the north, south, and west, are the finest of their type. The walls, three feet thick, are laid in Flemish bond with glazed headers. There are twelve large arched windows, two lighting the chancel and five on each side. The interior arrangement has been changed to one central aisle. Originally there were two side aisles covered with flagstone between the pews at the sides and those in the center, and a cross aisle before the chancel, connecting the north and south doors. A high pulpit stood near the south door. When

the interior was renovated in 1854, the congregation objected to the modern pews which were substituted for the medium-high box pews. At that time a floor was installed to replace the flagstone aisles at the level of the pew floor, and it was carried out over the tombs in the floor at the east end of the church. A vestibule was made of the space under the gallery, and a modern pulpit was placed in the chancel. The church now owns part of the set of communion silver that was given to Poplar Spring Church, Petsworth Parish, by Augustine Warner before 1681; he was a great-grandfather of George Washington.

318

Abingdon Church (1754)

Gloucester County, Virginia

After the downfall of Charles I, who was beheaded in 1649, many of his party, the Cavaliers, left England under pressure from the Puritans and came to Virginia, many of them settling in Gloucester County. In 1651 the county was laid off from Charles River County (later York). Abingdon Parish was established about 1655, covering the southeastern part of the county. Mobjack Bay, a great arm of the Chesapeake, lay on the east, the York River on the south, and the parishes of Petsworth and Ware on the west and north, making the total length of the boundaries thirty or forty miles. It was at Purton Bay of the York River that the Indian chief, Powhatan, had his main residence, at Weworocomico, and here Pocahontas saved the life of Captain John Smith. Many Indian middens of oyster shells mark Indian settlements in the county; and the "War Path", or "Indian Road," passed within a few miles of Ware and Abingdon churches, on the way to Page Rock and across the river to "Indian Fields," their settlement in York County. Tyndall's Point, now Gloucester Point, across the river from Yorktown, originally was in Kiskyache Parish (see Grace Church, Yorktown, No. 313).

In a walnut grove on the road between Gloucester Courthouse and Gloucester Point, the foundation of the first church lies close by the present building. The church was built in a region of large plantations. Early records of the parish and county were lost in a series of fires — at Jamestown in 1676, during Nathaniel Bacon's Rebellion of a century before the Revolution; at Williamsburg in 1776, during the Revolution; at the county seat of Botetourt, now Gloucester, in 1820; and at Richmond in 1865, during the Civil War, after the records had been taken there for safe keeping. Bacon's last stand was in Gloucester County, and he died here of malaria in 1676. Parish records here and elsewhere were affected by his rebellion; vestry books contained possible evidence of treason, and many such records antedating the rebellion were deliberately destroyed. It is more than coincidence, therefore, that the vestry book of Petsworth Parish commences in 1677. It is assumed that the first church, which was smaller than the present building, was built in the early days of the parish. The plot of half an acre, on which the first church and the cemetery were located, was given by Colonel Augustine Warner, of near-by Warner Hall. His daughter Mildred, who was brought up as a member of this church, married Lawrence Washington, of Westmoreland County, and became a grandmother of George Washington.

The present beautiful church was begun in 1754 and finished in 1755. It is one of the eight churches of colonial Virginia built in the form of

488

a Latin cross. It measures eighty-one by seventy-six feet, with brick walls over two feet thick laid in Flemish bond. The gables are pedimented, with dentilated cornices. The twelve windows are arched, with the arches framed in rubbed brick conforming to the curve. The three doorways are pedimented, the main doorway with a segmented arch. The interior has been changed to some extent. The modern pulpit has been restored to the southeast corner of the crossing, where the original stood, and the galleries in the transepts have been retained, with their original high-backed pews. The large reredos was installed in the chancel in 1841. During the Civil War, the large box pews were used as horse stalls by Federal troops; in 1867, in the course of repairs, they were replaced with modern pews, and the flag-stone aisles were floored over with the new flooring. In 1897 the building again was repaired and restored. The set of communion silver, still in use, was made in London in 1702 and presented to the church, in 1703, by Major Lewis Burwell of Carter's Grove. In that year George Keith, the first missionary of the Society for the Propagation of the Gospel, preached here. The Burwell, Lewis, Page, and Thruston families had large plantations in the parish, and they occupied the galleries in the north and south transepts. In the absence of many of the parish records, the Thruston family Bible is a source of valuable information in the eighteenth century.

319

Upper Church (c. 1725)
Old Church

King and Queen County, Virginia

The march of English settlement up the York River was marked by the formation of King and Queen County. The York is formed by the confluence of the Mattaponi River and the Pamunkey River at the present town of West Point. In 1651 the area north of the York and the Mattaponi was laid off from Charles River County (which had been one of the eight original shires and later was named York) to form Gloucester County; in 1654 the region of the two forks was laid off from York and Gloucester to form New Kent County; in 1691 the area between the Pamunkey and Dragon Swamp (the present boundary with Middlesex County) was laid off from New Kent to form King and Queen County; and in 1701 the area between the Pamunkey and the Mattaponi was laid off from King and Queen to form King William County. Of the nine colonial houses of worship built in the area of the original King and Queen County, six are still standing — two in the present King and Queen County and four in King William. The two in King and Queen are this third Upper Church of Stratton Major Parish and the second Mattapony Church (No. 320).

Stratton Major Parish was coextensive with King and Queen County. All of the parish records are lost except one vestry book, which begins in 1729. Then there were two churches in the parish, the Upper and the Lower churches, at which vestry meetings alternated. The present third building of the Upper Church was erected about 1725. It and its predecessor were located over eight miles below (downstream from) King and Queen Courthouse, and about four miles above (upstream from) Shackelford's. The first Upper Church, which was located above King and Queen Courthouse, had been included in the new St. Stephen's Parish, when it was laid off from Stratton Major Parish some time before 1674. The second Upper Church was built about 1675. The Lower Church stood below Shackelford's at Buena Vista. Of the three Upper and one Lower Church buildings, the present building is the only one to survive.

This third Upper Church, according to George C. Mason, in his *Colonial Churches of Tidewater Virginia*, evidently was built between 1724 and before 1729, when the surviving vestry book began. It is a beautiful example of the rectangular church. The colonial brick is laid in Flemish bond, with dark glazed headers. The upper walls are two feet thick, or two and a half brick lengths. The inside measurements are sixty feet-four inches by thirty feet, the conventional proportion of length twice the width. The building was oriented, with the chancel at the east end. A central aisle ran from the main entrance at the west end to the chancel, and a cross aisle from the pulpit on the north to the south door. There are three windows on each side of the nave, one on each side of the chancel, two in the east end, and circular windows in both gables. In 1739 a gallery was built in the west end. In 1730 Colonel Garvin Corbin, of a prominent family in the parish, gave a marble font to the church.

To serve the entire parish, a New Church was built at a point just north of Shackelford's, between the Upper and the Lower churches. The land was given by Richard Corbin, a member of the council and the receiver-general of Virginia. When it was completed in 1768, the New Church was the largest and the most costly in the colony. The two older churches then were abandoned; the Upper Church was boarded up, and the Lower Church was allowed to go to ruin. The New Church, however, was used for only nine years. In 1777, when there was opposition

to both the Crown and the Church of England, services were ended. The fine building was sold, and in 1825 it was pulled down and the bricks were taken for other uses.

After the disestablishment of the Church of England, following the Revolution, this one surviving building was put to use by a branch of the Lower King and Queen Baptist Church. In the early nineteenth century, other denominations contended for the use of the building, and in 1842 the congregation built the Olivet Baptist Church near by. The abandoned church building was used as a school taught by Robert Stubbs, until it was gutted by fire. In 1850 it was restored, and for some years thereafter it was used by both Baptists and Methodists. The property finally was bought by the Methodists, who had recorded it in their Gloucester Circuit from 1818 to 1826, and it has continued in their possession.

320

Mattapony Church (c. 1755)
Lower Church of St. Stephen's Parish

King and Queen County, Virginia

The present beautiful Mattapony Church (pronounced locally, Mat'-ta-po nī') was built as the second church on the site. The first was built about 1664, as the first Upper Church of Stratton Major Parish. Some time before 1674, the upper part of Stratton Major was laid off to form St. Stephen's Parish, and the first Upper Church of the old parish became the first parish church and the first Lower Church of St. Stephen's. The present Mattapony Church was built as the second church of St. Stephen's on the site of its predecessor, and it is the only colonial church of the parish to survive. It was located at the head of Mantapike Creek, on what was called "Church Road," on the south side of State Route 14, about eight miles north of King and Queen Courthouse. The Upper Church of St. Stephen's was known as the Apple Tree Church. It was a brick building located about six miles above Walkerton and southwest of the town of St. Stephen's Church. After the Revolution it was abandoned and destroyed.

The date of Mattapony Church is not known, but it was erected probably between 1720 and 1760. The date 1733 is on the cover of a Bible of "The Lower Church St. Stephen's Parish," but George C. Mason, in his *Colonial Churches of*

Tidewater Virginia, suggests that the Bible might have belonged to an earlier church, and he is led to believe that this one was built about 1755, because of its similarity to Abingdon Church (1754) in Gloucester County (No. 318), both of which were built in the form of a Latin cross. Mattapony was a large church for its time, measuring eighty-five by sixty-five feet outside the upper walls. The plan was conventional, with the brick walls laid in Flemish bond and glazed headers, the main entrance at the west end of the nave, the chancel at the east end, and doors in the north and south transepts. There are two windows in each side of the nave, one in each side of the other three arms of the cross, two in the east end, and none in the gables. The interior, which has been modernized, originally had a three-decker pulpit with a sounding board at the north angle of the crossing; the reredos in the chancel carried the Lord's Prayer, the Apostles' Creed, and the Ten Commandments; the high box pews had seats on three sides and the aisles were paved with marble.

After the disestablishment of the Church of England, Mattapony Church was abandoned. About 1803 it was taken over by Baptists and repaired. It served as the Lower King and Queen Baptist Church until 1828, when the congregation was organized as Mattapony Baptist Church. In 1834 the interior was modernized. As the Baptists had no use for a vessel of such a scale, the original baptismal font was given to Old Fork Church in Hanover County (No. 315). In 1922 the interior was gutted by fire, but the building was restored promptly, and it continues in use by the Baptist organization.

321   *(See photo on following page)*

St. John's Church (1732)
Lower Church of St. John's Parish

King William County, Virginia

In 1691, when it was laid off from New Kent County, King and Queen County extended from the Pamunkey River across the Mattaponi River to Dragon Swamp, where it has a common boundary with Middlesex County. In 1701 the area between the Pamunkey and the Mattaponi was laid off from King and Queen to form King William County. In the original King and Queen County, of the nine houses of worship built during the colonial period, six are still standing. Two of them are in the present King and Queen County, as we have just seen, and the remaining four are in King William — St. John's, Acquinton, Cattail, and Mangohick. Although they all were built as Anglican churches, of the six still standing, St. John's is the only one to be retained by the Episcopal Church. According to George C. Mason, in his *Colonial Churches of Tidewater Virginia,* St. John's Parish was formed in 1680, from the southern parts of Stratton Major and Stephen's parishes; and in 1691, upon the formation of King and Queen County, the part of St. Peter's Parish, New Kent (No. 314), between Pamunkey Neck Ridge and the Pamunkey River was added to St. John's.

The present St. John's Church was begun about 1732 and finished in 1734, as the second Lower Church of St. John's Parish. It is located between the Pamunkey and the Mattaponi rivers, about nine miles above their confluence at West

Point. The first Lower Chapel had been built at West Point about 1665. In 1732 the council had ordered the vestry of St. John's Parish to proceed with their plan to build two churches, and the present St. John's and Acquinton churches were the result.

The original rectangular building was oriented. A wing was added subsequently on the north side, giving the building its present T-form. The brick was laid in Flemish bond with glazed headers. The doorways in the west and north ends have pedimented enframents. The pediments were both triangular, but in recent times the north wing was enlarged, and an arched pediment was installed in molded brick, with rubbed brick forming the arch. When the north wing was added, the south doorway was closed up, the reredos and altar were moved from the east end to the south side, and a small doorway was made in the east end. The brick bearing the date 1734 and the initials "I. H.," which was in the pediment of the south doorway, was moved to the north entrance. The reredos does not fit the spaces between the windows in this church, and it is believed that it came from Acquinton Church (No. 322). The original gallery is in the west end, with two windows in the gable to light it. The church is now furnished with plain, unpainted benches. The church was idle for many years. An association was formed to preserve it, and the building was repaired. It is used occasionally for memorial services.

322

Acquinton Church (c. 1760)
Upper Church of St. John's Parish

King William County, Virginia

The second Upper Church of St. John's Parish was finished in 1734. The structure that still stands was a later addition to that church. It was located in the rich Pamunkey Neck area, just west of King William Courthouse. This Acquinton Church occupies the site of frontier Acquinton Chapel, on one of the tributaries of Acquinton Creek referred to in old deeds as "Chappell branch." The council had ordered, in 1732, that the vestry of St. John's Parish proceed to build two churches in the parish; St. John's (No. 322) and Acquinton churches were the result. During the decade from 1755 to 1765, the parish increased in population until it became necessary to enlarge the church, and a wing was added to the north side of the rectangular brick building. This wing, which in the absence of specific records we assume was built about 1760, is the only part of the colonial structure that still stands. Under the last colonial rector, Parson Henry Skyren, the attendance was so great that, even in the enlarged church, many parishioners brought seats and sat in the aisles.

The original rectangular building measured fifty-eight by twenty-nine feet inside of walls

twenty-two-and-one-half inches thick. The wing was twenty-six feet wide and extended thirty-four feet from the north wall. The brick was laid in Flemish bond. About 1800, after the disestablishment of the Church of England, the building was abandoned by the Episcopal parish and became a free church. It was used by Baptists, Methodists, Christians, and only occasionally by Episcopalians. After the Civil War the building became dilapidated. In 1875 a congregation of Methodists bought out the interests of the Episcopalians. They tore down the original body of the church, which was not worth saving, and remodelled the north wing. Bricks from the demolished walls were used to extend the wing by fourteen and one-half feet to close the south end, making a rectangular building of about fifty by thirty feet, outside. The lancet windows, which obviously are not colonial, date from this later period. The level top of the end wall indicates that the roof formerly was hipped. The walls were covered with stucco some years later. The colonial furnishings were retained, with the high-backed pews and the high pulpit at the left of the new south door. The building finally was abandoned, and in 1932 the Methodists deeded the property back to the Episcopalians, with the intention of having it preserved. However, it has been stripped of all furnishings and allowed to go to ruin.

323

Mangohick Church (c. 1730)
Chapel of St. Margaret's Parish
Upper Church of St. David's Parish

King William County, Virginia

In 1720 the upper part of St. John's Parish, which was coextensive with King William County, was laid off by Act of Assembly to create St. Margaret's Parish; and as the remaining St. John's would contain both churches, the old parish was ordered to contribute 25,000 pounds of tobacco and cask, a portion of the cost, for building a church in the new parish. The result was the present Mangohick Church, which evidently was built as a chapel of ease in St. Margaret's Parish. The second Colonel William Byrd of Westover (see No. 311), who passed this way in 1732 on his return journey, referred to it, in his journal of "Progress to the Mines," as the New Brick Church. With this and other evidence as clues, it is assumed by George C. Mason, in his *Colonial Churches of Tidewater Virginia*, that Mangohick was built about 1730. The new church was located at the head of Mangohick Creek, from which it assumed the Indian name. The creek is a tributary of the Pamunkey River. The building is on County Route 638, just off State Route 30.

In 1738 the history of the chapel was enlivened by a petition that throws additional light on the operation of the Church of England in a region where there were more houses of worship than ministers. Each parish had a paid clerk, whose duty it was, in addition to recording the affairs of the parish, to read services in the absence of a minister. The petition complained "that John Brunskill, Clerk Minister of said Parish hath Neglected to perform Divine Service at a Chapel of Ease built several years agoe for the Convenience of a great number of Families living remote from the Church of said parish and refusing to preach or Read prayers there as by Law he is obliged."

In 1744, when St. David's Parish was formed from a part of St. Margaret's, Mangohick became the Upper Church of St. David's Parish. As Mangohick was built as a chapel, the oriented, rectangular building is plain in style. It is unusually long in proportion to the width, sixty-two by twenty-eight feet outside the upper walls. The brick is laid in Flemish bond, with glazed headers, and the plan also is conventional — doorways in the west end and south side, two windows on each side of the nave and in the east end, one on each side of the chancel, and a gallery in the west end, lighted by two windows. All doors and windows are plain and rectangular; originally the doorway in the west end had a relieving arch, and the smaller brick of a later period can be seen where it filled in the space at the time of the alteration. A small window in the north side, nearer the chancel than the point opposite the south door, indicates that there was a great pew between the pulpit and the chancel, in addition to the customary two on the sides of the communion table.

After the Revolution, Mangohick was abandoned by the parish, and it became a free church. In 1825 the Union Baptist Church, with white and Negro members, was organized here. The white members moved to a new building in 1854, and since that time this has been the Mangohick Baptist Church, with a Negro congregation.

324

Cattail Church (1748)
St. David's Parish Church

King William County, Virginia

Among the tributary streams of the Pamunkey River, at a point between Mangohick and Acquinton churches (see Nos. 323 and 322), lies Cattail Swamp. In 1744 an Act of Assembly created St. David's Parish from the upper end of St. John's Parish and part of St. Margaret's Parish below Caroline County. The same act ordered the vestry of St. Margaret's to carry out their agreement by building a church in the new parish within four years, and without taxing the tithables of St. John's. The new church was to have the dimensions of the "middle church." George C. Mason, in his *Colonial Churches of Tidewater Virginia*, assumes that the middle church referred to was Reedy Church, apparently built in 1740, between the parish church of St. Margaret's, near Penola, and Mangohick Chapel, and not standing now. The result of that Act of 1744 evidently was the first St. David's Parish Church, which took the name Cattail from the near-by swamp. It stands two and a half miles

from Ayelett; William Ayelett was one of the churchwardens of St. John's Parish in whose name land was obtained by the parish in a patent of 1720, probably this site. This was the last colonial church built in King William County, and one of the four still standing. To meet the requirements of the act, building must have begun by 1748. The year of completion, 1751, appears on a brick, which was over the west doorway, and which was set as a cornerstone when the building was remodeled.

After the disestablishment of the Church of England, following the Revolution, Cattail Church was abandoned by the Episcopalians, and it became a free church, used by any denomination. The old building received no repairs or maintenance until the roof fell in, and the property was turned over to the Mt. Sinai Baptist congregation of Negroes. The building has been so remodeled that it cannot be recognized as a colonial church. Ten feet were cut off from the east end of the original length of sixty feet, buttresses were constructed to shore up the weakened brick walls, two steeples were added at the west end, a new tin roof was built, and the walls were stuccoed. Thus modernized, the colonial structure continues in active use as a church.

325

Christ Church (1712)

Middlesex County, Virginia

The present Christ Church, Middlesex, located two and a half miles south of Urbanna and the same distance east of Saluda, the county seat, was begun in 1712 and finished in 1714. It was the second parish church, the middle church of three houses of worship in Christ Church Parish. The parish and the county continue to be coextensive, as they have been since they were laid out. Middlesex County evolved through a series of divisions from the original Lancaster County, which was laid out in 1651, covering both sides of the Rappahannock River from its mouth upstream and westward indefinitely. In 1657 Lancaster was divided into two parishes separated by the river, and the parish on the south side was subdivided into an upper parish, named Lancaster, and a lower parish, named Peanckatanck (for the river on the southern boundary). In 1666 Lancaster and Peanckatanck parishes were united to form Christ Church Parish, and thereafter the

precincts were Upper, Lower, and Middle. In the Upper Parish three colonial chapels were built in succession — in 1667, 1712, and 1773. In the Lower Parish two chapels were built, in 1666 and 1714. In the Middle Parish two mother churches were built, in 1667 and 1712. Until 1949 there stood one surviving colonial house of worship in each of the three sections, but then the third Upper Chapel, at Church View, was destroyed by fire. Begun in 1772 and finished in 1773, it had been built as a cruciform brick church; early in the last century it had been taken over by Baptists, who converted the transepts to a rectangular building, after removing the nave and chancel, and used it as the Hermitage Baptist Church. After the fire, in which the old brick crumbled, the congregation built anew. That left two surviving colonial buildings, the second Lower Chapel (No. 326) and the present Christ Church.

Unlike those of many colonial parishes, the records of Christ Church Parish are intact, and a vestry book, which has been published, runs from 1663 to 1767. It is the only vestry book in Virginia antedating Bacon's Rebellion of 1676. In 1710 the vestry, noting that two of the buildings were unserviceable, ordered three new churches to be built, and included in the order several interesting architectural features which are mentioned below. In 1712 it was ordered specifically that a new church be built as soon as possible in "Middle Precinct in the same place where the old one now stands." Replacing the one of 1667, the present building was begun under that order, and it was finished in 1714, as required by the order. Three bricks inscribed with the year, as evidence that the building was finished on time, were moved during restoration from the side wall to a position over the doorway. Two "undertakers" had contracts for different parts of the work, John Hipkins and Alexander Graves. The former, whose initial "H" appears on two of the bricks with the date, had the undertaking for plumbing and glazing, "plumbing" in those days referring to lead work for gutters and leaders and possibly the sealing of glass panes. The brick of the rectangular building was laid in Flemish bond, with glazed headers, but many of the original features no longer exist in the present remodeled building. The original specifications called for dimensions of sixty by thirty feet in the clear; walls fourteen feet high (increased later by five courses of brick); a half-hipped or clipped-gable roof (as seen in Lower Chapel); a large arched window in the chancel end, ten feet wide and six feet high; a door in the south side of the chancel opposite a long, single-benched, box pew on the north side; and a rood screen between the chancel and the nave. The pulpit stood before the chancel in the middle of the aisle, with two boxed-in desks before it facing the congregation. On both sides of the pulpit were two large, double, box pews, with benches on three sides, and the remaining pews were long, single-benched box pews separated by the aisle. The rood screen was specified in 1710 for all three churches, but not one has survived in a colonial church in Virginia. The large window has been reduced considerably in size (it was similar to one in St. Peter's, New Kent, which was filled in, see No. 314). In 1719 a cupola was built on the west end to house a bell presented the year before by the Bishop of London. In 1731 the vestry made an appropriation for paving the aisles with stone in all three churches, and in 1733 to build brick walls around their churchyards. In 1762 the final colonial change called for the single pews in this church to be converted to double pews.

In his *Old Churches and Families of Virginia*, Bishop William Meade wrote that Christ Church

was abandoned for half a century. In 1848, when it was restored, a huge sycamore stood inside the open walls, and two feet of loam covered the flagstones of the aisles. No attempt was made to restore the building to its original design. In 1900 the building again was repaired and remodeled. Among the changes made, the entrance vestibule was added. Under the chancel is the grave of Sir Henry Chicheley, governor from 1678 to 1680, who died in 1682 and was buried here in the first building of the parish church. Part of an early communion set is still in use here. On land adjoining the churchyard is Christ Church School, a preparatory school for boys operated by the Episcopal Diocese.

326 (See illustration on following page)

Lower Chapel (1717)
Middlesex County, Virginia

The present Lower Chapel was the second building here, in the lower section of Christ Church Parish. It was a chapel of ease to the parish church, Christ Church, which was located in the middle section of this region between the Rappahannock and the Piankatank rivers. As noted in the account of Christ Church (No. 325), this region south of the Rappahannock was subdivided, in 1657, into Lancaster Parish and Peanckatanck Parish (the Indian name is spelled thirteen different ways in twenty-nine entries in the old vestry book), and when the two were united to form Christ Church Parish, in 1666, Peanckatanck Church became the Lower Chapel of Christ Church. The old Peanckatanck building was the first church in the region of the present county, and it probably had been the parish church of the lower parish of Lancaster County, formed in 1654, on both sides of the Rappahannock. It stood at the head of Scoggins' Creek, which flows into the Piankatank River, at the site where Lower Chapel now stands, about six miles below Christ Church.

In 1710 the vestry ordered the building of three new churches in the parish. In 1714 it ordered specifically, "That a New Church be built as Soone as conveniently may be in the Lower Precincts on the North Side of the old Church . . . fifty foot Long in the cleare and five and twenty foot wide in the cleare . . . the Roofe of the sd. Church be hipped above the wind beams." Later that year the vestry changed the measurements to fifty-two

by thirty feet, which fit the present building. The new chapel replaced the ancient Peanckatanck Church on the same site. The new mother church was nearing completion when the Lower Chapel was begun. This chapel was the smallest and the lowest in cost of the three churches. In their order the vestry set the costs of the three in sweet-scented tobacco, as follows: 126,000 pounds for the Parish Church, 110,000 pounds for the Upper Chapel, and 90,000 pounds for the Lower Chapel; the equivalent at prevailing prices of tobacco was £1060, £925, and £757 respectively. The work was undertaken by Captain Henry Armistead and Major Edmond Berkeley. It was ordered to be finished by 1717, and in October of that year the rector of the parish, Bartholomew Yates, conducted the first service in the new building.

The brick was laid in English bond, in which courses of stretchers alternate with courses of headers, and the headers are not dark or glazed. English bond was older than the popular Flemish bond, and this was one of only four surviving colonial churches in Virginia in which it was used — the others being the tower of the Jamestown Church (No. 293), St. Peter's, New Kent (No. 314), and Yeocomico Church (No. 331), the last two of which were contemporary. These bricks are unusually large, 10 by 4¾ by 3¼ inches, making a wall 27 inches thick. At the west end, to the left of the door, is a brick inscribed "17A15," the "A" probably being the initial of Armistead and the date midway in the course of construction. In the chancel end, over the table, was an unusually wide window, which had been specified in all three of the new churches. In 1750 a gallery was added in the west end. The hip roof was specified in all three churches, but this

is the only one to survive. The only other roof of the type on a colonial church in Virginia is that of Old Stone Church, Augusta (No. 343). The "wind beams" mentioned in the vestry book are called "collar beams" today. The inside arrangement used in the mother church was modified for this smaller building. At the south end of the cross aisle before the chancel there was a door, opposite the pulpit against the north wall; a rood screen separated the chancel and nave, and within the chancel the table was railed in, and there were long box pews on both sides of it, with single benches facing inward; and of the two banks of box pews separated by the aisle, the two front pews were double, having benches on three sides. The entrance portico is a later addition.

After the Revolution, when the building was abandoned, it was taken over by Methodists. All Episcopalian furnishings were removed, including the rood screen, the pulpit and the box pews; and the great window in the east end gave way to a chancel recess. Only a carved oak chest remains, before the chancel where it has always stood. It was bought in 1677 to hold altar linen, and it now is nearly three centuries old. The communion silver, which was presented to the Lower Chapel in 1722, now is in use at St. Paul's, Richmond. This Old Church, as it sometimes is called, is still active in the Methodist Lower Circuit, as Methodist Lower Chapel.

327

Vauter's Church (c. 1719)
St. Anne's Parish Church

near Loretto, Essex County, Virginia

Old Lancaster County originally lay on both sides of the Rappahannock River. In 1656 the upper part of the county was laid off to form Rappahannock County, which in turn was divided, in 1692, to form Richmond County of the territory on the north side of the river and Essex County on the south. That Rappahannock County — the present one lies four counties away to the northwest — contained Sittenbourn Parish, co-extensive with the county on both sides of the river. That extensive Anglican parish was divided, when the new counties were formed, into North Farnham Parish, Richmond County (see No. 328), and two parishes in Essex County — South Farnham Parish in lower Essex, and St. Anne's Parish in upper Essex County, both formed in 1692.

According to P. S. Hunter, in his account in *Colonial Churches in Virginia,* St. Anne's Parish had two churches. The lower of the two has been destroyed. It stood about eight miles downstream from Vauter's Church, and a quarter of a mile above the modern St. Matthew's Church (1860), in the Occupacia Creek section; its foundation remained visible on the site after the building materials had been carted away for other uses. Vauter's Church was the upper and parish church of St. Anne's.

Vauter's Church was erected on a branch of Blackburn's Creek (formerly Lucas' Creek) known as Church Swamp, near the site of the present James Madison Memorial Bridge over the Rappahannock. It is a fine example of the T-form of colonial brick church. By 1719, and possibly earlier, it was built originally as a rectangular structure; the south wing was added in 1731, which date appears on a brick in the south wall. Early parish records are lost; traditionally the communion silver was given to St. Anne's Parish by Queen Anne, and, as she died in 1714, the church may have been built by then, but among these colonial churches there are many traditions of association of Queen Anne with gifts made years after her death. We know that the church was standing in 1719, when John Vauter, a surveyor, plotted a survey of land having a boundary at "church Land," and in 1722, when he drew another survey on which is marked a "road leading to the church." From the early 1700's, the Vauters, whose name has been associated with this church from the beginning, owned land on the creek here, which they had acquired by charter from the king.

The building is oriented, with the main entrance in the west end. The chancel in the east end now is furnished in modern style, but the original high pulpit and reading desk still stand at the north side. The original box pews survive, although their high sides have been cut down. The doorway in the south wing is of classic pedimented design, with Tuscan influence, a style which was fashionable among these colonial churches in the first half of the eighteenth century, and of which Ware Church affords the earliest example (see No. 317). In the two arched doorways are the original double, four-paneled doors, with HL hinges. The brick walls are laid in Flemish bond, with black glazed headers. In the walls above each door, small windows light the two galleries.

In 1724 the rector of St. Anne's Parish was John Bagge. He died soon after he took charge, and in 1725 he was succeeded by Robert Rose (1705-1751). Rose served the parish for twenty-one years and, in 1746, became the rector of St. Anne's Parish, Albermarle County. In 1751 he was invited to Richmond by the officials laying out the city, who wanted his counsel, and when he died there during the mission, he was buried in the sarcophagus that stands outside the main entrance of the church on Richmond Hill (see St. John's Church, No. 312). He had come from Nairnshire, Scotland, the seat of the Rose clan, to become an intimate friend of Governor Alexander Spotswood, another Scot. Spotswood brought to Virginia the privilege of *habeas corpus,* developed the iron mines and German colony in Spotsylvania County, which extended to the mountains and was named in his honor (see Hebron Evangelical Lutheran Church, No. 339), and opened the western frontiers of the Virginia colony. Rose served as his chaplain, and when Spotswood died in 1740, during Rose's rectorship here, Rose served as executor of his estate. In his *Old Churches, Ministers and Families of Virginia* (1857), Bishop Meade likens the character of Rose to that of General Spotswood, "being a man of great labour, decision, benevolence, and of extraordinary business talents." He kept a journal during his last five years, which gives a vivid picture of his activities — traveling extensively in Essex and Nelson counties and the six counties between — preaching, baptizing, marrying, examining and settling accounts and consulting in regard to farms of the inhabitants, and even settling family disputes. Meade records that a brother, Charles Rose, was rector of Yeocomico Church, Cople Parish, Westmoreland County (No. 331), from 1754 to 1758.

328

North Farnham Church (c. (1737)

Farnham, Richmond County, Virginia

North Farnham Parish was formed in 1692, when Richmond County was created out of the territory of old Rappahannock County on the north side of the Rappahannock River and Essex County out of that on the south side (see Vauter's Church, No. 227). The parish was named North Farnham to distinguish it from South Farnham Parish in Essex, formed in the same year. Old Rappahannock County had been laid off from the upper part of old Lancaster County (the present Rappahannock lies four counties away to the northwest). The town of Farnham, where the parish church was built, is in the lower section of the county, on the main highway between the county seats of Richmond and Lancaster.

Evidently Farnham Parish was on both sides of the river before the county was divided. In this parish, there was a sidelight on the rebellion of Nathaniel Bacon against the government of Virginia under Berkeley, in 1676, which involved the Established Church. Some ministers were loyal to the governor, while others sided with the frontier people in their cause. The Reverend Thomas Gordon, of Farnham Parish, was convicted in 1677 and disbarred from ever serving again as a parish priest. He was ordered by the assembly, "... on his bended knees, before the right

honourable the governour and councell, with a rope about his neck, acknowledge his treasons and rebellions and beg his life, and in the like manner acknowledge his crimes in Rappahannock Court ..." When Gordon repeated his sentence in the frontier county court at Tappahannock, it was in an atmosphere of hilarity and contempt for a cynical government, which did not protect its frontier people and ignored their needs.

The present North Farnham Church was built about 1737, a brick building in the form of a Greek cross, with a single tier of windows. The colonial building suffered a series of catastrophies, and only the original walls survived. Their brick is laid in English bond up to the water table and in Flemish bond above. Newer brick is apparent in the gables and over the doorways, where the old walls were restored. During the difficult years for the Episcopal Church, following the Revolution and the disestablishment of the Church of England, the building was abandoned for many years. The bricks from the churchyard wall were taken for other uses, and the building was used as a granary, a stable, and a distillery. In the War of 1812, during a skirmish with raiders from Admiral Cockburn's British fleet, in 1814, bullets struck the building and left marks by the south door. In 1820 the building stood in ruins, but in 1835 it was restored. During the Civil War it was stripped of furnishings and used by troops of both armies. After the war, the building was restored; it burned again in 1887 and once more was restored in 1922.

329

Christ Church (1732)

Lancaster County, Virginia

Christ Church, Lancaster, is one of the finest examples of colonial church architecture which survives in Virginia. It retains its original design and stands practically as it was built. This is the second church on the site, and both of them were built by members of the Carter family. The Carters, who were active in the parish for many generations, had great wealth and prestige in the region. They came to own an estate of 8,000 acres on the Corotoman River, with a three-mile lane lined with cedars and leading straight from Corotoman House on the Rappahannock (now disappeared) to the church. Robert Carter, who became known as "King" Carter, and who built the present church, served as agent and representative for the Culpeper and Fairfax families in the Northern Neck of Virginia. Under Charles II, Lord Culpeper had been granted proprietorship of Virginia. The privilege was withdrawn later, and confined to the Northern Neck, the territory lying between the Potomac and the Rappahannock rivers, and extending from the Chesapeake Bay to their head waters in the Alleghany Mountains.

When it was formed in 1651, from parts of Northumberland on the north and York to the South, Lancaster County covered both sides of the Rappahannock and extended northwestward indefinitely into the wilderness. In a series of divisions, new counties were laid off from it, until the pres-

ent Lancaster was confined to the north side from the bay to Richmond County. Before 1666, when Middlesex County was laid off on the south side, Lancaster County contained four smaller parishes — two on the "South Side," Peanckatanck and Christ Church, and two on the "North Side," St. Mary's White Chapel (see No. 330) and Christ Church. During that period, the parishes on each side had wardens and a "sidesman" to represent the interests of both parishes on his side of the river; this is the only use of the English term that we have found in Virginia. In 1652, for example, it was recorded in court that William Chapman, Jr., was sidesman and John Taylor and Edmund Lum were wardens for North Side. In 1654 another division was made in Lancaster County Parish, with the present Richmond and Essex counties constituting the Upper Parish and the present Lancaster and Middlesex counties the Lower Parish. In 1666 the two parishes of South Side, Middlesex, merged as Christ Church (No. 325); in 1752 the two in the present Lancaster County merged also as Christ Church Parish. It is customary, therefore, to name the distinguishing county with Christ Church.

The histories of St. Mary's White Chapel and Christ Church, Lancaster, have been practically the same. Even before their merger, the two parishes shared one minister, and the separate vestries sometimes met together as a general vestry. The early vestry books have been lost, but Bishop Meade, who had seen the early vestry book of Christ Church, recalls in his *Old Churches, Ministers, and Families of Virginia*, that Colonel

John Carter, the immigrant founder of the distinguished family in America, headed the vestry list of Christ Church in 1654. He had settled first in Upper Norfolk, now Nansemond County, and both there and in Lancaster he was elected to the House of Burgesses. He served also as commander of the forces sent against the Rappahannock Indians. Both he and his son John were serving on the vestry when he undertook, by contract, to build the first Christ Church on this site. In 1669 he died, and six months later, in 1670, the completed building was received by the vestry from John Carter, Jr. The father was buried in the east end of the church, at the north side of the chancel, together, under one stone, with the three of his wives who predeceased him and a son and two daughters.

Among the ministers who served the parishes, was one Andrew Jackson. He may have been of the same family as the one who became President of the United States — his connections are not known. He was not Episcopally ordained, and he may have been a Presbyterian. He served here for more than twenty-five years, and he was so highly regarded and beloved that the vestry pleaded with the governor to make an exception to the law requiring all holders of a living in the Church to be ordained by an Anglican bishop. He was succeeded by John Bell, who was minister in 1713.

By 1728 the congregation had outgrown the first church, and the building of a larger one, at a site more convenient to the parishioners, was considered. Robert Carter, son of John Carter, Jr., provided in his will dated that year that if the vestry undertook to build a new brick church where the old one then stood, part of the cost would be paid from his estate. This provision for the growing needs of his family, tenants, and parish kept the grave of his grandfather in the same position in the present church, and it provided for the graves of himself and family. The vestry responded to his offer during his lifetime, and Robert (King) Carter paid the entire cost and added other donations. A large pew near the chancel was assigned to him and his immediate family, and the whole north transept was reserved for his tenants and servants. The building was completed in 1732; Robert Carter died on August 4 of that year, in his sixty-ninth year, and was buried in a large sarcophagus outside the east end of the church. Next to his is the sarcophagus of Betty Carter, his second wife, who died in 1710, and beyond it is that of Judith

Carter, his first wife, who died in 1699. A long inscription in Latin, accompanied by the family coat-of-arms, relates that Robert had served as rector of the College of William and Mary, speaker of the House of Burgesses for six years, governor of the colony for more than a year, and treasurer in the reigns of William, Anne, George I, and George II.

Located less than three miles south of Kilmarnock, in the lower precinct of the county, the beautiful brick church is in the form of a Greek Cross. It measures sixty-eight by sixty-eight feet, outside, with walls three feet thick and laid in Flemish bond, supporting a swag roof with four hips. The three doorways have classic pedimented enframements, with brick pilasters on each side. Over the doorways are small oval windows, framed in rubbed-brick arches with stone keys, and the semicircular arches of the tall windows are formed in the same style. The ceiling forms groined arches at the crossing. The aisles are paved with freestone. The wineglass pulpit, sounding board, walnut table, and marble font are all original. Meade records that the old box pews now stand without the brass rods and damask curtains which formerly divided them. The mortar and white plaster was clinched behind the thick laths, and the original walls have stood solid and intact. The building suffered occasional minor desecrations and vandalism during the years. From time to time, it has been repaired and painted, under the loving care of the parish, the Association for the Preservation of Virginia Antiquities, and friends.

330

St. Mary's White Chapel (1740)

Lancaster County, Virginia

The earliest records of Lancaster County Parish go back to 1650, when Lancaster and Middlesex were one, and the county covered both sides of the Rappahannock River. In that year Samuel Cole was appointed by the court as the Anglican minister to serve the whole parish, on both sides of the river. The two parishes of White Chapel and Christ Church (situated in the region on the north side that remained as Lancaster, after all the divisions had created new counties) had separate vestries for a century, but during that time they shared the minister's service and their histories were practically the same (see Christ Church, No. 229). In 1752 the two merged as Christ Church Parish. The vestry book for the early years and many county records were destroyed during the Civil War, and the history is fragmentary.

In the upper section of the county, at the present town of Lively, the first building of St. Mary's White Chapel was erected. In the absence of records, the date is not known, but it probably was before 1669, when the silver chalice was presented and inscribed. In his *Old Churches, Ministers, and Families of Virginia*, Bishop Meade states that, according to the vestry book, the old building was pulled down and a new one was built in 1740, under a contract with James Jones. This second building was cruciform, like its contemporary, Christ Church. In the course of repairing the building in 1830, after it had stood abandoned for many years, the building was remodeled; after the chancel and the nave wings had been removed, the transept was restored as a rectangular church, measuring sixty by thirty feet, which is the present building. The high pulpit originally stood at the north end facing the south door of the present building. The present long aisle, running from the south door to the north end, is crossed by a wider aisle from the door on the west side, which evidently was the main aisle in the nave of the cruciform building. Against the outside east wall, shown in the photograph, there are two chimneys, placed apparently at the joinings of the removed chancel walls.

The cruciform building had three galleries. Meade mentions that permission was given by the vestry, in 1740, for James and John Ball, of the predominant family in the parish, to build one of them, provided that it was finished with the building and conformed with the west gallery, and to two members of the Burgess family to build another under the same conditions. The third gallery, evidently in the west end, was for slaves. The only gallery remaining in the present structure is over the south door. The walls, which are twenty-four feet high, support a hipped roof and an oval ceiling. The furnishings have been modernized to some extent. Before the Civil War, the high box pews were cut down, and now they are open pews. The aisles paved with brick tile have been floored over and carpeted. In 1882 the high pulpit was removed, but in that year the four old walnut tablets, with lettering engraved and gilded, were restored to their places on the wall — two of them, with the Ten Commandments, were the gift of David Fox in 1702, and the two with the Apostles' Creed were the gift of his son William, in 1717. The Foxes and Balls were related The silver chalice, which is still used here, is inscribed, "The gift of David Fox, 1669." In 1691 another piece of communion silver was willed to the church by George Spencer. The silver salver still in use is unmarked, but it is worn by long service, and apparently dates from those early years. The old Bible here was a gift of Raleigh Downman, of Belle Isle, in 1838. The Downmans and Balls were related.

Most of the old tombstones in the churchyard carry names of the Ball family. The first of the family in Virginia was Colonel William Ball, who came from England with his family and settled at the mouth of the Corotoman River about 1650, and who died in 1669. The earliest name here is that of his grandson David Ball, born in 1686. The youngest daughter of Colonel William was Mary Ball, who became a grandmother of George Washington; she is buried about five miles from the church, at "Epping Forest." For a time she resided in Cople Parish and attended Yeocomico Church (No. 331).

331

Yeocomico Church (1706)

Westmoreland County, Virginia

There were two parishes in Westmoreland County, according to Bishop Meade in his *Old Churches, Ministers, and Families of Virginia*: Washington Parish in the upper section and Cople Parish in the lower. When Westmoreland was laid off from Northumberland County, in 1653, it covered the upper part of the Northern Neck as far as the Potomac Falls above Georgetown, and now, with its area reduced considerably, it still borders on both the Potomac and the upper Rappahannock at Essex County. Within the limits of the present county, there were two churches in Cople Parish, Yeocomico Church, which took its Indian name from the local creek, and Nominy Church, which acquired its name in the same way. The Nominy Church building was destroyed by fire soon after the War of 1812. Meade's records of ministers were not complete, and early parish records here have not survived; the earliest minister listed for Yeocomico Church was in 1754, when Charles Rose was rector. Charles was the brother of Robert, who was rector for many years at St. Anne's Parish, across the Rappahannock in Essex County (see Vauter's Church, No. 327). Robert Rose, like Meade, covered much ground, saw many people, and kept a detailed diary; from his diary one learns that Charles was rector here many years before 1754, the earliest record.

The first vestry of this parish was chosen in 1655, and the first church was built that year, a structure of oak timbers covered with clapboard. That was just two years after the formation of the county, and it was the usual practice to form parishes with the new counties. The second and present building was erected in 1706. This brick structure is the oldest of the T-form colonial churches, and among the oldest churches in Virginia. Its swag roof recalls that of earlier Merchant's Hope Church (No. 299). The lower half of the front wall is laid in Flemish bond, and the upper half, as well as the east end wall, is in English bond. At the top of the front wall, under the dentilated cornice, is a molded brick tile bearing the date 1706. The building has undergone several uses and considerable abuse. During the years following the Revolution it was used as a courthouse, a school, and a Methodist chapel. During the War of 1812, it was used as a barracks by soldiers stationed here to observe the movements of the British, and the high-backed pews were destroyed by Cockburn's raiders. The walnut communion table was used in the churchyard as a meat block, and the baptismal font served as a punch bowl, but both have been restored to use in the church. The font was rescued by a Mr. Murphy of Ayrfield, a Presbyterian who, at the proposal of W. L. Rogers of Princeton, New Jersey, in 1820, shared with him and others the task of restoring the building. The old pews have been replaced with modern ones, and the original pulpit and sounding board also have been replaced. During the Civil War the old building again was used as a barracks by the home guard.

For many years Mary Ball lived in this parish and attended church here. As we have seen, her father, Colonel William Ball, was a member of the Parish of St. Mary's White Chapel (see No. 330). Mary lived here while studying under the tutelage of Colonel George Eskridge of Sandy Point, from 1721 until her marriage with Augustine Washington in 1730. It was his second marriage. Their first child (one of six) was George Washington, who was born in Westmoreland County in 1732, the fourth generation of the Washington family in Virginia.

The photograph of the interior was made from a point near the main entrance, at the west end of the south side. The old communion table is seen before the east windows, in the normal place for the sanctuary, but the main aisle between the pews is in a north wing, which would be a transept if there were a similar south wing. This unconventional arrangement requires the congregation to pass by the lectern and pulpit on the way to the central aisle. In 1906, when the Bicentennial of the building was celebrated, a year before the Virginia Tricentennial, an association was formed to restore and preserve the church.

332

St. Paul's Church (c. 1766)

King George County, Virginia

St. Paul's Church is located in the Northern Neck, a mile and a half northwest of King George Courthouse, ten miles north of the Rappahannock River, and only a few miles south of the Potomac. In 1720 King George County was laid off from Richmond, as a narrow strip along the Potomac. In 1776 the boundaries of King George and Stafford were rearranged to make both counties border on both rivers, thereby transferring St. Paul's Parish to King George County, on the Potomac side, with Hanover Parish on the Rappahannock side. In 1732 Brunswick Parish was laid off from Hanover Parish. The Muddy Creek Church, Brunswick Parish, was succeeded by the present Lamb's Creek Church (No. 333). For many years during the nineteenth century, St. Paul's and Lamb's Creek shared one minister as a united parish. The Anglican Parish of St. Paul was formed from Potomac Parish before 1680. The available parish records are sketchy; there is a register with records of the parish beginning in 1722, which refers to earlier records. That was during the ministry of David Stuart, who had been the minister of St. Paul's for many years before 1722. He was a descendant of the royal family of Scotland, and according to the Reverend Robert Rose, of St. Anne's Parish in Essex County (No. 327), he was a man of high character, eloquence, and popularity. He died in 1749 and was succeeded by his son, William Stuart, who evidently had been serving as assistant to his father.

William served as curate until failing health led him to ask the vestry to relieve him of his duties, and in 1797 his successor, John Parsons, was received to officiate as deacon. Bishop Meade, in his *Old Churches, Ministers, and Families of Virginia,* whose mother attended church here during William's ministry, and who spoke of him in the highest terms, estimates that the combined ministry of the Stuarts, father and son, covered almost the whole eighteenth century. The father's ministry must have begun about the turn of the century, when William Fitzhugh, of Bedford (a vast estate on the Potomac River), wrote to the Bishop of London and requested that a minister be sent.

It was during the ministry of William Stuart that the present church was built. The exact date is not known; Meade records it as 1766, and others believe that it was earlier. The building is a large, cruciform structure in Georgian style. The brick is laid in Flemish bond, with headers matching the stretchers in type and color. There are two tiers of windows; those of the upper tier, which light the three galleries, are headed with semicircular brick arches. The doorways are framed in plain brick. The dentilated cornice is surmounted by a hip roof. A high, wineglass pulpit stands in the back of the chancel, in the front of which the communion rail forms a semicircle. With its three galleries, this large church seats 500 people.

Parsons died in 1808. He had been serving as deacon, but had not been ordained as a priest, and the parish had declined considerably. In 1812 or 1813, when Bishop Meade visited here, the church was in ruins. He held a service in the abandoned and stripped building, in which the roof was about to fall; there were no windows, doors, pews, or any interior woodwork. Proceeds from the sale of glebe lands, after the disestablishment of the Episcopal Church, were in a fund available for educational purposes, and the legislature then permitted the building to be repaired and converted for use, both as a house of worship and an educational institution. Methodists, and occasionally Baptists and Presbyterians, had stated appointments to preach at the academy. After a few years, the educational activity died out, and in 1830, after the legislature had returned the property to the Episcopal Church, the building was restored to its original use. There was temporarily an odd difference, however, for, while three arms of the cross were furnished as a fine church, the fourth (now a large vestry room) was divided into three small rooms to house the new minister.

Several treasures are still in the possession of the parish. The Bible, a Cambridge edition, was a gift of the rector, William Stuart, in 1762. Three pieces of old silver communion service, a flagon, a chalice, and a paten, were presented to the parish by Henry Fitzhugh. Among the vestrymen of the parish, after 1720, there were many members of the Washington family, including John, Samuel, Laurence, Robert, Thomas, J. K., Needham, Henry T., and John T. Washington.

333

Lamb's Creek Church (1769)

King George County, Virginia

As we have seen in the account of St. Paul's Church in King George County (No. 332), there was close co-operation between that church, on the Potomac side of the county, and Lamb's Creek Church, on the Rappahannock side. In the western part of King George, where Muddy Creek became the boundary with Stafford County in 1776, the Muddy Creek Church was in use in 1710. It was then in Hanover Parish and later in Brunswick Parish, which was laid off from Hanover in 1732, after which over half of Brunswick Parish remained in Stafford.

On a site west of Lamb's Creek, the present church was built in 1769. It replaced the old building at Muddy Creek as the Brunswick Parish Church. A stone in the yard states that the church was "removed" from Muddy Creek and "reerected," but the word "removed" in the early records did not mean that the same material was moved and used for rebuilding the structure. The vestry book was taken away by a Baptist minister, who used the building during the period of abandonment in the nineteenth century, and the history of the parish is not complete. According to the account in *The Colonial Churches in Virginia*, by Dr. George McLaren Brydon and Mary Goodwin, we know that the parish was active until 1797. In that year a lay delegate from Brunswick Parish attended the Diocesan Convention; thereafter the organized parish died out, and the church was abandoned. About 1825 there was a revival — the parish was reorganized, and the building was restored to use. The church continued active until the Civil War, during which the building was used as a stable by Union soldiers, and the interior was destroyed. After the war it was repaired and used as a church, but

in a short time the building again was abandoned. It was in the following period that the church was used by Baptists. In 1906, when great preparations were being made for the Virginia Tricentennial the following year, the building was restored, with new doors, windows, and roof, and services were resumed. In 1911, Dr. Brydon became rector of the churches in King George County and served for three years. During that time he organized a vestry and kept Lamb's Creek Church active as a parish church. Most of the congregation were poor whites, many of whom were illiterate. After Brydon had gone to Richmond as archdeacon, his successor did not maintain the work, and again this church became idle. The church then was placed in charge of the rector of the adjacent Hanover Parish, St. John's Church, King George. The only regular use in recent years is the annual meeting of the Historical Society. When Dr. Brydon gave the author this information in 1962, he was active at age eighty-seven as historiographer of the Diocese of Virginia. A great contribution to this field of history is his two-volume work, *Virginia's Mother Church and The Political Conditions Under Which It Grew* (1947). Lamb's Creek Church still owns a Bible printed in 1716, known as the "Vinegar" edition, and a Prayer Book printed in 1799, both of which came here from the Muddy Creek Church.

334

Aquia Church (1757)

Stafford County, Virginia

Aquia Church is situated on the east side of the Washington-Fredericksburg highway (U. S. Route 1), south of Alexandria, Mount Vernon, and the Pohick Church, and three miles north of Stafford Courthouse. Stafford County, the upper part of the Northern Neck, originally extended to the Blue Ridge Mountains, bordering on both the Potomac and the Rappahannock rivers. The early parish records are scanty, but two wardens of Potomac Parish are recorded in 1664, when the parish was coextensive with the county. In 1680 there were two parishes in the county, Stafford and Chotanck parishes. In that year appears the first record of a minister, John Waugh, and due to the general scarcity of clergymen, the two parishes evidently were served by one minister. Waugh's ministry was marked by his agitation of the concern over the promotion of Roman Catholicism by the reigning King James II; the tension in this county subsided after the accession of William and Mary. In 1700 the two parishes in Stafford were Overwharton and St. Paul's. In

that year John Fraser was rector, and in 1710 Alexander Scott began his ministry, both of them also serving the two parishes. In 1730 Prince William County was laid off from King George and Stafford, and that part of Overwharton Parish that lay in the new county was formed into Hamilton Parish. In 1777 a final change was made in the boundaries, bringing the counties to touch on both rivers, instead of being divided at the watershed between them. This final arrangement placed St. Paul's Parish in King George County (No. 332).

Alexander Scott (1686-1738) served Overwharton Parish for nearly twenty-eight years, until the time of his death. He was buried at Dipple, his estate on the Potomac. His successor was John Moncure, a Scot whose Huguenot ancestor had fled from France to Scotland at the time of the Revocation of the Edict of Nantes. Moncure had assisted Scott as curate; he served as minister until the time of his own death, in 1764, when he was buried beneath the chancel of the present building, which he had seen built. Many descendants of his have been active in supporting the parish, including the Reverend John Moncure, D.D., who wrote the account of Aquia Church in *Colonial Churches of Virginia* (1907). During the ministry of Scott, the Potomac Church evidently was the parish church of Overwharton; it was a large church on Potomac Creek, but after the disestablishment of the Episcopal Church, it went to ruin, and, after Bishop Meade had seen it in that condition in 1838, even the ruins vanished.

The present beautiful Aquia Church was built in 1757, on Aquia Creek. On a panel in the front of the west gallery, are recorded with that date the names of the minister, John Moncure, and ten vestrymen and the two wardens, who composed the vestry of twelve. This building replaced one which had been erected in 1751 and burned the same year. Over the south door are the names of Mourning Richards, who undertook the contract, and William Copein, the mason. This present cruciform brick church, with an upper tier of windows lighting the gallery, was unusually large for its time, and it has a number of interesting architectural features. The brick walls are finished with stone quoins, and the main doorway and the two at the ends of the transept are framed with the same stone, surmounted by classic pediments. The distinctive stone was quarried near by on Aquia Creek, where production was resumed in recent years. A unique feature of this building is the tower and cupola, based on

the western hip above the main entrance. From the cupola observatory there is a view of both the Potomac and the Rappahannock, which are not far apart at this point. The interior photograph shows the triple-decked pulpit, the box pews, and the walnut rails.

When Bishop Meade visited here in 1838, the church was neglected and the grounds were overgrown. When he returned in 1856, however, just before his famous book, *Old Churches, Ministers, and Families of Virginia*, was published, a transformation had taken place; the building had been repaired, and the congregation was good. During the Civil War the building was damaged and desecrated by soldiers. After the war, the minister, with a congregation of eight people, revived the parish and commenced the task of restoration, in which many members of the Scott and Moncure families took part. Overwharton Parish has continued active to the present day. The communion silver still in use is inscribed, "The gift of the Rev. Alexander Scott, A.M., late minister of this Parish Anno 1739."

A warm friend of the rector, John Moncure, and a kinsman of his wife was George Mason (1725-1792), the author of the Bill of Rights of Virginia. His beautiful Gunston Hall, overlooking the Potomac, is one of the many colonial plantation houses still standing in the Northern Neck.

Pohick Church (1769)

Fairfax County, Virginia

On the north side of Pohick Run, stands Pohick Church, near the old Alexandria-Fredericksburg highway (U. S. Route 1). It is six miles from both Gunston Hall and Mount Vernon, the estates on the Potomac of George Mason and George Washington respectively, and it was the parish church of both families. The first building stood on the south side of Pohick Run, at a point four miles from Gunston Hall. It was a frame structure, built about 1700 as an Upper Church of Hamilton Parish, which was coextensive with Prince William County. Truro Parish was formed in 1732, being laid off from Hamilton Parish, with boundaries on Occoquan River, Bull Run (of Civil War fame), the Blue Ridge, and the Potomac River. The vestry book of Truro Parish, now in the Library of Congress, commences in that year when the new parish was formed. Meetings were held in a church at the town of Occoquan, Hamilton Parish, until the Upper Church was built on Pohick Run. In 1730 the name was changed to the Church above the Occoquan, and in 1733, the year after Truro Parish was formed, the name became Pohick Church. In 1741 Fairfax County

was laid off from Prince William, and Truro Parish came in 1765, when the upper part was laid off as Fairfax Parish, including Alexandria (see Christ Church, No. 336), and the lower part remained Truro Parish.

Augustine Washington (1694-1743), the father of George, lived at Hunting Creek, the John Washington lands on the Potomac (later Mount Vernon), from 1734 to 1738. He was elected to the vestry here in 1735. In the following year, according to the minutes, he nominated Charles Green "as a person qualified to officiate in this church as soon as he shall receive orders from His Grace the Bishop of London." It is interesting to follow the procedure for placing a minister in an American colonial parish when the Church of England was the Established Church. The vestry commended Green to the Right Honorable Lord Fairfax, the principal landowner of the region, for an introduction to the Bishop of London, and Green then went to London for his ordination. Upon his return here in 1737, the vestry recorded "that the Rev. Charles Green, M.D., by a letter from the Hon'ble Wm. Gooch, Lieutenant Governor of Virginia, as by the letter of the Honourable James Blair, Commissary, is legally and regularly ordained, and it is therefore ordered by the vestry that the said Green be received and entertained as minister of this parish, and be provided for as the law directs." The first mention of Alexandria in the vestry book appears in 1753, when Green was ordered to preach there each third Sunday, presumably in the old Alexandria Church.

George Mason, of Gunston Hall, served on the vestry of Truro Parish for thirty-five years. He was an outstanding patriot and the author of the Declaration of Rights, the Constitution of the Commonwealth of Virginia, and the Fairfax Resolutions, as well as a member of the Constitutional Convention, over which his friend George Washington was president. He promoted the Act of Non-Importation of Slaves into the colony, and he manumitted his slaves, as did Washington in his will. The first mention of Mason in the vestry book was when he was appointed church warden for 1749-50. He continued to serve as a vestryman until after the Revolution, when the laws of Virginia dissolved all vestries and disestablished the Church of England, and he continued a member of the parish until his death in 1792. George Washington first became a member of the vestry in 1762, and in the following year he and Mason were appointed wardens.

As the old Pohick Church was in need of repair, it was decided to build a new and larger one. In 1769 plans were made and work was begun, but not until there had been some difference of opinion between these two friends over the selection of a site. Mason held that the new church should be built at the site of the old, near Gunston Hall, because of the burials there, but it was not convenient to all members of the parish. Washington made a survey of the parish on which he marked the residences of the congregation. At a vestry meeting he presented the plan, and the present site was chosen at the geographical center of the congregation. Washington then was appointed to a building committee, together with Mason, George William Fairfax, Daniel McCarty, and Edward Payne. At Christ Church, Alexandria, where Washington served on the vestry, building had begun two years before. The design for that building, drawn by James Wren, evidently was used by Washington as the basis for the plan which he drafted for Pohick Church (now in the Library of Congress). The scale was reduced for the new building, a south door was included, as was customary, although it was omitted at Christ Church, and two entrances still serve the west end, although a tower was added later at Alexandria. The contractor was Daniel French, of Rose Hill, who had deeded the land. The brick walls, laid in Flemish bond, are finished with quoins of similar white stone, but the semicircular window arches above and the flat arches below have no keystones. The same local sandstone was used in the pedimented door enframements and their Ionic pilasters. The building was finished in 1774, five years after it was begun. Pews No. 3 and 4 were bought by Colonel George Mason, and Nos. 28 and 29 by Colonel George Washington.

Before the Revolution, Washington attended church here regularly. After the war, when he was involved in the formation of the Republic, Washington was away from Mount Vernon much of the time, but when he was in residence there, he and Martha attended church at Alexandria. He resigned from the vestry of Truro Parish in 1782. The rector, Lee Massey, discontinued services soon after because of health, and the life of the church declined. "Parson Weems," Mason Locke Weems, a preacher and teacher from Maryland (see All Hallows Church, Anne Arundel, No. 55), who was the author of the famous story of the cherry tree in his *Life of Washington*, claimed in that book that he had been rector

here. During the Civil War, the church was damaged; one winter it was stripped of all furnishings and woodwork and used as a stable, and the soldiers used the east wall for target practice. The church was renovated in 1874, and in 1906 it was restored to its original condition for the Virginia Tricentennial.

Nearby is located Fort Belvoir, a large post of the Army Engineers, and the active congregation of about two hundred communicants is supplemented by the attendance of army officers and men. Belvoir was the plantation of William Fairfax, agent for the large tracts of Fairfax lands. The Fairfax family had acquired vast tracts of land through marriage in the Culpeper family, Thomas Lord Culpeper having been governor of Virginia and the proprietor of the Northern Neck. Lawrence Washington, a half brother of George and his guardian, was the son-in-law of Fairfax, with whom he had served at Cartagena. During that service he became acquainted with Admiral Edward Vernon, and after his return to Hunting Creek, the estate which he had inherited from their father Augustine, Lawrence changed its name to Mount Vernon. After leaving school in 1747, young George went to live with his guardian. The following year he was appointed surveyor of Fairfax lands, and soon after as public surveyor. When Lawrence died in 1752, his will made George his executor and residuary heir of Mount Vernon.

336

Christy Church (1767)
Alexandria Church, the Lower Church
Alexandria, Fairfax County, Virginia

Together with a number of men prominent in the affairs of the times, George Washington was active on the vestry of three Anglican churches in Fairfax County — Pohick Church (No. 335), Falls Church (No. 337), and Christ Church, Alexandria. Prince William County covered the south side of the Potomac River to its source in the Blue Ridge Mountains, until 1741 when Fairfax County was laid off. Truro Parish was coextensive with Fairfax County. The upper part of the county was laid off five years later, to form Loudon County, and thereafter Fairfax was confined to the region around the great bend of the Potomac. Within the area of the present Fairfax, there was a frame church near Gunston, the beautiful estate of the George Mason family on the Potomac. It was the predecessor of the present Pohick Church, which was designed and attended regularly by Washington, until after the Revolution, as the parish church of Mount Vernon. In 1765 a part of Truro Parish was laid off and Fairfax Parish was formed. In that year, at age thirty-three, George Washington was elected one of the twelve vestrymen of the new parish. Immediately the vestry undertook to repair the two old churches in the parish, and in 1766 it was decided to build two new churches, one at the Little Falls of the Potomac, Falls Church, the other here at Alexandria. The present church replaced the old frame building known as Alexandria Church, or Lower Church.

In 1767 work began on the church in Alexandria. The land was given by John Alexander, one of the landholders who developed the expansion of the town. The site was then in a dense wood, but it is now in the heart of the city, which grew so rapidly that it was considered for the location of the nation's capital. The plans were drawn by James Wren, who was reputed to be a descendant of Sir Christopher Wren, the designer of many famous London churches. The plans were used later by Washington in drafting his design of Pohick Church. The contract was let to James Parsons for £600, but he was unable to complete the work. After five years had elapsed and the work had come to a halt, in 1772, Colonel John Carlisle undertook to complete the work for an

additional £220. In February of 1773 the completed building was accepted by the vestry, and the cost was paid in choice Oronoko tobacco. The plain rectangular building had several changes made in the succeeding years. The gallery was installed in 1787, the west aisle in 1811, and the tower and steeple at the west end were added in 1818. In 1812 the chimneys were built, and the era of foot warmers ended for the congregation. Unusual features of the fine Georgian design are the white stone quoins which finish the brick walls of Flemish bond and emphasize their dark red color, the white keystones in the semicircular brick arches of the upper windows and in the flat arches of the lower ones, and the absence of a door in the south side. The continuous dentilated cornice is surmounted by a hip roof, which is now covered with slate. In the east end is a Palladian window, framed in square pilasters and a broken pediment. The pulpit, which stood originally at the north wall, now is centered before this east window. Not until 1813 was the building consecrated, by Bishop Claggett of Maryland,

with the name of Christ Church.

After services one Sunday in 1774, surrounded by the congregation of his friends in the churchyard, Washington advocated ending allegiance to King George and expressed his willingness to fight for independence. After the Revolution, when Washington attended services regularly here instead of at Pohick Church, the family was brought the ten miles north from Mount Vernon in the gold and green coach drawn by four horses. One of the treasures here is the Washington family Bible from Mount Vernon, given to the church in 1804 by the General's adopted son, George Washington Parke Custis. The beautiful chandelier of hand-wrought brass and glass, which hangs under the rear gallery, was bought in London and installed here in 1818.

Robert E. Lee spent his boyhood in the parish, and in 1853 he was confirmed here by Bishop Johns. It was in the churchyard, in 1861, that he agreed to take command of the Virginia forces, realizing that it meant the loss of Arlington, his home. During the Civil War, Alexandria was occupied by Federal troops, but Christ Church, unlike the others, was used for church services, with a chaplain in charge, and escaped damage. During that period, the parish register for 1765 to 1860 disappeared, as did the original silver plate marking Washington's pew. In 1866 the church was restored to the vestry, but services were not resumed until 1874, when the congregation revived and the building was repaired.

Among many distinguished ministers who served this parish, the first rector was Townsend Dade. After his death in 1778, he was succeeded by David Griffith, who had served as a chaplain in the Continental Army and was a close friend of Washington. In 1790, Bryan Fairfax became the rector; later he was made Lord Fairfax, Baron of Cameron. He was succeeded by Thomas Davis, who served from 1792 to 1811, and in 1799 conducted the funeral services of General Washington. From 1811 to 1813, William Meade was rector; he became Bishop of Virginia and author of the famous two volumes, *Old Churches, Ministers, and Families of Virginia* (1857). In 1860 Cornelius Walker became rector, and at the outbreak of the Civil War he became a chaplain in the Confederate Army. Christ Church has enjoyed close relations with the Theological Seminary, which was established after a Convention of the Diocese of Virginia in 1815, with a class at William and Mary College, and in 1823 was moved to Alexandria.

Falls Church (1767)
The Anglican Church
Falls Church, Fairfax County, Virginia

Falls Church was named for the Little Falls of the Potomac River (as compared to the Great Falls above Georgetown), and in colonial times it was called also "the Anglican Church." It is located about eight miles from both Alexandria and Georgetown. This church originally was in Truro Parish, in which it shared with Pohick Church (No. 335) and Chirst Church, Alexandria (No. 336), one minister and vestry. A number of prominent men served on the vestry, including George Mason; Augustine Washington and his son George; several of the Fairfax family, who were the principal landholders in the region; William Payne and his son William. (The colonial building of Payne's Church, or the Zion Church at Fairfax, Truro Parish, was destroyed in 1864 by Federal troops. It was rebuilt about 1930, to the original design.) In 1765 Truro Parish was divided, and the upper part was organized as Fairfax Parish, including Alexandria and Falls Church. The first church here was built about 1734, soon after Truro Parish had been formed from the upper part of Hamilton Parish. The builder was Colonel Richard Blackburn, of Ripon Lodge. Mount Vernon and Ripon Lodge were about twelve miles apart, and the two families were intimate; Judge Bushrod Washington, who inherited Mount Vernon from George, married a Blackburn. The deed to the land on which the church stood was recorded in the Fairfax courthouse in 1745, a decade after it was built. In 1750 the building was enlarged to accommodate the growing congregation, but it did not serve much longer. In 1763 the vestry, with George Washington present as a new member, found "that the Old Church is rotten and unfit for repair, but that a new church be built at the same place." Washington became a member of the building committee, and his diary for the following year records an advertisement for "undertakers to build Falls Church." Although Pohick was the parish church of Mount Vernon before the Revolution, and Christ Church after, as a vestryman Washington made it a rule to attend services at Falls Church four times a year.

As soon as Fairfax Parish was formed, the vestry undertook to build two new churches, at Alexandria and at Falls Church. Work on both

began in 1767. The old church here was torn down, and the new building here, as well as that at Alexandria, was undertaken by James Parsons. The design was the same as that drawn for Christ Church by James Wren, and used by the economical Washington as the basis of his drawing for Pohick Church — three churches for the cost of one design. This building differs from the other two in a few details. The enframement of the doorway on the south side is made of wood painted white, instead of white sandstone, and that at the west end is of brick. The gallery, provided in the design and included at the other two buildings, was never installed here. In the style of the period, the brickwork is laid in Flemish bond with black headers, and rubbed brick is used in the arches of the windows. Although the two were begun in the same year, Falls Church was completed several years before Christ Church.

The building suffered damage during two wars and abandonment between them. During the Revolution it was used as a recruiting headquarters, and occasionally army forces were encamped here. It was abandoned as a house of worship in 1787, when the Church of England had been disestablished, and the new Episcopal Church was struggling with the difficulties of the period, and it remained idle until 1830. During that time, the building was available to any denomination, and occasional services were held.

In the Civil War, the building was used first as a hospital for soldiers and then as a stable for cavalry horses. In 1865 the federal government appropriated funds for repairs. In 1906 a movement was started to restore the church for the Virginia Tricentennial of 1907. It took many years, but Falls Church was restored completely, and it continues active in the Diocese of Virginia.

338 *(See illustration on following page)*

Little Fork Church (1776)

Culpeper County, Virginia

The Little Fork Church stands in the present Culpeper County, named for Thomas Lord Culpeper, governor of Virginia and proprietor of the Northern Neck. St. Mark's Parish was formed when this region was a part of the frontier county of Spotsylvania. In 1730 an Act of the General Assembly at Williamsburg divided St. George's Parish, and the part laid off was formed as the new St. Mark's Parish. For the election of their first vestry of twelve outstanding parishioners, the meeting was held in the church in Germanna. The county was named in honor of Alexander Spotswood (1676-1740), who had served as governor from 1710 to 1722, and who was one of the first to open and develop this western frontier. In a part of his vast tract of 45,000 acres, Spots-

wood founded the town of Germanna, on the south side of the Raritan River, to settle the community of Germans who came to work in his iron industry. The site of the town is in the present Orange County. The great fork between the Rappahannock on the north and the Raritan on the south forms this region, which is now Culpeper County. In the northern section of this county, the Hazel River flows east into the Rappahannock, and in this section near Oak Shade, two miles from Rixeyville, stands the colonial brick building of the Little Fork Church.

The first building of this church was erected in 1731, the year after the formation of the Anglican Parish of St. Mark. It served for only two years, until it was destroyed by fire in 1733. In 1750 the vestry ordered a chapel to be built at the Little Fork, where the old chapel had stood. In 1752 the vestry changed the site for the building that had been ordered, to one in Freeman's old field, and it was ordered to be called a church. In 1760 an addition to this second building was ordered, to measure thirty-two by twenty-two feet, and in 1771 the vestry ordered another addition of the same dimensions. That building was replaced, in 1776, by the present brick structure in late Georgian style. With its hip roof, continuous cornice, and six arched windows on a single level on the south side, the design is similar to that of Lamb's Creek Church, which had been erected within the preceding decade (see No. 333). It lacks the doorway in the west end, and the pedimented enframements of brick, which are found at Lamb's Creek. The nature of the brickwork above the present arched doorway, which seems to have been repaired, suggests that it might have had originally a doorway of a dif-

ferent design. The building has been restored to good condition, after surviving the two wars. In the churchyard stands a monument to the memory of the Little Fork Rangers, 1861. The present pews are of the open slip type. Oil lamps are still used in the church.

For thirty-two years of the colonial period, from 1740 until his death in 1772, the rector of St. Mark's Parish was John Thompson. According to Bishop Meade, in his *Old Churches, Ministers, and Families of Virginia*, he was a Scot, who had taken a degree at the University of Edinburgh, and had received priest's orders from the Bishop of St. David's in the Chapel of St. James, in the palace royal of St. James of Westminster. The following year he came to St. Mark's Parish with the recommendation of Governor Gooch. In that year, 1740, ex-Governor Spotswood died. Two years later, Lady Spotswood, his widow, who lived in the mansion at Germanna, married the Reverend John Thompson. His suit was not won until after her long consideration of their different stations in life, and then her views were finally reconciled by the Reverend Robert Rose, family friend and adviser and executor of her late husband's estate (see Vauter's Church, No. 327).

339

Hebron Evangelical Lutheran Church (1740)

Madison County, Virginia

In Madison County, four miles south of Criglersville and a mile west of the highway, is the oldest church in America built by German Lutherans and still in use by that denomination. The building is older than the Trappe Church in Pennsylvania (No. 231); the older churches at Wilmington, Delaware (see Old Swedes Church, No. 13), and Philadelphia (see Gloria Dei, No. 202), were built by Swedish Lutherans and are now Episcopalian. The congregation here was formed by German Lutherans, who left Germany in 1717 for Pennsylvania, where they planned to join the many Germans who had preceded them. A storm drove their ship to the Virginia coast, and in that colony they were welcomed as a windfall by Alexander Spotswood, who was the governor at the time. He had brought other Germans from the Palatinate in 1714, only three years before, to establish an industry of iron mines and ore smelters in his vast tract of frontier territory in old Spotsylvania County, which had been named for him. The industry was appropriate for Lutherans, for Martin Luther had lived as a boy in Mansfeld, Germany, where his father leased three furnaces for smelting iron ore. Spotswood paid the captain for the passage of the Germans, and engaged them to work in his mines and vinyards at Germanna (see Little Fork Church, No. 338). That settlement of Germans was located on the Raritan River, in what is now Culpeper County.

In 1725, after working eight years for Spotswood, the group moved here and settled in the Robinson River Valley, in what is now the adjoining county of Madison. While their first church was being built here, the congregation sent a commission of two to Germany to seek a pastor, but they returned without success. In 1733, sixteen years after coming to Virginia, they settled their first pastor, John Casper Stoever. The congregation had grown to about three hun-

dred, and they needed a new building, but they lacked funds for such an undertaking. Another commission of two was sent to Germany, and this time it was highly successful. A fund of about £3,000, a number of books on theology for the pastor, and a library for the congregation were collected. At the same time a silver cup and plate were obtained, bearing the date 1729, to supplement the older pewter communion service which had been obtained in England by the first commission, and which is dated 1727.

Work on the present second building began after the commission had returned. In August of 1740, the completed building was dedicated, and a letter of thanks was sent to all contributors, in and outside of Germany. By the end of the century, the congregation had outgrown their second building, and about that time an addition was built, extending twenty feet from the middle of the south side, and measuring twenty-six feet in width. In this new wing of the T, the timbers are sawn, compared to those in the original structure, which were hewn. In the end of this new wing, an organ loft was built, facing the pulpit, and in 1802 a pipe organ was bought for £200 and installed. The organ was made by David Tannenburg, at Lititz, Pennsylvania, a town settled by Moravians from Bethlehem, Pennsylvania, where the manufacture of organs had begun in 1765, and it was brought here by wagon.

The church went through the two wars without damage, and the congregation, which is still active, has kept it in good repair, and has added some modern conveniences. In 1940 the Bicentennial of the building was celebrated, and for that occasion a historical account was published by William Harrison Lamb, of the fourth generation in the congregation.

340

Hopewell Friends Meeting House
(1759)

Frederick County, Virginia

Frederick County forms the northernmost county of Virginia, a spearhead thrust northward into West Virginia toward the northern bend of the Potomac River, which forms the border with Maryland, not many miles beyond which is the Pennsylvania line. The county was formed in 1738 from part of Orange County, which had covered all territory west of the Blue Ridge, and it was named for the Prince of Wales, the son of King George II and father of King George III. The county seat is Winchester, situated at the northern end of the Blue Ridge and the gateway to the Shenandoah Valley. Over this route into the mountainous frontier of Virginia and its beautiful valley, came pioneers from Pennsylvania — Quakers, Mennonites, German Baptists, and Scotch-Irish Presbyterians.

Not far from the West Virginia line, north from Winchester and near Clearbrook, stands the Hopewell Friends Meeting House in wooded country off the main highway. The site of this colonial building was within the vast grant of 100,000 acres near Opequan Creek, a tributary of the Potomac. The grant was made by the council at Williamsburg in 1732, to Alexander Ross, a Quaker, with the requirement that at least one family settle on each thousand acres. This inducement to pioneers was on a grand scale. Friends from Pennsylvania and Elk River, Maryland, migrated and settled here. The Meeting was established in 1734, and regular meetings for worship have been held ever since. Two years later, in 1736, a prominent Quaker from London visited the Meeting here, John Fothergill (1712-1780), a physician, writer, and botanist, who tried to negotiate peace between the British government and the colonies when the Revolution was brewing, through his good friend Benjamin Franklin. In 1744 Hopewell Monthly Meeting was established under Chester Quaterly and Philadelphia Yearly Meeting.

The oldest part of the present stone meeting house, the right half in the photograph, was built in 1759, with Thomas McClun acting as builder. The other half, on the left, was built in 1789. The rectangular building is constructed of the light gray limestone which runs all through the Blue Ridge. The repairs and remodeling of 1910 made no significant change in the style of the building, which was a large and handsome structure for a frontier meeting house. The records prior to 1759 were destroyed by fire; for the celebration of the Bicentennial of the founding of the Meeting, the *Hopewell Friends History, 1734-1934* was published in 1936.

341

Goose Creek Friends Meeting House (1765)

Lincoln, Loudon County, Virginia

Quakers were in Virginia at an early date. We have seen that they built meeting houses in Nansemond County, in the southeast corner of the colony, after George Fox, the founder of the Society of Friends, had preached effectively there in 1672 (see Glebe Church, No. 302). Here in the opposite corner of Virginia, in the county farthest upstream on the Potomac River, the colonial meeting house of Goose Creek Meeting still stands. It is in the hamlet of Lincoln, which was settled in the 1730's by Friends from Pennsylvania. The meeting was gathered under the leadership of Hannah, wife of Jacob Janney. The first meeting house was built about 1736, and the Meeting was organized about 1738. In 1775 it was made a Preparative Meeting, and in 1786 a Monthly Meeting, as part of Baltimore Yearly Meeting.

The stone structure, which is barely visible through the covering of ivy, was built as the Goose Creek Friends Meeting House in 1765, replacing the first building. In 1817 the red brick building across the street was built as the third meeting house, and the colonial stone building became a private residence.

342

Mill Creek Church (1770) Old Meeting House

Hamburg, Page County, Virginia

East of the Shenandoah Valley, on the western slope of the Blue Ridge, three miles west of Luray, stands the only colonial Baptist meeting house in Virginia. It is located only a few miles up the slope from the valley, through which came the flow of migration from Pennsylvania. The Church of England was the Established Church in Virginia, and as the frontier spread west to these mountains, Anglican parishes were

laid out with the new counties. The migration from Pennsylvania, however, was composed not of Anglicans, but of Dissenters of several different denominations. We have just seen that Quakers settled in the northern counties of Frederick and Loudon (see Nos. 340 and 341), and that in Madison County, German Lutherans settled, who accidentally had entered Virginia instead of Pennsylvania, for which they had sailed; and south of here we find settlements of Presbyterians from Pennsylvania.

The settlement here in Page County was composed mostly of Pennsylvania Germans, including Mennonites and German Baptists. John Koontz, a Baptist preacher, came to Mill Creek in 1770, and gathered most of the community into the Mill Creek Church which he formed, Mennonites and all. The present Old Meeting House was built in that year. It is a true product of this pioneer frontier, being constructed as a log house of hand-hewn square logs. The weatherboard covering on the outer walls was added later; the interior walls are still in their original state, with the logs exposed. There are galleries on two sides, with separate stairways. The old bare benches have been made slightly more comfortable by the addition of a back rail. The woodburning stove was cast with the inscription, "D. Pennybacker, 1799," an old Pennsylvania German name. The property was deeded to the people of Page County for tabernacle use forever. Once a year there is a gathering here for "a singing."

Augusta Church (1747)
Old Stone Church, Fort Defiance
Presbyterian Church

Fort Defiance, Augusta County, Virginia

Fort Defiance was the name given to the stone building of Augusta Church when palisades were erected on an embankment around the building, traces of which may still be seen, and it was fortified in 1753. It served for defense against Indian raids, when this whole western frontier was laid open to attack by the defeat of General Braddock, in 1755, near Fort Duquesne (now Pittsburgh, Pennsylvania) in the French and Indian War. Fort Defiance is now a small hamlet of scattered houses centered on the church and a school, beside the Lee Highway (U. S. Route 11) in the Shenandoah Valley north of Staunton. The region of wild mountains and the beautiful valley were first discovered in 1716 by Alexander Spotswood, while he was governor of Virginia. He claimed the region for the Crown, in the course of an expedition to protect this western frontier from encroachments of the French. They claimed by discovery all the vast region of the St. Lawrence, the Great Lakes, and the Mississippi basins, and therefore they threatened the western frontiers of the British colonies, which extended vaguely to the Southern Sea. This pressure extended around all the colonies, from what is now Maine to Georgia. After its discovery by Spotswood, the region of the Blue Ridge was defined as being part of Essex County, which had no specific western limits (see Vauter's Church, No. 327). In 1720 Spotsylvania County was laid off from Essex and named for the governor, and in 1734 Orange County was created to cover the western region (named for William, Prince of Orange, later King William III of England). In 1738 the General Assembly created in the parts of Orange west of the Blue Ridge the new counties of Frederick and Augusta, naming them for the Prince of Wales (the son of King George II and father of King George III) and his wife Princess Augusta. The new counties, however, were

to continue in Orange County and St. Mark's Parish (see Little Fork Church, No. 338) until they had "a sufficient number of inhabitants for appointing justices of the peace and other offices, and erecting courts therein." While the inhabitants were exempt from the taxes of Orange County and St. Mark's Parish, they were not to receive a bounty for killing wolves. Only seven years later, Augusta was organized as an independent county.

Although the county and coextensive parish were organized within the Established Church of England, exemption from parish taxes left the way open to Dissenters, and the region was populated early by Scotch-Irish Presbyterians. They had come from Northern Ireland via New Castle, Delaware (see No. 17), up the Susquehanna River to settle the Donegal Church, in Pennsylvania (see No. 251); and under the Donegal Presbytery they were the first settlers to recross the river and to enter the Cumberland Valley, where they settled Presbyterian churches, among others, at Silver Spring (see No. 257) and Carlisle (see No. 256); they moved south through the Cumberland Valley into the Shenandoah, and settled in this region.

From Augusta the Presbyterians sent supplications to the Donegal Presbytery for a pastor, and John Craig (1709-1774) was sent to this congregation. He was born in County Antrim, Northern Ireland, landed at New Castle in 1734, was licensed to preach in 1737, and in 1740 he came to Augusta. Here he "was set apart for the work of the gospel ministry in the south part of Beverley's Manor." It was not until seven years later, the year in which the Presbyterian church was built, that the first election was held in Augusta, to elect a vestry of the new Anglican parish, and that the first Anglican minister entered Augusta; and it was some years later that the first Anglican church was built in the county. In 1755 the first Presbytery in Virginia was founded, under the leadership of Samuel Davies, in Hanover County (see Fork Church, No. 315). Craig was of the Old Side Synod of Philadelphia, while Hanover Presbytery was New Side, and the Hanover Presbytery was a factor in the ministry of Craig in Augusta, after the factions united in 1758. Craig had a large parish, covering an area of thirty by twenty miles, which included the congregation at Tinkling Spring, in the valley east of the Blue Ridge. He reported that the inhabitants at Tinkling Spring were close-handed and perverse, and could not agree on a

site for a church, while here the inhabitants were fewer in number and poorer, but they co-operated to build their church and gave him no trouble. Men, women, and children took part in the building operations, hauling the sand from Middle River in bags on horseback. Craig walked the five miles to the church for services, which were held from ten to twelve on Sunday morning, and from one to sunset in the afternoon. His one published sermon contains fifty-five divisions.

The original building of logs stood in the burying ground. The present stone church was erected in 1747 and dedicated in 1749. In a colony where brick churches were the rule, the pioneers here brought from Pennsylvania their skill in adapting the local limestone to their meeting houses. The original building was a plain rectangle, with the front entrance in the end, as shown in the photograph. The front portico and the rear wings, which gave the building its T-form, were added in 1922. The old building has a gallery and a barrel ceiling. Over the present chancel and the transept, there is a vaulted ceiling.

344

Timber Ridge Church (1756) Old Stone Church

Timber Ridge, Rockbridge County, Virginia

The mountainous wilderness of Timber Ridge, now Rockbridge County, lying to the south of Augusta County, was settled after the region of the present Augusta, from which it was laid off in 1778, and the Presbyterian stone church here was built about a decade after Augusta Church (No. 343). In 1742 John McDowell and eight other early settlers were slain by Indians from Ohio, and he was buried in the family plot near the present church. The region was settled mainly by such Scotch-Irish Presbyterians, who came into the Shenandoah Valley from the Cumberland Valley of Pennsylvania, and whose pioneering instincts lead them to push on from here further west, into what is now West Virginia and Tennessee, and on into Texas.

In 1746 the second of two visits was made to this region by John Blair. He was a native of Northern Ireland who was serving as a Presbyterian minister in the Cumberland Valley. This was during the Great Awakening, and he was one of the New Side Presbyterians, inspired by the preaching of George Whitefield. He organized

here four Presbyterian congregations — Forks of James, Timber Ridge, New Providence, and North Mountain — but only the present Timber Ridge Church remains.

A leader in the Timber Ridge community was John Houston, great-grandfather of Sam Houston. In 1730, at forty-one years of age, he had come from Belfast to Philadelphia with his mother, wife, and six children. He lived in Pennsylvania long enough for three of the children to marry, and then he and his family joined others of Scottish descent in the migration into the Valley of Virginia. Here he was among the first citizens of "the new Presbyterian commonwealth beyond the Blue Ridge," as Marquis James called it in *The Raven*, his biography of Sam Houston. John acquired extensive land and established Timber Ridge Plantation, which extends southward from the present churchyard. He was a prime mover in the church, and he inspired the congregation to build this stone meeting house, where four generations of Houstons attended services.

Located seven miles north of Lexington, just off the highway, the Timber Ridge Church was erected in 1756. The women worked with the men in hauling sand by packsaddle from South River, as they had done at Augusta Church; and in the church a tablet, placed there by their descendants in 1904, pays tribute to the "Noble Women who Helped with their own Hands." Life here in the mountains of the frontier was quite different from that of the aristocrats on the plantations of Tidewater Virginia. At first the bare earth served as a floor, and the benches were of flat-hewn logs. The first flooring installed was also of puncheons, like the benches; tongue-and-groove flooring was installed much later. About the time of the Revolution, the log benches were replaced by box pews, and families were assigned pews located approximately where their benches had rested. After the Civil War, in 1871, the entrance on the side toward the burying ground was closed, and one was built with a vestibule at the north end. In 1900 two wings were added at the

523

end, making a T with the old rectangular building. At that time new modern pews were installed and, on Sunday, December 2, the building was rededicated.

At Timber Ridge, a school was started by Robert Alexander, in 1749, that was to become a university. In 1774, when the Reverend John Brown was teaching the school, it was taken over by the Presbytery. In 1776 it was moved to Mount Pleasant, where it occupied a new building, Liberty Hall, and after only a year there, it was returned to Timber Ridge. In 1780 Liberty Hall Academy was moved from Timber Ridge to Lexington, where it grew to become Washington and Lee University.

The stone church was used as a fort during Indian raids, as was that at Augusta. In 1763, when Cornstalk led his Shawnees to Kerr's Creek and massacred the inhabitants, those who were attending a religious meeting in the church escaped.

Robert Houston inherited Timber Ridge plantation from his father John, and built a fine house with a two-story gallery supported by square columns. It would have done credit to a Tidewater plantation. He married a Davidson, whose father was a man of wealth. Their son Samuel served in the Revolution in Morgan's Rifle Brigade in the Continental Army, and returned home as a captain. He continued to pursue the military life in the militia and was pro-

moted to major, but he wasted the fortunes of the family and the estate. He was interested in the Louisiana Purchase, and in Aaron Burr's abortive scheme for an empire beyond the Mississippi. Just before he died, in 1806, he negotiated for land in East Tennessee, and sold what was left of Timber Ridge Plantation. His son Samuel, who was to become teacher, soldier, senator, governor, president of the Republic of Texas, and an active citizen of the Cherokee Nation, was born in 1793 in the house on the hill, a hundred yards from the church. With his brothers and sisters, Sam attended a school started by Major Houston and a few neighbors, and built on forty acres of land near the church, which their father had donated for the purpose. They attended services regularly at this church, until their father died, when Sam was fourteen. The father was buried near the elaborate mansion of cousin Matthew Houston, in the churchyard of High Bridge (now Natural Bridge). Then their mother carried out her husband's last wish, by taking the children on the long journey up the valley into Tennessee, through the settlement of Knoxville and the hamlet of Maryville, up Baker's Creek Valley, up a branch; and there, with the Big Smoky Mountains in sight, she settled the family on the 419 acres that her husband had selected. Such was the heart of the pioneer; in a similar manner, across the whole land the settlement of the continent slowly proceeded.

WEST VIRGINIA

The one house of worship in the state, a Methodist church of wood,
is located on the map of Virginia.

345

Rehoboth Church (1785)

between Union and Gap Mills,
Monroe County, West Virginia

In a mountainous frontier west of the Alleghenies, in 1784 when the region was still a part of Virginia, Methodist pioneers organized Rehoboth Church. The organization took place several weeks before the Christmas Conference in Lovely Lane Chapel at Baltimore, at which the Methodist Church was made an institution separate from the Church of England. One of the pioneers, Edward Keenan, not only was active in building the church but deeded the land for the building and burying ground for "as long as grass grows and water flows." The Reverend Francis Asbury, who was then the first Methodist bishop in America, was present at the raising of the log church in 1785 (see Barrat's Chapel, Delaware, No. 24). In 1786 he dedicated the building, and in the three years 1792, 1793, and 1796 he held annual conferences here.

A log structure such as this, bare logs inside and out, had to be repaired from time to time, and the restoration of 1927 is memorialized on the bronze tablet over the door, dated August 30, 1930. Two of the photographs show the log house on the occasion of unveiling the tablet; they are included because later a tin roof was erected

above the entire historic building to preserve it, and in that state it is difficult to photograph. The building is now under the jurisdiction of the Historical Society of the West Virginia Conference, and it is used for worship occasionally by small groups. Rehoboth Church is one of ten National Methodist Shrines, marking the westernmost colonial house of worship still standing in America, in the path of migration which thrust steadily westward, to open new lands and to settle successively the territories that have become the United States.

526

APPENDICES

BIBLIOGRAPHY

and INDEX

APPENDICES

APPENDIX I

BUILDINGS IN ORDER OF DATE BY NAME, LOCATION, SERIAL NUMBER, ORIGINAL DENOMINATION, AND MATERIAL

Date	Name, Location	Serial No.	Denomination	Material
1632	Old Brick Church, Isle of Wight Cty., Va.	No. 297	Anglican	Brick
1639	Brick Church, Jamestown, Va.	No. 293	Anglican	Brick
1657	Merchant's Hope Church, Prince George Cty., Va.	No. 299	Anglican	Brick
c. 1675	Old Trinity Church, Dorchester Cty., Md.	No. 78	Anglican	Brick
1681	Old Ship M. H., Hingham, Mass.	No. 87	Congregational	Wood
1682	Third Haven Friends M. H., Easton, Md.	No. 76	Friends	Wood
c. 1685	Old White Marsh Church, Talbot Cty., Md.	No. 77	Anglican	Brick
c. 1690	Ware Church, Gloucester Cty., Va.	No. 317	Anglican	Brick
1694	Flushing Friends M. H., Flushing, N. Y.	No. 170	Friends	Wood
1695	Merion Friends M. H., Montgomery Cty., Pa.	No. 229	Friends	Stone
1696	Grace Church, Yorktown, Va.	No. 313	Anglican	Stone
1697	Gloria Dei Church, Phila., Pa.	No. 202	Swedish Lutheran	Brick
1697	Old Haverford Friends M. H., Oakmont, Pa.	No. 219	Friends	Stone
1698	Old Swedes Church, Wilmington, Del.	No. 13	Swedish Lutheran	Brick
1698	Christ Church, Accokeek, Md.	No. 47	Anglican	Brick
1698	Norriton Presbyterian M. H., Montgomery Cty., Pa.	No. 230	Presbyterian	Stone
1699	Sleepy Hollow Dutch Reformed Church, Scarborough, N. Y.	No. 178	Dutch Reformed	Stone
1699	Abington Friends M. H., Montgomery Cty., Pa.	No. 234	Friends	Stone
1699	Newport Friends M. H., Newport, R. I.	No. 266	Friends	Wood
1700	Portsmouth Friends M. H., Portsmouth, R. I.	No. 272	Friends	Wood
1701	St. Peter's Church, New Kent Cty., Va.	No. 314	Anglican	Brick
1703	Immanuel Church, New Castle, Del.	No. 16	Anglican	Brick
1703	Old St. Mary's Church, Burlington, N. J.	No. 159	Anglican	Brick
1703	Saylesville Friends M. H., Saylesville, R. I.	No. 262	Friends	Wood
1706	Rehoboth Church, Somerset Cty., Md.	No. 83	Presbyterian	Brick
1706	Pembroke Friends M. H., Plymouth Cty., Mass.	No. 90	Friends	Wood
1706	St. Andrew's Church, Charleston Cty., S. C.	No. 279	Anglican	Brick
1706	Yeocomico Church, Westmoreland Cty., Va.	No. 331	Anglican	Brick
1707	Old Presbyterian Church, New Castle, Del.	No. 17	Presbyterian	Brick
1707	St. Paul's Church, Wickford, R. I.	No. 265	Anglican	Wood
1709	St. Andrew's Church, Richmond, N. Y.	No. 169	Anglican	Stone
1709	Bristol Friends M. H., Bristol, Pa.	No. 235	Friends	Stone
1710	Old Kennett Friends M. H., Hamorton, Pa.	No. 225	Friends	Stone
c. 1710	Plymouth Meeting Friends M. H., Plymouth Meeting, Pa.	No. 233	Friends	Stone
1711	Trinity Church, Oxford, Phila. Cty., Pa.	No. 209	Anglican	Brick
1711	Newtown Square Friends M. H., Newtown Square, Pa.	No. 220	Friends	Stone
1711	Bruton Parish Church, Williamsburg, Va.	No. 294	Anglican	Brick
1712	Newington M. H., Newington, N. H.	No. 115	Congregational	Wood
1712	Christ Church, Middlesex Cty., Va.	No. 325	Anglican	Brick
1713	St. Paul's Church, Kent Cty., Md.	No. 72	Anglican	Brick
c. 1713	St. James' Church, Goose Creek, S. C.	No. 275	Anglican	Brick
1714	St. Michael's Church, Marblehead, Mass.	No. 110	Anglican	Wood

1714	Second Congregational Church, North Beverly, Mass.	No. 111	Congregational	Wood
1715	Woodbury Friends M. H., Woodbury, N. J.	No. 158	Friends	Brick
1715	St. David's Church, Radnor, Pa.	No. 222	Anglican	Stone
1717	Wye Church, Talbot Cty., Md.	No. 75	Anglican	Brick
1717	West Parish M. H., West Barnstable, Mass.	No. 91	Congregational	Wood
1717	Old Indian Church, Mashpee, Mass.	No. 92	Congregational	Wood
1717	Lower Chapel, Middlesex Cty., Va.	No. 326	Anglican	Brick
1718	Radnor Friends M. H., Ithan, Pa.	No. 221	Friends	Stone
1719	St. George's Church, Dorchester, S. C.	No. 280	Anglican	Brick
c. 1719	Vauter's Church, Essex County, Va.	No. 327	Anglican	Brick
1723	St. John's Church, Broad Creek, Md.	No. 48	Anglican	Brick
1723	Old North Church, Boston, Mass.	No. 96	Anglican	Brick
1724	East Nottingham Friends M. H., Calvert, Md.	No. 70	Friends	Brick
1724	Christ Church, Charleston Cty., S. C.	No. 281	Anglican	Brick
1724	St. Helena's Church, Beaufort, S. C.	No. 286	Anglican	Brick
1725	Matinecock Friends M. H., Nassau Cty., N. Y.	No. 172	Friends	Wood
1725	Providence Friends M. H., Providence, R. I.	No. 261	Friends	Wood
1725	Trinity Church, Newport, R. I.	No. 267	Anglican	Wood
1725	Strawberry Chapel, Berkeley Cty., S. C.	No. 278	Anglican	Brick
c. 1725	Upper Church, King and Queen Cty., Va.	No. 319	Anglican	Brick
1726	Stony Brook Friends M. H., Princeton, N. J.	No. 142	Friends	Stone
1726	French Chapel, Old Fort Niagara, N. Y.	No. 197	Roman Catholic	Stone
1726	East Caln Friends M. H., Chester Cty., Pa.	No. 228	Friends	Stone
1726	Old White Church, St. Helena Is., S. C.	No. 287	Anglican	Tapia
c. 1727	All Hallows Church, Anne Arundel Cty., Md.	No. 55	Anglican	Brick
1727	Doughoregan Manor, Howard Cty., Md.	No. 56	Roman Catholic	Brick
1727	Seaville Friends M. H., Seaville, N. J	No. 149	Friends	Wood
1727	Christ Church, Philadelphia, Pa.	No. 205	Anglican	Brick
1727	St. John's Church, Hampton, Va.	No. 310	Anglican	Brick
1728	First Reformed Dutch Church, Hackensack, N. J.	No. 131	Dutch Reformed	Stone
1728	Concord Friends M. H., Concordville, Pa.	No. 218	Friends	Brick
1728	Saponey Church, Dinwiddie Cty., Va.	No. 301	Anglican	Wood
1729	Old South M. H., Boston, Mass.	No. 94	Congregational	Brick
1729	Caroline Church, Setauket, N. Y.	No. 175	Anglican	Wood
1729	Cranston Friends M. H., Cranston, R. I.	No. 263	Friends	Wood
1729	Sabbath Day M. H., Newport, R. I.	No. 268	Seventh Day Baptist	Wood
1729	Dr. Hopkins' M. H., Newport, R. I.	No. 269	Congregational	Wood
1729	Wren Chapel, Williamsburg, Va.	No. 295	Anglican	Brick
1729	Slash Church, Hanover Cty., Va.	No. 316	Anglican	Wood
1730	First Congregational Church, Kittery Point, Me.	No. 31	Congregational	Wood
1730	Old St. Luke's Church, Church Hill, Md.	No. 74	Anglican	Brick
1730	Clapboardtrees M. H., Westwood, Mass.	No. 102	Congregational	Wood
1730	Old Stone Church, Red Hook, N. Y.	No. 188	German Lutheran	Stone
1730	Fort Herkimer Reformed Dutch Church, Herkimer Cty., N. Y.	No. 194	Dutch Reformed	Stone
c. 1730	Mangohick Church, King William Cty., Va.	No. 323	Anglican	Brick
1731	First Reformed Dutch Church, Fishkill, N. Y.	No. 182	Dutch Reformed	Stone
1731	Westover Church, Charles City Cty., Va.	No. 311	Anglican	Brick
1732	Durham Church, Charles Cty., Md.	No. 44	Anglican	Brick
c. 1732	Old North Vestry, Nantucket, Mass.	No. 93	Presbyterian	Wood
1732	Old M. H., Burlington, Mass.	No. 99	Congregational	Wood
1732	St. John's Church, King William Cty., Va.	No. 321	Anglican	Brick

1732	Christ Church, Lancaster Cty., Va.	No. 329	Anglican	Brick
1733	St. Paul's Church, Baden, Md.	No. 49	Anglican	Brick
1733	St. Thomas' Church, Croom, Md.	No. 50	Anglican	Brick
1733	Old Green Hill Church, Wicomico Cty., Md.	No. 79	Anglican	Brick
1733	Second Congregational Church, Newport, R. I.	No. 270	Congregational	Wood
1734	Christ Church, Dover, Del.	No. 23	Anglican	Brick
1734	St. Thomas' Church, Bath, N. C.	No. 198	Anglican	Brick
1735	Blandford Church, Petersburg, Va.	No. 300	Anglican	Brick
1735	Fork Church, Hanover Cty., Va.	No. 315	Anglican	Brick
1736	Christ Church, Chaptico, Md.	No. 42	Anglican	Brick
1736	St. Paul's Church, Edenton, N. C.	No. 199	Anglican	Brick
1736	Chester Friends M. H., Chester, Pa.	No. 216	Friends	Brick
1736	Donation Church, Princess Anne Cty., Va.	No. 306	Anglican	Brick
1737	Ye Old Yellow M. H., Imlaystown, N. J.	No. 145	Baptist	Wood
c. 1737	North Farnham Church, Richmond Cty., Va.	No. 328	Anglican	Brick
1738	Hockessin Friends M. H., New Castle Cty., Del.	No. 20	Friends	Stone
1738	Salem Town Hall, Salem, N. H.	No. 117	Congregational	Wood
1738	Glebe Church, Nansemond Cty., Va.	No. 302	Anglican	Brick
1738	St. George's Church, Pungoteague, Md.	No. 309	Anglican	Brick
1739	Trenton Friends M. H., Trenton, N. J.	No. 144	Friends	Brick
1739	St. Paul's Church, Norfolk, Va.	No. 304	Anglican	Brick
1740	First Presbyterian Church, Wilmington, Del.	No. 14	Presbyterian	Brick
1740	Friends M. H., Bordentown, N. J.	No. 166	Friends	Brick
1740	St. Philip's Church, Brunswick, N. C.	No. 200	Anglican	Brick
c. 1740	Donegal Presbyterian Church, Lancaster Cty., Pa.	No. 251	Presbyterian	Stone
1740	Paxton Presbyterian Church, Paxtang, Pa.	No. 258	Presbyterian	Stone
c. 1740	Elder Ballou M. H., Providence Cty., R. I.	No. 264	Six Principle Baptist	Wood
1740	St. Mary's White Chapel, Lancaster Cty., Va.	No. 330	Anglican	Brick
1740	Hebron Lutheran Church, Madison Cty., Va.	No. 339	German Lutheran	Wood
1741	St. Thomas' Manor House, Charles Cty., Md.	No. 46	Roman Catholic	Brick
1741	The Saal, Ephrata, Pa.	No. 248	Seventh Day German Baptist	Wood
c. 1741	Prince George's Church, Winyah, Georgetown, S. C.	No. 283	Anglican	Brick
1741	St. John's Church, Richmond, Va.	No. 312	Anglican	Wood
1742	Sater Baptist Church, Baltimore Cty., Md.	No. 57	Baptist	Brick
1742	St. Mary's Church, North East, Md.	No. 71	Anglican	Brick
1742	South Hingham M. H., South Hingham, Mass.	No. 89	Congregational	Wood
1742	Holden Chapel, Cambridge, Mass.	No. 97	Congregational	Brick
1742	Hungars Church, Northampton Cty., Va.	No. 308	Anglican	Brick
1743	St. Thomas's Church, Baltimore Cty., Md.	No. 58	Anglican	Brick
1743	Christ Church, New Brunswick, N. J.	No. 138	Anglican	Stone
1743	New Garden Friends M. H., New Garden, Pa.	No. 224	Friends	Brick
1743	Old Trappe Church, Trappe, Pa.	No. 231	German Lutheran	Stone
1743	Neshaminy Presbyterian Church, Bucks Cty., Pa.	No. 238	Presbyterian	Stone
1743	Chapel of St. Paul, Bally, Pa.	No. 246	Roman Catholic	Stone
1744	St. Peter's Church in the Great Valley, Chester Cty., Pa.	No. 223	Anglican	Stone
1745	Hampstead Town Hall, Hampstead, N. H.	No. 120	Congregational	Wood
c. 1745	Sheldon Church, Beaufort Cty., S. C.	No. 288	Anglican	Brick
1746	Welsh Tract Baptist Church, New Castle Cty., Del.	No. 21	Baptist	Brick
1746	Bird M. H., Nashua, N. H.	No. 123	Presbyterian	Wood
1747	First Parish M. H., Cohasset, Mass.	No. 88	Congregational	Wood

1747	Old School Baptist Church, Hopewell, N. J.	No. 141	Baptist	Stone
1747	Augusta Church, Fort Defiance, Va.	No. 343	Presbyterian	Stone
1748	Middleham Chapel, Calvert Cty., Md.	No. 53	Anglican	Brick
1748	All Hallows Church, Snow Hill, Md.	No. 85	Anglican	Brick
1748	Cattail Church, King William Cty., Va.	No. 324	Anglican	Brick
1749	King's Chapel, Boston, Mass.	No. 95	Anglican	Stone
1750	St. George's Church, Valley Lee, Md.	No. 40	Anglican	Brick
1750	Christ Church, Wayside, Md.	No. 45	Anglican	Brick
1750	St. James' Church, My Lady's Manor, Baltimore Cty., Md.	No. 59	Anglican	Brick
1750	Zion Lutheran Church, Oldwick, N. J.	No. 139	German Lutheran	Brick
c. 1750	Manhasset Friends M. H., Manhasset, N. Y.	No. 171	Friends	Wood
1751	Abington Congregational Church, Windham Cty., Conn.	No. 1	Congregational	Wood
1751	Tennent Church, Monmouth Cty., N. J.	No. 146	Presbyterian	Wood
1751	Old Chapel, Bethlehem, Pa.	No. 244	Moravian	Stone
1751	Lower Southwark Church, Surry Cty., Va.	No. 298	Anglican	Brick
1752	Old Stone Church, Frederick, Md.	No. 64	German Lutheran	Stone
1752	Makefield Friends M. H., Bucks Cty., Pa.	No. 242	Friends	Stone
1752	Plumstead Friends M. H., Bucks County, Pa.	No. 243	Friends	Stone
1752	St. Michael's Church, Charleston, S. C.	No. 274	Anglican	Brick
1752	Chuckatuck Church, Nansemond Cty., Va.	No. 303	Anglican	Brick
1754	Hampton Congregational Church, Hampton, Conn.	No. 5	Congregational	Wood
1754	Alloways Creek Friends M. H., Hancock's Bridge, N. J.	No. 153	Friends	Brick
1754	Chappaqua Friends M. H., Chappaqua, N. Y.	No. 180	Friends	Wood
1754	Eastern Shore Chapel, Princess Anne Cty., Va.	No. 307	Anglican	Brick
1754	Abingdon Church, Gloucester Cty., Va.	No. 318	Anglican	Brick
1755	St. Martin's Church, Worcester Cty., Md.	No. 86	Anglican	Brick
1755	First Parish M. H., Groton, Mass.	No. 100	Congregational	Wood
c. 1755	Mattapony Church, King and Queen Cty., Va.	No. 320	Anglican	Brick
1756	Old South Church, Newburyport, Mass.	No. 112	Presbyterian	Wood
1756	Community Congregational Church, Greenland, N. H.	No. 116	Congregational	Wood
1756	Timber Ridge Church, Rockbridge Cty., Va.	No. 344	Presbyterian	Stone
1757	Prince George's Chapel, Dagsboro, Del.	No. 25	Anglican	Wood
1757	Old M. H., Harpswell Center, Me.	No. 33	Congregational	Wood
1757	Nequasset M. H., Woolwich, Me.	No. 34	Congregational	Wood
1757	First Presbyterian Church, Carlisle, Pa.	No. 256	Presbyterian	Stone
1757	Aquia Church, Stafford Cty., Va.	No. 334	Anglican	Brick
1758	Randolph Friends M. H., Morris Cty., N. J.	No. 137	Friends	Wood
1758	St. Peter's Church, Philadelphia, Pa.	No. 206	Anglican	Brick
1758	Exeter Friends M. H., Berks Cty., Pa.	No. 247	Friends	Stone
1759	St. George's Church, Schenectady, N. Y.	No. 190	Anglican	Stone
1759	Touro Synagogue, Newport, R. I.	No. 271	Jewish	Brick
1759	Hopewell Friends M. H., Frederick Cty., Va.	No. 340	Friends	Stone
1760	Christ Church, Cambridge, Mass.	No. 98	Anglican	Wood
1760	Old Parish Congregational Church, Sheffield, Mass.	No. 108	Congregational	Wood
1760	Danville M. H., Danville, N. H.	No. 118	Congregational	Wood
1760	Mount Laurel Friends M. H., Burlington Cty., N. J.	No. 161	Friends	Stone
1760	St. James Church, Kingsessing, Phila., Pa.	No. 203	Swedish Lutheran	Stone
1760	Christ Church, Montgomery Cty., Pa.	No. 204	Swedish Lutheran	Stone
1760	St. Paul's Church, Philadelphia, Pa.	No. 207	Anglican	Brick
c. 1760	Acquinton Church, King William Cty., Va.	No. 322	Anglican	Brick
1761	First Church of Christ, Wethersfield, Conn.	No. 6	Congregational	Brick

532

1761	St. Paul's Church, Eastchester, N. Y.	No. 177	Anglican	Stone
1761	Trinity Church, Lancaster, Pa.	No. 249	German Lutheran	Brick
1761	St. John's Church, Berkeley Cty., S. C.	No. 277	Anglican	Brick
1762	St. James Church, Herring Creek, Md.	No. 54	Anglican	Brick
1762	First Church in Dedham, Dedham, Mass.	No. 101	Congregational	Wood
1762	Congregational Church, Park Hill, N. H.	No. 126	Congregational	Wood
1762	Peach Lake Friends M. H., Westchester Cty., N. Y.	No. 181	Friends	Wood
1762	Trinity Church, Portsmouth, Va.	No. 305	Anglican	Brick
1763	Trinity Chapel, Frederick, Md.	No. 65	German Reformed	Stone
1763	St. George's Church, Philadelphia, Pa.	No. 208	Methodist	Brick
1763	St. Mary's Church, Philadelphia, Pa.	No. 210	Roman Catholic	Brick
1763	Birmingham Friends M. H., Chester Cty., Pa.	No. 226	Friends	Stone
1763	Pompion Hill Chapel, Berkeley Cty., S. C.	No. 276	Anglican	Brick
1764	Priest Neale's Mass House, Harford Cty., Md.	No. 68	Roman Catholic	Stone
1764	Presbyterian Church of Lawrenceville, N. J.	No. 143	Presbyterian	Brick
1764	St. Paul's Chapel, New York, N. Y.	No. 168	Anglican	Stone
1764	Oblong Friends M. H., Quaker Hill, N. Y.	No. 184	Friends	Wood
1764	Marshallton Friends M. H., Chester Cty., Pa.	No. 227	Friends	Stone
1765	St. Andrew's Church, St. Mary's Cty., Md.	No. 41	Anglican	Brick
1765	All Faith Church, St. Mary's Cty., Md.	No. 43	Anglican	Brick
1765	Manokin Presbyterian Church, Princess Anne, Md.	No. 81	Presbyterian	Brick
1765	York Friends M. H., York, Pa.	No. 252	Friends	Brick
1765	Goose Creek Friends M. H., Lincoln, Va.	No. 341	Friends	Stone
1766	First Congregational Church, Shrewsbury, Mass.	No. 103	Congregational	Wood
1766	Pine Street Presbyterian Church, Philadelphia, Pa.	No. 211	Presbyterian	Brick
c. 1766	St. Paul's Church, King George Cty., Va.	No. 332	Anglican	Brick
1767	Blackwater Presbyterian Church, Sussex Cty., Del.	No. 26	Presbyterian	Wood
1767	Jerusalem Church, Ebenezer, Ga.	No. 28	German Lutheran	Brick
1767	St. Francis Xavier Church, St. Mary's Cty., Md.	No. 38	Roman Catholic	Wood
1767	Longmeadow M. H., Longmeadow, Mass.	No. 106	Congregational	Wood
1767	St. Peter's Church, Van Cortlandtville, N. Y.	No. 179	Anglican	Wood
1767	Falckner's Swamp Lutheran Church, Montgomery Cty., Pa.	No. 232	German Lutheran	Stone
1767	St. Peter's Church, Middletown, Pa.	No. 259	German Lutheran	Stone
1767	St. Stephen's Church, St. Stephen's, S. C.	No. 284	Anglican	Brick
1767	Christ Church, Alexandria, Va.	No. 336	Anglican	Brick
1767	Falls Church, Falls Church, Va.	No. 337	Anglican	Brick
1768	Old St. Anne's Church, Middletown, Del.	No. 22	Anglican	Brick
1768	Emmanuel Church, Chestertown, Md.	No. 73	Anglican	Brick
1768	Dover Friends M. H., Dover, N. H.	No. 114	Friends	Wood
1768	Tinicum Presbyterian Church, Bucks Cty., Pa.	No. 240	Presbyterian	Stone
1768	Buckingham Friends M. H., Bucks Cty., Pa.	No. 241	Friends	Stone
1768	St. James' Church, Santee, Charleston Cty., S. C.	No. 282	Anglican	Brick
1768	St. David's Church, Cheraw, S. C.	No. 285	Anglican	Wood
1769	Westminster Congregational Church, Westminster, Conn.	No. 2	Congregational	Wood
1769	Chestnut Hill M. H., Millville, Mass.	No. 104	Congregational	Wood
1769	First Church in Derry, Rockingham Cty., N. H.	No. 122	Presbyterian	Wood
1769	St. Thomas' Church, Hunterdon Cty., N. J.	No. 140	Anglican	Stone
1769	Christ Church, Shrewsbury, N. J.	No. 148	Anglican	Wood
1769	Charlotte Church, Oakdale, N. Y.	No. 176	Anglican	Wood
c. 1769	Trinity Church, Fishkill, N. Y.	No. 183	Anglican	Wood
1769	Indian Castle Church, Herkimer Cty., N. Y.	No. 193	Anglican	Wood
1769	Chichester Friends M. H., Delaware Cty., Pa.	No. 217	Friends	Stone

1769	Newtown Presbyterian Church, Newtown, Pa.	No. 239	Presbyterian	Stone
1769	Warrington Friends M. H., York Cty., Pa.	No. 253	Friends	Stone
1769	Lamb's Creek Church, King George Cty., Va.	No. 333	Anglican	Brick
1769	Pohick Church, Fairfax Cty., Va.	No. 335	Anglican	Brick
1770	First Congregational Church, Brooklyn, Conn.	No. 3	Congregational	Wood
1770	Old Trinity Church, Brooklyn, Conn.	No. 4	Anglican	Wood
c. 1770	German M. H., Waldoboro, Me.	No. 35	German Lutheran	Wood
1770	St. Andrew's Church, Princess Anne, Md.	No. 82	Anglican	Brick
c. 1770	St. Peter's Church, Freehold, N. J.	No. 147	Anglican	Wood
1770	Palatine Church, Montgomery Cty., N. Y.	No. 192	German Lutheran	Stone
1770	Mennonite M. H., Germantown, Pa.	No. 213	Mennonite	Stone
1770	Church of the Brethren, Germantown, Pa.	No. 214	Dunkard	Stone
1770	Mill Creek Church, Hamburg, Va.	No. 342	Baptist	Wood
1771	First Church of Christ, Farmington, Conn.	No. 7	Congregational	Wood
1771	Christ Church, Broad Creek, Sussex Cty., Del.	No. 27	Anglican	Wood
1771	Holy Trinity Church, Eldersburg, Md.	No. 63	Anglican	Stone
1771	Spring Hill Church, Hebron, Md.	No. 80	Anglican	Wood
1771	Congregational M. H., Amherst, N. H.	No. 124	Congregational	Wood
1771	Greenwich Friends M. H., Greenwich, N. J.	No. 151	Friends	Brick
1771	Deerfield Stone Church, Deerfield, N. J.	No. 152	Presbyterian	Stone
1772	Old Stone Church, East Haven, Conn.	No. 10	Congregational	Stone
1772	Kiokee Church, Columbia Cty., Ga.	No. 29	Baptist	Brick
1772	Walpole M. H., South Bristol, Me.	No. 36	Presbyterian	Wood
1772	Christ Church, Calvert Cty., Md.	No. 52	Anglican	Brick
1772	Congregational Church, Chester, N. H.	No. 121	Congregational	Wood
1772	Salem Friends M. H., Salem, N. J.	No. 154	Friends	Brick
1772	Rancocas Friends M. H., Rancocas, N. J.	No. 162	Friends	Brick
1772	Reformed High Dutch Church, Schoharie, N. Y.	No. 195	Dutch Reformed	Stone
1772	Unitarian Church, Charleston, S. C.	No. 289	Congregational	Brick
1773	Old Drawyers Church, Odessa, Del.	No. 18	Presbyterian	Brick
1773	First Parish Church, Kennebunk, Me.	No. 32	Congregational	Wood
1773	Gunpowder Friends M. H., Baltimore Cty., Md.	No. 60	Friends	Stone
1773	Little Falls Friends M. H., Fallston, Md.	No. 67	Friends	Stone
1773	Sandown M. H., Rockingham Cty., N. H.	No. 119	Congregational	Wood
1773	Union Church, West Claremont, N. H.	No. 128	Anglican	Wood
1773	Chesterfield Friends M. H., Crosswicks, N. J.	No. 167	Friends	Brick
1774	Kensington Congregational Church, Kensington, Conn.	No. 8	Congregational	Wood
1774	Old Congregational Church, Enfield, Conn.	No. 9	Congregational	Wood
1774	St. Barnabas Church, Prince George Cty., Md.	No. 51	Anglican	Brick
1774	German Reformed Church, Hagerstown, Md.	No. 66	German Reformed	Stone
1774	First Baptist Church, Providence, R. I.	No. 260	Baptist	Wood
1774	Hickory Neck Church, James City Cty., Va.	No. 296	Anglican	Brick
1775	Old M. H., Jaffrey, N. H.	No. 125	Congregational	Wood
1775	Mount Holly Friends M. H., Mount Holly, N. J.	No. 163	Friends	Brick
1775	Arney's Mount Friends M. H., Burlington Cty., N. J.	No. 164	Friends	Stone
1775	Old Springfield Friends M. H., Burlington Cty., N. J.	No. 165	Friends	Brick
1775	Frankford Friends M. H., Frankford, Pa.	No. 215	Friends	Stone
1775	First Reformed Church, Easton, Pa.	No. 245	German Reformed	Stone
1776	Little Fork Church, Culpeper Cty., Va.	No. 338	Anglican	Brick
1777	Creek Friends M. H., Clinton Corners, N. Y.	No. 186	Friends	Stone
1777	Old Sadsbury Friends M. H., Christiana, Pa.	No. 250	Friends	Stone
1779	Crum Elbow Friends M. H., Dutchess Cty., N. Y.	No. 185	Friends	Wood

1780	Barratt's Chapel, Frederica, Del.	No. 24	Methodist	Brick
1780	Fairfield Presbyterian Church, New England Crossroads, N. J.	No. 150	Presbyterian	Stone
1780	Nine Partners Friends M. H., Millbrook, N. Y.	No. 187	Friends	Brick
1781	Patapsco Friends M. H., Baltimore, Md.	No. 61	Friends	Brick
1783	Presbyterian Congregation of Connecticut Farms, Union, N. J.	No. 134	Presbyterian	Stone
1783	Free Quakers M. H., Philadelphia, Pa.	No. 212	Friends	Brick
1783	Silver Spring Presbyterian Church, Cumberland Cty., Pa.	No. 257	Presbyterian	Stone
1784	Deer Creek Friends M. H., Darlington, Md.	No. 69	Friends	Stone
1784	Rehoboth Episcopal Church, Somerset Cty., Md.	No. 84	Anglican	Brick
1784	Congregational Church, Phillipston, Mass.	No. 105	Congregational	Wood
1784	First Presbyterian Church, Elizabeth, N. J.	No. 133	Presbyterian	Brick
1784	Woodstown Friends M. H., Woodstown, N. J.	No. 155	Friends	Brick
1784	Trinity Church, Swedesboro, N. J.	No. 157	Swedish Lutheran	Brick
1784	Burlington Friends M. H., Burlington, N. J.	No. 160	Friends	Brick
1784	First Presbyterian Church, Huntington, N. Y.	No. 174	Presbyterian	Wood
1785	St. Paul's Church, Woodbury, Conn.	No. 11	Anglican	Wood
1785	Appoquinimink Friends M. H., Odessa, Del.	No. 19	Friends	Brick
1785	St. Ignatius Church, St. Mary's Cty., Md.	No. 39	Roman Catholic	Brick
1785	Otterbein Church, Baltimore, Md.	No. 62	United Brethren in Christ	Brick
1785	Rocky Hill M. H., Amesbury, Mass.	No. 113	Congregational	Wood
1785	Shaker M. H., Mount Lebanon, N. Y.	No. 189	Shaker	Wood
1785	Church of the Sacred Heart, Conewago, Pa.	No. 254	Roman Catholic	Stone
1785	Rehoboth Church, Monroe Cty., W. Va.	No. 345	Methodist	Wood
c. 1786	Christ Church, Middle Haddam, Conn.	No. 12	Anglican	Wood
1786	Southampton Congregational Church, Southampton, Mass.	No. 107	Congregational	Wood
1786	East Hoosac Friends M. H., Adams, Mass.	No. 109	Friends	Wood
1786	Washington Town Hall, Washington, N. H.	No. 127	Congregational	Wood
1786	Old Town House, Henniker, N. H.	No. 130	Congregational	Wood
1786	Moravian Church, Salem Cty., N. J.	No. 156	Moravian	Brick
1786	Reformed Dutch Church, Middleburg, N. Y.	No. 196	Dutch Reformed	Brick
1786	Conanicut Friends M. H., Jamestown, R. I.	No. 273	Friends	Wood
1787	First Presbyterian Church, Newark, N. J.	No. 132	Presbyterian	Stone
1787	Wrightstown Friends M. H., Wrightstown, Pa.	No. 237	Friends	Stone
1787	Great Conewago Presbyterian Church, Hunterstown, Pa.	No. 255	Presbyterian	Stone
1787	Rockingham M. H., Rockingham, Vt.	No. 291	Congregational	Wood
1787	First Congregational Church, Thetford Hill, Vt.	No. 292	Congregational	Wood
1788	Plainfield Friends M. H., Plainfield, N. J.	No. 136	Friends	Wood
1788	Jericho Friends M. H., Hicksville, N. Y.	No. 173	Friends	Wood
1788	Dutch Reformed Church, Stone Arabia, N. Y.	No. 191	Dutch Reformed	Stone
1788	Moravian Church, Bethabara, N. C.	No. 201	Moravian	Stone
1788	Ebenezer Church, Fairfield Cty., S. C.	No. 290	Presbyterian	Brick
1789	Asbury Methodist Church, Wilmington, Del.	No. 15	Methodist	Brick
1789	Alna M. H., Alna, Me.	No. 37	Congregational	Wood
1789	First Church, Hopkinton, N. H.	No. 129	Congregational	Wood
1789	Fallsington Friends M. H., Fallsington, Pa.	No. 236	Friends	Stone
1791	Springfield M. H., Springfield, N. J.	No. 135	Presbyterian	Wood
1792	Midway Church, Liberty Cty., Ga.	No. 30	Congregational	Wood

These last two buildings bear dates after the beginning of the Republic, but, as they were reconstructions of the colonial buildings, and are of special historic interest, they are included as exceptions to the 1789 limit.

SUMMARY OF BUILDINGS
BY DENOMINATION AND REGION
(for details see summaries by state, II A, B, C)

	South	New England	Mid-Atlantic	Total
Anglican	95	10	25	130
Baptist	3	1	3	7
Baptist, Six Principle		1		1
Baptist, Seventh Day		1		1
Baptist, German, Seventh Day			1	1
Baptist, German, Dunkard			1	1
Congregational	2	50		52
Friends	8	9	56	73
Jewish		1		1
Lutheran, German	3	1	7	11
Lutheran, Swedish			5	5
Mennonite			1	1
Methodist	1		3	4
Moravian	1		2	3
Presbyterian	5	5	23	33
Reformed Dutch			7	7
Reformed German	2		1	3
Reformed German, United Brethren	1			1
Roman Catholic	5		4	9
Shaker			1	1
20 Total	126	79	140	345

SUMMARY OF BUILDINGS IN THE SOUTH
BY DENOMINATION AND STATE

	Ga.	Md.	N.C.	S.C.	Va.	W.Va.	Total
Anglican		31	3	15	46		95
Baptist	1	1			1		3
Baptist, Six Principle							
Baptist, Seventh Day							
Baptist, German, Seventh Day							
Baptist, German, Dunkard							
Congregational	1			1			2
Friends		6			2		8
Jewish							
Lutheran, German	1	1			1		3
Lutheran, Swedish							
Mennonite							
Methodist						1	1
Moravian			1				1
Presbyterian		2		1	2		5
Reformed Dutch							
Reformed German		2					2
Reformed German, United Brethren		1					1
Roman Catholic		5					5
Shaker							
South Totals	3	49	4	17	52	1	126
New England							79
Mid-Atlantic							140
Grand Total							345

SUMMARY OF BUILDINGS IN NEW ENGLAND
BY DENOMINATION AND STATE

	Mass.	N.H.	Vt.	Me.	R.I.	Conn.	Total
Anglican	4	1			2	3	10
Baptist					1		1
Baptist, Six Principle					1		1
Baptist, Seventh Day					1		1
Baptist, German, Seventh Day							
Baptist, German, Dunkard							
Congregational	19	13	2	5	2	9	50
Friends	2	1			6		9
Jewish					1		1
Lutheran, German				1			1
Lutheran, Swedish							
Mennonite							
Methodist							
Moravian							
Presbyterian	2	2		1			5
Reformed Dutch							
Reformed German							
Reformed German, United Brethren							
Roman Catholic							
Shaker							
New England Totals	27	17	2	7	14	12	79
Mid-Atlantic							140
South							126
Grand Total							345

SUMMARY OF BUILDINGS IN THE MID-ATLANTIC
BY DENOMINATION AND STATE

	N.Y.	N.J.	Del.	Penn.	Total
Anglican	9	5	5	6	25
Baptist		2	1		3
Baptist, Six Principle					
Baptist, Seventh Day					
Baptist, German, Seventh Day				1	1
Baptist, German, Dunkard				1	1
Congregational					
Friends	10	18	2	26	56
Jewish					
Lutheran, German	2	1		4	7
Lutheran, Swedish		1	1	3	5
Mennonite				1	1
Methodist			2	1	3
Moravian		1		1	2
Presbyterian	1	8	4	10	23
Reformed Dutch	6	1			7
Reformed German				1	1
Reformed German, United Brethren					
Roman Catholic	1			3	4
Shaker	1				1
Mid-Atlantic Totals	30	37	15	58	140
South					126
New England					79
Grand Total					345

APPENDIX III
SUMMARY OF BUILDINGS
BY MATERIAL, REGION, STATE
(for details, see summary with each state)

		Brick	Wood	Stone	Tapia	Total
South						
Virginia		42	5	5		52
West Virginia			1			1
South Carolina		15	1		1	17
North Carolina		3		1		4
Maryland		38	3	8		49
Georgia		2	1			3
6	Total	100	11	14	1	126
New England						
Massachusetts		3	23	1		27
New Hampshire			17			17
Vermont			2			2
Maine			7			7
Rhode Island		1	13			14
Connecticut		1	10	1		12
6	Total	5	72	2		79
Mid-Atlantic						
New York		2	15	13		30
New Jersey		18	8	11		37
Delaware		10	3	2		15
Pennsylvania		14	1	43		58
4	Total	44	27	69		140
3 16	Grand Total	149	110	85	1	345

APPENDIX IV
BRITISH SOVEREIGNS AND AMERICAN COLONIAL HISTORY

Reign   PLANTAGENET KINGS

1377-1399 Richard II. 1383, marries Anne of Bohemia. Lollards and beginnings of Church reform. Writings of first reformer, John Wycliffe (c. 1320-1384), sent to Bohemia, where influenced reformer John Huss (c. 1374-1415).

1399-1413 Henry IV. 1415, John Huss of Bohemia martyred. Hussites and other Protestants grow to majority in Bohemia.

1413-1422 Henry V

1422-1461 Henry VI

1461-1483 Edward IV. Followers of Huss organize; 1467, as *Unitas Fratras*, Moravian Church fully organized with Apostolic succession, first Protestant Episcopal Church in Europe.

1483-2 mo. Edward V

1483-1485 Richard III

TUDOR KINGS

1485-1509 Henry VII. 1492, last Moorish kingdom in Spain conquered by Ferdinand and Isabella; discovery of America; Sephardic Jews dispersed. Reformer Ulrich Zwingli (1484-1531), Zurich. Reformer Martin Luther (1483-1546), Germany.

1509-1547 Henry VIII. 1517, Luther's theses posted at Wittenberg church, launch Reformation. Reformer John Calvin (1509-1564). 1533, Henry divorces Catherine; marries Anne Boleyn; Elizabeth born. 1534, Act of Supremacy makes King "Supreme Head of Church of England under Christ."

1547-1553 Edward VI. Calvin at Geneva; beginnings of Presbyterianism. Reformer John Knox (c. 1505-1572).

1553-1558 Mary I. 1554, marries Philip II of Spain. Restores Roman Catholicism in Church of England. 1557, Knox in exile, adviser to Protestant barons of Scotland, who enter first covenant, leading to Church of Scotland, Presbyterian.

1558-1603 Elizabeth I. Restores Protestantism in Church of England. 1559, Knox returns to Edinburgh. 1562, attempt of Huguenots to colonize in South Carolina. 1579, Union of Utrecht, independence of Protestant Holland. 1584, attempt of English to colonize in North Carolina. 1588, Battle of the Armada, climax in struggle between Catholic Spain and Protestant England. 1598, Edict of Nantes, concessions to French Protestants. Beginnings of Congregationalism; Robert Browne (1550-1638); Henry Barrowe (1550-1593). English Reformation completed at time of Council of Trent.

STUART KINGS

1603-1625 James I. 1604 negotiates treaty with Spain, permitting first Protestants to settle in North America. 1606, Virginia and Plymouth companies chartered. 1607, settlement of Jamestown. 1618, Thirty Years War begins in Bohemia. 1620, settlement of Plymouth. 1624, Virginia Plantation made a royal colony; settlement of Dutch New Netherland.

1625-1649 Charles I. 1642, Rebellion begins; Oliver Cromwell; Puritans. 1645, William Laud, Archbishop of Canterbury, beheaded. 1647, preaching of George Fox begins, leading to Religious Society of Friends. 1649, Charles beheaded. Cavaliers flee to Virginia, where province remains loyal to Crown. Puritans attempt to destroy Church and Crown.

1649-1660 Commonwealth. Virginia defies Puritans, gives allegiance to Charles II. Massachusetts and England under Puritan rule. 1650-58, Puritans temporarily hold government of Maryland from Catholic Lord Baltimore.

1660-1685 Charles II. Restoration of Crown and Church. 1676, Bacon's Rebellion, Virginia (100 years before Revolution). 1682, William Penn to America.

1685-1689 James II. 1685, Revocation of Edict of Nantes drives Huguenots to South Carolina, New York, New Jersey. 1688, English Revolution; King deposed, Roman Catholic.

1689-1694 William III and Mary II. Protestant reaction to Catholicism of James. Maryland made royal colony, Church of England established, ending Catholic government of Lord Baltimore. Massachusetts made royal colony, ending Puritan government.

1694-1702 William III. 1701, Act of Succession provides that all future sovereigns be members of Church of England; Bill of Rights protects Protestants from royal attack; organized Society for the Propagation of the Gospel in Foreign Parts; missionaries to Anglican churches in America.

1702-1714 Anne. 1702, George Keith to America, first missionary of S.P.G. Scotch-Irish Presbyterians to America; 1706, first presbytery formed, Philadelphia. 1707, Act of Union, uniting legislatures of England and Scotland, opens American colonies to Scots, thereafter "English" colonies are "British" colonies.

HANOVERIAN KINGS

1714-1727 George I. Elector of Hanover crowned King of England in preference to Roman Catholic Pretender. Emigration of Germans from the Palatinate to New York, Pennsylvania.

1727-1760 George II. 1733, Georgia founded, named for King. 1736, John and Charles Wesley to Georgia, followed by George Whitefield; beginnings of Methodism; Moravians to Georgia, then Pennsylvania, North Carolina.

1760-1820 George III. 1765, Stamp Act. 1776, Declaration of Independence. 1781, surrender of British at Yorktown, end of War of Independence. 1784, Church of England officially disestablished in Virginia, by incorporation of Protestant Episcopal Church. 1789, Protestant Episcopal Church in America organized, with constitution and revised Prayer Book; George Washington inaugurated first President of the United States of America.

APPENDIX V

SOME FIRSTS AMONG COLONIAL HOUSES OF WORSHIP

Oldest Protestant church building in North America; the only Gothic colonial church building in the United States; oldest church building in the English colonies of America; oldest Anglican church building in America; oldest church building in Virginia: *Old Brick Church, St. Luke's, Isle of Wight County, Virginia*, built 1632 (No. 297).

Remains of the church of the first parish established in the English colonies: *the brick tower at Jamestown, Virginia*, built 1639 (No. 293).

Oldest Anglican church building in America in continuous use: *Immanuel Church, New Castle, Delaware*, built 1703 (No. 16).

Oldest Anglican church in continuous use in Virginia: *Bruton Parish Church, Williamsburg*, built 1711 (No. 294).

Church of the first Anglican parish in New England, organized 1686; first Unitarian church in America, converted 1785: *King's Chapel, Boston*, built 1749 (No. 95).

Oldest Anglican church building in New England: *St. Paul's Church, Wickford, Rhode Island*, built 1707 (No. 265).

Oldest frame house of worship in America; oldest house of worship in America used continuously for services; oldest meeting house built by Congregationalists; only seventeenth-century house of worship in New England; oldest house of worship in Massachusetts: *Old Ship Meeting House, Hingham*, built 1681 (No. 87).

Oldest colonial house of worship built of stone; oldest house of worship in Pennsylvania: *Merion Friends Meeting House, Montgomery County*, built 1695 (No. 229).

Oldest Friends meeting house; second oldest frame house of worship in America; oldest house of worship in Maryland: *Third Haven Friends Meeting House, Easton, Maryland*, built 1682 (No. 76).

First Congregational church, oldest congregation of the denomination in America, organized in Southwark, London, 1616; moved to Scituate, Massachusetts, 1634; moved to Barnstable, 1639: present *meeting house of West Parish*, now *West Barnstable, Massachusetts*, built 1717 (No. 91).

Oldest meeting house in the country still in use by that denomination; oldest meeting house in New Hampshire: *Newington Meeting House*, built 1712 (No. 115).

Oldest Presbyterian church building in America: *Norriton Presbyterian Meeting House, Montgomery County, Pennsylvania*, built 1698 (No. 230).

First presbytery in America, the Presbytery of Philadelphia, organized 1706, with Francis Makemie as moderator; oldest Presbyterian church built by Presbyterians: *Makemie's Church (Rehoboth Church), Pocomoke, Somerset County, Maryland*, built in 1706 (No. 83).

Oldest Dutch Reformed church building in America: *Sleepy Hollow Church, Scarborough, New York*, built in 1699 (No. 178). [The First Reformed Dutch Church of Hackensack, New Jersey, was rebuilt in 1728 with some of the stone of the original building of 1696 (No. 131).]

Oldest German Reformed church building in America: *German Reformed Church, Hagerstown, Maryland*, built 1774 (No. 66).

First Church of the United Brethren in Christ, sect founded in 1789: *Otterbein Church, Baltimore, Maryland*, built 1785 (No. 62).

Oldest remaining church built by the Swedish Lutherans in America: *Old Swedes, Gloria Dei Church, Philadelphia, Pennsylvania*, built 1697 (No. 202).

Oldest German Luthern congregation in America: *Falckner's Swamp Lutheran Church, Hanover Township, Pennsylvania*, founded 1700 by Daniel Falckner; built 1767 (No. 232).

Oldest German Luthern church building in America: *Old Stone Church, Evangelical Lutheran Church of St. Peter the Apostle, Red Hook, New York*, built 1730 (No. 188).

Oldest German Lutheran Church in America built, owned, and still used by that denomination; oldest German Lutheran congregation and building in the South: *Hebron Evangelical Lutheran Church, Madison County, Virginia*, built 1740 (No. 339).

Oldest house of worship in America of the Moravian Church, the first fully organized (1467) Protestant Church in the world (except the Eastern Churches): *Old Chapel, Bethlehem, Pennsylvania*, built 1751 (No. 244).

Oldest Baptist Meeting House in America; oldest Baptist congregation: *First Baptist Church, Providence, Rhode Island*, founded 1638, built 1774 (No. 260).

Oldest Sabbath Day Meeting House in America: *Newport, Rhode Island*, built 1729 (No. 268).

The oldest meeting house of the Six Principle Baptists: *Elder Ballou Meeting House, Rhode Island*, built c. 1740 (No. 264).

Oldest German Baptist, or Dunkard, meeting house in America: *Church of the Brethren, Germantown, Pennsylvania*, built 1770 (No. 214).

Oldest Mennonite Meeting house in America: at *Germantown, Pennsylvania*, built 1770 (No. 213).

The first Protestant monastery in America; the oldest house of worship of the Seventh-Day German Baptists: *The Cloisters, Ephrata, Pennsylvania*, 1741 (No. 248).

Oldest Methodist church building in America; the first Methodist chapel to be called a church: *St. George's Church, Philadelphia*, dedicated by Methodists in 1769, though begun in 1763 but not completed by Dutch Reformed (No. 208).

First and only *Free Quakers Meeting House, Philadelphia*, built 1783 (No. 212).

The oldest, and only colonial, Shaker meeting house still standing: *Mount Lebanon, New York*, built 1785 (No. 189).

Oldest Roman Catholic chapel, private, in the British colonies: *Doughoregan Manor, Howard County, Maryland*, built 1727 (No. 56).

Oldest Roman Catholic parish chapel in the British colonies; first Roman Catholic parish school in the colonies, 1743: *St. Paul's Chapel, Bally, Pennsylvania*, built 1743 (No. 246.)

Oldest Jewish house of worship in America: *Touro Synagogue, Newport, Rhode Island*, built 1759 (No. 271).

The first Bishop of Connecticut and the first American Anglican Bishop, Samuel Seabury, was consecrated in 1784 at Aberdeen, Scotland, after having been elected at a meeting of Connecticut priests, at the *Glebe House of St. Paul's Church, Woodbury, Connecticut*. The present church was begun the following year, 1785 (No. 11).

First Episcopal Bishop consecrated in America, 1792, and the first Bishop of Maryland, Thomas Claggett, was rector of *St. Paul's Church, Baden, Maryland*, from 1780 to 1786, built 1733 (No. 49). He was rector also of Page's Chapel, at Croom, his family estate, which was a chapel of ease to St. Paul's and later was made *St. Thomas' Church*, built 1733 (No. 50).

Oldest church building in Delaware: *Old Swedes Church, Wilmington*, built 1698 (No. 13).

Oldest house of worship in Georgia, was built by Salzburgers: *Jerusalem Church, Ebenezer*, built 1767 (No. 28).

The first Episcopal ordination in the colonies took place at Savannah, Georgia, in 1736, when Bishop David Nitschmann ordained Anthony Seifferth as a deacon of the Moravian Church to serve the congregation there.

Oldest meeting house in Maine: *First Congregational Church, Kittery Point*, built 1730 (No. 31).

Oldest house of worship in New Jersey (not counting the First Reformed Dutch Church, Hackensack, rebuilt in 1728 from stone of the building of 1696): *Old St. Mary's Church, Burlington*, built 1703 (No. 159).

Oldest house of worship in New York: *Flushing Friends Meeting House*, built 1694 (No. 170).

Oldest house of worship, and only colonial church in Manhattan: *St. Paul's Chapel*, built 1764 (No. 168).

Oldest house of worship in North Carolina, where was also the first public library in the province: *St. Thomas' Church, Bath*, built 1734 (No. 198).

Oldest house of worship in Rhode Island: *Newport Friends Meeting House*, built 1699 (No. 266).

Oldest house of worship in South Carolina: *St. Andrew's Church*, built 1706 (No. 279).

Oldest houses of worship in Vermont: the two colonial meeting houses to survive, at *Rockingham* and at *Thetford Hill*, were both built in 1787 (Nos. 291, 292).

The oldest house of worship in West Virginia, and the only one west of the Alleghenies built in the colonial period: *Rehoboth Church*, a log church built in 1785 (No. 345).

BIBLIOGRAPHY

So many sources were used in this work that it would be difficult to present the reader with full references. Books have been published that are confined to the one subject of the date of a single building. An example is *The Brick Church, near Smithfield Virginia. Built in 1632*, by R. S. Thomas (1891), and yet it was not the last word. In the course of his thorough research on colonial churches of Virginia, George Carrington Mason developed the theory that the present building was erected as late as 1682, and he presents his reasoning, together with the arguments for the traditional date, in *Colonial Churches of Tidewater Virginia* (1945), Chapter IX, "Isle of Wight and Southampton County Churches." But *that* was not the last word. In the course of the restoration of the church, while Mason was serving as a member of the Restoration Committee, organized in 1953, a brochure was published, "Historic St. Luke's Restoration, Smithfield, Virginia." On page 8, a change in Mason's opinion is recorded as follows: ". . . he believed that St. Luke's was possibly built as late as 1682. After studying a deed of 1667, however, Mr. Mason now concludes that the building was certainly in existence in that year, and from references in the deed to earlier documents he conjectures that it may have been standing as early as 1638. In any event it is 'the oldest church building of English construction in America' and is 'undeniably the only Gothic Colonial church in the United States' (letter of George Carrington Mason, July 28, 1953)."

This gives some idea of the problem here of thorough documentation. One would think that colonial history might be static, but the example outlined above is only one in a field that is still very active. Should the author's work here be thoroughly documented, the volume of notes would be unreasonably great, and they still could not trace the reasoning as in the case above. The compromise offered here is a list of the principal published sources. In most cases the imprint gives the related significance; in others a parenthetical note mentions the connection.

Allen, The Rev. Ethan. *The Garrison Church: Sketches of the History of St. Thomas' Parish, Garrison Forest, Baltimore County, Maryland, 1742-1852.* (Ed. the Rev. Hobart Smith.) New York: James Potts & Co., 1898.

American Guide Series. Federal Writers' Project of the Works Progress Administration;

    Connecticut: A Guide to its Roads, Lore, and People. Boston: Houghton Mifflin Co. The Riverside Press Cambridge, 1938.

    Delaware: A Guide to the First State. New York: The Viking Press, 1938.

    Georgia: A Guide to its Towns and Countryside. University of Georgia Press, 1940.

    Maine: A Guide Down East. Boston: Houghton Mifflin Co. The Riverside Press Cambridge, 1937.

    Maryland: A Guide to the Old Line State. Oxford University Press, 1940.

    Massachusetts: A Guide to its Places and People. Boston: Houghton Mifflin Co., The Riverside Press Cambridge, 1937.

    New Hampshire: A Guide to the Granite State. Boston: Houghton Mifflin Co., The Riverside Press, Cambridge, 1938.

    New Jersey: A Guide to its Present and Past. New York: The Viking Press, 1938.

    New York: A Guide to the Empire State. New York: Oxford University Press, 1940.

    New York City: A Comprehensive Guide to the Five Boroughs of the Metropolis. New York: Random House, 1939.

    New York, Dutchess County. (Sponsored by the Women's City and County Club of Dutchess County, N. Y.) Philadelphia: William Penn Association, 1937.

    New York, Story of Five Towns: Inwood, Lawrence, Cedarhurst, Woodmere and Hewlett, Nassau County, Long Island. Rockville Centre, N. Y.: Nassau Daily Review-Star, 1941.

    North Carolina: A Guide to the Old North State. University of North Carolina Press, 1939.

    Pennsylvania: A Guide to the Keystone State. New York: Oxford University Press, 1940.

    Rhode Island: A Guide to the Smallest State. Boston: Houghton Mifflin, 1937.

South Carolina: A Guide to the Palmetto State. Oxford University Press, 1941.

Vermont: A Guide to the Green Mountain State. Boston: Houghton Mifflin Co., The Riverside Press Cambridge, 1937.

Virginia: A Guide to the Old Dominion. Oxford University Press, 1940.

West Virginia: A Guide to the Mountain State. Oxford University Press, 1941.

Andrews, Edward Deming. *The People Called Shakers: A search for the perfect society.* New York: Oxford University Press, 1953.

Apes, William (Indian preacher of the gospel, born 1798). *Indian Nullification of the Unconstitutional Laws of Massachusetts, Relative to the Mashpee Tribe: or, The Pretended Riot Explained.* Boston: Press of J. Howe, 1835. Pp. 168. ["The real author of this book is said to William J. Snelling." — Sabin, *Bibliotheca Americana.*]

Archambault, A. Margaretta. *A Guide Book of Art, Architecture, and Historic Interest in Pennsylvania.* Philadelphia: The John C. Winston Co., 1924. (Cumberland County, 201.)

Aurand, A. Monroe, Jr. (member of Pennsylvania German Society). *Historical Account of the Ephrata Cloister and the Seventh Day Baptist Society.* Harrisburg: The Aurand Press, 1940.

Batchelder, Samuel F. *Bits of Harvard History.* Cambridge: Harvard University Press, 1924.

Bean, Theodore W. (ed.). *History of Montgomery County.* Philadelphia: Everts & Peck, 1884.

Beardsley, The Rev. William A., D.D. *A historical sermon preached in Old Trinity Church, Brooklyn, Connecticut, November 1, 1939.* Pp. 14.

Bohannan, A. W. *Old Surry: Thumbnail Sketches of Places of Historical Interest in Surry County Virginia.* Petersburg: Plummer Printing Co., Inc., 1927.

Book of Meetings. Young Friends Movement. Philadelphia, 1940.

Book of Meetings of the Religious Society of Friends Called Quakers: Showing all Meetings in New York State and Parts Adjacent. New York, 1924.

Bridenbaugh, Carl. *Peter Harrison: First American Architect.* University of North Carolina Press, 1949.

Briggs, Charles Augustus, D.D. *American Presbyterianism.* New York: Charles Scribner's Sons, 1885.

Briggs, Martin S. *The Homes of the Pilgrim Fathers in England and America.* London and New York: Oxford University Press, 1932.

Brigham, Harry Hillyer. *The Two Hundredth Anniversary of the First Meeting House in Sheffield, Massachusetts.* Sheffield: Privately printed, 1935.

Brown, Alexander (ed.). *Genesis of the United States: A narrative of the movement in England, 1605-1616, which resulted in the plantation of North America by Englishmen, disclosing the contest between England and Spain for possession of the soil now occupied by the United States of America; etc.* Boston: Houghton, Mifflin & Co., Riverside Press Cambridge, 1890.

Brydon, George MacLaren, D.D. *Virginia's Mother Church and The Political Conditions Under Which It Grew — The story of the Anglican Church and the Development of Religion in Virginia. 1727-1814.* 2 vols. Philadelphia: Church Historical Society, 1952.

———, and Miss Mary Goodwin. *The Colonial Churches in Virginia.* Richmond: Virginia State Chamber of Commerce, 1935. Pp. 15.

Buck, William J. (historian of Montgomery County, Pennsylvania). *The Early History of Abington Meeting House: A paper read at the Bicentennial, 1899.*

Bulletin of the Friends Historical Association, XVIII, 106, "East Hoosac Friends Meeting, Adams, Massachusetts."

Bunting, Samuel J., Jr. *Merion Meeting House, 1695-1945.* (A study of evidence relating to the date.) Pamphlet.

Burr, Nelson R. "The Early History of the Swedes and the Episcopal Church in America," *Historical Magazine of the Protestant Episcopal Church,* VII (June, 1938), 117-127.

———. *The Anglican Church in New Jersey.* Philadelphia: Church Historical Society (Publication No. 20), 1954.

Burt, Struthers. *Philadelphia: Holy Experiment.* New York: Doubleday, Doran & Co., Inc., 1945.

Burton, Asa. (pastor of the Church in Thetford, Vermont.) *A sermon Preached at Windsor before His Excellency Thomas Chittendon, Governor, His Honor Paul Spooner, Esq., Deputy-Governor, the Honorable Council, and the Honorable House of Representatives of the State of Vermont, on the day of the Anniversary Election October 13, 1785.* Windsor: Printed by Hough and Spooner, 1786. (Probably on the press of 1638, now in the Vermont Historical Society Library, Montpelier.)

Canby, Henry Seidel. *The Brandywine.* New York: Farrar & Rinehart, Inc., 1941. (Birmingham Friends Meeting House and Battle of the Brandywine, 208-215.)

Catholic Encyclopedia. "Calvert" (The Lords Baltimore). "Carroll, Charles" (Three — father, son, grandson). "Maryland." "Pennsylvania." New York: Robert Appleton Co., 1907.

Charlton, Edwin A. *New Hampshire as It Is* (2d ed.). Claremont, New Hampshire: Tracy & Sanford, 1855. In Three Parts: I A Historical Sketch of ———; II A Gazeteer of ———; III A General View of ———.

Chase, Benjamin. *History of Old Chester from 1719 to 1869.* Auburn, New Hampshire: Published by the author, 1869.

Clark, Calvin M. *History of the Congregational Churches in Maine.* 2 vols. Portland: Published by the author, 1926.

Clauson, J. Earl. *Cranston: A Historical Sketch.* Providence, Rhode Island: T. S. Hammond, 1904. Pp. 52.

Clay, Jehu C. *Annals of the Swedes on the Delaware.* Philadelphia, 1835.

Clute, The Rev. Robert F., rector (ed.). *Annals and Parish Registry of St. Thomas and St. Denis Parish, in South Carolina from 1680 to 1884.* Published 1884.

Coates, Robert M. "Pastoral, with Planes," *The New Yorker,* August 22, 1942. (Oblong Friends Meeting House, Quaker Hill, Dutchess County, New York.)

Cogswell, Leander W. *History of the Town of Henniker, Merrimack County, New Hampshire from the date of the Canada Grant by the Province of Massachusetts in 1735 to 1880,* etc. Concord: Republican Press Association, 1880.

Collins, The Rev. Charles (member of the Presbytery of Philadelphia North). *Norriton Presbyterian Church, Montgomery County, Pennsylvania: Regarded as the Oldest Church in Pennsylvania claiming connection with the Protestant Reformation,* etc. Norristown, Pennsylvania: Herald Printing Establishment, 1895.

Colonial Churches in the Original Colony of Virginia. (Series of historical articles from *Southern Churchman,* published in celebration of the Jamestown Tricentennial.) Richmond: Southern Churchman Co., 1908.

Cooke, John Esten. *Virginia: A History of the People.* Cambridge: Houghton Mifflin Co., Riverside Press, 1884.

Coyle, Mary E. "Churches of the Three Springs." (Lamberton and Hamilton Library Association Prize Essays, Vol. I.) Carlisle, Pennsylvania, 1910.

Curtis, Martha E. *Ye Old Meeting House: Addresses and verses Relating to The Meeting House, Burlington, Middlesex County, Mass., Built 1732, and other Historical Addresses.* Boston, 1909.

Dailey, The Rev. W. N. P. *History of Montgomery Classis.* 1,000 copies published 1916. *Fort Herkimer* (2d ed.). St. Johnsville (New York) News, 1928. Pp. 16.

Dalcho, The Rev. Frederick. *Church History: An historical account of the Protestant Episcopal Church in South Carolina from the first settlement of the Province to the War of the Revolution,* etc. Charleston: E. Thayer, 1820.

Davenport, Frances Gardiner. (ed.). *European Treaties Bearing on the History of the United States to 1648.* Vol. I, Document 27, 246.

(Treaty between Spain and Great Britain concluded at London August 18-28, 1604. Ratification by the King of Great Britain, August 19-29, 1604. Ratification by the King of Spain, June 5-15, 1605.) Washington, D.C.: Carnegie Institution, 1917.

Davies, A. Mervyn. *Foundation of American Freedom: Calvinism in the Development of Democratic Thought.* Nashville: Abingdon Press, 1955.

Dion, Frances. *Upon this Rock: A History of the Community Congregational Church, Greenland, New Hampshire.* Portsmouth: Strawberry Bank Print Shop, 1956.

Dixon, James. "An Historical Sketch of Third Haven Meeting House," read by the author and included in *Celebration of the Two Hundred and Fiftieth Anniversary of Old Third Haven Meeting House, October 23, 1932.* Pamphlet, 1-21. Easton, Maryland: Press of the Star-Democrat, 1932.

Earle, Swepson. *The Chesapeake Bay Country.* 3d ed., revised. Baltimore: Thomsen Ellis & Co., 1929.

Eberlein, Harold Donaldson, and Cortlandt Van Dyke Hubbard. *The Church of St. Peter in the Great Valley 1700-1940: The Story of a Colonial County Parish in Pennsylvania.* Richmond, Virginia: August Dietz & Son, 1944.

Eckman, Jeannette. *New Castle on the Delaware.* Dutch Tercentenary Edition, 1651-1951. New Castle Historical Society.

Ely, Warren S. "Presbyterian Church of Tinicum at Red Hill." A paper read at Red Hill Church meeting October 4, 1910, included in *A Collection of Papers Read Before the Bucks County Historical Society,* Vol. IV, 108-118. Easton, Pennsylvania: Press of the Chemical Publishing Co., 1917.

Elzas, Barnett A., M.D., L.L.D. *The Jews of South Carolina.* Philadelphia: J. B. Lippincott Co., 1905.

Embury, Aymar, II. *Early American Churches.* Garden City, New York: Doubleday, Page & Co., 1914.

Encyclopedia Britannica (11th ed.). Scores of articles were consulted throughout the present work.

Fahnestock, William. H., M.D. "An Historical Sketch of Ephrata." Hazard's *Register of Pennsylvania,* Vol. 15, No. 11, March 1835, 161-167.

Faris, John Thomson. *Old Churches and Meeting Houses in and around Philadelphia.* Philadelphia: J. B. Lippincott Co. 1926.

Ferguson, The Rev. Thomas J., D.D. (former pastor). "The Early History of Silver Spring Church." An address in a booklet published upon the occasion of restoration and rededication, *Silver Spring Presbyterian Church, May 23, 1929,* 20-40.

Foote, The Rev. William Henry. *Sketches of North Carolina, Historical and Biographical, Illustrative of the Principle of a Portion of her Early Settlers.* New York: Robert Carter, 1846.

Forman, Henry Chandler. *Jamestown and St. Mary's: Buried Cities of Romance.* Baltimore: Johns Hopkins Press, 1938.

———. *The Architecture of the Old South.* Cambridge: Harvard University Press, 1948.

Fortenbaugh, Robert. "Adams County Prepares for 150th Birthday." Part Two in a series, Pennsylvania Department of Internal Affairs, *Monthly Bulletin,* Vol. 18, No. 6, May 1950, 16-18. (Great Conewago Presbyterian Church, and Conewago Chapel, Church of the Sacred Heart.)

Fraser, Charles. *A Charleston Sketchbook — 1796-1806.* (Forty watercolor drawings of the city and the surrounding country, including plantations and parish churches. Reprint of Fraser's sketches, with an introduction and notes by Alice R. Huger Smith.) Charleston: Carolina Art Association, 1940.

Fries, Adelaide L. (archivist of the Moravian Church in America, Southern Province) and J. Kenneth Pfohl, D.D. (pastor of Home Moravian Church, Winston-Salem, North Carolina.) *The Moravian Church: Yesterday and Today.* Raleigh: Edwards & Broughton Co., 1926.

Froude, James Anthony. *The Spanish Story of the Armada.* New York: Charles Scribner's Sons, 1892.

Garth, The Rev. William H. *Historical Sketch of St. Marks.* (Caroline Church, Oakdale, Long Island, New York, 9-11.) Privately printed, 1928.

Gibbons, Hughes Oliphant. (8th pastor.) *A History of Old Pine Street: Being the record of an hundred and forty years in the life of a Colonial church, with seventy-two full page illustrations.* Philadelphia: The John C. Winston Co., 1905.

Gibbs, James. *Book of Architecture, Designs, and Ornaments.* London, 1728. (Plate No. 30 used in design of First Baptist Church, Providence, Rhode Island.)

Gilbert, Edgar. *History of Salem, New Hampshire.* Concord, New Hampshire: Rumford Printing Co., 1907.

Greenleaf, Jonathan. (pastor of the Church in Wells.) *Sketches of the Ecclesiastical History of the State of Maine, From the Earliest Settlement to the Present Time.* Portsmouth: Published by Harrison Gray, Printer R. Foster, 1821.

Hall, Clayton Colman, *The Lords Baltimore and the Maryland Palatinate.* Six lectures on Maryland Colonial History, Johns Hopkins University, 1902. (Land tenure by a church, 48.) Baltimore: John Murphy Co., 1902.

Hanson, Willis T., Jr. *A History of St. George's Church in the City of Schenectady.* 2 vols. Schenectady, New York: Privately printed, 1919.

Hawks, Francis Lister. *Narrative of Events Connected with the Rise and Progress of the Prostestant Episcopal Church in Virginia, to which is added an appendix containing the Journal of the Conventions in Virginia from the commencement to the present time.* Referred to as *Ecclesiastical History.* New York: Harper, 1836.

Hayes, Lyman Simpson. *History of the Town of Rockingham Vermont including Bellows Falls.* Published by the Town of Bellows Falls, 1907.

Hazard, Caroline. *The Narragansett Friends Meeting House in the Eighteenth Century.* Boston and New York: Houghton Mifflin and Co., 1899.

Headley, Joel Tyler. *The Chaplains and Clergy of the Revolution.* New York: Charles Scribner, 1864. (Account of James Caldwell, Pastor of First Presbyterian Church of Connecticut Farms, New Jersey, and chaplain in the battle at Springfield Meeting House.)

Hening, William Waller. *Virginia, Laws, Statutes, etc.: The Statutes at Large; being a collection of all the laws of Virginia from the first session of the Legislature, in the year 1692. Published pursuant to an Act of General Assembly of Virginia, passed on the 5th day of February one thousand eight hundred eight,* etc. 13 vols. Richmond, 1810-1823.

Hills, The Rev. George M. *History of the Church in Burlington.* (Old St. Mary's.) Burlington, New Jersey, 1885.

Horton, Lewis E. *A Brochure on the First Presbyterian Congregation of Connecticut Farms, Union, New Jersey.* 1935.

Hovey, Horace Carter, D.D. (pastor). *The House of God: Historical Discourse on the Sesqui-Centennial of the Old South Meeting-House of Newburyport, Massachusetts, December 16, 1906.*

Howe, George, D.D. *History of the Presbyterian Church in South Carolina.* Columbia, South Carolina, 1870.

Hume, Martin (Pembroke College Cambridge. Editor of the Calendars of Spanish State Papers of Elizabeth, Public Record Office). *The Year After the Armada.* New York: The Macmillan Co., 1896.

———. *Two English Queens and Philip.* New York: G. P. Putnam's Sons; London: Methuen & Co.; 1908.

Hurd, D. Hamilton (ed.). *History of Middlesex County, Massachusetts.* Philadelphia: J. W. Lewis & Co., 1890.

Inventory of the Church Archives of Rhode Island: Society of Friends. Historical Records Survey, Works Progress Administration. Providence, R. I. May 1939. (Moses Brown School: Depository for records of the Yearly Meeting of Friends for New England, 1661.)

Inventory of Church Archives: Society of Friends in Pennsylvania. Pennsylvania Historical Survey. Division of Community Service Programs, Works Progress Administration. Philadelphia, 1941.

Inventory of Diocese of Washington Archives, Vol. I, The Protestant Episcopal Church. Historical Records Survey, Works Progress Administration, 1940. (Includes Southern Maryland.)

Isham, Norman Morrison. *The Meeting House of the First Baptist Church in Providence: A History of the Fabric.* Issued by the Charitable Baptist Society on the one hundred and fiftieth anniversary of the dedication of the house, May 28, 1775. Providence: Printed by the Ackerman Standard Co., 1925.

———. *Trinity Church in Newport, Rhode Island: A History of the Fabric.* Boston, 1936.

James, Marquis. *The Raven.* (Biography of Sam Houston, boyhood in Virginia, Timber Ridge Presbyterian Church.) New York: Bobbs-Merrill Co., 1929.

Janney, Samuel M. *History of the Religious Society of Friends.* 3 vols. Philadelphia: T. Ellwood Zell, 1870.

Jarvis, Lucy C. (ed.). *Sketches of Church Life in Connecticut.* (Early beginnings of the Protestant Episcopal Church.) New Haven: 1902.

Jenkins, Arthur H. and Ann R. *A Short History of Abington Monthly Meeting.* An address read at the dedication of a new building 11th Month 9th, 1929, by Charles F. Jenkins, and printed.

Keith, The Rev. George. "The Journal of the Reverend George Keith 1702-1704." Edited by Edgar Legare Pennington. Part I. Introduction: "Keith the Quaker and Keith the Anglican." By Pennington, 346. "An Account of the State of the Church in North America" (November, 1702). By George Keith, Evan Evans, Alexander Innes, Edmond Mott, John Talbot, William Vesey, and John Bartow, 363. Part II "A Journal of Travels from New Hampshire to Caratuck on the Continent of North America." By George Keith, A.M. (with notes by Pennington), 373-479. *Historical Magazine of the Protestant Episcopal Church.* Vol. XX, No. 4 (December, 1951).

Kelly, John Frederick. *Early Connecticut Meeting Houses.* 2 vols. New York: Columbia University Press, 1948.

Kieffer, The Rev. Henry Martin. *Some of the First Settlers of the Forks of the Delaware.* Lancaster, Pennsylvania: The New Era Printing Co. (The First Reformed Church, Easton, Pa.)

Kimball, Fiske. *Domestic Architecture of the American Colonies and of the Early Republic.* New York, 1927.

Kimball, Marie. "The Old Trappe Church, 1743." *Architectural Forum,* New York, Vol. V, No. 50 (1929), 521-528.

Kinsolving, The Rev. Arthur B., D.D. (rector of St. Paul's Parish, Baltimore). *Address before the Convention of the Diocese of Maryland in Emmanuel Church, Baltimore, on January 24, 1934, on the 150th Anniversary of the Organization of the Diocese.* Pp. 39.

Klett, Guy Soulliard. *Presbyterians in Colonial Pennsylvania.* Philadelphia: University of Pennsylvania Press, 1937.

Kling, The Rev. George H. "Centennial at Breakabeen and Early Church History." Schoharie County Historical Society, *The Quarterly Bulletin* (July and October, 1944). (Early settlers and their Dutch and German Reformed and Lutheran churches in New York and Pennsylvania.)

Lamb, William Harrison. *Hebron Evangelical Lutheran Church: A Brief History* (4th ed). Madison, Virginia, 1940.

Land, W. G. (ed.). *Harvard University Handbook.* Cambridge: Harvard University Press, 1936. (Holden Chapel.)

Larned, Ellen. *The History of Windham County.* 2 vols. Published by the author, Vol. I 1874, Vol. II 1880. Printed by Charles Hamilton, Worcester, Mass.

Latham, The Rev. Robert, D.D. *History of the Associated Reformed Synod of the South.* To which is prefixed *A History of the Associated Presbyterian and Reformed Presbyterian Churches.* Harrisburg, Pennsylvania: Published for the author, 1882. (Ebenezer Church, South Carolina, 295.)

Lawrence, The Rev. Robert F. (pastor of Congregational Church, Claremont). *The New Hampshire Churches: Comprising Histories of the Congregational and Presbyterian Churches in the State with notices of other denominations.* Published for the author by Claremont Manufacturing Co., 1856.

Lawrence, Bishop William. *Memories of a Happy Life.* Cambridge: Houghton Mifflin Co., 1926. (Chap. XXIV, restoration of Old North Church, Boston.)

Leach, R. J. *Yearly Meetings of the Religious Society of Friends.* Pendle Hill, 1944.

Levering, Bishop J. Mortimer. *History of Bethlehem, Pennsylvania.* Bethlehem, 1903. (Moravian Community.)

Lincoln, Francis H. *History of the Town of Hingham.* Vol. I, Part II "Historical," Chap. 1, "Ecclesiastical History." Published by the Town, 1893. (Includes the churches in Hingham, South Hingham, Cohasset.)

Lippincott, Horace Mather. *Chestnut Hill. Springfield. Whitemarsh. Cheltenham.* Jenkintown, Pennsylvania: Old York Road Publishing Co., 1948.

———. *Abington Friends Meeting and School: 1682-1949.* Printed booklet, 1949.

———. "Old Conanicut Meeting." *Friends Intelligencer* (Eighth Mo., 12, 1950), 475-6.

———. *Quaker Meeting Houses and a Little Humor.*

Jenkintown, Pennsylvania: Old York Publishing Co., 1952.

Lippincott, William R. *Traditions of Old Evesham Township*. Pamphlet, 1911.

Livingstone, Sir Richard. *Education for a World Adrift*. ("Current Problems," No. 17.) Cambridge University Press, 1943.

Longmeadow Centennial, The: Proceedings of the Centennial Celebration of the incorporation of the Town of Longmeadow (Massachusetts), *October 17, 1883, with numerous historical appendices and a town genealogy*. Published by the Secretary of the Centennial Committee, under authority of the Town. Hartford: Press of Case Lockwood & Brainard Co., 1884.

Lord, William G. *Historical Address at the Celebration of the 150th Anniversary of the Incorporation of the Town of Phillipston, Massachusetts, Tuesday, August 18th, 1936*.

Loveland, Clara O. *The Critical Years: The Reconstruction of the Anglican Church in the United States of America: 1780-1789*. Greenwich, Connecticut: The Seabury Press, 1956.

McCulloch, Dr. Samuel Clyde. "The Foundation and Early Work of the Society for the Propagation of the Gospel in Foreign Parts." *Historical Magazine of the Protestant Episcopal Church*, Vol. XX, No. 2 (June 1951), 121-135.

Macon, George Champlin. *Annals of Trinity Church, Newport, Rhode Island*. Philadelphia, 1890.

Major, Howard. *The Domestic Architecture of the Early American Republic. The Greek Revival*. Philadelphia, 1926.

Mason, George Carrington (historiographer of the Diocese of Southern Virginia). *Colonial Churches of Tidewater Virginia*. Richmond: Whittet and Shepperson, 1945.

Matlack, T. Chalkley. "Brief Historical Sketches Concerning Friends Meetings." Typescript, 1938. (At the Friends Historical Library, Swarthmore, Pennsylvania.)

Meade, Bishop William. *Old Churches, Ministers, and Families of Virginia*. 2 vols. Philadelphia: Lippincott, 1878. (Entered 1857.)

Mercer, Henry C. "The Origin of the Log Houses in the United States." *Old Time New England*, Vol. XVII (1927), reprinted from the Bucks County Historical Society Papers, V, with additions.

Merritt, Elizabeth. *Old Wye Church, Talbot County, Maryland, 1694-1949*. Baltimore: Published by the Maryland Historical Society, 1949.

Michner, Ezra. *A Retrospect of Early Quakerism; Being Extracts From the Records of Philadelphia Yearly Meeting and the Meetings Composing It. To which is prefixed An Account of Their First Establishment*. Philadelphia: T. Elwood Zell, 1860.

Middleton, The Rev. Arthur Pierce, Ph.D. "Angli-can Contributions to Education in Colonial America." *Pennsylvania History*, Quarterly Journal of the Pennsylvania Historical Society, Vol. XXV, No. 3 (July, 1958), 251-268. (Includes King's College, now Columbia; William and Mary; Washington College, Chestertown, Md.; Dr. Thomas Bray.)

Moses, George H. "A Pine Crowned the Hill." (A sketch of Henniker, New Hampshire.) *The Granite Monthly*, Vol. XVII, No. 5 (November, 1894.)

Muhlenberg, Henry Melchior. *Journals*. Translated by Theodore G. Tappert and John W. Doberstein. 3 vols. Philadelphia: United Lutheran Publishers, 1942; Muhlenberg Press, 1945, 1950.

Nevin, Alfred. *Churches of the Cumberland Valley* (Pennsylvania). Philadelphia: J. M. Wilson, 1852.

New Hampshire, A Gazetteer of the State of. Concord: Jacob & Moore, 1823.

Nichols, Herbert B. *Historic Sites in Westchester*. No. 2 of the series, "Historic Westchester." Westchester County Publishers, Inc., 1933. (St. Paul's Church, Eastchester; Sleepy Hollow Dutch Reformed Church.)

Page, The Rev. I. Marshall. *The Life Story of the Reverend Francis Makemie*. Grand Rapids, Michigan: William B. Erdmans Publishing Co., 1938.

Parker, Edward Lutwyche. *History of Londonderry*. Boston: Perkins & Whipple, 1851.

Pitney, Henry C. (ed.). *A History of Morris County, New Jersey, 1716-1913*. 2 vols. New York, Chicago: Lewis Historical Publishing Co., 1914. (Randolph Friends Meeting House.)

Place, Charles A. (minister of The First Church, Lancaster, Mass.). "From Meeting House to Church in New England. 1. The Meeting House in the First Hundred Years." *Bulletin of The Society for the Preservation of New England Antiquities* (October, 1922). 77ff.

Plainfield Meeting, Historical Sketch of: 1686-1938. Prepared by the Advancement Committee of the Rahway and Plainfield Monthly Meeting of the Religious Society of Friends; in commemoration of the 150th Anniversary of the construction of the Plainfield Meeting House, 1788-1938.

Pleasants, Henry. *History of Old St. David's Church*. Philadelphia: John C. Winston Co., 1915.

Podmore, Harry J. *The Presbyterian Church of Lawrenceville, New Jersey: Commemorating the two hundred and fiftieth anniversary of the deed conveying the land for the erection of a church in Maidenhead, now Lawrence Township*. Princeton University Press, 1948.

Pomfret, John E. *The Province of West Jersey*. Princeton University Press, 1956.

Prime, Nathaniel S. *History of Long Island*. 1845. (Charlotte Church, Oakdale, N.Y.)

Purcell, The Rev. J. B. *History of the Parish of Holy Trinity Church, Eldersburg, Maryland.* Pamphlet, printed 1892.

Ravenel, Beatrice St. Julien. *Architects of Charleston.* Introduction by William Watts Ball. Photographs by Carl Julien. Charleston: Carolina Art Association, 1945.

Restoration of Williamsburg. Reprinted in book form by F. W. Dodge Corp., New York, from *The Architectural Record,* of December, 1935. (Wren Building, 365, including a reproduction of the Bodeleian Plate. Hugh Jones and Sir Christopher Wren, 369.)

Richard, Chauncey. *The Old Stone Church and Fortress.* Schoharie, New York: Schoharie County Historical Society, 1933.

Ridgely, Helen West. *The Old Brick Churches of Maryland.* New York: D. F. Randolph & Co., 1894.

Rines, Edward F. *Old Historic Churches of America: Their Romantic History and Their Traditions.* Published under the auspices of the National Society of Colonial Dames of America. New York: The Macmillan Co., 1936.

Roads, Hon. Samuel, Jr. *St. Michael's Church, Marblehead, Mass.: 1714-1924.* Marblehead: N. A. Lindsey & Co., 1924.

Roberts, Ellwood. *Plymouth Meeting: Its Establishment and the Settlement of the Township with Historical, Genealogical and Biographical Data from Records of Friends.* Norristown, Pennsylvania: Roberts Publishing Co., 1900.

Robinson, J. H. (member of The Nantucket Historical Association). *Guide to Nantucket.* 6th ed. 1945.

Rodgers, Francis S. *The Bells of St. Michael's: being the history of the bells in the steeple of St. Michael's Church, Charleston.* Charleston: Quin Press, 1935.

Rolt, Richard. *The Lives of the Reformers: both Englishmen and Foreigners comprehending the General History of the Reformation; from its beginning in 1360, by Dr. John Wickliffe, to its Establishment, in 1600, under Queen Elizabeth.* London, 1759.

Rupp, I. Daniel. *History of Religious Denominations in the United States.* Philadelphia, 1844. (The Ephrata Cloister.)

Sachse, Julius Friedrich. *German Pietists of Provincial Pennsylvania, 1694-1708: The German Sectarians of 1708; Pennsylvania, 1708-1800.* 2 vols. Philadelphia, 1895-1900.

————. *Music of the Ephrata Cloister.* Lancaster, 1903.

Scharf, John Thomas. *History of Western Maryland.* Philadelphia: L. H. Everts, 1882.

Scott, John Welwood. *An Historical Sketch of The Pine Street or Third Presbyterian Church.* Philadelphia, 1837.

Segelken, The Rev. C. Benjamin, D.D. (moderator). *The Donegal Presbyterian Church.* Compiled by order of the Session. Harrisburg, Pennsylvania: The Evangelical Press, 1935.

Severance, Frank H. *An Old Frontier of France. The Niagara Region and Adjacent Lakes under French Control.* 2 vols. Vol. I. Chap. XIII "A House of Peace." (The building of Fort Niagara.) New York: Dodd, Mead & Co., 1917.

Shoemaker, Robert W. *The Origin and Meaning of the Name "Prostestant Episcopal."* New York: American Church Publications, 1959.

Shurtleff, Harold R. *The Log Cabin Myth: A study of the early dwellings of the English Colonists in North America.* Edited with an introduction by Samuel Eliot Morison. Cambridge: Harvard University Press, 1939.

Skirven, Percy G. *The First Parishes of the Province of Maryland; wherein are given historic sketches of the ten counties and thirty parishes in the Province at the time of the establishment of the Church of England in Maryland, in 1692; also a short treatise on the religious situation before the establishment, together with 56 illustrations and a colored map.* Baltimore: The Norman Remington Co., 1923.

Slaughter, The Rev. Dr. Phillip. *The Colonial Church in Virginia.* An address. Richmond, 1885. (Includes Old Fork Church.)

Society for the Preservation of New England Antiquities. *Bulletin* (October 1922). (Includes Elder Ballou Meeting House, Rhode Island.

Speare, Eva Augusta. *Colonial Meeting Houses of New Hampshire: Compared with their contemporaries in New England.* Published under the auspices of the Daughters of Colonial Wars, State of New Hampshire. Littleton, New Hampshire: Printed by the Courier Printing Co., 1938. Revisesd edition published by the author. Littleton: Reginald M. Colby, Agent, 1955.

Stacy, James. *History of the Midway Congregational Church, Liberty County Georgia.* Newnan, Georgia, 1889.

Stackpole, Edouard A. *Rambling through the Streets and Lanes of Nantucket.* Inquirer and Mirror Press, 1947.

Stoney, Samuel Gaillard. *Plantations of the Carolina Low Country.* Edited by Albert Simmons, F.A.J.A. and Samuel Lapham, Jr. With an Introduction by John Mead Howells. Carolina Art Association, Charleston, South Carolina. 1st ed., 1938. Revised ed. (4th), 1955.

Styles, Dr. Ezra. "Diary." Central Baptist Church, Newport, R. I., 1758 to the Revolution.

Taylor, Charles J. *History of Great Barrington, Massachusetts.* (Includes Sheffield Congregational Church.) Published by the Town of Great Barrington, 1928.

Tees, Francis H. (pastor of St. George's Church.) *The Beginnings of Methodism in England*

and in America. Nashville: The Parthenon Press, 1940.

——. *The Story of Old Saint George's*. Written and published by the pastor. Philadelphia: Printed by The Message Publishing Co. 1st ed. 1931, revised ed. 1946.

Thomas, R. S. *The Brick Church, near Smithfield, Virginia. Built in 1632*. A paper read before the Virginia Historical Society Tuesday, December 22, 1891. Reprinted from *Virginia Historical Collections*, Vol. XI, 1892.

Torrence, The Rev. Clayton. (Written while rector of St. Andrew's Episcopal Church, Princess Anne, Somerset County, Maryland.) *Old Somerset on Eastern Shore, Maryland: A Study in Foundations and Founders*. Richmond: Whittet & Shepperson, 1935.

Touro Synagogue of Congregation Jeshuat Israel, Newport, Rhode Island. Chapters by D. de Sola Pool, Fiske Kimball, Dr. Morris A. Gutstein, Joseph M. Proskauer, Lee M. Friedman, Leon Huhner, The Reverend Isaac Leeser, Henry Wadsworth Longfellow Dana, Carl Van Doren, Thomas J. Allen. Designated as a National Historic Site, 1946. Published on that occasion by The Society of Friends of Touro Synagogue National Historic Shrine, Inc. Pp. 60.

Toynbee, Arnold J. *Civilization on Trial*. New York: Oxford University Press, 1948.

Trevelyan, George Macaulay (Fellow of Trinity College Cambridge). *England in the Age of Wycliffe*. 1899. New ed. New York: Longmans, Green and Co., 1904.

Trinterud, Leonard J. (Associate Professor Church History, McCormick Theological Seminary, Philadelphia.) *A Reexamination of Colonial Presbyterianism*. Philadelphia: The Westminster Press, 1949.

Turner, The Rev. D. K. *History of Neshaminy Presbyterian Church of Warwick, Hartsville, Bucks County, Pennsylvania. 1726-1876*. Published by request of the Session. Philadelphia: Culbertson & Bache, Printers. 1876.

Virginia Highway Historical Markers, Key to Inscriptions on. Pp. 167. Issued by State Commission on Conservation and Development, Richmond, Virginia.

Waddell, Joseph A. *Annals of Augusta County, Virginia*. Richmond: J. W. Randolph & English, 1888.

Walker, E. Virginia, and Dorothy G. Harris. "Old Friends Record Book Found." (Third Haven Friends Meeting, Easton, Maryland.) *Bulletin of Friends Historical Association*. Vol. 35, No. 1 (Spring 1946), 3.

Wallace, Philip B. *Colonial Churches and Meeting Houses of Pennsylvania, New Jersey, and Delaware*. Measured drawings by William Allen Drum. Introduction by Horace Wells. New York: Architectural Book Publishing Co., Inc., 1931.

Washburn, Louis C. (ed.). *Christ Church, Philadelphia*. A Symposium Compiled in Connection with the Two Hundred and Twenty-Fifth Anniversary. Philadelphia: Macrae, Smith Company, 1925.

Waterman, Thomas Tileston and John A. Barrows. *Domestic Colonial Architecture of Tidewater Virginia*. Introduction by Fiske Kimball. University of North Carolina Press, 1947.

Wayland, John W. (ed.). *Hopewell Friends History 1734-1934 Frederick County, Virginia*. Records of Hopewell Monthly Meeting and Meetings Reporting to Hopewell. Two Hundred Years of History and Genealogy. Compiled from official records and published by a Joint Committee of Hopewell Friends. Printed by Shenandoah Publishing House, Inc., Strasburg, Virginia, 1936.

Webster, The Rev. Richard. *History of the Presbyterian Church of America*. Published by The Presbyterian Historical Society. Philadelphia: Joseph M. Wilson, 1857.

Wight, Charles Albert. *Some Old Time Meeting Houses of the Connecticut Valley*. Chicopee Falls, Massachusetts: The Rich Print, 1911.

Williams, George W. *St. Michael's, Charleston, 1751-1951*. Columbia: University of South Carolina Press, 1951.

Williams, The Rev. Richard L. *Norriton Presbyterian Church*. (Author was pastor and working on history of the church when he died.) Pamphlet, 1940.

Williams, Roger. *George Fox digg'd out of his Burrowes, or an offer of disputation on fourteen proposals made this last summer, 1672 (so Call'd) unto G. Fox then present on Rode Island in New England, by R. W. As also how (G. Fox slily departing) the Disputation went on being managed three dayes at Newport Rode Island, and one day at Providence between John Stubs, John Burnet, and William Edmundson on the one part, and R. W. on the other. In which many quotations out of G. Fox & Ed. Burrowes Book in folio are alleged: with an appendix of some scores of G. F., his simple lame answers to his opposites in that book, quoted and replyed to by R. W. of Providence in N. E.* Boston: John Foster, 1676. (Original copy at Newport Historical Society.)

Willis, Howard S. (Chairman, Board of Selectmen, Salem, N. H.). "The Salem Town Hall." An address in the Town Hall before the Association of Historical Societies of New Hampshire, Inc. (June 27, 1959). Typescript, Pp. 4.

Worth, Henry Barnard. *Nantucket Lands and Land Owners*. Nantucket Historical Association, 1906. Republished 1928. (Old North Vestry, 235.)

Zebley, Frank B. *The Churches of Delaware*. Published by the author. Wilmington, Delaware, 1947.

INDEX

All 345 buildings have serial numbers, which appear with the titles in the photograph section and with text references and in the index. The denominations, locations, and building material of each are given in the Appendices, and they are not indexed except for special interest. As official titles of buildings in many cases are long or obscure, the name indexed is selected as the one most revealing; if more than one name is commonly used, a cross reference is indexed. References to subjects prevalent throughout the accounts, such as architectural features, the Revolution, and the Civil War, are not indexed except in cases of special interest. Not all interesting categories are indexed by the group subject, but some special subjects are selected.

Abbreviations that may not be obvious: Bap., Baptist. Ch., Church (Chapel spelled). Co., Company (not County). Congl., Congregational. Cr., Creek. Cty., County (City spelled). Epis., Episcopalian. Evangel., Evangelical. F., Friends. H., House. M., Meeting. N., New and North. No., Number. Penn., Pennsylvania (not in general use, but it should be, as the province was named for the father of the founder). Presbyn., Presbyterian. R., River. R.C., Roman Catholic. S., South. St., Saint (Street spelled). So., Society.

A

Abbey, Thomas, 126
Aberdeen, Scot., 41, 128, 542
Aberdeen Univ., 155
Abingdon Ch. (No. 318), 94, 486, 488-89
Abington Congl. Ch., 116
Abington F.M.H. (No. 234), 346, 352, 369-71, 376
Academy, the, Phila., 84, 344
Accokeek, Md., 167
Accomack County, Va., 119, 473-74
Accomack Parish, 474
"Ace of Clubs" Ch. See Pongoteague Ch.
Acquackanock (Passaic), 53, 263
Acquinton Ch. (No. 322), 491-93
Acrelius, the Rev. Israel, 133
Act Concerning Religion (Md.), 33
Act of Supremacy, 4, 58
Adams, Azariah, 120
Adams, Pres. John, 240, 341, 348
Adams, Joseph (uncle of Pres.), 240
Adams, Mass., 231
Adams, Samuel, 213
Adirondacks, 106
Africa, 47
Agape (love feast), 76, 386
Age of Anxiety, XV
Agnew, Brig. Gen., 351
Agnew, the Rev. John, 468
Agrippa, Brother, 387
Albany Post Road, 308
Albany, N.Y., 54, 314
Albemarle, N.C., 22, 328
Alethians, 86
Alexander the Great, XIV, 44
Alexander, John, 513
Alexander, Robt., 524
Alexandria Ch. (Va.), 513
Alexandria, Egypt, 84
Alexandria Township, N.J., 272
Alexandria, Va., 512, 514-15

Alleghenies, 106, 501, 525, 542
Allen's Creek Ch. (Va.), 484
Allentown, Penn., 81, 342, 367
All Faith Ch. (No. 43), 163-64
All Friends Quarterly M., 270
All Hallows Ch., South River (No. 55), 172
All Hallows Ch., Snow Hill (No. 85), 200-01
Allin Congl. Ch., 223
All Saints Ch., Hickory Neck (No. 296), 457
All Saints Parish, Waccamaw, 435
Alloways Creek F.M.H. (No. 153), 280-81
Almodington (estate) Md., 198
Almohades, 46
Almonry, 387
Alna M.H., Me. (No. 37), 100, 157
Alsbuern, Reichert, 368
Amboy, N.J., 269
Amen corner, 134
Amer. episcopacy, 15
American Shearer Co., 250
Amer. Unitarian Assn., 39
Amesbury, Mass., 237, 246
Amherst Congl. Ch. (No. 124), 250-51
Amherst, Gen. Jeffery, 250
Amish, the, 75
Ammon, Jacob, 75
Amos, "Blind" Jos., 42, 211
Amsterdam, Holland, 38, 46, 49-50, 79, 414-15
Amwell, N.J., 272
Ancocas, N.J. See Rancocas
Andalusia, 47
Anderson, the Rev. James, 397
André, Maj. John, 297, 322
Andrews, the Rev. Jedidiah, 67
Andrews, Rev. Wm., 316
Andros, Sir Edmund, 40-41, 213, 410
Anglican Communion, 18-19, 27, 128, 454
Anglicans: 9-10, 13-26; chs., parishes,

20; 28, 33-34, 40, 43, 64, 74, 82, 87-90, 119, 135, 213, 219, 255, 315, 322, 325, 422, 425, 540
Anglo-Saxon, 275
Anabaptists, 19, 26, 75, 350, 438
Annapolis, Md., 18, 33, 35, 169, 173, 201
Anne of Bohemia, 78
Anne of Eng. See Queen Anne
Anne, ship, 23
Antinomians, 19, 418
Antwerp, Belgium, 383
Apes, the Rev. Wm., 211
Apostolic Church, 27, 80, 85
Appoquinimy, the Church of, 137
Appoquinimy Church, 140
Appoquinimink F.M.H. (No. 19), 98, 138
Apostolic succession, 128
Appalachian Range, 105
Apple Tree Ch. (Va.), 490
Appling, Ga., 26
Appomattox, R., 464-65, 477
Apse: semi-circular, 94, 188, 196, 435, 439, 474-75; octagonal, 366
Apthorp, the Rev. East, Charles, and Grizel, 218
Aquia Ch. (No. 334), 94-95, 508, 510
Aquidneck Is., R.I., 418
Aquinas, St. Thomas, 64
Arabs, 46
Aragon (Sp.), 3, 46-48
Archbishop of Canterbury, 11, 15, 128, 445
Archbishop of Sweden, 339
Archbishop of Tarsus, 32
Archbishop Uno von Troil, 63
Archbishop of York, 14
Arches, segmental, 172
Architects, 50, 94, 101-02, 104, 213, 215, 218, 248, 255, 287, 295, 297, 305, 340, 342, 348, 403-04, 410, 412, 415, 423, 441, 455, 483, 511, 513, 515

Architecture, church, 7
Arch Street Friends, 74, 353, 372
Arden, Joannes, 161
Argall, Gov. Samuel, 14, 61
Argall's Church (Va.), 450, 476, 478
Armistead, Cap. Henry, 498
Aristocrats (Va.), 523
Aristotle, XIV, 45, 64
Ark, ship, 19, 29-30
Arlington Plantation (Va.), 514
Armada, the, 5. *See also* Battle of
Arminian, 175
Arney's Mount F.M.H. (No. 164), 107, 290
Arnold, Gen. Benedict, 236, 322, 481
Articles of Confederation, 341
Arundel, Anne, 171
Asbury, Bishop Francis, 84, 134, 141, 344-45, 525
Asbury Methodist Epis. Ch. (No. 15), 85, 97, 134
Ashkenazim, 44
Ashland, Va., 484
Ashley, Father, S.J., 34, 161
Ashley, John, 230
Ashley River (S.C.), 21, 147, 422, 431-32
Assawaman Ch. (Va.), 474
Associate and Reformed Presbyns., 442
Assn. for the Presvn. Va. Antiquities, 451, 502
Astronomers, 9, 364, 403
Atomic Age, XIII, XV
Augsburg Confession, 58, 145, 180, 366
Augusta Ch. (No. 343), 17, 68, 106, 390, 395, 498, 521
Augusta County, Va., 521-22
Augustine, St., 64
Augustus Lutheran Ch. (No. 231), 365
Aureen, the Rev. Jonas, 62
Austin, Ann, Quaker, 70
Austria, 1, 26, 79, 145
Autocratic, 37
Autumn Pilgrimage in Va., 463
Avalon, Newfoundland, 28-29
Axson, the Rev. Dr. I.S.K., 148
Axson, Wm., 428, 436
Ayelett, Va., 495
Aylett, Wm., 495
Ayrfield (Va.), 505
Azores, 4

B

Babylonia, 44-45
Bach *B Minor Mass*, 380
Back Creek (N.C.), 327
Back River (S.C.), 423, 426, 428
Bacon's Castle (Va.), 461
Bacon's Rebellion, 16, 451, 461, 488, 496, 500
Baden, Md., 168
Bagge, the Rev. John, 499
Baker's Creek Valley (Tenn.), 524
Bally, Penn., 383
Bally, Father Augustin, S.J., 383
Ballou family, 407
Ball, Mary, 504-05
Ball, Keating Simons, 429, 431
Ball, Col. Wm., 504-05

Baltimore, Lords, 9, 14, 18-19, 27-29, 31-35, 162, 166, 168, 171, 186
Baltimore, Md., 19-20, 35, 49, 58, 141, 176-77, 348, 414
Baltimore oriole, 29
Baltimore Yearly M., 73-74, 185-86, 390-91, 519
Balzius, the Rev. John Martin, 145
Bancroft, Hubert Howe, 32
Bank of England, 217
Baptist Ch., First, Prov., R.I. (No. 260), 39, 101, 209, 403-04, 410, 541
Baptists: 8, 17, 20, 38-40, 42-43, 77-78, 86, 139, 175, 179, 209, 211, 223-24, 314, 406, 413, 422, 435, 437, 469, 485, 489, 491, 493, 496, 506-07, 520, 541; General, 175; Particular, 175
Barbados, Barbadians, 21, 262, 425
Barclay, the Rev. Thomas, 315
Bare Cove (Mass.), 204
Barker, Wm., 462
Barlow, the Rev. Henry, 472
Barnes, John, 370
Barnstable, Mass. 39, 209
Barnwell, John, 439
Baron of Cameron, 514
Baronet, 150
Barr, the Rev. David, 460
Barratt, Philip, 141
Barratt's Chapel (No. 24), 84-85, 141
Barron, Commodore Jas., 470, 477
Barrowe, Henry, 38
Barrowists, 13, 19, 38
Barry, Commodore John, 348
Bartram, John (botanist), 146, 331, 361
Bass River (Mass.), 233
Bass violin, 242
Batchelder, Samuel F., 217, *544*
Bath, Me., 153
Bath, N.C., 23, 325, 327-28
Battle of the Armada, 1, 5, 49, 438
Battle of Bothwell Bridge, 442
Battle of the Brandywine, 339, 356, 359-61, 367, 387, 390
Battle of Bunker Hill, 118, 221, 233, 242, 252, 417
Battle of Culloden, 440
Battle of Germantown, 351, 367
Battle of Gettysburg, 393
Battle of Lake Erie, 417
Battle of Lexington, 118, 126, 219, 236
Battle of Cooch's Bridge, 139
Battle of Monmouth, 66, 276-77, 291
Battle of Oriskany, 319
Battle of Pell's Point, 305
Battle of Princeton, 273, 343
Battle of Springfield, 267-68
Battle of Stone Arabra, 317
Battle of Trenton, 233, 375
Battle of White Hill (Bohemia), 79
Battle of White Plains, 306-07, 309
Baumstown, Penn., 384
Bavaria, Germ., 26, 145
Beach, the Rev. Abraham, 89
Beale, Othniel, 423
Bear Clan, Mohawk, 318
Beardsley, the Rev. John, 309

Beasley, John, 329
Beaufort, S.C., 2, 427, 438, 440
Beaufort River (S.C.), 438
Beaver Dam (Va.), 484
Beaver Pond, Brook, 248
Bedford, N.Y., 374
Bedford Plantation (Va.), 506
Beissel, the Rev. Johann Konrad, 77, 385-87
Belcher, Governor of Conn., 119
Belfast, N.Ire., 523
Belgium, 49, 54
Bell, the Rev. John, 502
Belle Isle plantation, 503
Bellinger, Landgrave Edmund and Elizabeth, 440
Bells: 117-18, 121-22, 124, 127, 129, 146, 161, 170-71, 178, 215, 223, 231, 251-53, 297, 301, 305, 327, 340, 342, 383, 387-88, 404, 408, 410, 423, 432, 445, 454, 470, 482-83, 497; Paul Revere, 152, 215, 229, 232, 236, 246, 253, 256. *See also* Liberty B.
Belvoir plantation (Va.), 512
Benburg, Thomas, 329
Bengal, India, 16
Benjamin, Asher (archit.), 104, 255
Benjamin Franklin Bridge, Phila., 345
Bennett, Richard, 14-15, 466-67
Bennett's Creek Ch. *See* Glebe Ch.
Bennett, Wm., 329
Bensalem, Penn., 374
Berbers, 46
Beresford, Richard, 428
Beresford's Bounty tract, 428
Bergen Dutch Ch. (N.J.), 56, 263
Berkeley County, S.C., 430-32
Berkeley, Maj. Edmond, 498
Berkeley, George, Lord Bishop of Cloyne, 411
Berkeley, Mass., 411
Berkeley plantation (Va.), 479
Berkeley, Gov. Sir. Wm., 451, 453, 500
Berks County, Penn., 76
Berkshire County, 230-31
Berkshire Hills (Mass.), 41, 85, 230, 314, 413
Bermuda Hundred (Va.), 477
Bermuda Is., 16, 411
Berthelsdorf estate, 79
Berthelsdorf Lutheran Ch., 80
Bertholf, the Rev. Guilliem, 56-57, 263, 366
Bertram, the Rev. Wm., 68, 397
Berwick, and S. B., Me., 150
Berwyn, Penn., 356-57
Bethabara, N.C., 9, 331
Bethania, N.C., 81
Bethany, 332, 387
Bethesda Orphanage Asylum, 25, 81
Bethlehem, Palestine, 77, 380, 385
Bethlehem, Penn., 9, 81, 283, 332, 379
Bethlehem Bach Festival, 380
Bethlehem Chapel, Natl.Cath., 168
Bethlehem Choral Union, 380
Bethpage Meeting, 300
Betty's Cove, 193
Bevan, John, 354, 355
Beverly (Burlington), N.J., 72

Beverly, Mass., 233-34
Beverly's Manor (Va.), 522
Bible Commonwealth, 37, 39, 40-41
Bibles: Kralitz, 79; 200, 278, 283, 297, 327; Sauer, 351; 382, 435, 463, 477, 489-90, 507, 514
Biddle, Col. Clement, 350
Biggin Ch. (No. 277), 428. See also St. John's, Berkeley
Biggin Hill, Kent, Eng., 428
Big Spring (Newville, Penn.), 393
Billings, the Rev. William, 121
Bill of Rights, (U.S.), 305
Bill of Rights (Va.), 510
Birch, Harvey, 308
Birckhead, Christopher, 171
Bird M.H. (No. 123), 250
Bird, the Rev. Samuel, 250
Birmingham F.M.H. (No. 226), 360-61
Bishop, Anglican, in Amer., 7
Bishop Luke of Prague, 78
Bishop, Methodist, 141
Bishop of Aberdeen, Scot., 128
Bishop of Conn., 41, 128-29, 542. See also Seabury, S.
Bishop of London, 11, 15-16, 128, 232, 272, 327, 340-41, 344, 410, 455, 482, 497, 506, 511
Bishop of Md., 168, 542
Bishop of Penn., 340
Bishop of Ross and Moray, Scot., 128
Bishop of St. David's (London), 516
Bishop Stephen (Bohemia), 78
Bishop of United Brethren Ch., 178
Bishop of Va., proposed, 15, 486
Bishopric of Durham, 28
Bishop, R.C., Amer., 35
Bishop's commissary, 16, 327, 428, 455, 480, 511
Björck, the Rev. Eric, 62, 132, 338
Blackbeard, pirate, 23, 327
Blackburn, Col. Wm., 514
Blackburn's Creek (Va.), 499
Blackfoot Town (Del.), 142
Blackler, Capt., 233
Blackstone, Mass., 226
Blackwater District (Va.), 471
Blackwater Presbyn. Ch. (No. 26), 69, 143, 375
Blackwater R. (Va.), 460
Blackwell, the Rev. Robt., 341
Blair, the Rev. James, 16, 454, 480, 511
Blair, the Rev. John, 522
Blair, the Rev. Samuel, 281
Blanchard, Joshua, 213
Bland, Theodorick, 479
Blandford Ch. (No. 300), 464-65
Blisland Parish (Va.), 457
Blue Ridge Mts. (Va.), 17, 68, 106, 390, 508, 510, 512, 518, 521-23
Boardman, the Rev. Richard, 84, 344-45
Bodlein Library, Oxford, 456
Boehm, the Rev. Martin, 58, 178
Boels, Thomas, 277
Bog-iron, 290
Bohemia, 25, 38, 78-79, 379
Bohemia (Md.), 35-36, 78, 332, 392
Bohemian Brethren, 78-79

Bohler, Peter, 25, 81-82, 379
Boleyn, Anne, 4
Bolles, John (Md.Sec.), 30
Bonner, Thomas, 329
Book of Common Prayer, 20, 40, 64, 90, 128, 189, 271, 304, 341, 435. See also Prayer Book
Boone, Daniel, 99, 384
Bordentown F.M.H. (No. 166), 290
Boston Common, 40
Boston Latin School, 218
Boston, Mass.: 16, 39, 41, 70, 88, 120, 148, 208-09, 213, 215, 232, 410; British occupation of, Tea Party, 213; Siege of, 220
Boston Port Act, 23, 328, 423
Boston Post Road, 304
Botanists, 146, 361, 388, 518
Botetourt, Gov. Lord, 457
Botetourt (Va.), 488
Bottle Alley, Charleston, 441
Boucher, the Rev. Jonathan, 169
Boudinot, Elias, 287
Boundaries: Conn-N.Y., 310; Del.-Penn., 142-43, 392; E.-W. Jersey, 72; Ga.-Fla., 23; Md.-Penn., 9, 28; Mass.-N.H., 243, 246; N.C.-Va., 465-66, 479; N.C.-S.C., 21; N.Y.-N.H.-Vt., 444
Bourdillon, the Rev. Benedict, 175
Bourne estate, L.I., 303
Bousch, Cap. Samuel, 468
Bowie, the Rev. John, 201
Bowne, John, 298
Boyd, the Rev. Adam, 397
Boyd, Mary (Penn.), 397; Wm., 397
Boyd, Wm. (N.C.), 329
Boyle, Robert (Brit. scientist), 455
Boxwood, 364
Braddock, Gen. Edward, 521
Bradfoot, the Rev. John, 470
Bradford, the Rev. James, 231
Bradford Monthly M., 361
Bradford, Gov. William, 287
Brainerd, the Rev. David, 264, 276, 281
Brainerd, the Rev. John, 264, 281
Braintree, Mass., 240
Bramfield, Betsy, 424
Brandon plantation. See Martin's B.
Brady photograph, 483
Brandywine Creek, Penn., 134, 359
Branford, Conn., 41-42, 65, 264, 267
Brant, Joseph, 318-19, 322
Brant, Molly, 318-19
Brantford, Ont., 319
Bray, the Rev. Dr. Thos., 16, 327
Brazil, 2, 414
Bremen, Germ., 178
Breton Bay (Md.), 161
Bretton, Wm. & Temperance, 34, 162
Brick: 91-98; English type, 92-93; Holland type, 92; inscribed, 96; from Eng., 92; molded, 95; tile, 96
Brick: kilns, 137, 145, 473, 477; water-rubbed, 95, 439, 489, 492, 502
Brick Market, Newport, 415
Brick Meeting House, Society, 186
Bridge, Thomas, 279
Bridger, Col. Joseph, 460
Bridgeton, N.J., 279-80

Bridlington, Yorkshire, 287
Brinton's Ford (Penn.), 360
Brinton, Wm., 360
Bristol F.M.H. (No. 235), 371
Bristol, Me. and Eng., 155
Bristol Parish (Va.), 463-65
Britt, John, 132
Broad Creek Hundred (Del.), 143
Broadway, 295, 308
Brookhaven, L.I., 302
Brookings, Robert, Richard, 187
Brookings Institution, 187
Brooklyn Congl. Ch. (No. 3), 118, 120, 124
Brooklyn, Conn., 118-120, 411
Brotherhood of mankind, XV
Broughton, Gov. Thos., 431
Brown, David, 50, 414
Brown, the Rev. Isaac Van Arsdale, 274
Brown, the Rev. John (Mass.), 206
Brown, Col. John (N.Y.), 317
Brown, the Rev. John (Va.), 524
Brown, the Rev. Jonathan, 248
Brown, Joseph (archit.), 102, 403, 410
Brown's Ferry (S.C.), 435
Brown Univ., 102, 404
Browne, Robert, 38
Brownell, the Rt. Rev. Thos. C., 129
Brownists, 13, 19, 38
Brunskill, John, 494
Brunswick, N.C., 22, 330
Brunswick R. (N.C.), 22
Brunswick Parish (Va.), 506-07
Brussels, 48
Bruton Parish Ch. (No. 294), XIV, 93-94, 96, 451, 453-55, 540
Bruton Parish, Somerset, Eng., 453
Bryan, the Rev. C. B., D.D., 472
Bryants Neck, Mass., 211
Brydon, the Rev. Dr. Geo. MacLaren, 486, 507, 544
Buccaneers, 411. See also Pirates
Bucer, Martin (reformer), 64
Buchanan, James, 388
Buck, the Rev. Richard, 450-51, 476
Buck Hole Creek (N.J.), 275
Buckingham F.M.H. (No. 241), 105, 291, 376
Bucks County, Penn., 69, 76
Buena Vista, Va., 490
Buffer colonies, 23, 41
Buffington's Ford (Penn.), 361
Bulfinch, Charles, 103, 215
Bull, family (S.C.), 439-41
Bull, William, Jr., 423
Bull Run (Va.), 510
Bullets, 219, 278, 303, 356, 440, 500
Bunker Hill Monument, 417
Bunting, Samuel J., 363, 544
Burgess, the Rev. Henry John, 468
Burgess family (Va.), 503
Burgoyne, Gen., 213
Burke, Edmund, 213
Burlingham, Roger, 406
Burling, Wm., 298
Burlington F.M.H. (No. 160), 282, 287-89, 372
Burlington, N.J., 277, 283, 286-89
Burlington Meeting House (No. 99), 220

Burlington, Mass., 220
Burlington Monthly M., 72
Burlington Yearly M., 72
Burnet, John, 409
Burnett, Henry, 423
Burnham, William, 125
Burnyeate, James, 404
Burr, the Rev. Aaron, Sr., 65, 265-66
Burr, Aaron, Jr., 265-66, 305, 524
Burr, Nelson, 272, 346, *544*
Burton, the Rev. Dr. Asa, 445
Burwell, Maj. Lewis, 489
Bush River Meeting, 185
Butler's Rangers, 318
Buttressed style, 93, 169, 195, 451, 453, 459
Butts, Sherebiah, 117
Byberry F.M., 346, 352
Byllinge, Edward, 71, 282, 289
Byrd family (Va.), 479; Col. Wm. II, 464-66, 479-80, 494
Byzantium, 46

C

Cabin Point chapels, 461, 463
Cadiz, Sp., 46
Cain Hoy Plantation (S.C.), 427
Calais, France, 4
Caldwell, the Rev. James, 66, 267-68
California, 3, 27
Caln F.M.H. *See* East Caln
Caln Quarterly M., 361-62
Calvary Epis. Ch., Flemington, 273
Calver, Sister Amelia, 315
Calvert family, 20, 29, 164
Calvert, Benedict Leonard, 29
Calvert, Cecilius (Cecil) 18, 27-28, 31-33, 169, 171
Calvert, Charles, 29, 33
Calvert, Charles, Jr., 29
Calvert, George, 27
Calvert, Leonard, 18-19, 29, 31, 32
Calvert, Philip, 29
Calvert County, Md., 33
Calverton Manor (Md.), 34
Calvin, John (reformer), 54, 64
Calvanism, 4, 13, 40-42, 57, 63, 89, 136, 175, 234, 250, 264, 301, 344, 364
Calvinistic Communion, 48, 58
Calvinistic Congl. So. of Henniker, 258
Calvinists, 19, 48, 53, 66, 83, 199, 280
Cambridge, Md., 195
Cambridge, Mass., 118, 208, 217-18, 264, 445
Cambridge Univ. 14, 218-19
Camden, N.H., 254
Camisards, 86
Campbell, the Rev. Jas., 69, 376
Canada, 35, 250, 315, 318-19, 325, 444
Canby, Henry Seidel, 361, *544*
Cannon balls, 117, 139, 291, 322, 424, 469
Canterbury, Conn., 117-18, 413
Canton, Mass., 215
Cantwell's Bridge, 138
Cape Charles, Va., 472, 474
Cape Cod, 12-14, 39
Cape Fear R. (N.C.), 22

Cape Henry (Va.), 6, 450, 470, 476
Cape May Meeting, 279
Cape May, N.J., 284
Cape Fear, R., 330, 435
Captain's walk, 204
Captivity, XIV
Cardozo, Justice Nathan, 49
Cardy, Samuel, 423
Carey, Gov. Thomas (rebellion), 327
Carleton, Sir Guy, 297
Carleton, Joseph, 157
Carlisle, Col. John, 513
Carlisle, Penn., 387, 394-95
Carlisle Indian School, 394
Carlisle Presbyn. Ch. (No. 256), 67, 106, 390, 393-94
Carnegie, Andrew, 305
Carolina, Province of: 6, 21-24, 422, 425, 430, 442; constitution of, 422, 428
Carolina Society, 441
Caroline Ch. (No. 175), 64-65, 302-03
Caroline County, Md., 191
Carpenter, Samuel and Edward, 371
Carroll family (Md.), 34-35
Carroll, Charles, from Eng., 35
Carroll, Charles, of Annapolis, 35
Carroll, Charles, of Carrolton, 35, 173
Carroll, Bishop John, 35
Cartagena, Colombia, 512
Carter family (Va.): Robert ("King"), John, John Jr., 501-02; John, Eliza, 479
Carter's Grove plantation (Va.), 489
Carteret, Sir George, 54
Cary, Henry, 477
Cary, Thomas, 156
Casco Bay, Me., 152
Castile (Sp.), 3, 46-48
Castile soap, 414
"Cathedral of Methodism," 345
Cathedral, R.C., Phila., 348
Cathedrals, 94, 287
Catherine of Aragon, 3-4
Catskill Mountains, 106, 321
Cattail Ch. (No. 324), 491, 495
Cavaliers, 15, 486, 488
Cecil County, Md., 35
Cedar, 101, 176, 213, 279, 360, 428, 501
Ceiling: barrel, 164, 187, 473-74, 522; cove, 437
Centennial (1876), 340, 357
Central Amer., 2
Central Bap. Ch., Newport (No. 270), 413
Central Moravian Ch. (Penn.), 380
Centurian, H.M.S., 88
Chads (Chadds) Ford, Penn., 360
Chamber of Amsterdam, 54
Chamberlain, John, 445
Champlain, Samuel de, 56
Chapel of Henry VII, Westminster Abbey, 441
Chapel Hill (S.C.), 430
Chapel Point, Md., 166
Chapel Royal, 215, 330, 453-54
Chapin, the Rev. Sewell, 479
Chaplains, 120, 206, 242, 267, 281, 341, 343, 348, 470, 499, 514
Chapman, John, 373

Chapman, Wm., Jr. (Va.), 501
Chapman, Wm., 424
Chapman & Mears, London (founders), 424
Chappaqua F.M.H. (No. 180), 307, 310
Chaptico Ch. (No. 42), Md., 164
Chaptico Manor (Md.), 164
Charles I, 14, 21, 28, 488
Charles II, 14-15, 21, 33, 54, 72-73, 340, 422, 486, 501
Charles V, Emp., I of Sp., 3-4
Charlemagne, XV, 46
Charles City County, Va., 462, 477, 478, 479, 486
Charles City corp. (Va.), 14, 450, 462, 477
Charles County, Md., 33
Charles River (Mass.), 223
Charles River County (later York), Va., 488-89
Charlesfort (S.C.), 438
Charleston, S.C., XIV, 2, 16, 21, 49, 414, 422-24
Charlestown, Mass., 147, 432
Charlestown, Penn., 357
Charlotte Ch. (No. 176), 303
Chase, Benjamin, 247, 545
Chase, Samuel, 35
Chatham, Conn., 129
Chelsea Hospital (Eng.), 455
Cheltenham F.M., 369
Cheraw, S.C., 437
Cherokee Indians, 423, 524
Cherry tree legend, 511
Chesapeake, warship, 274, 470
Chesapeake Bay, 18, 30-31, 177, 187, 191, 195, 198, 470-71, 473, 476, 482, 486, 488, 501
Chester, John, 122
Chester, Md., 190
Chester Ch. (Md.), 191
Chester Congl. Ch. (No. 121), 247
Chester County (Penn.), 73
Chester F.M.H. (No. 216), 352-54, 358, 362, 391, 518
Chester R. (Md.), 18
Chester Valley (Great Valley), Penn., 357
Chesterfield County, Va., 464, 480
Chesterfield Monthly M., 273, 274
Chesterfield F.M.H. (No. 167), 291
Chestertown, Md., 189
Chestnut, 397
Chestnut Country (tract), 247
Chestnut Hill M.H. (No. 104), 226
Chicheley, Gov. Sir Henry, 497
Chichester F.M.H. (No.217), 105, 353
Chickahominy R. (Va.), 478-79, 483
Child, James, 430
Childbury, S.C., 430
Chiquesalunga Creek (Penn.), 389
Chipman, the Rev. Mr., 234
Chipman's Pond, Del., 143
Choptank, R., 193
Chotank Parish (Va.), 508
Chowan Parish, 328
Christ Ch., Accokeek (No. 47), 167
Christ Ch., Alexandria (No. 336), 510-14
Christ Ch., Boston (No. 96), 215

Christ Church, Broad Creek (No. 27), 143, 197

Christ Ch., Calvert (No. 52), 169-70

Christ Church, Cambridge (No. 98), 217-19, 415

Christ Church, Chaptico, Md., (No. 42), 164

Christ Ch., Dover, Del. (No. 23), 140

Christ Ch., Eastville, Va., 474

Christ Ch., Lancaster, Va. (No. 329), 94-95, 501-503

Christ Church, Middle Haddam (No. 12), 129

Christ Ch., Middlesex (No. 325), 95, 484, 496-97, 501

Christ Ch., New Brunswick (No. 138), 89, 107, 270-71

Christ Ch. Phila. (No. 205), 62, 74, 84, 90, 95, 189, 305, 340, 342; Hospital, 343; Burial ground, 349; 356-57, 388

Christ Ch., Savannah, 24-25, 82

Christ Ch., Shrewsbury (No. 148), 89, 278

Christ Ch., S.C. (No. 281), 21, 97, 422, 433

Christ Ch., Upper Merion (No. 204), 338-39, 460

Christ Ch., Wayside, Md. (No. 45), 165

Christ Church School (Va.), 497

Christendom, XV, 37, 44-45

Christian, Dr. J. Loomis, 397

Christian Church, the, 44, 46-47

Christian Empire, the, 46

Christian fellowship, 76, 81

Christian brotherhood, XV

Christiana, Penn., 389

Christianity, XIII, XIV, 25, 27; primitive C., 37-38, 45-47, 64, 81-82, 414

Christians, XV, 5, 19, 29, 31, 37, 46

Christians (Disciples of Christ, denom.), 493

Christina, Queen (Sweden), 61, 132

Christina (Wilmington, Del.), 61-62, 132, 284

Christmas Conf., Meth., 85

Christmas Cove, Me., 155

Chrysler, Walter Percy, 196

Chuckatuck Church (No. 303), 466-68

Chuckatuck F.M. (Va.), 466

Church, a, 404

Church Act, the (S.C.), 21, 422

Church archit., derivation, 94

Ch. of the Blessed Sacrament (No. 246), 383

Church of the Brethren (Dunkard): Germantown (No. 214), 8, 76-77, 108-09, 351, 385, 541; Conestoga, 77

Church Creek, Md., 195

Church of Eng.: 2-4, 8-11, 13-15, 18-23, 25-27, 29, 33-34, 37-38, 40-42, 58, 60, 64, 73, 78, 84, 87-90, 97, 100, 119, 126, 128, 176, 189, 209, 213, 232, 234, 248, 278, 297, 302, 318, 327, 332, 338-40, 342-44, 346, 422, 425, 442, 454, 466, 472, 485, 494, 520; proposesd Amer. episcopate, 486. See also Disestablishment

Church on the Hill, 190

Church Neck (Va.), 473

Church party, 14

Church Point (Va.), 471

Church property law, Md., 199

Ch. of the Sacred Heart (No. 254), 35

Church Swamp (Va.), 499

Church View (Va.), 496

Circular Congl. Ch., 441

City of London, 39

City Point, Va., 464

Civil rights, liberties, 45, 75, 347

Civil War: S.C. and the, 22; refs. throughout, not indexed

Claggett, Bishop Thos. John, 168, 513, 542

Claggett, Wm. (clockmaker), 412

Claiborne, Cap. Wm., 18, 31

Clapboarding: 122; beaded, 231; graduated, 124, 224; scarf-jointed, 244-45

Clapboardtrees M.H. (No. 102), 223

Clapp, Nathaniel, 412

Claremont, N.H., 255

Clarke, John, 418

Clarksville, Del., 143

Classic Revival, 7, 95

Classis, the, 63

Clearbrook, Va., 518

Clinton, Gen. Sir Henry, 66, 276

Clinton Corners, N.Y., 312

Clive, Lord, 255

Clocks, 412, 423

Cloister, Ephrata (No. 248), 9, 77, 385-87, 412, 542

Clover Sunday, 137

Clymer, George (signer), 274, 388

Cobb, Gen. Simeon, 253

Cocalico Cr. (Penn.), 77, 385

Cocclestown, Staten Is., 297

Cochico R. (N.H.), 241

Cockburn, Admiral (raids), 500, 505

Cockeysville, Md., 176

Coddington, Wm., 408-09, 418

Coffee Run Ch. (Del.), 90

Cogswell, Leander W., 258, 545

Cohansey, N.J., 279

Cohasset M.H. (No. 88), 13, 206-07, 209

Coke, the Rev. Dr. Thos., 84, 141

Colby, Lester A., 244

Cold War, XIII

Cole, the Rev. Samuel, 503

College, only colonial state, 57

College of N. J. (Princeton), 11, 64, 68, 89, 263, 265-66, 375, 485

Colleges, 10, 11. See also by name

Colleges, Presbyn. (a list), 69

Collegiate Church (N.Y.), 55

Collegiate School (Yale), 264

Collegium Musicum, 380

Colleton, Sir John, 428-29

Colleton County, S.C., 431, 438

Collin, the Rev. Dr. Nicholas, 63

Collins, Henry, 412

Collins Mill, Md., 190

Collins, the Rev. Samuel, 126

Colonial Dames of Delaware, 134

Colonial Dames, Society of, 432

Colonial policy, 81

Colonization, 1-3, 5, 10, 18, 21, 27, 38, 47-48, 53, 55, 60-61, 70

Color, colonial paints, 102, 118-19,

121, 125, 154, 275

Columbia, S.C., 424

Columbia College, 297

Columbus, Christopher, 2-3, 47, 414

Combahee River (S.C.), 438

Comenius, Bishop Johann Amos, 79-80

Comingtee Plantation (S.C.), 429

Committees of Safety, 33, 309, 350

Commonwealth Fund, 463

Communes, 314, 385

Communion Office, Prayer Book, 128

Communistic societies, 85

Community Congl. Ch. (No. 116), 242

Conanicus, Chief, 419

Conanicut F.M.H. (No. 273), 101, 419

Conant, John, 5, 253

Conant, Roger, 233

Concord F.M.H. (No. 218), 353, 355, 360, 362

Concord Quarterly M., 138

Concordat of Aberdeen, 128

Concordville, Penn., 353

Conestoga, Penn., 385

Conestoga Creek, 389

Conestoga wagon, 76

Conewago, Penn., 347, 392

Conewago Creek, Great, 392-93

Conewago Creek, Little, 392

Conewago Presbyn. Ch., Great, (No. 255), 393

Confirmation: Anglican, 16; R.C., 34

Conformation (conformity), XV, 4, 14, 33, 47

Congdon Hill (R.I.), 408

Congregatio de Propaganda Fide (Rome), 31

Congregation Jeshuat Israel (Newport), 9, 49, 51, 414

Congregation Neveh Shalom, 50

Congregation Shaar Hashamayim, Jamaica, London, 50

Congl. Christian Chs., the, 182

Congl. (Independent) Chs., 63

Congregationalists: 10-11, 21, 26, 38, 42-43, 118-19, 122, 126, 128, 213, 217, 219, 233, 255, 278, 345, 442, 444

Congregationalists with Presbyn. leanings, 26, 40-41, 148, 248, 250, 264, 266-67, 302, 432, 442

Congregationalism, 8, 10, 37-39, 41-42, 209, 221, 232, 264, 413

Conjurer's Neck (Va.), 464

Connecticut: summary, 114; map, 115; 41-42, 64, 87, 279-80, 303, 382

Conn. Farms, N.J., 264, 279

Conn. Farms Presbyn. Ch. (No. 134), 65-66, 267-68

Conn. R., Valley, 41, 54, 104, 122, 129, 229, 253, 255, 444-45

Conodoguinet Creek (Penn.), 394

Conrad Weiser Park, 59

Consecration, churches, 7

Consecration, Ang. bishops, 15, 16

Consecration of a ch., 7, 433

Consistorial polity, 58

Constitution of Geneva, 64

Constitution of U.S.A., XV, 7, 34-35, 70, 90, 242, 309, 341, 347, 388

Constitution of Va., 511
Constitution of West Jersey, 287
Constitutional Conv., 6, 35, 511
Consubstantiation, 54
Contentment, Mass., 223
Continent, the, 4, 13, 24
Continental Army, 348, 356, 470
Continental Congress, 35, 287, 340, 348, 431
Contookook River (N.H.), 257
Convulsionnaires, French, 86
Conyngham, Cap. Gustavus, 343
Cooch's Bridge, Del., 139
Cook, Joseph, 407
Cook, the Rev. Samuel, 278
Cooke, John Esten, 485, *545*
Coombe, the Rev. Thomas, 343
Cooper, James Fenimore, 308
Cooper, the Rev. Robt., 424, 440
Cooper R., 21, 422, 427, 430, 433-34, 438
Coosaw R. (S.C.), 440
Coosawhachee R. (S.C.), 440
Copany F.M.H. (No. 165), 290
Copein, Wm., 508
Cople, Parish (Va.), 504
Copley, Gov. Lionel, 20
Copley, Thomas, 34, 166
Copp's Hill, Boston, 215
Corbin, Col. Garvin, 490
Corbin, Richard, 490
Cornbury, Lord, Gov. 89, 286
Cornice: 129; cove, 140, 201; bracketed, 169
Cornick, Wm., 472
Cornstalk, Chief, 524
Cornwall, Eng., 232, 457
Cornwall Plantation, 272
Cornwallis, General Charles, 6, 139, 205, 360, 437, 454, 470, 482
Corotoman R. (Va.), 501, 504
Corp. for Relief of Widows, etc., 89, 271
Cosby, Gov. Wm., 305
Cossitt, the Rev. Ranna, 255
Council of State for Va., 460
Council of Va., 31
Counties (Va.), the, 15
County Antrim, N. Ire., 522
Covenanters, Scottish, 63, 66, 276, 442
Covenants, 39
Coventry, R.I., 406
Coventry Parish Ch. (No. 84), 200
Cow March, Del., 78, 139
Cowes, Isle of Wight, 30
Cox, John, Jr., 298
Craddock, the Rev. Thomas, 175
Craig, the Rev. John, 522
Craighead, the Rev. Alexander, 393-94
Crane Hook Ch., 61-62, 132, 337
Cranston F.H.M. (No. 263), 406
Crater, the, Petersburg, 465
Craven County, S.C., 434, 437
Crawford, Col. Wm., 470
Creeds, 27, 58
Creek F.M.H. (No. 186), 108, 312
Crefeld, Germ., 75, 351
Creighton, the Rev. Jas., 85
Creitz, the Rev. Geo. A., 382
Criglersville, Va., 516
Crispin, William, 350

Croatan Indians, 3
Cromwell, Oliver, 14-15, 18, 33, 37, 40, 119
Croom, Md., 168
Crosby, Enoch, 308
Crossing of the Dela., 233
Crosswicks, N.J., 291
Cruciform chs.: style, 18, 93-94; Latin cross, 135, 168, 170, 175, 188, 195, 287, 316, 339, 346, 363, 392, 426, 431, 454, 474, 476, 481, 489-90, 496, 503; Greek cross, 94, 232, 500, 502, 506, 508
Cruck construction, 450
Crum Elbow F.M.H. (No. 185), 311
Crusades, 46
Culpeper County, Va., 515-17
Culpeper family (Va.), 501, 512, 515
Cumberland, R.I., 407
Cumberland County, Eng., 394
Cumberland Valley (Penn.), 17, 57, 67, 106, 136, 390, 393-95, 522
Curaçao, 49, 414
Curle's Ch., Richmond, 480
Currie, the Rev. Wm. 356-58
Currituck Sound, 470-71
Cushing, the Rev. Job, 225
Custis, John, 473-74
Custis, Col. Daniel Parke, 473, 483
Custis, Martha (Dandridge), 473, 483
Cutler, the Rev. Timothy, 216
Cypress, 96, 148, 199, 423, 428, 430, 460, 427
Cypress Ch. (Va.), 461

D

Dade, the Rev. Townsend, 514
Dado, 117
Dagsboro, Del., 142
Dagworthy, Gen. John, 142
Dalcho, the Rev. Frederick, 426, 428, 430, 432-33, *545*
Dale, Sir Thos., 450, 477, 486
Dale Parish (Va.), 480
Damariscotta River, 155
Danboro, Penn., 378
Dandridge, Major John, 483
Dandridge, Martha (Custis, Washington), 483
Danvers, Mass., 234
Danville, M. H. (No. 118), 244
Danville, N. H., 244, 246
Darien, 148
Darlington, Md., 185
Darragh, Lydia, 350
Darrow, George, 87, 314-15
Darrow School, 87, 315
Dartmouth College, 157, 318, 445
Day, Henry Mason, 460
Day, William, 263
Daye, Stephen, 445
Davenport, F. G., 5
David, Christian, 79
David, Robert ap, 362
Davies, the Rev. Samuel, 485
Davis, the Rev. Samuel, 67
Davis, the Rev. Thos., 468-69, 514
Dayton's Col., N. J. regiment, 267-68
Deacons' seats, benches, pews, 156,

226, 237, 244, 247-48, 258, 407
Decatur, Stephen, 343
Declarations of independence: 23, 329; Amer., 6, 35, 340-42, 348, 454, 469
Dedham Meeting House (No. 101), XIV, 223
Deep Run Ch. (Penna.), 376
Deer Creek (Md.), 34, 184-85
Deer Creek F.M.H. (No. 69), 185
Deerfield Massacre, 444
Deerfield Presbyn. Ch. (No. 152), 42, 66, 107, 280
de la Warr, Lord, Sir Thos. West, 61, 450-51
Delaware, 1, 9-10, 28, 57, 66, 73, 77-78, 90; summary, 130; map, 131; 142, 542
Delaware Bay, 137
Delaware County, Penn., 73
Delaware Indians, 373, 380
Delaware R., 1, 42, 54, 56, 60-62, 281, 284-85, 287, 337, 353, 372-73, 379-80
de Lery, Gaspard Chassegros, 325
Democracy, XIII, 42
Democratic, 37, 80
Denonville, Marquis de Jacques Dené de Brisay, 325
Derry, N. H., 246, 248
Derry Ch. (No. 122), 248-49
Derryfield, N. H., 248
Derry linen, 248
Derry Presbyn. Ch. (Penn.), 68, 249, 397
Dewey, Thomas E., 310
Dewitt, Va., 465
Diaper pattern, brickwork, 97, 122
Diaspora, XIV, 44, 81
Dickens, John, 345
Dickinson College, 394
Dickinson, the Rev. Jonathan, 65, 265-66
Dickson (Dixon), the Rev. Robert, 471-72
Digsby, Admiral, 301
Dillenburg, Germany, 178
Dilton, Gen., 348
Dinwiddie County, Va., 465
Dipple plantation (Va.), 508
Diocese of Baltimore (R.C.), 348
Diocese of Va., 17, 481, 507, 514
Diocese of Washington, 165
Disciples of Christ (denom.), 486
Discovery, age of, 1, 3, 13
Discovery, pinnace, 6, 61, 450, 458
Disestablishment: 17, 24; in Amer., 460, 467, 474-75, 490-91, 495, 500, 508, 511
Dispersion, 44-46, 48
Disraeli, Benj., 49
D'Israeli, Isaac, 49
Dissenters: 17, 19-22, 26, 34; N.E., 37-43, 53, 73, 88, 100; Irish, 119; 213, 217, 286, 327, 422, 472, 520, 522
Diversity, XV
Doane, Bishop Geo. Washington, 287
Dobbs, Gov. Arthur, 331
Dock Creek, Phila., 345
Doctor's Creek (N.J.), 275
Don Juan of Austria, 48

Dollington, Penn., 378
Dominion of N. Eng., 40-41, 410
Donegal Presbytery, 67-68, 390, 393-95, 397, 522
Donegal Presbyn. Ch. (No. 251), 67, 96, 108-09, 136, 389-90, 393, 396
Donation Ch. (No. 306), 470-72
"Don't give up the ship!", 274
Doorways, 95
Dorchester, Eng., Mass., S.C., Ga., 26, 40, 42, 147, 250, 432, 442
Doughoregan Manor (No. 56), 34-25, 173, 542
Dover, Del., 140
Dove, ship, 19, 29, 30
Dover, F. M. H. (114), 240
Dover, N. J., 270
Dover Point, Mass., 240-41
Downing, Col. John, 241
Downington, Penn., 362
Downingtown, Penn., 362
Downman Family (Va.), 504
Dragon Swamp (Va.), 489, 491
Drake Family (N.Y.), 305
Drake, Francis, 5
Drawyers, Old, Ch. (No. 18), 67, 137
Driver, Chas., Thos., 460
Driver, Va., 466
Drum: call to meeting, 123, 125, 127, 223; disrupted m., 126
Dublin F.M. (Penn.), 369
Duché, the Rev. Jacob, 342-43
Dudley, Gov. Joseph, 242
Duffield, the Rev. George, 348
Duke of Alva, 48
Dulany, Daniel, 181
Dunkards, 76, 351, 541
"Dunkerstown" (Penn.), 385
Dunn, N. P., 463
Dunstable, N. H., 250
Dunster, the Rev. Henry, 41, 220
Durham Ch. (No. 44), 165
duPont, Pierre Samuel, 359
Dutargue, Mr., 426
Dutch, the, 1, 41, 48-49, 53-58, 62, 69, 87, 90, 136, 262, 284, 298, 306, 308-09, 313, 315-16, 321, 350, 364, 414
Dutch Colonial style, 96, 109, 134
Dutch Gap Canal, Richmond, 480
Dutch Guiana, 50, 414
Dutch Reformed Church, the, 8, 10-11, 49, 53-57, 64, 67, 178, 263-64, 266, 270-71, 278, 295, 305, 315-16, 364, 380, 382, 541-42
Dutch West India Co., 305, 313
Dutch West Indies, 49, 414
Dutchess County, N. Y., 310

E

Eaglesham and Eastward, ship, 442
Earle, the Rev. Daniel, 23, 328
Earthquake, 424
East Caln F. M. H. (No. 228), 362
Eastchester, N. Y., 304
East Haven Congl. Ch., Conn., (No. 10), 107, 127
East Hoosac F. M. H. (No. 109), 231
East Jersey Province, 88, 269, 272, 277, 286
East Park, N. Y., 311

East Nottingham F. M. H. (No. 70), 185-86
Eastern Shore Chapel (No. 307), 471-73
Easter sunrise service, 380
East India Co., Dutch, 60
Easton, Md.
Easton Reformed Ch. (No. 245), 56, 58, 380-81
Easton-Weston, Northamptonshire, 382
Eastville, Va., 473-74
East Whiteland, Penn., 357
Eaton, Thos., 477
Ebenezer Ch. (Ga.) (No. 28), 26, 59, 145
Ebenezer Ch. (S.C.) (No. 290), 442
Echaw, S. C., 434
Eckerlein, Emanuel, 385
Ecumenical, XIV, XV, 81, 83
Eden, Gov. Chas. (N. C.), 23, 328
Edenton, N. C., 23, 328, 332
Edict of Nantes, 5
Edinburgh Univ., 516
Edmundson, Wm., 352, 409
Education, "Father of Modern E.", 79
Edward VI, 341
Edwards, the Rev. Jonathan, 26, 42, 65, 126, 413, 230, 343, 485
Egan, Bishop Michael, 348
Elbert, Wm., 191-92
Elder Ballou M. H. (No. 264), 39, 407, 541
Elder, the Rev. John, 397
Eldersburg, Md., 179
Elders' seat, 247-48, 258
Eldridge, John, 72
Elections, 43, 422
Eliot, John, 42
Eliot, Me., 150
Elk R., Md., 518
Ellicott City, Md., 173
Elmwood estate, Md., 198
Elizabeth I, 2-5, 13, 26, 49
Elizabeth City (Va.), 450, 466, 470, 476
Elizabeth City corporation, 14
Elizabeth City County, Va., 476, 482
Elizabeth, N. J., 265-67
Elizabeth Presbyn. Ch. (No. 133), 11, 65, 265-66, 268
Elizabeth River Parish (Va.), 468, 470, 471
Elzas, Barnett A., 422, 545
Emanuel I (Portugal), 48
Emmanuel Ch., Chestertown (No. 73), 89, 189
Emmanuel Ch., Kempsville, Va., 472
Emmanuel College, Cambridge, Eng., 11
Emerson, James, 345
Empire of the U. S., 349, 350
Enfield, Conn., 86, 126, 230
Enfield, Old Congl. Ch. (No. 9), 42, 103, 126
England, 1, 3-5, 8, 13, 15-16, 18-19, 24-29, 31-35, 37-42, 48-49, 70, 78-79, 83, 93
England, 120, 169; laws of, 287; 313, 342, 345, 414, 423, 445, 451, 459, 480
English, earliest settlers, 476

English, the, 1-2, 21, 23-24, 27, 41, 49, 56, 62, 87, 90
English bond, 92, 146, 391, 451, 456, 483, 498, 500, 504
English Catholics, 27
English Channel, 5
English Civil War, 486
English Reformation, 38
English Santee (S.C.), 434, 436
Enlargements of building, 103, 124, 138, 151, 176, 180, 190, 193, 209, 219-20, 223, 229, 232, 248, 255, 263, 273, 282, 285, 288, 297-98, 303, 307, 313-14, 320, 340, 348, 358, 360, 362, 370, 374, 378, 382, 386, 391-92, 405-06, 409, 454, 473, 480, 492, 523
Enoch, Brother, 387
"Enthusiasm," 83
Episcopacy: 38, 58, 60, 80; Amer. birthplace, 128
Episcopalians, 18, 120, 172, 213, 413
Episcopalianism, 9, 10, 37, 40
Episcopate for Amer., 286
Ephrata, Penn., 9, 385
Ephrata House, Nazareth, 379
Ephrata Academy, 387
E Pluribus Unum, XV, 45
Epping Forest plantation, 504
Equality, democratic principle of, 72
Erie, Penn., 357
Escorial (Sp.), 5
Eskimos, mission to, 25, 81
Eskridge, Col. Geo., 505
Essex County, 498-501, 504, 521
Essington, Penn., 61, 337
Established Church of England, 8-9, 17, 19, 21-24, 26, 29, 37
Established Church of Va., 455, 500
Established Order, the (N.E.), 10, 42-43, 70, 422
Ettwein, Bishop J., 283
Europe, 1, 2, 5, 24
Evangel. Luth. Ch. of St. Paul the Apostle (No. 188). See Old Stone Red Hook, N.Y.
N. Y.
Evangelical Luth. Ch., Frederick (No. 64), 59, 108, 180-81
"Evangeline," 340, 344
Evangelist. See Whitefield
Evangelization: 24; of heathen, 81
Evans, the Rev. David, 397
Evans, the Rev. Edward, 84, 345
Evans, the Rev. Evan, 356-57
Evans, William, 288
Everittstown, N.J., 272
Eversfield, the Rev. John, 168
Evesham Meeting. See Mount Laurel
Exeter F.M.H. (No. 247), 108, 384
Exploration, age of, 1, 47

F

Fabritius, the Rev. Jacob, 61-62, 338
Fairfax family (Va.), 501, 511-12, 514
Fairfax County, Va., 510, 512
Fairfax Parish (Va.), 510, 512
Fairfax Resolutions, 511
Fairfield County, Conn., 280, 304
Fairfield County, S. C., 442

Fairfield Presbyn. Ch. (No. 150), 42, 66, 107, 279
"Fair Harvard," 441
Fair Hill F.M., 352
Fairlee, Md., 188
Falckner, the Rev. Daniel, 368
Falckner, the Rev. Justus, 338
Falckner's Swamp Ch. (No. 232), 60, 107, 368, 541
Falls Ch. (No. 337), 95, 512-15
Falling Spring (Chambersburg, Penn.), 393
Falls Monthly M., 372, 378
Fallsington F.M.H. (No. 236), 372
Fallston, Md., 183
Faneuil Hall, Boston, 213
Farmington, Conn., 118, 123-25
Farmington Congl. Ch., Conn. (No. 7), 101, 123-24
Farmington School, 124
Farnham Parishes, N. and S. (Va.), 498
Farnham, Va., 500
Fawn Grove Meeting, 185
Federal Hill (N.H.), 253
Fenwick, Edward, Fenwick Hall (S. C.), 423
Fenwick, John, 282
Ferdinand III (Sp.), 47
Ferdinand V and Isabella (Sp.), 3, 44, 47-48, 414
Ferry Chapel (Va.), 464-65
Ferry Farm (Va.), 471
Ferry toll (S.C.), 426, 430, 467
Fetter Lane, London, 83
Field, Dr. David D., 129
Fighting parsons, 242, 268, 397
Fighting Quakers. See Q.
Finns, 90
Fir, 100
Fireplaces, 231, 273
First Ch. of Boston, 213
First Day Baptists, 77
First Parish Ch., Cambridge, 219
Fisher, Father Philip, S. J., 34, 47
Fisher, Geo. and Hannah, 399
Fisher, Mary (Quaker), 70
Fishermen, 232
Fishkill, N. Y., 55
Fishkill Dutch Ch. (No. 182), 55, 308-09
Fishing Creek, Md., 195
Fishing Point (Va.), 473
Fisk, the Rev. Jonas, 243
Fitch, John, 431
Fitz Randolph. See R.
Fitz, Richard, the Rev., 38
Fitzhugh, Henry, 507
Fitzhugh, William, 506
Five Nations (Iroquois), 73. See also Six Nations
Flagg, the Rev. Ebenezer, 247
Flags of three nations, 27
Flagstone, 96
Flanders, 54
Flat Creek Chapel (Va.), 464
Flemington, N.J., 272
Flemish bond (brickwork); 49, 92-93, 134, 137, 139, 162-65, 168, 169, 188, 190, 196-98, 201, 213, 328, 338, 346, 358, 451, 466, 468, 473, 479, 485, 487, 489-94, 497, 499,

500, 502, 505-06, 511, 513, 515
Florida, 2-3, 23, 27, 81, 379
Florida Campaign, 423
Flushing F.M.H. (No. 170), 298, 542
Flushing, Holland, 56, 263
Fogg, the Rev. Daniel, 120
Fogg, the Rev. Ezekiel, 195
Fontaine, the Rev. Francis, 482
Fork Ch. (No. 315), 484-85
Forks of the James Presbyn. Ch., 523
Fork Ch., Presbyn. (Va.), 485
Forman, Henry Chandler, 18, 451, 546
Fort Amsterdam Church (N.Y.), 55
Fort Anderson (N.C.), 331
Fort Belvoir (Va.), 512
Fort Caroline (Fla.), 2
Fort Casimir (Del.), 57, 67, 136
Fort Charles (S.C.), 2
Fort Christina (Del.), 62, 132
Fort Conty (Conti), (N.Y.), 324
Fort Defiance (Va.), 521
Fort Denonville, 325
Fort Dorchester (S.C.), 432
Fort Duquesne (Penn.), 521
Fort Frontenac (Ont.), 325
Fort Golgotha (N.Y.), 301
Fort Hendrick (N.Y.), 318
Fort Henry (Va.), 464
Fort Herkimer Dutch Ch. (No. 194), 55, 106, 320
Fort Motte (S.C.), 435
Fort Niagara (N.Y.), 3, 56, 316, 320, 325
Fort Niagara Assn., Old, 325
Fort Orange (Albany) church, 55
Fort Plain, N.Y., 318
Fort Stanwix (N.Y.), 319
Fort Ticonderoga (N.Y.), 219
Fort Wetherill (R.I.), 419
Forts, stockades, 2, 27, 55-57, 62, 99, 264, 316, 320-22, 325, 521, 524
Forty-five Mile House (S.C.), 430
Forty Fort (Penn.), 382
Foster, the Rev. Anthony, 441
Fothergill, John, 518
Fountaine, the Rev. Jas. Maury, 486
Four Mile Run Ch. (Md.), 163-64
Fowler, Robert, 408
Fox family (Va.), 504
Fox, Geo., 19, 70-71, 74, 169, 193, 277, 404, 408-09, 466
Fox Point, N.H., 241
France, 1-5, 23, 35, 54, 64
Franciscans, 33
Francke, August Hermann, 60, 80, 365-66
Francke' sche Stiftungen. See Orphanage, Halle
Frankford F.M.H. (No. 215), 107, 346, 352, 369-71
Frankfort (Frankfurt) Land Co., 75, 351
Franklin, Benjamin: 35, 83, 213, 340-41, 344, 349, 364, 387-88, 394, 518; lightning rod, 413; William, 278
Franklin and Marshall College, 388
Franklin Park, Phila., 84, 344-45
Fraser, the Rev. John, 508
Frazer, the Rev. Wm., 272
Frederica, Del., 141
Frederick, Md., 58, 178, 180-81

Frederick County, Md., 35
Frederick County, Va., 518
Fredericksburg, N.Y., 310
Fredericksville Parish (Va.), 484
Freedom of the press, 88, 305
Frelinghuysen, the Rev. Theodore Jacobus, 89, 271
French, the, 1, 3-4, 21, 23-24, 27, 35, 56, 73, 232, 324-25, 348, 394, 422, 427-29, 521
French, Daniel, 511
French Chapel, Castle, Fort Niagara (No. 197), 3, 27, 56, 107, 324-25
French and Indian War, 3, 23, 33, 118-19, 122, 124, 180, 229-30, 242, 256, 305, 316, 318, 320, 322, 324, 380, 397, 414, 423, 479, 521
French Settlement, French Santee (S. C.), 434, 436
French War Dept., Colonial Archives, 325
Freedom, XV, 44, 46-47
Freedmen, 404
Freedom of religion, conscience, worship, XV, 5, 8, 19, 21, 23-24, 27-28, 32, 34-36, 39-41, 45, 48-50, 70, 72, 88, 287, 347, 350, 403, 405, 409, 414, 417, 422, 454-55
Freehold, N.J., 16, 74, 89, 276-77, 286
Freeman, the Rev. James, 215
Freemasons, 417, 428, 436
Free Quakers M.H. (No. 212), 73, 349-50, 542
Fresh Kills, Staten Is., 297
Fresh Water Plantation (Conn.), 126
Frey, George, 399
Friends: 8-10, 17, 19-20, 28, 43, 70-75; reunion, 371-72; birthright, convinced, 391. See also Quakers
Friends Alms House, 344
Friends Hist. Assn., 355, 359
Friends meeting house, the, 100
Frobisher, Martin, 5
Frogmore, S.C., 439
Full Gospel Tabernacle, Penn., 353
Fultonham, N.Y., 322

G

Gables: corbie, 49, 93, 96, 451, 459; curvilinear, 95, 435-36, 483; seven, 232; hooded. See Roof
Gaddis, Robert, 198
Gainsborough, Eng., 38-39
Galbreath, Andrew, 390
Galleons, 5
Gaonate (Babylonia), 44
Gap Mills, W. Va., 525
Garbisch, Col. Edgar Wm., Bernice (Chrysler), 196
Garden, the Rev. Alexander, 428
Garden Week in Va., 463
Gardenia, 428
Gardenville, Penn., 378
Gardner, Bishop Wallace John, 287
Garfield, Pres. Jas. A., 407, 437
Garrison Forest (Md.), 175
Gates, Gen. Horatio, 350
Gay, Eben Howard, 205
Gay, the Rev. Dr. Ebenezer, 205-07

Gemein Haus, 332, 380
Gen. Convention Prot. Epis. Ch., 341
Gen. Court of Va., 459
Gen. Meeting of Friends in Amer., 40, 71, 73, 408
Gen. Synod of Mass., 312
Geneva (Switz.), 4, 13-15, 26, 54, 64
Geneva Catechism, 54
Georg Kirche, Phila., 345
George Keith, 16
George I, 425-26
George II, 23, 243, 276, 303, 328, 518
George III, 142, 303, 399, 518
George's Creek, N.H., 138
Georgia: 3, 9, 23-26, 42, 78-80, 82; summary, map, 144; 542
Georgian style, 169, 217, 266, 295
Georgetown, S.C., 435, 437
Georgetown College, Univ., Seminary, 35
German Baptists, 76-78, 518, 520
German Flatts, N.Y., 320
German Lutherans, 8, 17, 20, 24, 43, 55-57, 60, 263, 284, 313, 321-22, 368, 516-17, 541
German M.H., Waldoboro (No. 35), 43, 59, 154
German Reformed, 8, 10, 20, 49, 53, 55, 57-59, 77, 84, 181, 345, 382, 385, 541
German Reformed Ch., Hagerstown (No. 66), 106, 182
Germanna, Va., 515-17
Germans, 55, 57-58, 75-76, 90, 317, 350, 358, 383, 499, 516, 520. *See also* Palatines
Germantown, Penn., 75-77, 350-51, 385
Germantown F.M., 352, 370-71
Germany, 1, 4-5, 25, 56, 58, 79, 83, 146, 178, 180, 277, 351, 379, 386, 414, 517
Gerry, Gov., V.P., Elbridge, 227
Gerrymandering, 227
Gersdorf, Baroness von, 79
Ghettos, 44, 47
Ghost towns, 18, 22, 85, 146, 148, 197, 330, 385, 430, 432, 450-51
Gibbs, James (archit.), 101, 214, 295, 404, 423, *546*
Gibson (archit.), 423
Gilbert, Benjamin, 378
Gill, Henry, 433
Gillespie, the Rev. Geo., 390, 397
Gilman, the Rev. Dr. Samuel and Caroline, 441
Gilmanton, N.H., 256
Gingerbread style, 413
Girard Stephen, 344
Girard College, 344
Girelius, the Rev. Lawrence, 133
Glad Tidings Plain, 207
Glasgow, Scotland, 357, 442
Glass: 92, 122, 129, 133, 135, 226-27, 245, 255, 273, 281, 286, 382, 423, 514; panes, diamond, 232, 242, 251, 356, 460; panes, small, 122, 190; stained, 122, 129, 167, 190, 198, 232, 234, 242, 339, 348, 374, 382, 395, 404, 460; Waterford, 295
Glazier, 132

Glazing, 497
Glebe Ch. (No. 302), 14, 17, 466-68
Glebe House, Woodbury, Conn., 41, 104, 128-29, 542
Glebe houses, 472, 479-80
Glebe lands, 17, 426, 428, 432, 463, 467, 476
Glebe Point (Va.), 487
Glen, Gov. John (S.C.), 423
Gloria Dei Ch. (No. 202), 62-63, 92, 132, 337-39, 346, 417, 541
Gloucester, Eng., 215
Gloucester, Mass., 441
Gloucester Circuit, Methodist (Va.), 490
Gloucester County, Va., 486, 488-89
Gloucester Point (Va.), 488
Gloucestershire, Eng., 459
God Speed, ship, 6, 450, 458
Gold, 5
Golden age, Jews, 44, 47, 50
Gooch, Gov. Wm. (Va.), 511, 516
Goochland County (Va.), 480
Goodrich, Col. Elizur, 122
Goodwin, Mary, 507, *544*
Goodwin, the Rev. Dr. W.A.R., 454
Gookin, Gov. Charles, 135
Goose Creek Ch. (No. 275). *See* St. James', G.C.
Goose Creek F.M.H. (No. 341), 17, 106, 519
Gordon, the Rev. Thos., 500
Goshen F.M. (Penn.), 355
Goshenhoppen, Penn., 383
Gothenburg, Sweden, 61
Gothic Revival, 94, 180, 263, 287, 295, 441
Gothic style: 93, 96, 100, 168, 196, 303, 339, 451, 453, 458-59, 540, 543; "carpenter," 277; perpendicular, 441
Government, principle of, 1
Grace Ch., Yorktown (No. 313), 97, 109, 482-83
Granada (Sp.), 3, 46-47, 414
Granite, Quincy, 106, 214
Granville County, S.C., 438
Graves, Alexander, 497
Graves, the Rev. Matthew, 129
Grave robbery, 194
Great Awakening, the, 26, 42, 62, 68, 83, 126, 136, 230, 234, 248, 250, 263, 343, 366, 397, 413, 522
Great Barrington, Mass., 230, 413
Great Bay, N.H., 240, 242
Great Birmingham Rd. (Penn.), 360
Great Debate, the (Unitarian), 205
Great Dispersion, the, 44
Great Egg Harbor Monthly M., 279
Great Fire, the, Manhattan, 295
Great Highway, 274
Great Lakes, 3, 324
Great Meadows, N.H., 253
Great Michael (first bell of the peal), Charleston, 424
Great South Bay, L.I., 303
Greaton, Father Joseph, S.J., 36, 347, 392
Greece, 46
Greek civilization, XIV, 45
Greek Revival, 94, 103, 117, 121, 124,

126, 129, 221, 234, 413
Green, the, or common, 123, 135, 213, 220, 223, 229, 247, 250, 254, 263, 305
Green, the Rev. Chas., 511
Green, the Rev. Enoch, 281
Green, the Rev. Joseph, 234
Green Hill Ch. (No. 79), 197
Green Spring Valley, Hunt, Md., 175
Green Street Monthly M. (Penn.), 352
Greenland, N.H., 242
Greenwich Monthly M., 405-06
Greenwich, Conn., 310
Greenwich F.M.H. (No. 151), 280
Gregorian calendar, 7
Griffin, ship, 39
Griffith, the Rev. David, 514
Grip, ship, 61
Griscom, Elizabeth. *See* Betsy Ross
Griswold, Isaac, 122
Grosman, I. N., 366
Groton Congl. Ch. (No. 100), 221
Ground rent, 345
Ground Squirrel Bridge (Va.), 485
Guernsey, Isle of, 232
Guggenheim, Harry F., 427
Gulf of Mexico, 3
Gundalows, 208
Gunpowder F.M.H. (No. 60), 176
Gunston Hall (Va.), 510-12
Gwinnett, Button (signer), 148
Gwynn, the Rev. John, 486

H

Habeas corpus, 499
Hackensack Dutch Ref. Ch. (No. 131), 12, 56, 262-63
Haddonfield Quarterly M., 280, 288
Hadrian, Emp., 45
Hager, Jonathan, 182
Hagerstown, Md., 182
"Hail Columbia," 341
Hale, Edward Everett, 229
Hale, the Rev. Enoch, 229
Hale, the Rev. Moses, 247
Hale, Nathan, 229
Half Moon, ship, 60
Half-Yearly Meetings, 282
Halifax, Nova Scotia, 215
Hall, Daniel, 344
Hall, the Rev. Henry, 171
Hall, Dr. Lyman, 148
Halle, Germany: 59-60, 80, 365; Orphanage *(Francke' sche Stiftungen)*, 80-81; Univ., 60, 80
Hambleton, Md., 194
Hamburg, Va., 17, 520
Hamilton, Alexander, 266
Hamilton, Andrew, 305, 340
Hamilton Parish (Va.), 508, 510, 514
Hampton, N.H., 247
Hampton, Va., 18, 476-77
Hampton, the Rev. Thos., 451
Hampton Congl. Ch., Conn. (No. 5), 102, 121
Hampton Normal School (Institute) (Va.), 477
Hampton Parish, York, 482
Hamorton, Penn., 359

Hampstead Town Hall (No. 120), 246
Hancock, John, 431
Hancock Shaker Community (Mass.), 87, 315
Hancock's Bridge, N.J., 281
Hanover, Penn., 368
Hanover County, Va., 484-86
Hanover Parish (Va.), 506-07
Hanover Presbytery (Va.), 17, 485, 522, 524
Hanukah, 415
Hancock, John (signer), 469
Harding, Thomas, 288
Harford County, Md., 34
Harlem, Manhattan, 56, 263
Harmon's Manor (Md.), 35
Harpswell Center M.H. (No. 33), 152
Harris, John: 396-97; Ferry, 396
Harrisburg, Penn., 68, 395-97
Harrison, Benjamin, family (Va.), 437, 461, 463, 479
Harrison, Peter (archit.), 50, 97, 102, 213, 218, 410-12, 415
Harrop Parish (Va.), 453
Hart, Abraham, 50, 414
Hart, John (signer), 273
Hartford, Conn., 54, 123
Harun al-Rashid, 46
Harvard, John 11
Harvard College, Univ.: 41-42, 120, 204, 206, 217, 225, 240, 242, 246, 255-56, 264, 441, 454-55; Yard, 11
Harvey, Gov. (Va.), 31
Hasell, the Rev. Thos., 428
Hass, H., 366
Haste's Creek, Md., 197
"Hat in the ring," 43
Hatcher's Run Chapel (Va.), 464-65
Haverford, Penn., 73
Haverford, Old, F.M.H. (No. 219), 108, 354-55, 362-63
Haverhill, Mass., 243, 246-47
Hawke, N.H., town and Admiral, 244
Hawkins, John, 5
Hyde Park, 311
Hazel R. (Va.), 516
Heager, the Rev. Johann Friederich, 322
Hebron, Conn., 255
Hebron Lutheran Ch. (No. 339), 17, 59, 516, 541
Heidelburg Univ., 77, 385
Heilman, A., 366
Helen Creek (Md.), 170
Hellenic period, 45
Helmer, Adam, 320
Hemingway, Daniel, 225
Hemingway, the Rev. Samuel, 127
Hermitage Baptist Ch. (Va.), 496
Hermits, 77, 385
Hermits of the Wissahickon, 338
Henderson, the Rev. Joseph, 393
Hendrick, "King" (Mohawk Chief), 318
Henniker Old Town House (No. 130), 257
Henniker, Baron John, 258
Henrico, Henrico Parish, Henricopolis, Henricus, 14, 450, 477, 480-81
Henry IV (Fr.), 5
Henry VIII, 3, 4, 27

Henry, John, 485
Henry, Patrick, 454, 481, 485-86
Henry, the Rev. Patrick, 486
Heresy, 48, 70
Heretics, 3-4, 19, 38, 47
Herkimer, Johan, 320
Herkimer, Gen. Nicholas, 319-20
Herring Creek (Md.), 171
Herring Creek (Va.), 479
Herrnhut, Saxony, 24-25, 80, 82, 383
Herrnhutters, 24, 383
Hershey, Penn., 68, 397
Hess family, 318
Hessian soldiers, 267, 291, 305, 359, 367, 375, 418
Hewes, Joseph (signer), 341
Heyniger Memorial Library, 315
Hibernia, Md., 191
Hickory Grove F.M.H., 138
Hickory Neck Academy (Va.), 457
Hickory Neck Church (No. 296), 457
Hicks, Elias, 74, 300
Hicksite Friends (liberal faction), 300, 313, 352
Hicksville, Long Is., 300
"Hidden Seed," 79
Higbee, the Rev. Daniel, 273
High Dutch, 56-57, 322
High Dutch Church of Foxendorf, 322
Hill, Aaron, 329
Hilton, James, 44
Hingham, Mass., 204, 206-07
Hinton, Wm., 329
Hipkins, John, 497
Historic Amer. Building (designation), 269
Hist. Societies of N.H., 243
Hist. Society of Delaware, 134
Hist. So. of Penn., 387
Hobart, the Rev. Peter, 204, 206
Hobart, the Rev. Nehmiah, 206
Hobbs, John 197
Hockessin F.M.H. (No. 20), 138
Hocknell, John, 86
Hog Island Creek (Va.), 460
Hoge family (Penn.), 394-95
Holden Chapel (No. 97), 97, 217
Holden, Mr. and Mrs. Samuel, 217
Holden, Mass., 217
Holladay, Anthony, Esther, 468
Holladay's Point plantation (Va.), 468
Holland, 1, 13, 38, 46, 48-49, 55-57, 61, 132, 178, 262-63, 277, 322, 351, 414, 423
Hollis Prof. of Divinity (Harvard), 42, 205
Holliman, Ezekiel, 403
Hollowing Creek Ch. (Va.), 484
Holmes, the Rev. Dr. Abiel, 40, 148
Holmes, Oliver Wendell Holmes, 40, 148
Holy Catholic Church, 27
Holy Rollers, 86
Holy Roman Empire, XV, 2, 4, 37, 45-46
Home Moravian Ch., 332
Honeyman, the Rev. James, 410
Hood, Hope (Indian chief), 241
Hood, Robin (Indian chief), 241
Hoopsa Neck (S.C.), 440

Hoosic River (Mass.), 231
Hoover farm (Penn.), 395
Hope, Mrs. Jane Barron, 477
Hopewell, N.J., 273
Hopewell F.M.H. (No. 340), 17, 106, 518
Hopkins, Dr. Samuel, 413
Hopkins, Stephen, 341
Hopkins, Dr., M.H., (No. 269), 412-13
Hopkinsian theology, 413
Hopkinson, Francis (signer), 341
Hopkinson, Judge Joseph, 341
Hopkinton Congl. Ch. (No. 129), 256
Horton, the Rev. Simon, 65, 267
Hoskins, Reded, 329
Hough, George, 445
Houghton, Arthur A., Jr., 192
Housatonic Townships, 230
House of Burgesses (Va.), 14, 451
House of Peace, 325
Housertown (N.C.), 332
Houston, Robert, 143
Houston, Sam, family, 397, 523-24
Howard, A., 436
Howe, Bishop W.B.W., 433
Howe, Gen. Wm., 295, 297, 350, 360-61
Hubbard, the Rev. Jonathan, 230
Hudson, Henry, 56, 60
Hudson R.: 41, 54-56, 59; discovery, 60; 108, 262, 295, 308-09, 311, 313, 315-16
Huguenot Ch., Charleston, 2, 22, 64
Huguenots, 1, 2, 5, 21-22, 56, 63-64, 86, 194, 263, 297, 422, 426-29, 431, 434-37
Hughes, Will, 483
Human rights, 287, 298
Hungars Ch. (No. 308), 95, 473-74
Hunter, the Rev. Andrew, 281
Hunter, Father George, S.J.
Hunter, Jacob, 329
Hunter, P. S., 499
Hunterstown, Penn., 393
Huntersville, Md., 164
Hunting Creek plantation (Va.), 511-12
Huntington, L.I., 301, 303
Huntington Presbyn. Ch. (No. 174), 65, 301
Hurricanes, 103, 117, 127, 216, 225, 234, 423, 424
Huron Indians, 56, 325
Huse, Thomas, 246
Huss, John (reformer), 25, 38, 78, 332, 379
Hussey, Abigail, 240
Hussite wars, 78
Hutchinson, Anne, 418
Hutchinson River (N.Y.), 304

I

Iberian Peninsula, 44
Idolator, 19
Imlaystown, N.J., 275
Immanuel Ch., New Castle (No. 16), 62, 90, 135, 540
Import duties, 435
Independence, principle of, 22, 63-64

Independence of Amer. and R.C. Ch., 35
Independence Hall, 90, 305, 340-41, 344, 350
Independence Natl. Park, 350
Independent Congl. and Presbyn. Ch., Charleston, 441
Independents (Congl.), 13, 19, 39-40, 248, 278, 302, 466
Indiana, 87
Indigo, 436
Indian Castle Ch. (No. 193), 318-20
Indian Ch., Mashpee (No. 92), 42, 211
Indian interpreter. *See* Conrad Weiser, Jr.
Indians: 3, 11, 16, 23-25, 31-34, 42, 55-56, 59, 73, 80-82, 147, 162, 175, 183, 187, 211, 221, 229-30, 240-42, 264, 266, 276, 281, 284, 287, 290-91, 315-19, 325, 328, 332, 339, 357, 373, 380, 382, 392, 396, 404, 432, 444, 450, 454-55, 458, 465, 473, 476-77, 482, 488, 521-22, 524; treaties, 373, 382, 394
Individualism, 39-40, 405, 454
Infanta (Sp.), 27
Infant baptism, 41
Infidels, 46
"In God We Trust," 45
"Instruction," by Lord Baltimore, 30
Ingle, Richard (pirate), 31
Innes, the Rev. Alexander, 88
Interior, Dept. of the, 338, 417
Intolerance, 40, 46
Interdependent churches, 63
Inquisition, the Spanish, 3, 47-48, 50, 414-15
Ireland, 439
Iron, 423
Iron Hill (Del.), 139
Iron mines, indy., 17, 499, 516, 517
Ironsides, Md., 165
Iroquois. *See* Five, Six Nations
Irving, Washington, 55, 305
Isabella, the Catholic (Sp.), 3-4, 47
Isabella, dau. of I. the Catholic, 48
Isabella, granddau. of I. the Catholic, 48
Islam, 46
Isle of Wight County, Va., 458, 460, 543
Isle of Wight Plantation, 458
Islip, L.I., 303
Israel, 44, 417
Israelites, 63
Ithan, Penn., 355
Ivy, 140, 452, 519
Izard, Ralph, 426

J

Jablonsky, Bishop Daniel Ernst, 80
Jackson, the Rev. Andrew, 502
Jackson, Thos., 483
Jacksonville, N.J., 290
Jacob, the Rev. Henry, 39, 209
Jacobean style, 93, 95, 366, 435-36, 451, 457, 484
Jaffrey, George, 252
Jaffrey M.H. (No. 125), 252-53

Jamaica, 50, 417
James I (Eng., V of Scot.), 5, 13-14, 26-27, 38
James II, 19, 33, 86, 90, 128, 508
James City (borough corp., Va.), 14, 450, 458
James City County, Parish, Va., 453, 457, 460, 476-77
James, Duke of York and Albany, 54
James, Marquis, 523, *547*
James, the Rev. Richard, 18
James Madison Mem. Bridge (Va.), 499
James R. (Va.), 6, 15, 92, 153, 450, 453, 458, 460-62, 464, 466-68, 470, 475, 477-80, 482
James Town, S.C., 434
Jamestown, R.I., 408
Jamestown, Va., 6, 9, 13, 18, 26, 28, 61, 93, 450-51, 453-54, 457, 470, 476-88
Jamestown Ch., Va. (No. 293), 6, 14, 92-93, 450-51, 453, 456, 459-60, 540
Jamestown Exposition (Va.), 468
Jamestown F.M. (R.I.), 419
Janney, Jacob and Hannah, 519
Japan, XIII, chap. 5, 46, 63
Jarvis, the Rev. Dr. Abraham, 129
Jay, John, 308
Jednota Bratrska (Unity of Brethren), 78
Jefferson, Thomas, 454-56, 481
Jenkintown, Penn., 369
Jenkinsville, S.C., 442
Jericho F.M.H. (No. 173), 74, 299-300
Jersey, Isle of, 232
Jerusalem, Palestine, 44-45, 81, 380
Jerusalem Ch. (No. 28), 26, 59, 92, 145-46, 542
Jesuit Chapel. *See* French Chapel
Jesuits, 19, 30-35, 107, 161-62, 184, 324-25, 347, 383, 392
Jesus College, Cambridge Univ., 218
Jet Age, 473
Jewish Cemetery, Newport, 417
Jews, 3, 9, 24, 40, 44-53, 412, 414-17, 422, 542
John, Lord Berkeley, 54
John Street Society, N.Y., 84
Johns, Bishop (Va.), 514
John's Is. (S.C.), 423
Johnson, Sir Wm., 316-19, 324
Johnson, Sir John, 317-19, 322, 324
Johnston, Gov. Gabriel, 330
Johnston, Wm. W., 198
Johnstown, N.Y., 316
Jones, the Rev. Hugh, 455-56
Jones, Inigo (architect), 248
Jones, James, 503
Jones, John, 409
Jones, Peter, 464
Jones, Robert, 140
Jones, the Rev. Rowland, 453
Jones, the Rev. Wm. G. H., 459
Jones' Ford (Penn.), 360
Jones' Hole Creek Chapel (Va.), 464-65
Joppa, Md., 176
Jordon's Mile Hill (Va.), 466
Jordon's Parish (Va.), 478
Judaism, XIV, chap. 5, 46, 63

Judas, Iscarist, 47
Judd, the Rev. Jonathan, 229
Julian calendar, 7
Jumpers, Welsh, 86

K

Kalmar Nyckel, ship, 61
Kearsley, Dr. John (archit.), 340, 342
Kebner, G., 366
Kecoughtan (Va.), 476-77
Keeling, the Rev. Jacob, 467
Keenan, Edward, 525
Keith, the Rev. George, 74, 88-89, 272, 277-78, 286, 302, 346, 457, 477, 481, 489
Keithian Controversy, 74, 269-70, 277, 346, 352
Kelly, J. Frederick, 118, *547*
Kelly, the Rev. John, 246
Kennebec R., 153, 343
Kennebunk Ch. (No. 32), 103, 151
Kennett, Old, F.M.H. (No. 225), 109, 358-59
Kennett Square, Penn., 359
Kensington Cong'l. Ch., Conn. (No. 8), 125
Kent, ship, 72, 287
Kent, William, 415
Kent County, Md., 18, 188
Kent Is., Md., 18, 20, 31
Kenton, Del., 78, 139
Kentucky, 6, 87, 357
Kerr's Creek (Va.), 524
Key, Philip (high sheriff of Md.), 164
Kidder, Col. Reuben, 254
Killingworth, Conn., 264
Kilmarnock, Va., 502
Kilpatrick, Gen. Hugh Judson, 148
Kimball, Fiske, 415, 417, *547*
Kincaid's Bridge (S.C.), 442
King, Whittington, 198
King Geo. County, Va., 506-07
King George's Parish (Md.), 167
King Philip's War, 250
King and Queen County, Va., 489-91
King and Queen Parish, 164
King William County, Va., 489, 491-92, 494-95
King's Chapel, Boston (No. 95), 7, 40-41, 95-96, 106, 213-15, 218, 232, 415, 540
King's Chapel (Manhattan), 295
King's College (Columbia), 88, 295
King's Creek (Md.), 198
King's Guard, Boston, 208
King's Highway: N.J., 282-85, 287; Penn., 362
King's Mill Chapel, Somerset, 198
Kingsessing, Phila., 338-39
Kingston, N.H., 245
Kingston, Ontario, 325
Kingston, R.I., 408
Kingston Ch. (Va.), 486
Kingswood, N.J., 272
Kingswood Manor, 118-19
Kiokee Ch. (No. 29), 26
Kirchehoek, N.Y., 313
Kirkpatrick, the Rev. A.G., 442
Kiskyache Parish (Va.), 482

Kittery Point, Congl. Ch. (No. 31), 150, 542
Knights of Columbus, 413
Knott's Is., N.C., 471
Knoxville, Tenn., 524
Knyphausen, Gen. Wilhelm, Baron von, 360
Kocherthal, the Rev. Joshua, 322
Koontz, the Rev. John, 520
Korean War, XIII

L

L-form churches, 94
Lafayette, Gen.: 186, 341; Cemetery, 361, 470
Laggan Presbytery, N. Ire., 199
Lahaska, Penn., 376
Laing, John, 269
Lake Champlain, 56
Lake George (N.Y.), 316, 318
Lake Ontario, 3, 5, 6, 324-25
Lamb, Wm. Harrison, 517, 547
Lamball, Thomas, 441
Lambert, Thomas, 291
Lambertville, N.J., 272
Lamb's Creek Ch. (No. 333), 95, 506-07, 516
Lamech, Brother, 387
Lancaster, Penn., 57, 387-88
Lancaster County, Penn., 73, 76
Lancaster County, Va., 496-98, 500-01, 503
Lancet windows, 93, 195-96, 232, 263, 277, 374, 459, 493
Landed gentry (Va.), 17
Landgrave (S.C. title), 428
Langhorne F.M. (Penn.), 373
Langley, Batty, 415
Language: Bohemian, 78; Dutch, 56, 69, 263, 322; English, 22, 62, 82, 322, 339, 357-58, 388, 427; French, 21-22, 263, 427-28; German, 56, 69, 182, 322, 332, 357-58, 388; Indian, 42, 318; Swedish, 62, 338-39
La Rochelle, France, 428, 431
LaSalle, René Robert Cavelier de, 324-25
"Last Supper, the" (painting), 383
Latrobe, Benjamin, 94
Laud, Wm., Archbishop of Canterbury, 15
Laurens, Henry, 431
Lawndale, Penn., 346, 352
Lawne, Sir Christopher, 458, 460
Lawne's Creek (Va.), 458-59
Lawne's Creek Parish, 460-61
Lawrence, Amos, 417
Lawrence, Cap. Jas., 66, 274-75
Lawrence, Robert F., 243, 248, 547
Lawrence, Bishop Wm., 216
Lawrenceville Presbyn. Ch. (No. 143), 66, 274
Lawrenceville School (N.J.), 274
Lawry, Gawen, 72
Learning, 1, 10-12, 46-47
Leasehold system, 55, 59, 313
Lebanon School (N.Y.), 87, 315
Lee, Mother Anne, 86, 314
Lee family, 384
Lee, Francis D. (archit.), 441

Lee, Gen. Henry, 435
Lee, Robert E., 465, 514
Lee, the Rev. Wm. Byrd, 487
Lee, Wm. R., 233
Lee Highway (Va.), 521
Leeds, William, 278
Leeland, Md., 169
Lehigh River (Penn.), 81, 379-80
Lehigh University, 380
Le Jau, the Rev. Francis, 425
L'Enfant, Pierre Charles (archit.), 295, 297
Lenni-Lenape Indians, 360
Leon (Sp.), 3
Leonardstown, Md., 163
Lesesne, Isaac, 423
Leslie, the Rev. Geo., 255
Lester & Pack, London (founders), 287, 305, 340, 342, 423-24
Le Tort, James, 395
Lewes, Del., 67
Lewis, F., 479
Lewis family (Va.), 489
Lewis, Wm., 354
Lexington, war ship, 348
Lexington, Mass. See Battle of
Lexington, Va., 523-24
Leyden (or Leiden), Holland, 13, 38
Liberal faction, Friends (Hicksite), 371
Liberty Bell, 287, 305, 340, 342, 424
Liberty County, Ga., 147
Liberty Hall Academy, 524
Liberty of conscience, religion. See Freedom
Libraries, 16, 264, 327, 517
Library of Congress, 269, 387, 510-11
Lightwood, Light'ard, Lighterknot, 143
Lime from shells, 95, 107, 109, 127, 264, 328, 423, 439
Lincoln, Abraham, 205, 384
Lincoln, Benjamin, 205
Lincoln, Mordacai, 384
Lincoln, Samuel, 205
Lincoln, R.I., 406
Lincoln, Va., 519
Linen manufacture, 248
Linesborough, N.H., 256
Lisbon, 48, 50
Litchfield, Conn., 230
Lititz, Penn., 81, 388, 517
Little Bretton Manor (Md.), 34, 162
Little Creek (Va.), 471
Little Choptank R. (Md.), 195
Little Egg Harbor, N.J., 72
Little Falls F.M.H. (No. 67), 183
Little Falls of the Potomac, 513-14
Little Fork Ch. (No. 338), 515-16
Little Fork Rangers (Va.), 516
Little River (S.C.), 442
Littleton, N.J., 270
Liturgy, Anglican in the Revolution, 233
Lively, Va., 503
Liverpool, frigate, 469
Livingston, Gilbert, 59, 313
Livingston, Philip, 308
Livingston, Robert, 308
Livingston, Gov. Wm. (N.Y.), 289
Livingston Manor, 55, 59, 305, 313, 316, 321, 323
Livingstone, Sir Richard, XIII, 548

Locke, John, 422
Log College (Penn.), 11, 65-66, 68, 264, 374-75
Log College Ch. See Neshaminy Ch.
Log structures, 6, 61-62, 75, 99-100, 122, 132, 139-41, 154, 164-65, 181, 183, 186, 258, 272, 279-80, 283-84, 290, 312, 316, 320, 322, 338, 340, 351-52, 354, 356-58, 360, 363-64, 368, 374, 380, 384, 389-92, 394-95, 397, 430, 445, 450, 520, 522, 525
Lollards, 37-38, 78
Longmeadow Hist. So. (Mass.), 229
Longmeadow M.H. (No. 106), 103, 229
London, Eng., 13, 31-32, 40, 49-50, 59, 71, 82, 95, 156, 168, 200, 209, 217, 233, 358, 287, 313, 323, 340, 460, 475, 477, 479, 518
London Bridge (Eng.), 460
London Bridge, Va., 473
London Yearly M. (Eng.), 74, 277, 352
Londonderry, N.H., N.Ire., 248, 257
Longfellow, Henry W., 216, 340, 344, 357, 414
Long Island, N.Y., 64, 301, 303, 310
Long Valley, N.J., 271
Longwood Gardens (Penn.), 359
Lopez, Aaron, 415
Lopez, Abraham, 50
Lopez, Moses, 50, 414, 417
Lord, the Rev. Joseph, 147, 432
Lothrop, the Rev. John, 39, 209
Lothrop's Hill (Mass.), 39, 209
Lottery, 340, 348, 364, 375, 394
Loudon County, Va., 512, 519
Louis XIV (Fr.), 324, 427
Louis XV (Fr.), 325
Louisa County, Va., 484-85
Louisburg, Nova Scotia, 150
Louisiana, 35, 324
Louisiana Purchase, 524
Lovefeast (agape), 76, 386
Lovely Lane Chapel, 19, 85, 141
Lovewell, Jonathan, 250
Low Country, the (S.C.), 21-22, 433, 442
Low Dutch, 57, 322
Lower Chapel, Middlesex (No. 326), 92, 96, 456, 481, 496, 497-98
Lower Dublin F.M., 346
Lower Southwark Ch. (No. 298), 460-61
Lowndes, Christopher, 169
Loyalists (royalists), 120, 128, 215, 424, 469
Lucas, Nicholas, 72
Lucena, Jas., 50
Ludwell family, Williamsburg, 453
Lum, Edmund, 501
Luther, Martin (reformer), 25, 37, 56, 64, 78-79, 146, 263, 517
Lutheran Ch., the, 57-58, 60, 178, 316, 321, 365-66
Lutheranism, 366
Lutherans, 2, 8, 19, 48, 54, 56-60, 79-80, 145, 180, 376, 387, 422
Luther's Catechisms, 58
Luray, Va., 520
Lusby, Md., 170
Lyall Memorial Federated Ch. (N.Y.), 313

Lynam, the Rev., Sion, 242
Lynch, Thos., Jr. (signer), 435
Lynn, Mass., 208
Lynn, Norfolk, Eng., 471
Lynnhaven Parish (Va.), 468, 470-73
Lyon, ship, 362

Mc

McBean, Thomas (archit.), 295
McCarty, Daniel, 511
McClenachan, the Rev. Wm., 343-44
McClintock, the Rev. Samuel, 242
McClun, Thos., 518
McCormick, Henry and Annie (Criswell), 395, 397
McCormick, Henry B. and Mary (Boyd), 397
McDowell, John, 522
McGregor, James, 248
McKean, Thomas (signer), 388
Mackenzie, the Rev. Aeneas, 297
McLain, the Rev. Alexander, 155-56
McNish, the Rev. George, 200

M

Madison, Dorothea (Payne), Dolly, 485
Madison, Pres. James 227
Madison, Bishop James (cousin of Pres.), 455, 547
Madison County, Va., 516-17
Magnein, Col. Bernard, 470
Mahew, Thomas, 42
Mahogany, 436
Mahwah, N.J., 271
Maidenhead, N.J., 274
Maimonides, 46
Maine: 41, 87; summary, map, 149; 252, 542
Makefield F.M.H. (No. 242), 378
Makemie, the Rev. Francis, 19, 67, 136, 198-200, 541
Makemie's Ch. (No. 83). See Rehoboth Ch.
Malaria, 145, 451, 488. *See also* mosquitoes
Malbone, Godfrey, family, 118-20, 411, 415
Malbone, Peter, 472
Malcolm, the Rev. Alexander, 232
Malden, Francis, 169
Mammy Morgan's Hill (Penn.), 380
Manchester, Eng., 86, 314
Manchester, N.H., 248
Mangohick Ch. (No. 323), 494-95
Mangohick Baptist Ch. (Negro), 494
Manhasset F.M.H. (No. 171), 299
Manhattan, N.Y., 54, 262, 295, 542
Manigault, Gabriel, 423, 428
Manning, the Rev. James, 404
Manokin Presbyn. Ch. (No. 81), 198
Manor Ch. (No. 59), 176
Manorial system: Md., 28, 34; N.Y., 55
Mansfeld, Germ., 517
Mantapike Creek (Va.), 490
Marblehead, Mass. 232
Marcus Hook, Penn. 353

Marion, Gen. Francis, 431, 435, 437
Marion, Gabriel, 437
Markeley's Old Field (S.C.), 430
Market Street Ch., Phila., 348
Marl, 97, 109, 482
Marlborough, Mass., 258
Marranism, 47
Marranos, 47-48, 50, 414
Marrett, the Rev. John, 220
Marshall, Abraham, 361
Marshall, Christopher, 350
Marshall, the Rev. Geo., 26
Marshall, Humphrey and Abraham, 361
Marshall, Chief Justice John, 388, 455, 457, 581
Marshall, the Rev. John Rutgers, 128
Marshallton F.M.H. (No. 227), 361
Marsteler, F., 366
Marston, the Rev. Edward, 433
Marston Parish (Va.), 453
Martin, John, 462
Martin's Brandon Parish, 462-64
Martyrdom, 40, 70
Martyrs, 4, 38, 40, 75, 78, 86
Mary I, Tudor, 4, 13, 28, 48
Mary II, 455
Mary Stuart, Queen of Scots, 5
Maryland: 3, 8-9, 16, 18-21, 27-29, 31-35, 58-59; summary, 158-60; map, 159; 186, 189, 232, 347, 518
Maryland Charter, 18, 27-29, 31
Maryland Hunt, 176
Maryland Yearly M., 19
Marybone Chapel (London), 102, 404
Maryville, Tenn., 524
Mason (stone, brick), 122, 127, 132
Mason, George, 454, 510-12, 514
Mason, George Carrington, 451, 474, 477, 484, 490-91, 494-95, 543, *548*
Mason, John, 252
Mason and Dixon Line, 9, 186
Masonian Grant, 252, 254, 257
Masonic. See Freemasons
Mass house, 8, 184, 392
Massachusetts: 14, 37, 39-41, 87; summary, 202; map, 203; 215, 253, 255, 314
Mass. Bay Colony, 39, 147, 209, 403
Massacres, 2, 23, 48, 56, 256, 263, 280, 315, 328, 382, 436, 444, 458, 477-78, 480, 522
Massey, the Rev. Lee, 511
Masson (so spelled in history of St. Michael's Marblehead). See Mossom
Mather, Cotton, 41
Mather, Increase, 41
Matias, Jacob Ebli, 368
Matinecock F.M.H. (No. 172), 299
Matisse, Henri, XI, XII
Matlack, Col. Timothy, 350
Mattacopany, 290
Mattaponi R. (Va.), 484, 489, 491
Mattapony Ch. (No. 320), 94, 485, 489-91
Mattapony Bap. Ch. (Va.), 491
May, Robert, & Co., London (designers of houses), 137
Maybank, David and John F., 433
Mayflower, ship, 14, 38
Maynadier, the Rev. Daniel and wife,

Hannah (Martin), 194
Maytown, Penn., 390
Maxcy's Pond, 212
Meacham, Jos., 86-87, 314
Meade, Bishop Wm., 461, 497, 499, 501-04; mother, 506; 508, 510, 514, 516, *548*
Mears & Stainbank, London (founders), 424
Mease, the Rev. Wm., 476
Meaux, France, 64
Medfield, Mass., 223
Medomak R. (Me.), 154
Medway R. (Ga.), 148
Meeting House Cove (Me.), 154
Meeting House Spring (Carlisle, Penn.), 67, 393-95
Meeting house, the N.E., 43
Mendez, Simon, 50, 414
Mendham F.M.H., N.J., 270
Mendon, Mass., 226
Menendez, Don Pedro de Aviles, 2
Menno Simons (reformer), 75
Mennonite M.H. (No. 213), 75, 107, 350-52
Mennonites, 8, 58, 75-76, 178, 350, 364, 383, 518, 520
Mercersburg, Penn., 388
Merchants Club of Baltimore, 141
Merchant's Hope Ch. (No. 299), 94, 96, 462-66
Merion F.M.H. (No. 229), 73, 109, 354-55, 362-63, 541
Merrimack (Merrimac) R., 234, 243-44
Meshanticut F.M. (R.I.), 406
Methodism, 24-26, 42, 78, 80, 82-84, 263, 343-45, 379
Methodist Church, the, 8
Methodist conferences, 141, 345
Methodist Epis. Ch. in Amer., the, 19, 24, 84-85, 134, 141, 343-45, 366, 525, 542
Methodist Lower Chapel. See Lower Chapel (No. 326)
Methodists, 6, 8, 19, 82-85, 179, 242-44, 422, 490, 492, 498, 505-06
Methuen, Mass., 243
Metropolitan Museum of Art, 297, 328
Metapannay (Mattapany) plantation, 31
Mexico, 3
Mexican War, 397, 437
Michael, M.M., 368
Mid-Atlantic, 53-90
Middens, Indian (shell), 107, 423, 488
Middle Ages, 10
Middle Haddam, Conn., 129
Middle Plantation, Parish (Va.), 453
Middle R. (Va.), 522
Middle Spring (Penn.), 393
Middleburg, N.Y., 59, 322-23, 367
Middleburg Dutch Ch. (No. 196), 55, 59, 323-24
Middleham Chapel (No. 53), 169-70
Middlesex County, Va., 489, 491, 496, 501
Middleton, Arthur, 425
Middleton, Thos., 423
Middleton Place (S.C.), 431
Middletown, Conn., 129

Middletown, Del., 140
Middletown, Penn., 399
Middletown F.M. (Penn.), 373
Midway Ch. (No. 30), 26, 147-48, 432
Mifflin, Gen. Thomas, 388
Mikveh Israel Synagogue, 49-50, 414
Mill Brook (N.J.), 270
Mill Creek Ch. (No. 342), 17, 99, 520
Millbrook, N.Y., 312
Millennial Church, 86
Miller, John, 358
Miller, The Rev. John, 221, 315
Miller, Peter, 386
Millstone, 196, 275
Millville, Mass., 226
Minaquas Indians, 61
Minuit, Peter, 61
Mispillion, Del., 78, 139
Missions, 34-35, 56, 60, 62, 64, 66, 74, 80-81, 88, 133, 230, 346, 380
Mississippi R., 3, 324, 524
Mitchell, Joseph, 472
Mobjack Bay (Va.), 486, 488
Mohammed, 46
Mohammedans, 46-47
Mohawk castles, the, 318
Mohawk, N.Y., 318, 320
Mohawk Indians, 59, 315-16, 323
Mohawk reservation, Canada, 319
Mohawk R., 41, 55-56, 59, 313, 315-18, 320-21
Monadnock No. 8 (tract), 254
Monastery, 385
Monck's Corner, S.C., 428
Monckton, Lt. Col., 277
Moncure, the Rev. John, and family (Va.), 508, 510
Monocacy Cr. (Penn.), 81, 379
Monocacy R. (Md.), 180
Monroe County, W. Va., 525
Monroe, Pres. James, 455
Montgomery County, Penn., 69, 73, 76
Montgomery (linen weaver), 248
Moore, Bishop (Va.), 477
Moore, Justice Alfred, 331
Moore House, Yorktown, 482
Moorestown, N.J., 288
Moorish kingdoms (Sp.), 3, 44, 46
Moors, the, 3, 46-47, 414
Moor's Indian Charity School, 318
Moravia, 1, 79, 332, 379
Moravian Burying Ground, 380
Moravian Ch., the: 24, 57, 62, 78; catechism, 78; 263, 283, 366, 379, 541-42
Moravian Chapel, Bethlehem (No. 244), 25, 57, 80-81, 379-80, 541
Moravian Ch., Central, Bethlehem, 380
Moravian Ch., Bethabara (No. 201), 9, 23, 81, 331, 380
Moravian Ch., N.J. (No. 150), 81, 283
Moravian College and Theo. Sem., 380
Moravian Provinces, North, South, 81
Moravians, 9, 23-25, 53, 57, 78, 82-83, 331-32, 379-80, 517
Moray, the Rev. Alexander, 486
More, Father Henry, S.J., 32
Morgan family, 305
Morgan's Rifle Brigade (Va.), 524

Morris, Robert, 194, 308, 341, 388
Morrison, Joseph, 248
Morritt, the Rev. Thos., 435
Mortlake Manor, 119
Mortmain (Eng. law), 32
Morton, the Rev. Andrew, 272
Moses Brown School, 418
Moses, George H., 256, 548
Moslems, 46
Mosley, the Rev. Richard, L.L.B., 120
Mosquitoes, 22, 330, 433
Mossom, the Rev. David, 232, 480, 483
Mother Ann. See Lee
Motte, Jacob, 435
Motte, Rebecca (Brewton) (heroine of Revolution), 435
Mount Air plantation (Va.), 485
Mount Holly F.M.H. (No. 163), 289
Mount Laurel F.M.H. (No. 161), 107, 288
Mount Lebanon, N.Y., 9, 85, 314-15
Mount Pleasant, S.C., 433
Mount Pleasant, Va., 524
Mount St. Alban (D.C.), 168
Mount Vernon (Va.), 167, 483, 508, 510-12, 514
Moultrie, Gen. Wm., 431
Moved buildings, 103, 121, 154, 227, 229, 231, 253, 412, 418, 445
Moylan, Gen. Stephen, 348
Mt. Greylock (Mass.), 231
Mt. Monadnock, 252, 254
Mt. Sinai Bap. Ch. (Va.) (Negro), 495
Muddy Cr. Ch. (Va.), 506-07
Mueller, I., 366
Muhlenberg family, 60
Muhlenberg, Anna Maria (Weiser), 367, 387
Muhlenberg, the Rev. Frederick Augustus (speaker of the House), 367
Muhlenberg, the Rev. Gotthilf Henry Ernst, 388
Muhlenberg, the Rev. Henry Melchior, 56, 59-60, 80, 180, 263, 358, 364-67, 388, 399
Muhlenberg, the Rev. Gen. Peter Gabriel, 367
Muhlenberg College, 366
Muller, David, 318
Mullion brick, 18, 93, 95, 129, 459
Mumford, Stephen, 412
Munday, Richard (archit.), 102, 410, 412
Munich, Germ., 460
Murray, John, Lord Dunmore, 469
Musconetcong, N.J., 272
My Lady's Manor (Md.), 176
Mystics, 77, 338, 385

N

Nain, Penn., 380
Nairnshire, Scotland, 440, 482, 499
Namozine Chapel, Creek, 464
Nandue Ch. (Va.), 474
Nansemond County, Va., 14, 17, 466-67, 470, 472, 476
Nantucket Is., Mass., 211
Napoleon Bonaparte, XV

Narcossee, Fla., 87
Narragansett Indians, 419
Narragansetts No. 6 (tract), 227, 250
Narragansett Parish (No. 265), 408
Naraticon, N.J., 284
Nashua, N.H., 250
National Cathedral, Wash., D.C., 168
National Historic Site, 305, 338, 417
National Museum, Wash., D.C., 340
National Shrine, 341, 460
Nationalism, 1, 2, 5, 45, 49
Natural Bridge, Va., 524
Naval stores, 59, 313, 321
Navarre, 46
Navigation, 47
Nazareth, Penn., 81, 379-80
Neale, Father Bennett, S.J., 184
Neale, Sister Emma, 315
Negroes, 81, 119-20, 142, 148, 308, 310, 352, 379, 422, 425, 431, 461, 469, 494-95. See also Slaves
Nehardea, Babylonia, 45
Neher, Carl, 313
Neiser, Wensel, 82
Neisser family, Moravians, 79
Nelliston, N.Y., 318
Nelson County, Va., 499
Nelson family (Va.), 483, 485
Nequasset M.H. (No. 34), 153
Nero, Emperor, 45
Neshaminy Ch. (No. 238), 11, 65-66, 68, 109, 136, 265, 374-75
Neshaminy Monthly M. (Penn.), 373
Netherland Dancers, 86
Netherlands, 4, 5, 33, 48-49, 75, 93
New Amsterdam, 49, 284, 295, 304
New Bedford, Mass., 208
New Beverly, N.J., 287
New Britain, Conn., 125
New Brunswick, N.J., 57, 136, 263, 270-71
New Building, the (Phila.), 83, 344
New Castle, Del., 56-57, 135-36, 359, 389, 396, 485, 522
New Castle, Me., 150
New Castle, N.Y., 307
New Castle Dutch Church, 263
New Castle Presbyn. Ch. (No. 17), 57, 67, 69
New Ch., King and Queen, 490
New England, 1, 7-8, 11, 14, 40-43, 147, 232
New Eng. church society, the, 8
New Eng. Cross Roads, N.J., 279-80, 304
New Eng. town, the, 8
New England Way, the, 40
New England Yearly M., 73-74
New France, 3, 27, 325, 438
New Garden F.M.H. (No. 224), 358
New Hampshire: 7, 87-88; summary, 238; map, 239; 445
New Haven, Conn., 127; First Ch., 250
New Jersey: 1, 10, 14, 40-42, 54, 56-57, 59, 64, 66, 70-71, 77-78, 155; summary, 259-60; map, 261; 271, 286-87, 542
New Kent County, Va., 483-84, 486, 489, 491
New Lebanon, N.Y., 314

New (now Mount) Lebanon Society (N.Y.), 86-87
New Lights, 68, 83, 234, 250, 344, 374, 394, 397
New Marlborough, N.H., 258
New Milford, Me., 157
New Netherland, ship, 54
New Netherland, province of, 56, 60, 62, 87-88
New Old South Third Ch., Boston, 213
New Orleans, La., 3, 27, 417
New Providence Ch. (No. 231), 365-66
New Prov. Presbyn. Ch. (Va.), 523
New School (faction). See New Lights, New Side
New Side (faction), 26, 60, 62, 68, 276, 281, 366, 397, 485, 522
New Sweden, 61, 79, 132-33, 284, 237
New World, 2, 414
New York City, 16, 49-50, 86, 120, 295, 314, 323, 414, 542
New York Monthly M., 298-99
New York Provincial Council, 308-09
New York State: 1, 3, 10, 23, 27, 40-41, 54, 57, 59, 70, 74, 87, 180, 232, 271; summary, 292, 294; map, 293; 298, 329, 445, 542
New York Yearly M., 73-74, 231, 270, 312
Newark Monthly M. (Del.-Penn.), 359
Newark Preparative Meeting, 138
Newark Presbyn. Ch. (No. 132), 11, 41, 65, 107, 264-66, 281
Newburgh, N.Y., 308
Newbury, Mass., 232, 234, 247
Newburyport, Mass., 25, 42, 234, 413
Newfoundland, 28
Newington M.H. (No. 115), 240-41, 541
Newlin, Nicholas, 353
Newmarch, the Rev. John, 150
Newport, R.I., 43, 49, 50-51, 57, 118-20, 213, 232, 408, 412-14, 418
Newport, Cap. Christopher, 458, 480
Newport F.M.H., Old (No. 266), 19, 40, 101, 408-09, 419, 542
Newport Hist. So., 101, 412
Newport, Isle of Wight, Eng., 458
Newport Parish (Va.), 458-59
Newport River (Ga.), 148
Newton, F.M. (N.J.), 282
Newton Manor (Md.), 34, 161
Newton Presbyn. Ch. (No. 239), 69, 107, 375
Newton Square F.M.H. (No. 220), 108, 354-55
Niagara R. (N.Y.), 56, 324-25
Nicholas, the Rev. Mr., 356
Nicholson, Gov. Sir Francis, 41, 175, 232, 410, 474, 482
Nicholson, Samuel and Ann, 282
Nine Partners F.M.H. (No. 187), 312-13
Niskayuna (N.Y.), 86
Nitschmann, Bishop David, 80-81, 379, 542
Nockamixon, Penn., 376
Nominy Ch. (Va.), 504
Non-Conformists (Non-Cons), 19, 40, 70, 119, 422
Non-Jurors, 16, 128
Norfolk, Va., 468, 469
Norfolk County, Va., 466, 468-69, 476
Norris, Isaac, 364
Norristown, Penn., 364
Norriton Presbyn. M.H. (No. 230), 69, 105, 108, 364, 541
North Africa, 46
North America, 1, 2, 5, 13, 49
North Anna R. (Va.), 484
North Beverly Cong'l Ch. (No. 111), 233-34
North Carolina: 9, 22, 23, 81; summary, map, 326; 328, 330-32, 542
North Carolina Yearly M., 73
North Ch., Congl., Nantucket, 211
North Congl. Ch., Portsmouth, N.H., 242
North Elk Parish, Md., 187
North Farnum Ch. (No. 328), 94, 500
Northampton, Mass., 230, 413
Northampton County, Penn., 76
Northhampton County, Va., 473-74
Northeast Creek, River, (Md.), 187
Northern Ireland, 1, 19, 67, 68-69, 136, 199, 249, 255, 280, 374, 376, 389-90, 394, 396-97, 522
North Mountain Presbyn. Ch. (Va.), 523
North Pembroke, Mass., 208
North R. (the Hudson), 56, 60
North Salem, N.Y., 307
North Shore M.H., Nantucket, 211
North Vestry, Nantucket (No. 93), 211
North Virginia (territory), 5, 13
Northern Neck of Va., 501, 504, 506, 508, 510, 512, 515
Northumberland County, Va., 501, 504
Norton, the Rev. John, 204
Norwood, Mass., 223
Notley, Gov. (Md.), 33
Nottingham Lots, 186
Nottingham Monthly Meeting, 185
Nova Caesarea (New Jersey), 54
Nova Scotia, 232-33, 258
Nowadaga Creek (N.Y.), 318
Number 6 tract, N.H., 257
Nuremberg, Germ., 79
Nuswattocks Parish (Va.), 473
Nutfield, N.H., 248
Nys, Joannes (silversmith), 140

O

Oak Lawn Bap. Ch. (R.I.), 406
Oak Shade, Va., 516
Oak Timbers, 100, 124
Oakdale, L.I., 303
Oakmont, Penn., 354
Oaks: St. Anne's, 140; St. George's, 163; Wye, 191; live, 254, 440; Crosswicks, 291; Witness, 390
Oaks Plantation (S.C.), 423
Oath of loyalty, 128
Oaths of allegiance and supremacy, 28
Oblong F.M.H. (No. 184), 310
Occahannock Ch. (Va.), 474
Occoquan, Va., 510
Occupacia Creek (Va.), 499
Occupation, British, 24, 343-44, 348, 388, 413, 417, 419, 435, 441, 469
Oceana Naval Air Base (Va.), 473
Ockanickon, Indian Chief, 287
Odenheimer, Bishop Wm. H., 287
Odessa, Del., 137-38
Offley Plantation (Va.), 485
Oglethorpe, Gen. Jas. Edward, 23-24, 26, 145, 148, 423
Ohio, 6, 73, 87, 357, 376, 394, 522
Ohio Yearly M., 409, 418
Old Brick Ch., Isle of Wight (No. 297), XIV, 92-93, 95, 451, 453, 458-60, 540, 542
Old Lights (faction), 68, 234, 250, 374, 394, 397
Old North Ch., Boston (No. 96), 97, 102-03, 215-16, 410
Old Point Comfort, Va., 476-77
Old School Bap. Ch. (No. 141), 78, 273
Old Session House, Hershey, Penn., 397
Old Ship M.H. (No. 87), 11, 42, 100, 193, 204-06, 225, 246, 303, 541
Old Side (faction), 26, 42, 68, 397, 485
Old South Ch., Newburyport (No. 112), 25, 42, 103, 234
Old South M.H., Boston (No. 94), 26, 40, 97, 101, 124, 213, 215, 227
Old Stone Ch., Red Hook (No. 188), 59, 108, 313, 541
Old Stone Church, Schoharie (No. 195), 107, 321-22
Old Swedes, Wilmington (No. 13), 61, 109, 132-33, 284, 338, 542
Old Town Cr. (N.C.), 327
Old White Ch. (No. 287), 95, 109, 439, 423
Oldfield plantation (S.C.), 437
Oldwick, N.J., 271
Oley, Penn., 384
Oliphant's Hill, 283
Olivet Baptist Ch. (Va.), 490
Ompompanoosuc R. (Vt.), 445
Onancock Ch. (Va.), 474
Onderdonk, Bishop Benjamin Treadwell, 303
"One in Many," principle of, XIV, XV, 45
Onions, 122
Opechancanough, Chief, 477
Opequan Cr. (Va.), 518
Orange Quarter (S.C.), 427
Orange County, Va., 516, 518, 521-22
Oratam, Indian Chief, 262
Orchestra, 338
Ordination, Episcopal, 15, 542
Organs, 124, 342, 388, 404, 411, 423, 435, 439, 454, 474, 481, 517
Orphanage (Missionary training school), Halle, 60, 80, 365-66
Orphanages, 24-26, 80-81, 145, 365, 379
Orthodox Friends (conservative faction), 300, 352, 371
Orton Plantation (N.C.), 330
Oswego, N.Y., 325
Otterbein, Bishop Philip Wm., 58, 178
Otterbein Ch. (No. 62), 20, 58, 97, 178, 541

Ottsville, Penn., 376
Overwharton Parish (Va.), 508, 510
Oxen, 120, 208
Oxenstjerna, Axel, 61, 79
Oxford F.M. (Penn.), 346, 352, 369
Oxford Univ., 14, 16, 82, 119, 204, 411, 546
Oyster Bay, L.I., 299

P

Page County, Va., 520
Page, Francis, 453
Page, John, 453-54
Page, the Rev. John, 244
Page family (Va.), 485, 489
Page's Chapel (Md.), 168, 542
Paine, Thomas, 382
Painters, 342-43, 392, 417
Palfrey, Col., 219
Palmer, Cotton, 412-13
Palmer, Evans, 440
Palestine, XIV, 45-46
Palladian windows, 95, 140, 163, 342, 348, 435-36, 513
Palladio, Andrea (archit.), 248
Palatinate of Md., 28
Palatinate, Rhine, 59, 77
Palatine Bridge, N.Y., 59, 316
Palatine Ch. (No. 192), 59, 107, 109, 318-19
Palatines (Rhine Palatinate), 59, 271, 305, 313, 316, 318, 320-23, 385, 517
Pamlico R., Sound, 327
Pamticoe Parish, 327
Pamunkey R. (Va.), 483-84, 489, 491-92, 494-95
Paper mill, first, 350
Papist Priest, 19
"Paradice" tract, 184
Paramaribo, 50, 414
Parish clerk, Anglican, 494
Parishes (Va.), 15
Park Hill Congl. Ch. (No. 126), 103, 253
Parker, the Rev. Samuel, 120
Parliament, 14, 19, 25, 27, 78-80, 128, 217
Parnassus Plantation (S.C.), 423, 426, 428
Parochial chapel of ease, 428, 430, 434
Parsons, Jas., 513, 515
Parsons, the Rev. John, 506
Parsons, the Rev Jonathan, 234, 236
Parsons, Maj. Gen. Samuel Holden, 236
"Parsons Cause," the, 485
Parris Is., S.C., 438 (misspelled)
Pasteur, Jas., 468
Passaic, N.J., 56
Pastorius, Francis Daniel, 75, 351
Patapsco F.M.H. (No. 61), 177
Patapsco R., 177, 179
Paton, the Rev. Anthony, 482
Patriarch, 180
Patronage of chs., 28
Patroonships, 55, 305, 313
Patterson, N.Y., 310
Patuxent Indians, 31

Patuxent R. (Md.), 164
Pawlett, Cap. Thos., 479
Paxtang, Penn., 68, 395-97
Paxton: Presbyn. Ch. (No. 258), 68, 106, 396-97; family, 397
Payne, Dorothea (Dolly Madison), 485
Payne, Edward, 511
Payne, Wm. Sr., 514
Payne's Ch. (Va.), 514
Peanckatanck Parish (Va.), 496, 498, 501
Peace with Great Britain, 229
Peach Lake F.M.H. (No. 181), 307
Peale, Charles Wilson (painter), 343
Pearson, L., 166
Peck, the Rev. Jeremiah, 266
Pee Dee R., Great, 437
Peekskill, N.Y., 306
Pelham, N.Y., 304
Pelican symbol, 426
Pell, Thomas, 304
Pell's Point, N.Y., 304
Pellentz, Father James, 392
Pemberton, N.J., 290
Pembroke Cr. (N.C.), 328
Pembroke Farm (Va.), 476
Pembroke F.M.H. (No. 90), 208
Pencader Hundred (Del.), 139
Pendleton, Edmund, 454
Peninsula, the, Del., 141
Penn family, 9, 28, 341-42, 364, 382, 394
Penn, James, 287
Penn, Gov. John, 281, 341, 399
Penn, Richard, 342
Penn, Thomas, 342, 382, 390
Penn, Admiral Sir Wm. (Sr.), 72
Penn, Wm., 9-10, 33, 35, 70-74, 77, 139, 186, 193, 277, 282, 287-89, 340, 350, 354-55, 360, 362-63, 372-74
Penn Charter, the, 36, 70, 72, 347
Pennamite-Yankee War, 382
Pennsborough, Penn., 393-95
Pennsbury Manor (Penn.), 372
Pennsylvania: 8-10, 17, 19-20, 25, 28, 35-36, 58-59, 66, 68, 70, 72; the Great Law of, 72; 77, 80-82, 139, 178, 185, 271, 332, 342, 347, 351-52; summary, 333-34, 336; map, 335; 364, 382, 388, 397, 517-20
Pennsylvania College, University, 84, 344
"Pennsylvania Dutch," 58, 76, 350
Penn. Hist. and Museum Com., 77, 387
Pennsylvania Railroad, 133
Pennybacker, D., 520
Penobscot Bay, 13
Penola, Va., 495
Pentacostal, 353
Peppercorn, 353
Pepperell, Sir. Wm., Lady, 150
Pepper's Branch, 142
Pequot Indian, 211
Perkiomen Valley, 366
Perry, Commodore Matthew, 81
Perry, Commodore Oliver Hazard, 417
Persecution, 2, 4, 13, 21, 24-26, 35, 38, 40-41, 44, 46-47, 64, 70-71, 73, 76, 78-81, 145, 351, 379, 427
Persia, 44-45

Perth Amboy, N.J., 269, 271, 278, 286-87
Peru, 2
Peters, James, 257
Peters, the Rev. Samuel, 255
Peter's Point (Va.), 464
Petersburg, Va., 464-65
Petersburg Ladies Memorial Assn., 465
Petsworth Ch., Parish (Va.), 486-88
Pew: building private, 129; — ground, 227, 241, governor's 230, 331
Pewter, 156, 382, 395, 397, 472, 517
Phila., Penn. 1, 17, 36, 49, 62, 66, 70, 74, 76, 81, 83-84, 137, 140, 288, 337-38, 340, 342-49, 355, 362, 379, 414, 419, 483, 485, 523
Phila. Gen. Meeting of Friends, 371
Phila. Militia, 348
Phila. Museum of Art, XI, 415
Phila. Prot. Epis. City Mission, 344
Phila. Quarterly M., 352, 363, 370
Phila. Synod, 374, 485
Phila. Yearly M.: 72-75, 138, 185, 270, 288, 355, 371; reunion, 371, 518
Philharmonic Society, 380
Philip of Burgundy, 48
Philip II (Sp.), 3-5, 48-49
Philipsburgh Manor, 55, 305
Philipse family, 305
Philipse, Frederick, 55, 305
Phillips, Lt. Gov. Wm., 227
Phillipston Congl. Ch. (No. 105), 227
Philosophical So., Newport, 50, 414
Piankatank R. (Va.), 496-97
Piedmontese, 24
Pierson, the Rev. Abraham, Sr. and Jr., 11, 41-42, 65, 264, 267
Pietetism, Pietists, 56-60, 77, 79-80, 83, 178, 263, 276, 365-66, 379-80, 385
Pilgrim Fathers, 13-14, 37-38
Pilgrims, 8, 39, 100, 204, 206, 403
Pilmoor, the Rev. Jos., 84, 344-45
Pinckney family, 305, 423
Pine, 59, 143, 323
Pine Street Presbyn. Ch. (No. 211), 67, 348
Pioneers' Village, Salem, Mass., 99
Pirates, 23, 31, 327. See also Buccaneers
Piscataqua, Me., 150
Piscataway, N.J., 269
Piscataway Indians, 31
Piscataway Parish, Md. (No. 48), 167
Pitman, the, 99
Pitt, William, 213
Pittsburgh, Penn., 521
Pittstown, N.J., 272
Plainfield F.M.H. (No. 136), 269
Plantation, the (Va.), 477
Plate, collection, 192
Plater, George, 163
Plato (philosopher), XIV, 45
Plymouth, Eng., 147
Plymouth, Mass., 14, 18, 37
Plymouth, N.H., 157
Plymouth Colony, 38-41, 208-09, 403
Plymouth Company, 5, 38
Plymouth Meeting F.M.H. (No. 233), 108, 369

Plumstead F.M.H. (No. 243), 378-9
Pocahontas, 450, 473, 476, 480, 488
Pocomoke R. (Md.), 199-200
Pocotaligo, S.C., 440
Poetquesink F.M., 346
Pohick Ch. (No. 335), 95, 508, 510-15
Poland, 79, 414
Polity, church gov., 9-11, 14-15, 37-38, 53, 58, 63, 80
Pomfret, 116, 118-19
Pomfret, Lord, 382
Pompion Hill Chapel (No. 276), XIV, 2, 21, 422, 426-28, 430, 436
Pongoteaque Ch. (No. 309), 94, 474-75
Poole, Md., 184
Pope, the, 2-4, 27
Pope John XXIII, XV
Pope Leo III, XV
Pope Pius VII, 348
Popery, 19
Popham, Sir John, George (colony), 153
Poplar Hill Ch. (No. 40), 163
Poplar Hundred (Md.), 163
Poplar Spring Ch. (Va.), 474, 487
Poquoson Parish (Va.), 482
Porcher, Philip, 437
Port Royal, Acadia, 230
Port Royal Harbor (S.C.), 2
Port Royal Is. (S.C.), 21, 438
Port Royal R. (S.C.), 440
Port Republic, Md., 169
Porter, the Rev. Noah, Sr. (pastor), 124
Porter, the Rev. Noah, Jr. (pres. of Yale), 124
Porter, Miss Sarah (Miss Porter's School), 124
Porticos, pillared, 7, 94-95, 103, 215, 423, 434, 439-40
Portsmouth, N.H., 150, 242, 247
Portsmouth, R.I., 408, 418
Portsmouth F.M.H. (No. 272), 418
Portsmouth Parish (Va.), 468, 470
Portugal, 1-4, 44, 46-48
Portuguese, the, 2, 47, 414
Portuguese Jews, 24, 44
Potash, 414
Potomac Parish (Va.), 506, 508
Potomac R., 28, 30, 161-62, 166-67, 501, 506-08, 510-12, 514, 518-19
Potts, Frederick A.
Powel, Samuel, 343
Powhatan, Chief, 450, 480, 488
Powhatan County, Va., 480
Powhatan R. (the James), 6, 475
Pownalborough, Me., 157
Poughkeepsie, N.Y., 309-10
Prague Univ., 79
Prayer Book, 15, 278, 297, 302, 318, 507. *See also* Book of Common Prayer
Prayers for the king, 129, 309, 343, 356, 358, 408, 426
Prelacy, 19
Presbyn. Ch. in Amer., 199-200, 264
Presbyn. Ch., New Castle (No. 17), 96, 136-37
Presbyn. Ch., First, Wilmington (No. 14), 96, 134
Presbyterians, 8, 10-11, 16-17, 19-21, 26, 40, 42-43, 53, 57, 63-69, 83, 198-99, 211, 247, 263, 271, 304, 344-45, 364, 374, 394, 422, 437-38, 442, 483-84, 505-06, 521-22, 541
Presbyterianism, 10-11, 14, 37-38, 42, 53, 63
Presbytery, 13, 17, 63
Presbytery of Carlisle, 393
Presbytery of the Eastward, 236
Presbytery of Hanover. *See* H.
Presbytery of James Is. (S.C.), 442
Presbytery of Laggan, 67
Presbytery of New Castle, 67, 136, 390
Presbytery of N.Y., 68
Presbytery of Phila., 19, 67, 136, 199, 264, 375, 541
Presiding Bishop, 340
Prevent Danger (tract), 169
Price, Wm., 215
Priest Neale's Mass House (No. 68), 34, 184
Priest's house, 8
Primitive Baptists, 78, 139
Primitive Meeting of Friends, 372
Prince Charles (Scot.), 440
Prince Charles County, Va., 461
Prince Frederick Parish, 435, 437
Prince George County, Va., 462, 478
Prince George's Chapel (No. 25), 142-43, 201
Prince George's Ch., Winyah (No. 283), 434-35, 437
Prince of Orange, Wm. III, 33
Prince Wm. County (Va.), 508, 510-12
Prince Wm., Duke of Cumberland, 440
Prince Wm.'s Ch., Sheldon (No. 288). *See* Sheldon Ch.
Princess Anne, Md., 198
Princess Anne County, Va., 470-72
Princeton College, Univ., 11, 65, 68, 242, 264-65, 281, 375, 485. *See also* College of N.J.
Pringle, Robert, 423
Printing: 77, 79, 83, 344-45, 351, 380, 387, 445; press, 387, 445
Prinzhof, Penn., 337
Printz, Gov. Johan, 61, 337
Prisoners of war, 146, 308, 375
Privateering, 119, 411
Privy Council, com. on Amer. plantations, 29
Prof. of Medicine, 348
Prophesy, 86
Protectorate, the, 40
Protector and Supreme Head, Eng. Ch., 27
Protestant, XV, 1, 5
Protestant Assn., the, etc. (Md.), 33
Protestant Epis. Ch., ancient, 25, 78, 80, 332, 541
Prot. Epis. Ch. in Amer.: 17, 63; name, 89; 90, 128, 189, 270-71, 283-84, 338-40, 454, 481
Protestant Monastery, 77, 541
Protestantism, 4, 27, 33, 48-49
Protestants, 1-6, 13, 17, 24-26, 29, 33, 49, 53-90, 438, 541
Providence (Annapolis), Md., 33
Providence, R.I., 39, 208, 403-05
Providence Ch. (Penn.), 364
Providence County, Md., 172
Providence F.M.H. (No. 261), 404-06
Providence Plantation (Province of R.I.), 405, 408
Provincial Congress, Mass., 233
Pulaski, Gen. Count Casimir, 361
Pulpits, three-decker, 411, 491, 502, 510
Puncheons, 397, 450, 523
Pungo Chapel (Va.), 471
Pungoteague, Va., 474
Puritan Commonwealth of Eng., of Mass., 70
Puritan Presbyn. Ch., 64-65. *See also* Congl. with Presbyn. leanings
Puritanism, 14, 37, 39-40, 43, 63-64, 148, 209
puritans, 13-14, 25-26, 38-39, 41
Puritans, 8, 11, 14-15, 17, 19, 29, 33, 40, 42, 100, 172, 213, 215, 218, 232-34, 248, 264, 279, 301-02, 403, 466, 472, 488
Purton Bay (Va.), 488
Putnam, Gen. Israel, 118-20, 308
Putnam, Col. Daniel, 120
Putney Hill, 256
Putney's Fort, 256
Putlogs, 141

Q

Queen Anne: 29, 59, 89, 286, 313, 323, 327, 462; gifts, 135, 140, 171, 187, 200, 278, 286, 297, 340, 408, 410, 474, 499
Queen Anne Parish (Md.), 169
Queen Anne's Bounty, 327
Queen Anne's County, Md., 191
Queen Anne's Creek, 328
Queen Anne's Town, 328
Queen Anne's War, 221, 425, 444
Queen's Chapel, Boston, 40
Queen's College (Rutgers), 12, 57, 263
Queen's Light Dragoons, 213
Queenstown, Md., 192
Quaker burying ground, 176-77, 419
Quaker Hill, N.Y., 310
Quakerism, 10, 70-72, 405, 409
Quakers: 16, 22, 34, 36, 40, 53, 70-75, 81, 86, 88-89, 171, 193, 208, 211, 310, 342-43, 345-46, 360, 362, 392, 408, 422, 466, 485, 518-19; birth-right, convinced, 74; execution of, 208; free, fighting, 186, 349-50, 419; Hiksite (liberal faction), or-thodox (conservative faction), 74; Irish, 391. *See also* Friends
Quebec: 3, 27, 324; expedition, 236, 257
Quincy, Josiah, 213
Quiney, Richard and Thomas, 462
Quinnipiac River, 127

R

Raccoon (N.J.), 62
Raccoon Creek, N.J., 284

Race Street Friends (liberal faction, Hicksite), 352, 372
Race St. Yearly M., 74-75
Radical party (Penn.), 73
Radnor (Penn.), 73
Radnor F.M.H. (No. 221), 354-55, 362-63
Raikes, Robt. (Sunday school, Eng.), 25
Raising of frame: 7, 120, 204, 225, 230, 234, 243, 258; hazards, 124
Raleigh, Sir Walter, 2, 13, 22, 153, 438
Rancocas F.M.H. (No. 162), 93, 288
Randolph family (Va.): Edmund, 481; Sir John, 457, 480; Peyton, 454, 457; Richard, 480
Randolph, Fitz, family (N.J.): Edward, 270; Hartshorn, 270
Randolph F.M.H. (No. 137), 270
Rappahannock County, Va., 498-500
Rappahannock Indians, 502
Rappahannock R. (Va.), 496-99, 501, 504, 506-08, 510, 516
Raritan Ch. (N.J.), 57
Raritan Dutch Ch. (N.J.), 263
Raritan R. (N.J.), 57
Raritan R. (Va.), 516-17
Ratcliffe, the Rev. Robt., 213
Ravanel, Beatrice St. Julien, 431, *549*
Read, George (signer), 135
Reading desk, 124
Reading, Pa., 59, 367, 387
Rebellion, Eng., 14, 33, 40, 79, 100, 466
Reber family, 318
Rectangular style, 93-94
Red Hill Ch. (Tinicum Ch., No. 240), 376
Redwood Library, 50, 412, 414-15, 417
Reed, Thomas, 246
Reedy Ch. (Va.), 495
Rees, Edward ap, 362
Reese, Catherine, 363
Reform, 37
Reformed Ch., Easton (No. 245), 366
Reformed Ch. of Poland, 79
Reformed churches, 8, 10, 57, 79, 178, 316, 322, 376
Reformed High Dutch Ch. (No. 195), 321-22
Reformation, ship, 31, 37
Reformation, the XV, 1, 4-5, 25, 49, 57-58, 63-64, 75, 78-79, 366
Reformers, 25
Rehoboth Ch. (Makemie's) (No. 83), 19, 67, 198-200, 541
Rehoboth Spis. Ch. (No. 84), 200
Rehoboth Ch., W.Va. (No. 345), 6, 85, 99, 525, 542
Rehoboth plantation (Md.), 199-200
Religion, XV, 1, 2, 4, 5, 12, 24, 27, 32, 37, 45, 48
Religious liberty. *See* Freedom of
Religious Society of Friends, 16, 19, 70-71, 73, 75, 169, 408
Religious Toleration, Act of, 19
Renaissance, the, 1, 5
Renaissance style, 93
Rensselaerswyck Manor (N.Y.), 55, 305

Republican polity (representative), 10, 63, 80
Reredos, 232, 425, 489, 492
Restoration, Eng., 15, 19, 33, 40, 73, 119
Restorations: Williamsburg, XIV; 136, 192, 195, 201, 205, 210-11, 216, 234, 266, 268, 303, 325, 382, 427, 433, 460, 463, 465, 484, 505
Revere, Paul, 216
Revere & Sons, Paul. *See* bells.
Revival, 475. *See also* the Great Awakening
Revocation of the Edict of Nantes, 2, 86, 194, 427, 434, 508
Revolution, Amer., 17, 22, 24, 26, 29, 35, 119, 124, 126, 146, 148, 169, 194, 213, 219-20, 225, 233, 236, 268, 340, 348, 397, 437, 451, 466. *See also* War of Independence
Revolution, Eng., 19, 33, 86
Reynolds, Deacon Daniel, 248
Rhinelander family (N.Y.), 305
Rhode Island: 8, 10, 19, 37, 39-41, 43, 50, 70; summary, 400; map, 401; 403, 410, 413, 542
Rhode Is. Charter, 414, 422
Rhode Is. College (Brown), 403-04
Rhode Is. Monthly M., 418
Rhodes, Samuel (archit.), 342
Ribaut, Jean, 2, 438
Rice, David, 329
Rice, the Rev. Jacob, 258
Richard II, 78
Richards, Mourning, 508
Richardson, Joseph, 132
Richelieu, Cardinal, 429
Richmond, Staten Is., 297
Richmond, Va., 49, 414, 464, 479-81, 488-99, 507
Richmond County, Va., 498-99, 501, 506
Richter, Schulius, 82
Riddle, the Rev. Willis, 155
Ripon Lodge plantation (Va.), 514
Rittenhouse, David, Matthias, 364
Rittenhouse, the Rev. Wm., 350
Rivera family (Newport), 50
Rivera, Jacob Rodriguez, 414, 415
Rivers, Robert, 423
Rixeyville, Va., 516
Roan, the Rev. John, 397
Roanoke Is., N.C. (settlement), 2, 153, 438
Roberts, Hugh, 355, 363
Roberts, Justice Owen J., 363
Roberts, Wm., 329
Robertson, the Rev. Geo., 464
Robinson, John, 38, 39
Robinson, Mrs. Mary (Ramsay), 478
Robinson, R. (Va.), 517
Rochambeau, general, 122, 348
Roche, Jordon, 423
Rockbridge County, Va., 522
Rockefeller, John D., Jr., 454
Rockingham M.H. (No. 291), 444-45, 542
Rocky Hill M.H. (No. 113), 100, 237
Rocky Pine Plain, Mass., 225
Rockyana, John, Bishop of Prague, 78

Rodgers, Francis S., 423, *549*
Rogers, Abner, 246
Rogers, the Rev. James, 442
Rogers, Cap. Mose, 437
Rogers, W. L., 505
Rolfe, Cap. John, 450, 473, 476, 480
Roman Catholic Ch., 2, 4-5, 13, 19, 26, 48, 50, 64, 70, 75, 79, 248, 347-48
Roman Catholicism, 4, 33, 86-87, 90, 508
Roman Catholics, 3-5, 8, 18-20, 23, 25, 27-36, 40-41, 49, 56, 64, 90, 166, 173, 184, 324, 383, 392, 422, 542
Roman civilization, XIV
Roman Empire, XIV, 45-46
Rome, N.Y., 319
Romeyn, the Rev. James V.C., 263
Rood screen, 297 (photo), 498
Roofs: 96; bonnet, jerkin head, hooded gable, 96, 109, 133, 366, 425, 428, 430, 497; gambrel, 109, 134, 190, 390; hip, 96, 120, 123, 169, 308, 322, 364, 376, 409, 433, 493, 497-98, 506, 510, 516; hip-gambrel, 109, 474; Mansard, 96; swag, 96, 109, 167, 463, 502-4
Roosevelt, Pres. Franklin D., 311, 338
Roosevelt, Pres. Theo., 148
Roosevelt family, 305
Rose, the Rev. Chas., 481, 499, 504
Rose, the Rev. Robt., 481, 499, 504, 506, 516
Rose, Thomas, 431
Rose clan, Scot., 499
Rose Hill plantation (Va.), 511
Rosemary (herb), 472
Roses of Sharon, Sisterhood of, 385
Rosetti, Dom, Archbishop of Tarsus, 32
Ross, Alexander, 518
Ross, Betsy, 341, 350
Ross, George (signer), 341
Rope maker, 348
Rough cast. *See* Stucco
Roundheads, 19, 466
Royal arms, 232, 425
Royal colony, 33, 35, 41
Rudhall, Abel, 215
Rudman, the Rev. Andrew, 62, 346
Rudolph II of Bohemia, 79
Ruins of churches, 179, 194, 198, 200, 362, 428-29, 432, 439, 450-51, 461, 493
Rum, 225, 230, 253, 258, 366
Rumford, Count, 301
Running bond (brickwork), 168
Rush, Dr. Benj. (signer), 341, 348, 388, 394 (misspelled)
Russell, the Rev. Samuel, 264
Russia, 258, 414
Rutgers College, Univ., 12, 57, 263, 266

S

Saal, the (No. 248). *See* Cloister, Ephrata
Sabbatarians, 412

Sabbath Day M.H. (No. 268), 101, 412, 541
Sabin, Jonathan, 412
Sacred Heart Ch. (No. 254), 107, 347, 392
Sadler, John, 462
Sadsbury F.M.H., Old (No. 250), 108, 389
Safford, John, 255
St. Albans School, XIV
St. Andrew's Ch., N.Y. (No. 169), 64, 108, 297
St. Andrew's Ch., St. Mary's (Md.) (No. 41), 163-64
St. Andrew's Ch., Somerset (Md.), (No. 82), 198
St. Andrew's Ch. (S.C.) (No. 279), 21, 97, 422-23, 431-32, 438, 542
St. Andrew's Ch. (Va.), 461
St. Anne's Ch., Burlington, N.J., 89, 286
St. Anne's Ch., Middletown, Del., 140
St. Anne's Ch., Old (No. 22), 140
St. Anne's Parish, Albermarle, 481, 499
St. Anne's Parish, Essex, 498-99
St. Augustine, Fla., 2
St. Barnabas Ch. (No. 51), 96, 169
St. Bartholomew Massacre, 2
St. Bartholomew's Ch. (No. 79), 197
St. Bride's, Berkeley, Parish (Va.), 468
St. Clements Is. (Md.), 30
St. David, 437
St. David's Ch., Cheraw (No. 285), 437
St. David's Ch., Radnor (No. 222), 107, 109, 356-7
St. David's Parish (Va.), 494-95
St. Denis, 21, 427
St. Francis Xavier, 56, 161, 325
St. Francis Xavier Ch. (No. 38), 34, 161
St. George, 432
St. George's Ch., Accomack. See Pongoteague ch.
St. George's Ch., Dorchester (No. 280), 92, 431-32
St. George's Ch. (Md.), (No. 40), 163
St. George's Ch., Phila. (No. 208), 84, 344-45, 366, 542
St. George's Ch., Schenectady (No. 190), 88, 106, 315-16
St. George's Parish, Spotsylvania, 515
St. Helena Is., S.C., 439
St. Helena's Ch. (No. 286), 97, 438-40
St. Hugo, 64
St. Ignatius Ch. (No. 39), 34, 162, 166
St. Inigoes, Md., 34, 162
St. James, Court of, 366
St. James' Chapel of Ease (S.C.), 426
St. James' Ch., Goose Creek (No. 275), XIV, 21, 77, 422-23, 425-26, 431
St. James Ch., Herring Creek (No. 54), 171
St. James' Ch., Kingsessing (No. 203),

62, 107, 338-39
St. James' Ch., My Lady's Manor (No. 59), 176
St. James' Ch., Perkiomen, 356, 358
St. James' Ch., Santee (No. 282), 21, 95, 422-23, 434-36
St. John's Ch., Berkeley (No. 277), 21, 422, 428-9, 430
St. John's Ch., Broad Creek (No. 48), 167
St. John's Ch., Chuckatuck, see C. Ch.
St. John's Ch., Hampton (No. 310), 17, 94, 476-78
St. John's Ch., King Geo. (Va.), 507
St. John's Ch., King Wm. (No. 321), 95, 491-2, 494-95
St. John's Ch., Oakdale, 303
St. John's Ch., Richmond (No. 312), 455, 457, 480-81, 486, 499
St. John's Parish, Baltimore, 176
St. John's Parish (Ga.), 26, 147-48
St. John's Parish, New Kent, 483
St. John's R., Fla., 2
St. Jones' Ch. (No. 23), 140
St. Joseph, 325
St. Joseph's Chapel, Phila., 35, 56, 347-48, 392
St. Lawrence R., 3, 56, 324
St. Luke's Ch., Church Hill (No. 74), 190
St. Luke's Ch., Isle of Wight (No. 297) See Old Brick Ch.
St. Luke's Ch., Wye (No. 75), 191
St. Margaret's Parish, 494-95
St. Mark's Parish (S.C.), 437
St. Mark's Parish (Va.), 515-16, 521
St. Martin-in-the-Fields, London, 214, 295, 404, 423, 484
St. Martin's Ch. (No. 86), 142, 200, 201
St. Martin's Parish, Hanover, 484-86
St. Mary Anne's Parish, Md., 187
St. Mary-le-bourne Chapel, London, 404
St. Mary-le-Strand, London, 423
St. Mary's Ch., Baltimore, 94
St. Mary's Ch., Burlington, 287
St. Mary's Ch., Old, Burlington (No. 159), 94, 97, 272, 277, 286, 542
St. Mary's Ch., North East (No. 71), 187
St. Mary's Ch., Phila. (No. 210), 36, 347-48
St. Mary's Ch., St. Mary's City, Md., 18, 31, 93, 95
St. Mary's Ch., Smith's Hundred (Va.), 478
St. Mary's City, Md., 18, 20, 31, 35, 161-62
St. Mary's County, Md., 30, 33-34
St. Mary's Parish (Md.), 18
St. Mary's R. (Ga.-Fla.), 23
St. Mary's White Chapel (No. 330), 501, 503-04
St. Matthew's Ch., Essex, 499
St. Michael's Ch., Charleston (No. 274), XIV, 95-96, 422-24, 426, 428, 436, 440
St. Michael's Ch., Marblehead (No. 110), 232-33
St. Michael's Ringers, 424

St. Paul, 45
St. Paul's Chapel, Bally (No. 246), 36, 109, 383, 542
St. Paul's Chapel, N.Y.C. (No. 168), 88, 94, 105, 295, 542
St. Paul's Ch., Baden (No. 49), 168-69, 542
St. Paul's Ch., Baltimore, 175, 179
St. Paul's Ch., Colleton, 433
St. Paul's Ch., Edenton (No. 199), 16, 23, 328
St. Paul's Ch., Eastchester (No. 177), 88, 105, 108, 304-05, 417
St. Paul's Ch., Kent (No. 72), 188-89
St. Paul's Ch., King Geo. (No. 332), 94, 96, 506-08
St. Paul's Ch., London, 425
St. Paul's Ch., Norfolk (No. 304), 94, 468-69
St. Paul's Ch., Petersburg, 465
St. Paul's Ch., Phila. (No. 207), 84, 343-45
St. Paul's Ch., Schoharie, 322
St. Paul's Ch., Spring Hill, 197
St. Paul's Ch., Suffolk, Va., 467-68
St. Paul's Ch., Wickford (No. 265), 103, 408, 540
St. Paul's Ch., Woodbury (No. 11), 16, 41, 104, 120, 128-29, 542
St. Paul's Parish, Chester, Md., 191
St. Paul's Parish, Hanover, 484, 486
St. Peter's Ch., Freehold (No. 147), 16, 74, 89, 277
St. Peter's in the Great Valley (No. 223), 109, 356-58, 366
St. Peter's Ch., Middletown (No. 259), 60, 107, 399
St. Peter's Ch., New Kent (No. 314), XIV, 92, 96, 164, 232, 456-57, 483-84, 491
St. Peter's, Kent, Eng., 484
St. Peter's Ch., Perth Amboy, 477
St. Peter's Ch., Phila. (No. 206), 342-44
St. Peter's Ch., Rome, XV
St. Peter's Ch., Van Cortlandtrille (No. 179), 55, 306
St. Peter's Ch., White Marsh (No. 77), 194
St. Philip's Ch., Brunswick (No. 200), 22, 330-31
St. Philip's Ch., Charleston, 422-24, 440
St. Philip's Ch., Southport, N.C., 331
St. Stephen's Parish, King and Queen, 490-91
St. Stephen's Ch. (S.C.) (No. 284), 95, 428, 434, 436-37
St. Thomas' Ch., Alexandria, N.J. (No. 140), 272-73
St. Thomas Ch., Bath (No. 198), 23, 120, 327-28, 542
St. Thomas' Ch., Croom (No. 50), 168, 542
St. Thomas' Ch., Garrison Forest (No. 58), 175, 179
St. Thomas' Ch., Pompion Hill (No. 276). See Pompion Hill
St. Thomas' Ch., Whitemarsh, 346
St. Thomas' Manor House (No. 46), 34, 166

St. Thomas and St. Denis Parish, 22, 427
Salem, Mass., 213, 232-34, 403, 472
Salem, N.J., 71, 282-83, 287
Salem, N.C., 23, 81, 332
Salem F.M.H. (No. 154), 282
Salem Town Hall (No. 117), 243
Salem Monthly M., 283
Salem Quarterly M., 279-81, 288
Salisbury, H.M.S., 120
Salisbury, Mass., 237
Salisbury Plantation (Va.), 472
Salmon Brook, 250
Saltbox style, 100, 193, 241, 264
Saluda, Va., 496
Salvation by faith, 82
Salzburg, Austria, 26, 145
Salzburgers, 24, 26, 145-46, 542
Sanders, Henry, 243
Sandown M.H. (No. 119), 100, 237, 244-45
Sandy Hook, N.J., 276
Sandy Point Plantation (Va.), 505
Sandys, Sir Edwin, 14
San José Mission, Texas, 417
Santee River (S.C.), 434-35
Saponey Church (No. 301), 464-65, 486
Saratoga Monthly Meeting, 231
Saron (Sister House), 386-87
Sater, Henry, 175
Sater Baptist Ch. (No. 57), 175
Sauer, Christopher, Sr. (printer), 351, 387
Sauer, Bishop C., Jr., 351, 387
Saumaine, Simeon, 135
Savannah, S.S., 437
Savannah, Ga., 23, 25, 49, 78, 81-82, 145, 148, 379, 414, 440, 542
Savannah R., 23, 26, 145, 438
Sawyer, the, 99
Sawyer, the Rev. Moses, 258
Sawshin, Mass., 220
Saxony, Germ., 25, 60, 79-80, 82, 332
Sayles family (R.I.), 406
Saylesville F.M.H. (No. 262), 405-06
Scales, the Rev. Jacob, 258
Scales, the Rev. James, 256-57
Scarborough, Joseph, 118
Scarborough, N.Y., 55, 305
Schenectady, N.Y., 315, 323
Schenectady Dutch Ch., 263
Schenectady Massacre, 56, 263
Schismatic, 19
Schisms, 16, 68, 74, 223-34, 258, 300, 374, 397, 412-13, 441, 469. *See also* Separation and Keithian Controversy
Schlatter, the Rev. Michael, 56, 58, 263, 366, 380
Schlatter Fund, 382
Schob, Detrick, 399
Schoharie County Hist. So., 322
Schoharie Cr. Valley, 55-56, 59, 313, 316-17, 322-24
Schoharie Dutch Ch. (No. 195). *See* Old Stone Ch.
Scholasticism, medieval, 47
Schooley, Wm., Robt., 270
Schools: 35, 81, 87, 154, 161, 274, 288, 312-13, 315, 318, 339, 344, 366-67, 374, 379, 382, 387-88, 390,

397, 418, 428, 457, 468, 471-72, 477, 490, 497, 505-06, 524; parochial, 383, 542
Schuyler, the Rev. Johannes, 322
Schuylkill, 61-62, 339, 354-55, 363
Scituate, Mass., 39, 208-09, 541
Scoggins' Creek (Va.), 497
Scotch-Irish, 22, 53, 72, 136, 247-49, 257, 280, 364, 374, 393-96, 518, 522
Scotland, 1, 16, 120, 128, 248, 442, 472, 499, 506
Scots: 16, 22, 24, 53, 155, 199, 277, 295, 376, 390; banished, 442; 454, 486, 499, 508, 516, 523
Scott, the Rev. Alexander, 508, 510
Scott, the Rev. Jonathan, 157
Scottish Covenanters, 276
Scriven, Elisha, 435
Scriven, the Rev. Wm., 435
Scrooby Manor House, Eng., 38
Seabury, the Rev. Samuel, Sr., 309
Seabury, Bishop Samuel, 16, 41, 89, 104, 120, 128, 233, 271, 286, 303-04
Seabury, the Rev. Chas. (son of Bishop S.), 303
Sea Islands (Ga.), 25
Seary, Sarah, 352, 369
Seaville F.M.H. (No. 149), 101, 279
Second Baptist Church, Newport, 413
Second Congl. Ch., Newport (No. 270), 412-13
See (Episcopal), 348
Seifferth, Anthony (first Amer. epis. ordination), 81, 542
Seixas, Moses, 51, 417
Seminole War, 437
Seneca Indians, 183
Separation, the Great (Friends), 300, 310, 313, 352, 371
Separation of ch. and state, 45, 88
Separatism, 39, 209
Separatists, 13-14, 19, 37-38, 49, 100, 286, 403
Sepharad, 44
Sephardic Jews, 9, 22-23, 44-52, 414, 422
Sephardim, 44
Setauket, N.Y., 64, 302-03
Seventh Day Bap. Ch. (No. 268), 39, 101, 412
Seventh Day Germ. Bap., 9, 77, 385, 542
Severn R., Md., 33
Sewall, Father Charles, S.J., 166
Sewall, Judge Samuel, 213
Sewell's Point (Va.), 468
Sexes separated, 71, 134, 176, 226, 231, 267
Shaco's (Va.), 464
Shackelford's (Va.), 490
Shaker Community, Inc., 87, 315
Shaker M.H. (No. 189), 9, 85-87, 314-15, 542
Shakespeare, Wm., and Judith, dau., 462
Shaver, Wm., 355
Shaw, the Rev. Wm., 232
Shay's Rebellion, 230
Shannon, ship, 274
Sharptown, N.J., 283

Shawnee Indians, 524
Shea, Thomas, 184
Sheffield Congl. Ch. (No. 108), 41, 230, 413
Sheldon Ch. (No. 288), 95, 423, 435, 440-41
Sheldon Hall (S.C.), 423, 440-41
Sheldon Parish, Warwickshire, 440
Shenandoah Valley, Va., 17, 57, 106, 390, 395, 397, 518, 520-23
Sherley (Shirley), Ceciley, 478
Sherman, Gen. Wm. T., 424, 440
Sherwood Forest plantation (Va.), 479
Sherwood, Grace, 472
Shield, ship, 287
Shipbuilders, 143, 204, 208, 303
Shippen, Wm., 343
Shippen, Dr. Wm., Jr., 348
Shires (Va.), 15, 450, 458, 460, 466, 470, 477
Shirley, Mass., 315
Shirley plantation, 479
Shrewsbury, N.J., 278
Shrewsbury Congl. Ch. (No. 103), 225
Shrewsbury Quarter, 270
Shute, the Rev. Daniel, 207
Sidesman, 501
Signers of Decl. Ind., 35, 148, 173, 249, 273-74, 341, 388, 435, 457, 463, 469, 483
Silver, church, 135, 140, 163, 171, 215; money, 258; 284, 286, 297, 303, 327, 340, 408, 426, 428, 431, 433, 435, 437, 439-40, 451, 454, 463, 472, 474-75, 477-78, 481-82, 485, 487, 489, 499, 503-04, 507, 510, 514
Silk culture, 146
"Silk Stocking Ch." (Va.), 461
Silver, James, 67, 394
Silver Spring Presbyn. Ch. (No. 257), 67, 105-06, 390, 393, 394-95, 397
Singers Galleries, seating, 127, 156, 161, 219, 242, 258
Singing, 77, 366, 380, 387, 520
Sipple, Waitman, 141
Sister Emma Neale, 87
Sister Amelia Calver, 87
Sister House (No. 248), Ephrata, 9
Sisterhood of the Spiritual Virgins, 387
Sittenbourn Parish, Essex, 498
Sitkorvius, Bishop Christian, 80
Six Nations (Iroquois), 23, 316, 318-19, 325, 328, 373, 382, 394. *See also* Five Nations
Six Principle Bap. Ch., the, 39, 101, 407, 541
Skinner, the Rev. Wm., 271
Skye, Isle of, 155
Slash Ch. (No. 316), 486
Slate, 96, 423
Slater, Richard, 275
Slavery, 75, 298, 310, 371, 413, 511
Slaves, 25, 81, 142, 161, 213, 359, 404, 454, 463
Sleepy Hollow Dutch Ch. (No. 178), 55, 108-09, 305, 541
Slocum, Ebenezer, 419
Smallwood, Gen. Wm., 165, 186
Smallpox, 244

Smart, John, 132
Smith, Benjamin, 423
Smith, Cap. John, 5, 12-13, 15, 93, 206, 450, 462, 476, 480, 488
Smith, Joseph (iron plow), 378
Smith, Robert, 342, 348
Smith, the Rev. Dr. Wm., 172, 189
Smithfield, Penn., 374
Smithfield, Va., 460
Smithfield Monthly M., 405-06
Smith's Cr. (Md.), 18
Smith's Hundred(Va.), 477, 480
Smoky Mountains, 524
Snow Hill, Md., 200, 474
Snow Hill Parish (Md.), 200-01
Society for the Promotion of Christian Knowledge, S.P.C.K., 16, 327
Society for the Propagation of the Gospel in Foreign Parts (S.P.G., the Society, the Venerable Society), 16, 62, 74, 82, 88-89, 120, 128-29, 140, 218, 255, 271-72, 277-78, 286, 297, 303, 327, 356, 408, 410, 425-26, 428-29, 431-32, 457, 477
Society for the Preservation of N.E. Antiquities, 237
Society of Friends. See Religious So.
Society of Jesus, 31, 162
Society of the Solitary, 77, 385
Somerset County, Md., 197, 200
Somerset Parish Ch., Md., 198
Sons of Liberty, 468
Souhegan West No. 3, (tract), 250
South, 13-26
South America, 2, 49
South Anna R. (Va.), 484
South Carolina: 2, 9, 232; summary, 420; map, 421; 423, 542
South Ch., Old, Newburyport (No. 112), 234
South Company, 61
South Hingham M.H., (No. 89), 207
South River Ch. (No. 55), 172
South R., the (Delaware), 56, 60
South River (Va.), 523
South Virginia (territory) 5, 13-14
Southampton, Eng., 30
Southampton, Long Is., 65
Southampton Congl. Ch. (Mass.) (No. 107), 229
Southampton County, Va., 458
Southampton Hundred (Va.,), 477-78
Southern Sea, 6
Southold, Long Is., 65
Southwark Eng., 39, 209, 460, 541
Southwark Bridge (London), 460
Southwark Parish (Va.), 460-61, 463. See also Lower S. Ch.
Spain, 1-3, 5, 23, 27, 44, 46-49, 414
Spangenberg, Bishop Augustus Gottlieb, 81, 283, 332, 380
Spanish, the, 3, 5, 23-25, 27, 48, 81, 324
Speaker of the House, U.S., 367
Speare, Eva A., 256, 549
Speedwell, ship, 38
Spencer, Geo., 504
Spencer, Wm., 473
Spener, Philip Jacob, 60, 366
S. P. G. See Society for the Propagation of the Gospel

Spiket River, N.H., 243
Spinoza, Baruch (philosopher), 46
Spirit, XV
Spooner, Alden, 445
Spotswood, Gov. Alexander, 454-55, 499, 515-17, 521
Spotsylvania County, Va., 499, 515, 517, 521
Spring Hill Ch. (No. 80), 197
Springfield, Mass., 229-30
Springfield F.M.H., Old (No. 165), 290
Springfield Presbyn. Ch. (No. 135), 42, 66, 268
Spruce, 100
Stacy, James, 148, 549
Stafford County, Va., 506-08
Stage, John, 263
Stairway, outside, 109, 133, 351, 376, 467
Stamford, Conn., 310, 413
Stamp Act, 468
Stamper's Hill (R.I.), 405
Staten Is. N.Y., 64, 267-68
Staunton, Va., 521
Stecher, Franz (painter) 392
Steichen, Edward, XIV
Stepney Parish (No. 80), Md., 143, 197
Sterling Memorial Library, Yale, 264
Stevens, the Rev. Dr. Benj., 150
Stevens, John, Lewis, 272
Stevens, Col. Wm., 67, 199
Stevenson, Thos. H., 474
Stewart, Gen. Daniel, 148
Stewart, Robert, plantation (Penn.), 376
Stiles, Henry R., 122
Stith, the Rev. Wm., 480
Stockbridge Congl. Ch., 230, 413
Stockbridge Indians, Mission, 230
Stockton, Richard (signer), 273
Stoever, the Rev. John Casper, 517
Stoke Orchard, Gloucestershire, 369
Stone, 105-109
Stone Arabia Dutch Ch. (No. 191), 55, 107, 316-17
Stone Ch., Old, Frederick (No. 64), 180
Stonersville, Penn., 384
Stoney, Samuel G., 425-26, 428, 549
Stono R. (S.C.), 431
Stony Brook F.M.H. (No. 142), 273
Storrs Parsonage, Longmeadow, 229
Story, Thomas, 354
Stratton Major Parish (Va.), 489-91
Strawberry Bank, N.H., 242
Strawberry Chapel (No. 278), XIV, 21, 97, 422, 429-31
Strawberry ferry (S.C.), 426, 428, 430-31
Strasbourg, France, 64
Stretcher bond (brickwork), 93
Stringer, the Rev. Wm., 344
Stuart, the Rev. David, 506
Stuart, Gilbert (painter), 417
Stuart, the Rev. Wm., 506-07
Stuart line, 16, 128, 506
Stubs, John, 409
Stubbs, Robert, 490
Stucco (rough cast), 96-97, 108, 134-

35, 138, 169, 178, 273, 308, 313, 348, 357, 363, 366, 371, 378, 390, 423, 425, 430, 433, 439, 482, 493, 495
Styles, the Rev. Ezra, 413
Stuyvesant, Peter, 62
Suffolk County, L.I., 64, 303
Suffolk Parish (Va.), 466-67
Suffolk, Va., 466
Sumner, the Rev. Clement, 445
Sumner, Maj. Gen. E. V., 483
Sumner, James, 404
Sumner, the Rev. Joseph, 225
Sunbury, Ga., 148
Sunday school, first, 24-25
Sunderland, Mass., 230
Superimposed orders, 214, 216, 411, 417
Superintendent, Methodist, 85, 141
Surinam, 50, 414
Surrey, Eng., 459-60
Surry County, Va., 460
Surry Courthouse, Va., 460
Susan Constant, ship, 6, 450, 458
Susquehanna Manor (Md.), 186
Susquehanna R., 57, 67, 136, 185-86, 389-90, 393, 395-96
Susquehannock Indians, 187
Sussex County, Va., 460
Swamp Fox, the, 431, 437
Swan emblem, 146
Swan, frigate, 301
Sweden, 1, 79, 132
Sweden, Lutheran ch. of, 58, 60-63. See also Swedish Lutherans
Swedes, the, 53, 60-63, 72, 90, 99, 132, 284, 337-39
Swedesboro, N.J., 62, 284
Swedish Lutherans, 8, 60-63, 132, 346, 517, 541
Swedish Mission in Amer., 62-63, 133, 346
Swiss, the, 24, 54, 58, 380
Switzerland, 1, 79
Sycamore trees, 473, 475, 497
Symms, Benj., 477
Symms, Eaton Free School (Va.), 477
Synagogue, 43, 49-50, 414, 542. See also Jews
Synod of the Carolinas (A.R.P.), 442
Synods of Holland, 57-58, 380, 382
Synod of N.Y., 68, 266
Synod of Paris, 64
Synod of Phila., 67-68, 390
Synod of the South (A.R.P.), 442
Syrians, 46

T

T-form churches, 94, 176, 188, 195
Tabor, Church, 255
Tabor, Joseph, 255
Tacony Monthly M., 352
Talbot, George, 186
Talbot, the Rev. John, 88-89, 272, 277, 286-87
Talbot County, Md., 191
Tannenburg, David (organ maker), 388 (misspelled), 517
Tappahannock, Va., 500

Tapia ("tabby"), 91, 94-95, 109, 432, 439
Tarleton, Co., 460
Tarrytown, N.Y., 305
Taschemaker (Thessehenmaecher), the Rev. Petrus, 56, 262-63
Taunton, Mass., 412
Taxes, 33, 36-37, 75, 118-22, 124, 213, 223, 227, 247, 251, 255
Taylor, Benjamin, 378
Taylor, Daniel, 118
Taylor, George, 382
Taylor, John, 501
Taylor, the Rev. Nathaniel, 67
Taylor, Samuel, 129
Teach, Edward (pirate "Blackbeard"), 23, 328
Teacher (asst. min., Congl.), 39, 234, 403
Teedyuscung, Chief of Delawares, 382
Temple Farm, Yorktown, 482
Temple of Jehovah, 45
Temple of Jupiter, 45
Templeton, Mass., 227
Tennent Ch. (No. 146), 66, 276-77, 375
Tennent family, 11, 66, 144, 276, 366, 374-75
Tennent, the Rev. Chas., 143, 276
Tennent, the Rev. Gilbert, 68, 83, 89, 136, 271, 276, 281, 344, 375, 485
Tennent, the Rev. John, 68, 276, 375
Tennent, the Rev. Wm., Sr., 60, 68-69, 136, 374-75
Tennent, the Rev. Wm., Jr., 276-77, 375
Tennessee, 6, 522, 524
Test Oath (Md.), 34
Texas, 522
Thames R. (Eng.), 39, 209, 460
Thanksgiving, 118, 348
Thanksgiving Day, 289
Thatch, 223
Theocratic, 37
Theological seminaries, 11, 263, 514
Thetford Congl. Ch. (No. 292), 445, 542
Thetford Hill, Vt., 445
Third Haven F.M.H. (No. 76), 19, 100, 193, 541
"Thirty days has Sep.," 313
Thirty Years War, 25, 79, 83
Thomas, Lowell, 310
Thomas, R. S., 543, 550
Thompson, the Rev. John, 516
Thompson, the Rev. Samuel, 394
Thornton, Matthew, 249
Thoroughgood, Adam: 470-72; house, 93
Thurston family (Va.), 489
"Test, the," 328
Tidewater Va., 463, 470, 479, 523
Tiffany, 424
Tillinghast, the Rev. Pardon, 403
Tilly, Thos., 467
Timber Lane, N.H., 246
Timber Ridge Presbyn. Ch. (No. 344), 17, 68, 106, 390, 395, 397, 522-24
Timothy, Lewis, 83
Tinicum Is., Penn., 61, 337

Tinicum Presbyn. Ch. (No. 240), 69, 109, 376
Tinkling Spring Ch. (Va.), 522
Tiot Parish, 223
Tipicop-Haw Hill (S.C.), 428
Tissot, the Rev., 428
Tithes, 171, 192
Tittermary, John, 348
Titus, Roman General, 44-45
Tobacco (currency), 167, 170-71, 188, 192, 198, 474, 494, 498, 513
Tobacco colonies, the, 455
Toleration, 40, 47, 73
Toleration Act: Eng., 40; Md., 32-33, 253, 258
Topanemus, N.J., 277
Tories, 119, 169, 207, 255, 266, 320, 322, 382, 411, 440
Torkillus, the Rev. Reorus, 61, 132
Tornado, 424
Torrence, the Rev. Clayton, 198, 550
Toughkenamon, Penn., 358
Touro, Abraham, 415, 417
Touro, the Rev. Dr. Isaac de Abraham, 415, 417
Touro, Judah, 417
Touro Synagogue (No. 271), 9, 22, 43, 49, 51-52, 97, 414-17, 542
Tower of London, 431
Toynbee, Arnold, XIV, 550
Trade, 1, 5, 22, 46-50, 54-56
Trading Post, 27, 31, 56, 315, 320, 325, 394, 396
Tranhook. See Crane Hook
Transubstantiation, 54
Trappe Ch. (No. 231), 60, 80, 108-09, 180, 365-67, 517
Trappers, 284
Treaties: Eng.-Amer. (1783), 6; of Ghent (War of 1812), 324; Eng.-Spain (1605), 5, 438
Tred Avon, 193
Tredyffrin, Penn., 357
Trent, William, 364
Trenton F.M.H. (No. 144), 274, 167
Trevelyan, Geo. Macauley, 38
Trevett, Samuel R., 233
Tricentennial (Va.), 17, 451, 457, 463, 505, 507, 512, 515
Trinitarian, 39, 220-21
Trinity Chapel, Frederick (No. 65), 8, 58, 181
Trinity Ch. (Old), Brooklyn (No. 4), 118-20, 411
Trinity Ch. (New), Brooklyn, 120
Trinity Ch., Dorchester (No. 78), 93, 195
Trinity Ch., Eldersburg (No. 63), 175, 179
Trinity Ch., Fishkill (No. 183), 309
Trinity Ch., Lancaster (No. 249), 60, 387-88
Trinity Ch., N.Y.C., 88, 94, 287, 295, 303
Trinity Church, Newport, R.I. (No. 267), 102, 118-20, 408, 410-12
Trinity Ch., Oxford (No. 209), 62, 74, 92, 346, 352
Trinity Ch., Portsmouth (No. 305), 97, 470

Trinity Ch., St. Mary's City, Md., 18-19
Trinity Ch., Swedesboro (No. 157), 284
Trinity Ch., Wilmington. See Old Swedes, Wilm.
Trinity Parish, Hanover, 484
Triune baptism, 76, 351
Trombone choir, 380
True, the Rev. Henry, 246
Trumbull, John (painter), 242
Truro Parish (Va.), 510-12, 514
Truth, 305
Tryon, Gov. Wm., 331
Tuckahoe, Md., 193
Tuckahoe Chapel (Md.), 191
Tucker, Bishop Beverley Dandridge, 469
Tunnell, William, 143
Tunxis R., valley, 123
Turned structures, 117, 121, 247
Tuscan style, 423, 499
Tuscarora Indians, 23, 325, 328, 439
Tustian, the Rev., 432
Twelves, Robert, 213
Tyburn, the (Eng.), 404
Tyler, Pres. John, 479
Tyndall's Point (Va.), 488

U

Underdaubing, 122
Underground Railroad, 359
"undertakers" (contractors), 497
Union, N.J., 264, 267
Union, W.Va., 525
Union Baptist Ch. (Va.), 494
Union Church (N.H.), (No. 128), 255
Union of Utrecht, 49
Unitarian Ch., Charleston (No. 289), 97, 441
Unitarian Controversy, 205
Unitarian So., American, 205
Unitarianism, 11, 39
Unitarians, 42, 118, 152, 204, 207, 213, 215, 220-21, 223, 233-34, 413, 441
Unitas Fratrum (Church of the Brethren), 379. See also Unity of Brethren
United Baptists, 413
United Brethren in Christ, the, 21, 58, 178, 541
United Church of Christ, 182
United Meeting of Friends, 372
United Meetings of Friends, 74-75
United Nations, XV
United Society of Believers in Christ's Second Appearing, 86
United States, founding of, XV, 1, 4, 12, 22, 37, 51, 60, 64, 70, 119, 148, 340
United States Senator, 35
United Yearly M., 74
Unity of Brethren, 24-25, 78-80
Upjohn, Richard (archit.), 94, 287, 295
Upland (Chester, Penn.), 72, 352
Up River Chapel (Md.), 190

Upper Ch., King and Queen (No. 319), 95, 489
Upper Flanders, N.H., 250
Upper Merion, Penn., 339
Uppsala (Sweden), Archbishop, Consistory of, 62
Urbanna, Va., 496
Urmston, the Rev. John, 328
Usselinx, Wm., 61
Usurpation, 29, 33-34

V

Valley Forge (Penn.), 277, 281-82, 341, 344, 355, 364
Valley Lee, Md., 163
Valley of Virginia, the. See Shenandoah
Van Cortlandt Manor, family, 55, 305-06, 308
Van Dussen, Alexander, 423
Van Rensselaer, Col. Robert, 308, 322
Van Tassel, Katrina, 305
Vasey, the Rev. Thos., 85
Vatican Council, XV
Vaudreuil, Marquis de, 325
Vauter, John, 499
Vauter's Ch. (No. 327), 481, 498-99
Veeder, Col. U., 322
Vendue, 121
Venerable Society. See Society for the Propagation of the Gospel
Vermont Historical So., 445
Vermont: summary, map, 443; 542
Vernon, Adm. Edward, 512
Vespasian, Roman Gen., Emperor, 45
Victorian style, 198, 219, 234, 303, 472
Villepontoux, Francis, 436
Villepontoux, Zachariah, 423, 426, 428, 436
Virginia: 1, 5-6, 9, 13-17, 19, 22, 24, 29, 31, 33, 40, 88, 119, 206, 232, 286; summary, 446, 448-49; map, 447; 477, 540, 543
Virginia Company (Va. Council of London, "London Company"), 5, 13-14, 18, 29, 38, 477
Virginia Yearly M., 73
Vitrified forts, 482
Voorseler (clerk, Dutch parish), 263

W

Waccamaw River, 435
Wachau (Austria), 332
Wachovia (N.C.), 332
Wadboo Baroney (S.C.), 428
Wade, Robert, 352-53
Waldo, Gen. Samuel, 154
Waldoboro, Me., 43, 154
Waldrum's Old Fields, 163
Wales, 1, 77, 139, 354, 356
Walker, Benjamin, 391
Walker, the Rev. Cornelius, 514
Walkerton, Va., 490
Walking Purchase (Penn.), 373
Wall, Richard, 369

Wall House (Penn), 369
Wallingford Parish (Va.), 463, 478
Walloons, the, 54
Walpole M.H. (No. 36), 155
Walton, George, 382
Walton, Father James, S.J., 162
Walton, Pelatiah, 329
Wambaw Ch. See St. James', Santee
Wambaw Lodge, Freemasons, 436
Wampanoag Indians, 211
Wando Ch., 427
Wando R. (S.C.), 427
Wanton, Edward and Michael, 208
Wappinger Indians, 310
War of 1812, 164, 324, 343, 437, 477
War of Independence: Amer., 16, 118-19, 514 (See also Revolution, Amer.); Dutch, 48
Ward, Gen. Artemus, 225
Ward, the Rev. Jonathan, 157
Wardley, James and Anne, 86
Wardman, Adam, 368
Ware, the Rev. Henry, 42, 205
Ware, Isaac, 417
Ware Ch. (No. 317), 95, 486-88, 499
Warner, Augustine, Mildred, 487-88
Warner, Edmund, 72
Warner Hall (Va.), 488
Warren, R.I., 404
Warrington F.M.H. (No. 253), 108, 390-91
Warrosquyoake (Va.), 458
Warwick County, Va., 476
Warwick Presbyn. Ch. See Neshaminy
Washington, Augustine (father of Geo.), 505, 511, 514
Washington, Judge Bushrod (of Mount Vernon), 514
Washington, Geo.: army, 60, 66, 139, 215, 268-69 (W.Rock), 276-77, 281, 307-10, 348, 350, 360-61, 364, 367, 375, 382; attended services, 122, 165, 167, 219, 297, 306, 340; cherry tree, 172; Diocese of Va., 481; College of Wm. and Mary, 455; crossing of the Del., 233; draftsman, ch. designs, 511, 515; family, 507 (9 W's. one vestry), 487-88, 504-05, 510-12, 514; funeral, 514; linen, 248; marriage, 483; Pres., 7, 51-52, 287, 341, 343; surveyor, 511-12; towns named for, 254; vestryman, 454, 511-12, 514; visited, 236, 417
Washington, Martha (Dandridge) (Custis), 219, 340, 453
Washington, D.C., 297
Washington, N.H., 254, 256
Washington (N.H.) Town Hall (No. 127), 254
Washington, N.C., 254
Washington College (Md.), 189
Washington and Lee Univ., 524
Washington Parish (Va.), 504
Water table, 95, 167
Waterford, Me., 257
Watervliet, N.Y., 86-87, 314
Wattle and daub, 122, 450
Watts' hymnal, 268
Waugh, the Rev. John, 508
Waugh, the Rev. Samuel, 395

Wayne, Gen. Anthony, 146, 282, 348, 357
Wayne, Anthony, Sr., 356
Wayside Ch. (No. 45), Md., 165
Webb, the Rev. Jos., 65, 264
Webb, Cap. Thos., 84, 134, 345
Webb house (Conn.), 122
Webster, Daniel, 223
Weeks, Abel, 307
Weeks, the Rev. Joshua, 233
Weems, John, 171
Weems, the Rev. ("Parson") Mason Locke, 171-72, 511
Weiser, Anna Maria, 59, 367, 387
Weiser, John Conrad, Sr., 59, 323, 367
Weiser, John Conrad, Jr., 59, 323, 367, 387, 394
Weiser Park, Conrad, 367, 387
Weiser's Dorf (Middleburg, N.Y.), 59, 323-24
Welcome, ship, 363
Wells, Me., 150-51
Welsh, the, 53, 73, 77, 90, 362
Welsh Tract, Barony, 73, 77, 139, 339, 354-57, 362
Welsh Tract Bap. Ch. (No. 21), 77-78, 96, 139
Wentworth, Gov. Benning, 243, 246, 252, 255, 444
Wentworth, Gov. Sir John, 247, 252, 254-55, 258
Wesley, Chas., 24, 82-83
Wesley, John, 24-25, 42, 78, 80, 82-85, 141, 344-45, 366, 379
West, Thos., Lord de la Warr, 450, 478
West, Francis, 478
West, Harry, 478
West Barnstable M.H. (No. 91), 39, 209-10
West Caln F.M.H. (Penn.), 362
West India Co., Dutch, 54-55, 61
West Indies, 2-4, 6, 25, 49, 80
West Jersey (province): 1, 42, 62, 70-72, 88, 277, 279, 282, 284, 286; constitution (the "Concessions"), union with E.J., 287; 288-89, 405
West Parish M.H., Mass. (No. 91), 209-10, 541
West Point, N.Y., 322
West Point, Va., 489-91
West Port, N.H., 255
West and Shirley Hundred, 477-78
West Virginia; 6; map, 447; 518, 522, 525, 542
West Va. Conference (Meth.), 525
Westbury Monthly M., 299
Western Europe, XV, 1
Western Quarterly M., 358-59
Westminster Congl. Ch., 103, 117
Westmoreland, N.H., 253
Westmoreland County, Va., 488, 504-05
Westover Ch. (No. 311), 477-79
Westover Parish (Va.), 463, 477
Western Quarterly Meeting, 138
Westrope, John, 463
Westwood, Mass., 223-24
Wetherill, Fort (R.I.), 419
Wetherill, John Price, 350

Wetherill, Samuel, Jr., 350, 419
Wethersfield Congl. Ch. (No. 6), 92, 97, 101, 122, 124
Wetmore, the Rev. James, 303
Weworocomico (Va.), 488
Weyanoke Parish (Va.), 463, 478
Weyanoke plantation (Va.), 477-79
Whatcoat, the Rev. Richard, 84-85
Whigs, 207, 440
Whitaker, the Rev. Alexander, 476, 480
Whitaker, Jas., 86
Whitaker, Father James, 314
White, Father Andrew, 30-31, 162
White, the Rev. John, 147
White, the Rev. Wm., 340-41, 343, 348
White Hill (N.J.), 276
White House (Va.), 483
White Marsh Ch., Old (No. 77), 194
White Marsh plantation (Va.), 460
Whitefield, the Rev. Geo., 25-26, 42, 60, 68, 81-84, 89, 136, 234, 248, 250, 271, 276, 281, 343-45, 366, 374, 379, 413, 522
Whitefield House (Penn.), 81, 379
Whitemarsh, Penn. 350
Whittier, John Greenleaf, 240
Wicaco (Phila.), 62, 132, 338-40
Wickford, R.I., 408
Wicomico R., Md., 197
Wilkins, the Rev. Daniel, 250
Willard, Samuel, 213
Willets, Jacob and Deborah, 313
William I (Prussia), 26
William III, 295, 521
William III and Mary II, 11, 20, 28, 33, 41, 90, 188, 508
William and Mary College, XIV, 11, 16, 454-56, 480-81, 502, 514
William and Mary Parish, 163, 165
William of Nassau, Prince of Orange, 48
Williams, David, 322
Williams, Geo. W., 423, 550
Williams, the Rev. John, 444
Williams, the Rev. Roger, 39, 50, 403-05, 408-09, 414, 419, 550
Williams R. (Vt.), 444
Williamsburg, Va., 11, 451, 453-56, 464, 467, 481, 488, 515, 518
Williamsburg restoration, XIV, 195
Willing's Alley, Phila., 343-44, 347
Willis, Howard S., 243, 550
Willistown F.M., 355
Wilmington, Del., 132, 134, 139, 284
Wilmington, N.C., 22, 330-31
Wilmington Monthly Meeting, 138
Wilmington Parish (Va.), 478

Wilson, David, 138
Wilson, James (signer), 341
Wilson, the Rev. John (Del.), 137
Wilson, the Rev. John (N.H.), 247
Wilson, the Rev. Thomas, 198
Wilson, Woodrow (Gov. N.J.), 263
Wilson, the first Mrs. Woodrow, 148
Wiltshire, Eng., 237
Wiltshire Manor (Conn.), 119
Winchester, Va., 518
Windham, N.H., 248
Windsor, Vt., 445
Winship, the Rev. Josiah, 153
Winston-Salem, N.C., 23, 332
Winter's Run, 175
Winthrop, Gov. John (N.H.), 213
Wiscasset, Me., 157
Wissahickon Creek, Penn., 350
Witch Duck (Va.), 472
Witches, 213, 472
Withers, James, 423
Wittenberg, Germ., 25
Wittenberg Univ., 80
Woburn Congl. M.H. (Mass.), 220
Wolfe, General, Tavern (Conn.), 118
Wolle, Dr. J. Frederick, 380
Wolves, 522
Woltz, Peter, 399
Womelsdorf, Penn., 367
Wood, 99-105
Wood, Abraham, 464
Wood, carved, 423, 428, 498
Wood, Jackanias (or John), 283
Wood's Ch. (Va.), 464
Woodbridge, N.J., 269-70
Woodbridge, the Rev. Benj., 66
Woodbury (N.J.) F.M.H. (No. 158), 285
Woodham Walter Ch., Essex, Eng., 459
Woodhouse, ship, 408
Woodruff, Judah, 101, 123-24
Woodruff, Matthew, 124
Woodstock, Va., 367
Woodstown F.M.H. (No. 155), 93, 283
Woolman, John, 288-89
Woolwich, Me., 153
Woonsocket F.M., 405
Worcester Parish, County, Md., 200-01
World community of Jews, 45-46, 49
World War II, XIII, 338, 437
World Wars, 397, 437
Worthington, Conn., 125
Wrangel, the Rev. Chas. Magnus, 339
Wren, Sir Christopher, 97, 101-02, 295, 404, 410, 423, 455-56, 513
Wren, James, 511, 513, 515

Wren Building (Va.), 454-57
Wren Chapel (No. 295), XIV, 11, 97, 102, 454-57
Wrightstown F.M.H. (No. 237), 373
Wycliffe, John (reformer), 25, 37-38, 78, 379
Wythe, George (signer), 454, 457, 481
Wye Ch. (No. 75), 191-92
Wynne, Dr. Thomas, 363
Wyoming Massacre (Penn.), 382
Wyoming, R.I., 407

Y

Yadkin River (N.C.), 332, 384
Yale College, Univ., 11, 41-42, 64-65, 215, 225, 230, 264, 267, 413
Yamasee War, 425, 436, 438-41
Yard, Joseph, 132
Ye (thorn, rune) 275
Ye Old Yellow M.H. (No. 145), 78, 275
Yeardley, Gov. Sir George, 451, 458, 477
Yeocomico Ch. (No. 331), 92, 96, 456, 481, 504-05
York, Me., 150
York County, Va., 483, 501
York F.M.H. (No. 252), 390
York Parish (Va.), 482
York R. (Va.), 453, 476, 482, 484, 486, 488-89
Yorkshire, Eng., 72, 213, 287
Yorktown, Va., 205, 470, 482
Yorktown Capitulation, 6, 205, 482
Youngstown, N.Y., 324
Y.W.C.A., Burlington, 288

Z

Zedek ve Shalom Synagogue, 50, 414
Zenger, John Peter, 305, 340
Zinzendorf, Nicholas Ludwig, Count von, 25, 57, 80-81, 263, 332, 366, 379-80, 383
Zion Ch., Fairfax, Va., 514
Zion Ch., Lancaster, 388
Zion Epis. Ch., N.J. (No. 156), 81, 283
Zion Germ. Ref. Ch., Hagerstown (No. 66), 58, 182
Zion Hill, Ephrata, 386, 387
Zion Luth. Ch., Oldwick (No. 139), 59, 271
Zion Reformed Ch., Allentown, 342
Zurich, Switz., 64, 75
Zwingli, Ulrich (reformer) 54, 64, 75

DATE DUE
